GREAT MILITARY LEADERS
AND THEIR CAMPAIGNS

GREAT MILITARY LEADERS
AND THEIR CAMPAIGNS | EDITED BY JEREMY BLACK

With 545 illustrations, 440 in color

Thames & Hudson

Contents

Half-title: The uniform worn by Napoleon at the battle of Marengo (1800).

Title page: Moltke and his staff watch Prussian infantry and artillery converging on Paris, 19 September 1870, during the Franco-Prussian War.

Contents pages: Mosaic of Alexander the Great on horseback from the House of the Faun, Pompeii; section of the Bayeux Tapestry showing William the Conqueror lifting his helmet to prove to his men he has not been wounded; Gustavus Adolphus's hard-won victory at the battle of Lützen (1632); American infantry landing on the Gilbert Islands in World War II.

First published in 2008 in hardcover in the United States of America by Thames & Hudson Inc., 500 Fifth Avenue, New York, New York 10110

thamesandhudsonusa.com

Library of Congress Catalog Card Number 2007910200

ISBN 978-0-500-25145-4

Printed and bound in Singapore by Tien Wah Press (Pte) Ltd.

▶ An adept battlefield commander, the Duke of Wellington, here shown in an 18th-century portrait by Sir Thomas Lawrence, ably executed a form of contracted fire-and-movement tactics, balancing the well-drilled line with the extensive use of light infantry, the conservatism of an emphasis on linear firepower formations with a greater role for manoeuvrability. He was also a fine judge of terrain and adept at controlling a battle as soon as it developed.

campaigning in what they saw as the crucial zone of operations – one in which their presence could influence events in a critical way. When Süleyman the Magnificent (pp. 108–11) chose to campaign in Hungary in the 1520s and 1530s, it helped make that front more important than the Persian one.

The political importance of campaigning became even more relevant as the contrast between what was seen as civilian and military leadership increased. Until early modern times the two were usually fused in rulers, such as Alexander the Great (pp. 18–23), the Roman emperors, the Mongol clan leaders, the Turkish sultans or European monarchs. The kings of England (and subsequently Britain) continued to lead their armies into battle until 1743, when George II commanded at Dettingen. His second son, William, Duke of Cumberland, was in command three years

later at Culloden, the key battle in the defeat of the Jacobite claim on the British throne. For most rulers, military success was a crucial source of prestige, which helped ensure the respect and support of their subordinates and subjects. Victory was the facilitator of obedience, and this helps explain the great concern taken to ensure a favourable 'spin' on campaigns. Proclaiming victory and associating it with a leader was a central feature of politics, as demonstrated by Julius Caesar and Napoleon.

At the strategic level, the key ability is that of defining realizable goals, ensuring the necessary domestic and international support (or, at least, acceptance), and distributing resources between different campaign fronts. These are complex and difficult tasks, and most commanders and politicians struggle to complete all three. Civilian politicians

◄ Eisenhower and his men. The supreme commander talks to soldiers from the US 82nd Airborne Division, a key unit in the attack on German forces in Normandy on D-Day, 6 June 1944. Eisenhower was an able political general, whose broad-front approach to the exploitation of the battle of Normandy has been a cause of controversy. Given the resistance of the German military and Allied supply problems, both Eisenhower's approach and Montgomery's methodical warmaking were sensible options. Eisenhower was to go on to command NATO and become a two-term President.

frequently do not understand the nature of risk that is inherent in military operations, nor how to manage it. Moreover, many military commanders are only suited to operational command; they lack the skills of coalition maintenance required for alliance politics, including the 'alliances' within their own forces that have become increasingly important as a result of joint operations. Furthermore, the military mindset is frequently not suited to the ambiguities and difficulties bound up in the term 'realizable goals' when 'realizable' extends to domestic constituencies of support.

Once these points are appreciated, it becomes difficult to decide how best to define the most impressive military leaders. Success would seem to be an obvious factor, but would exclude a defeated figure such as Napoleon. The latter indeed raises a number of key questions, as his campaign failures between 1812 and 1815 were arguably the consequence of his strategic overreach. It is also important to determine where the focus of attention should rest, particularly in terms of strategic motivation: did Julius Caesar conquer Gaul and invade Britain in part to win prestige in the competitive politics of the late Roman Republic, as well as to build up a loyal army for political ends? From this perspective, is he to be seen as a success because he gained power, or a failure because his reliance on force helped lead to the conspiracy that claimed his life?

Such points may seem far removed from the classic understanding of what military leadership entails. However, this political dimension has always been central, playing a crucial role in the framing of strategic goals, the maintenance of support and dealing with the aftermath of war. Thus, Ulysses S. Grant and Eisenhower (pp. 218–25; pp. 258–67) emerge as more successful figures than Cromwell (pp. 142–47) because they gained and exercised power peacefully – although we should recognize that Cromwell also faced very difficult domestic circumstances.

These points need to be borne in mind when considering what constitutes a successful military leader, but they must be complemented by an understanding of the factors that make for success in the field. Such factors include the ability to appreciate problems, to devise workable plans, to understand enemy objectives, to respond rapidly and effectively to events in order to gain the tempo that permits their management, to prepare for successful exploitation and to learn the lessons necessary to secure best practice and improved planning.

These criteria can be expanded, but even in this reduced form they help explain why different readers and scholars propose their own lists and indicate the complexity of the subject. That is also a measure of its importance.

1

The
Ancient
World

◄◄ Alexander the Great (r. 336–323 BC) of Macedonia, here represented on horseback in a detail from the battle of Issus mosaic from the House of the Faun at Pompeii, conquered the Persian empire, an astonishing achievement. He developed the army of his father Philip, and proved a vigorous commander, risking his own life in key battles. Although the army had a core of pikemen, Alexander was primarily a cavalry general, as he showed at his victory at Gaugamela in 331 BC. Alexander's success at siegecraft was shown in 332 at Tyre and Gaza.

▼ Augustus, the first emperor of Rome, established himself as commander-in-chief of a new professional standing army. Although, as emperor, he was not a field commander, he at least partly owed his longevity as leader to his close association with (and supreme command of) a loyal army. Through subordinate commanders he was able to continue the expansion of the empire.

Some of the military leaders to best grasp the imagination of contemporaries and subsequent ages alike lived in the ancient world, notably Alexander the Great (pp. 18–23), Hannibal (pp. 32–35) and Julius Caesar (pp. 36–41). Such leaders were expected to be able to fight, and war was crucial to the careers of many, often requiring their personal involvement in battle. This was true, for example, of Augustus (pp. 42–47), Caesar's adopted son and heir. He campaigned against Mark Antony in 43 BC, defeated Brutus and Cassius at the First and Second Battles of Philippi (42 BC), overcame Antony's brother Lucius Antonius at Perusia (41 BC), campaigned against Sextus Pompey (40–36 BC), pacified Dalmatia, Illyria and Pannonia

(34 BC), took a personal command role in Antony's defeat at Actium (31 BC), and invaded Egypt (30 BC). Thus, the possibility of delegation did not preclude a direct role.

For some rulers, the available information is less plentiful, but it is apparent that both Chandragupta (pp. 24–25) and Shi Huangdi (pp. 26–31) were state builders for whom conflict was crucial. It was necessary to be forceful against domestic opponents, but even more so in the face of an inherently volatile political situation. The threat posed by nomadic or less settled peoples was particularly acute, as they were able to operate very effectively and were less ready to respect borders. Cyrus the Great of Persia (pp. 16–17), who had considerable success in conquering settled states, was killed by the nomadic Massagetae when he campaigned in Central Asia in 529 BC.

Ancient world leaders had to be able to mould possibilities and circumstances to their own design. Those we know most about did so in the context of state power, such as the Roman empire, chiefly because the records of their activities survive best (certainly in comparison with nomadic leaders). In addition, the opportunities available to them, as heads of well-developed military systems, were greater. The Roman ability to create and maintain records was such that we also know a reasonable amount (albeit from the Roman viewpoint) about their opponents, such as Hannibal (pp. 32–35) and also Julius Caesar's rival in Gaul, Vercingetorix (p. 38).

Leaders tended to take existing military systems and push them further. Thus, Alexander built on the foundations laid by his father Philip (p. 19), while Belisarius (pp. 52–53) indicated the potential of the Byzantine development of the later-Roman army. The Byzantine recapture of North Africa, Italy and the south coast of Spain revealed the range of skills that Belisarius had to master: amphibious capability was a prerequisite, while siegecraft was also necessary, as shown by the capture of Palermo (AD 535) and Ravenna (AD 539). Victory in battle required the ability to gain the initiative and to maintain pressure on the enemy, as demonstrated against the Vandals of North Africa at Tricamerum (AD 533), a struggle decided by Byzantine cavalry charges.

Equally, even highly successful commanders could face serious problems. Hannibal was defeated by the Romans at Zama (202 BC), became an exile from Carthage, and ended up committing suicide. The emperor Augustus had to cope with the crushing defeat of Varus in the Teutoburg Forest (AD 9), and Trajan (pp. 48–51), having overcome Parthian resistance and advanced to the Persian Gulf in AD 116, faced serious revolts and southern Mesopotamia, part of modern Iraq, was lost the following year. This was a reminder that all empires were restricted by their own limits, and that perseverance, endurance and success could only achieve so much in the face of determined opponents and pressing events.

▲ A battle between Romans and Gauls represented in high relief on a 2nd-century AD Roman sarcophagus. The fighting effectiveness of the Romans was particularly evident in the range of their operations. Aside from tactical skill and weaponry, they also had superior manpower, resources, willpower and organization, and they mastered a range of physical and military environments.

Cyrus the Great

Founder of the Achaemenid Persian Empire

'Men in the mass, when aflame with courage, are irresistible, but when their hearts fail them, the more numerous they are the worse the panic that seizes them.' CYRUS THE GREAT

A Life in Brief

c. 598 BC
Born in Anshan, son of Cambyses I and Mandane, daughter of Astyages the Mede

c. 578 BC
Marries Cassandane, who bears him a son, Cambyses II

c. 558 BC
Ascends the throne

c. 529 BC
Dies in battle

▼ The so-called 'winged genius' from Gate R at Persepolis. The figure in fact probably represents the 'Fortune' of Cyrus the King, for he wears an Egyptian-Phoenician royal crown, and the Elamite royal robe. It is therefore possible that the facial features of this figure are those of Cyrus himself.

Cyrus the Great was an extraordinary general, and a master of lightning campaigns and of ruses and stratagems. His principal virtue was his skill in handling his men, earning their love and trust. Under his rule, the Persians ceased to be vassals of the Medes, and created a vast empire. History is obscured by contradictory legends, but sufficient material survives to give an outline of the life of this outstanding leader.

The region of Persis lies in southwest Iran. At the beginning of the 1st millennium BC the area lay under the domination of Elam, and the ethnic composition of its population is unknown. Iranian tribes, including the Persians, started to move into the region and fell under the political domination of the Elamites. Their chief city, Susa, fell to Assyria in 646 BC. Henceforward, the eastern Elamite city of Anshan, now located at Tal-e Malyan, became the most important political entity in the area. The inscriptions on the Babylonian Cyrus Cylinder record Cyrus as king in Anshan, son of Cambyses, grandson of Cyrus, and great-grandson of Teispes – all kings in Anshan. It is possible that Cyrus was of Elamite origin.

The Median king Cyaxares (625–585 BC) overthrew Assyria and Anshan came under his control. His successor Astyages (585–550 BC) married his daughter to Cyrus' father Cambyses. Cyrus, however, revolted. The sources are divided as to the exact sequence of events. Cyrus suffered a number of reverses and withdrew to Pasargadae. According to the Cyrus Cylinder, when Astyages invaded Anshan his army mutinied. Cyrus spared the life of his father-in-law – a precedent for his humane treatment of defeated enemies. Cyrus spent the next two years consolidating his position, conquering Hyrcania and Parthia.

In 547 BC Cyrus marched to the River Halys, the border with Lydia, whose king Croesus marched into Cappadocia (central Turkey). An indecisive battle took place at Pteria, with Croesus withdrawing behind a screen of cavalry. Cyrus pressed on towards Sardis, and met Croesus again in a small plain east of the city. Cyrus stationed his camels in front of the line, and the Lydian horses fled at their sight. This may have convinced Cyrus to form an efficient force of cavalry. Croesus retired to Sardis, but after a 14-day siege the supposedly impregnable acropolis was taken, probably in 546/45 BC. Croesus was spared, becoming an adviser to Cyrus. Cyrus treated the Lydians mildly, leaving them governed by a Lydian named Paktyas, who later revolted. Cyrus sent Mazares back with the army to destroy Lydians' military capability. A number of Greek and other cities were also brought back under Persian rule.

Cyrus now conceived a programme of world conquest, and his patchily attested campaigns in eastern Iran probably took place at this point. Bactria, bordering with the nomadic Sakai of Central Asia, was probably subjugated in this period, and Cyropolis was founded to stabilize the border. Further south in Drangiana (modern Helmand, Afghanistan) the army ran out of food and resorted to cannibalism until the Ariaspi provided for them. Further to the north and east, Cyrus destroyed the city of Kapisa, near modern Kabul. The historians Berosus and Herodotus assert that Cyrus possessed all the rest of Asia when he eventually attacked Babylon – perhaps confirmation that Cyrus conquered the eastern Iranian peoples in the late 540s. Syria may also have been conquered in 541 BC before the invasion of Babylonia.

In 540 BC Cyrus moved against Babylon, whose king, Nabonidus, had built another capital at Teima in Arabia, leaving his son Belshazzar in Babylon. Cyrus defeated the desert rulers around Teima, and Nabonidus was forced to leave. Cyrus won a great victory at Opis, and Gubarru, an important Babylonian governor, defected. Cyrus diverted the Euphrates and marched down its riverbed. Without water to drink, the Babylonians surrendered. Cyrus entered Babylon in triumph, probably on 29 October 539 BC.

In 538 BC Cyrus occupied Jerusalem and allowed the Jews to return. Phoenicia and Palestine were probably annexed at this point, and Cyrus adopted the title 'Cyrus, king of the world, great king, mighty king, king of Babylon, king of Sumer and Akkad, king of the four quarters'.

Possibly during the 530s, Cyrus attempted to conquer India. He suffered a disaster crossing the Gedrosian desert, escaping with only seven men. According to Strabo this occurred as Cyrus returned, but Arrian states that the disaster prevented an invasion. Cyrus's failure makes the achievements of Alexander (pp. 18–23) all the more remarkable.

One critical aspect of Cyrus's character was his abundant energy. It was a key factor in the Persian overthrow of Median supremacy, and the creation of the empire. His energy allowed him to operate successively on widely separated fronts, and set the tempo of his operations.

Cyrus managed to win the unswerving loyalty of the Persians, for which his insight into human psychology, preserved in the legends that Xenophon wrote down in his *Cyropaedia*, was indispensable. However, he perhaps deserves most credit for the creation of the Persian cavalry, which became the most effective mounted force in the ancient world.

Before his last campaign, against the Sakai of Central Asia, Cyrus returned to Persia for only the seventh time during his reign. Croesus warned him: 'You think that you are immortal, and that you command an army that is so.' The criticism was timely; in his 70th year, Cyrus was killed in battle fighting the most important of the Sakai tribes, the Massagetae.

▲ **The Cyrus Cylinder.** This is the most detailed historical record of Cyrus's conquest of Babylon in 539 BC. Written in cuneiform, it records how Cyrus restored the worship of the chief Babylonian god Marduk, and how he returned to their true homes other gods and peoples deported by the Late Babylonian kings.

▼ **Brick frieze** from the later king Darius's palace at Susa, showing the famous 10,000 elite Persian infantry known as the 'Immortals'. Two different regiments, each numbering 1,000 men, are shown. The different badges they wear as appliqués on their robes were probably repeated on square regimental standards.

Key Campaigns

The Conquest of Media, 550 BC
Median troops mutiny when they invade Persis. Cyrus spares the life of the Median king Astyages, setting the precedent for the humane governance of the Persian empire in the future.

The Defeat of Lydia, 547–45 BC
A decisive battle takes place in the 'Plain of Cyrus' at Thymbrara near Sardis. Sardis falls after a siege. The life of the Lydian king Croesus is spared.

The Defeat of Babylon, 539 BC
Following an initial victory at Opis on the Tigris, Cyrus captures Babylon by a stratagem, by diverting the river.

Eastern Campaigns, 538–28 BC
In a series of campaigns in the eastern Iranian plateau, Cyrus bends the remaining Iranian nations to Persian rule, although a number of reverses are suffered. An attempt to invade India is unsuccessful.

Defeat in Central Asia, 529 BC
An attempt to stabilize the central Asian border ends in disaster when fighting an enemy with superior mobility and able to shoot from the saddle.

▼ At the death of Cyrus the Persian empire had practically achieved its widest extent, with the exception of Egypt, conquered by his successor Cambyses.

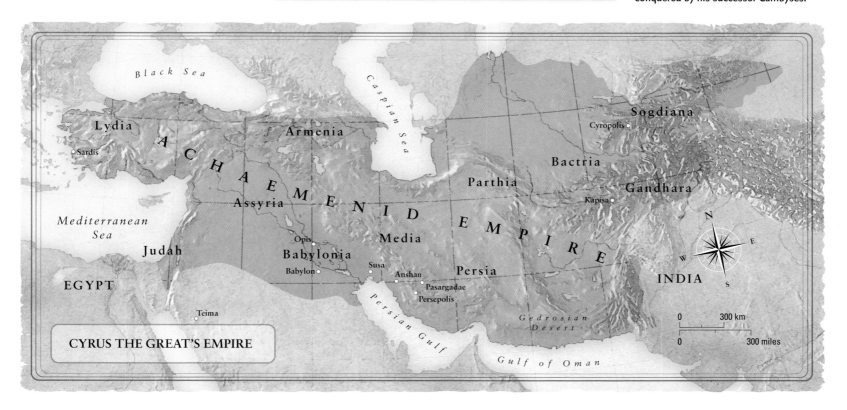

CYRUS THE GREAT'S EMPIRE

Alexander the Great

Macedonian Conqueror of Western Asia

'The end and object of conquest is to avoid doing the same as the conquered.'
ALEXANDER THE GREAT

A Life in Brief

356 BC
Born in the Macedonian capital of Pella

338 BC
Commands the cavalry in his father's army at the battle of Chaeronea

334 BC
As King of Macedon, commands the Macedonian–Greek invasion of Persia

323 BC, June
Dies in Babylon (Iraq)

▶ Alexander's conquest of Asia in the 4th century BC established the largest empire the world had yet seen.

▲ Marble head of Alexander. A copy of the idealized image established by Alexander's favourite sculptor, Lysippus, which showed the king gazing upwards as a sign of his divine connections.

Alexander was the greatest military commander of the ancient world, and arguably of all time. In four years of campaigning (334–330 BC) he defeated the Persian empire through confident leadership, brilliant tactics, and sheer determination. After assuming the Persian crown, he enforced his control over all its eastern territories, and at his death in 323 BC, aged only 33, he was planning further conquests. Although his empire quickly fragmented, his charismatic image of youthful world-conqueror remained to inspire, and frustrate, subsequent leaders.

THE GREEK CRUSADE

At the assassination of his father Philip in 336 BC, Alexander inherited the leadership of the Greek world and of the planned invasion of Persia. First, he had to convince the neighbouring powers that he fully matched Philip's abilities. In 336 and 335 BC lightning campaigns took him to the Danube, deep into the Illyrian mountains, and finally to Thebes in Greece, which was razed to the ground as a ruthless warning to opponents. In 334 BC he crossed the Hellespont to avenge the Persian invasions of Greece in the 5th century BC. Victory over local forces at the River Granicus that year allowed him to take control of the Greek cities of the Aegean coastline, though not always peacefully, since some of the local rulers preferred Persian control. In 333 BC he crossed Asia Minor to Cilicia, while the powerful Persian fleet manoeuvred in the Aegean and threatened Greece. Victory (in person) over the Persian king Darius at the battle of Issus confirmed Alexander's position and permitted his annexation of the Levant during 332 BC, although this involved difficult sieges at Tyre and Gaza. A diversion

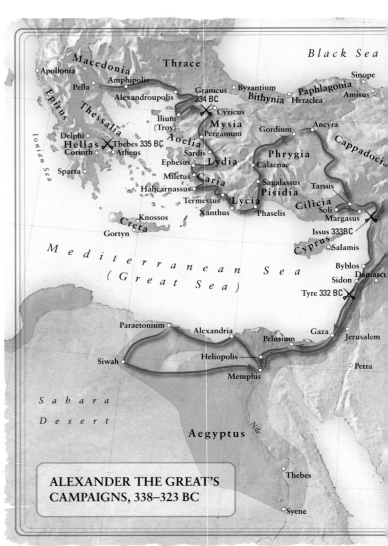

ALEXANDER THE GREAT'S
CAMPAIGNS, 338–323 BC

to Egypt in winter 332/331 BC completed the acquisition of Persia's Mediterranean territories, preparing the way for the decisive march east in 331 BC. Victory at Gaugamela that year gave Alexander control of Persia's capital and central treasuries. Alexander now dismissed his Greek allies, a sign that future conquests were being undertaken in his role of Lord of Asia, and in 330 BC Darius's death, after an exhausting chase across central Iran, left Alexander the acknowledged ruler of a massive empire.

Philip of Macedon (382–336 BC)

In 359 BC Philip became regent of a fractious country dominated by tribal neighbours in the west and threatened by Greek states eager to control its coastal settlements and mineral wealth. Philip, who soon claimed the throne, transformed Macedon into the most powerful state in Greece and was praised, even by enemies, as one of the greatest of men. Key to his success was the creation, through rigorous training, of an effective army, with a core of pike-wielding infantry and a strike force of cavalry. The kingdom maintained a standing army that expanded as Philip extended his authority over neighbouring Thrace and Thessaly. The increased wealth from Thracian mines and the availability of fertile land to bestow on loyal followers consolidated royal control internally. Diplomacy enabled Philip to divide and conquer enemies, or mislead them before striking rapidly, and a network of marriages cemented agreements. Details of his individual battles are scarce, though we know he was not always victorious, ambushed by the Phocian Onomarchus in 352 BC and failing to capture Perinthus in 340 BC. However, at Chaeronea in 338 BC he defeated Athens and Thebes, his major Greek enemies. He organized the Greek world for an invasion of Persia, but was assassinated just before departure. Various objects, including a miniature ivory portrait and a sword, were found in the Tomb of Philip at Vergina.

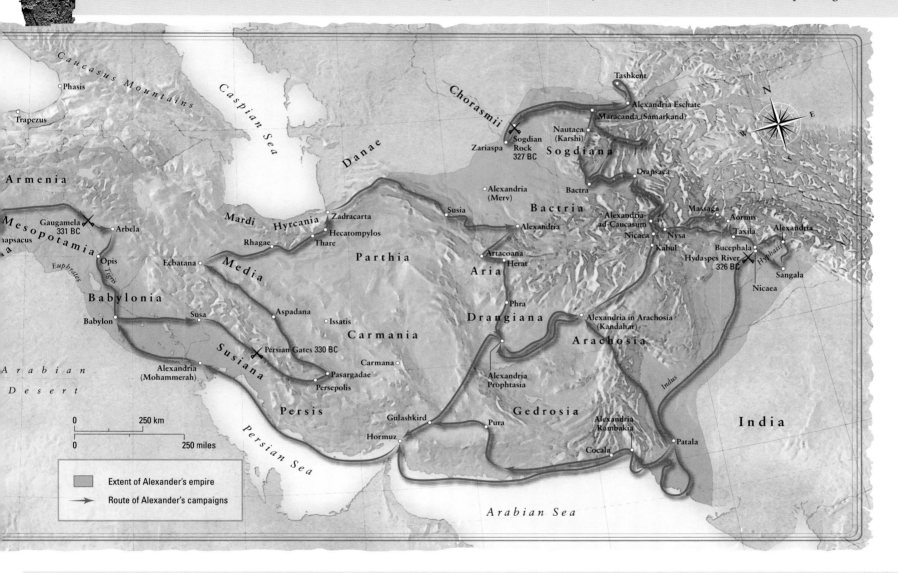

Key Battles

The Battle of Granicus, 334 BC
Alexander is victorious against Memnon of Rhodes, Arsites, and other Persians. He leads a cavalry attack across the riverbed and forces his way up the east bank in a fierce struggle, during which he was almost killed. Thereafter he annihilates the Persian army including its substantial contingent of Greek mercenaries.

The Battle of Issus, 333 BC
Alexander's outnumbered force triumphs over King Darius of Persia. Darius occupies a defensive position on the Pinarus stream behind Alexander, who responds confidently, adjusting his deployment as Persian dispositions became clearer. Alexander then delivers the decisive attack on the right wing at the head of the heavy cavalry. The Persians suffer greatly, Darius flees the battlefield, and his wives are captured.

The Siege of Tyre, 332 BC
Alexander's capture of the island city entails construction of a substantial causeway, neutralization of the superior Tyrian fleet through acquisition of naval allies, deployment of advanced siege engines, and sheer determination to overcome ferocious and inventive defence. The siege lasts six months and demonstrates Alexander's resourcefulness, powers of motivation and commitment to finishing what he has begun.

The Battle of Gaugamela, 331 BC
Some 18 months after Issus, King Darius has assembled troops from the eastern provinces and has chosen a suitable battlefield. Alexander confronts the challenge confidently on the right, dragging the Persians from their chosen positions by a diagonal advance and then charging their fragmenting formation. Fighting on the Macedonian left is fierce, and Alexander abandons pursuit of the fleeing Darius to ensure complete victory.

The Battle of the Hydaspes River, 326 BC
King Porus relies on the swollen river Hydaspes (Jhelum) in India to defend his territory, but Alexander leads a daring night crossing. Not even the unfamiliar threat of elephants, which disconcerts the cavalry, thwarts Alexander and his superior forces from destroying the Indian army.

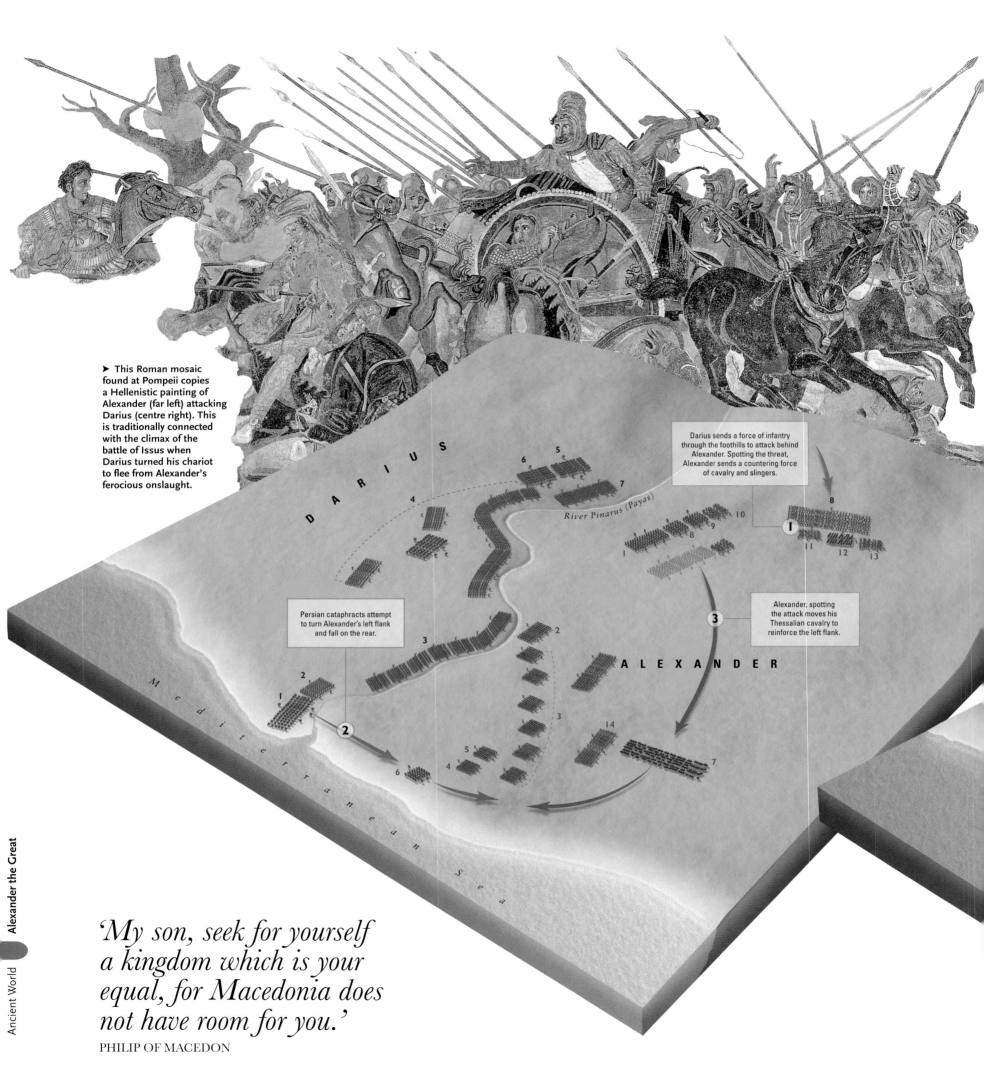

▶ This Roman mosaic found at Pompeii copies a Hellenistic painting of Alexander (far left) attacking Darius (centre right). This is traditionally connected with the climax of the battle of Issus when Darius turned his chariot to flee from Alexander's ferocious onslaught.

DARIUS

River Pinarus (Payas)

Darius sends a force of infantry through the foothills to attack behind Alexander. Spotting the threat, Alexander sends a countering force of cavalry and slingers.

Persian cataphracts attempt to turn Alexander's left flank and fall on the rear.

ALEXANDER

Alexander, spotting the attack moves his Thessalian cavalry to reinforce the left flank.

Mediterranean Sea

'*My son, seek for yourself a kingdom which is your equal, for Macedonia does not have room for you.*'
PHILIP OF MACEDON

Eastern Adventures

Alexander's first task was to reassert central control over the eastern satrapies (or provinces) of Bactria (Afghanistan) as far as the Jaxartes (Syr Darya) and India. Tough campaigning ensued against guerrilla resistance in Bactria (330–328 BC); he reduced mountain strongholds in the Himalayan foothills (327 BC), and quashed substantial opposition in the Indus Valley. Alexander's determination drove his troops on through frostbite in the Hindu Kush and thirst in the Uzbek deserts, and an alliance with the ruler of Taxila and conquest of the neighbouring king Porus provided him with a foothold in the Indus Valley (326 BC). His own ambitions increased with every success, and his new goal was the Ganges Valley and the encircling ocean, which marked the world's end in Greek thought; but two months of monsoon rains, rumours of even mightier armies ahead and thoughts of home led his troops to mutiny and refuse to cross the River Hyphasis (Beas). After some sulking, Alexander had to concede; a fleet was constructed, and he led his army down the Indus. Fierce fighting continued as Alexander crushed opponents through ruthless massacres, but he almost died from a chest wound while assaulting a local fortress. At the mouth of the Indus he sacrificed in the ocean to indicate the terminus of his conquests in this direction (325 BC), and prepared to return to Babylonia. The journey for the main party on land became a nightmare; Alexander had decided to cross the Gedrosian (Makran) desert, partly because this had never been achieved by an army before. Thousands perished, especially among the camp followers, and the fleet's journey along the barren coast fared only slightly better.

Back in Babylon, now the effective capital of the empire, Alexander punished provincial governors for misdeeds during his long absence, and planned fresh campaigns. Arabia was the first goal, to be invaded in mid-323 BC; further plans probably included the circumnavigation of Africa and an attack on Carthage, the western enemy of the Greeks. In June 323 BC, a week of illness, perhaps brought on by heavy drinking and exacerbated by repeated serious injury, ended in Alexander's death at Babylon, opening a protracted struggle to control his inheritance.

The Battle of Issus, 333 BC	
Macedonians	Persians
Alexander the Great	**Darius III**
25,000 infantry, 5,000 cavalry	60,000 infantry, 10,000 cavalry
Casualties: c. 500–1,200	Casualties: c. 45,000

▲▼ At the battle of Issus Alexander and Darius confronted each other across the Pinarus. Some detail is known of the complex structure of the two armies: the Macedonian army (shown in red) consisted of (1) companion cavalry; (2) hypaspists (shield-bearing infantry); (3) Macedonian phalanx; (4) Cretan archers; (5) Thracian javelinmen; (6) allied Greek cavalry; (7) Thessalian cavalry; (8) *prodromoi* (light cavalry); (9) Paeonian cavalry; (10) Macedonian archers; (11) Agrianian javelin-men; (12) 300 cavalry; (13) some of the Macedonian archers (ex 10); and (14) Greek mercenary infantry. The Persians (in blue) consisted of (1) Persian cataphracts (armoured cavalry); (2) slingers and archers; (3) Greek mercenary infantry; (4) reserves; (5) Hyrcanian and Median cavalry; (6) Persian cavalry; (7) javelinmen and slingers; (8) detached infantry.

Alexander's cavalry push back the Persians under cover from archers and infantry. The Companions then break through the dispersing Persians and wheel round to Darius's centre.

Alexander reorganizes his right flank by bringing up the *prodromoi*, Paeorians, and Macedonian archers.

Alexander's force holds off the flank threat and some units regroup elsewhere.

The Persian cataphracts begin to break up as they attempt to fall on the Macedonian rear. The Thessalian cavalry then strike their flank, putting the Persians to flight.

The Macedonian phalanx advances across the Pinarus and the Persians are enveloped. Darius himself flees the field.

DARIUS

ALEXANDER

River Pinarus (Payas)

> *'What great or noble success could we have achieved, if we had sat at home in Macedonia and thought it enough to guard our homeland without effort?'*
>
> ALEXANDER THE GREAT

The Battle of the Hydaspes River, 326 BC	
Macedonians, Greek, Persian and Indian allies	Hydaspes (Punjabi Indian Kingdom)
Alexander the Great	**Porus**
6,000 infantry, 5,000 cavalry	20,000 infantry, 2,500 cavalry, 60 chariots, 50 war elephants
Casualties: 900 infantry, 300 cavalry	Casualties: Almost all killed or captured

SUCCESS, SELF IMAGE, AND A LASTING LEGACY

There is no single key to Alexander's extraordinary successes, but the experienced officers and disciplined army that he inherited from Philip were crucial. Both groups, however, needed to accept Alexander's leadership. The soldiers were easier, since youthful charisma, shared campaigning, victories and booty secured their devotion. Alexander's early years witnessed a competition for authority and glory with the powerful Parmenio family; this only ended with the executions in 330 BC of Parmenio and his son Philotas, respectively second and third in the military hierarchy. The army initially fought as it had under Philip, with the cavalry as the key offensive element and the infantry phalanx as the holding unit. The only significant addition was the appearance of stone-throwing catapults at Halicarnassus in 334 BC. Torsion artillery had

evolved rapidly during the 4th century BC; Philip had failed to reduce Perinthus (in Thrace, Greece), whereas Alexander captured even the toughest fortifications, such as Tyre and Gaza. After Gaugamela there began a gradual but radical change in the composition of the army with the progressive incorporation of non-European elements. This process started in the cavalry, where eastern elites could be assimilated, but by 324 BC Alexander was restructuring the phalanx so that Macedonian pikemen were brigaded with oriental missile troops.

Alexander was driven by a Homeric desire for glory – the *Iliad* was his favourite book – and he could not resist a challenge. First, he had to outdo his father, but this family rivalry soon incorporated remote ancestors:

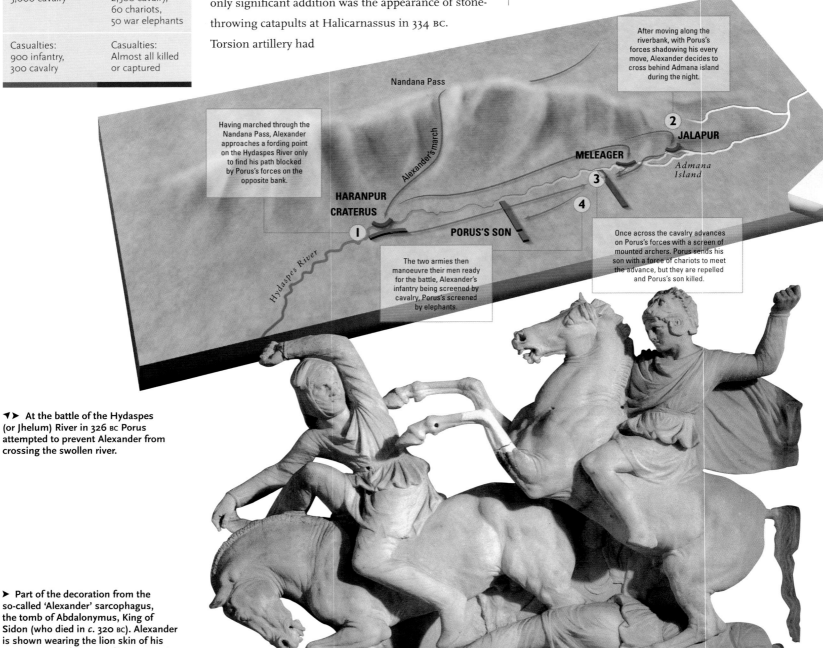

Having marched through the Nandana Pass, Alexander approaches a fording point on the Hydaspes River only to find his path blocked by Porus's forces on the opposite bank.

After moving along the riverbank, with Porus's forces shadowing his every move, Alexander decides to cross behind Admana island during the night.

The two armies then manoeuvre their men ready for the battle, Alexander's infantry being screened by cavalry, Porus's screened by elephants.

Once across the cavalry advances on Porus's forces with a screen of mounted archers. Porus sends his son with a force of chariots to meet the advance, but they are repelled and Porus's son killed.

Nandana Pass

JALAPUR

Admana Island

MELEAGER

HARANPUR
CRATERUS

PORUS'S SON

Hydaspes River

Alexander's march

◄► At the battle of the Hydaspes (or Jhelum) River in 326 BC Porus attempted to prevent Alexander from crossing the swollen river.

► Part of the decoration from the so-called 'Alexander' sarcophagus, the tomb of Abdalonymus, King of Sidon (who died in c. 320 BC). Alexander is shown wearing the lion skin of his ancestor Heracles, trampling on Persian corpses and about to spear another rider.

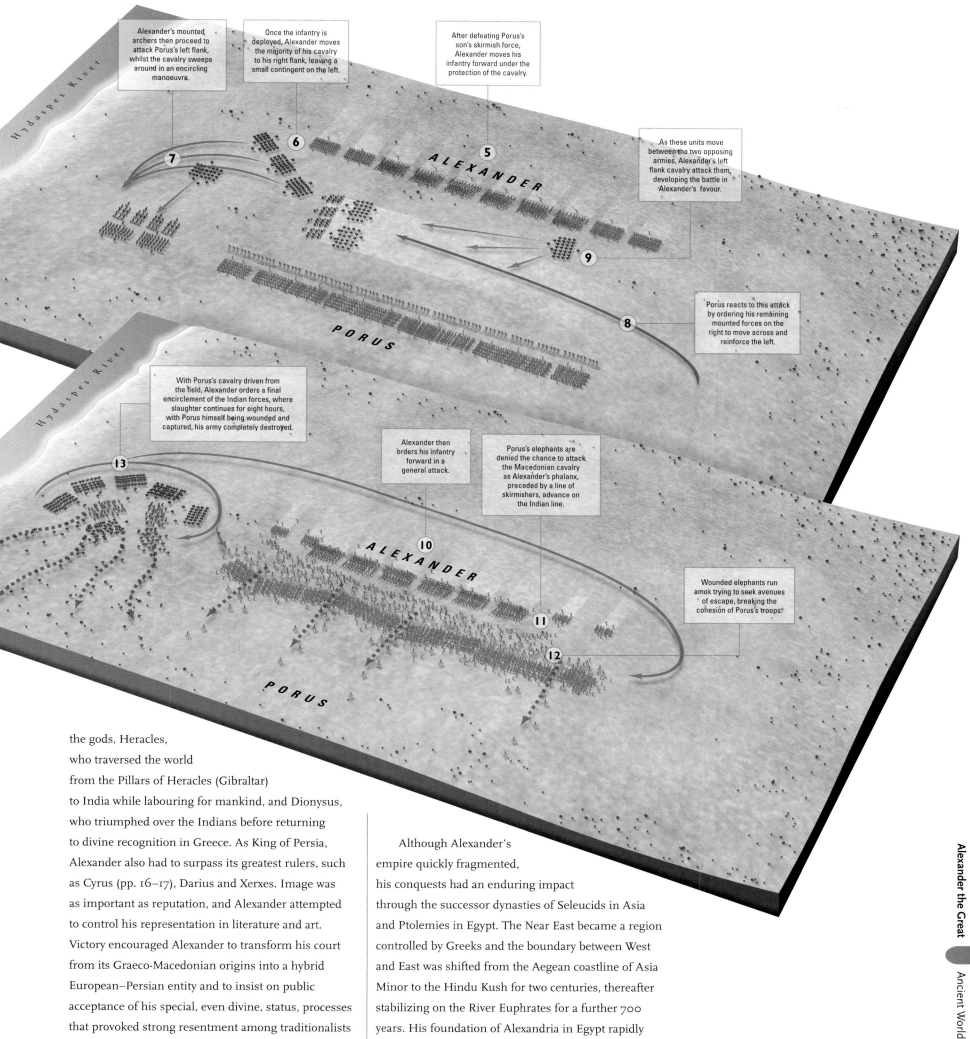

Alexander's mounted archers then proceed to attack Porus's left flank, whilst the cavalry sweeps around in an encircling manoeuvre.

Once the infantry is deployed, Alexander moves the majority of his cavalry to his right flank, leaving a small contingent on the left.

After defeating Porus's son's skirmish force, Alexander moves his infantry forward under the protection of the cavalry.

As these units move between the two opposing armies, Alexander's left flank cavalry attack them, developing the battle in Alexander's favour.

Porus reacts to this attack by ordering his remaining mounted forces on the right to move across and reinforce the left.

With Porus's cavalry driven from the field, Alexander orders a final encirclement of the Indian forces, where slaughter continues for eight hours, with Porus himself being wounded and captured, his army completely destroyed.

Alexander then orders his infantry forward in a general attack.

Porus's elephants are denied the chance to attack the Macedonian cavalry as Alexander's phalanx, preceded by a line of skirmishers, advance on the Indian line.

Wounded elephants run amok trying to seek avenues of escape, breaking the cohesion of Porus's troops.

Hydaspes River

ALEXANDER

PORUS

the gods, Heracles, who traversed the world from the Pillars of Heracles (Gibraltar) to India while labouring for mankind, and Dionysus, who triumphed over the Indians before returning to divine recognition in Greece. As King of Persia, Alexander also had to surpass its greatest rulers, such as Cyrus (pp. 16–17), Darius and Xerxes. Image was as important as reputation, and Alexander attempted to control his representation in literature and art. Victory encouraged Alexander to transform his court from its Graeco-Macedonian origins into a hybrid European–Persian entity and to insist on public acceptance of his special, even divine, status, processes that provoked strong resentment among traditionalists and occasioned plots against his life.

Although Alexander's empire quickly fragmented, his conquests had an enduring impact through the successor dynasties of Seleucids in Asia and Ptolemies in Egypt. The Near East became a region controlled by Greeks and the boundary between West and East was shifted from the Aegean coastline of Asia Minor to the Hindu Kush for two centuries, thereafter stabilizing on the River Euphrates for a further 700 years. His foundation of Alexandria in Egypt rapidly emerged as one of the world's great cities.

Chandragupta

Creator of the Mauryan Empire in India

'The conqueror shall think of the circle of states as a wheel – himself as the hub and his allies, drawn to him by the spokes though separated by intervening territory, as its rim.' THE *ARTHASHASTRA*, 4TH-CENTURY BC TREATISE ON STATECRAFT

A Life in Brief

c. 350 BC
Born (location unknown)

c. 326 BC
Attends Alexander's court

321 BC
Becomes King of Magadha

c. 293 BC
Dies at Sravana Belgola, 50 miles northwest of Mysore, India

In the wake of the invasions of Alexander the Great, a young warrior of humble background named Chandragupta Maurya set about challenging Macedonian power in the Indian subcontinent. Over the course of the next 22 years, using a unique blend of military and political strategy, he went on to create South Asia's largest historical empire, stretching from the Ganges to the Indus.

Chandragupta Maurya was born into a rapidly changing world, as the smaller republics and kingdoms based around the Indus and Ganges rivers were absorbed by their larger neighbours in the mid-4th century BC. The most aggressive of the latter was the kingdom of Magadha, centred on the city of Pataliputra on the Ganges in northeast India. Ruled by the Nanda dynasty, Magadha had annexed much of the lower Ganges and acquired a sufficiently formidable reputation to force Alexander to abandon his eastern campaign in 326 BC.

Although there are conflicting accounts of his birth and training, Plutarch records that the young Chandragupta closely observed Alexander on his Indian campaigns. The impact of Alexander's death in 323 BC created a power vacuum in the Macedonian-held Punjab. Megasthenes – the Seleucid ambassador to Pataliputra – later recorded that Chandragupta

▶ A Mauryan silver punch-mark coin, from the 3rd century BC, displaying elephant and wheel motifs. Such symbols represented royal insignia or were the mark of the guild that struck the coin.

mobilized an alliance of disaffected leaders in the Punjab against their occupiers and established his own authority in their place.

Chandragupta then embarked on a campaign against the Nandas, ably assisted by Kautiliya, a Brahmin and once the Nandas' chief minister. It is said that Chandragupta developed his offensive strategy after observing a mother chiding her son for eating the hottest part of his meal (the centre) first. Chandragupta would thus attack the weaker, outer towns before drawing the Nanda king into a disastrous series of engagements. Following the murder of Dhana Nanda in *c.* 321 BC, he entered Pataliputra as first king of the Mauryan dynasty.

Expanding the territories of Magadha westwards into Seleucid lands and southwards into the Deccan, Chandragupta's campaigns were reliant on the mass of his standing army, which Megasthenes estimated to be 600,000 infantry, 30,000 cavalry and 9,000 elephants. Chandragupta's tax regime allowed supplements of mercenaries and allies to be rapidly raised. His forces were trained to respond to separate calls for use, at differing places and times. Chandragupta augmented traditional methods of war with diplomacy, propaganda, treachery and even assassination.

In 305 BC Seleucus Nicator, Alexander the Great's leading successor, attempted to recapture the lost provinces of the east, but failed to defeat Chandragupta. Seleucus was forced to cede four provinces to him, and perhaps even a Seleucid bride. Eight years later, Chandragupta abdicated and became a Jain ascetic, renouncing all worldly goods for the remainder of his days.

Key Campaigns

The Reconquest of Macedonian India, c. 323 BC
Chandragupta leads a confederacy against Macedonian control of the Punjab, overthrowing the governing satraps.

The Conquest of the Nanda Empire, c. 323–321 BC
Chandragupta leads a confederacy against Magadha. After four years of fighting 'from the edges to the centre', he defeats the Nanda army and has Dhana Nanda assassinated.

War against Seleucus Nicator, 305 BC
Seleucus Nicator invades Chandragupta's northwestern territories, but fails to defeat him. Chandragupta receives the provinces of Arachosia, Gedrosia, Paropamisadae and, perhaps, Aria in exchange for war elephants.

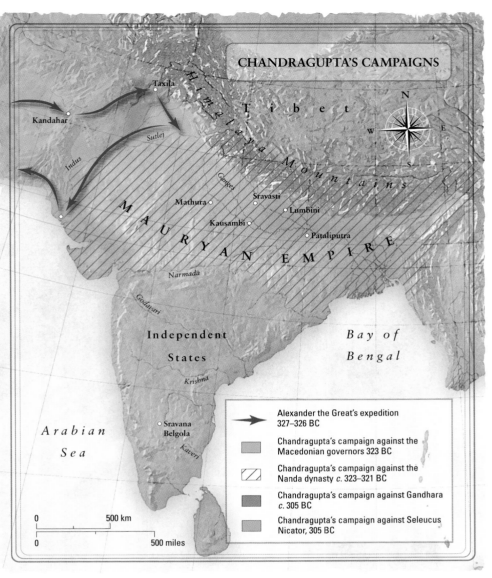

CHANDRAGUPTA'S CAMPAIGNS

Taxila
Kandahar
Tibet
Himalaya Mountains
Indus
Sutlej
Ganges
Mathura
Sravasti
Lumbini
MAURYAN EMPIRE
Kausambi
Pataliputra
Narmada
Godavari
Independent States
Bay of Bengal
Krishna
Arabian Sea
Sravana Belgola
Kaveri

Alexander the Great's expedition 327–326 BC

Chandragupta's campaign against the Macedonian governors 323 BC

Chandragupta's campaign against the Nanda dynasty c. 323–321 BC

Chandragupta's campaign against Gandhara c. 305 BC

Chandragupta's campaign against Seleucus Nicator, 305 BC

0   500 km
0   500 miles

▶ The remains of a timber rampart in what was Pataliputra, which lay at the heart of the Mauryan empire.

▲ Chandragupta greatly expanded his empire in the late 4th century BC.
▼ Detail of a Mauryan chariot from a relief sculpture on a torana – or gateway – at the Great Stupa of Sanchi, India.

Shi Huangdi

First Emperor of China

'Our growing might shook the four corners of the earth and brought down the six princes; we then unified the country, uprooted evil, and put an end to war.' SHI HUANGDI

A Life in Brief

259 BC
Born in Handan (Zhao)

246 BC
Ascends the throne of Qin

238 BC
Assumes full control of government

230–221 BC
Conquers the six independent kingdoms ruling over China, creating a unified country

210 BC
Dies, in Shaqiu prefecture

▶ **No contemporary likenesses exist of Shi Huangdi. This image is characteristic, however, of later depictions.**

Shi Huangdi (Chinese for 'First Emperor' – his birth name was Ying Zheng) ruled the Chinese state of Qin between 246 and 221 BC, before unifying China through conquest. The empire he founded would endure, in one form or another, until AD 1912. Although he never commanded his armies on campaign or on the field of battle, he was the strategic architect of Qin's triumph over its rival powers.

Scion of the Qin royal line, Zheng was born into the brutal Warring States period (403–221 BC). The numerous states that made up ancient China had been in competition for decades, constantly reshaping the political landscape. As the larger states gobbled up the smaller ones and sought to increase their power and resources, armed conflict developed on a much greater scale. The new armies formed were based on a professional core. They featured shock (or heavy) infantry, archers (equipped with the traditional Asian reflex bow), and crossbowmen (a critical development). These armies were overwhelmingly infantry based, with cavalry and chariots playing minor roles, and those sent out on campaign might number 100,000 or more. Higher figures are given in contemporary sources, though these appear exaggerated.

By *c.* 250 BC seven states were vying for supremacy, but none had gone further in refashioning its institutions, acquiring more resources and building up its army than the state of Qin. Based in the Wei River Valley (its capital lay near modern Xi'an), Qin had spent the preceding century expanding to the north against nomadic tribes, to the south against the state of Chu, and to the southwest into the northern part of modern Sichuan. This last acquisition was particularly important in providing Qin with additional agricultural products, raw materials and manpower. Upon Zheng's accession to king in 246 BC, Qin was unquestionably the most powerful state and the likeliest candidate to achieve unification. Yet conditions were not propitious for the immediate execution of such an ambitious programme. Although Qin had benefited from stability under the long reigns of recent rulers, Zheng was the third to ascend the throne within a five-year period. Moreover, as a youth of 14, he was obliged to accept a regent, who handled the reins of government until 238 BC.

By this juncture, strategy, in practice if not in theory, had had a long history in China, dating back centuries to when there were many more, individually weaker states. Strategy revolved primarily around ideas of balance of power. Amid constant diplomatic manoeuvring, alliances were made and then broken as each state pursued its own interests. During the first half of the 3rd century BC, however, a change occurred, no doubt related to the higher stakes now in play among the much larger states. A new objective became destruction of the enemy in the Clausewitzian sense, rather than the simple occupation of territory or manoeuvring for better position; contemporary sources record the mass slaughter of prisoners at this point. There was also a more systematic effort to absorb and to integrate newly acquired territories into one's own,

rather than treating them as bargaining chips. In Qin, specifically, there was a shift from a broad divide-and-conquer kind of strategy to one formulated as 'ally with those distant, attack those nearby'. This appears to have been the basic strategic line pursued by King Zheng down to final victory in 221 BC.

While sporadic warfare took place from the beginning of his reign, the king began a series of offensives in the mid-230s against the northern state of Zhao, perhaps the most militarily potent of the other six states. Victories are recorded in 236 and 234 BC, but reverses followed in 233 and 232 BC, one of which even cost the life of the Qin field commander. There was a redirection of effort to the immediate east in 230 BC against Han,

Key Campaigns

The Conquest of Zhao, 236–222 BC
Zheng's strategy of reducing this northern state first is frustrated by stout resistance. In 229 BC, the Qin general Wang Jian invades Zhao, capturing King Youmiu the following year. Prince Jia leads the last Zhao forces against the Qin at the battle of Dai in 222 BC, where final resistance to Qin rule is crushed.

The Conquest of Han, 230 BC
Qin's strategic position is improved by its seizure of this centrally located state.

The Conquest of Qi, 221 BC
The last and most easterly lying of the six states is reduced by Qin, leading to the unification of China.

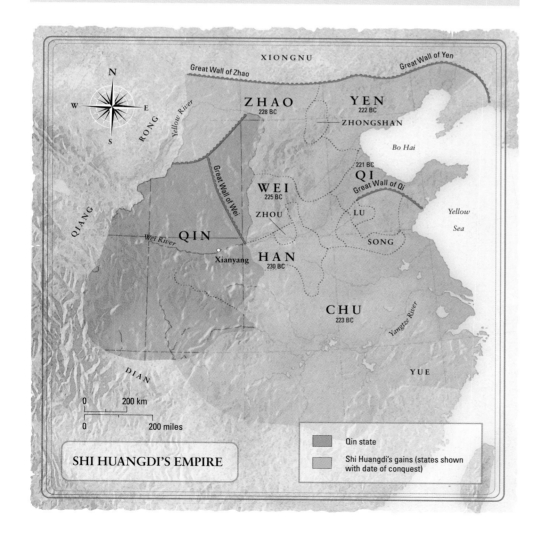

SHI HUANGDI'S EMPIRE

| | Qin state |
| | Shi Huangdi's gains (states shown with date of conquest) |

◄▲▼ The stone helmet (copying a bronze original) is one of a huge number to be excavated from Shi Huangdi's tomb. The wire that bound the stone plates together has mostly decayed, leaving a jumbled mass of plates for the archaeologist to piece back together. Also shown are various bronze weapons, including (clockwise from above) a halberd, spearhead, small spearheads and a sword.

◄ Between 230 and 221 BC, Shi Huangdi conquered six neighbouring states and a number of smaller territories to create the unified Qin empire.

resulting in a quick conquest and the death of this state. Its central position no doubt opened up additional options to Qin. But in 229 BC King Zheng ordered a resumption of attacks against Zhao that, evidently after serious fighting, led to complete success the following year. The state of Wei, now boxed in by Qin territories on three sides, was doomed but remained independent (at its neighbour's pleasure) until 225 BC. To the southeast, Chu was still a formidable enemy, as it demonstrated in the major defeat inflicted on a Qin army in 224 BC. But by the next year it too had succumbed. The two surviving states of Yen and Qi, though located furthest from the Qin homeland, posed few problems and were conquered and absorbed in 222 and 221 BC respectively.

Remarkably, after centuries of division and contention, Qin had achieved the conquest of all its rivals within barely a decade. The military means employed – primarily a well-equipped, well-trained and large-scale infantry – had been developed over the past century and before. But the sure hand of King Zheng, now assuming the title of First Emperor (Shi Huangdi), and his ability to manage his generals were essential as well. As emperor, one of his first orders of business was external security. He dispatched one of his most able generals and a large army to the northern frontier to counter the nomadic Xiongnu tribes. Having enjoyed considerable success, his forces, supported by large peasant levees, were then ordered to construct a physical barrier demarcating the limits of Chinese settlement and control – the precursor of the Great Wall. While parts of this 1,500-mile barrier were new, the remainder actually comprised walls built previously by the individual northern states. In the creation of the first comprehensive static defence system in China, Shi Huangdi left an impressive mark.

Following his death in 210 BC, Shi Huangdi's successor could not preserve his legacy and the empire all but collapsed within four years. In 1974 Shi Huangdi's remarkable tomb was discovered outside Xi'an, containing over 8,000 terracotta figures – a unique source of information on his army. His career bears some resemblance to that of another great conqueror and empire builder, Alexander the Great (pp. 18–23). Both men inherited kingdoms long regarded as backward, but which had become cohesive and powerful; both were heir to potent, modern armies; and each ascended his throne amid expectations of conquest and expansion. Although Alexander has received infinitely better treatment from subsequent historians than Shi Huangdi, they both changed history in dramatic fashion.

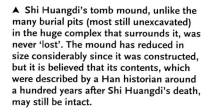

▲ Shi Huangdi's tomb mound, unlike the many burial pits (most still unexcavated) in the huge complex that surrounds it, was never 'lost'. The mound has reduced in size considerably since it was constructed, but it is believed that its contents, which were described by a Han historian around a hundred years after Shi Huangdi's death, may still be intact.

◄▲ Each of the more than 8,000 figures that make up the terracotta army was mass-produced using a selection of moulds for different body parts. The moulded parts were then joined to form a slightly larger than life-sized figure and sculpted with individual facial features, hairstyles, beards, accoutrements, folds in clothing and so on. A variety of ranks and types of soldier is represented: the figures below are, from left to right, a standing archer, a kneeling archer, a cavalryman with mount, a general, and a chariot driver. Other types of figure include officials, musicians, acrobats and stable boys.

▶▶ A small section of one of the terracotta army burial pits, with the figures standing as they were found. Behind the ranks of soldiers lie collapsed horses and chariots.

Hannibal

Daring Carthaginian General who Challenged the Might of Rome

'I am that Hannibal who after the battle of Cannae became master of almost the whole of Italy.' HANNIBAL

A Life in Brief

247 BC
Born, probably in Carthage

221–218 BC
Commander in Spain

218–202 BC
Supreme commander of Carthaginian armies against Rome

201–195 BC
Peacetime politician in Carthage, following the treaty with Rome

195–183 BC
Exiled from Carthage, mercenary commander in the eastern Mediterranean

183 BC
Commits suicide at Libyssa (modern Gebze, Turkey)

▲ This silver double shekel coin in the British Museum depicts a Carthaginian war elephant with rider. It was probably minted by the Barcids (Hannibal's family) in Spain during the period of Punic rule there, and formed part of a coin-hoard found in Valencia.

◄ This marble bust purportedly depicting Hannibal came from Capua, a city south of Rome that defected to the Carthaginians and was retaken by the Romans after a lengthy siege. The sculpture is now in the Museo Nazionale in Naples.

Hannibal was the principal Carthaginian military commander in the Second Punic War against Rome (218–202 BC). He showed genius in welding together diverse elements into an effective fighting force, exploiting the strengths and weaknesses of his heterogeneous army. He was a battlefield commander of rare ability, winning several apparently decisive victories over the Romans and their allies, but ultimately he was unable to conquer them or even defend his own homeland.

The Punic Wars of the 3rd and 2nd centuries BC saw over a hundred years of conflict between the two great powers of the central and western Mediterranean. Rome had grown from a central Italian city-state to control Italy. Carthage (located in the suburbs of the modern Tunisian capital, Tunis) was originally a colony of the Phoenician (Latin, *punicus*) city of Tyre (Lebanon). The First Punic War (264–241 BC) was a Roman victory, largely fought over Sicily, in which Rome developed its naval power. The Second Punic War was a struggle for Italy and eventually the Carthaginian heartland in Africa, dominated by the personality and generalship of Hannibal. The Third Punic War (146 BC) saw the destruction of Carthage.

Hannibal was a member of the Barca family, part of the ruling elite of Carthage. Much of Hannibal's early life was spent in Spain, where first his father Hamilcar, then his brother-in-law Hasdrubal, commanded armies engaged in the expansion of the Punic empire. On Hasdrubal's death in 221 BC, Hannibal took command of the army in Spain. A treaty with Rome allowed the Carthaginians to control Spain south of the River Ebro, but when Hannibal laid siege to Saguntum, south of the river, the Romans extended

their protection to the town, precipitating the Second Punic War. The Romans controlled the sea, and so Hannibal led his army overland from Spain, through southern Gaul (France) and across the Alps into northern Italy. This unexpectedly bold move typifies Hannibal's operational style with swift and sudden movement, often through difficult terrain, to get the better of his opponents.

The army that he led to Italy was diverse and multi-ethnic, including mercenaries and subject peoples. Libyans made up the core of the infantry and fought hand-to-hand, often using captured Roman equipment. Spanish and Gallic infantry also fought at close quarters but were less predictable in their behaviour. Skirmishing infantry included slingers from

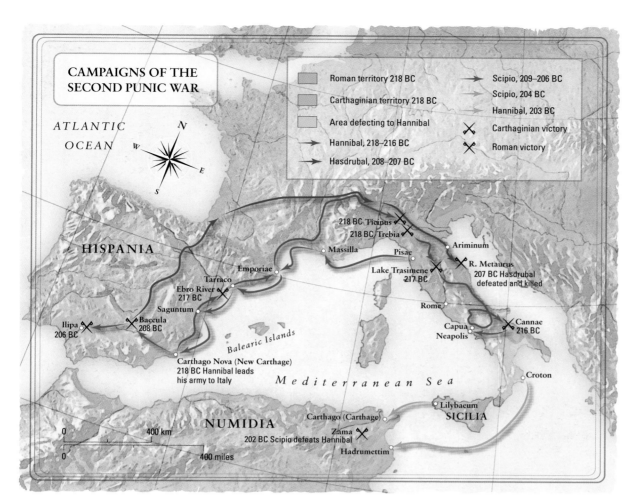

CAMPAIGNS OF THE SECOND PUNIC WAR

Roman territory 218 BC

Carthaginian territory 218 BC

Area defecting to Hannibal

Hannibal, 218–216 BC

Hasdrubal, 208–207 BC

Scipio, 209–206 BC

Scipio, 204 BC

Hannibal, 203 BC

Carthaginian victory

Roman victory

ATLANTIC OCEAN

N
W   E
S

HISPANIA

Massilla

Emporiae

Tarraco

Ebro River
217 BC

Saguntum

Ilipa
206 BC

Baecula
208 BC

Balearic Islands

Carthago Nova (New Carthage)
218 BC Hannibal leads
his army to Italy

218 BC Ticinus
218 BC Trebia

Pisae

Ariminum

R. Metaurus
207 BC Hasdrubal
defeated and killed

Lake Trasimene
217 BC

Rome

Capua
Neapolis

Cannae
216 BC

Croton

Mediterranean Sea

Lilybaeum
SICILIA

NUMIDIA

Carthago (Carthage)

Zama
202 BC Scipio defeats Hannibal

Hadrumetim

0   400 km

0   400 miles

◄ This map shows the decisive campaigns and battles of the Second Punic War. Starting in Spain, Hannibal crossed the Alps and won victories at the Ticinus, Trebia, Lake Trasimene and Cannae. However, he was unable to capture Rome itself, and a relieving army, commanded by his brother Hasdrubal, sent from Spain was defeated at the Metaurus. Meanwhile, the Romans struck back at Carthaginian territories in Spain. Ultimately Scipio Africanus attacked the Carthaginian heartland in Africa, forcing Hannibal to return to face defeat at Zama.

► This short-bladed sword, designed more for stabbing with its point rather than cutting with its edge, was found in Spain and is now in the Museo Archeológico Nacional in Madrid. Similar swords were used by Spanish auxiliary troops serving in Hannibal's army, and the design so impressed the Romans that they adopted a version of it called the *gladius hispaniensis* ('Spanish sword').

Key Battles

The Battle of Trebia, December 218 BC
Hannibal defeats a Roman army under the rash consul Tiberius Sempronius Longus, provoking him to attack across the freezing river and employing elephants and an ambush by concealed Numidians to disorder the Roman army.

The Battle of Lake Trasimene, June 217 BC
Hannibal lures a Roman army under the consul Gaius Flaminius into an ambush, trapping it between the lake (in north-central Italy) and his army, and then destroying it.

The Battle of Cannae, August 216 BC
Hannibal defeats a Roman army under the consuls Gaius Varro and Lucius Paullus in Apulia (southeast Italy). Hannibal's Gallic and Spanish troops give way before the Roman attack, drawing the enemy into the centre of Hannibal's formation, where they are encircled by Libyan infantry and Carthaginian cavalry.

The Battle of Zama, October 202 BC
Drawn back to Africa by the Roman threat to Carthage, Hannibal is defeated by Scipio Africanus at Zama (Tunisia). Hannibal's opening massed elephant attack is thwarted by Scipio's deployment. Unusually, the Romans are superior in cavalry, which forces the vanguard of Hannibal's triple-lined infantry back on their own comrades.

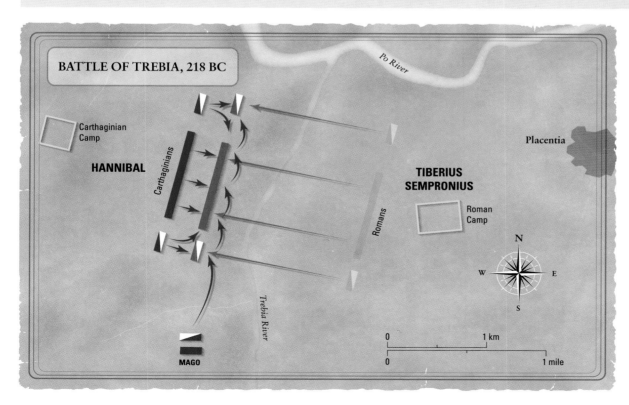

BATTLE OF TREBIA, 218 BC

Po River

Carthaginian Camp

HANNIBAL

Carthaginians

Placentia

TIBERIUS SEMPRONIUS

Romans

Roman Camp

N
W   E
S

Trebia River

MAGO

0   1 km

0   1 mile

◄ The battle of Trebia illustrates Hannibal's genius for forcing his enemies to fight on terms and terrain of his choosing. Having used Numidian skirmishers to provoke the Romans into attacking across a freezing cold river while still hungry, he also set an ambush on his right (under Mago) that attacked and broke the Roman army while engaged with his main force.

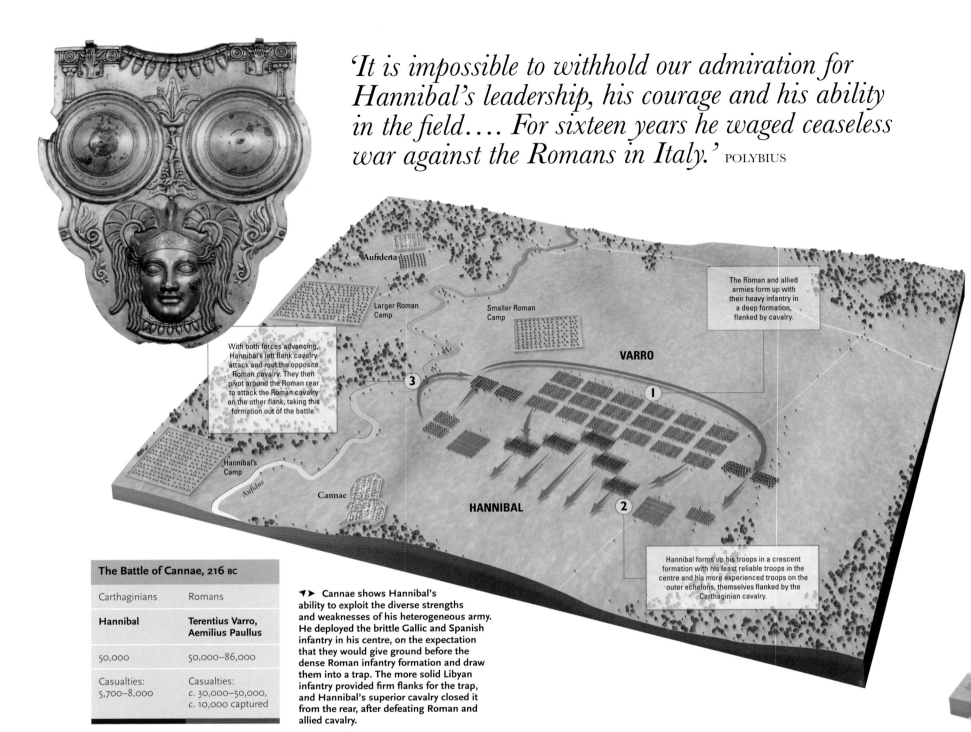

'It is impossible to withhold our admiration for Hannibal's leadership, his courage and his ability in the field…. For sixteen years he waged ceaseless war against the Romans in Italy.' POLYBIUS

With both forces advancing, Hannibal's left flank cavalry attack and rout the opposite Roman cavalry. They then pivot around the Roman rear to attack the Roman cavalry on the other flank, taking this formation out of the battle.

The Roman and allied armies form up with their heavy infantry in a deep formation, flanked by cavalry.

Aufidena

Larger Roman Camp

Smaller Roman Camp

VARRO

3

1

Hannibal's Camp

Aufidus

Cannae

HANNIBAL

2

Hannibal forms up his troops in a crescent formation with his least reliable troops in the centre and his more experienced troops on the outer echelons, themselves flanked by the Carthaginian cavalry.

The Battle of Cannae, 216 BC

Carthaginians	Romans
Hannibal	**Terentius Varro, Aemilius Paullus**
50,000	50,000–86,000
Casualties: 5,700–8,000	Casualties: *c.* 30,000–50,000, *c.* 10,000 captured

◀▶ **Cannae shows Hannibal's ability to exploit the diverse strengths and weaknesses of his heterogeneous army. He deployed the brittle Gallic and Spanish infantry in his centre, on the expectation that they would give ground before the dense Roman infantry formation and draw them into a trap. The more solid Libyan infantry provided firm flanks for the trap, and Hannibal's superior cavalry closed it from the rear, after defeating Roman and allied cavalry.**

▲▲ A bronze breastplate, perhaps Carthaginian and from the time of the Punic Wars, now in the Bardo Museum in Tunis. However, its general appearance, with the disc-shaped pectorals, finds numerous parallels in Italy and other parts of the central and western Mediterranean in the 4th and 3rd centuries BC.

the Balearic Islands and Moorish troops. Cavalry was more important to Carthaginian armies than to the Romans, and comprised Libyans, Gauls, Spaniards and, crucially, Numidian light cavalry. Like many contemporary Mediterranean armies, Hannibal's included war elephants. However, these played a significant role in only two of his battles (Trebia 218 BC and Zama 202 BC) and only one of the beasts survived for long after the crossing of the Alps.

Hannibal skilfully exploited the strengths and weaknesses of his different troops. At Cannae (216 BC) he deployed his army so that the gradual retreat of his relatively weak Spanish and Gallic infantry drew the Romans into his centre, where they were trapped by the more solid Libyan infantry

on the flanks. He employed the scouting abilities of his Numidians to observe enemy movements and ascertain their intentions. Intelligence gathered on enemy commanders enabled him to exploit their rashness and any dissent: at Lake Trasimene (217 BC), he goaded Gaius Flaminius into pursuing him blindly into an ambush, and at Cannae he exploited political and personal conflicts between the two Roman commanders. Such knowledge also meant that he was often able to fight on ground and terms of his own choosing, as at Trebia and Lake Trasimene.

Hannibal's outnumbered army won a series of crushing victories over the Romans (Trebia, Trasimene and Cannae). However, he was unable to win a final decisive victory. The Romans continued to resist and

Scipio Africanus (236–c. 183 BC)

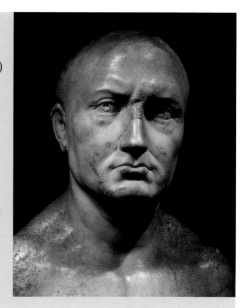

Publius Cornelius Scipio defeated Hannibal at Zama in 202 BC, gaining the victory title 'Africanus' from that battle. A member of an aristocratic Roman family, the young Scipio survived Hannibal's major victories in Italy; after his father was killed fighting the Carthaginians in Spain in 211 BC, he assumed command in his place. He remained there until 205 BC, capturing the major Punic base of New Carthage (modern Cartagena) and winning two important battles at Baecula (208 BC) and Ilipa (206 BC), eventually driving the Carthaginians from Spain. His success was based on rigorous training of his men, and the exploitation of the flexibility of the maniples (sub-units of 60 or 120 men) of the Roman legions on a tactical level.

After holding the consulship in Rome in 205 BC, Scipio raised an army and crossed to Africa in 204 BC. By military and diplomatic means he won the support of Carthage's former Numidian allies, gaining superiority in cavalry for the Romans. At Zama in 202 BC Scipio adapted the arrangement of his maniples to defeat Hannibal's massed elephant attack, used his multiple lines to support and relieve his tired infantry and exploited his cavalry superiority to attack the Carthaginians from behind.

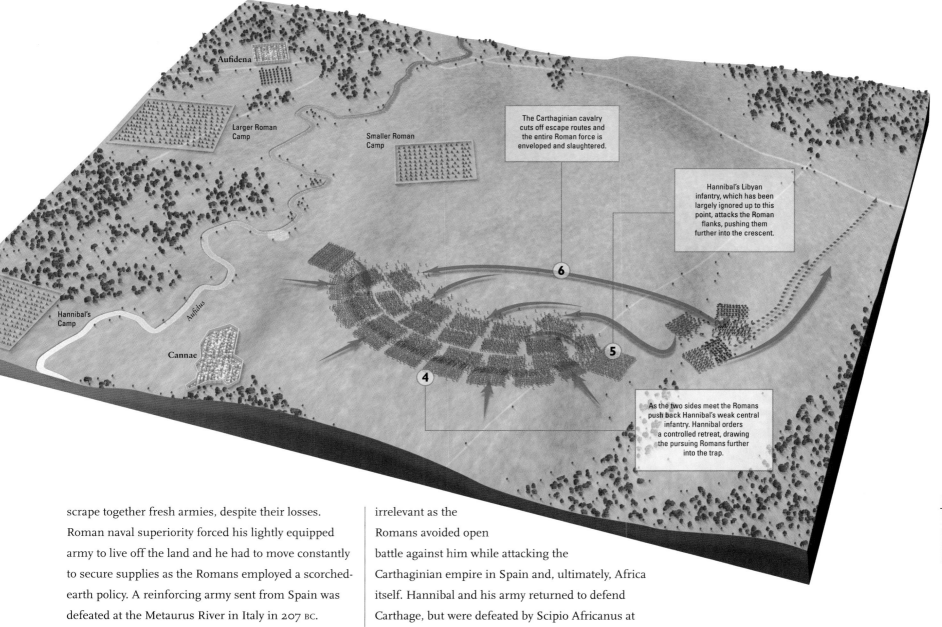

Aufidena

Larger Roman Camp

Smaller Roman Camp

The Carthaginian cavalry cuts off escape routes and the entire Roman force is enveloped and slaughtered.

Hannibal's Libyan infantry, which has been largely ignored up to this point, attacks the Roman flanks, pushing them further into the crescent.

Hannibal's Camp

Aufidus

Cannae

6

5

4

As the two sides meet the Romans push back Hannibal's weak central infantry. Hannibal orders a controlled retreat, drawing the pursuing Romans further into the trap.

scrape together fresh armies, despite their losses. Roman naval superiority forced his lightly equipped army to live off the land and he had to move constantly to secure supplies as the Romans employed a scorched-earth policy. A reinforcing army sent from Spain was defeated at the Metaurus River in Italy in 207 BC. Finally, despite coming within a few miles of Rome, Hannibal lacked the siege equipment to capture the walled city itself. Hannibal's army became increasingly irrelevant as the Romans avoided open battle against him while attacking the Carthaginian empire in Spain and, ultimately, Africa itself. Hannibal and his army returned to defend Carthage, but were defeated by Scipio Africanus at Zama (October 202 BC), where Hannibal's tactics, though innovative (including a massed elephant attack), were unsuccessful.

Julius Caesar

'I came, I saw, I conquered.'

JULIUS CAESAR

A Life in Brief

100 BC, 13 July
Born in Rome

59 BC
Elected to his first consulship

58–49 BC
Commander in Gaul

49–44 BC
Appointed dictator of Rome

44 BC, 15 March
Assassinated in the Senate on
the Ides of March

▶ A marble bust of Julius Caesar, now in the Pio-Clementino Museum in the Vatican. Given his fame as a military commander and the fact that he was adoptive father of Augustus, the first Roman emperor, the image of Julius Caesar was widely reproduced and disseminated after his death as well as during his lifetime.

▶▶ These maps show both Caesar's campaigns in Gaul, Germany and Britain, and the subsequent civil war against his political and military rival Pompey the Great, culminating in the battle of Pharsalus.

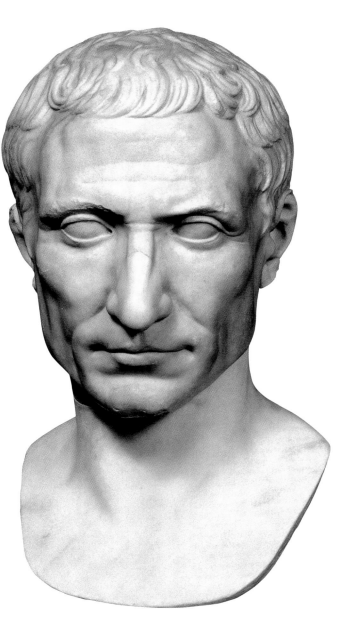

Julius Caesar is the best-known Roman military commander of the late Republican period. His foreign conquests (especially of Gaul) extended the Roman empire and enhanced his own reputation in domestic politics, and his victory over Pompey in civil war gave him complete control over the Roman state. The war commentaries he wrote maintained his reputation as a commander and influenced later commanders and military thinkers.

Military success was one of the qualities required to achieve high political office, and foreign conquest was an important means by which Roman politicians demonstrated their martial ability and won popularity for themselves and their families. Thus, domestic politics drove imperial expansion. During the late Republican period (*c.* 107–31 BC) the common soldier became more loyal to successful commanders than to the state as a whole. Ancient writers blamed this on increasing enlistment of the poor in place of the landed middle class, who previously had formed the core of the army. As the empire expanded, it became impossible for the Senate and magistrates in Rome to exercise close control over armies in distant frontier areas like Syria and Gaul (modern France), and commanders in those areas tended to act independently. The result was the rise of a sequence of great Republican generals (Marius, Sulla, Pompey and Julius Caesar) who used their military reputations and the personal loyalties of their troops to achieve supreme political power in Rome by violent and unconstitutional means, including civil war against their rivals.

Gaius Julius Caesar was born into an old aristocratic Roman family, but adopted a radical stance in his early political career. In 60 BC he formed an informal political alliance (known to modern scholars as the First Triumvirate) with Gnaeus Pompey ('the Great') and Marcus Licinius Crassus. In 59 BC he was made consul, one of the two annually appointed magistrates with supreme political and military authority, and exploited popular political agitation and the threat of violence to achieve his political agenda. One aspect of this was his appointment as governor and military commander in Gaul.

The Romans only controlled part of the south of France ('The Province', hence modern Provence)

Key Battles and Campaigns

The Battle of the Sambre, 57 BC
During Caesar's campaigns against the Belgic tribes in northern Gaul, his army is ambushed in hilly, wooded terrain while setting up camp after crossing the River Sambre. Unable to form a proper battle line, the Roman cavalry and light infantry are routed, but Caesar moves from legion to legion encouraging his men, eventually fighting in the front rank of the XII Legion. A relief force arrives and the Nervii are defeated and forced to surrender.

The Invasion of Britain, 55–54 BC
In the autumn of 55 BC, Caesar takes a small force (two legions plus auxiliaries) across to Britain, landing with difficulty against opposition near Deal (in Kent). A storm prevents his cavalry arriving and wrecks his own fleet. Having returned to Gaul, Caesar launches a five-legion expedition in July 54 BC. The Romans manage to force a crossing of the River Thames and bring the British leader Cassivellaunus to terms before returning to Gaul. However, a permanent Roman presence in Britain will not be established until Claudius's invasion nearly a century later.

The Siege of Alesia, 52 BC
After defeat in open battle, the Gallic rebel leader Vercingetorix and his men are besieged by Caesar and 12 legions in the hilltop fortress of Alesia (in Burgundy). Caesar's men build a double circuit of elaborate and impressive fortifications to hold off any Gallic relief force and to surround Alesia itself. The relieving force arrives and attacks the Romans, but Caesar leads a decisive counterattack as the Gauls are about to break through. The relieving army is defeated, and Vercingetorix surrenders shortly afterwards.

The Battle of Pharsalus, August 48 BC
After his failed siege of Pompey's army at Dyrrhachium (modern Durrës, Albania), Caesar leads his army to Thessaly (Greece) followed by his enemy. The two armies meet just west of the town of Pharsalus. While the main clash takes place in the centre, Pompey's numerically superior cavalry threaten to attack the right flank of Caesar's engaged infantry, but are driven off by an infantry reserve Caesar has kept for this purpose. Caesar then commits the third line of his infantry and routs Pompey's main force.

CAESAR'S CAMPAIGNS IN GAUL, 58–50 BC

55 BC: After British tribes give aid to Gallic rebels, Caesar sends a reconnaissance mission. The following year a full scale expedition defeats Cassivellaunus north of the Thames.

56 BC: After crossing the Rhine Caesar campaigns against Germani.

56 BC: Veneti defeated by Caesar's fleet in a sea battle.

58 BC: Caesar supports allied Aedui and defeats Helvetii migrating west

Approximate site of the defeat of Ariovistus.

English Channel (Oceanus)

MORINI · NERVII · EBURONES · ADUATUCI · BELGAE · REMI · TREVERI · CALATES · Samarobriva (Amiens) · Bratuspantium · VENETI · LEXOVII · BELLOVACI · Durocortorum (Réims) · CORIOSOLITAE · AULERCI · SUESSIONES · PARISII · LINGONES · SENONES · Cenabum (Orleans) · Alesia · SEQUANI · VENETI · CARNUTES · Avaricum (Bourges) · PICTONES · BITURIGES · Bibracte (Mont Beuvray) · AEDUI · Matisco (Macon) · HELVETII · Lemonum (Poitiers) · LEMOVICI · ARVERNI · Uxellodunum · AQUITANI · Tolosa (Toulouse) · Narbo (Narbonne) · Aquae Sextiae (Aix-en-Provence) · Massilia (Marseille) · Antipolis (Antibes)

Sambre 57 BC

51–50 BC

0   100 km
0   100 miles

CAESAR'S CAMPAIGNS, 58–44 BC

Nervii 57 BC · Eburones 54 BC · Agedincum 52 BC · Alesia 52 BC · Avaricum 52 BC · Gallia · Bibracte 58 BC · Transalpina · Gergovia 52 BC · Lugdunum 58 BC · Vindobona · Mediolanum · Aquileia · Verona · Dacia · Olbia · Heraclea · Black Sea (Pontus Euxinus) · Tyras · Tomi · Trapezus · Provincia Romana · Caesar crosses the river Rubicon 49 BC · Salonae · Narona · Sinope · Heraclea Pontica · Narbo · Pisae · Dyrrhachium 48 BC · Byzantium · Nicomedia · Zela 47 BC · Hispania · Ilerda 49 BC · Salamantica · ROME · Italia · Macedonia · Asia · PARTHIAN EMPIRE · Tarraco · Dertosa · Toletum · Palma · Valentia · Puteoli · Neapolis · Brundisium · Tarentum · Thessalonica · Pergamum · Iconium · Tarsus · Munda 45 BC · Corduba · Caralis · Pharsalus 48 BC · Smyrna · Ephesus · Attalea · Side · Antioch · Carteia · Carthago Nova (New Carthage) · Lilybaeum · Corinth · Athenae · Halicarnassus · Syria · MAURETANIA · Catana · Syracusae · Sparta · Rhodes · Salamis · Thapsus 46 BC · Mediterranean Sea (Mare Internum) · Gortyn · EMPIRE · Africa · Cyrene · Cyrenaica · Alexandria 48–47 BC · PTOLEMAIC KINGDOM OF EGYPT · Memphis

0   250 km
0   250 miles

Julius Caesar

Ancient World

The Siege of Alesia, 52 BC	
Romans	Gallic tribes
Julius Caesar	**Vercingetorix**
30,000–60,000	80,000 besieged, 80,000–250,000 relief forces
Casualties: 12,800	Casualties: c. 45,000

➤▲ A three-dimensional reconstruction shows the importance of terrain at the siege of Alesia, with both Alesia itself and Caesar's siege lines located to dominate the high ground. Roman armies were known for their engineering skills, and the Roman siege-works at Alesia are described in some detail by Caesar. The modern reconstruction shows ditches, palisades and towers, supplemented by smaller pits with spikes.

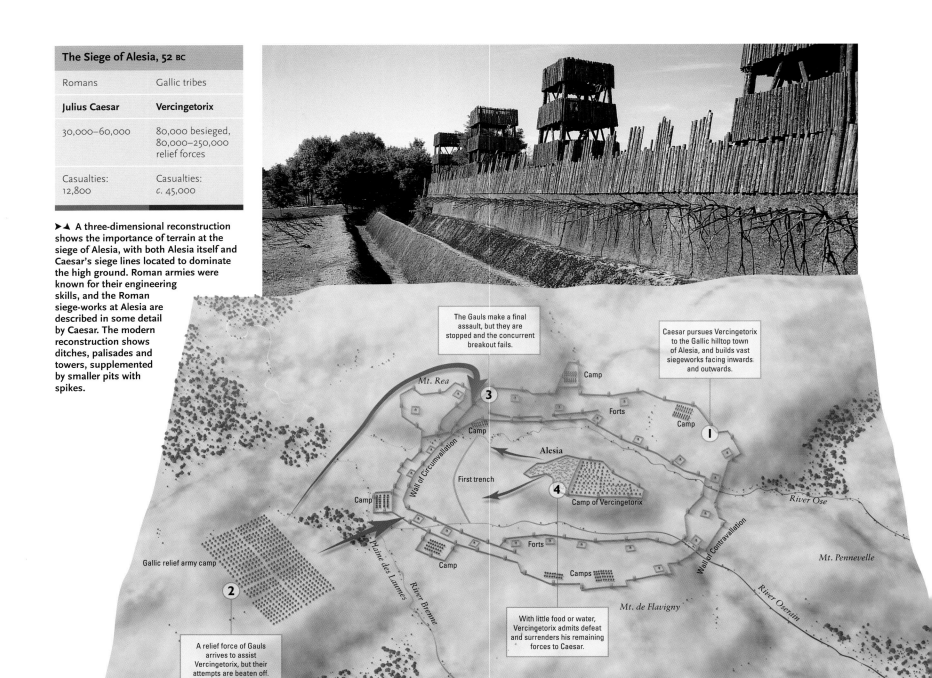

The Gauls make a final assault, but they are stopped and the concurrent breakout fails.

Caesar pursues Vercingetorix to the Gallic hilltop town of Alesia, and builds vast siegeworks facing inwards and outwards.

Mt. Rea

3

Camp

Forts

Camp

1

Alesia

Camp

Wall of Circumvallation

First trench

4

Camp of Vercingetorix

River Ose

Camp

Gallic relief army camp

Plaine des Laumes

Forts

Camp

Wall of Contravallation

Mt. Pennevelle

River Brenne

Camps

2

A relief force of Gauls arrives to assist Vercingetorix, but their attempts are beaten off.

With little food or water, Vercingetorix admits defeat and surrenders his remaining forces to Caesar.

Mt. de Flavigny

River Oserain

Vercingetorix (d. 46 BC)

Vercingetorix was a noble of the Arverni of south-central Gaul (the Auvergne). Caesar's account suggests he usurped power to become king among his people after his calls for revolt against the Romans were opposed by the existing ruling class. Caesar characterizes Vercingetorix as a commander of boundless energy, and the success with which he unified Gallic resistance suggests he was a skilled (but ruthless) diplomat. Vercingetorix's rebellion met with mixed success at first, with the loss of the important centre of Avaricum (Bourges) after a siege, while a later, rash, Roman assault on the

mountain fortress of Gergovia was defeated.

Gallic armies were strong in cavalry, and on a number of occasions Caesar depicts Vercingetorix leading a predominantly mounted force in the field. One such force was defeated in battle (in modern Burgundy) in the late summer of 52 BC, leading Vercingetorix to withdraw to the nearby hilltop

stronghold of Alesia, where Caesar's 60,000-strong army besieged him and his 80,000-strong force. Despite the arrival of a relief force, Vercingetorix was forced to surrender. He was imprisoned in Rome until 46 BC, when he was displayed in the triumphal procession to celebrate Caesar's Gallic victory, and then subsequently executed.

These two gold coins from Gaul, both depicting Vercingetorix, show that far from being the primitive place imagined by some, Gaul at the time of Caesar's conquest was increasingly sophisticated in political and economic terms.

but Caesar used this as a springboard for expansion. From 58 to 49 BC, he engaged in a grand programme of conquest that enlarged the Roman empire, gained him a popular reputation as a successful general and increased not only his army's fighting efficiency but also its loyalty to Caesar himself. Over his nine years in Gaul, Caesar not only conquered all of modern France and Belgium up to the Rhine, but also suppressed a number of revolts, local and widespread, defeated migrations and invasions by Gauls and Germans, crossed the Rhine twice on punitive campaigns and launched two expeditions to Britain. The culmination of his campaigning was Caesar's defeat of the uprising led by Vercingetorix in 52 BC. Having besieged the main rebel force in the fortress of Alesia, Caesar defeated a relieving army and a break-out attempt, compelling Vercingetorix to surrender.

During the last years of the Gallic wars, Caesar became estranged from his former political ally, Pompey, who now allied himself to conservative members of the traditional ruling class hostile to Caesar. When in 49 BC they called for Caesar to be recalled and disarmed, he led his army across the River Rubicon in northern Italy (the southern boundary of his command) and instigated civil war, relying on the loyalty and fighting qualities that he had forged in his army in Gaul. Caesar's typically bold advance into Italy caught his opponents off guard and forced them to abandon first Rome, then Italy. In 48 BC Caesar crossed into Greece after Pompey, and, after near defeat at Dyrrhachium on the west coast, ultimately defeated Pompey at Pharsalus in Thessaly. With typical energy and speed Caesar pursued Pompey

to Alexandria in Egypt, but Pompey was murdered by agents of the Egyptian king before Caesar arrived. Caesar then fought in the civil war there and met Cleopatra, followed by a brief campaign in Asia Minor and victories over Pompey's supporters in Spain and modern-day Tunisia – all before the end of 46 BC. Caesar enjoyed a brief spell of total dominance of domestic politics at Rome, but, accused of increasingly tyrannical behaviour, was assassinated on 15 March 44 BC by a conspiracy that included a number of former opponents from the civil wars whose lives he had spared.

LEADING THE ARMY

The core of Caesar's army was composed of legions of about 5,000 men recruited from Roman citizens, men with full Roman political and legal rights. They were equipped as heavy infantry, wearing armour (typically chainmail), carrying a large oval shield and fighting with the *pilum* (a heavy throwing spear) and a short stabbing sword. Supporting ('auxiliary') cavalry and lighter infantry were provided by allies, subject peoples and mercenaries. Caesar's army in Gaul included not only Gallic auxiliaries but also German cavalry, Numidians and Balearic slingers like those used by Hannibal (pp. 32–35) 150 years earlier. The construction of elaborate marching camps had been a feature of Roman armies in the Punic Wars, but Caesar's forces in Gaul demonstrated a remarkable range of engineering skills, constructing bridges across the Rhine, large fleets of ships to fight the Veneti and cross to Britain, and elaborate siegeworks at Alesia and elsewhere.

▲ Part of a 1st-century BC marble relief, depicting Roman legionaries participating in a sacrifice for the war god Mars. While the sculpture (the 'Altar of Domitius Ahenobarbus', in the Louvre, Paris) probably dates to a few decades before Caesar's campaigns, the appearance of the soldier here is typical of Roman legionaries of the Republican period. He wears a chainmail tunic and helmet, and carries the elongated oval shield (*scutum*).

Pompey (106–48 BC)

In the Roman Civil War, Pompey raised three legions, and, after the resolution of the fighting in Italy, he was successful in the mopping up operations in Africa and Sicily. In 77 he suppressed a revolt and was dispatched to subdue Sertorius in Spain. He was defeated several times by the latter, but following Sertorius's assassination Pompey quickly concluded the campaign. He claimed the credit for subsequent victory in the Third Servile War (73–71 BC). He was at his best in the suppression of piracy in the Mediterranean – exhibiting his powers of organization – and in the conclusion of the Third Mithridatic War (75–65 BC), when he intervened in the Judaean civil war and captured Jerusalem (63 BC). In the civil war against Caesar, Pompey was constrained by senators, and was defeated at Pharsalus (48 BC).

'They brought it on themselves. They would have condemned me regardless of all my victories — me, Gaius Caesar — had I not appealed to my army for help.'
JULIUS CAESAR ON HIS CIVIL WAR OPPONENTS

► At Pharsalus, both armies were drawn up in deep formations, especially Pompey's, which was superior in both infantry and cavalry. With a river to the south (Caesar's left) decisive action took place on Caesar's right where (phase 1) Pompey's massed cavalry drove off Caesar's cavalry. The main infantry clash initially was indecisive, but (phase 2) Caesar's right flank infantry reserve drove off Pompey's victorious cavalry, and then hit his infantry in the flank, undermining the Pompeians' resistance.

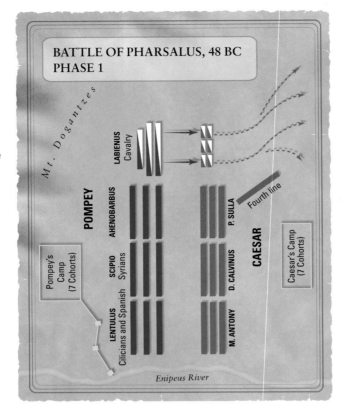

BATTLE OF PHARSALUS, 48 BC
PHASE 1

Mt. Dogantzes

LABIENUS Cavalry

POMPEY

AHENOBARBUS

SCIPIO Syrians

LENTULUS Cilicians and Spanish

Pompey's Camp (7 Cohorts)

P. SULLA

Fourth line

CAESAR

D. CALVINUS

M. ANTONY

Caesar's Camp (7 Cohorts)

Enipeus River

PHASE 2

N
W E
S

Mt. Dogantzes

LABIENUS Cavalry

POMPEY

AHENOBARBUS

SCIPIO Syrians

LENTULUS Cilicians and Spanish

Pompey's Camp (7 Cohorts)

P. SULLA

Fourth line

CAESAR

D. CALVINUS

M. ANTONY

Caesar's Camp (7 Cohorts)

Enipeus River

Caesar wrote commentaries on his wars in Gaul and on the civil war against Pompey, the most detailed accounts of any of the Roman wars. However, we must bear in mind that Caesar wrote them to justify his actions. For example, he cites only military motives for his expeditions across the Rhine and to Britain, but it is likely that his main reasons were to win glory and enhance his domestic political reputation by doing something no other Roman commander had done. The size of the army he took on his second expedition to Britain implies a desire for long-term conquest, but he plays down his failure to achieve this.

As a general, Caesar showed tremendous energy, confidence and decisiveness. His commentaries depict him as being everywhere at once on the battlefield, moving from region to region within Gaul and beyond, travelling between different elements of his command and leading forced marches to catch his enemies unawares. He is depicted as a soldier's general. The Roman biographer Suetonius records that he was a skilful swordsman and horseman who marched alongside his army on foot, bareheaded in all weathers, and swam across rivers like his men. At the Battle of the Sambre against the Nervii in 57 BC, when his right flank was in difficulties, Caesar fought in the front rank himself, calling the centurions (lower-ranking officers) by name and encouraging the men. On the other hand, one might criticize him for being over-confident, and even rash. His first expedition to Britain was a near disaster, and was undertaken with inadequate preparation and intelligence. The repeated revolts and unrest he faced in Gaul suggest a failure to consolidate superficial and rushed military conquests. The Dyrrhachium campaign in the civil war also shows how Caesar tended to put himself and his men in danger and then had to expend considerable effort extracting them. Caesar made much of his clemency towards defeated enemies, especially other Romans, but even in his own commentaries he admits to the deliberate massacre of non-combatants.

► The Dying Gaul depicts a warrior with distinctive hair, beard and Celtic torque. His heroic nudity would not be typical of the Gauls encountered by Caesar, commemorating instead an earlier (3rd- or 2nd-century BC) struggle between eastern Celts ('Galatians') and the kingdom of Pergamon in modern Turkey. Nevertheless this Roman copy of a Greek sculpture vividly demonstrates how Romans perceived their Celtic enemies.

►► This full-length statue of Julius Caesar depicts him in military dress, and is situated in the Roman theatre at Orange (Roman Arausio) in the south of France. While Arausio itself was founded as a Roman colony a few years after Caesar's death, this southern part of ancient Gaul was under Roman control at the time of Caesar's campaigns to the north, and provided him with a logistical and recruiting base.

Augustus

The First Emperor of Rome

'I waged many wars, by land and sea, against domestic and foreign enemies, in every part of the world. As victor I pardoned all citizens who sought mercy.' AUGUSTUS

▶▶ A detail of the famous statue of Augustus from the villa at Prima Porta, just north of Rome, now in the Vatican Museum. It depicts the emperor as commander-in-chief of the Roman army, wearing military dress. The cuirass Augustus wears presents a rich selection of propaganda images, including (not visible in this picture) the return of a captured Roman military standard by the Parthians, commemorating Augustus's diplomatic settlement with Parthia in 20 BC.

▶ This onyx cameo, the Gemma Augustea, depicts Augustus (seated, with bare chest, in the upper register) crowned as conqueror of the known world, and perhaps dates to just after his death in AD 14. The lower register shows soldiers raising a trophy and barbarian prisoners, probably celebrating a victory in the Balkans by Tiberius (Augustus's general and imperial successor).

Augustus (great-nephew and adopted son of Julius Caesar, pp. 36–41) was the first Roman emperor. He rose to political supremacy in Rome by the threat and use of military force. However, his great strengths were not as a field commander but as an organizer and politician. His reforms of the Roman army established it as a professional standing force with Augustus himself as commander-in-chief, creating a relationship between emperor and army that was to endure for centuries.

Augustus was the last of a series of leaders who exploited their popularity with veteran soldiers to achieve political supremacy in Rome. However, unlike earlier Republican military leaders, his power endured. Instead of being assassinated or overthrown in a civil war, Augustus established a new imperial system of government with himself as sole ruler under the

title of 'emperor'. An important part of this system was the emperor's position as commander-in-chief of a professional standing army created by Augustus himself. Supreme command of this army helped Augustus retain lifelong power and enabled him (through loyal subordinate commanders) to continue the expansion of empire begun in the Republican period, at least until Roman imperialism suffered setbacks late in his reign.

When Julius Caesar was assassinated in 44 BC, he had no surviving children; his will nominated his sister's 19-year-old grandson Octavian (as the young Augustus was known) as adopted son and heir. With virtually no political or military experience, Octavian threw himself into the struggle to succeed Caesar as the dominant force in Roman politics. He had to contend with Caesar's assassins and their sympathizers among the Senate and traditional magistrates, and the older and more experienced Mark Antony (Marcus Antonius), who saw himself as Caesar's true political and military heir. Octavian cleverly exploited the name of his adoptive father to win the support of Caesar's veterans. Backed by this army, he used the threat of force to seize the consulship (an elected office normally held by men twice Octavian's age) in 43 BC. One Roman writer claims that when the Senate hesitated, one of Octavian's officers displayed his sword, and threatened, 'If you don't make him Consul, this will.'

Later that year Octavian and Mark Antony patched up their differences temporarily, for mutual advantage, forming the 'second triumvirate', an unconstitutional government exercised by themselves with a third man, Lepidus.

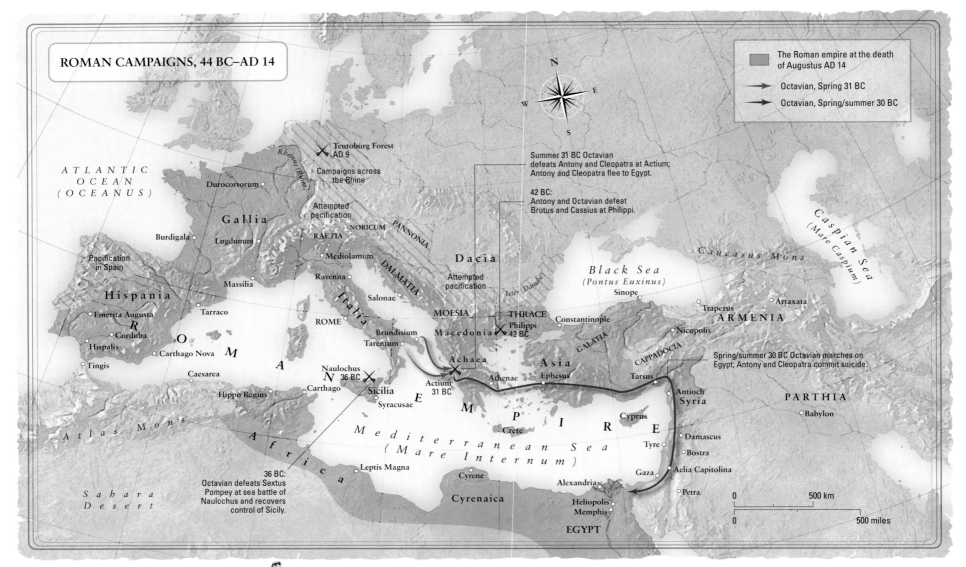

ROMAN CAMPAIGNS, 44 BC–AD 14

The Roman empire at the death of Augustus AD 14

→ Octavian, Spring 31 BC

→ Octavian, Spring/summer 30 BC

ATLANTIC OCEAN (OCEANUS)

Teutoburg Forest AD 9

Summer 31 BC Octavian defeats Antony and Cleopatra at Actium; Antony and Cleopatra flee to Egypt.

42 BC: Antony and Octavian defeat Brutus and Cassius at Philippi.

Campaigns across the Rhine

Durocortorum

Gallia

Attempted pacification

Rhenus (Rhine)

RAETIA NORICUM PANNONIA

Caspian Sea (Mare Caspium)

Burdigala

Lugdunum

Mediolamum

Caucasus Mons

Pacification in Spain

DALMATIA

Dacia

Black Sea (Pontus Euxinus)

Hispania

Massilia

Ravenna

Salonae

Attempted pacification

Ister (Danube)

Sinope

Trapezus

Artaxata

Emerita Augusta

Tarraco

Italia

ROME

MOESIA

THRACE

Constantinople

ARMENIA

Corduba

Brundisium

Macedonia

Philippi 42 BC

GALATIA

Nicopolis

Hispalis

Carthago Nova

Tarentum

Achaea

Asia

CAPPADOCIA

Tingis

Caesarea

Naulochus 36 BC

Actium 31 BC

Athenae

Ephesus

Tarsus

Spring/summer 30 BC Octavian marches on Egypt; Antony and Cleopatra commit suicide.

Antioch

PARTHIA

Atlas Mons

Carthago

Sicilia

Syracusae

EMPIRE

Syria

Babylon

Hippo Regius

Africa

Mediterranean Sea (Mare Internum)

Crete

Cyprus

Damascus

Tyre

Bostra

Leptis Magna

Cyrene

Aelia Capitolina

Sahara Desert

36 BC: Octavian defeats Sextus Pompey at sea battle of Naulochus and recovers control of Sicily.

Cyrenaica

Alexandria

Gaza

Petra

Heliopolis Memphis

EGYPT

0   500 km

0   500 miles

▲ Augustus's campaigns were quite widely split in terms of time and geography. This map shows the major battles of the civil wars against Caesar's assassins (Philippi), Sextus Pompey (Sicily) and Mark Antony (Actium), as well as major areas of military activity after he became emperor (in 31 BC) in Spain, Germany and the Balkans.

▶ A marble relief sculpture, probably of the 2nd century AD, depicting officers and soldiers of the Praetorian Guard. The establishment of this imperial guard on a permanent basis was an important Augustan innovation in securing his own military dominance over the Roman state.

Key Battles and Campaigns

The Battle of Philippi, October 42 BC
Octavian (Augustus) and Mark Antony confront Brutus and Cassius, the assassins of Caesar, near Philippi in Macedonia. In the first battle early in October, Mark Antony defeats Cassius while on the other flank Brutus beats the forces of Octavian (laid low by illness). In the second battle (23 October) the triumvirs' troops drive back the enemy and a rout ensues.

The Sicilian Campaign, 36 BC
Octavian seeks to defeat Sextus Pompey in his Sicilian stronghold. Lepidus lands in the west and Agrippa wins a naval battle in the northeast, but Octavian suffers a naval defeat off the east coast. Both sides converge on northeast Sicily, where Agrippa wins a decisive naval victory on 3 September 36 BC.

The Battle of Actium, 31 BC
Mark Antony brings his fleet and army to western Greece, but Octavian and Agrippa, crossing from Italy, succeed in blockading his forces near Actium. Mark Antony attempts to break out by sea on 2 September, but most of his fleet (about 300 ships) is sunk or captured.

Campaigns across the Rhine, 12 BC–AD 9
Tiberius continues his brother's attempts to pacify the tribes in this troublesome province. However, in September AD 9, the Roman governor Varus is ambushed by a German army in the Teutoburg Forest (north of Osnabrück) leading to the destruction of three legions.

This coalition led to the battle of Philippi in October 42 BC, where Octavian and Mark Antony combined to defeat Brutus and Cassius, the assassins of Caesar. Philippi highlights a theme of Octavian/Augustus's military career – his poor reputation as a commander in his own right. He was in poor health at the time of the first battle, and his wing of the army was routed while Mark Antony's was victorious. The picture painted of Octavian as a bad commander who lacked personal courage partly derives from Mark Antony's hostile propaganda, but his talents lay in appointing capable subordinates and in organization rather than in field command. This was certainly true of his next campaign, a combined naval and land effort against Sextus Pompey (son of Pompey the Great) in Sicily. Again, reliance on subordinates (particularly his old friend Marcus Agrippa) and good organization were more important than Octavian's personal role as commander.

The year 36 BC also saw a split between Octavian and Mark Antony, with Octavian based in Italy and the western part of the empire and Mark Antony, with his Egyptian lover Cleopatra, in the east. A final, decisive clash between them took place at Actium (western Greece) in 31 BC, with Agrippa once more playing a leading role. Mark Antony (and Cleopatra) fled to Egypt, where they committed suicide.

Augustus as Emperor and Commander-in-Chief

The victory at Actium left Octavian in sole control of the Roman world. He now faced the problem of how to maintain power, when others (like Caesar) had been

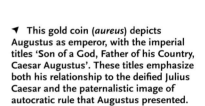

overthrown quickly. Part of his solution was political, the creation of a new system of government (the Principate, or imperial system) in which Republican government was replaced by autocratic rule by an emperor, namely Augustus (the honorific title, meaning 'revered one', by which he was known from 27 BC). Another part of the solution was military. To prevent other military commanders becoming too powerful and thus a threat, Augustus established himself as commander-in-chief. Commanders of major military units were no longer as independent as Julius Caesar had been in Gaul. Henceforth, they were mostly direct appointees of the emperor, commanding in his name, and the victories they won were his. He also established the army and navy as a regular, standing, professional force, with its loyalty focused on the state and the emperor as head of state, instead of on individual commanders. He set up regular terms of service and standardized pay, and provided retirement bonuses (previously irregular and often dependent on the influence of individual commanders) from a state military treasury. He also established the Praetorian Guard. This was an imperial guard based in and around the city of Rome, supplemented by a bodyguard of German mercenaries. This formula established by Augustus for the relationship between army and emperor remained in force for over two centuries after his death. However, while Augustus himself remained in power until his death from (probably) old age, he did

◄ This gold coin (*aureus*) depicts Augustus as emperor, with the imperial titles 'Son of a God, Father of his Country, Caesar Augustus'. These titles emphasize both his relationship to the deified Julius Caesar and the paternalistic image of autocratic rule that Augustus presented.

► A silver tetradrachm coin of 5 BC from the eastern, culturally Greek, part of the Roman empire, bearing a portrait of Augustus. The legend describes him as Sebastos, the Greek translation of 'Augustus', meaning, roughly, 'Revered One'.

Arminius (16 BC–AD 21)

Arminius (Hermann) was a Cheruscian noble. Early in his life he commanded German auxiliary troops in the Roman army and gained Roman citizenship as a result. He exploited this knowledge on his return to Germany, and formed an alliance with other German tribes: the Chatti, Marsi and Bructeri. In AD 9 he ambushed and destroyed Varus's army of three legions and supporting troops on the march in the Teutoburg Forest, east of the Rhine. This was by far the worst defeat the Romans suffered in Augustus's reign, and

was the main reason he advised his successors to bring expansion of the empire to an end. While the Romans subsequently abandoned direct control of Germany east of the Rhine, between AD 14 and 16 the Roman general Germanicus launched punitive expeditions across the river and inflicted several defeats on Arminius. However, Arminius was eventually killed (in AD 21) not by the Romans, but by political enemies in Germany.

The massive and heavily romanticized statue of Arminius (the 'Hermannsdenkmal')

shown here was set up near Detmold in Germany in the 19th century to celebrate his victory in the Teutoburg Forest. It also demonstrates the later importance of Arminius/Hermann in the creation of German national identity.

Marcus Agrippa (c. 63–12 BC)

Marcus Vipsanius Agrippa was a Roman general and statesman, born into a family of equestrian status. A companion of Octavian at the time of Caesar's assassination, Agrippa played a crucial role in his rise to power and the establishment of imperial rule. Ancient and modern writers attribute Octavian's early military success to Agrippa's leadership qualities. Agrippa won two major naval battles in the Sicilian campaign of 36 BC, and his bold and aggressive seizure of Mark Antony's bases in western Greece closed the net on the latter's forces at Actium, where Agrippa commanded Octavian's fleet in the ensuing battle. Agrippa subsequently fought campaigns in Spain and Pannonia, engaged in diplomatic activity on the emperor's behalf, and attended to the administration of Rome and the empire as a whole. He married Augustus's daughter Julia, and for a while he may have been Augustus's intended successor. However, he predeceased Augustus in 12 BC.

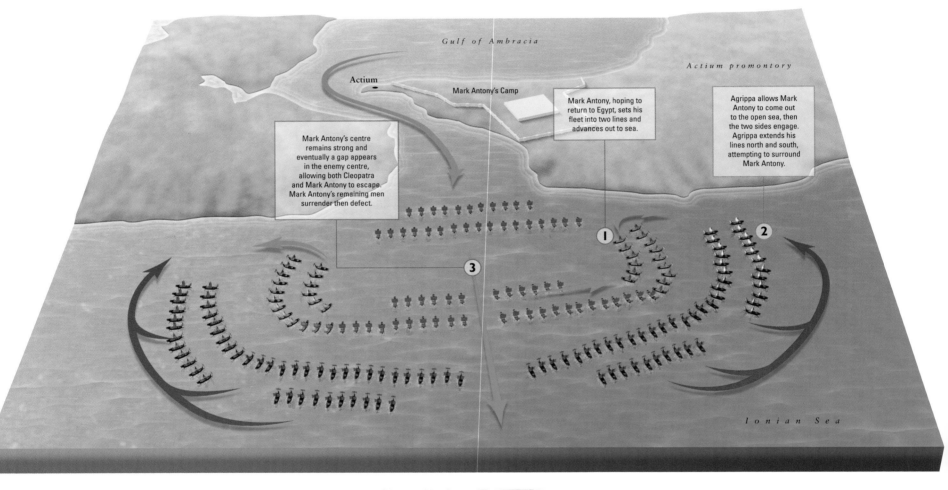

Gulf of Ambracia

Actium promontory

Actium

Mark Antony's Camp

Mark Antony, hoping to return to Egypt, sets his fleet into two lines and advances out to sea.

Agrippa allows Mark Antony to come out to the open sea, then the two sides engage. Agrippa extends his lines north and south, attempting to surround Mark Antony.

Mark Antony's centre remains strong and eventually a gap appears in the enemy centre, allowing both Cleopatra and Mark Antony to escape. Mark Antony's remaining men surrender then defect.

Ionian Sea

1

2

3

The Battle of Actium, 31 BC

Mark Antony's supporters	Octavian's supporters
Mark Antony	**Marcus Vipsanius Agrippa**
230 warships, 60 Egyptian warships, 20,000 legionnary marines, 2,000 archers	400 warships, 16,000 legionnary marines, 3,000 archers
Casualties: almost all ships captured	Casualties: unknown

▲ This reconstruction of the naval battle of Actium shows Mark Antony's attempt to break out his fleet from its blockaded position in the face of opposition from Octavian's fleet (commanded by Agrippa).

▶ A marble relief depicting Roman marines or legionaries on board a warship. Besides raising the naval force that won at Actium, as part of his reform of the Roman armed forces Augustus also created standing fleets based at Misenum and Ravenna, on the west and east coasts of Italy. The crocodile in the sculpture alludes to the Nile and Egypt, and hence, perhaps, to Actium.

not succeed in taking the Roman army out of politics, as many subsequent emperors came to power or were overthrown by elements of the army, both Praetorians and frontier armies. While Augustus reformed the army's structure and terms of service, he made no great innovations in tactics and equipment. Roman legions under Augustus continued to fight in more or less the same way they had under Julius Caesar.

AUGUSTUS'S FOREIGN WARS

Augustus continued the expansion of the Roman empire that had typified the Republican period, but, again, with trusted subordinates to command his armies in the field. Marcus Agrippa remained important in this role until his death in 12 BC, but Augustus increasingly employed his stepsons Drusus and (his ultimate successor) Tiberius as his main military

commanders. Augustus was cautious in his use of military power, likening rash generals to men who fish with a golden hook, in the full knowledge that nothing they catch could ever compensate for its loss. Thus, his success in resolving disputes with Armenia and Parthia in 20 BC, which relied on diplomacy and the threat of force, was the perfect Augustan victory, and was advertised on coins and other media as if it were a military victory.

However, other campaigns were more costly. Between 12 BC and AD 9 Tiberius extended Roman control to the Danube, but only after suppressing a large-scale revolt in Pannonia (modern Hungary) in AD 6–8. In Germany, Drusus (until his death in 9 BC) and then Tiberius extended Roman power across the Rhine to the River Elbe. However, long-term Roman ambitions beyond the Rhine were ended by the destruction of Publius Quinctilius Varus's army in the battle of the Teutoburg Forest in AD 9. While foreign expansion on an Augustan scale would not occur again until the reign of Trajan, the link between imperial power and the army was established in Augustus's reign, and it was Tiberius, an experienced general, who succeeded Augustus on his death in AD 14.

▲▶ The Altar of Augustan Peace commemorates the establishment of peace in Gaul and Spain after Augustus's diplomatic and military successes in 13 BC. Processional friezes around the outside of the altar wall depict members of the imperial family and Rome's religious and political elite. Augustus himself is the wreathed, damaged figure to the left of the intact panel illustrated in the detail above.

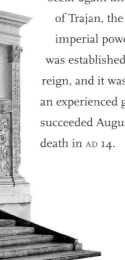

Trajan

Roman Emperor who Expanded the Imperial Domains to their Greatest Extent

'[Trajan] used to say that he had advanced further than Alexander the Great, although he could not retain control even of the territory he had conquered.' CASSIUS DIO

A Life in Brief

AD 53, 18 September
Born at Italica, Spain
(near modern Seville)

AD 91
First consulship

AD 98, 28 January
Becomes emperor

AD 117, 9 August
Dies at Selinus, Cilicia
(southern Turkey)

Marcus Ulpius Traianus, better known as Trajan, was one of the last and greatest exponents of the old Roman ideology of boundless imperial expansion, and a self-conscious emulator of Alexander the Great (pp. 18–23). He led Roman armies across the Danube to conquer Dacia, and eastward through modern Iraq to the shores of the Persian Gulf, and in his reign the Roman empire achieved its greatest extent. However, many of his conquests proved untenable, and were abandoned by his successor Hadrian.

Despite the advice from Augustus (pp. 42–47) to his successor Tiberius to limit expansion of the empire (perhaps influenced by late reverses in his reign, such as the Teutoburg Forest disaster in AD 9), military conquest remained an activity that a Roman emperor was supposed to undertake, and one he advertised prominently. Nevertheless, relatively few emperors of the 1st century AD regularly commanded troops themselves, relying on subordinates, as Augustus had done. This was true even of emperors who were good generals before their accession, such as Tiberius and Vespasian. Trajan, however, spent a good portion of his imperial reign engaged in direct command of conquering armies.

Trajan was born into an upper-class family in the Roman colony of Italica in Spain in AD 53. He followed the mixed military-political career typical of male members of the senatorial class, serving as a legionary tribune (middle-ranking officer in a legion) and legionary legate (commanding a legion) before becoming consul (by now a largely honorific position) in AD 91. In AD 97 he was made imperial governor of Upper Germany, an important military command, with three legions (about 15,000 men) and a similar number

▶ **This statue, now in the Louvre, depicts Trajan wearing a cuirass, emphasizing his role as commander-in-chief of Roman armies and as a general. While it was normal to depict Roman emperors in a military guise (see Augustus, pp. 42–47), few actually commanded troops in battle as regularly as Trajan.**

of supporting auxiliary troops. He was adopted as son and heir of the ruling emperor, Nerva, who used Trajan and his troops to counterbalance pressure exerted on him by the Praetorian Guard, which remained loyal to his predecessor Domitian. Nerva died, apparently of natural causes, early in AD 98, and Trajan became emperor – the first born outside Italy.

Key Campaigns

The First Dacian War, AD 101–2
Concerned by the Dacians' past encroachments on Roman territory and the amount of tribute paid to pacify them, Trajan crosses the Danube. After a close victory at Tapae (in Transylvania), Trajan advances to the Dacian capital Sarmizagethusa. The Romans capture some Dacian mountain fortresses and recover booty taken in past Roman defeats. The Dacian king Decebalus sues for peace and the Romans agree terms.

The Second Dacian War, AD 105–6
Decebalus breaks the terms of the treaty, and Trajan leads his army across the Danube again, on a bridge constructed by the architect Apollodorus. The Roman army overruns Dacia, and Sarmizagethusa is destroyed. Decebalus commits suicide rather than be captured, and his head is taken to Rome for display.

The Parthian War, AD 114–16
In response to the accession of a pro-Parthian king of Armenia, Trajan attacks Armenia and deposes the king. He undertakes operations in Mesopotamia (the modern Kurdish areas of Iraq and Turkey), conquering the cities of Singara, Nisibis and Batnae and the kingdom of Adiabene. Next, Trajan leads his army along the Euphrates Valley to Babylon, apparently without much Persian resistance, and enters the Parthian capital of Ctesiphon. Finally, Trajan advances downstream to the mouth of the Persian Gulf.

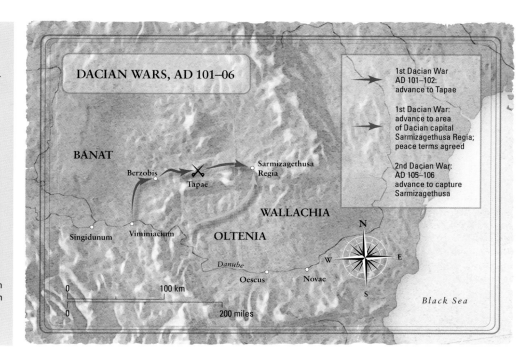

Trajan commanded field armies in two wars (AD 101–2, and AD 105–6) to conquer Dacia (essentially modern Romania) and in the conquest of the kingdom of Armenia and the western part of the Parthian Persian empire (AD 114–16). Modern scholars have debated whether Trajan's conquests were motivated by a rational strategic plan, but ancient writers emphasize his desire for glory and emulation of the conquests of Alexander the Great. Certainly, the Romans only retained control of his conquests for a short period. Shortly after his expedition to the Persian Gulf (in AD 116) revolts broke out in Trajan's newly created provinces of Armenia and Mesopotamia, along with a Jewish uprising in existing parts of the empire. Trajan's eastern conquests became untenable, and were abandoned by his successor Hadrian. Hadrian also contemplated abandoning Dacia,

▲ Trajan's Dacian Wars were fought largely in mountainous terrain within modern Romania. Ancient sources provide us with relatively little detail on the course of the campaigns, although these are fleshed out by the depictions on Trajan's Column.

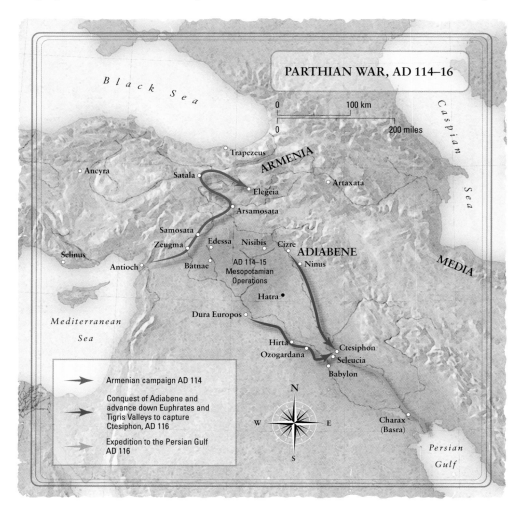

◄ The course of Trajan's eastern wars against Rome's long-standing Parthian enemies. After Roman successes in the kingdom of Armenia (traditionally a focus of conflict between the two powers) and northern Mesopotamia, Trajan led his army south to sack the capital of Ctesiphon, then to the Persian Gulf. However, a subsequent revolt meant that most of this territory was lost before the conquests were consolidated.

▼ A terracotta plaque showing chained captives being displayed in a triumphal procession. The triumph, a formal parade in which a victorious general led his army, prisoners and spoils of war through Rome, was a set-piece of Roman culture enabling emperors (and earlier Republican commanders) to enhance their reputations by a display of military prowess.

▲ Trajan's Column is a 38-m high monument to the emperor's Dacian campaigns that forms part of Trajan's Forum in Rome. The column is decorated with a sculpted spiral frieze depicting military activities in some detail, including not only the battles themselves, but also aspects of military routine.

Hadrian (AD 76–138)

Publius Aelius Hadrianus, Trajan's successor, was a man of great military experience, who spent much of his reign visiting frontiers and training the army. However, he took a very different approach from that of Trajan, preferring to consolidate the empire rather than engage in expansion. Later writers criticized him for abandoning what Trajan had conquered, indefensible though it may have been.

Hadrian was related to Trajan, and the latter served as Hadrian's guardian after the death of his father. Before his own accession, Hadrian followed the usual mixed military-political career of a member of the senatorial class, but with a particular emphasis on military positions. He was tribune (junior officer) in three different legions, unusual for someone of his status. He commanded the First Minervan Legion in Trajan's Second Dacian War and accompanied the emperor on other campaigns, ending up as governor of Syria (with a substantial army under his command) at the time of Trajan's death in AD 117.

He was apparently adopted by Trajan (although there were rumours that the adoption was faked by members of the imperial court) and thus became emperor.

Despite (or perhaps because of) his military experience, Hadrian abandoned Trajan's eastern conquests and concentrated on consolidation and rationalization. His reign saw the development of frontier systems in Germany and Britain (Hadrian's Wall, shown above), and while these were not intended as hard-and-fast defensive barriers, they mark at least a psychological departure from the past ideology of boundless expansion. Hadrian travelled from province to province, inspecting frontiers and military units. An ancient biography describes how he loved peace but trained his men for war, and an inscription from the legionary base at Lambaesis (in modern Algeria) records a speech he gave to the troops there, assessing their performance in training exercises with the eye of an experienced soldier.

but it remained under Roman control until the reign of Aurelian (AD 270–75). Symptomatic of the frustrations of the last year of Trajan's reign was his unsuccessful siege of Hatra (in modern northern Iraq), where he caught a disease that led to his death in August AD 117, while he was travelling back to Rome.

Like other Roman emperors, Trajan presented his image as a conqueror to the Roman people through titles, coins and monuments. Victory titles with references to defeated peoples formed a regular part of an emperor's name, and Trajan was called Germanicus ('Conqueror of the Germans'), Dacicus ('Conqueror

of the Dacians') and Parthicus ('Conqueror of the Parthians'). Coins bore legends like 'Dacia captured' and 'Armenia and Mesopotamia brought under the control of the Roman People'. The famous sculpted frieze of Trajan's Column depicts the emperor leading the army to victory in Dacia, and provides a wealth of detail about the army's activities, not just fighting but also construction and caring for the wounded. Relatively little detail about Trajan as a commander has survived, beyond the sort of clichés about the emperor sharing the hardships of his troops that were a mark of written accounts of popular Roman generals.

Belisarius

Byzantine General who Conquered Italy and North Africa

'Whoever of you has hopes of setting foot in Rome without a fight is mistaken in his judgment, for as long as Belisarius lives, it is impossible for him to relinquish this city.' BELISARIUS

A Life in Brief

c. AD 500
Born at Germania (Saparevska Banya, western Bulgaria)

529–31, and 533–42
Magister Militum per Orientem (General in the East) – also used to cover his reconquests of Vandal Africa (533) and Ostrogothic Italy (535–40)

544–49
Becomes Sacri Stabuli (Count of the Imperial Stable)

565, March
Dies in Constantinople

▶ A mid-6th century mosaic from the church of San Vitale, Ravenna. Commissioned by the banker Julius Argentarius, this depicts the emperor Justinian in the centre and archbishop Maximianus, flanked by ecclesiastical and secular leaders, with bodyguards further back. Belisarius may be the bearded figure immediately to the emperor's right.

Flavius Belisarius is associated with the greatest military successes of the East Roman emperor Justinian (AD 527–65), whom he served loyally in all major sectors: the eastern frontier (repulsing the Persians in 530 and 542), Africa (reconquered from the Vandals in 533), Italy (overthrowing the Ostrogothic kingdom in 540), and finally the Balkans (driving Hun invaders back from Constantinople in 559).

Belisarius's first command was as an officer in Justinian's bodyguard conducting raids into Armenia in 527–28. He rapidly moved up the eastern command structure, becoming the senior general for the Persian campaigns in 529. Blame for defeat at Callinicum in 531 led to his recall, but at Constantinople in January 532 his loyalty to Justinian during fierce rioting returned him to favour. Victory in Africa over the Vandals in 533 led to the campaign to seize Italy from the Ostrogoths in 535. By 540 the Ostrogoths were penned in at Ravenna, and surrendered in the hope that Belisarius would become their ruler. His subsequent career, in the East (541–42) and then back in Italy (544–49), was beset by frustrations over limited resources and uncertain imperial support. During the 550s he remained in Constantinople in honourable retirement until the Kutrigur Hun invasion of 559 led to a final recall.

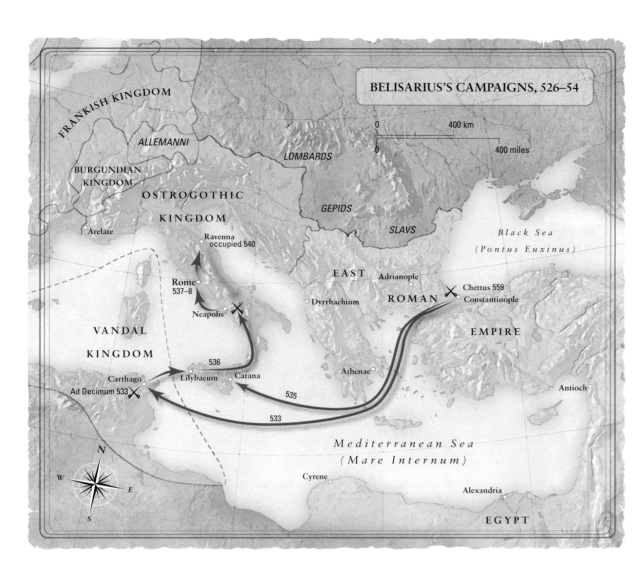

BELISARIUS'S CAMPAIGNS, 526–54

FRANKISH KINGDOM

ALLEMANNI

LOMBARDS

BURGUNDIAN
KINGDOM

OSTROGOTHIC

KINGDOM

GEPIDS

Arelate

SLAVS

Ravenna
occupied 540

Black Sea
(Pontus Euxinus)

EAST

Adrianople

Rome
537–8

ROMAN

Chettus 559
Constantinople

Neapolis

Dyrrhachium

VANDAL

EMPIRE

KINGDOM

536

Carthago

Ad Decimum 533

Lilybaeum

Catana

Athenae

Antioch

535

533

Mediterranean Sea
(Mare Internum)

Cyrene

Alexandria

EGYPT

0   400 km
0   400 miles

N
W   E
S

◄ Belisarius's campaigns in the west included the reconquest of North Africa from the Vandals and protracted struggles against the Ostrogoths in Italy.

Key Battles

The Battle of Dara, 530
Belisarius protects a defensive position outside his base at Dara (in southeast Turkey) with a staggered ditch. This, combined with skilful deployment of Hunnic allies, allows him to repulse the superior Persian army, inflicting heavy losses.

The Battle of Callinicum, 531
Belisarius fails to restrain his troops' belligerence while shadowing Azarethes's Persian army withdrawing down the Euphrates. The Lenten fast and an adverse wind weakens Roman efforts and, after the rout of their Arab allies, they are forced to withdraw across the Euphrates.

The Battle of Ad Decimum, 533
Gelimer's Vandals attempt to disrupt Belisarius's advance on Carthage, but poor timing leads his fellow commanders to attack too soon. Gelimer initially puts to flight Belisarius's cavalry, but news of his brother's death demoralizes him. Belisarius reorganizes his forces, routs the Vandals and recovers Carthage.

The Defence of Rome, 537–38
Belisarius sustains civilian morale and disrupts Witigis's superior Ostrogothic besiegers through frequent skirmishing. The arrival of Roman reinforcements, and developments elsewhere in Italy, persuade the Ostrogoths to withdraw.

The Battle of Chettus, 559
Belisarius is summoned from retirement to lead a scratch force against Zabergan's 7,000 Kutrigur Huns, who have overrun the Long Walls of Constantinople. Despite being outnumbered, Belisarius uses ambushes and deception to repulse the invaders.

▲ Copy of a gold medallion, probably struck to commemorate the triumph over the Vandals, showing Justinian in military equipment on horseback preceded by a winged figure which combined the attributes of an angel and the pagan goddess of victory.

▼ The northeastern section of the defences of Dara, the major fortress on the Roman eastern frontier whose construction was begun in 505 under Anastasius and carried on by Justinian. The massive horseshoe-shaped towers, which currently stand at about 10 metres, would originally have been at least twice as high.

Belisarius repeatedly had problems in controlling subordinate officers, and on occasion he bowed to the wishes of his troops. He was capable of tactical ingenuity, appreciated the advantages of his (primarily Hunnic) mounted archers, and showed considerable organizational vision in outmanoeuvring the Ostrogoths in the late 530s. He appears, however, not to have valued the capacity of Roman infantry, and his greatest victories owed much to luck (Ad Decimum) and the errors of opponents who were demoralized or incompetent.

2

The Medieval World

◄◄ A small section of the Bayeux Tapestry, an embroidered history of the events leading up to and during the Norman Conquest of England by William, Duke of Normandy (later 'the Conqueror'). In this scene, William raises his helmet during the battle of Hastings to show his troops, who rally around him, that he has not been wounded as they thought.

▼ French representation of the great Muslim leader Saladin's army. This focus on French-style cavalry was misleading as the prime emphasis in Saladin's cavalry was on mounted archers who played an important harassing role. Not all Arab cavalry, however, was light cavalry. For example, the Khurasaniya, on whom the Abbasid caliphs (750–1258) relied, were heavy cavalry, equipped with armour and armed not only with bows but also with curved swords, clubs and axes. During the First Crusade (1097–9), the Crusaders encountered Agulani (probably drawn from Persia), with armour of plates of iron, which also covered the horses.

Command in the medieval period was generally synonymous with rule, given that the willingness and ability to lead into battle were seen as crucial political attributes. Serious problems arose if the ruler was unable to provide adequate military leadership, or was judged as being so by his subjects. The contrast in fortune of the kings of England provides a clear example of this: Richard I (p. 70), Edward I (pp. 84–87), Edward III and Henry V were great war-leaders who won prestige through conflict, while Edward II and Henry VI proved cruelly disappointing in this light.

The gains made through war brought rulers and their dynasties to the fore, and the most spectacular occurred in Eurasia. Using the opportunities provided by the effective use of mobile horse-archers, Saladin (pp. 68–71), Chingiz Khan (pp. 76–79) and Timur (pp. 80–83) created far-reaching empires, and in doing so defeated powerful opponents. In the 12th century, Saladin became the dominant ruler in the Near East as a result of his success against the Crusaders. In the following century, Chingiz Khan launched the Mongols on a rapid series of conquests that were to take their forces across much of Europe. China and Persia fell and the Mongols advanced into Eastern Europe; however, their attacks on Japan and Java were less successful. Timur conquered Persia, captured Delhi and defeated the Ottoman Turks.

The rapid establishment and promotion of dynasties also took place at a more modest level, notably in England. The successors of Alfred the Great established the Old English state by defeating the Danes in the late 9th and early 10th centuries, before Sweyn and Cnut of Denmark established Danish rule. The Old English dynasty returned briefly, but in 1066 William of Normandy (pp. 64–67) conquered the country, not only through his victory at Hastings but also by his successful exploitation of it.

Success in battle was but one goal that leaders sought to achieve; they also strove to derive political benefits from campaigning. This was a matter not only of directing and sustaining the coalitions (comprising clan heads, aristocrats, subordinates and allies) that were vital to their cause, but also ensuring that opponents accepted the verdict of defeat and transferred their loyalty. This could entail taking over new roles as leader, as Charlemagne (pp. 58–61) did when he became Holy Roman Emperor in AD 800, or when the Mongols established themselves on the throne of China. An understanding of political opportunities and outcomes, and of how best to translate

campaign success into permanent advantage, proved crucial to military leadership. As with prowess on the battlefield, the onus lay on the individual ruler. He could not rely on subordinates or on a staff; he had to prove himself a true leader.

All the commanders in this section are generals. The potential for naval warfare in this period was constrained by the technological limitations of ships, affected as they were by the pressures of wind and wave and without the great advantages that were subsequently presented by cannon. Furthermore, most states were ruled by monarchs and elites who focused on conflicts over control of land. Nevertheless, it would be a mistake to assume there was no naval conflict, nor any related command skills. In some cases, the ability to move troops across the sea

was critical, as with the Viking landings, the Danish invasions of England in the 9th and 11th centuries, the Norman invasion of England in 1066, the Crusades and the two unsuccessful Mongol invasions of Japan. In contrast, Chingiz Khan and Timur – the two commanders whose forces ranged the farthest afield – had no need of navies. The steppes across which they advanced and in which they operated were in some respects land oceans, comprising large, open and difficult areas. However, their forces were particularly well attuned to this combat environment.

▼ Crusades against the Hussites in Bohemia in 1420–31, shown here in a contemporary manuscript, ultimately failed. The Hussites held off the attacks of Holy Roman Emperor Sigismund thanks to excellent leadership – by commanders such as Jan Žižka – and innovative infantry tactics, including the use of fortified wagons to create defensive boundaries. The wagon fortresses (wagenburgen) were defended with crossbows and also handguns and cannon, the latter signs of a receptiveness to new armaments.

▲ The campaigns of Timur (1336–1405) were all characterized by careful planning, including thorough reconnaissance. His forces were highly organized and well-disciplined, and this helped him execute such methods as rapidly changing the direction of march. These were not just predatory raids; supplies were raised on the march and efforts were made to use existing structures by levying tributes.

Charlemagne

Leader of the Franks and First Holy Roman Emperor

'Then came in sight… Charlemagne, topped with his iron helm, his fists in iron gloves…, an iron spear raised high against the sky he gripped in his left hand, while in his right he held his still unconquered sword.'

NOTKER THE STAMMERER, 9TH-CENTURY MONK

A Life in Brief

AD 742, 2 April
The traditional date of Charlemagne's birth

768
Becomes joint king of the Franks with his brother Carloman

771
Becomes sole king of the Franks

774
Becomes king of the Lombards

800, 25 December
Crowned 'Emperor of the Romans' by the Pope in Rome

814, 28 January
Dies at Aachen

Charlemagne (also known as Carolus Magnus, or Charles the Great) is often described as the 'father of Europe'. The grandson of Charles Martel, he rose to power as sole king of the Franks in AD 771, and went on to conquer most of the Continent. In the year 800 he founded the Holy Roman Empire, a political entity that would endure until 1806. Through these achievements, Charlemagne bequeathed to posterity a notion of European unity, which has strong resonances to this day.

The Franks lived between the Rhine and the Loire, and under their Merovingian kings traditionally dominated neighbours like Aquitaine, Bavaria and Saxony. However, weakness in the ruling house led to civil wars, out of which Charlemagne's father, Pepin the Short (714–68), emerged as victor; Pepin eventually persuaded the Pope to confirm him as King of the Franks in 751. Military triumphs were vital to the security of the new dynasty; the king led his aristocrats on profitable raids, extorted tribute from neighbours and distributed it amongst his aristocrats or gave them land and office in conquered territories. For this reason, Charlemagne quickly completed his father's conquest of Aquitaine and set out to reaffirm Frankish domination over the peoples who had drifted from subservience during the internal conflicts of the Franks.

Amongst these were the Saxons, a pagan, warlike people whose expansionist tendencies threatened the Frankish lands. Charlemagne's Saxon campaigns would dominate his reign, and their eventual conquest was his greatest military achievement. In a major expedition in 772,

Charlemagne destroyed their sacred oak, the Irminsul, and received the homage of their leaders. He may have intended to return, but in the following year the Pope asked for his help against Desiderius (r. 756–74), king of the Lombards in northern Italy, who was threatening to annex Rome. Charlemagne and his dynasty owed their royal status to papal approval, and he was thus obliged to respond,

▶ Charlemagne portrayed as a conquering emperor, splendidly mounted and holding the orb of the world in his hand. This bronze, gilded 10th- to 11th-century figurine was made long after Charlemagne's death and shows the long-lasting impact of his conquests.

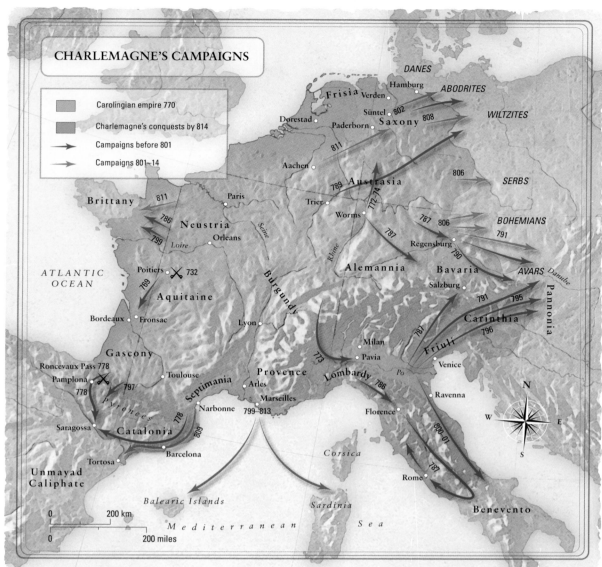

CHARLEMAGNE'S CAMPAIGNS

Carolingian empire 770

Charlemagne's conquests by 814

Campaigns before 801

Campaigns 801–14

▲ Charlemagne's 'Talisman', allegedly made at the court of the Caliph Haroun el Raschid in Baghdad. It is a sapphire in a gold setting decorated with jewels and pearls and originally held a sliver of the Holy Cross. It was an important status-symbol worn to impress his followers and visitors. Found in Charlemagne's tomb by the emperor Otto III (980–1002) in 1000, it was given to the empress Josephine and now forms part of the French national collection.

◄ Charlemagne was occasionally able to mobilize large armies, and up to 800 he personally commanded a campaigning army almost every year. Any ruler needed successful leadership in war so that he could seize plunder – slaves, treasure and land – to distribute to his chief followers. But Charlemagne was an ambitious conqueror, seeking to incorporate potential enemies into his own kingdom. The secret of his success was meticulous and elaborate planning and organization.

deposing Desiderius and himself assuming the Lombard crown in 774. Italian troubles often diverted him from other campaigns, notably embroiling him in war with the Byzantine empire over control of Venice and southern Italy after 786. The Saxons took advantage of Charlemagne's troubles on this occasion and rebelled, and it was not until 777 that he was able to impose a peace at Paderborn.

Charlemagne also had to face the threat of raids from Muslim Spain on his southern lands, and in 778 allied with the Caliph of Baghdad, who disliked the independence of the Cordoban Umayyad dynasty. That same year, he led an expedition to Spain, no doubt in an attempt to establish a defensive zone (or 'march'), but enjoyed only limited success. As his army returned, its rearguard was destroyed by the Basques at the battle of Roncevaux Pass and a senior leader, Roland, was killed. It would not be until 801, with Charlemagne's conquest of Barcelona, that a strong March of Spain would be established to protect his southern lands.

Key Campaigns

The Subjugation of the Saxons, 772–804
In 772 Charlemagne launches his first campaign against the troublesome Saxon tribe in northwest Germany, invading their territories and desecrating the sacred Irminsul. Over the following 30 years, Charlemagne is forced to devote much attention to subduing rebellion in his new domain. He also converts this pagan culture to Christianity in the process.

The Spanish Campaign, 778
Charlemagne leads an army over the Pyrenees to aid Moorish rulers in their struggle against the Umayyad emir of Cordoba. Fearing betrayal, Charlemagne decides to withdraw over the mountains, and his rearguard is ambushed by Basques at the battle of Roncevaux Pass. Charlemagne's paladin Roland, who is killed there, later becomes a key figure in medieval and Renaissance literature.

Charlemagne's distraction over Spain provoked unrest in Aquitaine, and revolt in Saxony, which he was forced to suppress. The Franks were defeated by the Saxons at Süntel in 782, following which an alleged massacre of 4,500 rebels took place by the Frankish army (led by Charlemagne) at Verden. The Saxons

▲ Charlemagne reformed the Frankish currency and based it on silver. Each pound was divided into 12 pennies (denarii). Here his image is portrayed in imitation of a Roman emperor. The new coinage fostered the economic growth of Charlemagne's empire and, at the same time, made excellent propaganda for the ruler.

Charles Martel (AD 686–741)

Charles Martel ('the Hammer') succeeded his father as Mayor of the Palace of the Frankish Kings by defeating his rivals for power at the battles of Amblève (716) and Vincy (717). By 730 he had established Frankish dominance over the Saxons, Bavarians and various peoples of western Germany. In 732 the Muslim governor of al-Andalus led a major raid into Aquitaine. Charles defeated him at the battle of Poitiers (shown below in a manuscript illustration)

that October, but was unable to pursue the retreating Muslims. The importance of the victory has been much debated. Some see it as a decisive moment in European history, when the tide of Islam was halted and western Christendom saved. Others dismiss the Arab expedition as a mere raid. What is clear is that Charles had plenty of enemies throughout Gaul; had the Arabs been victorious at Poitiers, they might well have exploited rifts in the Frankish aristocracy.

▼ There is no better symbol of conquest than a sword, and this splendidly jewelled example – according to legend belonging to Charlemagne – serves the role magnificently. For long held in the royal abbey of St Denis, it was used in the coronation ceremonies of the French kings to link them to the glory of Charlemagne.

had no central authority, and defeating one group simply led to war with another. The bitter fighting evolved into a holy war, with Charlemagne attempting to impose Christianity as a means of pacification. Only a terrible winter campaign in 784–85 broke major Saxon resistance, though intermittent rebellion continued until 804.

The conquest of the Saxons brought new enemies. The Avars were Asian horse-borne raiders based in Hungary. In 788 they invaded Bavaria, but Charlemagne was unable to deal with them immediately. From 790 he began a careful programme of fortification of the frontier, before launching

numerous punitive raids against them, eventually securing their submission in 796. At the same time, Charlemagne campaigned against the Slav tribes on his eastern borders.

By 800 Charlemagne ruled so much of Europe that the Pope considered him to be the true 'Emperor of the Romans', crowning him thus on Christmas Day during his visit to Rome. However, successive Byzantine emperors challenged this apparent transfer of power away from them, and fought a series of campaigns against Charlemagne in Italy until peace was made in 812.

Charlemagne's extraordinary success can be accounted for in several ways. The Frankish lands Charlemagne inherited were richer than those of his neighbours, producing more and better-quality iron weapons and armour, the export of which was prohibited to enemies. Charlemagne was an organizational genius who united the Franks, recruited large armies and paid careful attention to logistics. His large, well-equipped armies overwhelmed and destroyed his enemies, particularly in set-piece attacks. A favourite tactic of his was to launch simultaneous attacks, as exemplified during the Avar campaign, where the enemy was eventually destroyed in 796 by attacks from several armies. It used to be thought that the Franks invented shock cavalry and that Charlemagne exploited the mobility and effectiveness of this military innovation, but this has recently been called into question. Charlemagne did make mistakes, as at Roncevaux Pass in 778, but he had great resolve, campaigning virtually every year of his life down to 800, and his leadership skills drove his armies on to victory.

◄ Charlemagne is portrayed alongside his wife in this manuscript illustration dating to shortly after his death. Charlemagne took his first wife, Desiderata, as part of an alliance with the Lombards, but when he made war upon them he set her aside. She was succeeded by Hildegard, daughter of an important and well-connected Swabian family, who gave him three sons who lived into adulthood. On her death in 783 Charlemagne married Fastrada who is said to have wielded considerable political influence. She died in 794 and Charlemagne took as his wife Liutgard, after whose death in 800 he did not remarry. The marriages all served political purposes and none prevented Charlemagne from enjoying the pleasures of numerous concubines.

The Avar Campaign, 791	
Franks and Allies	Avars
Charlemagne	**Unknown**
c. 20,000 troops	c. 15,000 troops
Casualties: unknown	Casualties: unknown

▼ The resources at Charlemagne's disposal meant that he was sometimes able to launch an attack with two converging armies – and he did this to great effect in his campaign against the semi-nomadic Avars. A planned follow-up attack in 792 was not put into operation, and it was not until 796 that their power was finally destroyed. Although a huge treasure was captured, the Avar lands remained outside the Carolingian kingdom.

➤ A soldier from the time of Charlemagne: the steel shirt or 'byrnie' is made of plates sewn or riveted to a leather or cloth backing. In many cases such shirts would have been made of chainmail over a cloth jacket. The crested iron helmet was made in two parts hammered together along the central ridge. A round shield of wood bound with metal completed his defensive array. The spear was his main offensive weapon, though the better-off could supplement this with a sword or dagger.

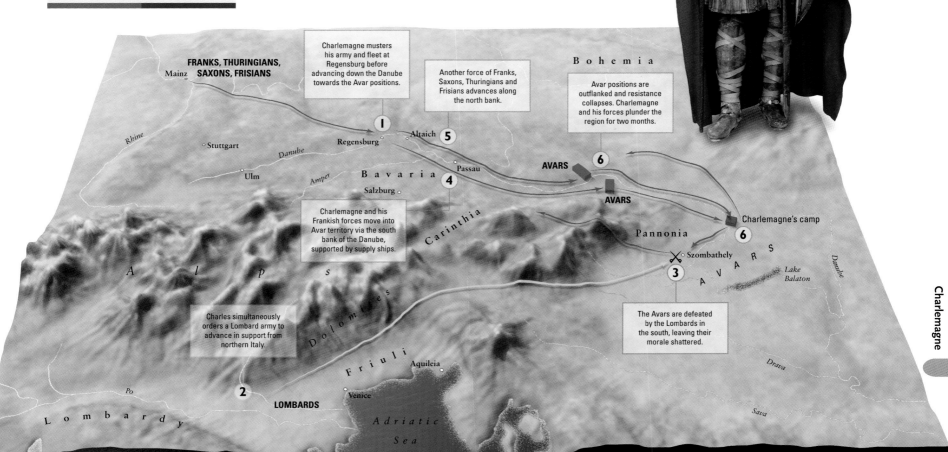

FRANKS, THURINGIANS, SAXONS, FRISIANS
Mainz

1 Charlemagne musters his army and fleet at Regensburg before advancing down the Danube towards the Avar positions.

B o h e m i a

5 Another force of Franks, Saxons, Thuringians and Frisians advances along the north bank.

6 Avar positions are outflanked and resistance collapses. Charlemagne and his forces plunder the region for two months.

Rhine

Stuttgart

Danube

Regensburg

Altaich **5**

AVARS **6**

Ulm

Amper

B a v a r i a

Passau

Salzburg

4

AVARS

A l p s

4 Charlemagne and his Frankish forces move into Avar territory via the south bank of the Danube, supported by supply ships.

C a r i n t h i a

P a n n o n i a

Charlemagne's camp **6**

D o l o m i t e s

Szombathely

3

A V A R S

Lake Balaton

Danube

2 Charles simultaneously orders a Lombard army to advance in support from northern Italy.

3 The Avars are defeated by the Lombards in the south, leaving their morale shattered.

F r i u l i

Aquileia

Drava

Po

2

Venice

L o m b a r d y

LOMBARDS

A d r i a t i c S e a

Sava

Otto the Great

German Holy Roman Emperor who Defeated the Magyars

'Let us confer with the enemy with our swords rather than with our tongues.' OTTO THE GREAT

A Life in Brief

912, 23 November
Born in Wallhausen, Saxony

936, 7 August
Crowned King of the East Franks in Aachen

951, October
Marries Adelaide, widow of King Lothar of Italy, securing the Italian crown

962, 2 February
Crowned Holy Roman Emperor in Rome

973, 7 May
Dies in Memleben, near Naumburg, Germany

▲ Stone statue of Otto and his first wife Edita in the archiepiscopal centre of Magdeburg that was established after the battle of Lechfeld for the purpose of converting Eastern Europe.

Otto is primarily known for his victory over a large army of mounted Magyar archers at the battle of Lechfeld in August 955. Barring the Mongol incursions in the 1240s, Otto's crushing victory over the Magyars ended the invasions by steppe warriors into Europe, which had begun with the advent of the Huns in the 4th century AD. The prestige that Otto gained from this triumph led to his coronation by the Pope as Holy Roman Emperor.

After inheriting the title of German king from his father Henry I in 936, Otto honed his tactical and operational skills by facing down numerous rebellions that were led by the dukes of Lothringia and Franconia and his brothers Thankmar and Henry. Like other medieval leaders Otto relied on manpower resources of ecclesiastics as a counterweight to those of secular vassals. In 939 Otto won a battle against rebels at Andernach, where the dukes Giselbert and Eberhard perished in an ambush at a Rhine crossing. This was a harbinger of things to come; ambushes at river crossings became a favoured tactic of Otto and his subordinates, and he employed such tactics against the Magyars.

From his father Otto inherited a grand strategy of defence in depth. His forces did not simply huddle inside fortresses; they were able to defeat interlopers in the field whenever invaders lost momentum. In addition to well-trained local defence units, Otto's army included a following of professionals and expeditionary forces that were capable of operations far from their home bases. These soldiers fought as cavalry or infantry, depending upon the tactical situation.

During the Lechfeld campaign, Otto demonstrated his tactical and operational skills. The Magyars laid siege to Augsburg, hoping to lure Otto's relief forces onto the treeless Lechfeld plain that surrounded the city on three sides, an environment that favoured the tactics of mounted archers. The king, however, foiled them by concentrating his army at Ulm and marching it through the rough and forested terrain west of Augsburg. When the Magyars attempted to use the cover of woodlands to slip behind the relief column, Otto's (previously rebellious) son-in-law Conrad countered and destroyed these forces. Otto then deployed his men to attack the main Magyar army in front of him. The Magyars realized that they could not stand their ground against a charge of heavy cavalry, and feigned a retreat to draw Otto's men out and destroy them with arrow fire. The king, however, did not take the bait. He pursued them for only a short distance, thus avoiding traps and ambushes. Otto knew that he had forces stationed in fortifications along the enemy's lines of retreat, and these forces were able to destroy the Magyars.

Key Battles and Campaigns

Campaigns in Italy

During Otto's first Italian campaign of 951–52, he defeats the usurper Berengar II and seizes the Italian crown, marrying Adelaide of Italy. In 961, he crosses the Alps for a second time. He passes much of his last decade there, suppressing rebellions and engaging in the politics of the papacy.

The Battle of Lechfeld, August 955

During the final Magyar retreat, heavy rains cause flooding. Otto dispatches couriers to the men who control the river crossings, ordering them to fall upon the enemy trapped by the inundations. Few Magyars survive.

The Battle of Lechfeld, 955

Germans and Bohemians	Magyars and Slavic subjects
Otto the Great	**Horka Bulksu and Lel**
8,000 plus 4,000 at river crossings	10,000 mounted archers, 5,000 foot
Casualties: 4,000 killed	Casualties: almost total annihilation

▲ A 9th-century illumination showing a king leading Western-style heavy cavalry to attack mounted archers (probably Avars), forcing them to flee.

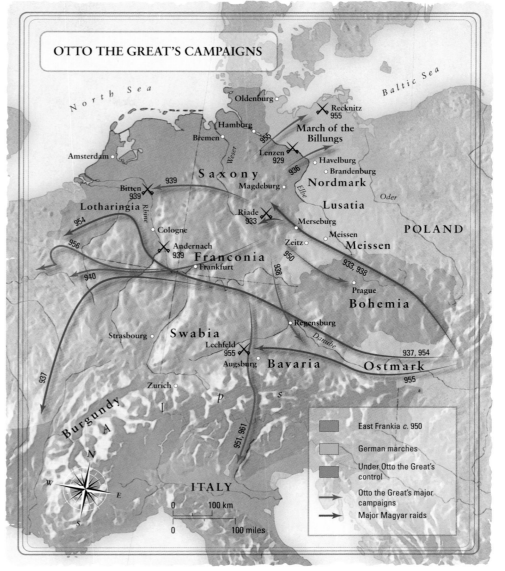

OTTO THE GREAT'S CAMPAIGNS

North Sea · Baltic Sea
Oldenburg · Recknitz 955
Hamburg · March of the Billungs
Bremen · Weser · Lenzen 929 · Havelburg · Brandenburg
Amsterdam · Saxony · Nordmark
Bitten 939 · Magdeburg · Elbe · Oder
Lotharingia · Rhine · Riade 933 · Merseburg · Lusatia · POLAND
Cologne · Zeitz · Meissen · Meissen
Andernach 939 · Franconia · 950 · 933, 938
Frankfurt · 938 · Prague · Bohemia
940 · 956 · Regensburg · Danube
Strasbourg · Swabia · Lechfeld 955 · 937, 954
Zurich · Augsburg · Bavaria · Ostmark 955
Burgundy · 937 · ALPS · 951, 961
ITALY

Legend:
- East Frankia c. 950
- German marches
- Under Otto the Great's control
- → Otto the Great's major campaigns
- → Major Magyar raids

0 — 100 km
0 — 100 miles

▲ Otto's Campaigns: Otto conducted far-reaching military operations against rebellious underlings, the Slavs of eastern Europe, the kingdoms of France and Italy, as well as against the Magyars.

[Battle of Lechfeld diagram]

Rauherforst

2 Otto approaches Augsburg through the Rauherforst, screened from skirmish attacks by the Magyar mounted archers.

Conrad · OTTO · Augsburg

Schmutter

4 Otto launches his main attack: a heavy cavalry charge.

3 A Magyar force attempts to encircle the Germans, but Otto's son-in-law, Conrad, launches a successful counterattack.

The Magyars lift their siege on Augsburg and deploy forces to meet Otto's relief column.

LEL · Lech

HORKA BULKSU

5 The Magyars attempt to draw the German forces out onto the Lechfeld (where the dispersed heavy cavalry will be easier targets for the Magyar mounted archers) with a feigned retreat.

1

6 Otto does not take the bait, knowing that the retreating enemy will be trapped by flooded rivers to the east and destroyed by his forces stationed there.

Lechfeld

Magyar Camp

◀ Otto's strategy of defence-in-depth allowed him to use Bavaria's geography to annihilate the Magyars at river crossings, such as at the battle of Lechfeld.

William the Conqueror

Norman Invader of England

'If you fight manfully, victory, honour and riches will be yours; otherwise you will be slain or, as captives, you will serve the whims of a most cruel enemy.' WILLIAM THE CONQUEROR

A Life in Brief

c. 1027/28
Born at Falaise, Normandy, the illegitimate son of Duke Robert II

1035
Becomes Duke William II of Normandy, aged seven

1066
Seizes the English throne after victory at Hastings

1087, 9 September
Dies near Rouen, France, after falling from his horse at Mantes

▶ William I of England enthroned, from a 12th-century manuscript of the chronicle of Battle Abbey. The abbey was founded by William on the site of the battle of Hastings as a form of penance. The high altar of the abbey was said to be on the very place that King Harold was slain.

▼ The reverse side of William's seal, showing him mounted. On the obverse he is shown enthroned.

Victory at the battle of Hastings in 1066 has ensured William the Conqueror a place among the great commanders of English history. Yet the battle was close fought, and it was but one example of William's military genius. Prior to the Norman Conquest, as William II of Normandy, he fought numerous campaigns in France to secure his territories from the threat of rebellion and invasion, and after Hastings expended much time and effort securing England, particularly the north.

William was a Norman, one of a people attuned to war and astonishingly successful in all the conquests they attempted, from England to southern Italy and Sicily. His first martial experience came when he fought rebel barons, led by Guy of Brionne, at the battle of Val-ès-Dunes (near Caen) in 1047, but as a 20-year-old it is unlikely that the responsibility of command fell upon such young shoulders. It was not long, however, before his ability began to show. In the early 1050s he successfully resisted the invasion of Normandy by Geoffrey II of Anjou. In 1063 he masterminded the conquest of the County of Maine, and conducted an effective campaign in Brittany. His strategy was not to seek battle, but to seize castles and terrorize the countryside. Realizing the importance of good intelligence, William himself took part in scouting missions. During one siege, William 'went out riding by day and night, or lay hidden under cover, to see whether attacks could be launched against those who were attempting to bring in supplies'. Surprise attacks were important: in 1051 he took Alençon by a dawn assault, after riding through the night. By 1066 William was a highly experienced soldier. It was not just that he knew how to fight. The task of assembling a force to invade England demanded administrative skills of the highest order; ships had to be acquired and built, and supplies needed to be organized. Recruitment needed diplomatic skills to persuade men, not all of them his Norman subjects, to join in what must have seemed a highly risky enterprise.

Hastings was the one major battle in which William had command, although purportedly his nerves led him to put his hauberk (a chainmail shirt) on the wrong way round. The surviving chronicles record, no doubt with much artistic licence, his speech before the battle, but we can be sure that at this point he demonstrated his capacity to inspire. At a vital moment of the battle, he rallied his men as they withdrew from an initial attack on the shield-wall of the Anglo-Saxons under Harold. The Bayeux Tapestry shows him raising his helmet so he could be recognized, an incident also recorded in other sources. The battle was a long one, and the advantage that the Norman mounted and armoured knights possessed was only marginal. William himself had three horses killed under him, showing that he was a commander who led by example, and was prepared to take great personal risks. The battle, however, was not won by bravery alone. It took great skill to organize

Key Battles and Campaigns

The Defence of Normandy, 1051–60
Geoffrey II of Anjou invades Normandy in 1051 and seizes the towns of Domfront and Alençon. William successfully retakes them, and drives Geoffrey back over the border into Maine. Geoffrey attempts a further invasion in 1054 with King Henry I of France, along the River Seine, but is forced to retreat. William moves to the offensive against Geoffrey in Maine, who attempts a third invasion with Henry in 1057. William defeats them at the River Dives in a surprise attack.

The Battle of Hastings, 14 October 1066
In the course of the long and hard-fought battle, the English form a strong defensive shield wall. The Normans attack in successive cavalry charges, and their archers fire rain arrows down on the English. The deaths of Harold Godwinson, and his brothers Gyrth and Leofwine, cause a collapse in the English morale, and the Normans break through the shield wall.

The Harrying of the North, 1069–70
William's campaign against the northern English rebels takes place in winter. There is extensive destruction of territory, crops and livestock, and many thousands die. William's tactics eventually force the population to accept him as king.

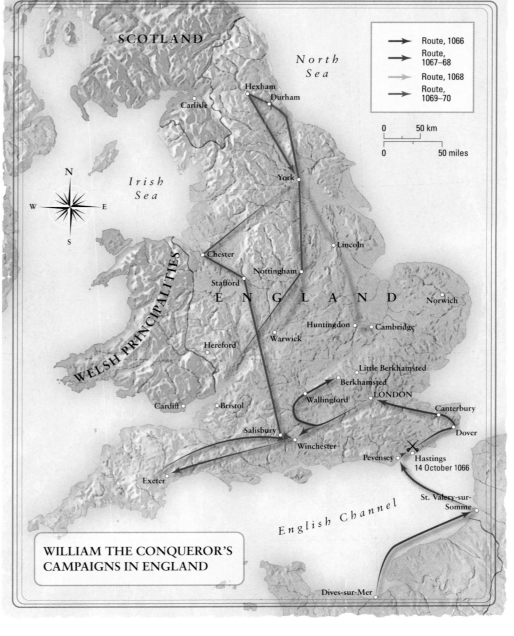

WILLIAM THE CONQUEROR'S CAMPAIGNS IN ENGLAND

the successive waves of attacks that characterized William's tactics. Most notable was the use of feigned retreats, which encouraged the English under Harold to break ranks.

Hastings was an exceptional moment in William's military career. His enterprise in invading England depended on defeating Harold, and battle was unavoidable. In his other campaigns, William avoided set-piece engagements, in which the risks were great and the rewards uncertain, preferring instead surprise attacks on his enemies. As Duke of Normandy, William had already demonstrated his acceptance of the brutality of war, capturing castles, firing towns and destroying villages. At the siege of Exeter in 1068, where he rode ahead of his main army to investigate the defences, he cruelly blinded a hostage in full sight of the citizens. During the Harrying of the North in

1069–70, as his army headed for northern England, his men carved out a great swathe of destruction, echoed in the form of reduced valuations in Domesday Book 20 years later. The northern campaign was savage in the extreme; it ground down the English, and frightened off their Danish allies. It was also hard going for the Norman soldiers, to whom William was a constant inspiration in the cold of winter. The chronicler Orderic Vitalis tells how, 'remarkably sure-footed, [he] led the foot-soldiers, readily helping them with his own hands when they were in difficulties'.

However, much remains unknown about William's generalship. There is surprisingly little evidence about the composition and size of his armies, though it is clear that the members of his household provided the core of his forces. Mercenary and paid troops were important; such men garrisoned the castles (a new

▲ William is famous for the battle of Hastings but, as this map shows, he campaigned extensively throughout England.

▼ The White Tower (part of the Tower of London) was the greatest castle built by William I. It was intended to overawe the citizens of London, and was complete by 1100.

The Battle of Hastings, 1066

Normans	Anglo-Saxons
William	**Harold Godwinson**
5,000–7,000 troops	7,000–8,000 troops
Casualties: *c.* 2,000 killed or wounded	Casualties: *c.* 4,000 killed or wounded

▼ At Hastings the Anglo-Saxons under Harold, all on foot, held the hilltop. William's men, in three divisions, had to advance up the slope, shown in the main picture, to attack them. The Norman technique of feigned retreat was vital in breaking the Anglo-Saxon shield wall.

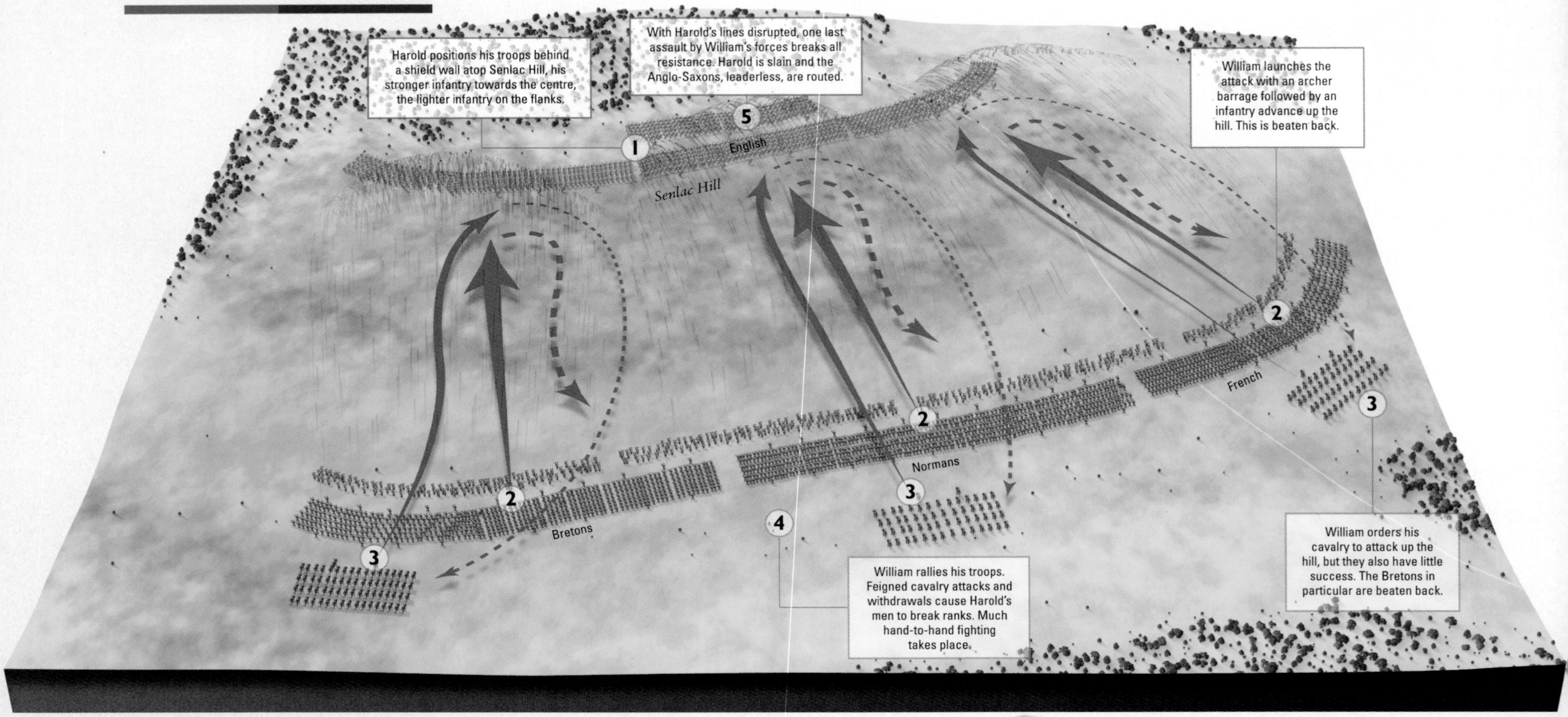

Harold positions his troops behind a shield wall atop Senlac Hill, his stronger infantry towards the centre, the lighter infantry on the flanks.

With Harold's lines disrupted, one last assault by William's forces breaks all resistance. Harold is slain and the Anglo-Saxons, leaderless, are routed.

William launches the attack with an archer barrage followed by an infantry advance up the hill. This is beaten back.

William orders his cavalry to attack up the hill, but they also have little success. The Bretons in particular are beaten back.

William rallies his troops. Feigned cavalry attacks and withdrawals cause Harold's men to break ranks. Much hand-to-hand fighting takes place.

Senlac Hill

English

Normans

Bretons

French

introduction to England and Wales) the Normans built. The significance of troops serving under a feudal obligation for periods of 40 days is controversial. William's armies were not large; it is estimated he had between 5,000 and 7,000 men under his command at Hastings. The armies were well trained and disciplined; when Exeter fell to the king in 1068, the troops were prevented from looting the place.

William remained active as a soldier into the 1080s, when he was in his 50s, though, as Orderic Vitalis noted, in the last 13 years of his life he won no battles and captured no castles. At Dol in 1076 Philip I of France forced William's troops into ignominious retreat; at Gerberoi in 1079 he was wounded and unhorsed in the course of a defeat at the hands of his own son Robert. Over a long military career, however, William showed a complete mastery of the arts of command. He had the ability to inspire his men at a personal level, recognized the importance of good intelligence, and had a clear strategic grasp.

▲ The Bayeux Tapestry was produced in England, under Norman direction. Some of the images were copied from Anglo-Saxon manuscripts at Canterbury. This scene shows the Norman cavalry assault on the Anglo-Saxon shield wall at Hastings.

▼ This sword is typical of the kind of weapon used at Hastings. The Normans also used lances, and the Anglo-Saxons axes. Both sides had archers.

Saladin

Muslim Victor over the Crusaders

'European merchants supply the best weaponry, contributing to their own defeat.' SALADIN

A Life in Brief

c. 1138
Born into a Kurdish family in Tikrit, in modern-day Iraq

1169
Succeeds his uncle as Vizier of Egypt

1174
Assumes title of Sultan of Egypt

1193, 4 March
Dies in Damascus

The most famous Muslim warrior of the High Middle Ages, Saladin al-Din Yusuf ibn Ayyub was a ruler who came to power through force. He achieved great distinction as the creator of a major Islamic state and as a result of his struggles with the Crusaders, notably against his Christian foe Richard the Lionheart. The range of the opponents he faced, and the way he transformed the fortunes of his people from defeat to triumph, are clear indications of his ability. Whilst some consider Saladin to have been a paragon of virtue, quiet and deeply religious, others see him as ruthless and devious, and a less capable military commander than he might at first appear.

Saladin was a Muslim Kurd, of the Ayyubid family, who rose to prominence in the service of his uncle Shirquh. Shirquh was the governor of Egypt, and was in turn in the service of Nur al-Din, the Turkish ruler of Syria, northern Iraq and Egypt. Saladin's formative military experiences came in the campaigns in Egypt between 1164 and 1169, which were provoked by the three failed invasions of the Fatimid state by Crusader forces. Egypt was crucial to the geopolitical

position of the Crusader states, and the Kingdom of Jerusalem made a major attempt to influence the situation there. The conflict involved clashes with fellow Muslims as well as with Crusaders. A result of Saladin's contributions to victory in Egypt was that he learnt how best to fight the Crusaders, which would play a key role in his eventual defeat of the latter. In 1169, following the death of his uncle, Saladin became the Vizier of Egypt – in effect, its ruler – a move that would lead directly to the end of the Fatimid Caliphate in 1171, when Saladin founded the Ayyubid sultanate there. In 1173, Nur al-Din died, creating an opening for Saladin gradually to seize control of the deceased's realm. One of his first moves was to create an army loyal to himself – which comprised Turkish, Armenian, Arab and Kurdish soldiers, among others – and he also changed the faith of Egypt from Shi'a to Sunni Islam. The mainstay of Saladin's army was the light cavalry, comprising Turcoman horse archers.

From Egypt, Saladin's forces pushed west along the North African coast to Gabès (in modern Tunisia), and, under his brother, Turan Shah, south up the Nile

▶ Saladin, Sultan of Egypt and Damascus, holding a scimitar, from a 15th-century European illuminated manuscript.

▶▶ Illustrations of a shield-cum-bow and a lance-and-bow combined from a treatise on arms and armour written for Saladin.

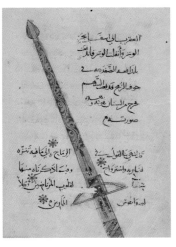

Medieval World | Saladin

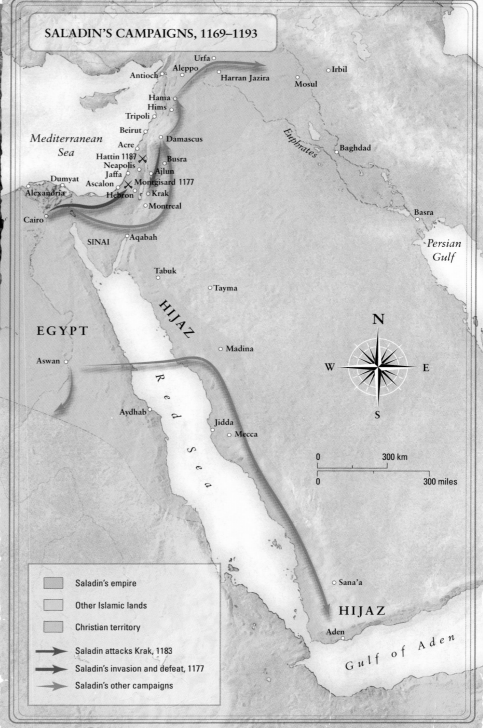

SALADIN'S CAMPAIGNS, 1169–1193

Urfa
Irbil
Antioch
Aleppo
Harran Jazira
Mosul
Hama
Hims
Tripoli
Baghdad
Beirut
Damascus
Mediterranean
Sea
Acre
Hattin 1187
Neapolis
Jaffa
Busra
Ajlun
Ascalon
Montgisard 1177
Dumyat
Hebron
Krak
Alexandria
Montreal
Basra
Cairo
Persian
Gulf
SINAI
Aqabah
Tabuk
Tayma
EGYPT
HIJAZ
N
Aswan
Madina
W
E
S
Red
Sea
Aydhab
Jidda
Mecca
0   300 km
0   300 miles
Saladin's empire
Other Islamic lands
Christian territory
Sana'a
→ Saladin attacks Krak, 1183
→ Saladin's invasion and defeat, 1177
→ Saladin's other campaigns
HIJAZ
Aden
Gulf of Aden

Key Battles

The Battle of Montgisard, 25 November 1177
In a pitched battle near Ramla (Israel), Saladin is defeated by the Crusader forces of Baldwin IV of Jerusalem, Raynald of Châtillon and the Knights Templar. The Muslim forces suffer heavy casualties and Saladin only narrowly avoids capture.

The Battle of Hattin, 1187
Saladin entices the Crusader forces of Raymond III of Tripoli and Guy of Lusignan from the fortress stronghold of Sephoria into a field battle in Galilee, knowing that this will be to his advantage. He surrounds the isolated Crusader army, and his archers inflict heavy casualties. The Crusader defeat leads to the virtual collapse of the Crusader states and the fall of Jerusalem in October.

The Siege of Acre, 1189–91
The Muslim forces in Acre are besieged by Guy of Lusignan and the Knights Templar. On 4 October 1189 Saladin reaches the city's outskirts, and his light cavalry inflicts heavy losses on the Crusaders. Crusader reinforcements arrive, but Saladin also increases his forces, and sets a second siege around them. The arrival of Richard the Lionheart and Phillip II of France in April 1191 spells the end for the Muslim defenders, though, and Saladin withdraws.

The Battle of Arsuf, 7 September 1191
The Crusader forces under Richard the Lionheart defeat Saladin at Arsuf, just to the north of the vital port of Jaffa. The Knights Hospitaller charge into Saladin's right flank, and rout his troops. The battle provides a crucial boost to Crusader morale.

into Nubia and across the Red Sea into Yemen. This was an impressive extension of power.

Saladin expanded his forces as he moved, increasing the diversity of his army, and thus its strength. He extended his grasp over much of the Arab world, including Syria, where Damascus was captured in 1174 and Aleppo in 1183, and parts of Iraq, including Mosul. This was an age-old geopolitical goal of the Egyptian rulers, but one that Saladin proved particularly successful in achieving. His was an adroit linkage of military, political and diplomatic strategies, each designed to be mutually supportive.

Saladin then turned on the Crusader states. Proclaiming a jihad in 1187, he smashed the Crusader army at Hattin that year. The predominantly infantry forces of the Kingdom of Jerusalem were out-generalled, advancing in the July heat under the fire of Saladin's mounted archers before being surrounded and defeated. The destruction of the field army left most of the fortress garrisons in too weak a position to hold out, and Saladin was able to overrun most of the Kingdom of Jerusalem, including Acre and Jerusalem, although the mighty fortress of Krak des Chevaliers successfully held out.

▲ Between 1174 and 1186 Saladin spent 33 months asserting his authority over other Muslim rulers, and only 13 months campaigning against the Christians. It was not until he controlled the region between Mosul and Egypt that he attacked the Crusader kingdom of Jerusalem, which culminated in the battle of Hattin.

▼ Ruins of Qalat al-Gundi, a fort in the Sinai region of Egypt built by Saladin.

The Battle of Hattin, 1187

Ayyubids	Kingdom of Jerusalem
Saladin	**Guy of Lusignan**
c. 12,000–20,000 troops	*c.* 20,000 troops
Casualties: unknown	Casualties: heavy

▶ Guy of Lusignan staked everything on confronting Saladin at Hattin, near Lake Tiberias. His defeat left the Kingdom of Jerusalem open to invasion.

▼ A Christian-Muslim joust from a manuscript dating to *c.* 1340: the contest is between a Crusader (right) and a Saracen (left), interpreted as Richard the Lionheart and Saladin, who did not in fact joust.

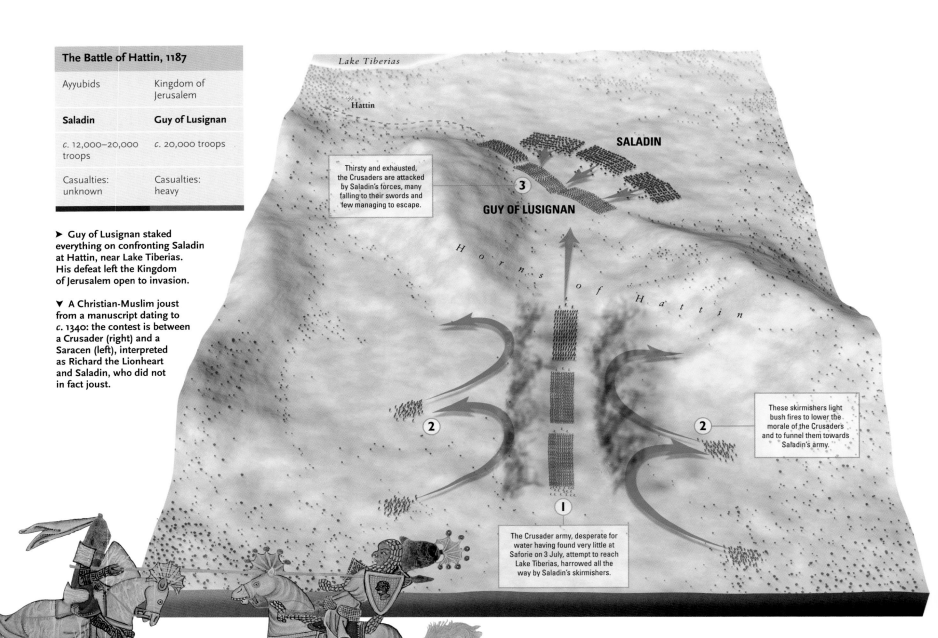

Lake Tiberias

Hattin

SALADIN

3 Thirsty and exhausted, the Crusaders are attacked by Saladin's forces, many falling to their swords and few managing to escape.

GUY OF LUSIGNAN

Horns of Hattin

2 These skirmishers light bush fires to lower the morale of the Crusaders and to funnel them towards Saladin's army.

2

1 The Crusader army, desperate for water having found very little at Saforie on 3 July, attempt to reach Lake Tiberias, harrowed all the way by Saladin's skirmishers.

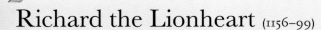

Richard the Lionheart (1156–99)

The bellicose second son of Henry II of England, Richard the Lionheart was involved in conflict for much of his youth, both in rebellion against his father, and then in maintaining, especially against baronial rebellions, the Duchy of Aquitaine in France, over which his father had given him authority. Becoming king in 1189, he launched the Third Crusade alongside Philip Augustus of France and Frederick Barbarossa, fighting in Sicily and Cyprus en route. Following the death of Frederick and the return home of Philip after the capture of Acre in 1191 (in which Richard played a leading role), Richard became the most important leader fighting to retake the Holy Land. Like Saladin, Richard's most remarkable achievement was to maintain cohesion within a widely disparate force during a prolonged campaign. He defeated Saladin at Arsuf, but was unable to capture Jerusalem. Imprisoned by the Austrians on his return home, he was ransomed, and then began a conflict with Philip Augustus, with whom he had competed for leadership of the crusade. Killed as result of a crossbow wound, he was buried at Fontevraud Abbey in Anjou. His tomb effigy is shown here.

The fall of Jerusalem led to the launching of the Third Crusade in 1189, which represented a formidable challenge to Saladin's control of Palestine, not least because of the range of the participants. The most vigorous leader in the crusade, Richard I of England, the Lionheart, captured Acre in 1191 and defeated Saladin at Arsuf that year, but Saladin was able to prevent Richard from exploiting his success and, in particular, he stopped him from besieging Jerusalem. The two men agreed an armistice in 1192 that acknowledged Saladin's control of the interior.

However, Saladin died suddenly at Damascus the following year.

Strategically adroit, Saladin was effective as both a military commander and a political leader, most notably in the way that he kept large and disparate forces in the field during extensive campaigning. His successes in Syria and Iraq tend to be overlooked by Western commentators, who focus on his clashes with the Crusaders, but they were a formidable achievement and he devoted more of his time to them than to the struggle for control of the Holy Land.

▲ At the battle of Hattin, Saladin cut the Crusaders off from the Tu'ran springs and waited until they were weakened by thirst before launching his attack, evoked here in a 15th-century French manuscript. The depiction is highly misleading, not least for the presence of the city and absence of horse-archers.

Frederick Barbarossa

German Holy Roman Emperor who Died on Crusade

'God granted us complete victory over Crema… and yet we have granted the wretched folk that were in the city their lives. For both divine and human law demand that the utmost clemency should ever dwell in the prince.'
FREDERICK BARBAROSSA

A Life in Brief

c. 1122
Born (location unknown)

1152
Becomes King of Germany

1154
Crowned Holy Roman Emperor

1190, 10 June
Dies at the River Saleph in Cilicia (Turkey)

Frederick I 'Barbarossa' (so-called because of his red beard) was the first Holy Roman Emperor of the Hohenstaufen family. He was an able soldier whose wars in Italy impressed contemporaries, despite mixed success. His army seemed so powerful on the Third Crusade (1189–92) that the Muslims saw his accidental death as an act of God. He was, in many ways, an unlucky commander.

Since Charlemagne (pp. 58–61), the Holy Roman Empire had encompassed Germany and Italy, and with the accession of Otto the Great (pp. 62–63) the imperial title was acquired by the German kings. Recent conflicts over the succession in Germany had weakened control over northern Italy, and, following his accession as King of Germany, Frederick was

determined to restore it. He should have been assisted in this by the divisions between the major trading cities of the Lombard Plain, most notably the fact that many disliked the domination of Milan, by far the greatest amongst them. However, Frederick could not count on unlimited support from German magnates, while all the Italian cities strongly disliked German overlordship and were heavily fortified. In 1154 Frederick entered Italy for his imperial coronation in Rome, but the Lombard cities resisted and, after a long siege, he destroyed Tortona. On his return from Rome, he had to fight his way back across the Lombard Plain. In 1158 he returned to Italy with a large army and forced Milan, which had not prepared for a siege, to surrender, though its fortifications remained intact. At the Diet

▶ Cloister of the Augustinian Church of St Zeno, Bad Reichenhall, Germany. The relief of Frederick Barbarossa is from the 12th century but it is intended to portray his majesty rather than a likeness.

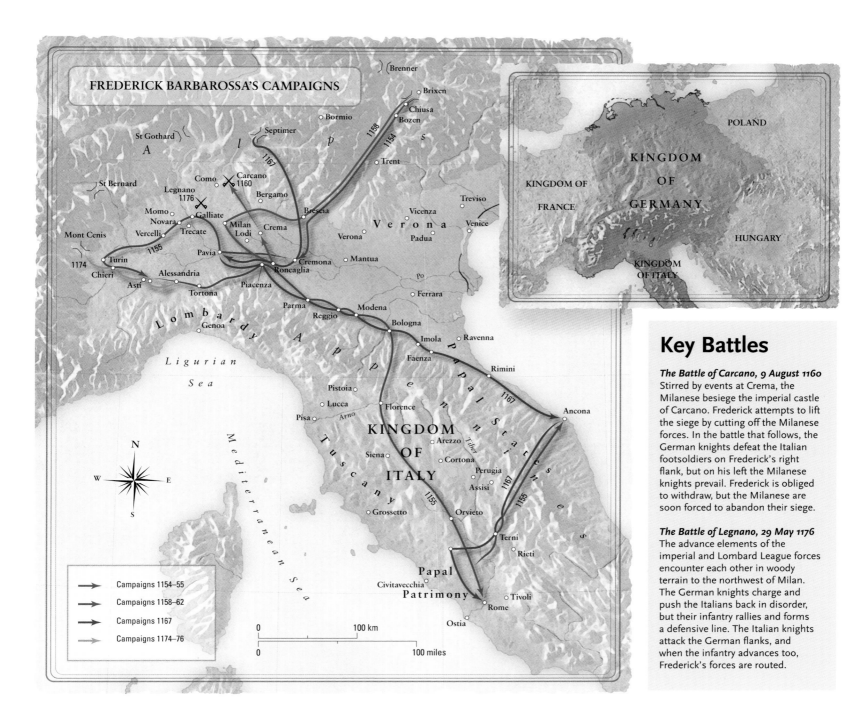

KINGDOM OF FRANCE

KINGDOM OF GERMANY

POLAND

HUNGARY

KINGDOM OF ITALY

Campaigns 1154–55
Campaigns 1158–62
Campaigns 1167
Campaigns 1174–76

0   100 km

0   100 miles

Key Battles

The Battle of Carcano, 9 August 1160
Stirred by events at Crema, the Milanese besiege the imperial castle of Carcano. Frederick attempts to lift the siege by cutting off the Milanese forces. In the battle that follows, the German knights defeat the Italian footsoldiers on Frederick's right flank, but on his left the Milanese knights prevail. Frederick is obliged to withdraw, but the Milanese are soon forced to abandon their siege.

The Battle of Legnano, 29 May 1176
The advance elements of the imperial and Lombard League forces encounter each other in woody terrain to the northwest of Milan. The German knights charge and push the Italians back in disorder, but their infantry rallies and forms a defensive line. The Italian knights attack the German flanks, and when the infantry advances too, Frederick's forces are routed.

of Roncaglia (1158) he reasserted imperial rights of taxation over the Lombard cities, but once his army had departed many of them rebelled.

Frederick also tried to assert his power over lands claimed by the Pope, and as a result at the papal election of 1159 backed the anti-Pope Victor IV (1159–64) against Alexander III (1159–81), who enjoyed widespread recognition. At the same time his ambitions in southern Italy alarmed the Norman Kingdom of South Italy and Sicily. In 1159 he attacked the small but strongly fortified city of Crema (near Cremona), and, despite a huge army and the deployment of all the latest siege devices, it resisted from July 1159 until January 1160. Frederick's army then melted away and the Milanese defeated him at the battle of Carcano on 9 August 1160. However, he

gathered reinforcements, besieging Milan itself in May 1161. The great city was formidably fortified and fell only in March 1162, when it was razed to the ground and its citizens dispersed. Imperial taxation, however, alienated the other cities, which rebelled again and ignored Frederick's attempts to impose peace on his third journey to Italy in 1163.

By 1165 the Pope was again in defiant mood. In 1166 Frederick gathered a great army, overawed the Lombards, and captured Rome, forcing the Pope to flee to southern Italy. Frederick was preparing a campaign to the south when a great plague decimated his army, obliging him to retreat and enabling all his enemies to unite against him. He prepared another expedition, but many of the German nobles were reluctant. Even during the 1161–62 siege of Milan some had not

▶ The Alps were a formidable barrier to Barbarossa's hopes of controlling Rome and the wealthy cities of Italy. The sheer difficulty of crossing such a barrier explains why the emperor found it hard to raise and maintain armies.

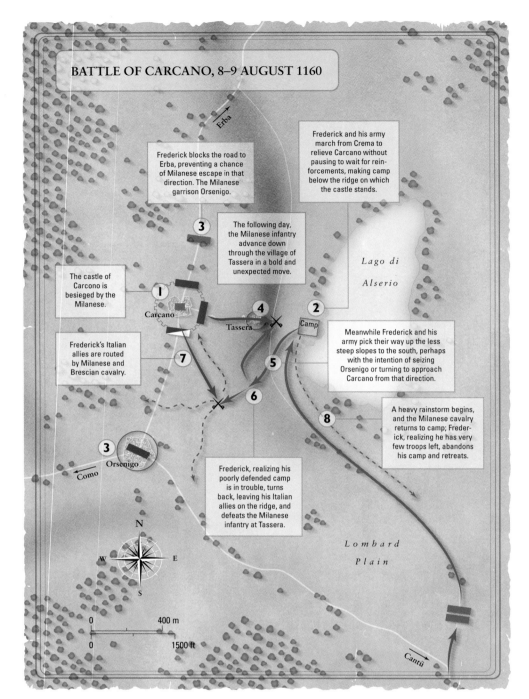

BATTLE OF CARCANO, 8–9 AUGUST 1160

Frederick blocks the road to Erba, preventing a chance of Milanese escape in that direction. The Milanese garrison Orsenigo.

Frederick and his army march from Crema to relieve Carcano without pausing to wait for reinforcements, making camp below the ridge on which the castle stands.

The following day, the Milanese infantry advance down through the village of Tassera in a bold and unexpected move.

The castle of Carcono is besieged by the Milanese.

Frederick's Italian allies are routed by Milanese and Brescian cavalry.

Meanwhile Frederick and his army pick their way up the less steep slopes to the south, perhaps with the intention of seizing Orsenigo or turning to approach Carcano from that direction.

Frederick, realizing his poorly defended camp is in trouble, turns back, leaving his Italian allies on the ridge, and defeats the Milanese infantry at Tassera.

A heavy rainstorm begins, and the Milanese cavalry returns to camp; Frederick, realizing he has very few troops left, abandons his camp and retreats.

Lago di Alserio

Lombard Plain

Carcano · Tassera · Camp · Orsenigo · Como · Erba · Cantù

N W E S

0 400 m
0 1500 ft

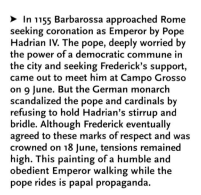

▲ Barbarossa, with a small army, challenged the Milanese siege of Carcano castle on 9 August 1160. In the subsequent battle the Germans killed many of the Milanese infantry, but their cavalry were ambushed and the Emperor was forced to withdraw.

► In 1155 Barbarossa approached Rome seeking coronation as Emperor by Pope Hadrian IV. The pope, deeply worried by the power of a democratic commune in the city and seeking Frederick's support, came out to meet him at Campo Grosso on 9 June. But the German monarch scandalized the pope and cardinals by refusing to hold Hadrian's stirrup and bridle. Although Frederick eventually agreed to these marks of respect and was crowned on 18 June, tensions remained high. This painting of a humble and obedient Emperor walking while the pope rides is papal propaganda.

wanted to fight, and now, led by Henry the Lion, Duke of Saxony, there was outright refusal to serve. Because of this, Frederick could bring only limited forces on his fifth expedition to Italy in 1174. The cities of northern Italy united in the Lombard League, and, with the support of the papacy and the Normans, fielded larger armies than the emperor. Frederick was unable to capture Alessandria (in Piedmont), a strategic fortress built across his line of approach, and in 1176 he was defeated by the Lombard League at the battle of Legnano. This led to peace with Rome and imperial recognition of Pope Alexander III, but the Lombard cities fought on until 1183 and the Peace of Constance. Frederick was able to exploit internal divisions to obtain a degree of rule over them, but not to the extent that he had claimed at Roncaglia in 1158.

In 1187 Saladin (see pp. 68–71) captured Jerusalem and in May 1189, at the age of 67, Frederick took the cross. He had participated in the Second Crusade (1145–49), when the German army had been poorly organized. Now he asserted tight control over a 100,000-strong force, which was said to have taken three days to pass a single point. He marched down the Danube and brushed aside Byzantine resistance. He crushed the Turkish Sultan of Iconium, becoming the first Christian leader since the First Crusade to force the passage of Asia Minor. However, with his enemies trembling before him, Frederick fell into the River Saleph (modern Göksu) in Cilicia and died. His army immediately dissolved.

'What [the people of Milan] have done to injure us… and the glory of the Roman empire will be visited with such penalties that no hope may spring up among the base and seditious.'

FREDERICK BARBAROSSA

◄ This 14th-century stained glass image of Barbarossa from St Stephen's in Vienna is much less stylized than the other pictures, but, of course, is purely imaginative. We have descriptions of Barbarossa, but no real idea otherwise of what he looked like. Realistic portraiture only develop in the late 13th century.

▼ This portrait bust from Cappenberg is of gilded bronze and was probably made between 1150 and 1160 when Barbarossa was at the height of his power. It is tempting, therefore, to see this as a real likeness, but again it is an effort to portray greatness and power.

Barbarossa was a master of 12th-century warfare. His armoured knights were superb, and even at Legnano swept the Milanese cavalry from the field. However, he and his noble followers were contemptuous of the Italian footsoldiers, partly because of disdain for social inferiors. This element of class hostility may account for the cruelty of the fighting in the Lombard Plain: at one stage Barbarossa proclaimed that anyone captured fighting against him would have their right arm cut off. He also faced the usual problems of medieval generals. Armies could only be raised by persuading great magnates to join, and they tended to go home as soon as possible. In Italy Frederick was fighting far from his bases and it was exceptionally difficult to establish a party amongst the shifting allegiances of the northern Italian cities. He overplayed his hand in 1164 when a peace seemed possible and again in 1166 when he contemplated conquest of southern Italy, and until his defeat at Legnano he consistently failed to use diplomacy to support his military efforts. On the Third Crusade he commanded a large and enthusiastic army that he organized and led superbly, only for fate to strike him down at the Saleph.

Chingiz Khan

Fearsome Mongol Leader who Created the Largest Empire in Europe

*'I am the scourge of God. If you had not committed great sins,
God would not have sent a punishment like me upon you.'* CHINGIZ KHAN

A Life in Brief

1162
Born in the Onan–Kerulen river basin, Mongolia

1183
Enters service of Toghril Ong-Khan, ruler of the Kereits

1184
Begins military apprenticeship under Jamuqa

1206
Officially named ruler of the Mongolian steppes

1227, 18 August
Dies during the Western Xia campaign, in northwest China

▶ Chingiz Khan, painted by an unknown artist on silk canvas. The painting comes from the Yuan period (1265–1368), well after Chingiz Khan's death, so is at best a representation of the Mongol leader in a Chinese manner.

Chingiz Khan (or as he is less correctly known in the West, Genghis Khan) is the embodiment of the Mongol empire and the Mongol art of war. Not only did he conquer more territory than any other single commander, he also created the most powerful military force of the pre-Modern period. His key achievement, which allowed him to establish the Mongol empire, was the creation of a highly disciplined army, staffed by trained officers.

Chingiz Khan was born as Temüjin in the 1160s, the eldest son of Yesügei and Hö'elün, minor nobility of the Borjigin Mongols in the Onan–Kerulen river basin. Yesügei was murdered by Tatars, the ancestral enemies of the Mongols, when Temüjin was only eight or nine years old. Temüjin began his rise to power by becoming the *nökör* or bondsman of Toghril Ong-Khan, the head of the powerful Kereit confederation in central Mongolia. It was here that he first learned about leadership, under the guidance of Toghril's war chief, Jamuqa – a former childhood friend of Temüjin. Following their joint involvement in the rescue of Temüjin's wife, Börte, from kidnappers, the two renewed their friendship. Temüjin served as Jamuqa's apprentice in the ways of war and military leadership, including the use of decimally organized military units.

However, tensions arose between the charismatic and talented Temüjin and his mentor. When the two parted company, many from Jamuqa's camp followed Temüjin. Most were commoners who valued emphasis on talent and merit, rather than birth, for privileges – a practice that defied tradition among the nomads.

THE UNIFICATION OF MONGOLIA

As Temüjin came into his own as a tribal leader he attracted more supporters from other tribes. Among the reasons for this was that he would divide any plunder among all those who participated in a raid, rather than only to the nobility who then distributed it as they desired. He also instilled discipline among his troops, punishing anyone who stopped fighting in order to gather booty; victory, he stressed, was the most important thing, and there would be plenty of time to plunder afterwards.

Temüjin remained Toghril's *nökör* for several years. During this time he suffered only one defeat, to Jamuqa, in 1187 at the battle of Dalan Balzhut. Eventually, Temüjin and Toghril also parted ways, as the former's prestige and power began to eclipse the latter's. In 1203 the two fought: Temüjin emerged victorious, and gained control over eastern and central

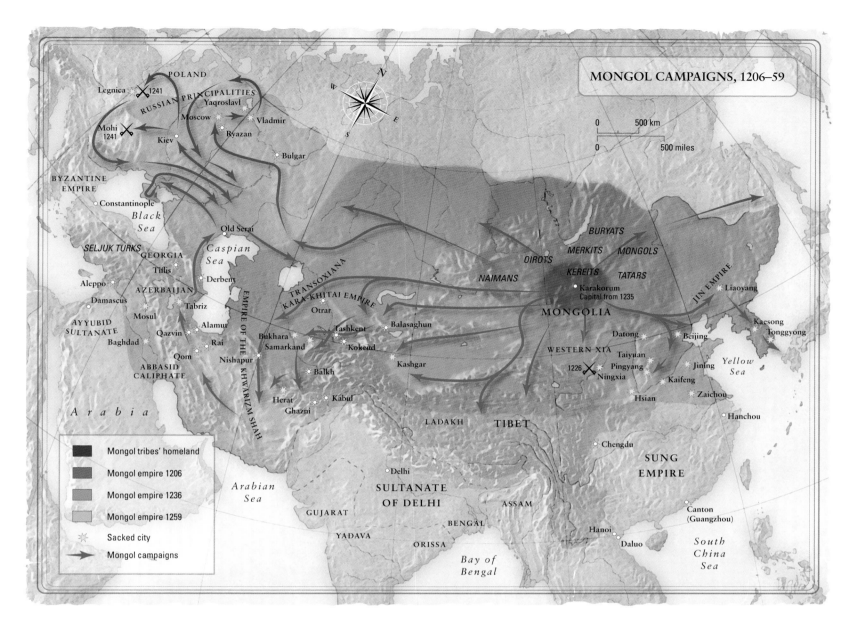

Mongol tribes' homeland
Mongol empire 1206
Mongol empire 1236
Mongol empire 1259
✳ Sacked city
→ Mongol campaigns

Mongolia. Next he defeated the remaining threat to his power, the Naiman confederation in western Mongolia, using a combination of deception and innovative tactics that became the Mongol hallmark.

The Mongols organized their forces in decimal units of tens, hundreds and thousands. Their disciplined troops could thus march in loose formation and in several columns, which allowed them to move much more quickly. Scouts operated in all directions, keeping them informed of potential danger. Furthermore, they used psychological warfare, including feeding the enemy misinformation. When attacking, the Mongols always sought to encircle or outflank their opponents. Their preferred tactic was

▲ While earlier campaigns were little more than large-scale raids, the Mongols gradually turned to permanent conquests. By the time of his death in 1227, Chingiz Khan had conquered more territory than any ruler in history; his successors expanded the empire still further.

▲ This Mongolian dagger would probably have been used to aid quick repair of equipment in the field, rather than for fighting. Weapons for combat included the battle-axe, the lance and the recurved bow.

Key Battles

The Battle of Chakirmaut, 1204
In the war with the Naiman confederation, Chingiz Khan launches an attack in early spring – even though his horses have not fully recovered from the hardships of winter – thus gaining the element of surprise. On the eve of battle, the Mongols deceive the Naiman by lighting extra camp fires to disguise their inferior numbers. The Mongols use the 'chisel' formation to achieve victory.

The Siege of Zhongxiang, 1209–10
During the Western Xia campaign (1207–10), the Mongols fail to capture Zhongxiang by direct assault, and are forced to lay siege to the city. Their lack of experience in siege warfare almost costs them dearly, when they divert a river

to flood the city: their dykes break and flood the Mongol camp. However, Western Xia is eventually overrun.

The Siege of Zhongdu, 1214–15
During the conquest of the Jin empire (1211–34), Chingiz Khan first blockades the city of Zhongdu and then subjects it to continuous bombardment from catapults. Meanwhile, Mongol field armies roam the region to prevent any relief forces from aiding the city, which eventually submits.

The Siege of Bukhara, 1220
During the Khwarezmian War (1219–23) Chingiz Khan arrives at Bukhara, 300 miles behind the front line, by marching through the Kizil Kum desert. The Mongols allow a sortie by the garrison to break through their ranks, and then follow and destroy the fleeing troops. The city is invested and taken.

Chingiz Khan

Medieval World

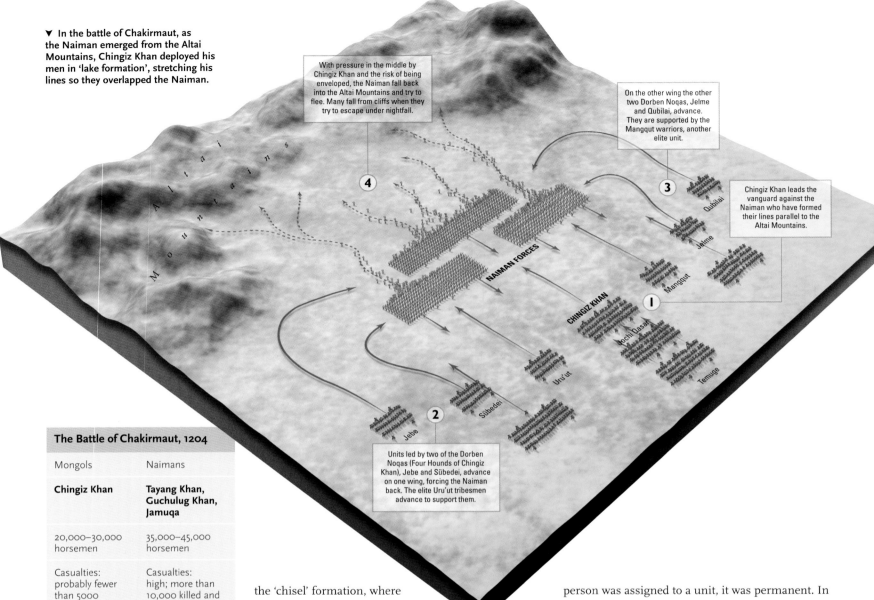

▼ In the battle of Chakirmaut, as the Naiman emerged from the Altai Mountains, Chingiz Khan deployed his men in 'lake formation', stretching his lines so they overlapped the Naiman.

With pressure in the middle by Chingiz Khan and the risk of being enveloped, the Naiman fall back into the Altai Mountains and try to flee. Many fall from cliffs when they try to escape under nightfall.

On the other wing the other two Dorben Noqas, Jelme and Qubilai, advance. They are supported by the Mangqut warriors, another elite unit.

Chingiz Khan leads the vanguard against the Naiman who have formed their lines parallel to the Altai Mountains.

Units led by two of the Dorben Noqas (Four Hounds of Chingiz Khan), Jebe and Sübedei, advance on one wing, forcing the Naiman back. The elite Uru'ut tribesmen advance to support them.

The Battle of Chakirmaut, 1204

Mongols	Naimans
Chingiz Khan	**Tayang Khan, Guchulug Khan, Jamuqa**
20,000–30,000 horsemen	35,000–45,000 horsemen
Casualties: probably fewer than 5000	Casualties: high; more than 10,000 killed and 10,000–20,000 captured

▼ The lamellar armour of a Mongol heavy cavalryman. Lamellar was made from lacquered leather by the Mongols themselves and offered better protection against arrows than other armours, including chainmail.

the 'chisel' formation, where mounted archers attacked in single file, with each member charging and shooting their arrows, before wheeling back around, still shooting, and returning to the rear of the file. The enemy was thus subjected to continuous attack. This was often used in conjunction with other tactics, such as feigning retreat to lure enemy troops out from their lines and then ambushing them.

CREATING AN EMPIRE

By 1206, Temüjin had gained complete control over Mongolia, and he ascended the throne as Chingiz Khan, meaning 'firm or resolute ruler'. He then set about organizing his empire and army. He assigned commanders to each unit of 1,000 men (a *mingan*), and each unit of 10,000 men (a *tümen*), a structure mirrored in civil society too. Many of the commanders of these units had risen through the ranks during the wars of unification, such as the great general Sübedei. Defeated tribes were dispersed among the *mingans* to remove any threat of organized rebellion. Once a

person was assigned to a unit, it was permanent. In doing so, the old tribal structure disappeared and a new 'super tribe' came into being, eventually known as the *Yeke Mongol Ulus*, or Great Mongol Nation.

In addition, Chingiz Khan developed the *keshik*, or bodyguard, of the khan. It numbered 10,000 men, and recruits were brought in from throughout Mongolia. Later, the sons of vassal rulers would be enrolled in its ranks, as both security and potential replacements should their fathers ever rebel. The *keshik* also served as an officer training school. All the major generals and governors who emerged after 1206 served therein. Furthermore, a commander in the *keshik* always outranked his peers in the regular Mongol army.

THE WORLD CONQUEROR

After uniting Mongolia, Chingiz Khan conquered much of northern China and Central Asia. His wars were usually motivated by revenge or to nullify threats to stability in Mongolia. Indeed, his initial invasions involved little territorial acquisition, save for control of mountain passes leading to Mongolia. However, as

Medieval World — Chingiz Khan

time went on rulers, governors and generals offered their vassalage, and the empire evolved. In the case of the Jin empire in northern China, continuous Mongol raiding weakened the state to such an extent that conquest took place *ipso facto*, in the ever-expanding quest for plunder.

In 1207 the Mongols invaded the kingdom of Western Xia, which comprised much of northwestern China and parts of Tibet; it eventually submitted to Chingiz Khan in 1210. In 1211 he led his armies against the Jin dynasty in northern China. Its forces resisted for over 20 years, before succumbing in 1234. At the same time, a front opened in Central Asia after a Mongol-sponsored caravan was massacred in Otrar, a city of the empire of Khwarezm, in 1219.

So launched one of the most brilliant campaigns in history, lasting from 1219 to 1223, which demonstrated the independence that Chingiz Khan allowed his commanders. Chingiz Khan left a token force in China under Muqali, a trusted general, while he marched 1,000 miles to Central Asia. His armies struck from five different routes, and Chingiz Khan himself led an army through the Kizil Kum desert to appear at Bukhara (Uzbekistan), 300 miles behind enemy lines. Although the Khwarezm empire was overrun, Chingiz

Khan kept only the territories north of the Amu Darya river, so as not to overextend his armies.

In 1226 his armies again invaded Western Xia, to quell an uprising there. While hunting in Western Xia, Chingiz Khan fell from his horse and later died from internal injuries. His followers completed the destruction of Western Xia and then buried Chingiz Khan in a secret location that has yet to be found.

LEGACY

At its height, the Mongol empire stretched from the Sea of Japan to the Carpathian mountains. The military practices in organization, tactics and overall strategy that Chingiz Khan instituted were standardized and maintained. As the Mongols often fought on multiple fronts, the example set by Chingiz Khan ensured that they did not overextend their forces. In both its organization and the role of its commanders, the Mongol army functioned in ways more similar to that of a modern army than a medieval one, and the horse archer became one of the most infamous fighting men in world history. Some commentators have even drawn parallels between Mongol battle tactics and those of the German Panzer commanders in the blitzkrieg years of World War II.

> *'With Heaven's aid I have conquered for you a huge empire. But my life was too short to achieve the conquest of the world. That task is left for you.'*
> CHINGIZ KHAN TO HIS SON

Kublai Khan (1215–94)

Kublai Khan, a grandson of Chingiz Khan, was the founder of the Mongol Yuan dynasty, which ruled over most of eastern Asia until 1368. In many ways Kublai, shown here with two attendants, was the antithesis of his grandfather, as his

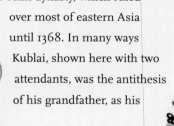

accession to power led to the splitting of the Mongol empire. Whereas his grandfather had created a Mongolian state, the nomadic Mongols of the steppes did not view Kublai as a true Mongol, as he spent most of his time in China.

Kublai came to power after a civil war with his brother, Ariq Böke, following the death of their elder brother, Möngke, in 1259. Both claimed the title, but it was not until 1264–65 that Kublai emerged victorious. However, the empire he won consisted only of Mongolia, Korea and modern China. The rest of the Mongol territories drifted away, with some fighting Kublai and others recognizing him as their overlord.

Kublai's greatest military achievement was the conquest, beginning in 1234, of the Song

empire in southern China. His ultimate success lay in the integration of the Mongol cavalry with Chinese infantry and naval troops, who were better suited to warfare in mountainous terrain and among the rice paddies. Kublai completed the conquest of the Song in 1279 with a naval victory at Yaishan. Throughout the war, Kublai also contended with frontier wars against his cousins.

Kublai's military reputation remains tarnished by his overambitious attempts to expand the empire. Two planned invasions of Japan (1274 and 1281) ended in disaster when typhoons destroyed the Mongol fleets. His attempts to expand into Southeast Asia also failed, and the Mongols were forced to abandon Java and Vietnam. Only in Burma did the Mongols succeed in obtaining tribute. Nevertheless, Kublai Khan remains a great commander, owing to his dynamism and his ability to integrate different military systems, with his fame immortalized in *The Travels of Marco Polo* and Coleridge's poem *Kubla Khan*.

Timur

Creator of a Great Central Asian Empire

'I smiled that God should have given the mastery of the world to a lame man like me.' TIMUR

A Life in Brief

1336
Born near Samarkand

1360
Made Lord of Kesh by
Chaghatayid Khan

1370
Ruler of Mawarannahr

1405, 19 January
Dies at Otrar while marching on
the Ming empire of China

▶ A reconstruction of Timur's head made by M. M. Gerasimov, a Soviet scholar. It was based on Timur's actual skull which was found after his mausoleum was opened in 1941. Gerasimov pioneered the science of reconstructing faces from skulls, a common forensics technique today. According to legend the tomb had a curse stating that if anyone desecrated it, a worse calamity than Timur would invade their country. Three days after Gerasimov opened the tomb, Hitler's armies invaded the Soviet Union.

In the late 14th century Timur (also known as Tamerlane or Tamberlaine) attempted to resurrect the Mongol empire, and very nearly succeeded. He conquered an empire stretching from the Syr Darya river in Central Asia to the Mediterranean, defeating the major powers of his day – the Mamluks, Ottomans, the Sultanate of Delhi, and the Golden Horde khanate – and all despite the fact that he was lame on the right side of his body.

Born near the town of Shakhrisyabz near Samarkand in 1336, like many Central Asian conquerors Timur's career began as a minor leader and occasional bandit during the unrest that accompanied the unravelling of the Mongol empire during the mid-14th century. Timur's detractors gave him his sobriquet *Timur-e Leng* (Timur the Lame) as a result of arrow wounds to his right hip and elbow sustained during one of his bandit forays.

With the collapse of the Mongol states, new opportunities arose for those with ambition. Timur took advantage of the situation, becoming the lieutenant of his brother-in-law Emir Husain. Despite a devastating loss against the Chaghatayid Mongols at the Battle of the Mire in 1365, they won control of Mawarannahr ('the land across the river', also known as Transoxiana) before rivalry surfaced in 1370. Ultimately, Timur emerged as victor from this struggle.

After establishing himself as ruler of Mawarannahr, Timur consolidated his control over the region and defended it from nomadic attacks. Then, in 1380, he became involved in the politics of the wider world. Timur supported Tokhtamysh, a prince in the Golden Horde, in his ultimately successful bid to seize control of the khanate's throne.

Using an army similar to that of Chingiz Khan (pp. 76–79) based around highly disciplined nomadic horse archers, Timur expanded beyond Mawarannahr in 1383. By the middle of the next decade, his empire stretched from the Syr Darya to the River Tigris and the Caucasus mountains. For the most part, Timur rarely established effective administration in his conquered territories. Instead, he seemed to delight in suppressing rebellions and plundering the regions again. With the plunder, he raised the cities of Bukhara and his capital of Samarkand to an almost unimaginable splendour. Some of the outlying sections were named after cities he had sacked.

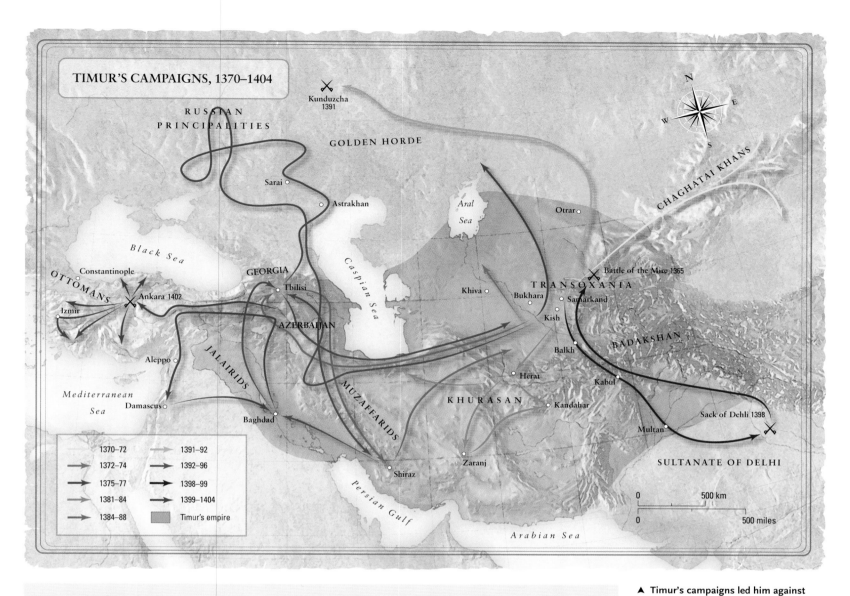

TIMUR'S CAMPAIGNS, 1370–1404

	1370–72		1391–92
	1372–74		1392–96
	1375–77		1398–99
	1381–84		1399–1404
	1384–88		Timur's empire

Key Battles

The Battle of the Mire, 1365
Emir Husain and Timur attempt to wrest control of Mawarannahr from the Chaghatayid Mongols. The two forces collide at the Battle of the Mire during a storm, which the Chaghatayids have used shamans to summon. Timur and Husain are defeated, and thousands of their troops are swept away or drown in the mire.

The Battle of Kunduzcha, 1391
During the war against the Golden Horde, Timur crosses the Syr Darya river and pursues Tokhtamysh after his raid on Mawarannahr. Tokhtamysh tries to draw out Timur's line by continually retreating. Timur's army maintains its discipline and finally defeats Tokhtamysh near the confluence of the Kama and Volga rivers in the forests of Siberia – a far from ideal place for two horse-archer-based armies.

The Sack of Delhi, 1398
During the invasion of India, Timur's armies meet the forces of the Sultanate of Delhi 6 miles from the city. Despite being heavily outnumbered, Timur prevails. He defeats the Sultanate of Dehli, breaking the Indian lines by releasing water buffalo carrying flaming bundles, which terrifies the Indian elephants, and scattering caltrops (metal spikes) on the ground. His more disciplined troops then annihilate the Indian army and pillage the city.

The Battle of Ankara, 1402
In the struggle for domination of Eastern Anatolia, Timur and the Ottoman Sultan Bayezid clash at Ankara. Timur ultimately prevails as thousands of nomads desert to his side, an opportunity that Timur has cultivated. Bayezid's European troops fight loyally, but ultimately his Janissaries are annihilated and he is taken prisoner.

▲ Timur's campaigns led him against every major power in Eurasia in the 14th and early 15th centuries. Through them he defeated the Golden Horde, north of the Caspian and Black Seas, the Sultanate of Delhi in India, the Mamluks in Syria, and the Ottomans in modern Turkey. The only state to escape his wrath was the Chinese Ming empire as he died in 1405 before he could complete his march to China.

▶ This stone commemorates Timur's march against Tokhtamysh, ruler of the Golden Horde, in 1391. The rock was inscribed in Arabic and Chaghatay Turkic (the language Timur spoke). Only a fragment of the stone exists today, now located in the Hermitage Museum in St. Petersburg, Russia.

▶ The battle of Ankara was a cataclysmic battle that set the Ottoman empire back for 50 years. Sultan Bayezid rushed to relieve the city of Ankara from Timur's siege. Timur outmanoeuvred Bayezid with a strong defensive position and also poisoned the wells on Bayezid's route. Thus they positioned themselves by the Kizilcakoy stream on a series of hills. In the battle, the Ottoman sipahis or cavalry broke before Timur's attack on the Ottoman left. Timur then struck the Ottoman Serbian cavalry on the right wing. The Serbs fell for a feigned retreat. The mortal blow for the Ottomans was when the nomadic Turkic auxiliaries abandoned the Ottomans and joined Timur. With the loss of most of his cavalry, Bayezid made a last stand on a hill called Catal Tepe, where he was captured.

▼ The later Timurid period was known for its excellence in artistry. This 15th-century dragon-headed sabre, made from watered steel and white jade inlaid with gold, along with dragon-headed hilt and scabbard, is a fine example. It was a weapon that was once carried by a Timurid prince.

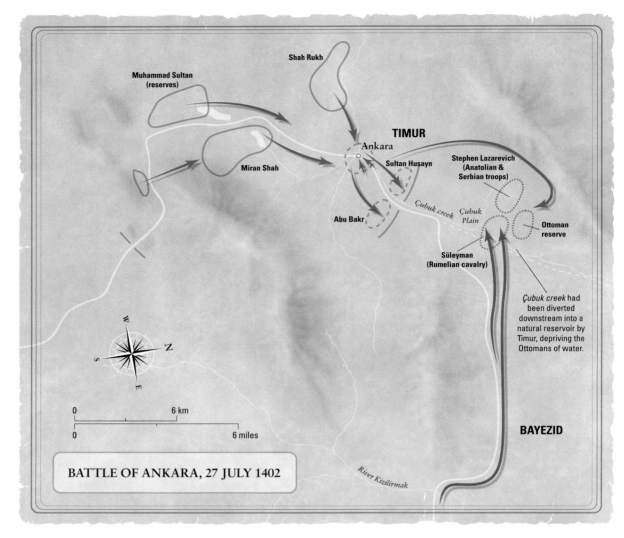

BATTLE OF ANKARA, 27 JULY 1402

Meanwhile, Timur's protégé Tokhtamysh had risen to challenge his authority. Tokhtamysh defeated Timur's generals during invasions in 1385 and 1388, but could not stand before the fury of Timur, who defeated Tokhtamysh by pursuing him into the steppe and then into the forests at Kunduzcha. Despite the apparent foolishness of pursuing nomads into the steppe, where they could vanish and then return to attack the pursuer's overextended supply lines, Timur prevailed. In 1395, Timur defeated Tokhtamysh again at the River Terek, this time conclusively. Tokhtamysh survived, but Timur sacked his capital city of Sarai. This not only ruined Tokhtamysh militarily, but also economically. With the destruction of the important cities on the Volga (including Astrakhan), Timur shifted the trade routes south to his empire and away from his rival.

Timur sought to justify his actions on religious grounds as jihads. Although many considered him an infidel, Timur was a Muslim who followed the teachings of the Naqshbandiyya Sufis. When he invaded India in 1398, he accused the Sultanate of Delhi of excessive tolerance towards its Hindu subjects. The city was subsequently sacked.

Timur did not tarry long in his capital. In 1399, he marched west against the Mamluk sultanate in Egypt and Syria and the Ottoman empire. Both had previously made alliances with Tokhtamysh and other rebels. With his intelligence network keeping him informed of the whereabouts of his enemies, Timur dealt with both through lightning attacks. He invaded Syria in 1401 and defeated the Mamluks, sacking Aleppo and Damascus in the process. He then invaded Anatolia, and defeated the Ottomans at the battle of Ankara in 1402.

Timur reached Samarkand in 1404. Now, in his 70s and often confined to his litter due to his age and the injuries suffered in youth, he planned to invade China and overthrow the Ming dynasty. However, Timur died on 19 January 1405 at the city of Otrar (Kazakhstan), where his army had assembled for the invasion. His empire quickly crumbled after his death, as his sons and grandsons quarrelled over control of the empire.

Although Timur did not develop revolutionary tactics, he was a highly creative commander and

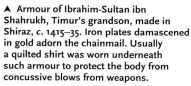

▲ Armour of Ibrahim-Sultan ibn Shahrukh, Timur's grandson, made in Shiraz, c. 1415–35. Iron plates damascened in gold adorn the chainmail. Usually a quilted shirt was worn underneath such armour to protect the body from concussive blows from weapons.

◄ The Gur-e Amir, the Mausoleum of the Great Emir Timur in Samarkand. Constructed in 1404, this octagonal tomb with its decorative tile mosaic work is a brilliant example of Timurid architecture. Timur was buried alongside his grandson Muhammad Sultan. Nearby is the tomb of a Sufi saint and adviser to Timur.

was brilliant at adapting to changing circumstances and inspiring his men. Timur's legacy is characterized by both his conquests and his cruelty. Massacres were a tool to terrorize and intimidate, and the skulls of his victims were often built into towers.

Timur brought about the decline of five major states, although the Byzantine empire was spared for 50 years due to the chaos that arose from the Ottomans' defeat. The defeat of the Mamluks did not destroy them, but it exposed the slow decay of their once grand military might. Tokhtamysh's defeat eroded the strength of the Golden Horde and accelerated the rise of the Grand Duchy of Moscow. Finally, the destruction of Delhi was something from which the Sultanate of Delhi never recovered. Indeed, one of Timur's direct descendants, Babur (pp. 116–19), supplanted the Sultanate with the Mughal empire in India.

Edward I

King of England who Conquered Wales and Campaigned in Scotland

'When you get rid of a turd, you do a good job.'
EDWARD I, ON HANDING OVER AUTHORITY IN SCOTLAND TO JOHN, EARL WARENNE, 1296

A Life in Brief

1239, 17 June
Born at Westminster

1263–65
Fights for his father in the civil war

1272, 20 November
Becomes King of England

1307, 7 July
Dies at Burgh-on-Sands, Cumbria

Edward I's reputation as a military leader rests largely on his achievement in conquering Wales. In contrast, his apparent success in Scotland turned to dust at the end of his reign, and he achieved little campaigning on the Continent and on crusade in the early 1270s. His main achievements lay in successfully mobilizing military resources on an impressive scale, and organizing his campaigns in a systematic and efficient manner.

Edward's military career began before his accession, with the civil war of 1263–65 against Simon de Montfort. He learnt much from this conflict, not least from defeat at Lewes (1264) where he failed to control his troops. He made no mistake at Evesham in 1265, where his opponent de Montfort was slain. On crusade (1270–72) Edward achieved little, due to the inadequacy of his forces.

In Wales Edward showed an excellent understanding of strategy. The three main campaigns (1277, 1282–83 and 1294–95) followed similar plans. Edward advanced in the north, close to the coast, while in central and south Wales troops under the command of Marcher lords would also engage the Welsh. Forces were sent by sea to take Anglesey; in 1277 they were equipped with sickles to collect the harvest. Edward overpowered the Welsh with massive military force; in 1282 the Welsh prince Llywelyn ap Gruffydd broke out of the north and was defeated by a Marcher force in mid-Wales at the battle of Irfon Bridge. In 1295 the stranglehold Edward had over Snowdonia compelled the rebel leader Madog ap Llywelyn to move south, to be defeated by the Earl of Warwick at the battle of Maes Moydog. The great castles

▶ Edward I shown seated on a simple throne, being addressed by bishops and others present in his court. It was a brave cleric who opposed the king, who is said to have frightened both a dean of St Paul's and an archbishop of York to death.

Key Battles and Campaigns

The Battle of Lewes, 1264
Edward commands one division of the royal army, and routs the Londoners of Simon de Montfort facing him. However, by the time his troops reform, the battle is lost.

The Battle of Evesham, 1265
After clever manoeuvring, Simon de Montfort is surrounded by royalist troops, and his forces are crushed.

The First Welsh War, 1277
A march along the coast of North Wales, and a naval expedition to Anglesey, leads to the surrender of Prince Llywelyn ap Gruffydd without a real fight.

The Second Welsh War, 1282–83
Edward advances in the north, while other English forces operate in the centre and south. Prince Llywelyn ap Gruffydd is defeated and killed at Irfon Bridge in December 1282; Edward is not present at the battle.

The Welsh Rebellion, 1294–95
Edward follows a familiar strategy, advancing from Chester, and wintering at Conwy. In March 1295 a force led by the Earl of Warwick defeats the Welsh leader Madog ap Llywelyn.

The Battle of Falkirk, 1298
The Scots, under William Wallace, are drawn up in solid formations (schiltroms), which are broken and routed by the English infantry.

The Siege of Caerlaverock, 1300
Edward's campaign in southwest Scotland achieves limited success. The capture of Caerlaverock Castle, immortalized in a medieval French poem, provides a highlight for him.

The Siege of Stirling, April 1304
Edward conducts a four-month siege of the castle, the last stronghold of anti-English resistance. The Scots under William Oliphant surrender just as Edward's latest siege engine, the huge and terrifying War Wolf, is readied for action.

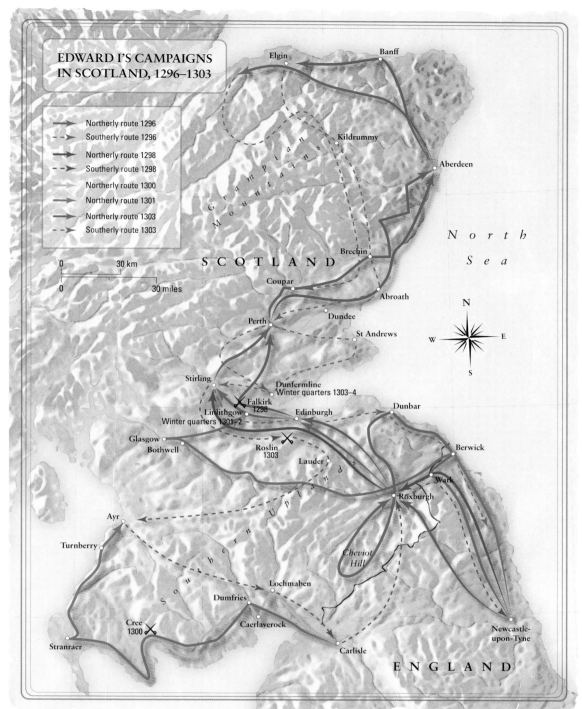

➤ Edward I's expeditions to Scotland met with mixed success, though by 1304 and the siege of Stirling success seemed to have been achieved. Campaigning was largely in southern and central Scotland.

EDWARD I'S CAMPAIGNS IN SCOTLAND, 1296–1303

Northerly route 1296
Southerly route 1296
Northerly route 1298
Southerly route 1298
Northerly route 1300
Northerly route 1301
Northerly route 1303
Southerly route 1303

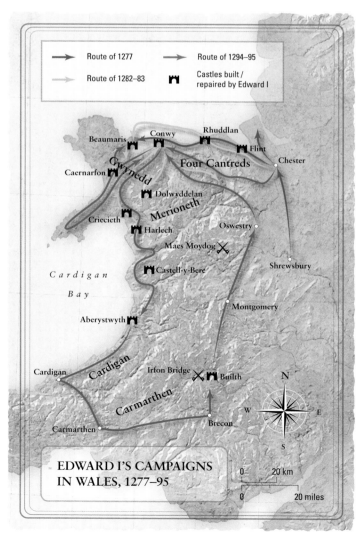

Route of 1277
Route of 1282–83
Route of 1294–95
Castles built / repaired by Edward I

EDWARD I'S CAMPAIGNS IN WALES, 1277–95

◄ Edward I's Welsh campaigns were concentrated on Gwynedd, in the north, the heartland of the Welsh prince Llywelyn ap Gruffudd. His armies advanced from Chester, assisted by naval support.

Harlech ▲ and Caernarfon ▼ are two of the great castles built by Edward I after the campaign of 1282–83 to consolidate his conquest of Wales. They were built under the direction of an expert from Savoy, Master James of St George.

The Battle of Evesham, 1265

Royalists	Rebels
Edward, son of King Henry III	**Simon de Montfort**
c. 10,000 troops	*c.* 5,000 troops
Casualties: limited	Casualties: *c.* 4,000 (at least 30 knights, and many others).

▼ At Evesham, royalist forces under the command of Edward and the earl of Gloucester trapped Simon de Montfort's army, allowing no opportunity for escape. The battle was fought during a storm. De Montfort's forces briefly forced Edward to pull back, but as the wings of the royalist army closed in, his forces were encircled. Slaughter followed.

▲ Evesham was a savage, bitter battle. A special 'hit squad' was created to kill the rebel leader, Simon de Montfort. This illustration from a Rochester chronicle shows his death. Contrary to all conventions, his corpse was beheaded; his hands, feet and genitals were cut off. Such extreme barbarity was rare in this period.

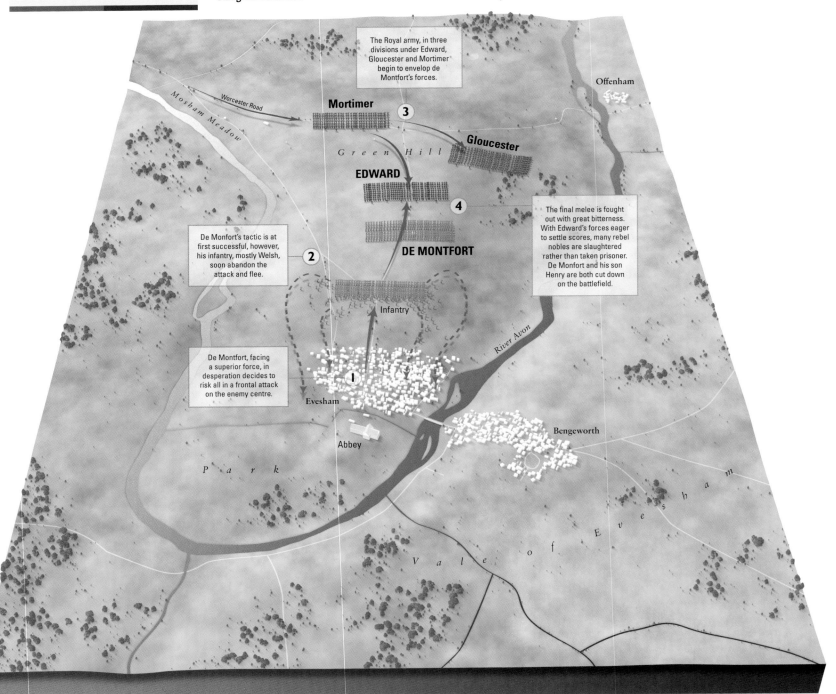

The Royal army, in three divisions under Edward, Gloucester and Mortimer begin to envelop de Montfort's forces.

Mosham Meadow

Worcester Road

Mortimer (3)

Offenham

Green Hill

Gloucester

EDWARD

(4)

The final melee is fought out with great bitterness. With Edward's forces eager to settle scores, many rebel nobles are slaughtered rather than taken prisoner. De Monfort and his son Henry are both cut down on the battlefield.

De Monfort's tactic is at first successful, however, his infantry, mostly Welsh, soon abandon the attack and flee.

(2)

DE MONTFORT

Infantry

River Avon

De Montfort, facing a superior force, in desperation decides to risk all in a frontal attack on the enemy centre.

(1)

Evesham

Bengeworth

Abbey

P a r k

V a l e   o f   E v e s h a m

Edward I

that Edward built to cement the conquest of Wales (such as Beaumaris, Conwy and Caernarfon) demonstrated his sense of strategy: they were all carefully sited so that they could be supplied, and relieved if need be, by sea. The integration of castle walls and urban defences, as seen at Conwy, facilitated the settlement of Wales.

In the early 1290s Edward became increasingly involved in the struggle of succession between the Scottish barons, seeking to dominate the kingdom. War broke out and in 1296 Edward invaded. In March the inhabitants of Berwick were massacred by English forces, and in April the Scots were defeated at Dunbar. Further victory in 1298 at the battle of Falkirk (the only battle Edward fought as king) was followed by a series of campaigns that eventually ground the Scots into submission by 1304. In 1306, however, Robert Bruce (pp. 88–89) rebelled, and Edward's achievement began to unravel. Correspondence with the Exchequer in 1301 suggests that Edward's strategic concept consisted of little more than a hope that if he crossed the Firth of Forth he would be able to bring the Scots to heel. The large armies that Edward marched north failed to engage an enemy who,

after 1298, was extremely reluctant to face the English in battle.

Edward is often credited with transforming English forces from an ill-organized feudal host into a well-managed, paid army. This should not be exaggerated; even by the end of his reign most of the cavalry were not paid by the crown, and the infantry were poorly equipped and prone to desertion. If there was a military revolution in his reign, it was with the recruitment of far larger numbers of troops (up to 24,000 at Falkirk) than had been possible in the past, and the establishment of effective arrangements for victualling and supply. The king himself was not a man to engage with the detailed administrative work that was needed, in contrast to his grandson Edward III. Such instructions from him as survive show that he expected others to do this, namely household clerks and Exchequer officials. He was capable of giving orders that bore little relation to reality, such as a request for funds sufficient to pay 60,000 troops for his Scottish campaign in 1296. He had, however, the ability to see the big picture, to realize what was needed, and to identify the right men to help him achieve his ambitious goals.

▲ This imaginary battle scene, from a life of St Edward, shows mounted kings and nobles in conflict, with swords, lances and chainmail armour that are just what would have been used on the Evesham campaign in 1265.

Robert Bruce

Scottish King who Defeated the English

'You could have lived in serfdom, but, because you yearned to have freedom, you are gathered here with me.' ROBERT BRUCE, TO HIS TROOPS BEFORE BANNOCKBURN

A Life in Brief

1274, 11 July
Born, probably at Turnberry

1292
On the resignation of his father, becomes Earl of Carrick

1306, 25 March
Enthroned as King of Scots

1329, 7 June
Dies at Cardross, Scotland

Robert Bruce was a charismatic leader, and one of Scotland's most famous warriors. Although he was fortunate in facing an incompetent opponent in Edward II, he was nonetheless a man of undoubted military genius who secured independence for Scotland from the English crown.

By 1304, Edward I (pp. 84–87) appeared to have conquered Scotland. Yet, in the years that followed Bruce succeeded in undoing all the English king had achieved there. Enthroned as King of Scots in 1306, he set about waging war against English rule. However, his defeat at the battle of Methven in June 1306 forced him to adopt guerrilla tactics. As one English chronicler put it, 'Robert Bruce, knowing himself unequal to the King of England in strength or fortune, decided that it would be better to resist our king by secret warfare rather than to dispute his right in open battle.' Bruce's guerrilla tactics were brilliantly successful. English-held castles fell to a series of surprise attacks. By 1311 Bruce, ably assisted by his lieutenant James Douglas, was in a position to take the war to England, launching swift destructive raids into the north, to which the English had no answer.

In 1314 he achieved his greatest triumph in battle, with the defeat of a large English army at Bannockburn. The battle was not of Bruce's choosing; it was the result of a deal struck by his brother, which effectively challenged the English to relieve the siege of Stirling castle by midsummer, and which gave Bruce little option other than to fight a battle. He was able to select ground highly unsuitable for the English cavalry, and his infantry forces, drawn up in solid formations known as schiltroms, routed Edward II's troops. Despite this success, Bruce chose not to challenge the English again on the battlefield.

Bruce was a master of unconventional warfare, who made conditions impossible for his opponents. In 1322, for example, rather than confront the English in battle when they invaded Scotland, he emptied the land of all supplies, forcing Edward II to withdraw in disarray. Instead of garrisoning castles taken from the English, Bruce slighted them, rendering them useless.

► Robert Bruce is unlikely to have looked like this 16th-century interpretation of him with his first wife, Isabella of Mar. Her early death meant that the marriage lasted no more than six years; Bruce's second marriage was to Elizabeth, daughter of the Earl of Ulster.

> With the feeble Edward II on the English throne, the Scots made frequent devastating raids into the north of England. Bruce's main lieutenants, James Douglas and Thomas Randolph, often led the armies south. The map also shows the sites of the main battles fought by Robert Bruce in Scotland.

Key Battles

The Battle of Methven, 19 June 1306
Surprised in his camp at Methven by an early-morning English cavalry charge, Bruce is roundly defeated in his first battle as king by Aymer de Valence.

The Battle of Loudoun Hill, 10 May 1307
Bruce prepares his position well, using ditches to hinder the English cavalry charges. Aymer de Valence's men are forced to attack along a narrow front, and the Scottish pikemen exorcise their defeat at Methven with a decisive victory.

The Battle of Bannockburn, 23–24 June 1314
Bruce selects a strong position near Stirling castle on boggy ground, which puts the English cavalry of Edward II at a disadvantage. Edward has a far larger army than the Scots, but makes little use of his archers, and cannot break the Scottish infantry, drawn up in schiltroms. On the first day of fighting, Robert Clifford's cavalry force is defeated. On the second, after a failed attack by the English vanguard, the Scots drive the English back; many are drowned in the Bannock Burn stream.

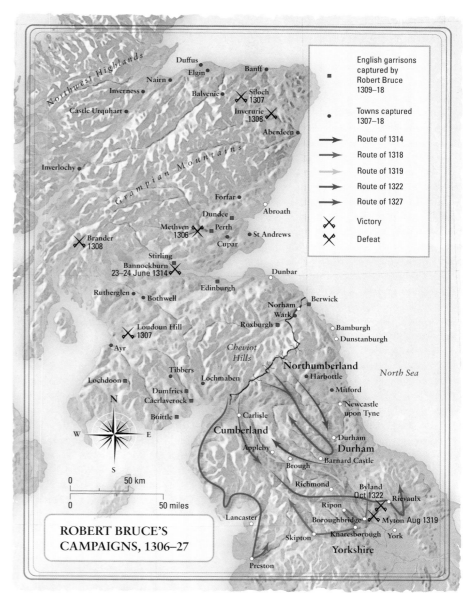

ROBERT BRUCE'S CAMPAIGNS, 1306–27

Key to map legend:
- ■ English garrisons captured by Robert Bruce 1309–18
- • Towns captured 1307–18
- → Route of 1314
- → Route of 1318
- → Route of 1319
- → Route of 1322
- → Route of 1327
- ⚔ Victory
- ⚔ Defeat

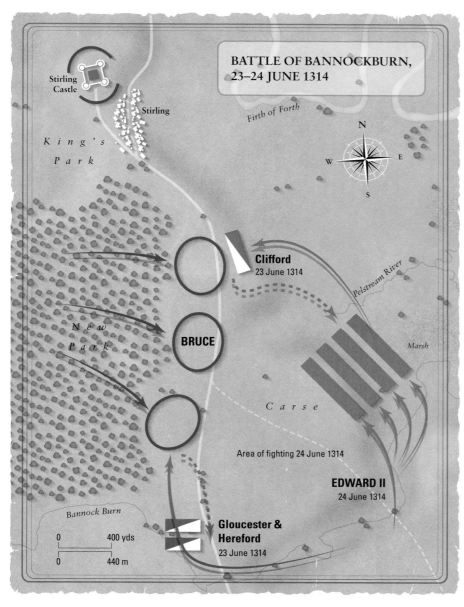

BATTLE OF BANNOCKBURN, 23–24 JUNE 1314

Stirling Castle
Stirling
Firth of Forth
King's Park
New Park
Pelstream River
Marsh
Carse
Clifford 23 June 1314
BRUCE
Area of fighting 24 June 1314
EDWARD II 24 June 1314
Bannock Burn
0   400 yds
0   440 m
Gloucester & Hereford 23 June 1314

◀ The key to the battle of Bannockburn was Bruce's choice of terrain. The Scots fought in schiltroms, tight infantry formations bristling with spears, and were probably in three main divisions. The English outnumbered the Scots, but were demoralized by incidents such as the death of Henry de Bohun at the hands of Bruce himself, and by the death of the Earl of Gloucester in a suicidal charge.

▼▼ This image, below, from the Holkham Picture Bible Book shows knights and men-at-arms fighting in battle, using a range of weapons such as swords, battle-axes and spears. The artist could have had Bannockburn in mind. At top left, in another image from the same source, common soldiers are shown fighting on foot. They are using swords, a long-handled axe, while two have bows and arrows. Small round bucklers are used for defence.

Jan Žižka

'Remember your first fight, which you – small against large, few against many, unarmed against armed – fought with bravery. Therefore, trust in God, and be ready!' JAN ŽIŽKA

A Life in Brief

c. 1360
Born in Trocnov
(southern Bohemia)

1419
Elected one of the four Hussite leaders

1424, 11 October
Dies of plague outside Přibyslav

▶ Though painted long after his death, this German portrait of Žižka does show him holding a mace, one of the weapons associated with his soldiers. Few of his troops would have worn as much armour, however.

▼ The Hussites made good use of both crossbows and handguns that were still in an early stage of development. This contemporary woodcut shows squads of spearmen covering troops with missile weapons during an attack on a fortified town.

Žižka was one of the most successful leaders of the Hussite insurgency, and won each of the ten battles in which he commanded troops. He moulded an unpromising band of Bohemian peasants into a force capable of defeating the best armies of the day, and came to symbolize the Hussite way of waging war.

Žižka (who lost sight in one eye when only a youth) had his formative military experiences as a mercenary of the Polish king in the wars against the Teutonic Order (1409–11). On his return from Poland he served as a palace guard in Prague, and gradually fell under the influence of the movement led by Jan Hus that promoted religious and cultural revival in Bohemia. Hus was sentenced to death by the Council of Constance in 1415, and in July 1419 the Hussite revolt erupted. Žižka played a leading role in the attack on the aldermen of Prague. When King Wenceslas IV died two weeks later, his brother Sigismund, King of Hungary and of the Romans, mounted a crusade to restore Catholicism and the old political order. Žižka was compelled to improvise resistance from the Hussite base at Tábor in southern Bohemia.

Having repelled Sigismund's initial invasion in 1419–20, Žižka fought against the Bohemian Catholics from 1420 to 1421. In 1421, he suffered an injury to his remaining eye whilst besieging Rabí, eventually turning him completely blind. A second invasion from Germany was stemmed that autumn by Žižka's counterattack at the battles of Kutna Hora and Jihlava, and he defeated Sigismund at the battle of Deutschbrod on 6 January 1422. However, the Hussite movement began to fragment, and Žižka's later years were spent attempting to reunite the factions. In 1423

he established a permanent field army, known as Žižka's Military Order. In 1424 he defeated a combined army of Bohemian Catholics and moderate Hussites at Malešov, but died soon after whilst besieging Přibyslav.

Žižka's army mostly comprised peasant and burgher infantry, and he made particular use of innovative and highly effective defensive tactics. Although such forces were particularly vulnerable to heavy cavalry charges in the open, they used war wagons as mobile defences from which to repel such attacks. These wagons could be corralled, with fire from arquebuses and small cannon unleashed on the enemy. Žižka was also careful to make use of natural terrain features such as ponds, hillocks and other obstacles, to hinder enemy attacks. Such tactics continued to influence military practice long after his death.

Key Battles

The Battle of Sudoměř, 25 March 1420

Žižka defeats a force of Bohemian Catholics five times his strength by skilful use of the terrain; he forces his opponents to dismount and attack his infantry, who are protected by war wagons. The victory turns him into a national hero and ensures the Hussite movement's further development.

The Battle of Vítkov (Prague), 14 July 1420

Sigismund's 30,000-strong force attempts to trap Žižka in Prague, but the Hussites fortify the Vítkov hill to the east, which secures their supply lines. A large cavalry assault is repulsed, prompting the besiegers to retreat and ending the first crusade.

The Battle of Malešov, 1424

A coalition of Catholics and moderate Hussites forces Žižka to assume a defensive position at Malešov, overlooking his opponent's line of approach through a narrow river valley. Žižka disorders their army by gunfire and by rolling wagons loaded with rocks down the slope, and then completes his victory with a charge.

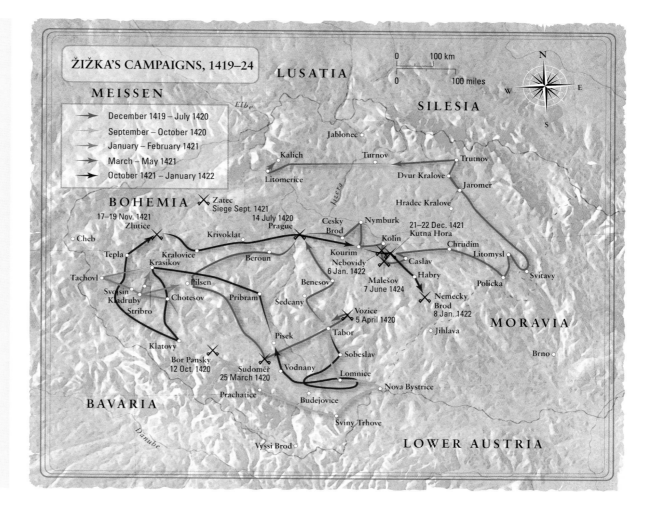

ŽIŽKA'S CAMPAIGNS, 1419–24

→ December 1419 – July 1420
→ September – October 1420
→ January – February 1421
→ March – May 1421
→ October 1421 – January 1422

0   100 km
0   100 miles

LUSATIA
MEISSEN
SILESIA
BOHEMIA
Zatec Siege Sept. 1421
17–19 Nov. 1421 Zlutice
14 July 1420 Prague
Cesky Brod
Nymburk
21–22 Dec. 1421 Kutna Hora
Cheb
Krivoklat
Kolin
Chrudim
Tepla
Kralovice
Krasikov
Beroun
Kourim
Nebovidy
6 Jan. 1422
Caslav
Litomysl
Tachovl
Pilsen
Benesov
Malesov
7 June 1424
Habry
Svitavy
Svojsin
Kladruby
Chotesov
Pribram
Sedcany
Nemecky Brod
8 Jan. 1422
Policka
Stribro
Tabor
MORAVIA
Klatovy
Pisek
Vozice
5 April 1420
Jihlava
Brno
Bor Pansky
12 Oct 1420
Sudomer
25 March 1420
Vodnany
Sobeslav
Lomnice
BAVARIA
Prachatice
Budejovice
Nova Bystrice
Sviny Trhove
LOWER AUSTRIA
Vyssi Brod

Jablonec
Kalich
Turnov
Trutnov
Litomerice
Dvur Kralove
Jaromer
Hradec Kralove

▲ Žižka was a skilled tactician, especially in defence, meaning that despite the disadvantage of an army largely formed of infantry he never lost a battle.

◄ This rather fanciful depiction of the Hussite wagon castle dates from around 1450, but does give an indication of how mobile and improvised fixed defences could be used to protect their largely infantry army from the Catholic heavy cavalry.

János Hunyadi

Hungarian National Hero who Defeated the Turks

'Are you terrified? Is it just the Turks you now see? ...If God is with us, this enemy can easily be crushed.' JÁNOS HUNYADI

A Life in Brief

1407
Born (location unknown),
the son of a lesser nobleman
from Wallachia

1431–33
In the service of the Duke of Milan

1439–56
Commander of the frontier
province of Szörény

1441–56
Royal governor of Transylvania, and
commander of Temesvár, Belgrade
and the River Danube castles

1444–46
Captain-general

1446–53
Regent of the Kingdom of Hungary

1456, 11 August
Dies of plague at Zemun, Serbia

➤ **In this late 15th-century miniature from**
*La chronicque du temps de roy Charles
VII de France*, **Hungarian knights gain
victory over the Turkish cavalry, with
the Turkish fleet shown waiting in the
distance. Although the miniature shows
heavy cavalry, light cavalry of mounted
archers comprised a substantial part of the
Hungarian army in Hunyadi's lifetime.**

János Hunyadi won several battles against the Ottoman Turks between 1441 and 1444, and thwarted their advance into Hungary and Central Europe by defending Belgrade in 1456 against Sultan Mehmed II (r. 1444–46, 1451–81). Despite two significant defeats in 1444 and 1448, his victories against the Ottomans made him a Hungarian national hero and a celebrated military commander throughout Christian Europe.

Hunyadi learned the basics of contemporary warfare in the service of Sigismund of Luxembourg, Holy Roman Emperor (r. 1433–37), and in Italy, serving the Duke of Milan in the early 1430s. It was during Sigismund's 1436–37 campaign against the Hussites in Bohemia that Hunyadi studied the Hussite use of armed wagons, which he in turn would deploy to great effect against the Ottomans.

As royal governor of Transylvania and commander of Belgrade, Hunyadi thwarted several Ottoman raids in the early 1440s. In the winter of 1443/44 the Hungarian army, led by King Wladislas of Poland and Hunyadi, invaded the Balkan provinces of the Ottoman empire as far as Sofia (Bulgaria), defeating the enemy in several battles. Hunyadi's victories prompted the Pope to forge a new anti-Ottoman Christian coalition. After the papal legate declared the Ottoman-initiated Hungarian–Ottoman peace treaty of 1444 void, Hungarian forces crossed the Ottoman border. However, on 10 November 1444 they suffered a major defeat at the battle of Varna. Hunyadi's second attempt to defeat the Ottomans in the Balkans ended with failure at the second battle of Kosovo Field in 1448.

Hunyadi achieved his greatest victory in 1456, when he defended the key fortress city of Belgrade during Mehmed II's siege. First, he coordinated an attack against the Ottoman fleet that was blocking the passage of his relief army, and then, in a five-hour battle on the River Sava on 14 July, destroyed the Ottoman river flotilla, thus bringing much needed reinforcements into Belgrade. On 22 July, Hunyadi joined in an opportunistic sortie, capturing the Ottoman cannon in front of the castle and turning them against the besiegers.

Hunyadi's aggressive defence of his kingdom, coupled with the military reforms instituted by his son King Matthias Corvinus (r. 1458–90), meant that the Ottomans would not attack Hungary again until 1521.

Key Battles

The Battle of Varna, 10 November 1444
In eastern Bulgaria, the entrapped 18,000-strong army of Hunyadi and King Wladislas of Poland clashes with the 40,000 troops under Murad II. Both sides lose heavily, and Hunyadi is forced to withdraw, barely escaping with his life.

The Second Battle of Kosovo Field, 16–18 October 1448
In southern Serbia, Hunyadi is defeated by the much larger forces of Murad II in a two-day battle. The Ottoman light cavalry turn the Christian flanks on the first day, and on the next, the final Ottoman assault smashes Hunyadi's army.

The Siege of Belgrade, 4–22 July 1456
Hunyadi leads a force to relieve the Ottoman siege of the key Hungarian border fortress in Serbia. At Zemun (14 July), Hunyadi's forces destroy the Ottoman river flotilla. On 22 July Hunyadi leads a sortie from the fortress and captures Mehmed II's cannon.

▶ Hunyadi's father Woyk, a Romanian nobleman, served Sigismund of Luxembourg, King of Hungary, and in 1409 was awarded the borough of Hunyad, from where the family name originates. Hunyadi repelled several Ottoman attacks against Hungary in the early 1440s, as well as launching his own campaigns, reaching the Black Sea in 1444.

▼ Hunyadi's victory at Belgrade in 1456, achieved through an attack by river and land, postponed the Ottoman advance in Central Europe until 1521, when they eventually conquered this key fortress of the medieval Hungarian defence system.

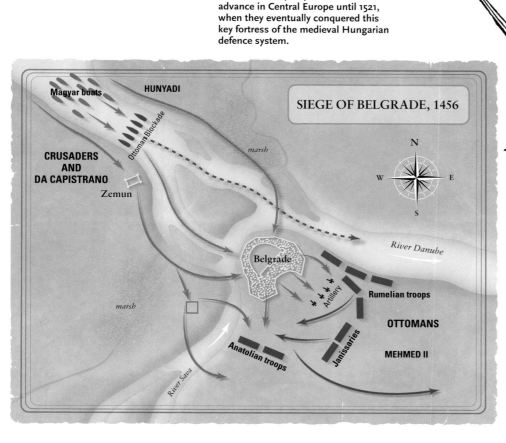

▲ János Hunyadi, woodcut from *The Chronicle of the Hungarians*, 1488.

3
The Age of Empires and Revolutions

◄◄ The battle of Lützen (1632) was a bitterly fought battle between the kingdom of Sweden and the Holy Roman empire that demonstrated the personal risks of leadership. The Swedes eventually won a cavalry confrontation on their right after Pappenheim, the Austrian cavalry general, who had initially turned the battle there and had seven horses shot from under him, was mortally injured by a cannonball. In the centre, the Swedish infantry led by their king, Gustavus Adolphus, who was shot in the arm but pressed on, were unable to drive back the main Austrian line. Gustavus died in the melee, shot three times. The Austrians eventually retreated.

▲ Süleyman the Magnificent besieges Rhodes (1522) in this Turkish miniature painting. Turbaned soldiers digging at the lower left indicate use of siege techniques such as mines and trenches. Many of the Turkish soldiers carry firearms, and the Knights of St John employed fortress artillery in their unsuccessful defence. The absence of a relief army doomed the fortress, unlike Malta in 1565.

In this period, command became increasingly separated from rule, as demonstrated by Turenne (pp. 138–41 – a marshal for Louis XIV of France), Marlborough (pp. 158–63 – a general for Queen Anne of Britain), and Nelson and Wellington (pp. 192–97 and pp. 198–203 – who both served George III of Britain). Furthermore, egalitarian and democratic ideals began to influence historical events, as the careers of both Oliver Cromwell (pp. 142–47) and George Washington (pp. 174–79) showed – a factor that would exert much more influence in the modern age.

Nevertheless, most of the key commanders of the period were also rulers. Some, such as Babur (pp. 116–19) and Charles V (pp. 112–15), created new empires, while others, such as Nader Shah of Persia (pp. 168–69), took over failing ones. While Hideyoshi (pp. 124–31) and Napoleon sought to create powerful empires through war, each failed to do so. Others still, notably Selim I (pp. 104–07), Süleyman the Magnificent (pp. 108–11), Akbar (pp. 120–23), Shah Abbas I (pp. 132–33), Gustavus Adolphus (pp. 134–37), Jan Sobieski (pp. 148–51), Peter the Great (pp. 152–57), Frederick the Great (pp. 164–67) and the Qianlong Emperor (pp. 170–73), inherited the right to rule, and then used war to protect and enhance their assets.

In each case, the ability of the individual emerged through the circumstances of conflict. A common requirement of the ruler-leaders in this era was the demonstration of both political and military skill; in short, the latter became closely associated with the former. Thus, it was necessary to divide opponents, to create tensions in their alliances and to fight them in sequence. This was a practice at which Frederick the Great was adept, and in which Napoleon was successful until 1812. It also became increasingly important to hold together constituencies of interest, be they alliances, as with Marlborough and Wellington, or the groups supporting a war effort.

Victory brought prestige, and this in turn was important in maintaining political support. In the light of this, the notions that glory, honour and prestige were somehow 'irrational' pursuits, and that opportunism and the absence of consistent policies demonstrated inferior intelligence to the formulation of long-term plans, can both be dispelled. *Gloire*, or national dignity, could serve to win support for a policy, and provide the emotional impetus that might carry a people to war. Prestige and glory were the basis of the power of early-modern monarchs, both domestically and internationally. They conferred a mantle of success and magnificence, which encouraged obedience in societies with poorly developed systems of administration – ones that essentially relied upon the willingness of the subjects.

War was regarded as the natural activity, indeed the 'sport', of rulers. Their upbringing conditioned them to accept such a notion, and most male leaders spent their years of peace in activities that were substitutes for, and which served to keep their minds on, military matters: manoeuvres, reviews and the cavalry exercises of hunting. The famous war games of Peter the Great were matched by those of other young princes too.

Military success was crucial to a leader's reputation, and especially to his personal and dynastic honour. This helps explain why their wars often involved a series of gratifying and valorous achievements. In contrast to today, the gains and *gloire* to be won from war were eagerly sought, and leadership of the time has to be understood, in part, in these terms. A further key to understanding is held within the dominant religious ideologies of the age, which manifested themselves in ceremonies to secure or give thanks for divine intercession during war. In the Christian world, such ceremonies included fast-day sermons, and the Te Deums, processions, fireworks and addresses that frequently followed victory.

▼ Napoleon on campaign, followed by his leading generals, in a 19th-century painting Ernest Meissonier. Napoleon was important in taking forward operational art by developing the rapid and decisive manoeuvre of autonomous forces, not least between a series of engagements, and so as to ensure that the engagements were a series with opponents fixed, outmanoeuvred and defeated. However, his political abilities did not match his zeal for battle.

Hernando Cortés

Spanish Conqueror of the Aztecs

'Seeing how determined [the Aztecs] were to die in their own defence, I concluded… that they gave us cause, and indeed obliged us, to destroy them completely.' HERNANDO CORTÉS

Empires & Revolutions

Hernando Cortés

A Life in Brief

1484 (or 1485)
Born in Medellín, Spain

1506
Settles on Hispaniola
(Haiti/Dominican Republic)

1511–12
Participates in Diego Velázquez
de Cuéllar's invasion and
conquest of Cuba

1521
Becomes effective ruler of
New Spain (the former Aztec
empire and adjacent regions
of Mesoamerica)

1522
Acknowledged by the king of Spain
as governor and captain-general
of New Spain

1528
Made Marqués del Valle, with vast
holdings in southern Mexico

1541
Accompanies the king of Spain
on an expedition to Algiers

1547, 2 December
Dies in Castelleja de la Cuesta,
Spain (en route to Seville
and Mexico)

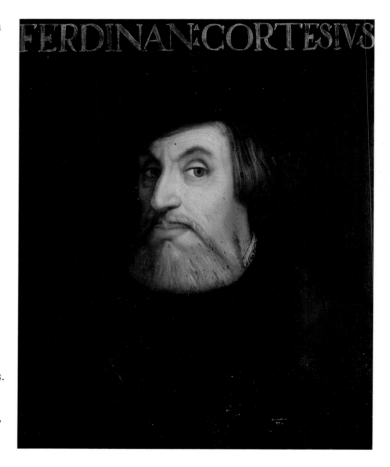

◀ Portrait of Hernando Cortés, painted
by the Italian artist Christofano di Papi
dell'Altissimo after a likeness of Cortés
that the conquistador himself had sent to
the collector and bishop Paolo Giovio.

Hernando Cortés was the most famous of the Spanish conquistadores, and the first governor of New Spain. He led the invasion of Mexico in 1519 and presided over the fall of the Aztec empire and the destruction of its great capital of Tenochtitlan in 1521. In the absence of any formal Spanish army in the Americas, armed entrepreneurs such as Cortés flourished. By seeking direct royal patronage, and by forming alliances with native peoples and deposing their rulers, Cortés followed the same procedures as other conquistadores. Arguably, he was more skilled in this, and had better luck.

Born to low-ranking noble parents, Cortés was a restless youth during the age of Columbus's transatlantic voyages. Defying his parents' wish that he become a lawyer, in his twenties he found fortune and preferment in the Caribbean, as Spanish companies explored, conquered and settled the islands. He also discovered his own ambition and gift for leadership, betraying his patron, the governor of Cuba, in 1519, and turning an exploration of the Mexican coastline into a two-year war of conquest against the Aztec empire.

On the verge of being defeated in 1519 by the Tlaxcala confederation, Cortés convinced the Tlaxcalans to join him in marching on Tenochtitlan, the capital of their enemy, the Aztecs. The city was set in a spectacular location on an island in Lake Texcoco, and with 200,000 inhabitants was larger than any European city of the day. Welcomed into the city by the emperor Motecuhzoma in an apparent act of surrender, Cortés found himself trapped and forced into a disastrous flight back to Tlaxcala in 1520. Cortés's finest moments came during the year

that followed; he combined focused military assaults and diplomatic initiatives to build a central Mexican alliance that gradually isolated the Aztecs on their island city, culminating in a bloody and destructive siege. In the wake of Aztec defeat in 1521, Cortés helped consolidate Spanish control over the Aztec empire and adjacent regions.

Even before his death, Cortés had come to symbolize the archetypal conquistador. His success is undeniable, and he acquired the kind of wealth and power that were the stuff of dreams during the age of European overseas expansion. His supposed

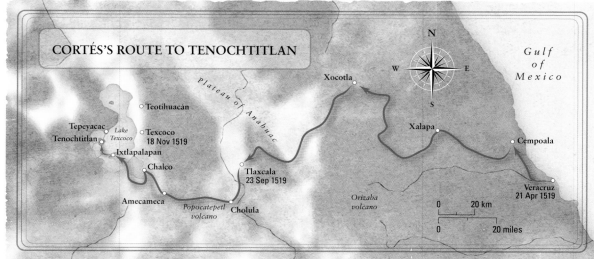

▲▲ The arrival of Cortés at Veracruz and his reception by Motecuhzoma's ambassadors is shown in this late 17th-century painting (one of a series of eight) by an unknown Mexican artist. These paintings are now held in the Jay Kislak Collection in the Library of Congress, Washington DC.

CORTÉS'S ROUTE TO TENOCHTITLAN

Teotihuacán
Tepeyacac — *Lake Texcoco* — *Texcoco 18 Nov 1519*
Tenochtitlan
Ixtlapalapan
Chalco
Tlaxcala 23 Sep 1519
Amecameca
Popocatepetl volcano — *Cholula*
Plateau of Anahuac
Xocotla
Xalapa
Cempoala
Orizaba volcano
Veracruz 21 Apr 1519
Gulf of Mexico

0   20 km
0   20 miles

▲ Cortés and his native allies marched from the Gulf of Mexico coast up to the Aztec imperial capital of Tenochtitlan in 1519.

Key Campaign

The Spanish Conquest of the Aztec Empire, 1519–21

On 10 February 1519 Cortés's fleet of 11 ships departs from Cuba on a purported voyage of exploration of the Mexican coast. Between 2 and 23 September 1519, his men clash several times with the warriors of the Tlaxcala confederation, but Cortés convinces the Tlaxcalans to join an alliance against their enemy, the Aztecs. In November 1519, Cortés arrives at the Aztec capital, Tenochtitlan. Initially welcomed, fighting soon breaks out. During the *Noche Triste* (30 June 1520), Cortés and his men are forced to flee Tenochtitlan, suffering heavy losses. Between 22 May and 13 August 1521, Cortés lays siege to and then assaults Tenochtitlan with an allied force of Spaniards, Tlaxcalans and others, bringing about the final Aztec surrender.

▲ Hernando Cortés's official Coat of Arms, granted to him by the Emperor Charles V at the time he was made Marquis of the Valley of Oaxaca.

▶ The Valley of Mexico, with the Aztec island-city of Tenochtitlan at its centre. Cortés first entered the city as a guest of Motecuhzoma in November 1519. In May–June of 1520 he left for the coast, quickly returned with more Spaniards, and was then forced to flee the city. The final siege began early in 1521, with the city falling in August.

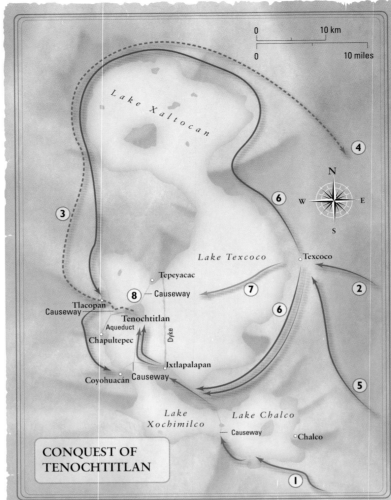

0 10 km

0 10 miles

CONQUEST OF TENOCHTITLAN

Lake Xaltocan

N
W E
S

Lake Texcoco

Texcoco

Tepeyacac

Causeway

Tlacopan
Causeway

Aqueduct
Tenochtitlan

Chapultepec

Dyke

Ixtlapalapan

Coyohuacán
Causeway

Lake Xochimilco

Lake Chalco

Causeway

Chalco

(1) Cortés's initial route; arriving at Tenochtitlan on 8 November 1519 he later returns to the coast to defeat a hostile Spanish force sent to return him to Cuba for violating orders.

(2) Cortés, hearing that the Spanish forces he left in Tenochtitlan are besieged in their quarters (after a massacre of thousands of Aztecs), returns to Tenochtitlan, 24 June 1520.

(3) Unable to calm the situation, surrounded and with supplies dwindling Cortés, on 30 June 1520 (the so-called *Noche Triste*), begins a fighting retreat towards Tlaxcala.

(4) After 11 days Cortés arrives in Tlaxcala.

(5) Cortés, bolstered by allied forces, re-enters the Valley of Mexico unopposed on 30 December 1520.

(6) Cortés's troops attempt to encircle and isolate the Aztecs, defeating nearby towns and cutting off the causeways and aqueduct (from February 1521).

(7) Cortés launches newly constructed ships on 28 April 1521 and, combined with attacks by troops on land, the siege proper begins.

(8) Tenochtitlan finally falls to the Spanish on 13 August 1521.

▶ Motecuhzoma kneels before Cortés in this fresco painting by Miguel Gonzalez — a creative rendering of a surrender by Motecuhzoma that never happened. However, the emperor did become Cortés's captive and was eventually killed during the *Noche Triste*, to be succeeded first by his brother (who died of smallpox brought by the Spanish soon after) and then his nephew, Cuauhtemoc.

military genius lay at the heart of some of the myths of the Spanish conquests in the Americas, most notably that he used superior European technology and manipulated both the credulous natives and a superstitious Motecuhzoma to lead a few hundred Spanish soldiers to daring victory over an empire of millions. While steel swords did give the Spaniards an advantage compared to native weapons, the Aztecs and other Mesoamericans were no more credulous than the Spaniards, and native leaders manipulated Cortés as much as he did them. The truth is that the Spanish invaders survived and triumphed because they were aided by tens of thousands of native allies, and an onslaught of epidemic diseases, which killed about half the central Mexican population during the 1519–21 war.

Cortés's gift lay in his understanding of the limitations of Spanish superiority and the vulnerability of invasion forces. Despite being called audacious, his strength lay in his generally cautious attitude. Although often considered a great general, he rarely relied on battle tactics and campaign strategy; instead, he was a successful captain who married diplomacy with the flash of display violence against his enemies. In waging war, he seemed to demonstrate just the right balance of prudence and valour. In the words of Pánfilo de Narváez, both a friend and foe, Cortés was 'steadfast, but not over prudent, very bold in fighting against the Indians, and perhaps against others as well'. The historian Hugh Thomas summarizes Cortés as a man who was 'decisive, flexible, and had few scruples'.

Hernando Cortés

Empires & Revolutions

101

Francisco Pizarro

Destroyer of the Inca Empire

'Pizarro raised a cloth, the signal to move against the Indians. Candia fired the shots, a novelty for them and frightening, but even more so were the horses.' PEDRO CIEZA DE LEÓN, CONQUISTADOR

A Life in Brief

c. 1478
Born in Trujillo, Spain, the illegitimate son of Captain Gonzalo Pizarro

1502
Leaves Spain for Hispaniola

1529, 26 July
Named Governor and Captain General of Peru

1541, 26 July
Killed by supporters of Diego Almagro in Lima, Peru

▲ The embroidered Battle Standard, with the royal arms of Charles V, that accompanied Pizarro and his men throughout the conquest.

◀ A contemporary portrait (by an unknown artist) of Francisco Pizarro.

Francisco Pizarro was the quintessential conquistador. The years he spent hunting for gold in hostile, tropical terrain made him a ruthlessly effective commander. He quickly grasped how native societies functioned, and exploited their weaknesses, one of which was a very different, often ritualistic approach to warfare. His use of shock tactics against indigenous forces was a trademark, and compensated for inferior troop numbers.

Pizarro was born around 1478 in Trujillo, Extremadura. He departed for the Caribbean in 1502, where he took part in numerous plundering expeditions. He gained a reputation for his leadership skills and the use of extreme brutality to cow native populations. In 1519 he became one of the founding fathers of the city of Panama. Pizarro was now in his forties and a wealthy man, but news of the conquest of Mexico by Hernando Cortés (pp. 98–101) prompted him to dream of greater things.

By the mid-1520s Spanish ships had begun to explore the west coast of South America, and rumours circulated of a rich land called Viru (Peru). Pizarro formed a syndicate with two other men, and they bought several ships. In 1527 they encountered a trading raft along the coast of Ecuador, coming from further south and laden with precious metals.

In 1528 Pizarro sailed back to Spain to secure royal assent to his rights of conquest. He returned quickly with his four half-brothers to prepare and recruit. On 27 December 1530, three ships containing 180 Spanish adventurers and some 30 horses left Panama.

After almost a year of acclimatization, marching slowly through Ecuador, Pizarro and his men reached the northern Inca town of Tumbez. From there they

headed inland to Cajamarca, where the Inca ruler Atahualpa and thousands of his troops were camped on the town's outskirts. The Inca ruler, who was engaged in a civil war, was well informed about the Spaniards but oblivious to any threat they might pose. Pizarro and his men were allowed to proceed into the town and occupy the main square. On 16 November 1532, Atahualpa and some 5,000 of his followers entered Cajamarca. The Spaniards, their horses and a few cannon were disposed around long Inca buildings on three sides of the square. After a brief, ineffectual exchange between Atahualpa and the Dominican friar

Key Campaign

The Conquest of Peru, 1532–33
Having secured royal assent for his plans to conquer Peru, Pizarro is granted a licence to do so on 26 July 1529. The expedition begins on 27 December 1530. On 16 November 1532 in the Inca town of Cajamarca, the Inca ruler Atahualpa is captured by Pizarro and thousands of his followers are killed. Pizarro and his men enter Cuzco, the Inca capital, on 15 November 1533, completing the conquest of the empire.

◄ A striking but fanciful 16th-century rendering by Theodor de Bry of the capture of Atahualpa and the slaughter of his retinue at Cajamarca.

Vicente de Valverde, who failed to convince the Inca leader to submit peacefully, Pizarro gave the order for cannon to be fired into the crowd. Spanish horsemen charged the largely unarmed Incas, and those that were not cut down were trampled to death. The ruthless massacre at Cajamarca and the capture of Atahualpa left the Inca empire paralyzed. It gave Pizarro time to await Spanish reinforcements and, critically, to form alliances with other ethnic groups hostile to the Incas. Eventually, accompanied by thousands of native allies, Pizarro was able to march south, take over the capital of Cuzco and seal the conquest.

▲ The massive walls of Sacsayhuaman, overlooking the Inca capital of Cuzco, where the last major military confrontation between Incas and Spaniards took place.

◄ Pizarro's three campaigns began with a brief initial foray into what is now Colombia in 1524, followed two years later by a much more ambitious voyage down the Pacific coast. This brought dramatic evidence of an unknown civilization possessing breathtaking quantities of gold and made a third, more systematic attempt at conquest inevitable.

Francisco Pizarro

Empires & Revolutions

103

Sultan Selim I

Ottoman Leader who Vanquished the Mamluks of Egypt

'The world is not enough for a sultan!'
SELIM I

A Life in Brief

1465, 10 October
Born in Amasya, northern Turkey
(some sources state he was born
in 1467 or 1470)

1512, 25 April
Ascends the Ottoman throne

1520, 22 September
Dies at Çorlu, Turkey

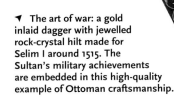

▼ The art of war: a gold inlaid dagger with jewelled rock-crystal hilt made for Selim I around 1515. The Sultan's military achievements are embedded in this high-quality example of Ottoman craftsmanship.

▶▶ Selim's coronation ceremony in 1512. The striking image of the mustachioed sultan is further enhanced by the size of his befeathered turban. Selim appears to be in complete control of the situation, as he receives humble homage from bearded officials.

Sultan Selim I is also known in Turkey by the sobriquet *Yavuz*, usually (if not completely accurately) rendered in English as 'grim'. The name is certainly appropriate for a man who liquidated his brothers and other close relatives who threatened his claim to the Ottoman throne. A tall, strong, brooding man with a wry sense of humour, Selim possessed an almost single-minded drive for conquest. Although he lasted only eight years as *padishah* (emperor) of the Ottomans, his expansion of the empire throughout the Middle East left a permanent mark on world history.

Selim came to the throne in the wake of a coup d'état of the Janissaries and the abdication of his father Bayezid II on 25 April, 1512. The Janissaries had become exasperated by what they considered Bayezid's dithering attitude towards the unrest caused in eastern Anatolia by the agents of the Safavid Shah Ismail I of Persia, the Ottoman empire's eastern neighbour and rival. In the brief civil war that followed Bayezid's overthrow, Selim captured and executed his brothers Kurkud and Ahmed, before launching a mopping-up campaign in Anatolia during which he executed Ismail's followers in their thousands. He then attacked the shah himself, with the excuse that Ismail's Shi'a religious beliefs ran contrary to orthodox Sunni Islam, defeating him at Chaldiran (in modern Iran) on 23 August 1514. The Ottomans' skilful use of firearms proved more than a match for the allegedly 80,000-strong Safavid cavalry. Despite their initial success against the Ottoman irregulars, when the Persians reached the main enemy line they were mown down in their hundreds by

Selim's artillery and the handgun-armed Janissaries. Selim followed up his victory by sacking the Safavid city of Tabriz, but when he wished to push on the Janissaries mutinied, forcing him to retreat to Amasya. Selim, however, continued to fight the Safavids for the next two years, annexing the mountainous area from Erzurum to Diyarbekir and bringing under his control the local warlike Kurdish tribes. By the time he had expelled the last Safavids from Anatolia, Selim had acquired in northern Syria a common border with the Mamluk Sultanate of Egypt.

Not surprisingly, Selim's next campaign, and possibly his masterpiece, was directed against the Mamluks. Having received intelligence about a possible anti-Ottoman alliance between the Egyptians and the Persians, Selim struck first by invading Syria in August 1516 and defeating the Mamluk Sultan Qansuh al-Ghawri at the battle of Marj Dabiq, north of Aleppo. Once again, superior Ottoman technology and discipline won the day, and following his victory Selim subjugated all Egyptian land down to Gaza. Thanks to the superb Ottoman logistical organization, Selim managed to cross the Sinai Desert, and on 23 January 1517 met Qansuh al-Ghawri's successor Tumanbay at al-Raydaniyya, outside Cairo. The Mamluks had learnt the lesson of Marj Dabiq and had entrenched their artillery with the intention of silencing the unprotected Ottoman guns. Selim, however, refused to be lured into the trap, executing instead an outflanking manoeuvre towards the enemy camp. Forced to revert to their traditional cold-steel tactics, the Mamluks faced the full brunt of Ottoman firearms, with very few falling to traditional weapons. The victorious Selim conquered the whole of Egypt, bringing under Ottoman control

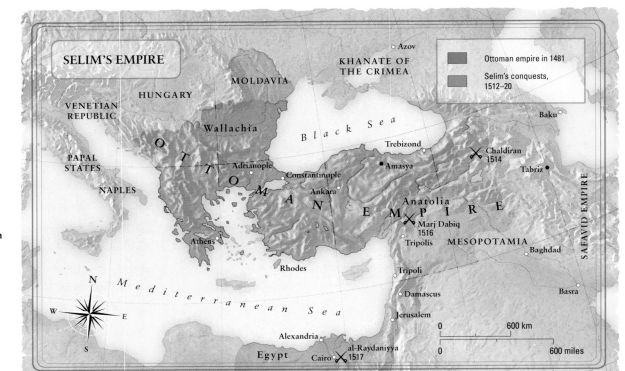

SELIM'S EMPIRE

Ottoman empire in 1481

Selim's conquests, 1512–20

► The Ottoman empire under Selim I. The pattern of Ottoman territorial conquests are evidence of the sultan's strategic goals. By the end of Selim's reign the Ottoman empire appeared like the open maws of a gigantic beast, poised to consume the entire European continent.

▲ Selim I at the battle of Chaldiran: the sultan rides a red caparisoned horse, shielded by the Janissaries in the foreground. The absence of firearms is misleading, the Ottoman victory over the Persians being largely the result of concentrated fire from the sultan's artillery and handgunners.

Key Battles

The Battle of Chaldiran, 23 August 1514
An Ottoman army of about 50,000 men faces a Safavid 80,000-strong force, which mostly consists of cavalry. Selim manages to repulse repeated Persian charges, mainly thanks to his army's superior discipline and firepower. The Ottoman victory gives Selim control over the eastern part of Anatolia, and clearly defines the Ottoman–Persian border.

The Battle of Marj Dabiq, 24 August 1516
Invading Syria, Selim meets a superior Mamluk army under Qansuh al-Ghawri at Marj Dabiq, north of Aleppo. The Mamluk attack is initially successful, but Ottoman firearms manage to stem the tide long enough to allow al-Ghawri's disgruntled Syrian and Lebanese troops to desert. Qansuh al-Ghawri dies on the field of battle, probably from a stroke.

The Battle of al-Raydaniyya, 22 January 1517
Invading Egypt with less than 20,000 men, Selim faces an entrenched Mamluk army under Sultan Tumanbay at al-Raydaniyya, east of Cairo. Executing a flanking attack towards the enemy camp, Selim forces the Mamluks to abandon their position. In the following struggle, the Egyptians are mown down by Ottoman gunfire, losing few men to traditional weapons.

'While unified, we have the means to repulse the enemy.' SELIM I

'I do not want my viziers to have any pull on me.'

SELIM I'S REPLY ON BEING ASKED WHY, CONTRARY TO TRADITION,
HE INSISTED ON SHAVING HIS BEARD

the main grain supplier of the Mediterranean plus nearly all the commercial routes to the Levant. The sultan next planned to finish off the Safavids for good, but when his army assembled on the Euphrates in May 1518, the Janissaries, tired by years of incessant campaigning, refused to move further.

Selim died in 1520 while busy preparing a large fleet in the arsenal of Istanbul, with the alleged intention of attacking Rhodes. Ottoman power had already expanded towards the western Mediterranean, with Selim bringing under his control the independent coastal cities of North Africa. In 1519 the ruler of Algiers, Hayreddin 'Barbarossa', sought the sultan's

protection to obtain aid against the Spaniards. By obliging, Selim not only acquired a new semi-autonomous province but also, in the person of Barbarossa, one of the ablest mariners of all times. With keen strategic sense, Selim understood that naval power would be a crucial element of Ottoman expansionism, given also that since 1517 the Portuguese had been active in the Red Sea and even threatened the Islamic holy cities of Mecca and Medina. Selim left his son Süleyman (pp. 108–11) an empire doubled in size and armed forces amongst the finest in the world. Thanks to the 'grim' sultan, Ottoman primacy in the Islamic world would last for another four centuries.

▲ Kaftans once worn by Selim I. Sumptuous as these clothes appear, Selim's personal frugality and administrative ability allowed him to fill the state's coffers to the brink. According to one story, 'the Grim' sultan decreed that until one of his successors managed to beat his financial achievements, the seal of Selim I should be used to lock the treasury. For the next 400 years, the seal of the Ottoman treasury never changed.

Süleyman the Magnificent

Supreme Ottoman Sultan who Conquered Hungary

'Whether it be day or night, my horse is saddled and my sword ready.'
SÜLEYMAN THE MAGNIFICENT

A Life in Brief

1494, 6 November
Born at Trebizond (modern-day Trabzon, northeast Turkey)

1520, 30 September
Ascends to the sultan's throne

1566, 5 September
Dies while besieging Szigetvár (southern Hungary)

▶ Süleyman is painted as a young man in this portrait, a copy of a work by Titian. Despite the seemingly lifelike representation, Titian and Süleyman never met. Later in life Süleyman would sport a beard, as a mark of authority.

Known in the West as 'the Magnificent', and in the Islamic world as *Kanuni* ('the Lawgiver'), Süleyman I came closest to bringing the whole of Europe under Islamic rule. During his fifty years as sultan, the Ottoman empire reached its peak of political and military power. When Süleyman succeeded his father Selim I (pp. 104–07) in 1520 at the age of 26, the Ottoman empire stretched from Serbia to Syria, including Egypt and most of the Greek Islands. By the time of his death, the borders ran from Hungary to Yemen, and from Algeria to Basra.

During Süleyman's reign, the empire expanded on four different fronts. Süleyman chose Hungary as his first target, on the pretext that King Lajos II had imprisoned the Ottoman ambassador. The 1521 campaign against Lajos proved inconclusive, although the Ottomans managed to capture Belgrade. In the summer of 1526 the sultan's army again invaded Hungary, and on 29 August won a resounding victory at the battle of Mohács (the only one fought by Süleyman in person). Concentrated fire from the Ottoman field guns and the Janissaries' arquebuses broke up the poorly coordinated Hungarian attacks, and King Lajos and 15,000 of his men were killed. Süleyman, however, decided to occupy only the south of the kingdom, and entrusted the central part to his vassal János Szapolyai – a move actively contested by Ferdinand of Habsburg, brother of the Holy Roman Emperor Charles V (pp. 112–15). Süleyman took umbrage and in 1529 invaded Austria and laid siege to Ferdinand's capital, Vienna. Bad weather and the stubbornness of the defenders eventually forced the Ottomans to retreat, and a second attempt in 1532 to take the city also failed. Süleyman was forced to accept

that a rapid conquest of Europe was impossible, and a year later the Habsburgs and Ottomans agreed an uneasy truce. War would erupt in southeast Europe between the two great powers four more times, in the course of which Süleyman annexed central Hungary and most of Transylvania, securing the western borders of his empire; however, the Hungarian problem remained unresolved at the time of his death.

Süleyman's Mediterranean front opened with the 1522 siege of Rhodes – the seat of the Knights Hospitaller and a hotbed of anti-Ottoman military activity. The fortifications of Rhodes were considered the most up to date in Europe, but after six months of relentless bombardment and assaults the few surviving defenders surrendered. Having been distracted by the wars in Hungary and Persia, Süleyman turned his

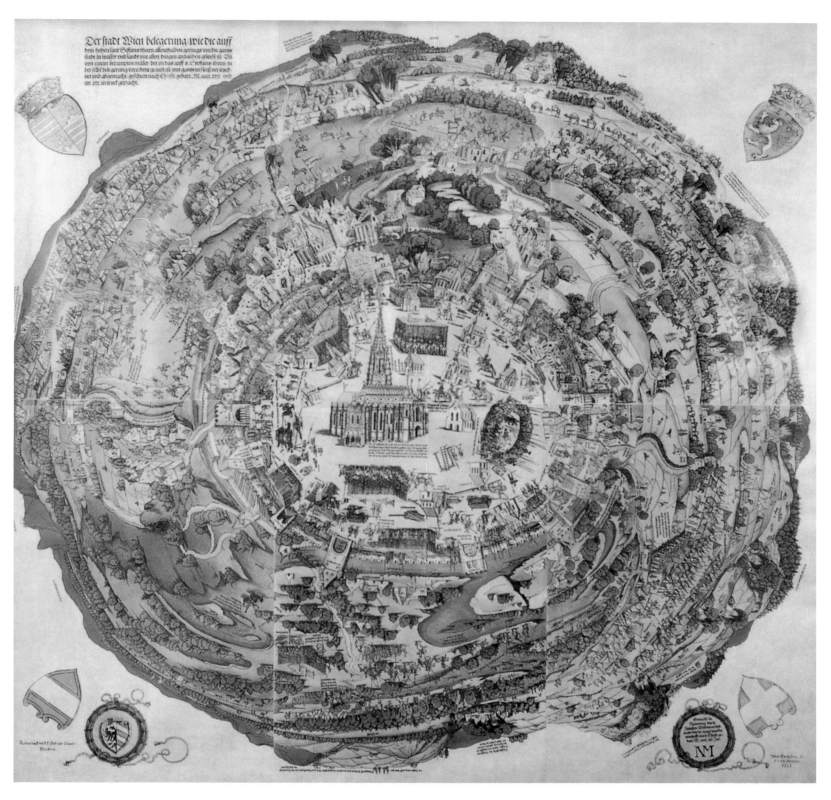

attention to the Mediterranean in the mid-1530s. After Charles V's conquest of Tunis in 1535, Süleyman struck an alliance with Francis I of France. The two sovereigns planned a combined attack on Habsburg territories in Italy in the summer of 1537, and when the French forces failed to materialize, Süleyman instead attacked the Venetian domains in Greece and the Aegean. A year later his grand admiral Hayreddin 'Barbarossa' defeated a Habsburg-Papal-Venetian fleet at the battle of Preveza. From this point onwards, Süleyman's fleet maintained the initiative in the Mediterranean,

although a lack of support from his French allies did not allow the Sultan to exploit this advantage to the full. Habsburg counteroffensives against Ottoman-controlled North Africa met with limited success, and occasionally ended in disaster. In 1560 grand admiral Piyale Pasha vanquished a Spanish expeditionary fleet at Djerba, north of Tunis. The internal rebellion of Süleyman's son Prince Bayezid did not allow him to make the most of this victory, and in 1565, when he finally decided to attack Malta, the stiff resistance of the Knights Hospitaller, aided by regular Spanish troops

▲ A circular panorama dating to 1530 of Vienna during the first siege by the Turks under Süleyman in 1529. Süleyman's failure to take Ferdinand of Habsburg's capital effectively stopped the Ottoman advance in central Europe.

Key Battles

The Battle of Mohács, Hungary, 29 August 1526
Süleyman's 50,000-strong force (equipped with 166 guns) is confronted by Lajos II's 25,000-strong army (with 53 artillery pieces). After initial success on their right flank, the badly coordinated Hungarians are subjected to withering Ottoman fire. A Janissary counterattack wins the day for the Ottomans, and Lajos is killed.

The Battle of Preveza, 28 September 1538
During Süleyman's Aegean and Ionian campaign, Hayreddin Barbarossa's outnumbered Ottoman fleet clashes with a large Holy League alliance of naval forces, comprising Spanish, Papal, Genoese, Venetian and Maltese contingents. The lack of wind plays into the Ottoman hands and Barbarossa gains a significant strategic victory. For the next 35 years the Ottomans dominated the Mediterranean.

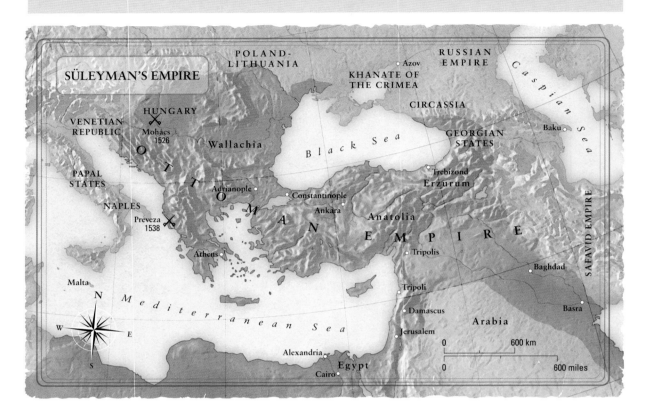

▶ The Ottoman empire at the time of Süleyman's death in 1566.

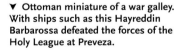

▼ Ottoman miniature of a war galley. With ships such as this Hayreddin Barbarossa defeated the forces of the Holy League at Preveza.

and ships, put a stop to the Ottoman advance towards the western Mediterranean.

Süleyman never managed to concentrate fully on his western fronts, being forced to deal with the Safavids in the east and the Portuguese in the Indian Ocean. Between 1533 and 1556 he conducted three campaigns in Mesopotamia, conquering most of present-day Iraq. However, the Safavids consistently avoided fighting against the full might of the Ottoman army, preferring instead to adopt a scorched-earth policy to repulse the invaders. They managed to capture a few frontier fortresses and on one occasion ambushed and destroyed an Ottoman force under the governor of Erzurum. Süleyman was content to sign the Treaty of Amasya in 1555, since it confirmed his conquests in Mesopotamia. He also hoped that, with the capture of Basra, he would manage to evict the Portuguese from the Indian Ocean and revive the spice trade towards the Mediterranean. In order to stop the Portuguese forays in the Red Sea, and to protect the sacred cities of Mecca and Medina, Süleyman sent expeditionary forces to occupy Aden, Yemen and parts of the Abyssinian coast, but failed to take the Portuguese stronghold of Hormuz. The Portuguese remained a problem for the rest of Süleyman's reign, but their limited resources never allowed them to become a serious threat.

Süleyman was compelled to keep his army occupied, in particular the standing forces, such as the Janissaries. These soldiers ultimately aspired to become holders of a *timar* (a land grant), forcing Süleyman to acquire more land for an ever-growing list of petitioners from the military and administrative classes, who formed the bedrock of the sultan's power. *Timar*-holding Sipahis (cavalrymen) formed the bulk of Süleyman's army, but since such fiefs were seldom hereditary, their sons had to prove their worth in the field before obtaining a *timar*. Süleyman's territorial expansionism became a socio-political necessity, fuelled also by his religious duty as a Muslim ruler to bring the lands of the infidels under the rule of Islam.

Süleyman himself stated that he did not fight 'for gold and treasures, but for victory, glory, renown and the increase of the empire'.

The need to acquire new land would heavily condition Süleyman's strategy. In 1537 he attacked Venice precisely because he was interested in acquiring Venetian possessions, and in 1541 Süleyman dismissed the grand vizier Lutfi Pasha (who favoured a focus on naval operations) for his opposition to the war in Hungary. Süleyman did understand the importance of the maritime front, as shown by his attack on Malta in 1565, but he was also distracted by enemies such as the Safavids, and internal disturbances, such as Prince Bayezid's revolt. One could argue that as a tactician Süleyman was inferior to his father Selim I, but his conquests alone make him one of the foremost military commanders of all time.

◄▼ The battle of Mohács, at left seen through Ottoman eyes. Despite the sultan appearing to be in complete control, at the beginning the fight was little less than a shambles.

▲ An Ottoman shield of the type carried by timar-cavalrymen or frontier raiders.

The Battle of Mohács, 1526

Ottomans	Hungarians
Süleyman	**Lajos II**
40,000 men (including 5,000–6,000 janissaries), 160 artillery pieces	25,000 men, 80 artillery pieces
Casualties: at least 5,000 killed	Casualties: at least 15,000 killed, 2,000 captured and beheaded

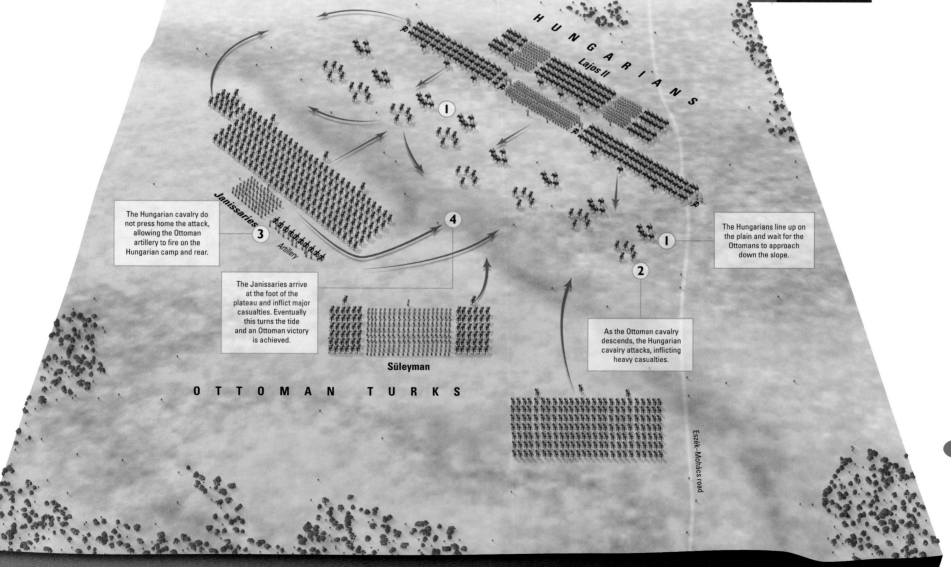

The Hungarian cavalry do not press home the attack, allowing the Ottoman artillery to fire on the Hungarian camp and rear. **3**

The Janissaries arrive at the foot of the plateau and inflict major casualties. Eventually this turns the tide and an Ottoman victory is achieved.

The Hungarians line up on the plain and wait for the Ottomans to approach down the slope. **1**

As the Ottoman cavalry descends, the Hungarian cavalry attacks, inflicting heavy casualties. **2**

Janissaries

Artillery

Süleyman

OTTOMAN TURKS

Eszék–Mohács road

HUNGARIANS

Lajos II

Emperor Charles V

Habsburg Ruler who Waged the Italian Wars

'I speak Spanish to God, Italian to women, French to men, and German to my horse.' CHARLES V

A Life in Brief

1500, 24 February
Born in Ghent

1506
Inherits his father's
Burgundian territories

1516
Becomes King of Aragon

1518
Becomes King of Castile

1519
Becomes King of the Romans
(Germany)

1530–56
Holy Roman Emperor

1558, 21 September
Dies at Yuste (Spain)

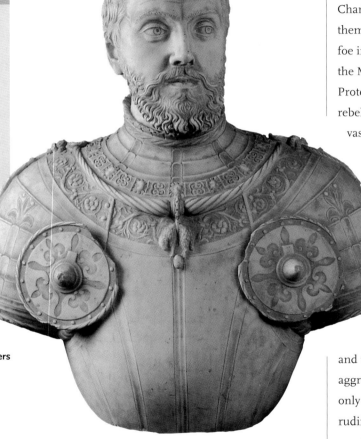

▶ Charles's mental outlook remained in many ways late medieval but, in keeping with late Renaissance style, he often had himself portrayed in the guise of a Roman emperor. Some of his major advisers and a number of writers and propagandists in Spain regarded his rule as a historical opportunity to reconstitute the old Roman empire and achieve European unity and peace. Ironically, his reign coincided with the rise of the nation-state and the onset of religious wars.

As a political and military leader, Charles V faced unprecedented challenges. He inherited history's first global empire spanning from the Iberian Peninsula to Transylvania, and from Sicily to the Netherlands, including outposts in North Africa and a growing dominion in the Americas. He had to manage the disparate political and military traditions of these states, as well as their often-diverging strategic interests. Overall, his record as a military leader is mixed, although he did manage to increase his holdings outside of Germany.

Although Italy remained the primary battleground, Charles faced a shifting list of enemies, among them the Valois dynasty in France, the old Muslim foe in the guise of the Ottoman emperor Süleyman the Magnificent (see pp. 108–11), and the rebellious Protestant princes of Germany. There was constant rebellion or war somewhere in his lands, and the vast distances separating them was an insoluble problem. Charles often had to make painful strategic choices between France, the Empire, Italy and the Mediterranean. His usual response was to concentrate forces on one or two fronts and maintain a defensive posture elsewhere. Yet, there were tensions between the notion of universal empire promoted by some counsellors, the medieval crusading ideal, noble concepts of honour and reputation and the more parochial drive toward the dynastic aggrandizement of his Habsburg family. Thus, it was only towards the end of his reign that he developed the rudiments of a cohesive strategic vision.

Charles only started campaigning at the age of 29, and faced further challenges as an operational commander. The spread of new 'Italian design' fortresses demanded an increase in artillery and manpower, as European warfare shifted its orientation from battle to siege. Charles learned to adapt. In 1536 he authorized the formation of Europe's first successful regimental organization, the Spanish *tercio*, with 20–25 per cent of firearms. Aided by the growing sophistication of cartography and with the assistance of the Duke of Alba, he became increasingly adept in manoeuvre warfare, designed to wear out an enemy

Key Campaigns

The French and Italian Wars, 1521–59
In the course of several wars, Charles retains Naples, gains Milan, turns Genoa and Florence into allies and manages to repel French invasions, while gaining territory in the Netherlands.

Wars with the Ottoman empire, 1529–41
Charles helps check the Ottoman advance into Central Europe, but fails to stop Muslim raids in the Mediterranean.

At Tunis (1535), Charles plans, directs and fights in the landing and attack on this Muslim base. In July his troops storm the fortress of La Goleta and capture the city, seizing its artillery as well as the entire enemy fleet and liberating thousands of Christian slaves.

Wars against the Protestants in the Holy Roman Empire, 1536–52
Charles attempts to stamp out Protestantism militarily end in failure. At the battle of Mühlberg (24 April 1547), Charles, assisted by the Duke of Alba, manoeuvres his numerically superior army along the River Elbe in pursuit of the Protestant forces of Johann-Friedrich, Elector of Saxony, who believes himself to be safe behind the river. Led by its Spanish contingents, the imperial host conducts a surprise crossing of the Elbe, and fights a running battle.

The Elector's army is destroyed, and he is captured.

Major rebellions, 1521–40
Charles manages to snuff out the Comunero uprising in Castile (1520–21), and a tax revolt in Ghent (1539). In both cases local freedoms are curtailed, and Charles's revenue is increased.

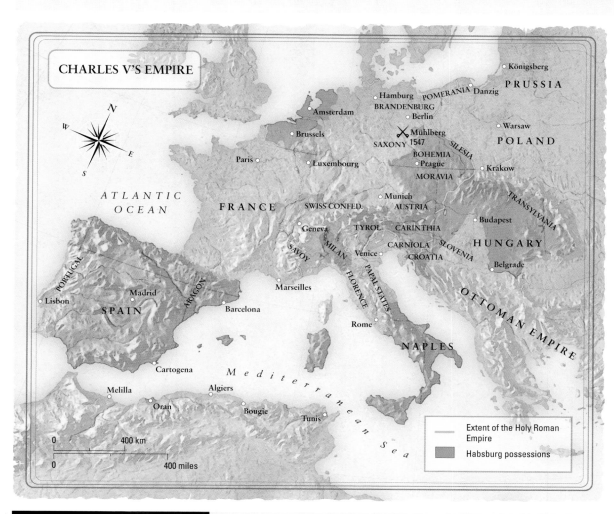

◄ The peculiar geographic disposition of Charles's European empire significantly conditioned his military career. Besides distance and the tenuous nature of his authority over a religiously and politically divided Holy Roman Empire, the major challenges were the inevitable enmity of France which saw itself surrounded and a growing Ottoman threat in the south and east. Charles's decision to divide his possessions between his brother Ferdinand and his son Philip after decades of war was in part a response to this intractable geopolitical situation. Charles's empire also included territory in the Americas.

William of Orange (1533–84)

The career of William of Orange exemplifies the triumph of strategic and organizational persistence over repeated tactical failure. He had limited military experience before the Dutch Revolt. In 1551 he became a cavalry captain and from 1555 to 1557 campaigned against the French in northeast France. A prince and a leading landowner, William headed the opposition to Spanish rule in the 1560s, and in 1568 sponsored a number of failed incursions. He finally led a large force into Brabant in October, but the governor, the Duke of Alba, outmanoeuvred William and defeated his rearguard at Jodoigne.

William withdrew with his army in tatters. Hopes of French support were dashed and William opted for a naval strategy: a small fleet of privateers engaged in abortive attempts to grab a foothold in the Netherlands. They finally succeeded in April 1572 at Brill, sparking a new uprising. The rebel seizure of Mons forced Alba to withdraw his troops from the north, and there the revolt expanded. William invaded Brabant in August, but was out-generalled by Alba, Mons surrendered, and William withdrew to Holland, never again to fight in person. He was assassinated in 1584.

▶ In one of the great equestrian portraits of all time, Titian depicts Charles V as a great Catholic fighter wearing the red sash of Spanish commanders, determinedly riding towards the unseen clash with heretics at Mühlberg; but sunset skies (the battle took place in the morning and afternoon) suggest that the emperor is in the twilight of a long and arduous career. Though he put up a brave front at Mühlberg, Charles was already prematurely aged and racked by gout.

▼ One of Charles V's swords. Charles took his roles as Holy Roman Emperor, Catholic king of Spain and Christian crusader quite in earnest. However, despite the Turkish danger and the ongoing Protestant Reformation, the Papacy, wary of the rise of Spanish power in Italy, sometimes sided with the French against him. In May 1527 his troops sacked Rome for days in one of the worst atrocities of the 16th century. Although Charles had not authorized the sack, the event preyed on his conscience and became a stain on his reputation.

without battle, as exemplified in Germany in 1546. From 1529 to 1553, over nine campaigns, he learned every aspect of tactical deployment. However, with the exceptions of Tunis (1535) and Mühlberg (1547), Charles was absent from his troops' greatest victories, such as those at Bicocca (1522), Pavia (1525) and

'*To endeavour to domineer over conscience is to invade the citadel of heaven.*' CHARLES V

Dinant (1554). In many ways Charles was a transitional figure between the medieval and the modern, often leading his troops personally into battle at great risk for the sake of honour, and twice challenging the king of France, Francis I, to personal combat to settle their disputes.

In 1556, Charles abdicated from the role of Holy Roman Emperor, and distributed his territories between his son Philip and his brother Ferdinand. He spent the last two years of his life in a monastery at Yuste in Spain, suffering from poor health. He died there two years later.

Fernando Álvarez de Toledo, Duke of Alba (1507–82)

Scion of one of Spain's most aristocratic clans, Alba received an exemplary military education. As a commander, he first distinguished himself in 1535 in Charles V's capture of Tunis and the following year he successfully led an independent army detachment in Charles's invasion of Provence. After a masterful defence of Perpignan in 1542, he conducted a brilliant campaign along the Danube against the German Protestant princes, becoming the emperor's top military adviser, a position he would maintain under his successor, Philip II. The Duke of Alba's strategy and tactics, which inspired many theoretical treatises and imitators, demonstrated an appreciation of the changing nature of warfare in the 16th century. He avoided battle unless overwhelmingly to his advantage, in order to preserve his soldiers for the lengthy sieges that sturdier fortifications had made much more common. He preferred dilatory manoeuvres and quick opportunistic thrusts, including commando-style night attacks, giving minute attention to logistics and to the appointment, quite rare for his period, of highly trained subordinates from all social classes. Alba was an excellent battle commander, as demonstrated at Mühlberg in 1547, crushing the Dutch rebels and their French allies in 1568, and leading the Spanish army that defeated the Portuguese pretender in 1580.

'I came, I saw, God conquered.'
CHARLES V

▼ Enjoying numerical superiority, expert subordinates and thousands of battle-tested Spaniards, Charles methodically subdued the Protestant cities of southern Germany in 1546 and in early 1547 moved into Saxony where he lulled the army of the Schmalkaldic League into a false sense of security through dilatory manoeuvres. After a surprise crossing of the Elbe his forces crushed the Schmalkalders at Mühlberg. However, in the aftermath, a lasting political and religious settlement proved unreachable and in 1552 the Protestants again rebelled.

The Battle of Mühlberg, 1547	
Holy Roman Empire	Schmalkaldic League
Charles V	**Philip of Hesse**
13,000 infantry, 4,100 cavalry, 20 guns	7,000 infantry, 3,000 cavalry, 21 guns
Casualties: 100–200 killed or wounded	Casualties: 8,000 killed or wounded

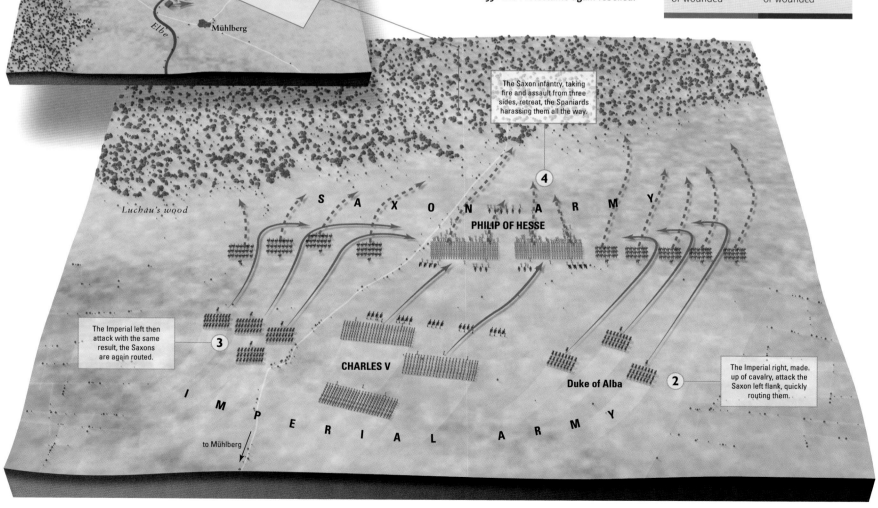

On 24 April the Imperial forces begin to cross the Elbe, the Saxon pickets defending retire to the main Saxon formation.

Belgern

Saxdorf

Elbe

Mühlberg

The Saxon infantry, taking fire and assault from three sides, retreat, the Spaniards harassing them all the way.

Luchau's wood

S A X O N   A R M Y

PHILIP OF HESSE

The Imperial left then attack with the same result, the Saxons are again routed.

CHARLES V

I M P E R I A L   A R M Y

Duke of Alba

The Imperial right, made up of cavalry, attack the Saxon left flank, quickly routing them.

to Mühlberg

Babur

Mughal Conqueror of Northern India

'When one has pretensions to rule or a desire for conquest, one cannot sit back and watch if events do not go right once or twice.' BABUR

A Life in Brief

1483, 14 February
Born in Andijan, Uzbekistan

1494
Succeeds his father as ruler of Ferghana, Uzbekistan

1530, 26 December
Dies in Agra

▶ Babur, founder of the Mughal dynasty in India. He strove for over 20 years to win an empire matching the achievements of his ancestors, Timur and Chingiz Khan. His memoirs reveal a life of extraordinary endurance and a mind of unusual sophistication.

Zahir al-Din Muhammad Babur was descended on his father's side from Timur (pp. 80–83) through his grandson Abu Said of Herat; his grandfather on his mother's side was Yunus Khan of Tashkent, Great Khan of the Mongols, and thirteenth in line of descent from Chingiz Khan (pp. 76–79). Babur was powerfully aware of his glittering ancestry and for the first two decades of his campaigning life set out to reconquer his patrimony, in particular Timur's capital of Samarkand. After his third attempt to keep hold of Samarkand failed, he turned his attention to northern India, which he conquered in two great battles in 1526 and 1527. The outcome was the establishment of the Mughal dynasty as rulers of India; they were to fashion the largest and richest of the Muslim gunpowder empires of their era.

After Babur's father died in 1494, when he was but 12, he found himself catapulted into the competition for power in Transoxiana in Central Asia, in part with his own relatives but increasingly with the Uzbek Turks. Babur aimed to recapture Samarkand, which, he declared in the *Baburnama*, 'for nearly 140 years... had been in our family'. In his first ten years of campaigning he besieged it three times and conquered it twice. But in this period he was little more than a 'political vagabond', as he described himself, subject to the fluid alliances and opportunism of the clan factionalism of the region. At one moment he might be master of a great city; at another fighting for his life with just a few followers. During this period he was advised in part by some of his father's old commanders, but in particular by his mother and grandmother. In 1501, after being blockaded in Samarkand for several months, he succeeded in escaping from the city with only his mother and two other women.

From 1504, when Babur captured Kabul and turned it into a permanent base, his position began to improve. From his base there, Babur was constantly engaged in campaigning. In 1507 he captured the strategically significant city of Kandahar, in modern-day Afghanistan. The Uzbeks had recently conquered Herat and the danger was that they would conquer Kandahar and threaten Kabul. In his first major pitched battle, Babur defeated the Arghun family, who technically owed feudal allegiance to the Timurid rulers of Herat. 'Although our men were few', he declared, 'I prepared an excellent battle order. Never before had I arranged things so well.' The key element in the victory was the Mongol cavalry, who were to play an important role in Babur's other great victories.

Most of Babur's fighting, however, was with the Uzbeks to the north and west, which led, at different times, to the capture of Herat and Bukhara. In 1511 he defeated the Uzbeks at Pul-i Sangin and was able for a third time to capture Samarkand, which he entered on 8 October. But in the summer of 1512 he was defeated by the Uzbeks at the battle of Kol-i Malik; a cunning ruse by the Uzbeks enabled them to overcome Babur's superior numbers, and he was forced to flee Samarkand for Kabul.

From the time of his capture of Kabul, Babur 'had craved Hindustan', but had been held back by the opposition of his officers. However, by 1519 he had succeeded in overcoming this opposition and began the first of five probing raids into India. Then, in 1523, he received a formal invitation to execute a full-scale invasion from Dawlat Khan, the governor of the Punjab. Opposition was growing towards the Afghan Lodi regime, which ruled much of northern India. Babur prepared for the invasion both by training his men thoroughly and by acquiring the latest gunpowder technology.

The future of India was decided in two great battles. On 20 April 1526 on the plain of Panipat, north of Delhi, Babur's army of 12,000 faced Ibrahim Lodi's 100,000 men supported by 1,000 elephants. He strengthened his position by using the town of Panipat to guard his right flank and by a system of ditches to

Key Battles and Campaigns

Campaigns in Central Asia and Afghanistan, 1496–1519
Babur fails to conquer permanently his patrimony of Samarkand, but establishes a secure base in Kabul.

The Invasion of India and the First Battle of Panipat, 1519–26
Babur makes five probing raids into India from 1519, followed by a full-scale invasion in 1526. On 20 April 1526 he defeats Sultan Ibrahim Lodi at the First Battle of Panipat; using his Mongol cavalry, Babur drives the Lodi forces into a funnel, where they are slaughtered by fire from bows, matchlocks, field guns and mortars.

The Battle of Kanwah, March 1527
Babur consolidates his position by defeating the Rajputs and Lodi Afghans at Kanwah, using the same tactics as at Panipat.

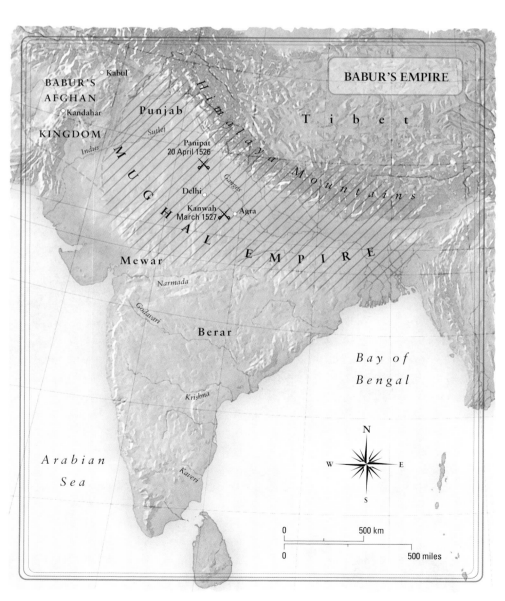

▲ A pre-gunpowder era battle scene. Babur's failure to be able to maintain the upper hand over the Shaibanid Uzbeks in Transoxiana led him to turn his attention to Hindustan.

▼ After failing to secure an empire in his family's traditional territories of Transoxiana, Babur built himself a bridgehead based on Kabul. From 1519 he began probing raids into India, and then took advantage of growing opposition to the Afghan Lodi regime to launch a full-scale invasion. He secured his conquest of Hindustan in two great battles, at Panipat in April 1526 and at Kanwah in March 1527.

117

Babur

Empires & Revolutions

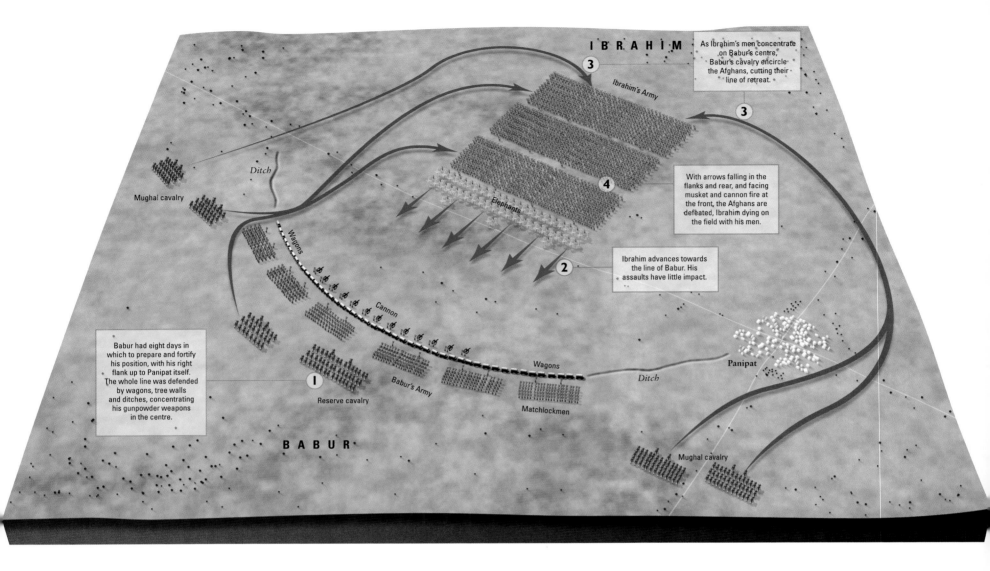

As Ibrahim's men concentrate on Babur's centre, Babur's cavalry encircle the Afghans, cutting their line of retreat.

With arrows falling in the flanks and rear, and facing musket and cannon fire at the front, the Afghans are defeated, Ibrahim dying on the field with his men.

Ibrahim advances towards the line of Babur. His assaults have little impact.

Babur had eight days in which to prepare and fortify his position, with his right flank up to Panipat itself. The whole line was defended by wagons, tree walls and ditches, concentrating his gunpowder weapons in the centre.

IBRAHIM

Ibrahim's Army

Elephants

Ditch

Mughal cavalry

Ditch

Panipat

Wagons

Cannon

Wagons

Babur's Army

Matchlockmen

Reserve cavalry

BABUR

Mughal cavalry

The First Battle of Panipat, 1526	
Mughals	Delhi Sultanate
Babur	**Ibrahim**
12,000 troops	100,000 troops, 1000 war elephants
Casualties: low	Casualties: 40,000–50,000

▲ At Panipat Babur faced the vastly superior forces of the Afghan Lodi ruler, Sultan Ibrahim. He created a funnel with his defences, 700 wagons being positioned along his centre, artillery in front, matchlockmen behind, and with gaps through which his cavalry could pour. The Mughal cavalry drove Sultan Ibrahim's army into the funnel where they were at the mercy of Babur's guns and archers.

the left. Across the centre of the battlefield he had 700 carts tied together in the 'Anatolian manner', with matchlockmen being placed behind the carts and the cannon in front. In the event, Babur used his Mongol cavalry on the wings to roll up the Afghan forces and to force them into the funnel he had created in front of his centre, where they were at the mercy of his arrows and his guns. By midday around 16,000 of the Afghan forces lay dead. In the second battle in March 1527 at Kanwah, just west of Agra, Babur faced Rana Sangar of Mewar, the leader of a confederation of Hindu Rajput princes, and Mahmud Lodi, the brother of Ibrahim. On this occasion the opposition fielded 200,000 men. Babur used the same tactics as at Panipat, which were again decisive. He ordered a tower of heads to be built in honour of his victory.

Gunpowder had been used in Indian siege warfare since the 14th century. Babur was the first in India to use gunpowder weapons on the battlefield, and in doing so his tactics were similar to those used by the Ottomans against the Safavids at Chaldiran in 1514 and by the Safavids against the Uzbeks at Jam in 1528. There is a debate about how important gunfire was in the two great battles to secure the conquest of India, but Babur himself had no doubt it was crucial at Kanwah. 'From the centre', he wrote, 'Mustafa Rumi brought forward the caissons and with matchlocks and mortars broke not only the ranks of the infidel army but their hearts as well.'

Babur left an autobiography entitled the *Baburnama*, a notable work of world literature. It shows him to be highly cultivated, humane and deeply curious about people and the world in which he moved. It also reveals, through its descriptions of skirmishes, set-piece battles and campaigns, the resilience, perseverance and intelligence that supported his military genius. Through his military leadership he was able to found a Muslim dynasty that was to rule India for more than three centuries, and which helped to provide the environment in which the subcontinent came to support one-third of the Muslim peoples of the world.

'Don't think [the Lodi Afghans] are like the Uzbeks! How would they know how to evaluate the odds of a battle?' BABUR

▲ An Uzbek prisoner in a yoke. When Babur was forced to retake Kabul in 1506, one of the rebels, Sultan Sanjar Barlas, was brought before him 'bound at the neck', very possibly after this fashion.

◄ Gunpowder weaponry played an important role in Babur's victories at Panipat and Kanwah. The first to use gunpowder weapons on the battlefield in India, Babur's three main weapons were the *kazan*, a form of mortar on a four-wheeled cart, a *zarbzan*, a light cannon on a two-wheeled cart, and the matchlock. Shown here are *zarbzan*s, above, and *kazan*s, below, at the battle of Panipat.

Akbar

'A monarch should ever be intent on conquest lest his neighbours rise in arms against him.' AKBAR

A Life in Brief

1542, 15 October
Born in Umarkot (Sind)

1556, 14 February
Enthroned as Mughal emperor

1605, 25 October
Dies in Agra

▶ Akbar was the greatest in the line of great Mughal emperors, which stretched from Babur to Awrangzeb (r. 1658–1707). Expander and consolidator of Mughal power in India, Akbar was deeply aware of his dynasty's heritage of empire which went back through Timur to Chingiz Khan. Here, he hands his imperial crown to his grandson, Shah Jahan, while his son, Jahangir, looks on.

▼ Portrait of Akbar in old age on a gold presentation coin minted by his son, Jahangir. The inscription says 'God is Great' and 'Auspicious Year 1'. Human images on Islamic coins are most unusual.

Jalal al-Din Muhammad Akbar is remembered as the most able of the gifted Mughal line of rulers and, with the 3rd-century BC emperor Ashoka, the greatest ruler India has seen. The grandson of Babur (pp. 116–19) through his son Humayun (1508–56), he was profoundly aware of the Timurid traditions of conquest and empire that reached back to his ancestor Chingiz Khan (pp. 76–79), and which were celebrated in Mughal painting and in the history of his reign that he commissioned from Abul Fazl as part of the *Akbarnamah* trilogy. He both consolidated the Mughal empire and expanded it, so that it came to stretch from Afghanistan's Helmand river in the west to Bengal's Brahmaputra river in the east, and from the

Deccan's Godavari river in the south to the Himalayan mountains in the north.

Akbar was 13 when he came to the throne, after his father had died by falling down the stone steps of his library in Delhi. Effective power was taken by Bayram Khan, whom Humayun had made Akbar's guardian. Immediately, they were threatened by a combination of Afghan and Rajput forces under the able generalship of Hemu, a former vegetable seller. On 5 November 1556 Bayram Khan and Akbar defeated Hemu's vastly superior forces at the Second Battle of Panipat.

As Akbar grew through adolescence he increasingly resented his guardian's authority. In 1560 he dismissed Bayram Khan. However, he was not

Key Battles and Campaigns

The Second Battle of Panipat, 5 November 1556
Together with his guardian, Bayram Khan, Akbar defeats Hemu and his Afghan and Rajput supporters. Although Hemu's war elephants dominate the battlefield, at a critical moment he is struck in the eye by an arrow and is rendered senseless. Hemu's forces panic, and the Mughals carry the field. Hemu is captured and executed.

The Siege of Chitor, 1567–68
The Rajput fortress of Chitor is besieged for 58 days, before succumbing to Akbar's siege operations. Akbar's sharpshooting skill picks off the Rajput general, Jaimal, causing Rajput morale to collapse as the Mughal forces charge through a breach in the walls. The fort's inhabitants are massacred.

The Conquest of Gujarat, 1571–73
Akbar's conquest of this independent sultanate in west India provides the emperor with access to the Arabian Sea.

The Conquest of Bihar and Bengal, 1574–76
The annexation of these rich eastern provinces removes the threat of further Afghan resistance in this region.

The Central Indian Campaigns, 1595–1601
Akbar's final campaigns to quash political turmoil in the Deccan, in which he annexes the sultanates of Ahmednagar and Khandesh. Unrest in the region continues after Akbar's death.

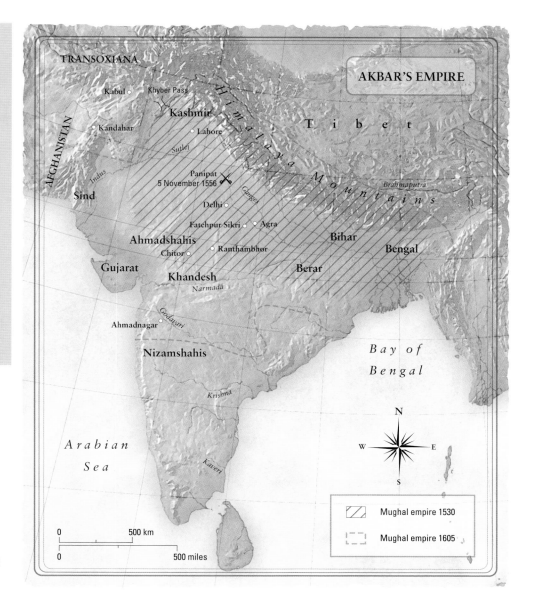

▲ Akbar expanded the Mughal empire so that it came to stretch from Afghanistan's Helmand river in the west to Bengal's Brahmaputra river in the east, and from the Deccan's Godavari river in the south to the Himalayan mountains in the north.

completely his own man until 1562, when he was able to throw off the political influence of his able foster mother, Maham Anaga, and kill her insolent son, Adham Khan.

Akbar spent much of his time in the field. War kept the treasury full, the army fit and the people reminded of his power. The Mughal court travelled with Akbar in his highly organized camp. The use of different bases at different times followed the changing strategic emphases in the expansion of Mughal power.

Down to 1571 Agra was Akbar's base. An early campaign began in 1564 when his Uzbek nobles revolted; in 1566 they invited his half-brother, Hakim, who ruled Kabul, to invade India. Akbar moved quickly, first to confront his half-brother at Lahore, forcing him to retreat to Kabul, then to drive the Uzbeks from the cities and fortresses they had occupied east of Agra. This convinced Akbar of the need to recruit nobles of Indian background. Some were recruited from Muslim families, but large numbers came from the heads of the Hindu Rajput clans, who in turn gave him their daughters as wives. The Rajputs surrendered all control over their territories, with the revenues from them being collected by Mughal administrators. Not all gave in without a fight. In 1567 Akbar had to besiege the Rana of Mewar in the great fortress of Chitor, and in 1569 Rai Surjan in Ranthambhor, which with Chitor controlled the trade route to the Arabian Sea.

In 1571 Akbar moved his capital westwards to Fatehpur Sikri, a city he was building to reflect the cultural inclusiveness and Islamic legitimacy of his regime. From here he pushed the empire's boundaries westwards through Gujarat to the Arabian Sea. By

1573 he had conquered the region and linked its busy ports to the agrarian wealth of the Indo-Gangetic Plain. He then turned eastwards to address the rich provinces of Bihar and Bengal. By 1576 these regions had been annexed, although resistance was not finally suppressed until the late 1580s.

In 1585 Akbar moved his capital northwards to Lahore. The death of his half-brother Hakim increased the threat to Kabul from Abdullah Khan, the leader of the Shaybanid Uzbeks. Akbar brought Kabul under imperial administration, negotiated a treaty with Abdullah Khan, and set about pacifying the Afghan tribes to enable India's rich caravan trade to flow through the Khyber Pass to central and west Asia. At the same time he turned his attention further northwards to Kashmir, which he had conquered by 1589, and then southwards to Sind, which acknowledged his suzerainty by 1593.

In 1598 Akbar returned to Agra. He had already turned his attention south to the Deccan in 1595, when he ordered the invasion of the sultanate of Ahmadnagar; as payment for lifting the siege of

'A night attack is the trade of cowards.' AKBAR

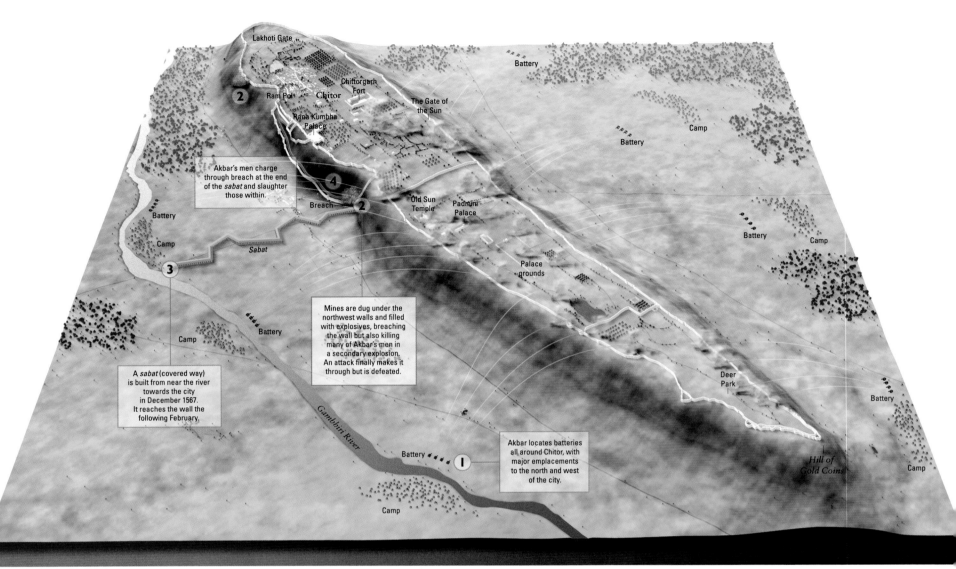

Lakhoti Gate

Battery

Ram Pol

Chitor

Chittorgarh Fort

The Gate of the Sun

Camp

Battery

Rana Kumbha Palace

2

Akbar's men charge through breach at the end of the *sabat* and slaughter those within.

4

Battery

Breach **2**

Old Sun Temple

Padmini Palace

Battery

Camp

Battery

Camp

Battery

Palace grounds

3

Camp

A *sabat* (covered way) is built from near the river towards the city in December 1567. It reaches the wall the following February.

Mines are dug under the northwest walls and filled with explosives, breaching the wall but also killing many of Akbar's men in a secondary explosion. An attack finally makes it through but is defeated.

Deer Park

Gambhiri River

Battery **I**

Akbar locates batteries all around Chitor, with major emplacements to the north and west of the city.

Hill of Gold Coins

Camp

Camp

The Siege of Chitor, 1567–68	
Mughals	Rajputs
Akbar	**Jaimal, Governor of Chitor**
Troop numbers unknown; at least 300 war elephants	8,000 troops
Casualties: unknown; *c*. 200 men killed daily at one stage	Casualties: *c*. 30,000

▲ The Rajput fortress of Chitor was invested on 20 October 1567. After two months of bombardment and mining, Akbar had made little progress. Two developments enabled him finally to succeed: his construction of a *sabat*, or covered way, which allowed his men to breach the walls under cover, and his good fortune in being able to kill, as a result of his own sharpshooting, the Rajput general, Jaimal. On 23 February 1568 the Mughal forces took Chitor.

▶ A two-page spread from the *Akbarnamah*, the history of Akbar's reign by Abul Fazl. On the left is an incident during the siege on 17 December 1567 when a second mine exploded as the Mughals poured through the breach created by the first; at least 100 notables were killed; Akbar directs the siege at bottom left. On the right, the *sabat* snakes its way to the foot of the walls of Chitor.

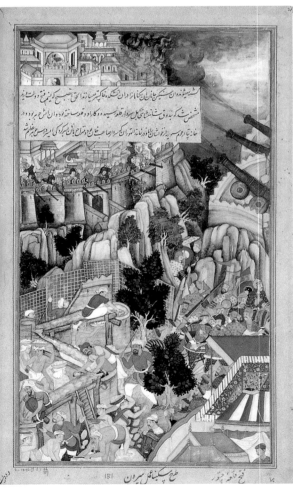

122

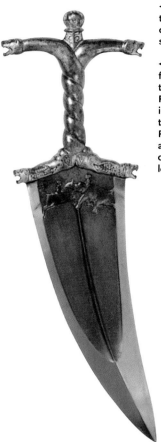

◀ Mughal dagger made of steel with traces of gilding, *c.* 1600. Mughal craftsmen brought the production of such weapons to a high level.

◀◀ After Akbar had conquered the Rajput fortress of Chitor in 1568, he laid siege to the second great Rajput fortress of Ranthambhor, which in 1569 he conquered in a month. Here, he can be seen receiving the surrender of the Rajput prince, Rai Surjan. Note the gun batteries around the fortress and the red tents of the royal encampment to the bottom left of the picture.

'Although knowledge of itself is regarded as the summit of perfection, yet unless displayed in action, it bears not the impress of worth.' AKBAR

Ahmadnagar, the province of Berar was ceded to Akbar. In September 1599 he took personal control of campaigning in the region, and through his energetic leadership the sultanates of Ahmadnagar (1600) and Khandesh (1601) were conquered.

In military terms the major contributions to Akbar's success comprised organization, discipline and gunpowder. Observers were astonished by the size and symmetry of the royal camp, which could contain up to 100,000 people. Ordered with streets and bazaars, it retained the same form wherever it was set up, with an immense, white royal pavilion at the centre – a clear statement of authority as it traversed the lands of India. Disobedience in the ranks of his army was met with instant and exemplary punishment. It was gunpowder technology, however, that provided the key to Akbar's success. The *Ain-i Akbari*, the third volume

of the *Akbarnamah* trilogy, describes Akbar's artillery as 'a wonderful lock for securing the august edifice of royalty and a pleasing key to the door of conquest'. There were heavy guns, mortars, and lighter field guns such as zarbzans and zamburaks. The royal household maintained a monopoly of such weapons, and their key role was symbolized by being parked in front of the emperor's pavilion when in camp. Musketeers were also vital for the preservation of power; in 1595 there were 35,000 in the imperial army, and the evidence indicates that they were employed by the royal establishment alone.

Through his genius as a military leader, and also as a monarch, Akbar secured Mughal rule in north and central India, entrenched his dynasty for a further 100 years and left a memory of good government that has been cherished down to the present.

Toyotomi Hideyoshi

Great Unifier of Japan

'I shall take China about the ninth month, and I shall receive your gift of formal clothing for the festival of the ninth month in the Chinese capital.'
TOYOTOMI HIDEYOSHI, LETTER TO HIS MOTHER

A Life in Brief

1537
Born at Nakamura in Owari province, Japan

1585, 6 August
Kampaku ('imperial regent')

1587, January
Dajo daijin
('great minister of state')

1598, 18 September
Dies at Fushimi Castle, Japan

▲ Many portraits of Hideyoshi were painted soon after his death while his image remained fresh in the minds of the people. This portrait is said to have been drawn by a painter, Kano Mitsunobu, who died in 1608.

Toyotomi Hideyoshi was responsible for ending the Warring States Period in Japan, and unifying the country. He did this by forbidding warlords from engaging in battle, preventing piracy and smuggling at sea, and disarming villagers. Hideyoshi's military ability was pre-eminent amongst his contemporaries, although he never received the title of shogun (supreme military leader) from the imperial court. He established a military, political, social and economic structure that would form the basis of the Tokugawa shogunate, and campaigned twice in Korea.

Hideyoshi was born in 1537 (all dates here are Gregorian, though Japan had its unique lunar calendar until the 19th century) of peasant stock and started his military career under Oda Nobunaga. He participated in numerous campaigns, earning victories as both a minor and major commander. One of his most favoured tactics was the rapid manoeuvre of his forces.

At the time Nobunaga was forced to commit suicide by Akechi Mitsuhide in Kyoto (the Honnoji Incident), Hideyoshi was engaged in the siege of Takamatsu Castle in Bicchu province. This was part of a military operation to subdue the Mori, among the strongest warlords ruling the Chugoku region. On hearing the news Hideyoshi made peace with Mori Terumoto, and hurried to Omi province to avenge his master. He defeated Akechi Mitsuhide 12 days later in what became known as the battle of Yamazaki, moving his forces to battle at astonishing speed.

The tensions between Hideyoshi and another influential commander, Shibata Katsuie, were so strong that their forces engaged in battle in Omi province the following year. Sakuma Morimasa, a nephew of Katsuie, surprised Hideyoshi's troops while Hideyoshi was in Mino province attacking Katsuie's ally, Oda Nobutaka. As soon as he heard the news of this, Hideyoshi rushed back accompanied by over 10,000 soldiers. His men covered the 30 miles in five hours, and struck Morimasa's troops in the middle of the night. Hideyoshi's rapid movement interfered with Morimasa's retreat to the main force, and thus broke the coherence of his army. Katsuie later committed suicide during the battle of Shizugatake. Within a year of Nobunaga's death, Hideyoshi had already destroyed two of his most powerful rivals.

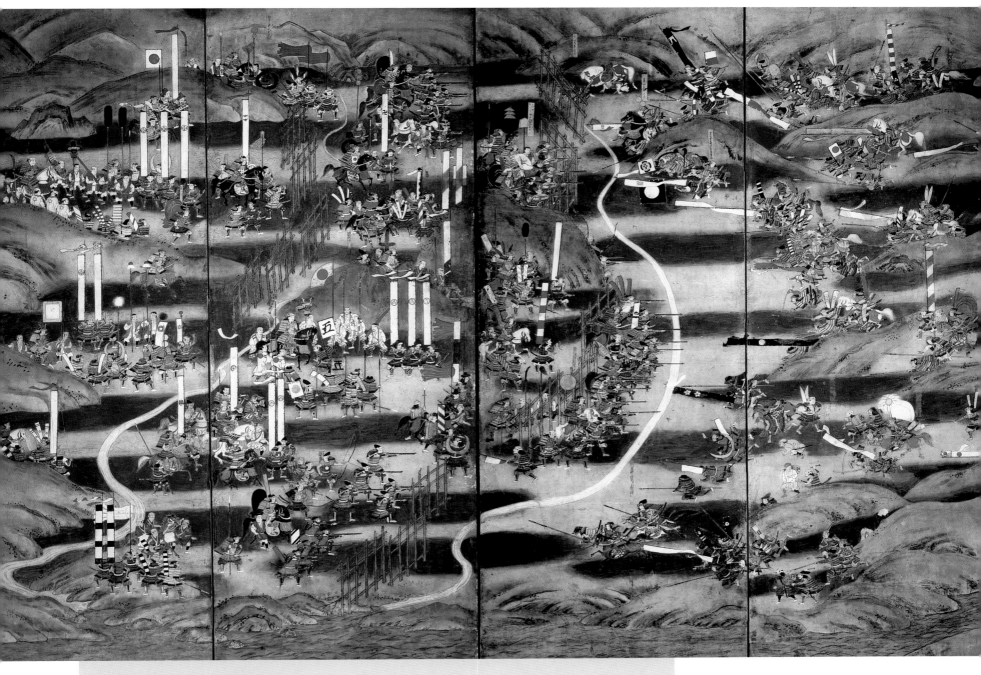

Oda Nobunaga (1534–82)

Oda Nobunaga was the first of Japan's three great unifiers, preceding Toyotomi Hideyoshi and Tokugawa Ieyasu. Utilizing the traditional authority of the imperial court and the shogun, Nobunaga triumphed over many warlords. He also challenged the power of religious institutions and ended the military rule of the Muromachi shogunate.

An esteemed commander, he sought victory through siege warfare and the rapid manoeuvre of his forces. During the battle of Nagashino (1575), he led a relieving force together with Tokugawa Ieyasu to lift the siege of the castle. The battle became famous for the innovative use of volley fire from thousands of arquebuses arranged in ranks. The scene above is part of a six-panel folding screen showing the battle: its theme is the decisive engagement fought at Shidaragahara. On the second panel from the right, ranks of arquebuses arranged by Nobunaga are drawn on the left bank of a river, while on the right bank, the forces of Takeda, Nobunaga's opponents, are pictured.

Nobunaga opened the way for the unification of Japan, and the key moments in this were his confrontations with the Honganji warrior-monks, his destruction of the temples of Enryakuji, and his forcing the 15th shogun into exile. He was made to commit suicide on 1 July 1582 by the samurai general Akechi Mitsuhide.

Key Battles and Campaigns

The Battle of Shizugatake, May 1583
In the struggle between Hideyoshi and Katsuie over Nobunaga's succession, Sakuma Morimasa captures two forts belonging to Hideyoshi in Omi province. Hideyoshi is fighting Oda Nobutaka in Mino province, but rushes back to Omi and routs Morimasa. Morimasa's forces retreat in disorder, which exposes Katsuie's army and leads to its collapse.

The Battles of Komaki and Nagakute, 1584
During the lengthy battle of Komaki, Hideyoshi tries to attack Tokugawa Ieyasu's forces from both sides simultaneously at Nagakute, but fails. Ieyasu finally agrees to peace talks with Hideyoshi, as the superior size of Hideyoshi's forces becomes evident.

The Invasions of Korea, 1592–98
Hideyoshi's initial invasion in 1592 is successful, but active guerrilla resistance, naval operations against his supply lines and attacks by Chinese forces lead Japan to the negotiating tent. A second invasion follows in 1597, but the death of Hideyoshi forces the Japanese to withdraw.

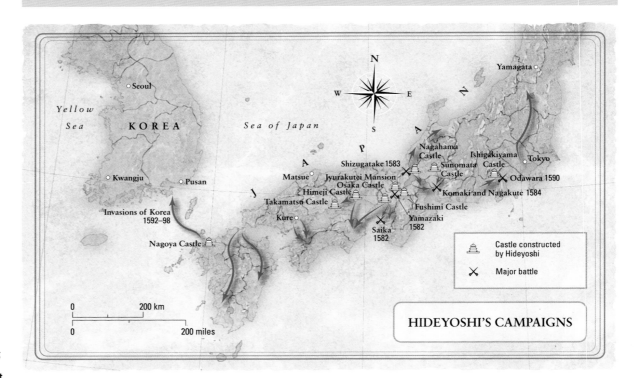

HIDEYOSHI'S CAMPAIGNS

▲ A lacquered war fan, used for signalling in battle, said to have been used by Hideyoshi and bearing the paulownia crest (the symbol still used by the government of Japan). The image of the crest is drawn on both sides of the fan, one is vermillion on a gold background, while the other is gold on silver.

◄ Conquering five provinces in the Chugoku area from 1577 to 1581, Hideyoshi made peace with the Mori and beat Akechi Mitsuhide at the battle of Yamazaki in 1582. The year after, Hideyoshi defeated Katsuie at the battle of Shizugatake and started constructing Osaka Castle, but failed to triumph over Ieyasu at the battles of Komaki and Nagakute in 1584. His military success in taking control of the Kishu, Shikoku and Hokuriku area in 1585, and the Kyushu area in 1587, and his victory at the battle of Odawara leading to control of the Kanto and Oshu areas in 1590, brought the unification of Japan. Hideyoshi twice invaded Korea in the 1590s without success.

▼ Trumpet shells like this one were used on the battlefield for signalling over long distances. They were usually made from giant triton shells, and were sounded in battle by specially trained Buddhist monks.

A MASTER OF SIEGE WARFARE

Hideyoshi was also an expert in besieging castles, and particularly favoured the use of floods: he took three castles by using this method (Takamatsu, Takegahana and Ota).

In 1582 Hideyoshi's 30,000-strong army besieged Takamatsu Castle, which was defended by approximately 6,000 soldiers. He ordered an embankment to be built around the castle in 12 days. It was 2.5 miles long, 21.7 m in breadth and 7.2 m high. Once completed, the castle was flooded, becoming an isle in a lake. A Mori army failed to relieve the besieged castle, and instead was forced to surrender to Hideyoshi. Hideyoshi's assault on Takegahana Castle in 1584 formed part of the battle of Komaki. The embankment built around this castle was said to be longer, broader and higher than that at Takamatsu.

One month after the start of the siege, the castle's lord capitulated. Ota Castle suffered a similar fate, with the besieged surrendering in 1585 within a month of the construction of an embankment.

Hideyoshi was also an expert in blockading castles. He besieged Miki Castle in 1578, and destroyed the minor forts surrounding it, preventing his force from being attacked on both flanks. The combined forces of the Mori and Honganji (a powerful warrior-monk sect) attempted to break the siege, but were defeated by Hideyoshi's forces. At the beginning of 1580, the castle commander surrendered to Hideyoshi and offered to commit hara-kiri (ritual suicide), on condition that this would guarantee the lives of his people.

In 1581 Hideyoshi surrounded Tottori Castle with 20,000 soldiers. He seized all the available supplies of rice in the surrounding area, and instigated a naval blockade at the mouth of the river to stop food from getting in. Some 65 ships, fully laden with rice that the Mori had sent, were attacked and sunk on Hideyoshi's orders.

THE UNIFICATION OF JAPAN

Tokugawa Ieyasu was the most powerful rival that stood in the way of his goal of unifying Japan. He faced him down in the Komaki campaign, which included the battle of Nagakute. In the battle, Hideyoshi deployed some of his 20,000 soldiers to Mikawa province in order to envelope Ieyasu's forces from both sides, but Ieyasu predicted this and won. After the Komaki campaign, Hideyoshi sent his aged mother to Ieyasu as a hostage, in an attempt to gain Ieyasu's trust and loyalty.

In 1590, after suppressing the warlords of Shikoku and Kyushu, Hideyoshi attacked Odawara Castle, the military base of the Hojo, who controlled the area around Kanto. Hideyoshi mobilized more than 210,000 men, surrounded the castle, and destroyed other Hojo fortresses. Lacking allies, the Hojo surrendered within three months. With the fall of the castle, and the suppression of all military groups around Oshu, Hideyoshi achieved his aim of unifying Japan. He now turned his attention to foreign conquest.

THE INVASION OF KOREA

In the latter part of the 16th century the established international order in East Asia, up to then dominated by the Ming dynasty of China, began to collapse. Korea was under the political hegemony and security system of China, and Hideyoshi assumed that Korea would wish to switch its allegiance to Japan – but

he was wrong. In 1590, in a meeting with Korean ambassadors, he demanded that Korea should open the way for Japan to conquer the Ming. He began his move by constructing a headquarters, a staging area, and a sizeable castle town in Nagoya in the Hizen province in Japan, all at huge expense.

The first Japanese offensive forces, numbering 160,000 in nine divisions, left for Korea in May 1592.

SIEGE OF TAKAMATSU CASTLE, 1582

▲ Takamatsu Castle in Bicchu province, surrounded by swamp, had a reputation for being impregnable. Hideyoshi ordered an embankment to be built, and, helped by the rainy season, succeeded in flooding the swamp and cutting off the castle. A Mori army failed to break the siege. To save the lives of the besieged, the castle lord Shimizu Muneharu and his three relatives, taking a sip of drink and composing their last words, committed hara-kiri (ritual suicide) in a boat on the lake in front of both armies.

Yi Sun-Shin (1545–98)

A Korean national hero, Yi Sun-Shin was born in Seoul (where the statue shown here stands). He won seven naval battles against the Japanese during the first invasion. At the battle of Sacheon in 1592, Yi attacked the Japanese navy using his 'turtle' ships, so-called because the ships' roofs were covered with iron plates. These ships were armed with 13 cannon each, fired through small openings. Yi knew the south Korean coast well, and often used the tides and narrow straits to his advantage. The Korean victories at sea forced Hideyoshi to change his strategy, and thereafter he avoided naval confrontation, preferring to bombard the Korean navy from his forts.

Yi was appointed commander of the Korean navy immediately after the second invasion began. He won three naval battles, including the battle of Myongryang, where his 13 ships defeated 133 of the Japanese fleet. Yi was killed in a naval battle in December 1598.

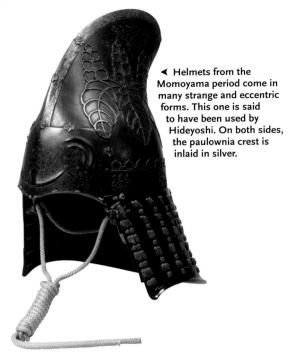

◀ Helmets from the Momoyama period come in many strange and eccentric forms. This one is said to have been used by Hideyoshi. On both sides, the paulownia crest is inlaid in silver.

▶ For his attack on the Chugoku area, Hideyoshi established a base at the strategically important town of Himeji in Harima province, building a three-storey castle tower in 1581. The castle, known for its beautiful layout and structure, was extended by another commander, Ikeda Terumasa, at the beginning of the 17th century.

▲ A lacquered saddle and stirrups inlaid with gold and silver, said to have been cherished by Hideyoshi. This luxurious and decorative set is indicative of the atmosphere of the Momoyama period in the 16th century.

It took only three weeks for Seoul to fall into Japanese hands. However, Korean guerrilla resistance and the success of Korean naval operations led by Yi Sun-Shin, eventually forced Japan to enter peace talks. Other contributing factors were the support given by Chinese reinforcements to the Koreans, the deviousness of the Ming ambassadors and a damaging raid on the huge Japanese supply base in Seoul, where two months' worth of food for all the Japanese forces in Korea was stored.

In 1597 the breakdown of negotiations between Japan and China led to a second invasion of Korea. Among the key engagements were the naval battle of Myongryang, from which the Korean navy emerged victorious after a ten-hour struggle, and the 1598 battle of Ulsan. Both sides were tiring of war, though, and the death of Hideyoshi in 1598 brought about the Japanese withdrawal from Korea. The restoration of peaceful relations with Korea was obtained by the subsequent regime, led by Tokugawa Ieyasu.

Tokugawa Ieyasu (1543–1616)

Tokugawa Ieyasu, founder of the Tokugawa shogunate, was born in Mikawa province. Two years after the death of his former ally Nobunaga, Ieyasu clashed with Hideyoshi at the battles of Komaki and Nagakute (1584). Ieyasu subsequently offered loyalty to Hideyoshi, and based himself in Edo. He became the most powerful lord under Hideyoshi's regime.

After Hideyoshi's death, Ieyasu formed relationships, through marriage, with other warlords. This enabled him to challenge the primacy of the Toyotomi clan. Ishida Mitsunari, and other vassals loyal to the Toyotomi clan, opposed Ieyasu. This led to the battle of Sekigahara (1600). Ieyasu's forces exceeded 75,000, while the enemy stood at 80,000. Some 20,000 enemy troops swore allegiance to Ieyasu and a further 28,000 refused to fight against him.

Ieyasu, wearing the armour shown here, won the battle, received the title of shogun, and in 1603 established the Tokugawa shogunate in Edo. At the battle of Osaka (1614–15) Hideyoshi's son, mother and 100,000 soldiers and independent samurai failed to hold the castle. Tokugawa's 200,000-strong army destroyed it. The dynasty he founded would continue for more than 250 years.

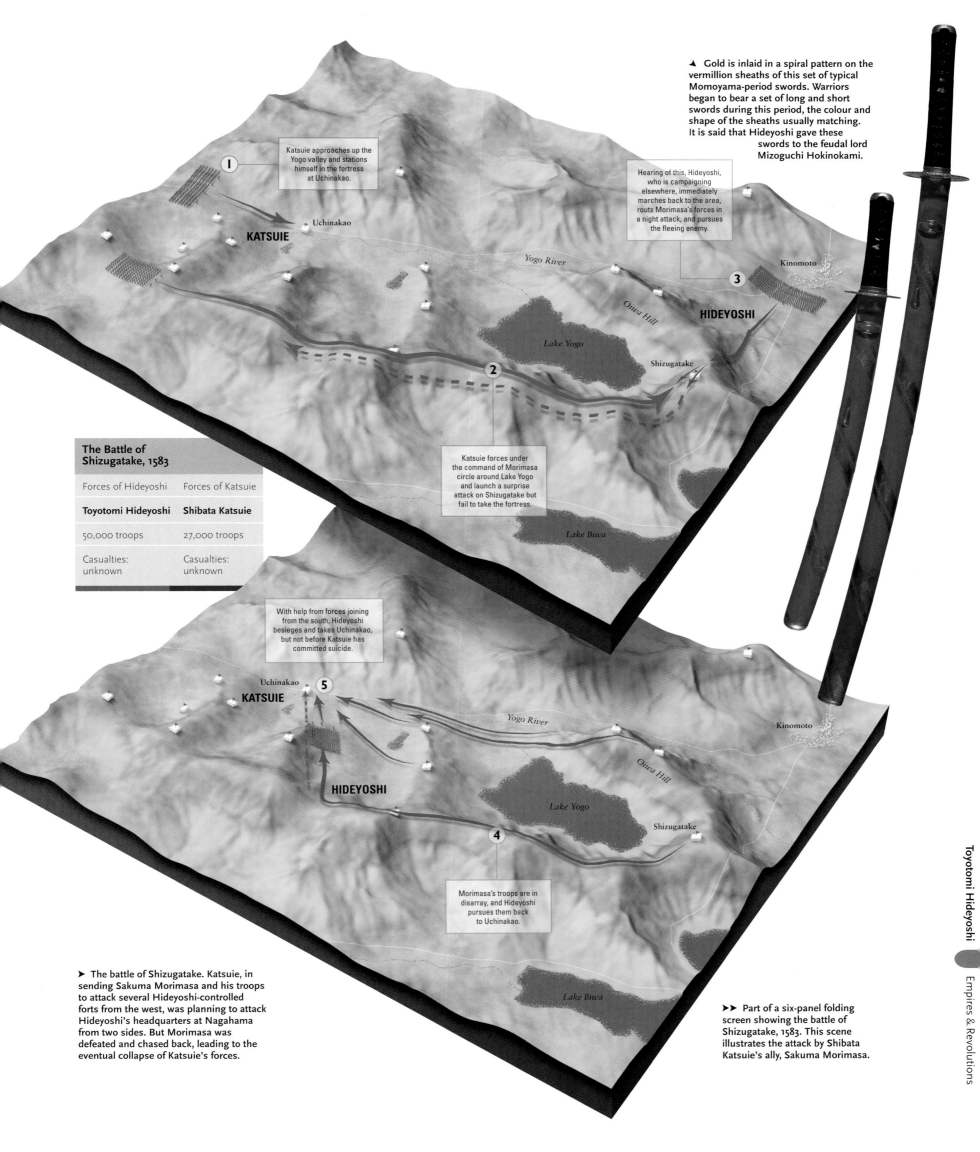

① Katsuie approaches up the Yogo valley and stations himself in the fortress at Uchinakao.

Uchinakao

KATSUIE

▲ Gold is inlaid in a spiral pattern on the vermillion sheaths of this set of typical Momoyama-period swords. Warriors began to bear a set of long and short swords during this period, the colour and shape of the sheaths usually matching. It is said that Hideyoshi gave these swords to the feudal lord Mizoguchi Hokinokami.

Hearing of this, Hideyoshi, who is campaigning elsewhere, immediately marches back to the area, routs Morimasa's forces in a night attack, and pursues the fleeing enemy.

Yogo River

Kinomoto

③

Oiwa Hill

HIDEYOSHI

Lake Yogo

Shizugatake

②

Katsuie forces under the command of Morimasa circle around Lake Yogo and launch a surprise attack on Shizugatake but fail to take the fortress.

Lake Biwa

The Battle of Shizugatake, 1583

Forces of Hideyoshi	Forces of Katsuie
Toyotomi Hideyoshi	**Shibata Katsuie**
50,000 troops	27,000 troops
Casualties: unknown	Casualties: unknown

With help from forces joining from the south, Hideyoshi besieges and takes Uchinakao, but not before Katsuie has committed suicide.

Uchinakao ⑤

KATSUIE

HIDEYOSHI

Yogo River

Kinomoto

Oiwa Hill

Lake Yogo

Shizugatake

④

Morimasa's troops are in disarray, and Hideyoshi pursues them back to Uchinakao.

Lake Biwa

▶ The battle of Shizugatake. Katsuie, in sending Sakuma Morimasa and his troops to attack several Hideyoshi-controlled forts from the west, was planning to attack Hideyoshi's headquarters at Nagahama from two sides. But Morimasa was defeated and chased back, leading to the eventual collapse of Katsuie's forces.

▶▶ Part of a six-panel folding screen showing the battle of Shizugatake, 1583. This scene illustrates the attack by Shibata Katsuie's ally, Sakuma Morimasa.

Shah Abbas I

Safavid Ruler who Built Iran into a Great Power

'If you hand over Khurasan [region] to my officers – then I am ready to make peace, too. If not, I am ready to fight, and have come from Iraq eager for such a fray; wherever we meet, God will decide between us.'
SHAH ABBAS I

A Life in Brief

1571, 27 January
Born in Herat (Afghanistan)

1588, 1 October
Becomes Shah of Iran in a rebellion against his father

1629, 19 January
Dies in Mazandaran (Iran)

▶▶ A late 16th- to early 17th-century fresco depicting a confrontation between Abbas I and the Uzbeks, from the Persian Palace of Chihil Soutoun, Isfahan, Iran.

▶ A detail from the portrait of Shah Abbas I by Bishn Das, an artist of the Mughal School. Objectivity was a prized aesthetic goal of Mughal art.

▶▶ A resourceful leader who introduced military reform, Abbas significantly extended the Iranian empire.

Abbas was the fifth shah of Iran's Safavid dynasty, who significantly extended the borders of the Iranian empire. He was a skilled diplomat as well as an effective administrator, and among his major achievements were the reorganizations of the Qizilbash tribal confederation and the military. However, many of the details of Abbas's life derive from sources produced at his own court, and so must be judged with care.

The years between the death of Abbas's grandfather, the second Safavid shah Tahmasp (r. 1524–76), and his own succession were rocked by civil war between members of the Qizilbash tribal confederation. These tribes had brought the Safavids to power, and had helped conquer a territory whose borders approximated those of modern Iran. As the civil war raged, Iran's enemies, comprising the Ottomans in the west and the Uzbeks in the east, seized the opportunity to encroach upon Iranian territory.

Abbas made three major changes to the structure of his military forces. First, and soon after his accession, he eliminated the most unreliable of the traditional Qizilbash confederates and their leaders. Secondly, he gradually incorporated into the confederation as Qizilbash subclans or subordinate tribes a number of non-Qizilbash tribal elements that had previously been on the politico-military fringe. These included Kurdish, Luri and Chagatai Turkish elements. Thirdly, Abbas increased the importance of previously underutilized, small *ghulam* ('servant') forces. The latter were composed of non-Qizilbash tribal volunteers together with captured Georgian, Circassian and Armenian youths who had converted to Islam.

The contemporary court chronicles extol Abbas's forced marches of small numbers of specialized bodies of troops. His ability to maintain his forces in the field during cold winter weather (Ottoman troops usually retired from the field in November) is also highlighted. He is said also to have made full use of excellent intelligence, especially on the Ottomans, and to have been astute at deploying his troops with great effect. The battle of Sufian (1603), fought against the Ottomans, is of particular note in this respect. Abbas was also adept at delegating powers widely, based solely on personal trust. Thus, key campaigns were undertaken by both tribal and *ghulam* commanders, individually or as co-commanders.

Abbas was politically astute, and was at ease moving between diplomacy and military force. He was willing and able to cooperate with the major European powers and even play them off against each other, as attested by the 1622 capture of Ormuz (Hormuz) with English assistance.

Key Battles and Campaigns

Campaign against the Uzbeks, 1597–98
Abbas finally retakes the city of Mashhad from the Uzbeks in 1597 after a hard struggle. In 1598, he defeats the Uzbeks at Herat, forcing them to withdraw beyond the River Oxus, and paving the way for the recapture of eastern Khurasan.

The Battle of Sufian, 1603
The battle against the Ottomans takes place near Tabriz (northwest Iran). Abbas's victory, achieved using both guile and a combination of forces, enables him to retake the former capital of the Safavid kingdom from the Ottomans.

The Capture of Ormuz (Hormuz), 1622
Abbas achieves the capture of this kingdom from the Portuguese, who wish to extend their influence in the Persian Gulf. Abbas achieves this with the help of English forces, demonstrating his diplomatic skills.

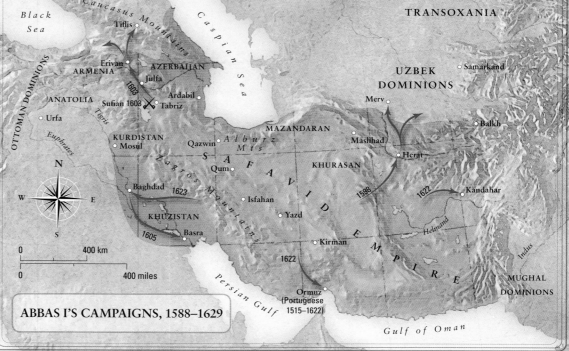

ABBAS I'S CAMPAIGNS, 1588–1629

TRANSOXANIA

Black Sea
Caucasus Mountains
Tiflis
Caspian Sea
Erivan
ARMENIA
AZERBAIJAN
Julfa
Ardabil
1603
Sufian 1603
Tabriz
Samarkand
UZBEK DOMINIONS
Merv
OTTOMAN DOMINIONS
ANATOLIA
Urfa
Tigris
Euphrates
KURDISTAN
Mosul
Qazwin
Alburz Mts
MAZANDARAN
Mashhad
Balkh
Herat
Zagros Mountains
Qum
SAFAVID
KHURASAN
1598
1622
Kandahar
Baghdad
1623
Isfahan
Yazd
EMPIRE
Helmand
N
W E
S
KHUZISTAN
1605
Basra
Kirman
Indus
1622
0 400 km
0 400 miles
Persian Gulf
Ormuz (Portuguese 1515–1622)
MUGHAL DOMINIONS
Gulf of Oman

Shah Abbas I

Empires & Revolutions

Gustavus Adolphus

Great Swedish Commander and King during the Thirty Years' War

'I hope to God that the Russians will feel it a bit difficult to skip over that little brook.' GUSTAVUS ADOLPHUS, AFTER EXCLUDING THE RUSSIANS FROM THE BALTIC

A Life in Brief

1594, 9 December
Born in Stockholm

1611, 30 October
Becomes King of Sweden

1632, 16 November
Killed in combat at Lützen

▶ **Gustavus Adolphus became ruler at the age of 17. Here shown towards the end of his life in a painting by Matthäus Merian, he combined his experience with well-directed political and administrative efforts to raise resources in Sweden for warfare.**

Gustavus Adolphus initiated and realized radical political, administrative and military reforms in his native Sweden. He made a deal with the aristocrats, who in return for working for the state received administrative power, and persuaded the peasants to accept increased conscription, which doubled the size of the national army to 40,000 men. His military achievements made permanent armies the main instrument of warfare in Europe.

In 1611, Gustavus inherited wars with Denmark–Norway, Russia and Poland–Lithuania. He bought off Denmark with a ransom in 1613 and concentrated on taking control of Russian-held territory, which closed Russia out of the Baltic for almost a century. From 1621 Gustavus launched attacks on Poland. The siege of Riga in 1621 secured a base for the conquest of Livonia (completed by 1625). In 1626 Gustavus invaded Prussia, so that Sweden could impose tariffs on Poland's trade with Western Europe. After intensive campaigning, a truce was concluded in 1629. Sweden retained the right to impose tariffs in Prussia, which was important for Gustavus's war in Germany.

These two decades of almost yearly campaigns were used by Gustavus to implement major reforms within a rapidly growing army. Between 1617 and 1630 Gustavus reorganized the army into permanent regiments of standardized size, structure and training, and increased the number of officers. Gustavus also increased the firepower, mobility and flexibility of his army. The infantry was intensively trained in Dutch-inspired linear formations, rapid fire and the preparation of field fortifications. Pike-men were trained to thrust into enemy ranks, disordered by salvoes from the musketeers. Cavalry tactics drew inspiration from the Polish enemy and emphasized edged weapons and the impact of attack in tight formations. The field artillery was provided with light, short-range guns that could follow the infantry and increase its firepower. Gustavus personally led all major operations and exercised command in combat. His reforms benefited from experiences gained during operations, and Gustavus could promote officers who performed well, understood his intentions and acted on their own initiative.

By 1629, the Imperial-Catholic forces had gained a victory in the 'German phase' of the Thirty Years' War. Gustavus saw this as a threat, but also as a challenging opportunity to use the army he had formed. From 1628 he raised several new Scottish and German mercenary

Key Battles

The Battle of Breitenfeld, 17 September 1631
A Swedish army of 23,000 men from seasoned regiments, and a hastily organized Saxon army of 18,000 men, both under Gustavus's command, are attacked by the experienced Imperial-Catholic army of 31,000 men. Tilly's centre and right wing charge the Saxons, who are put to flight, but the left wing is beaten back by Gustavus. Meanwhile, the Swedish left wing and reserve under Gustav Horn launches a devastating counterattack against the enemy's main force, which decides the battle.

The Battle of Lützen, 16 November 1632
Some 19,000 Swedes attack 17,000 Imperial-Catholic soldiers as they are being dispersed to winter quarters in Saxony (allied with Sweden). Wallenstein manages to gather his forces and fight an equal battle, but is forced to retreat to the emperor's territories in Bohemia.

regiments, which were trained in Swedish tactics and paid with Prussian tariff incomes. In mid-1630, when Gustavus secured a bridgehead in Pomerania by amphibious assault, his army had an effective strength of 72,500 men. His ability to mobilize a large army containing a high proportion of seasoned regiments made the intervention possible. Around 58,000 soldiers were sent to Germany from Sweden, Prussia and the British Isles, before any form of local recruitment was instigated.

Gustavus's army gradually penetrated Germany and on 17 September 1631 his forces met the opposing army at Breitenfeld (near Leipzig). Here his tactical reforms, aimed at achieving flexibility in uncertain conditions, proved their value. When the veteran troops of his enemy Count von Tilly routed the Saxon army, a sufficient number of Swedish cavalry, infantry and artillery units were able to redeploy rapidly and launch a counterattack against the enemy's exposed flank, before it could turn against the Swedish army. This ability, primarily executed at a low level of command, was quite unexpected and decided the battle.

After Breitenfeld, much more territory became available to support the army and many German military entrepreneurs organized new regiments for the Swedish forces. In 1632 Gustavus commanded around 150,000 men, including allied armies, but the lack of experience among many of these regiments was a drawback. However, the core of veteran regiments was still the decisive factor at the battle of Lützen on 16 November 1632. Gustavus was killed when he took tactical control of a cavalry regiment at a critical stage of the battle.

▲ By the time of his campaigns within the Holy Roman Empire, Adolphus had gained two decades of continuous experience in warfare and amassed an army with an effective strength of 72,500.

◄▲ Swedish cavalry sword, c. 1630. Gustavus Adolphus transformed the Swedish cavalry into an elite force, with the sword as its main offensive weapon.

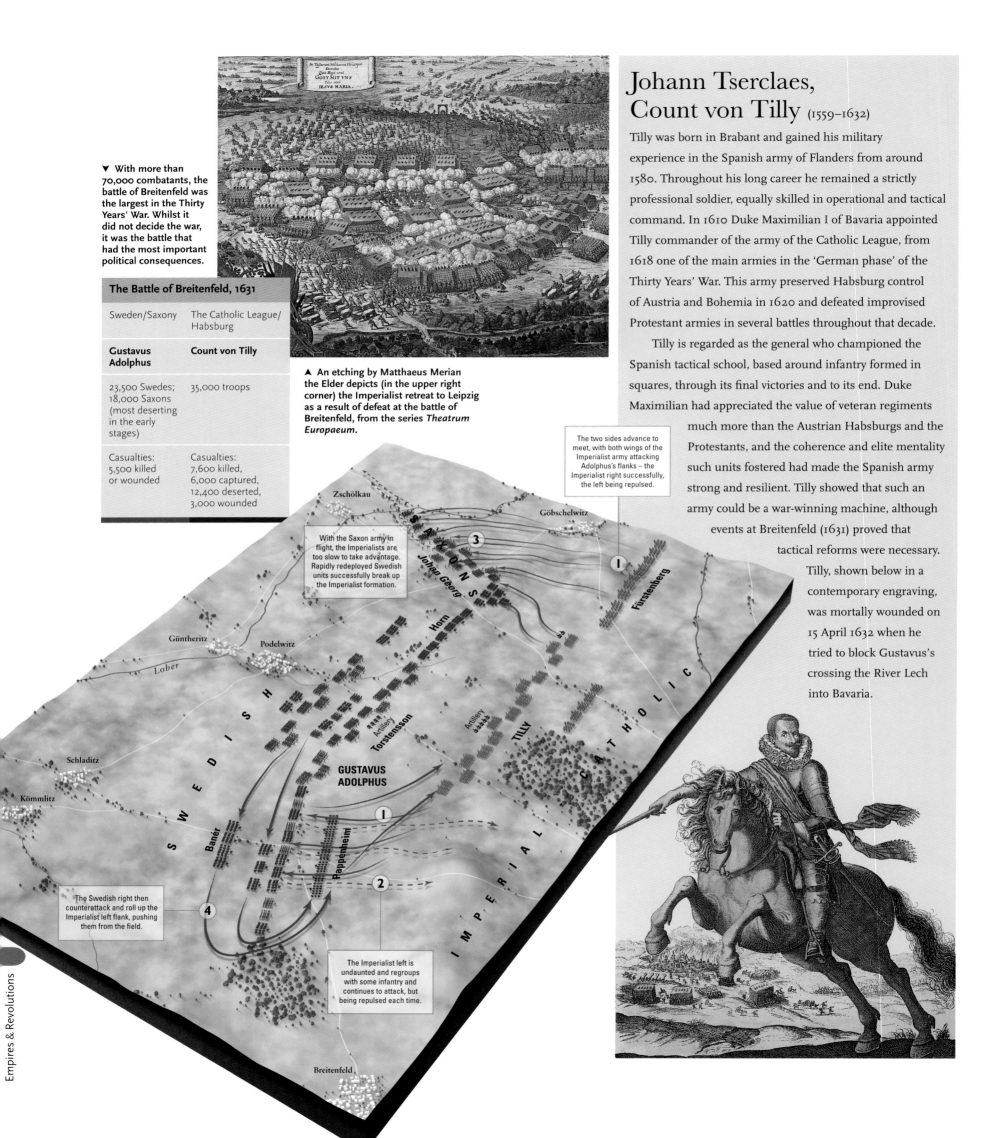

▼ With more than 70,000 combatants, the battle of Breitenfeld was the largest in the Thirty Years' War. Whilst it did not decide the war, it was the battle that had the most important political consequences.

The Battle of Breitenfeld, 1631

Sweden/Saxony	The Catholic League/ Habsburg
Gustavus Adolphus	**Count von Tilly**
23,500 Swedes; 18,000 Saxons (most deserting in the early stages)	35,000 troops
Casualties: 5,500 killed or wounded	Casualties: 7,600 killed, 6,000 captured, 12,400 deserted, 3,000 wounded

▲ An etching by Matthaeus Merian the Elder depicts (in the upper right corner) the Imperialist retreat to Leipzig as a result of defeat at the battle of Breitenfeld, from the series *Theatrum Europaeum*.

Johann Tserclaes, Count von Tilly (1559–1632)

Tilly was born in Brabant and gained his military experience in the Spanish army of Flanders from around 1580. Throughout his long career he remained a strictly professional soldier, equally skilled in operational and tactical command. In 1610 Duke Maximilian I of Bavaria appointed Tilly commander of the army of the Catholic League, from 1618 one of the main armies in the 'German phase' of the Thirty Years' War. This army preserved Habsburg control of Austria and Bohemia in 1620 and defeated improvised Protestant armies in several battles throughout that decade.

Tilly is regarded as the general who championed the Spanish tactical school, based around infantry formed in squares, through its final victories and to its end. Duke Maximilian had appreciated the value of veteran regiments much more than the Austrian Habsburgs and the Protestants, and the coherence and elite mentality such units fostered had made the Spanish army strong and resilient. Tilly showed that such an army could be a war-winning machine, although events at Breitenfeld (1631) proved that tactical reforms were necessary. Tilly, shown below in a contemporary engraving, was mortally wounded on 15 April 1632 when he tried to block Gustavus's crossing the River Lech into Bavaria.

The two sides advance to meet, with both wings of the Imperialist army attacking Adolphus's flanks – the Imperialist right successfully, the left being repulsed.

With the Saxon army in flight, the Imperialists are too slow to take advantage. Rapidly redeployed Swedish units successfully break up the Imperialist formation.

The Swedish right then counterattack and roll up the Imperialist left flank, pushing them from the field.

The Imperialist left is undaunted and regroups with some infantry and continues to attack, but being repulsed each time.

Zschölkau

Göbschelwitz

Güntheritz

Podelwitz

Lober

Schladitz

Kömmlitz

Banér

Pappenheim

GUSTAVUS ADOLPHUS

Torstensson

Artillery

Horn

Johan Georg

Artillery

TILLY

Fürstenberg

SAXONS

SWEDISH

IMPERIAL CATHOLIC

Breitenfeld

Albrecht Wenzel Eusebius von Wallenstein, Duke of Friedland (1583–1634)

Wallenstein (sometimes referred to as Waldstein) rose from being a minor Bohemian nobleman to commander of a large army through an unusual combination of entrepreneurial, operational and tactical skills. However, he lost his life through a lack of political judgment.

Wallenstein's formative experiences were in Habsburg service. The confiscations of the defeated Protestants' property in Bohemia after 1620 made him rich. He used this capital in a meteoric career as a military entrepreneur, exploiting Habsburg administrative inability to create a powerful army. From 1625 Wallenstein organized an Imperial army under his own control. He first recruited the army with loans, and then used it to enforce contributions from friend and foe. By 1630 this system had become intolerable to the German princes, who forced Emperor Ferdinand II to dismiss Wallenstein.

Wallenstein was recalled after Breitenfeld (1631). In summer and autumn 1632 he brought the Swedish offensive to a halt via a strategy of attrition. He successfully resisted Gustavus's attack on his fortified camp at Nuremberg, but after Lützen he was forced to retreat to Bohemia. A period of complicated negotiations and cautious operations followed. Wallenstein's ambiguous behaviour and harsh treatment of his officers created distrust, and the suspicious Habsburgs turned his officers against him. They murdered him on 25 February 1634 as he tried to escape.

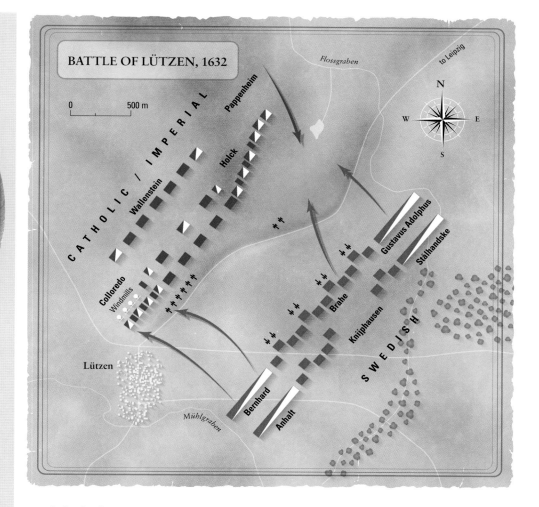

▲ The battle of Lützen was a hard-fought contest between two armies of veterans after months of strategic manoeuvres by Wallenstein and Gustavus Adolphus. The death of the Swedish king started a series of political negotiations which ended with the death of Wallenstein.

▼ The battle of Lützen, at which Adolphus was killed during a cavalry charge, in a copper engraving from *Theatrum Europaeum*, by Matthaeus Merian the Elder.

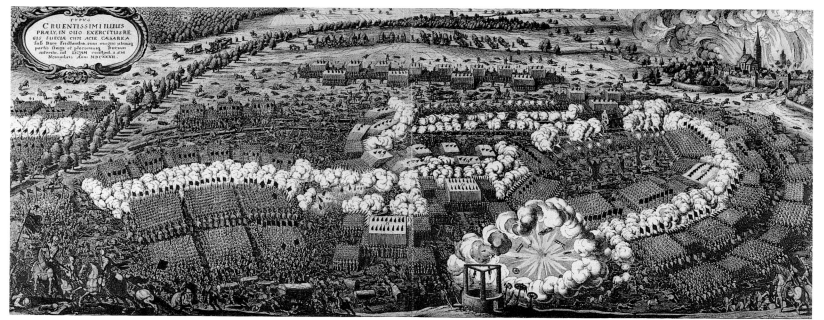

Turenne

Able French Marshal in the Age of Louis XIV

'Few sieges, but many skirmishes.'
TURENNE

A Life in Brief

1611, 11 September
Born in Sedan, northeast France

1643
Made Marshal of France

1675, 27 July
Dies at the battle of Sasbach, Germany

▶▶ Charles le Brun's portrait of Turenne, painted around 1665, shows the marshal towards the end of his life.

▼ Turenne enjoyed great success on the 17th-century battlefields of northwest Europe.

Henri de la Tour d'Auvergne, Vicomte de Turenne, was the most successful French commander of the 17th century. Together with his former superior, Condé, he exerted considerable influence on later generals, notably Marlborough (pp. 158–63), who served directly under him in 1673.

From a leading Huguenot (Protestant) aristocratic family, Turenne entered Dutch service as a cadet in 1625, gaining valuable experience under the brothers Maurice and Frederick Henry of Nassau against Spain. Transferring to France as a colonel in 1631, he fought Spain in Flanders, Italy and the Pyrenees, with a brief spell against the emperor

in Germany (1638). However, his refusal to convert to Catholicism until 1668 meant he was not fully trusted.

For this reason he was assigned to Germany in 1643, considered a secondary front, and was placed under Condé (1644–45). Although he made mistakes, notably at Mergentheim where he split his force, he also saved his chief from serious errors at Freiburg (1644) and Allerheim (or Nördlingen, 1645). Condé's

Key Battles

The Battle of Mergentheim (Herbsthausen), 2 May 1645
Turenne allows himself to be caught whilst dispersed in winter quarters, and only escapes after losing much of his army to a Bavarian surprise attack.

The Battle of Zusmarshausen, 7 May 1648
In the last major battle of the Thirty Years' War, Turenne, aided by a Swedish contingent, catches the Bavarian and Holy Roman imperial army as it retreats through difficult terrain in Bavaria, and breaks it by relentless pursuit.

The Battle of Porte Saint-Antoine, 2 July 1652
Turenne traps Condé's rebel army outside Paris and destroys most of it, effectively ending the Fronde.

The Battle of Arras, 25 August 1654
Turenne defeats the Spanish under Condé and relieves Arras (France).

The Battle of Valenciennes, 16 July 1656
Condé reverses their previous encounter, routing part of Turenne's army to relieve Valenciennes (France).

The Battle of the Dunes (Dunkirk), 14 June 1658
Turenne besieges Dunkirk, Spain's principal northern European naval base. Condé tries to relieve it, but Turenne blocks him on the beach before the fortress and routs him, in only an hour, in his greatest triumph. Dunkirk surrenders ten days later, and Spain opens peace talks.

The Battle of Sinsheim, 16 June 1674
Turenne defeats the imperial general Caprara, who is opposing the French invasion of the Rhineland.

The Battle of Enzheim, 4 October 1674
Turenne is fought to a standstill by a slightly larger imperial army, and is forced to abandon Alsace.

The Battle of Türkheim (Colmar), 5 January 1675
Having regrouped behind the Vosges, Turenne surprises the imperialists by advancing through the Belfort Gap, defeating one wing of their far larger army at Türkheim and forcing them out of Alsace.

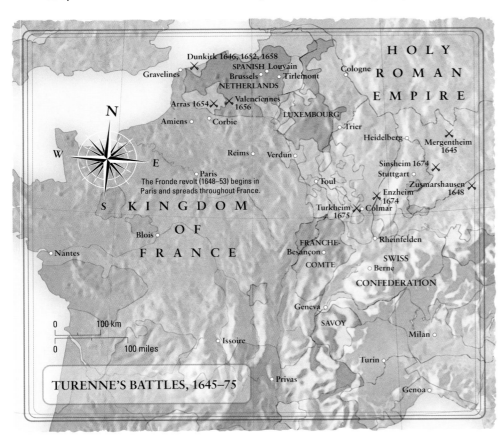

TURENNE'S BATTLES, 1645–75

Dunkirk 1646, 1652, 1658
SPANISH Louvain
Gravelines Brussels Tirlemont
NETHERLANDS
Arras 1654 Valenciennes 1656
Amiens Corbie LUXEMBOURG
Cologne
HOLY ROMAN EMPIRE
Trier
Heidelberg Mergentheim 1645
Reims Verdun
Paris The Fronde revolt (1648–53) begins in Paris and spreads throughout France.
Sinsheim 1674
Stuttgart
Toul Enzheim 1674 Zusmarshausen 1648
KINGDOM OF FRANCE
Turkheim 1675 Colmar
Blois
Nantes
FRANCHE-COMTE Besançon Rheinfelden
SWISS Berne CONFEDERATION
Geneva
SAVOY
Milan
Issoire
Turin
Privas
Genoa

0 100 km
0 100 miles

	French territory, 1618
	Huguenot-dominated area, 1618
	Spanish Habsburg territory, 1618
	Austrian Habsburg territory, 1618
	French gains, 1618–62
✕	Major battles involving Turenne

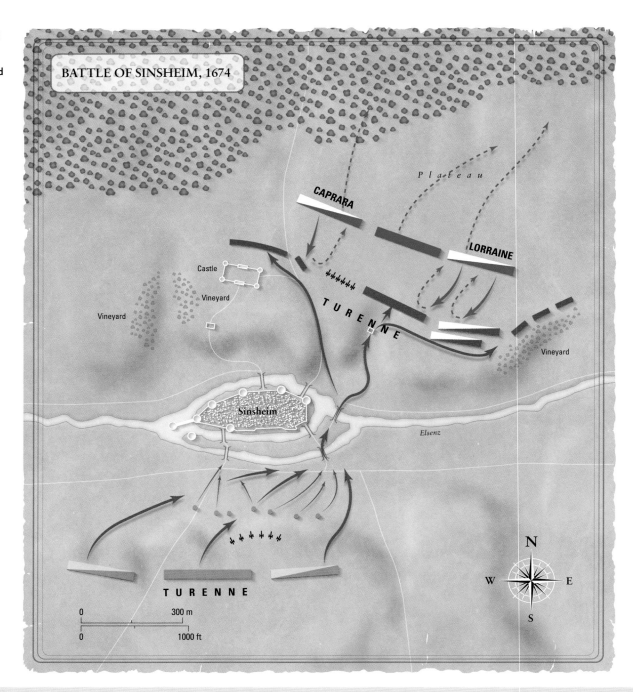

► Though Turenne had a slight numerical superiority at the battle of Sinsheim, he faced the difficult task of fighting his way across a river and seizing sufficient ground on the other side to deploy his troops. The imperial cavalry made repeated charges against the French infantry, but were ultimately repulsed once the rest of Turenne's army had crossed.

BATTLE OF SINSHEIM, 1674

CAPRARA

LORRAINE

Plateau

Castle

Vineyard

Vineyard

TURENNE

Vineyard

Sinsheim

Elsenz

TURENNE

0   300 m

0   1000 ft

N
W   E
S

Condé (1621–86)

Louis II de Bourbon, duc d'Enghien, prince de Condé was the most important French general of the first half of the 17th century. He owed his reputation to his family's eminence (he was fourth in line to the French throne) and how subsequent generations rated his first, spectacular victory, rather than his skills as a commander. Despite virtually no experience, he was given command of the main French army aged only 22 when the country faced invasion. Condé blocked the Spanish at Rocroi where he managed to rout their cavalry and force the infantry to surrender on 19 May 1643. His success led him to rely on shock tactics throughout his career, throwing his men's lives away in repeated frontal assaults. These worked at Freiburg (1644) only because the Bavarian commander was personally shaken and ordered a retreat. The same tactics nearly ended in disaster at Allerheim (1645), except this time the enemy lost cohesion after their general's death. Condé displayed considerable strategic skill on the Pyrenean front against Spain, but without major success. Resuming command in Flanders, he repeated Rocroi almost exactly at Lens (1648) with a similar outcome. These successes earned him renown as 'The Great Condé'

to distinguish him from his father, Henri II (1588–1646), France's principal general between 1635 and 1646.

Unlike many grandees, he initially remained loyal during the Fronde revolt, but rebelled at what he saw as insufficient reward. Turenne defeated him at Porte Saint-Antoine (Paris, 1652), but Condé was by now too heavily implicated to surrender and fought on until Spain made peace in 1659. He was pardoned by Louis XIV and entrusted with important commands against Spain (1667–68) and the Dutch (1672–79). His narrow victory over William III at Seneffe (1674) was typical of his reckless tactics in one of the bloodiest battles of the 17th century.

Vauban (1633–1707)

Sébastien le Prestre de Vauban was the foremost European military engineer of the 17th century, whose ideas influenced fortification design for 150 years after his death. Born in St-Léger de Fougeret in central France to noble but impoverished parents, he was orphaned at 10 and joined Condé's regiment at 17. Thanks to his engineering skills and assistance to Turenne, he enjoyed rapid promotion to brigadier (1676), chief military engineer (1678) and marshal (1703). He directed 53 sieges, of which 50 were successful, including Maastricht (1673). Vauban was a consummate artist and sketched the exploding mine shown here for one of his many publications on siege warfare.

He strengthened France's defences after 1678, although it is hard to give precise figures for how many new fortresses he designed, built and improved; estimates vary widely between 150 and 300, depending on differing assessments of his personal involvement. What is clear, though, is that he expended enormous amounts of time and energy travelling and surveying France, creating a chain of fortresses around the perimeter of Louis XIV's kingdom – forming what he called a *pré carré* (or 'protected meadow'). Vauban systematized existing practice rather than inventing entirely new techniques, relying on defence in depth with overlapping fields of fire to keep besiegers at a distance. He also planned and built several new towns, such as Charleroi and Neuf Brisach.

departure left him in sole command between 1646 and 1648, but with a difficult task. A large part of his small army consisted of politically unreliable Germans, and he was obliged to collaborate with the Swedes, whose war aims diverged from those of France. Turenne preferred to seek decisive battle, and, unlike Condé, eschewed frontal assaults in favour of skilful pre-battle manoeuvres intended to place his opponents at a disadvantage.

His participation in the Fronde rebellion (1648–53), provoked by heavy taxation and the increasing centralization of power, mirrored that of Condé. Having initially opposed the monarchy, Turenne changed sides in 1651 and became its principal commander, fighting his former superior. Louis XIV rewarded him with the important administrative post of Colonel General of the Cavalry in 1657. Turenne stood midway between tradition and modern professionalism. He improved royal authority over the officers, yet was still conscious of his own family heritage and personal reputation. This made for difficult relations with Michel le Tellier, war minister after 1643, and his son Louvois, who assumed this post after 1664 and eclipsed Turenne's influence in military administration by 1668.

◄ This portrait of Turenne by the Dutch artist Adam Frans van der Meulen shows him in the typical staged pose of a 17th-century commander. Few senior officers wore full armour in actual battles.

Turenne rapidly overran the Spanish Netherlands in the War of Devolution (1667–68) and held senior command against the Dutch after 1672. Acting as he had done in Germany 30 years earlier, he largely ignored Louvois. While this impaired central strategic control, his conduct of operations was widely admired. Although outmanoeuvred by Raimondo Montecuccoli (1609–80) in Germany (1673), he forced a far larger imperial army to evacuate Alsace in 1675, where he was killed in battle by a cannonball.

Oliver Cromwell

Victorious General in the British Civil Wars

'A few honest men are better than numbers.'

OLIVER CROMWELL

A Life in Brief

1599, 25 April
Born in Huntingdon, Cambridgeshire

1643
Attains rank of Colonel, Governor of Ely and is later promoted to Lieutenant-General

1645
Lieutenant General of Horse (second-in-command of the New Model Army)

1649
Lord Lieutenant of Ireland

1650
Captain General of the Commonwealth, replacing Fairfax who resigns

1653
Declared 'Lord Protector'

1658, 3 September
Dies in London – his body is later disinterred and hung on Tyburn gallows

▶▶ Portrait of Cromwell by Thomas Wyck painted around 1640 before his rise to prominence, but already showing him in the pose of a commander.

▶ A pair of cavalry stirrups associated with Oliver Cromwell, now in the collection of the Cromwell Museum, Huntingdon.

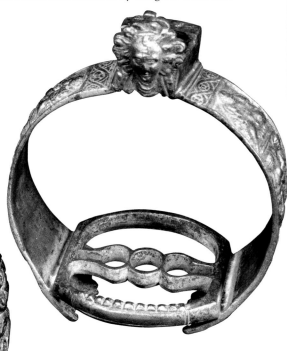

Cromwell remains one of the most controversial figures in British history. Arguably the founder of the modern British army, he was certainly the principal driving force behind Parliament's victory over King Charles I. Though noted as a successful general, he directed only three major battles. His main skill was as an organizer, and at the time of his death the country was considerably stronger and more respected internationally.

Cromwell began his military career late at the age of 43, but within 11 years was not only supreme commander, but ruler of the country. This dramatic rise led later generations, especially the Victorians, to exaggerate his importance and see his guiding hand behind every Parliamentarian victory. He remained overshadowed by the great lords like Essex, Manchester and Sir (later Lord) Fairfax until 1646, and owed his subsequent prominence as much to his political acumen as his military skill. From the minor Huntingdonshire gentry, Cromwell entered Parliament as a spokesman for local interests in 1628. His devout Protestantism inclined him against Charles I, but he remained a pragmatist throughout his career and opposed those who wanted to translate religious radicalism into egalitarianism.

Like many minor provincial European nobles, he started his military career by raising a troop of horse (1642), and secured promotion to colonel by expanding it to a full regiment (1643). However, his methods were substantially different from most of his contemporaries, since he stressed quality over quantity, attracting attention through the efficiency rather than the size of his unit. Though present at Edgehill (1642), Cromwell's first test as a unit commander came in a cavalry skirmish at Grantham on 13 May 1643, where, having plucked up the courage to charge, he drove the Royalists from the field. His new self-confidence was displayed in a more substantial action at Gainsborough ten weeks later; it signalled his rapid promotion and saw him commanding entire cavalry wings at major battles, notably Marston Moor (1644) and Naseby (1645). His strict discipline improved cohesion and control, enabling Cromwell to switch from simple frontal assaults to more complicated manoeuvres, notably holding back units that had just broken their opponents, instead of losing them in exhilarating yet tactically pointless pursuits of the enemy.

By 1644, Cromwell had become increasingly impatient with his superiors' conduct of the war. Whereas Essex, Manchester and others sought military

Key Battles and Campaigns

The Battle of Naseby, 14 June 1645

Cromwell commands the Parliamentarian cavalry on the right wing in the decisive victory over King Charles I's smaller army. Whereas the Royalist cavalry loots the Parliamentary baggage, Cromwell retains his own troops under control and, having driven the enemy horse from the field, uses them in support of the Parliamentary foot to defeat the enemy centre and clinch victory.

The Battle of Preston, 17 August 1648

Cromwell catches a much larger Anglo-Scottish army while it is strung out on its march into England, and defeats it in detail. His first victory as sole commander, the action ends the Second Civil War.

Campaigns in Ireland, 1649–50

Cromwell lands on the east coast and storms Drogheda (September 1649) and Wexford (October 1649), whereupon most of the other towns surrender. His attempt to repeat this at Clonmel (May 1650) proves costly when Hugh Dubh O'Neill ambushes the assault column. Despite Cromwell's heavy losses, Irish resistance largely collapses.

The Battle of Dunbar, 3 September 1650

Cromwell pre-empts a Scottish invasion by advancing on Edinburgh. He is blocked by David Leslie at Dunbar. Cromwell concentrates his force for a surprise attack at daybreak, routing the enemy.

The Battle of Worcester, 3 September 1651

Dunbar forces the Royalists back into England, where they take up a strong position at Worcester. For the first time, Cromwell deploys superior numbers and uses these to smash his opponents.

➤ Cromwell campaigned extensively throughout Britain and Ireland, safeguarding the Parliamentary regime and then giving it mastery over the whole British Isles.

CROMWELL'S BATTLES, 1645–51

SCOTLAND

North Sea

Inverkeithing 1651

Dunbar 1650

Edinburgh

Londonderry

IRELAND

Drogheda 1649

Irish Sea

York

Preston 1648

Rathmines 1649

Dublin

Limerick 1651

Kilkenny 1650

ENGLAND

New Ross 1649

Clonmel 1650

Wexford 1649

Naseby 1645

Worcester 1651

WALES

London

Celtic Sea

English Channel

0   100 km

0   100 miles

Langport 1645

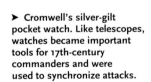

➤ Cromwell's silver-gilt pocket watch. Like telescopes, watches became important tools for 17th-century commanders and were used to synchronize attacks.

preponderance to induce the king to make concessions, Cromwell wanted decisive victory to depose Charles altogether. Disagreement over strategy compounded that over army reform. Cromwell emerged victorious in Parliament between December 1644 and April 1645. The army was remodelled, merging the regional armies with their numerous depleted units into a single force with fewer, but larger and more effective regiments. Totalling initially 22,000, this

New Model Army was expanded to 56,000 by 1650. Cromwell outmanoeuvred his political opponents as the Commons passed the Self-denying Ordinance removing the grandees from command. Though Fairfax was named commander, Parliament gave Cromwell special dispensation to continue serving. Cromwell's influence grew with the success of these reforms. He backed Pride's Purge, the military coup that broke Parliament's opposition to Charles's execution in 1649. The monarchy was replaced by the republican Commonwealth, which stirred considerable domestic and international opposition.

Cromwell now exercised full field command, making himself indispensable by defeating the Commonwealth's enemies. In each of his three major battles, Cromwell rapidly concentrated his forces for a decisive blow. Such energy proved less successful in Ireland, where his impatience led to costly assaults

Sir Thomas Fairfax (1612–71)

From a prominent Yorkshire family, Fairfax, shown here in a contemporary woodcut presiding over an army council, was the leading Parliamentarian general after Cromwell. After a decade of Dutch service, he returned to England where he was knighted for his role in the First Bishops' War (1639). He joined Parliament against Charles I in 1642, serving with distinction, especially at Marston Moor where he played a major part in the victory. Named commander-in-chief 1645, he remodelled the army and defeated Charles at Naseby, effectively ending the First Civil War. He opposed the king's execution and resigned over the invasion of Scotland in 1650.

▲ The metal and leather armour of a typical heavy cavalryman during the later stages of the Civil Wars. Cromwell had made his reputation commanding men equipped like this.

The Battle of Naseby, 1645	
Parliamentarians	Royalists
Oliver Cromwell, Sir Thomas Fairfax	Charles I
6,000 horsemen, 7,000 foot	4,100 horsemen, 3,300 foot
Casualties: 150	Casualties: 1,000 killed, 5,000 captured

▼ Cromwell's defeat of the Royalist cavalry clinched victory at the battle of Naseby, where two-thirds of the king's army were killed or captured, while Parliamentarian losses were around 150. This discrepancy in casualties shows the fatal consequences for a 17th-century army that had lost its cavalry during a battle.

▼ A cannonball now in the Cromwell Museum. Artillery was undergoing a transformation in this period with the development of lighter pieces used in close support of the infantry.

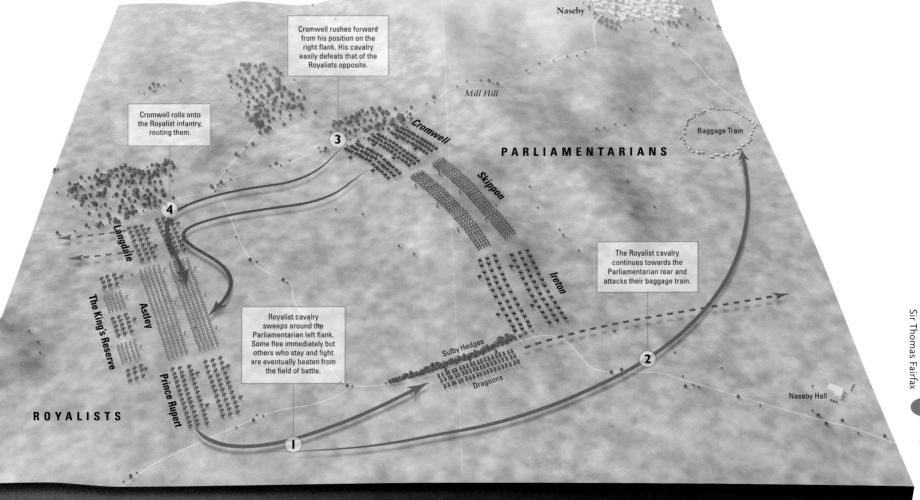

Naseby

Cromwell rushes forward from his position on the right flank. His cavalry easily defeats that of the Royalists opposite.

Mill Hill

Cromwell rolls onto the Royalist infantry, routing them.

3

Cromwell

Baggage Train

PARLIAMENTARIANS

Skippon

4

Langdale

Astley

Ireton

The King's Reserve

The Royalist cavalry continues towards the Parliamentarian rear and attacks their baggage train.

Royalist cavalry sweeps around the Parliamentarian left flank. Some flee immediately but others who stay and fight are eventually beaten from the field of battle.

Sulby Hedges

Dragoons

2

Naseby Hall

Prince Rupert

ROYALISTS

1

Oliver Cromwell
Sir Thomas Fairfax

Empires & Revolutions

➤ Known as 'Cromwell's crowning mercy', the battle of Worcester foiled Charles II's attempt to recover the throne with Scottish assistance. Cromwell's gamble of dividing his forces in the face of the enemy paid off, because the Scottish contingent largely failed to support the rest of Charles's troops.

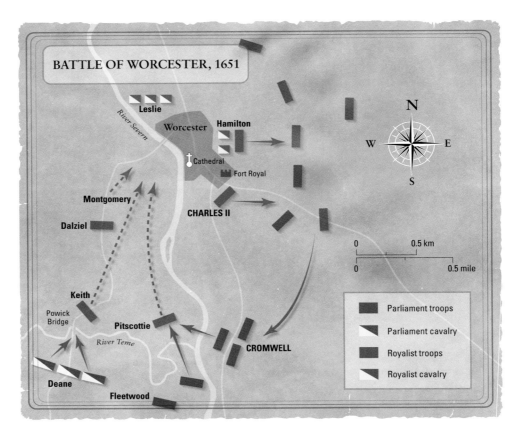

BATTLE OF WORCESTER, 1651

Leslie
River Severn
Worcester
Hamilton
✝ Cathedral
Fort Royal
Montgomery
Dalziel
CHARLES II
Keith
Powick Bridge
River Teme
Pitscottie
CROMWELL
Deane
Fleetwood

| | 0   0.5 km |
| | 0   0.5 mile |

■	Parliament troops
◣	Parliament cavalry
■	Royalist troops
◣	Royalist cavalry

▲▼ This sword is reputed to have belonged to Cromwell, but is typical of those carried by his troopers.

'I had rather have a plain russet-coated captain that knows what he fights for, and loves what he knows, than that which you call a gentleman and is nothing else.' OLIVER CROMWELL

Prince Rupert of the Rhine (1619–82)

Prince Rupert was the most daring and feared Royalist cavalry commander of the Civil Wars. He was born in Prague, the third son of Elizabeth (James I's daughter) and Elector Frederick V of the Palatinate – the 'Winter King and Queen' of Bohemia who were driven out of their home during the opening stages of the Thirty Years' War. After limited service with the Dutch and in Germany (where he was captured at Vlotho in 1638), he went to England (1642) and was made General of Horse by Charles I. He employed the shock tactics developed by the Swedes in the Thirty Years' War, which relied on cavalry charges instead of firepower. A string of victories ended with major defeats at Marston Moor and Naseby. He then entered French service as commander of the English troops (1646), before heading the fugitive Royalist navy (1648–52). After the Restoration (1660), he promoted British colonial and naval expansion, and commanded the fleet during the Second (1665–67) and Third (1672–74) Anglo-Dutch Wars. Gerrit van Honhorst's portrait of Prince Rupert captures something of his dash and self-confidence that so impressed contemporaries; it is painted around the time of his release from captivity after the battle of Vlotho shortly before he came to England.

Oliver Cromwell
Prince Rupert of the Rhine

on fortified towns. He massacred the defenders of the first two towns he took to terrify the remaining strongholds into surrendering. The tactic worked, and, technically, was in line with the prevailing laws of war, since in both cases the defenders refused to surrender after their walls were breached. Following long and mounting brutality, Cromwell's actions sullied his reputation and left a difficult legacy for English rule in Ireland.

Cromwell dissolved Parliament and had himself proclaimed Lord Protector in 1653 during the crisis of the First Anglo-Dutch War (1652–54). He appreciated sea power, which had already played an important part in his Irish and Scottish campaigns, and oversaw a major expansion of British naval power, defeating the Dutch and taking Jamaica from Spain (1655). However, the continued warfare and the cost of occupying Ireland and Scotland necessitated high taxes, undermining his diminishing political legitimacy. His successor, his son Richard (1626–1712), was unable to command authority and was deposed by a military coup in 1659. The monarchy was restored in 1660.

▲ Cromwell at the height of his political and military power in a portrait by Robert Walker painted in *c.* 1649. He is shown holding a baton in his right hand, the traditional symbol of the supreme commander.

Jan Sobieski

Polish King who Triumphed over the Turks at Vienna

'I came, I saw, God carried the victory.'

JAN SOBIESKI

A Life in Brief

1629, 17 August
Born in Olesko, Poland

1649
Regiment commander

1666
Field Hetman of the Southeast Frontier, later Grand Hetman

1674
Becomes King of Poland

1696, 18 June
Dies at Wilanów Palace outside Warsaw

➤ An anonymous portrait of Sobieski dressed as commander of the Polish hussars, or heavy cavalry. The breastplate of interlocking circular plates is typical of those worn by richer Polish horsemen in the later 17th century.

▼ Sobieski's travelling watch (made in London) and his silver mace, gilded and inlaid with turquoise. Though this decorated example was a symbol of command, many Polish cavalry troopers carried simpler maces as weapons.

Jan Sobieski was Poland's greatest warrior king. His spectacular victory against considerable odds at Chocim in 1673 made him a national hero, not least for the rich booty his subordinates looted from the enemy camp. However, his actions outside Vienna in 1683, when he arrived in time to save the city from the Ottoman siege, secured him international fame – something he worked assiduously to promote.

Born into a wealthy aristocratic family, Sobieski began his military career aged 20, leading a regiment sent to relieve Zbarazh (in western Ukraine) from the Cossacks. The death of his brother left him heir to a vast fortune, which he used to pay his troops once he had been named hetman (commander) of the southeastern frontier of the Polish–Lithuanian Commonwealth. However, his forces were insufficient to prevent Ottoman raids, which intensified from 1667 into open war in 1672.

Sobieski had become heavily involved in a struggle for national power, from which he emerged victorious in May 1674 when elected king by the Polish nobility. The ongoing conflict against the Ottoman Turks provided opportunities for further victories, notably against the Tatars in 1675, but it also prevented him consolidating political power. He was obliged to work with the nobles in the Sejm (parliament), which controlled the budget and could veto policy. Objections from the Sejm inhibited his efforts to reform the army. The latter remained dependent on the cavalry branch, and although Sobieski favoured an increase of infantry firepower, he was not a true modernizer. His own successes were achieved with traditional forces against the Commonwealth's traditional opponent, the Ottomans. At Vienna in 1683, although the Polish cavalry charge proved decisive, the German and other imperial infantry contributed significantly to the victory. Sobieski's actions at Párkány shortly afterwards indicate his limitations as a commander. He found it impossible to work with his allies, and after 1685 he concentrated on a futile attempt to conquer the Ottoman vassal state of Moldavia, before effectively withdrawing from the war in 1691.

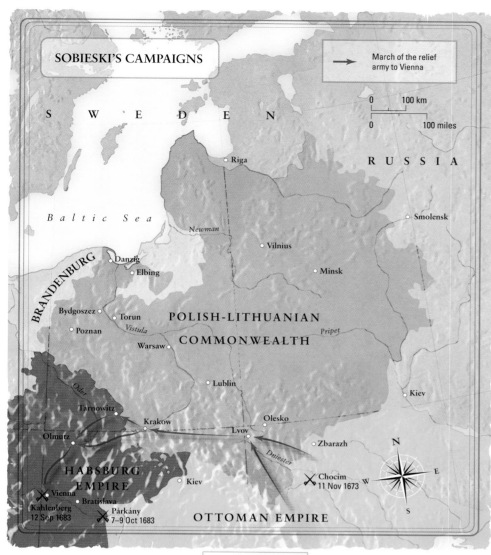

→ March of the relief army to Vienna

0 — 100 km

0 — 100 miles

S W E D E N

RUSSIA

Baltic Sea

Riga

Smolensk

Newman

Vilnius

BRANDENBURG

Danzig

Elbing

Minsk

Bydgoszez

Torun

POLISH-LITHUANIAN

Poznan

Vistula

Pripet

Warsaw

COMMONWEALTH

Odra

Lublin

Kiev

Tarnowitz

Krakow

Olesko

Olmutz

Lvov

Zbarazh

Dniester

HABSBURG

Kiev

Chocim

EMPIRE

11 Nov 1673

Vienna

Kahlenberg

Bratislava

12 Sep 1683

Párkány

7–9 Oct 1683

OTTOMAN EMPIRE

N S E W

Key Battles

The Battle of Chocim, 11 November 1673

Sobieski, with a small army consisting mostly of cavalry, confronts a much larger invading Ottoman force. He attacks their encampment outside Chocim (modern-day Khotyn in western Ukraine), and routs them.

The Battle of the Kahlenberg, 12 September 1683

Having collected around 30,000 men at Cracow, Sobieski races to relieve Vienna, besieged since July by the Ottoman Grand Vizier Kara Mustafa with around 90,000 troops. Having assumed nominal command over the German and imperial relief forces, Sobieski advances east along

the south bank of the Danube to attack the Ottomans deployed on the Kahlenberg hill outside the city. The Polish cavalry on the Christian right charges through the Ottoman left, pinning much of the remainder of Kara Mustafa's army against Vienna, where it is destroyed.

The Battle of Párkány, 7–9 October 1683

Racing after the retreating Ottomans, Sobieski attacks without waiting for the Germans to arrive, and is repulsed with heavy losses: the Turks send 1,000 severed Polish heads to the sultan as trophies. Sobieski renews the attack two days later with the Germans, and routs the enemy, whose troops are forced out of western Hungary.

The Battle of the Kahlenberg, 1683

Christians	Ottomans
Jan Sobieski	**Grand Vizier Kara Mustafa**
65,000 troops, 152 guns	75,000 troops, 180 guns
Casualties: 1500 killed, 2500 wounded (plus 5,000 killed during the siege)	Casualties: 10,000 killed and wounded, 5,000 captured

▼ This ceremonial hat was given to Sobieski by Pope Innocent IX after he crushed the Turks at Vienna.

▲ The Polish-Lithuanian commonwealth, led by Sobieski, shared a border with the Ottoman empire. The constant threat from the Turks gave Sobieski a series of chances to show his ability as a military leader.

▶ The battle of the Kahlenberg (also known as the Relief of Vienna) in 1683 was Sobieski's greatest military triumph. The decisive action in the battle was a Polish cavalry charge.

▶▶ This panoramic view by the Flemish painter Frans Geffels shows the battle of the Kahlenberg. Polish forces are attacking from the left, while the Turkish siege lines and Viennese defences can be seen in the middle distance.

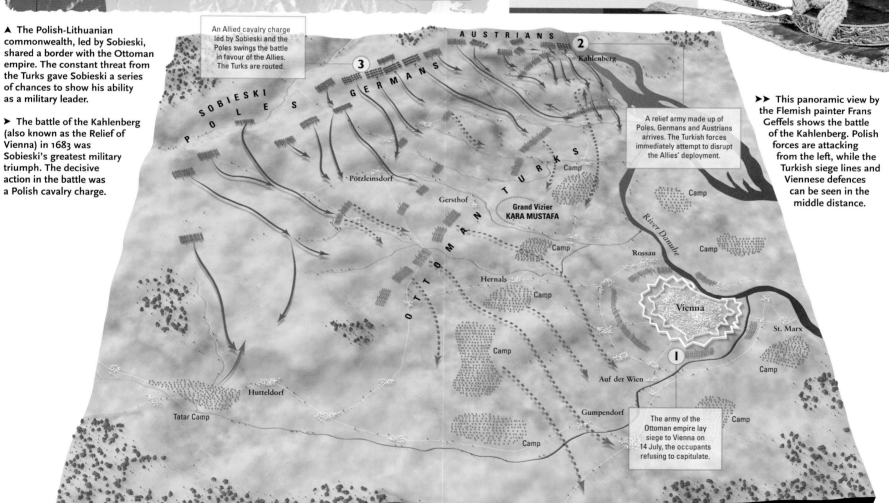

An Allied cavalry charge led by Sobieski and the Poles swings the battle in favour of the Allies. The Turks are routed.

AUSTRIANS

Kahlenberg

2

3

SOBIESKI POLES

GERMANS

A relief army made up of Poles, Germans and Austrians arrives. The Turkish forces immediately attempt to disrupt the Allies' deployment.

Pötzleinsdorf

OTTOMAN TURKS

Gersthof

Grand Vizier KARA MUSTAFA

Camp

River Danube

Camp

Camp

Rossau

Camp

Hernals

Camp

Vienna

St. Marx

Auf der Wien

Camp

1

Hutteldorf

Camp

Tatar Camp

Gumpendorf

Camp

The army of the Ottoman empire lay siege to Vienna on 14 July, the occupants refusing to capitulate.

Camp

Peter the Great

Russian Tsar who Defeated the Swedes in the Great Northern War

'I declare to you that the all-merciful God has granted us an unprecedented victory over the enemy.' PETER THE GREAT, AFTER POLTAVA

A Life in Brief

1672, 9 June
Born in Moscow

1682
Becomes tsar with his half-brother Ivan, under Regent Sophia

1696
Rules alone following Ivan's death

1725, 8 February
Dies in St Petersburg

▼ This portrait of Peter by the English artist Sir Godfrey Kneller presents him in the early 18th-century ideal of the warrior-king.

Tsar Peter the Great deserves his sobriquet as the 'founder of modern Russia'. He achieved his primary goals of stabilizing tsarist rule and securing access to the sea by founding St Petersburg, and his gains on the Baltic were to remain almost continuously in Russian hands until 1991. However, he lost the Black Sea foothold of Azov, and Daghestan would soon follow under his successor. A dynamic reformer, Peter modernized the army, created a navy and achieved Russia's breakthrough as a European great power.

As a child, Peter displayed a fascination with military tactics and technology, personally testing new weapons and techniques. His hostility to traditional methods stemmed from the revolt of the Streltsy infantry (provoked in part by the harsh conditions of service) a month after his accession. Too young to rule personally, government was entrusted to his jealous half-sister Sophia, while Peter spent his time at Preobrazhenskoe outside Moscow drilling a new regiment formed from young noblemen. The military exercises increased in scale, culminating in mock battles involving 30,000 men at Kozhukhovo in September 1694, intended as much to demonstrate the regime's power as to improve military efficiency. He exercised little influence over the first two campaigns of his reign against the Crimean Tatars (1687 and 1689), but used their failure to discredit Sophia, whom he imprisoned in a convent in 1689. He then consolidated his domestic position, especially after the death of his half-brother and co-ruler Ivan in 1696. He finally crushed the Streltsy when they rebelled again in 1698, paving the way for thoroughgoing reform.

Some commentators attribute Peter's success entirely to his desire for modernization (meaning 'westernization', or the adoption of British, Dutch, German and Scandinavian expertise and methods), symbolized by his 1698 order for the beards of the boyars (aristocrats) to be shaved off. Peter was indeed impatient with those unwilling to accept change, but he also combined foreign ideas with existing best practice and indigenous innovation. Russia had already introduced western infantry fire tactics in the 1630s. Peter now extended this to the entire infantry, which was reorganized into permanent regiments recruited by conscription. These did not entirely displace the cavalry that traditionally formed the backbone of all Eastern European armies. Cavalry still formed 56 per cent of the field army sent against Persia in 1722, for instance, but regular units drilled for shock tactics, rather than lighter irregulars or noble levies, now accounted for a higher proportion of the army.

Russia was nominally an ally of the Christian powers who had been fighting the Ottoman Turks since 1684, but did little until 1695, when Peter sent two armies to seize the lower reaches of the Dnieper and Don rivers. Whereas the still-traditionally organized army attacking the Dnieper was successful, the modern one failed on the Don. Determined that his reforms should be seen to succeed, Peter renewed the offensive the following year, this time sending pre-fabricated warships to support the assault on Azov, the great fortress at the mouth of the Don. Though successful, the subsequently expanded Azov fleet was destroyed when the fortress was returned to the Ottomans in 1711. A new Baltic navy was built after 1701, totalling 122 warships and 280 support vessels by 1725. Other ships were used on the Caspian Sea against Persia in 1722–23. Though unable to challenge

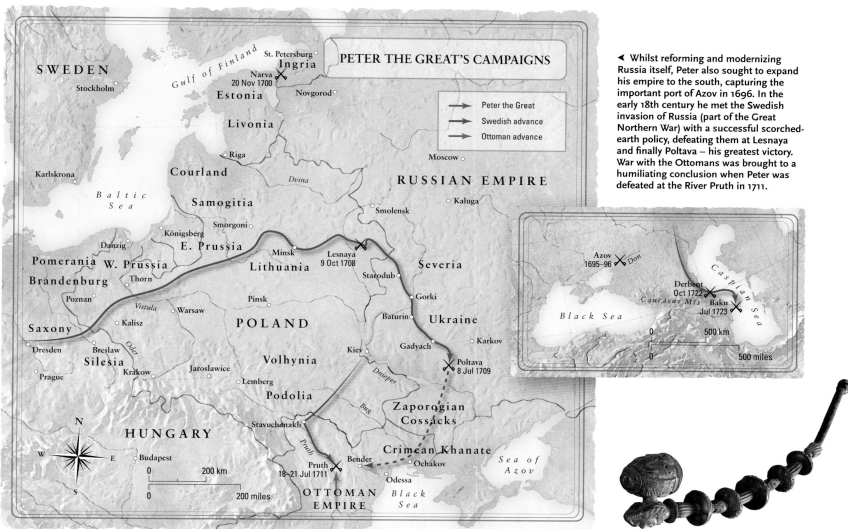

PETER THE GREAT'S CAMPAIGNS

Peter the Great
Swedish advance
Ottoman advance

◄ Whilst reforming and modernizing Russia itself, Peter also sought to expand his empire to the south, capturing the important port of Azov in 1696. In the early 18th century he met the Swedish invasion of Russia (part of the Great Northern War) with a successful scorched-earth policy, defeating them at Lesnaya and finally Poltava – his greatest victory. War with the Ottomans was brought to a humiliating conclusion when Peter was defeated at the River Pruth in 1711.

Key Battles and Campaigns

The Battle of Azov, 1695–96
Having failed to capture Azov from the Ottomans in 1695, the following year Peter returns with a larger army and naval support. This time he succeeds.

The Battle of Lesnaya, 9 October 1708
In the Great Northern War, Peter's 15,000 Russians defeat 10,000 Swedish reinforcements east of Minsk and capture their supply train. This strategic victory considerably worsens Charles XII's position in Russia, just as winter sets in.

The Battle of Poltava, 8 July 1709
Running short of supplies, the outnumbered Swedes are obliged to assault Peter's entrenched camp. However, the success of Peter's military reforms is demonstrated by his infantry, who leave their entrenchments and confront the Swedes in the open. Having shattered the Swedish assault, the Russian cavalry pursues the broken army, trapping most of it against a river, where it surrenders.

The Russo-Turkish War, 1710–11
Peter rushes to seize the mouth of the Danube, but a rapid Turkish counterattack traps him against the River Pruth (on the modern Romanian–Moldovan border). In 1711 he is forced to accept a humiliating peace.

The Russo-Persian War, 1722–24
Peter overcomes considerable logistical obstacles to advance down the western Caspian shore to take Derbent in October 1722, exploiting internal crisis in the Persian empire. A second advance to Baku fails after a storm disperses the supply fleet. A renewed amphibious expedition captures Baku in July 1723, and the following year Persia accepts these losses.

▲ Peter's pipe is preserved in his house in St Petersburg. Tobacco smoking was a habit he shared with his contemporary warrior-king, Prussia's Frederick William I, the 'soldier king' (r. 1713–40).

►► This rather stylized depiction of Poltava nonetheless gives a good impression of the formations well-drilled soldiers would adopt to maximize firepower. It was vital for success that individual units maintained such regular lines despite the smoke and confusion of battle.

◄ Artillery and infantry involved in the exercises of Peter's 'poteshnye' (play) regiments outside Preobrazhenskoe. This watercolour slightly postdates the events and shows the soldiers in the uniforms worn towards the end of Peter's reign.

▼ The commander as bureaucrat: a view of Peter's study in his house in Archangelsk. Much of Peter's importance stems from his work on reforming Russia's administration and armed forces.

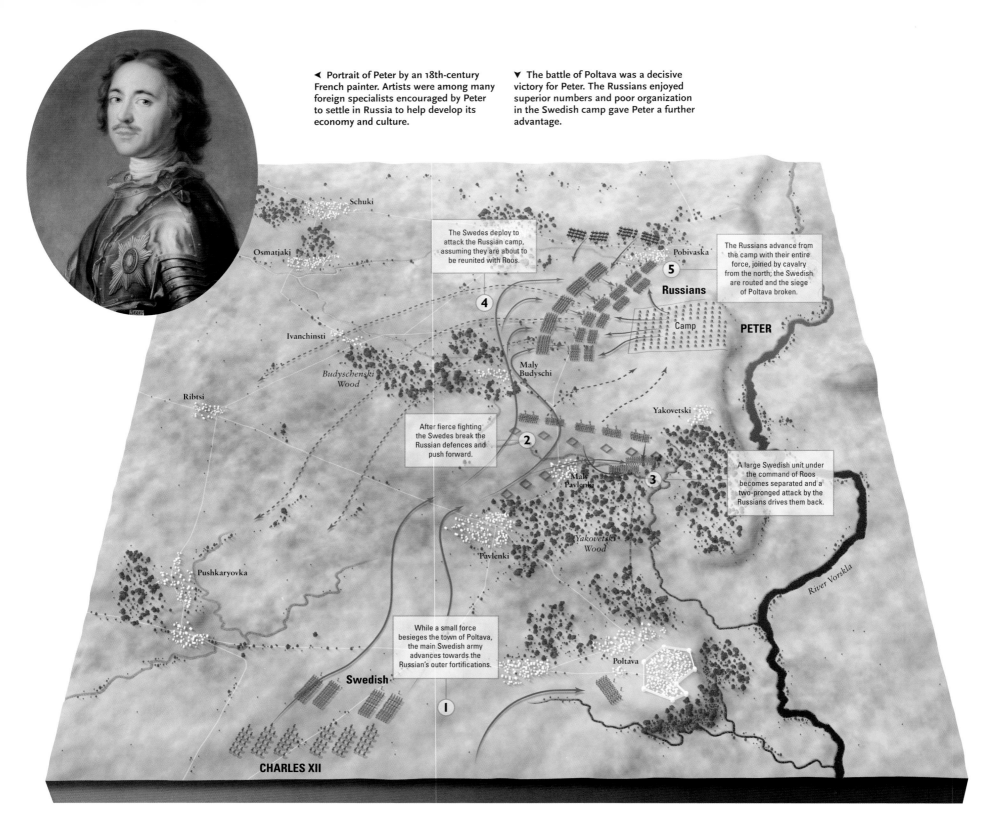

◄ Portrait of Peter by an 18th-century French painter. Artists were among many foreign specialists encouraged by Peter to settle in Russia to help develop its economy and culture.

▼ The battle of Poltava was a decisive victory for Peter. The Russians enjoyed superior numbers and poor organization in the Swedish camp gave Peter a further advantage.

The Swedes deploy to attack the Russian camp, assuming they are about to be reunited with Roos.

The Russians advance from the camp with their entire force, joined by cavalry from the north; the Swedish are routed and the siege of Poltava broken.

5

Russians

PETER

Camp

4

Pobivaska

Maly Budyschi

Ivanchinsti

Budyschenski Wood

Yakovetski

After fierce fighting the Swedes break the Russian defences and push forward.

2

A large Swedish unit under the command of Roos becomes separated and a two-pronged attack by the Russians drives them back.

Maly Pavlenki

3

Ribtsi

Yakovetski Wood

Pavlenki

Pushkaryovka

River Vorskla

While a small force besieges the town of Poltava, the main Swedish army advances towards the Russian's outer fortifications.

Poltava

Swedish

1

CHARLES XII

Schuki

Osmatjaki

The Battle of Poltava, 1709	
Russians	Swedes
Peter the Great	**Charles XII**
30,000 infantry, 9,000 cavalry, c. 3,000 Cossacks	9,500 infantry, 12,800 cavalry, up to 5,000 Cossacks
Casualties: 1,345 killed, 3,200 wounded	Casualties: 6,900 killed, wounded or missing, 2,800 prisoners

Europe's maritime powers for control of the world's oceans, Peter's fleets nonetheless played a major role in supporting his land conquests, notably in the Baltic.

Russia was vast, inhospitable, thinly populated and underdeveloped. Peter turned these disadvantages into strategic assets when confronted by Sweden after 1700 (the Great Northern War). The Swedish invasion of Russia was met by a scorched-earth policy after 1707, which thwarted King Charles XII's drive on Moscow. Poltava (1709), Peter's greatest victory, was also a defensive action where he played to his army's strengths. It represented a major improvement since

the First Battle of Narva (1700) where the Russians had been routed, despite sheltering behind earthworks. However, Poltava made Peter overconfident and the Ottomans defeated him on the River Pruth in 1711 after he advanced without adequate reconnaissance or supply arrangements. His real skill was as a strategist rather than as a field commander. His choice of subordinates was generally good and he was prepared to accept advice. Above all, his relentless energy forced his officials to find the men and materials necessary to sustain a prodigious and prolonged war effort.

▲ Poltava painted by Jean-Marc Nattier in 1717. Unlike the depiction on pp. 154–55, this version captures something of the confusion of battle, though in reality most of the fighting was away from the woods immediately north of Poltava itself.

Burkhard Christoph von Münnich (1683–1767)

Von Münnich was the principal Russian general and reformer after Peter the Great. Hailing from a family of drainage engineers in Oldenburg, he served in the Hessen-Darmstadt contingent with the imperial army against France between 1701 and 1712. He joined Saxony-Poland, rising to the rank of inspector general, until a dispute at court forced him to switch to Russia in 1721. A natural charmer, he won Peter the Great's confidence by building the Lagoda canal (1721–33) linking St Petersburg to the Volga. Peter II (r. 1727–30) made him a count, but his real influence came under Empress Anna (r. 1730–40), who made him field marshal, war minister and governor of St Petersburg in 1732. Having improved the professionalism of the officer corps and strengthened the infantry and light cavalry, he commanded Russia's field armies against Poland (1734) and the Turks (1735–39) with mixed success. Despite the loss of many men to disease and malnutrition, his soldiers loved him, calling him 'the Falcon'. He fell foul of political intrigues after Anna's death, but was reprieved from the death sentence at the last minute in 1742. He was fully pardoned on his return from exile in 1762.

Duke of Marlborough

English Victor of the Battle of Blenheim

'More than a match for all the generals of [France].'

CAPTAIN PARKER ON MARLBOROUGH

A Life in Brief

1650, 24 June
Born in Ashe, Devonshire
(different dates are also given)

1667
Commissioned as Ensign

1672
Captain

1674
Colonel

1688
Lieutenant-General; abandons
James II

1689
Fights the French at Walcourt;
created Earl of Marlborough

1692
Dismissed due to suspicion of
Jacobite leanings

1698
Restored to favour

1701
Captain-General of British forces
in Low Countries

1702
Created Duke of Marlborough

1711
Dismissed by the Tory
government

1714
The new king, George I,
reappoints him Captain-General

1716
Suffers a series of strokes

1722, 16 June
Dies at Windsor

◄ John Churchill, Duke of Marlborough,
as depicted by Adriaen van der Werff.
Sir Winston Churchill, in a four-volume
biography of his ancestor, was to
summarize the Duke's achievement of
having 'never fought a battle that he did
not win, nor besieged a fortress that he
did not take... He quitted war invincible.'

John Churchill, 1st Duke of Marlborough was
the most talented British army commander
between Oliver Cromwell and the Duke of
Wellington. Under Marlborough, the British
army reached a peak of success that it was
not to repeat in Europe for another century.
Cool and composed under fire, and brave to
the point of rashness, he was a master of the
shape and details of conflict. In the chaos
of battle, Marlborough was able to control
and commit his troops decisively at the most
appropriate moment.

MARLBOROUGH'S EARLY CAREER

Entering the English army in 1667, John
Churchill served in the garrison at Tangier
from 1668 to 1670, against the Dutch at
sea in 1672, and as part of the English
contingent sent to help Louis XIV of France
between 1673 and 1674. He rapidly acquired
a reputation for bravery in combat to match
the looks that served him well in the court of
Charles II. Subsequently, he rose through the
army and played the key role in the defeat of James,
Duke of Monmouth's rebellion at the battle of
Sedgemoor in 1685. The poorly organized rebel
army was defeated by the superior firepower of its
experienced opponents. In 1688, however, when
England was invaded by William III of Orange,
Churchill abandoned the Catholic James II. This
greatly weakened the morale of the army and
contributed to William's seizure of England without a
battle. Churchill served William in the Low Countries
in 1689 and in Ireland in 1690, capturing Cork.

Created Earl of Marlborough in 1689, he then fell from
favour in 1692 as William suspected him of conspiring
with the exiled James II. However, convinced of
Marlborough's competence, William brought him back
to favour at the close of his reign. As Captain-General,
Marlborough was commander of the army in the Low
Countries from 1702 to 1711.

THE WAR OF THE SPANISH SUCCESSION

The war comprised a wide-ranging conflict between
an alliance of Britain, Austria and the Dutch, and
Louis XIV of France, as the alliance sought to block

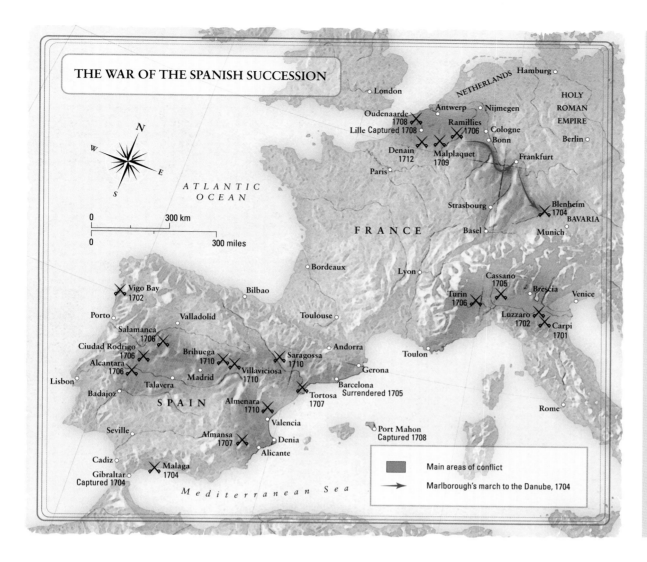

THE WAR OF THE SPANISH SUCCESSION

159

Key Battles

The Battle of Blenheim, 13 August 1704
The Anglo-Dutch-Austrian victory over the Franco-Bavarian army is largely due to the tactical flexibility Marlborough displays. His ability to retain control and manoeuvrability contrasts greatly with the failure of his opponents. The decisive factors are mastery of the terrain, the retention and management of reserves, and timing of the heavy strike in the centre, where the opposing line is broken.

The Battle of Ramillies, 23 May 1706
On a spread-out battlefield, Marlborough again obtains a victory by breaking the French centre. The centre has been weakened in order to support action against British attacks on the flanks.

The Battle of Oudenaarde, 11 July 1708
After several hours of fighting, the French position is nearly enveloped when Marlborough sends the cavalry on his left around the French right flank and into their rear. The move destroys his opponents' cohesion, and the French position collapses.

The Battle of Malplaquet, 11 September 1709
Responding to the increasingly formulaic nature of Marlborough's tactics, the French at first hold the British attacks on their flanks, but are finally pushed back. The battle exemplifies Marlborough's belief in the attack, but also indicates the heavy casualties that could be caused by the sustained exchange of fire between nearby lines of closely packed troops.

France's attempted domination of western Europe. Marlborough's skills in generalship were tested in a sequence of campaigns, in which he distinguished himself tactically, operationally and strategically. The battles he fought – particularly the major ones of Blenheim (1704), Ramillies (1706), Oudenaarde (1708) and Malplaquet (1709) – were fought on a more extended front than those of the 1690s (let alone the 1650s), and thus placed a premium on mobility, planning, and the ability of commanders to respond rapidly to developments over a wide front and to integrate and influence what might otherwise have been in practice a number of separate conflicts. Marlborough was particularly good at this and anticipated Napoleon's skilful and determined generalship in this respect. He was also successful in coordinating the deployment and use of infantry, cavalry and cannon, and in turning an army and system of operations developed for position warfare into a means to make war mobile. However, the combination of fortifications and field armies made France a serious challenge, and it was not possible to invade it to any great distance.

MARLBOROUGH'S GENERALSHIP

The combat effectiveness of British units, especially the fire discipline and bayonet skill of the infantry, and the ability of the cavalry to mount successful charges relying on cold steel, owed much to their extensive experience of campaigning and battles in the 1690s and 1700s. These also played a vital role in training the officers and in getting the troops accustomed to immediate manoeuvre and execution. The infantry, drawn up in three ranks, were organized into three firings, ensuring that continuous fire was maintained. British infantry fire was more effective than French fire, so that the pressure of battlefield conflict with the British was high. The inaccuracy of muskets was countered by the proximity of the opposing lines, and their close-packed nature. The cavalry was made to act like a shock force, charging fast rather than, as mounted infantry, relying on pistol firepower; indeed, Marlborough used a massed cavalry charge at the climax of his victories of Blenheim, Ramillies and Malplaquet. The artillery was well positioned on the field of battle, and the cannon were resited and moved forward to affect its development. As Marlborough was

▶ The wide-ranging nature of the War of the Spanish Succession posed major problems of command and control, not least in getting the anti-French alliance to coordinate operations.

▼ Coins such as this one showing Marlborough as victor were an established part of the pageantry of generalship.

> *'I… beg you will give my duty to the Queen, and let her know that her army has had a glorious victory. Monsieur Tallard and two other generals are in my coach.'*

DUKE OF MARLBOROUGH,
SHORTLY AFTER THE BATTLE OF BLENHEIM

The Battle of Blenheim, 1704

Allied forces of Kingdoms of England, Dutch Republic, Denmark and the Holy Roman Empire	Kingdom of France and Bavaria
Duke of Marlborough, Eugene, Prince of Savoy	**Duc de Tallard, Maximillian II Emanuel, Ferdinand de Marsin**
52,000 troops, 60 guns	56,000 troops, 90 guns
Casualties: 4,542 killed, 7,942 wounded	Casualties: 20,000 killed, drowned or wounded, 14,190 captured

▼ The battle of Blenheim, as portrayed by John Wooton, a major painter of battle scenes who was a protégé of William, Duke of Cumberland, the victor of Culloden. Marlborough's success resonated through the century.

➤ Marlborough and Colonel John Armstrong, a fortification specialist, discussing battle plans (for the siege of Bouchain, which Marlborough captured in 1711). Marlborough's wife commended the likeness.

At the battle of Blenheim, having pinned down most of the French infantry and reserves in defensive engagements, Marlborough launched the substantial force he had kept unguarded in the centre, achieving a local superiority in what he made a crucial part of the battlefield.

The Allied right under Eugene engage the Bavarian troops making up the French left. The fighting is fierce, but both forces are disordered and few gains are made.

1

With Oberglau and Blenheim besieged and the French left still fighting Eugene, Marlborough pushes his centre forward and the outnumbered French are eventually routed.

Although the village of Blenheim is not taken, the French commit their best troops to its defence, critically losing the advantage elsewhere on the battlefield.

2

Many retreating French troops are drowned in the Danube or cut down by pursuing cavalry.

3

4

Marsh

Lutzingen

Bavarians

Schwennenbach

Eugene

MARLBOROUGH

Wolperstten

Oberglau

Marsh

Unterglau

Marlborough

Augraben

TALLARD

French

Blenheim

Marsh

Danube

Eugene, Prince of Savoy (1663–1736)

Eugene was the French-born son of a member of a collateral line of the dukes of Savoy. He rose to be President of the War Council (1703–36) and commander-in-chief for three successive rulers of

Austria: Leopold I, Joseph I and Charles VI. Eugene was victorious against both the Ottomans and rival Christian powers (a skill that his contemporary Peter the Great could not match), was more triumphant than any other Austrian general before or since, and was the most successful European opponent of the Ottomans. In addition, his generalship was recognizably different from that of his French rivals.

Although he deployed his troops in the conventional manner, Eugene placed greater emphasis on manoeuvre on campaign and attack in battle than did his French rivals. His boldness was amply displayed in his struggle with the French in northern Italy (1701–06), in his surprise attack on Cremona (1702) and in the outflanking of the Duke of Vendôme, which was a vital prelude to the relief of Turin in 1706. In part, Eugene translated the mobility of warfare in Hungary to western Europe. He did not allow the French emphasis on the defence of river lines and fortified positions to

thwart his drive for battle and victory. In part, this was a consequence of Eugene's personality: the preference for excitement and acceptance of risk took him into the thick of the action.

Eugene's victories over the Ottomans at Zenta (1697), Peterwardein (1716) and Belgrade (1717), in which he employed effective offensive tactics, were instrumental in advancing Austria's frontiers. Zenta and Belgrade were particularly influential in helping bring two successive wars with the Ottomans to a close. His victories (either on his own or in linked command) over the French at Carpi (1701), Blenheim (1704), Turin (1706), Oudenaarde (1708), and Malplaquet (1709), shattered the French reputation for invincibility.

Eugene, however, proved a poor peacetime commander. He failed to sustain the Austrian army as an effective fighting force in the 1720s and early 1730s, and was substantially to blame for its poor state during the War of the Polish Succession.

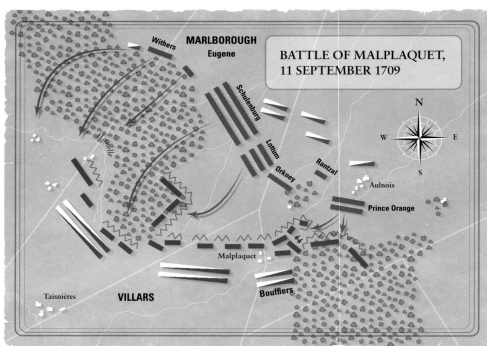

BATTLE OF MALPLAQUET, 11 SEPTEMBER 1709

▲ Villars's entrenchment at Malplaquet threatened the British forces besieging Mons, thus provoking an attack on terrain favouring the defence. Having withstood advances on their flanks, the French retained a substantial reserve to meet Marlborough's final central push. The French finally retreated in the face of sustained pressure on their left and centre, but it was not a rout — their retreat was in good order. The casualties were very heavy on both sides.

principalities functioning and militarily effective. Without the latter achievement, he would not have had the forces available to win the battles that stopped Louis XIV in the War of the Spanish Succession. The 1700s saw the failure of the French effort to achieve hegemony in western Europe, especially with defeat at Blenheim in 1704 – the key campaign. The danger that France would knock Austria out of the war was averted by Marlborough's bold advance, at the head of an Anglo-German army, from the Rhine to the Danube – the most decisive British military move on the Continent until the 20th century. His command skills proved crucial to France's defeat, and prevented the anti-French alliance collapsing. Marlborough won other battles, but none had the dramatic impact of Blenheim.

As a result of the battle, Marlborough, who had been made a duke in 1702, was granted the royal land and parliamentary funds to build a major palace at Woodstock (near Oxford) named after his great victory, a reward not granted to previous generals. By 1711, however, Marlborough could no longer deliver a major victory and support for the continuation of the costly war had eroded in Britain. Marlborough was dismissed by the new Tory government. He died in 1722.

Master-General of the Ordnance as well as Captain-General of the army, he was able to direct the artillery. Marlborough was also effective in siegecraft, as shown in the successful, although very costly, siege of Lille in 1709.

Strategically, Marlborough was adept at coalition warfare, taking great pains to keep the alliance of Britain, the Dutch, Austria, and various German

Claude, Duke of Villars (1653–1734)

One of the leading French generals of Louis XIV's later years, Villars, shown here in an 18th-century portrait after Hyacinth Rigaud, was more competent than most of his colleagues and contemporaries (such as Tallard and Villeroi), and his career continued right up until his death on campaign in 1734. He made his name in the cavalry and acquired key early experience of combat and command during the Dutch War (1672–78). In 1687, he accompanied the Elector of Bavaria in the successful Austro-German campaign against the Turks. He played a prominent role in the War of the Grand Alliance (1688–97), fighting at Fleurus (1690), Steenkirk (1692) and Neerwinden (1693), and during the War of the Spanish Succession (1701–14). In the latter he played a key role against Marlborough between 1709 and 1711, commanding at Malplaquet (1709), before defeating Eugene at Denain (1712) and Freiburg (1713). His final achievement was to conquer Lombardy (1733–34) in the opening stage of the War of the Polish Succession (1733–35).

◄ Tapestry showing the battle of Malplaquet. The 110,000-strong Anglo-Dutch-German army under Marlborough suffered 24,000 casualties, leading to acute political criticism in Britain and the Netherlands. After the battle, Marlborough went on to capture Mons and Ghent, but hopes of breaching the French frontier defences and marching on to Paris proved misplaced.

Frederick the Great

King of Prussia who Defeated the Austrians

'He who defends everything defends nothing.'

FREDERICK THE GREAT

A Life in Brief

1712, 25 January
Born in Berlin

1740, 28 May
Succeeds father as King of Prussia

1786, 17 August
Dies at his summer palace of Sanssouci, Potsdam

➤ In December 1777, General Nathanael Greene cited Frederick (shown as an old man in this contemporary painting by an unknown artist) 'the greatest general of the age' when attempting to dissuade George Washington (pp. 174–79) from attacking the British in Philadelphia. Frederick had become Europe's most famous general and those interested in military matters studied his campaigns.

The maker of modern Prussia, Frederick was regarded as the leading European warrior of his day. His innovations dominated the military imagination of Prussia, and subsequently Germany. At the time of his death in 1786, he was the most famous general in Europe.

Heir to the brutal Frederick William I of Prussia, the young Frederick was raised for a military life, serving in 1734 in the War of the Polish Succession. The Prussian army was second only to that of Austria in the Holy Roman Empire, and soon after succeeding to the throne, Frederick II brought it into action in December 1740 on the outbreak of the First Silesian War. He invaded the wealthy Habsburg province of Silesia (now in southwestern Poland), where his dynasty had territorial claims. Frederick hoped that Maria Theresa, the new ruler of Austria, would respond by buying him off, but initially this was not to be. The Austrians were defeated at Mollwitz (1741), and in 1742 Frederick invaded Bohemia, also part of the Austrian empire, defeating Prince Charles Alexander of Lorraine, Maria Theresa's brother-in-law, at Chotusitz. Keen to lessen the number of her opponents, as she was now under attack from France, Saxony, Bavaria and Spain as well, Maria Theresa bought peace by ceding most of Silesia.

The retention of Silesia was to be a major burden for Prussia, leading Frederick into the Second Silesian War (1744–45). Concerned about Austrian strength and intentions, Frederick invaded Bohemia again in 1744, capturing its capital Prague. However, there was no decisive battle, and Frederick's army was harassed

by Austrian light forces. At the end of the campaign, Frederick retreated, having suffered heavy losses.

In 1745, the Austrians took the offensive, only to be defeated by Frederick in a series of battles at Hohenfriedberg, Soor and Hennersdorf. Frederick had developed the 'oblique attack', whereby he concentrated his strength on one end of his attacking line, while holding back the other end, thus using a concentrated effort to shatter the opposing formation and roll up the enemy line. Prussian successes enabled Frederick to capture Dresden, the capital of Saxony, and to retain Silesia in the subsequent Peace of Dresden.

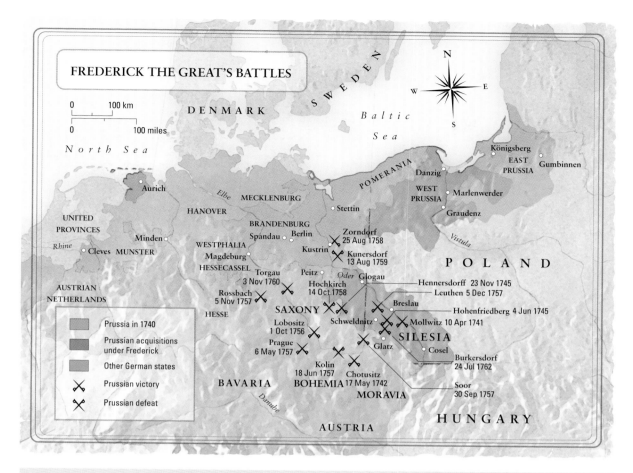

FREDERICK THE GREAT'S BATTLES

Prussia in 1740
Prussian acquisitions under Frederick
Other German states
⚔ Prussian victory
⚔ Prussian defeat

Zorndorf 25 Aug 1758
Kunersdorf 13 Aug 1759
Hennersdorff 23 Nov 1745
Leuthen 5 Dec 1757
Hohenfriedberg 4 Jun 1745
Mollwitz 10 Apr 1741
Hochkirch 14 Oct 1758
Torgau 3 Nov 1760
Rossbach 5 Nov 1757
Lobositz 1 Oct 1756
Prague 6 May 1757
Kolin 18 Jun 1757
Chotusitz 17 May 1742
Soor 30 Sep 1757
Burkersdorf 24 Jul 1762

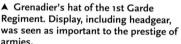

▲ Grenadier's hat of the 1st Garde Regiment. Display, including headgear, was seen as important to the prestige of armies.

▼ Threatened by Russia to the east, Austria to the south and France to the southwest, Prussia was in a vulnerable position.

Key Battles

The Battle of Mollwitz, 10 April 1741
In his first battle as king, Frederick's Prussians clash with the Austrians under von Neipperg for control of Silesia. The Austrians win the cavalry battle, but are outshot by the better Prussian infantry. The Austrians abandon the field, but the Prussians have taken higher casualties.

The Battle of Kolin, 18 June 1757
Frederick breaks off his siege of Prague and attempts to intercept Daun's relieving force. Attempts to outflank the Austrian defensive positions near Kolin on the River Elbe are met by stiff resistance, and the Prussians are forced back. The defeat forces Frederick to abandon Bohemia.

The Battle of Rossbach, 5 November 1757
Frederick moves quickly to surprise and attack his French–Imperial opponents under Charles de Rohan while they are on the march at Rossbach in Saxony. The outnumbered and highly disciplined Prussian cavalry and infantry prove superior, and the French are routed.

The Battle of Zorndorf, 26 August 1758
At Zorndorf (Sarbinowo, Poland), Frederick clashes with the Russian troops under Fermor, who are attempting to link up with the Austrians under Daun for a move on Berlin. The bloody, hand-to-hand fighting, which lasts until nightfall, inflicts tens of thousands of casualties on both sides, but prevents the Russians from linking up with Daun. Frederick loses a quarter of his force.

'Rascals, would you live for ever?'

FREDERICK TO HIS GUARDS, WHEN THEY HESITATED AT KOLIN

◄ Frederick reviewing troops: keen to respond to change, by 1768 Frederick was considering more flexible tactical ideas, in particular an advance in open order.

The Battle of Rossbach, 1757

Prussians	Holy Roman/ Austrian Empire and France
Frederick the Great	Charles, Prince de Soubise and Joseph Frederick William, Duke of Saxe-Hildburghausen
21,000 troops, 79 guns	42,000 troops, 45 guns
Casualties: 169 killed, 379 wounded	Casualties: 5,000 killed or wounded, 5,000 captured

▼ At Rossbach, Frederick, with 21,000 troops, attacked the French and Imperialists who had planned to turn the Prussian left flank. Responding rapidly, Frederick attacked his opponents on the march, screening his move behind a hill. Major-General Seydlitz surprised and defeated the opposing cavalry of the Allied advanced guard, attacking them in front and with a double-flanking movement. The Allied cavalry was pushed back and dissolved into a confused mass. The advancing columns of French infantry were rapidly brought low by salvoes of Prussian musket fire, supported by a battery of 18 Prussian heavy cannon. Seydlitz's cavalry then attacked the French infantry and was joined by the advancing Prussian infantry, firing as they moved. The French fled in confusion.

▲ Frederick at Rossbach. His ability to grasp and retain the initiative, and the disciplined nature of the Prussians, both infantry and cavalry, were decisive. The Prussians lost fewer than 550 men, their opponents more than 10,000 (half of them taken as prisoners).

The Franco-Imperial army, hoping to attack Frederick's flank, leave units on Gallows Hill whilst the remainder move to the south of Frederick's positions.

Eichstadt River

Kayna

Bedra
Braunsdorf

Schartau

Janus Hill

FREDERICK

Lundstedt

Gallows Hill

Gröst

IMPERIAL ARMY

Rossbach

Reichertswerben

Branderoda

①

Rustedt

Zouchfeld

Obschutz

Storkau

Frederick pulls his infantry behind the ridge of Janus Hill with his cavalry on his left flank. The Franco-Imperial army believes he is retreating.

Braunsdorf

②

FREDERICK

Janus Hill

Cavalry

Cavalry

Seydlitz

Frederick advances his infantry over Janus Hill and attacks the Imperial army whilst they are in a state of confusion still trying to form in line. His cavalry also attacks their flank. Victory is Frederick's.

Cavalry

Cavalry

Soubise

③

The Imperial cavalry is attacked and routed by their Prussian counterparts.

Lundstedt

④

Rossbach

Reichertswerben

IMPERIAL ARMY

Count Leopold Josef von Daun (1705–66)

Daun's Austrian forces defeated Frederick the Great at Kolin (1757) and fought well at Torgau (1760). A master of position warfare, Daun was more effective than Charles Alexander of Lorraine, who was beaten by Frederick at Prague (1757) and Leuthen (1757). Daun had earlier played a role in the professionalization of the Austrian army, becoming founding commandant of the military academy opened at Wiener-Neustadt in 1752. He also favoured appointment and recognition without regard to social rank. Daun played an important role in developing tactics designed to thwart those of Frederick. At Hochkirch in 1758, Daun used multiple columns to great effect in surprising Frederick, and showed that the armies of the period were not rendered inflexible by the use of linear tactics. Moreover, Daun's successful use of the defensive features of the North Bohemian and Moravian hills revealed defects in Prussian tactics and, in particular, Frederick's use of the oblique order (focusing the attack on a single enemy flank). However, at Burkersdorf (1762) Frederick defeated Daun by the use of dispersed columns, breaking Daun's will to continue the struggle with his old adversary.

'If my soldiers were to begin to think, not one would remain in the ranks.' FREDERICK THE GREAT

In 1756 the Seven Years' War broke out. Correctly fearing attack by Austria and Russia, Frederick invaded Austria's ally Saxony in 1756 in order to gain resources and room for manoeuvre, and to deny a base to his opponents. However, France, Sweden and most of the German rulers joined the alliance against Frederick, who was only supported by Britain.

In 1756, Frederick invaded Bohemia once more, but the Austrians put up unexpectedly strong resistance and he only won a limited victory at Lobositz. In 1757, Frederick was put under particular pressure, suffering defeat by the Austrians at Kolin, leading to the loss of large parts of Silesia. Frederick, however, saved the situation by defeating French forces at Rossbach, and the Austrians at Leuthen, where the oblique attack was once again used decisively. After the defeat, the Austrians abandoned most of Silesia.

In January 1758, the Russians, who had already overrun East Prussia, invaded Brandenburg, only to be blocked by Frederick at the battle of Zorndorf. In 1759, they defeated Frederick at Kunersdorf. He came under further pressure in 1760–61, but was helped by the failure of the Austrians and Russians to coordinate operations, and by the death of his most determined enemy, Tsarina Elizabeth of Russia, in January 1762. Frederick was then able to defeat the Austrians, who were happy to sign a peace treaty in 1763. The peace was on the basis of the *status quo ante bellum*, as things were prior to the war.

During the War of the Bavarian Succession (1778–79), which was touched off by the end of the main line of the Wittelsbach family that ruled Bavaria, and by the Prussian fear that this might lead to Austrian gains, Frederick once again invaded Bohemia. However, he was unable to force battle on the Austrians, and the war revealed serious weaknesses in the Prussian army. In some respects, the army Frederick had created was inferior to the one he had inherited from his father and used so successfully in the 1740s. Moreover, his aggressive stance on the battlefield, which he had employed so successfully in the Seven Years' War to repel attacks on Prussia, could not be repeated, because now the Austrians adeptly relied on active defence to protect their interest. Nevertheless, because the war was short and there were no battlefield defeats, the prestige of the Prussian military remained high. Thereafter, until his death in 1786, Frederick remained at peace.

Nader Shah

Iranian King and Great 18th-century Warrior

'I will place the collar of obedience on the necks of all the rebels of Iran and Turan.' NADER SHAH

A Life in Brief

1688, 22 November
Traditional date of Nader's birth

1736, February
Becomes Shah

1747, June
Assassinated by his own officers

▲ Nader Shah on horseback: a detail from a mid-18th-century opaque watercolour and gold-on-paper battle scene attributed to Muhammad 'Ali ibn 'Abd al-Bayg ibn 'Ali Quli.

Nader rose from humble origins to become the military commander and the self-proclaimed shah of Iran in 1736. He regained territory seized by the Afghans, Ottomans and Russians after the 1722 fall of the Safavids, invaded Afghanistan and India, and founded the Afsharid dynasty.

Key to Nader's early successes was his loyalty to the remaining Safavids and his efforts to restore them to the throne. He was thus in an excellent position to rally and organize tribal elements in his fight to recover territory lost to Iran's traditional enemies in the years following 1722. Following his appointment as shah, Nader sought legitimacy by stressing his ties to the noble Turkmen peoples of the Mughals, the Ottomans and the Uzbeks – even though the latter two were traditional enemies of the Safavids. He also sought to create parallels between himself and figures such as Chingiz Khan (pp. 76–79) and Timur (pp. 80–83). Nader also sought to downplay the position of the Shi'a faith in Iran established by the Safavids.

Contemporary sources indicate that the Qizilbash – Turkic tribal elements that brought the Safavids to power in Iran in 1501 – formed the backbone of Nader's armies. However, in the conquest of Kandahar, his forces included few of the original Qizilbash forces, and instead comprised an assortment of Kurds, Georgians, other Iranians and even Afghan and Uzbek tribesmen – the latter both former enemies.

The scholar Laurence Lockhart called special attention to Nader's successful use of swift cavalry attacks – as witnessed in the routing of Indian forces in the Khyber Pass – and musketeers. The latter were more than a match for the famed Janissaries of the Ottoman Turks, on more than one occasion. Nader was also very skilful at deploying his reserves.

By contrast, Nader had little success at siege warfare (as demonstrated at Baghdad, Mosul and Basra, for example). At Ganja (Azerbaijan), he succeeded only with Russian assistance, and at Kandahar (1738) he was helped from inside the city. His use of heavy artillery, given the distances in question, was not as effective as his use of light and medium guns, the command of which he entrusted to French officers.

Despite his impressive conquests, Nader failed to secure the long-term support of domestic tribal elements, and as his reign progressed rebellion and internal dissent increased, fuelled by heavy taxation. Only 11 years after his enthronement he was assassinated.

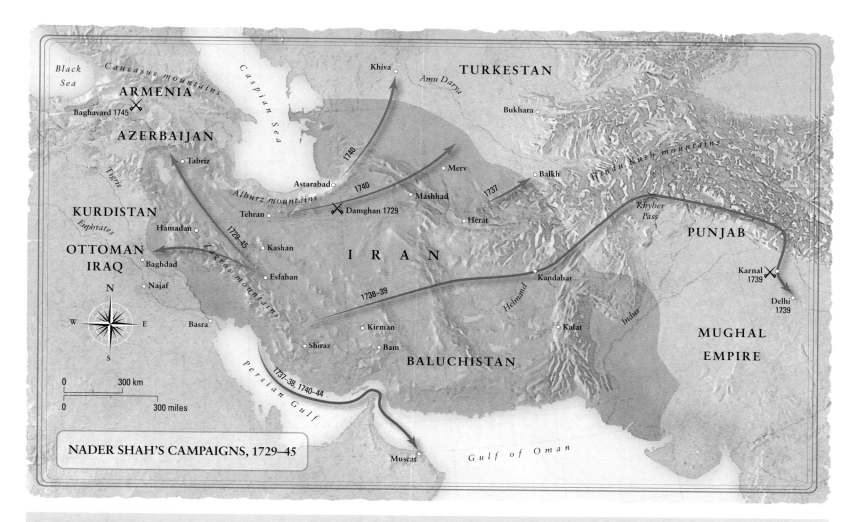

Black Sea
Caucasus mountains
ARMENIA
Baghavard 1745 ✕
AZERBAIJAN
Caspian Sea
Khiva
TURKESTAN
Amu Darya
Bukhara
Tabriz
Tigris
1740
Astarabad
1740
Merv
Balkh
Hindu Kush mountains
KURDISTAN
Alburz mountains
Tehran
Mashhad
1737
Khyber Pass
Euphrates
Hamadan
1729–45
Damghan 1729 ✕
Herat
PUNJAB
OTTOMAN IRAQ
Kashan
I R A N
Baghdad
Zagros mountains
Esfahan
Kandahar
Karnal 1739 ✕
Najaf
1738–39
Helmand
Delhi 1739
N
W E
S
Basra
Kirman
Indus
Kalat
MUGHAL EMPIRE
Shiraz
Bam
BALUCHISTAN
0   300 km
0   300 miles
1737–38, 1740–44
Persian Gulf

NADER SHAH'S CAMPAIGNS, 1729–45

Muscat
Gulf of Oman

Key Battles

The Battle of Damghan (Mehmandust), September 1729
Nader defeats the Ghilzai Afghans led by Ashraf Khan. This battle marks the downfall of the Hotaki dynasty, and the end of seven years of Afghan rule over Iran.

The Siege of Kandahar, 1737–38
Nader successfully carries the siege of the city, and razes it to the ground. The siege is the last act of defiance of the Ghilzai Afghans, who were responsible for ending the rule of the Safavid dynasty in 1722.

The Battle of Karnal, February 1739
During Nader's invasion of India, he defeats the Mughal emperor Muhammad Shah 70 miles north of Delhi. His victory, in which he uses camels to set panic among the Mughal elephants, secures his conquest of the country.

The Battle of Baghavard, August 1745
Nader is victorious over the Ottomans near Yerevan. This leads to new negotiations with the Ottomans, ending in the 1746 treaty in which the Ottomans finally recognize Nader's rule.

▲▲ In a short period Nader Shah managed to regain much territory which was lost in the years before he became shah.

◄ A dagger and scabbard from the second quarter of the 18th century, Iran. The weapon, 41.2 cm long, is made from damascened steel, gold, ivory and enamel.

◄ Nader Shah receiving an Ottoman envoy: detail from a 1730–40 watercolour and gold-on-paper work attributed to Muhammad Rashid Khan.

Qianlong Emperor

Expansionist Ruler of the Qing Dynasty

'It may be that soldiers are not mobilized for one hundred years, but they must not be left unprepared for a single day.' QIANLONG EMPEROR

A Life in Brief

1711, 25 September
Born in Beijing, with the name of Hongli

1735, 16 October
Enthroned as the Qianlong Emperor

1796, 9 February
Abdicates in favour of his son

1799, 7 February
Dies in Beijing

▶▶ **Perhaps to his regret Qianlong never personally rode to war, but he paid close attention to warfare and military preparation and presided regularly over ritual spectacles glorifying imperial military power. Here he is shown soon after becoming emperor, at a formal Grand Inspection of the troops. Reproduced from art catalogues to T-shirts, this view of the emperor has in modern times become the iconic image of the Qing empire.**

An intense focus on military power characterized the reign of the Qianlong Emperor, fourth emperor of the Manchu Qing empire (1636–1912). While this emphasis contrasted markedly both with the predominantly intellectual emphasis of earlier Chinese imperial regimes, and with China's later military weakness, it complemented rather than supplanted the well-known cultural, artistic and literary efflorescence of the Qianlong period. Near the end of his reign, in 1792, Qianlong hailed his military triumphs as one of the central accomplishments of his reign by assuming the designation 'Old Man of the Ten Great Victories'.

Most notable among the emperor's victories was the conquest (in a series of campaigns) of vast lands in Central Asia (later known as Xinjiang), which Qianlong achieved by exploiting shifting alliances among Zunghar and Mongol leaders in the region. Thus, in 1755 a famous Qing night attack at Gedengshan overwhelmed one Zunghar leader,

enabling imperial forces to pursue the others. No single engagement marked the Qing victory, indeed the Qing commander barely survived a protracted siege at Black Water Camp (1758). But ultimately the Qing exterminated the Zunghars, permanently ending the nomadic threat to China's northwest frontiers.

The conquest of Xinjiang enlarged an empire that already included China proper, Taiwan, Tibet, Mongolia and Manchuria, whereas other wars in the catalogue of ten suppressed resistance in various frontier regions. Though routinely glorified, most of these were as notable for their battle defeats as their overall victories, perhaps most markedly at Muguomu (1773) when the Qing commander Wenfu, Qianlong's son-in-law, perished ignominiously at the hands of Jinchuan rebels.

Qing military successes derived from a combination of three main factors. Firstly, the Qing's extraordinary logistical organization meant that their

▶ **The Manchus were well known for their mounted archery; Qianlong himself was said to be a crack shot. This Qianlong-period leather quiver and bow case is covered with embroidered satin and has gilded brass fittings. Annual month-long hunts, including archery displays, mock battles, and the pursuit of deer, tigers and other quarry, functioned to promote the Qing's martial ethos and demonstrate its military power as well as maintaining military skills in peacetime.**

▶ Especially well known among the paintings commemorating Qianlong's wars are the 16 illustrations executed by four foreign artist missionaries employed at his court. The emperor sent copies to Paris to have mass reproductions made in the form of copper engravings.

▼ Fine weapons fulfilled Qianlong's passion for collecting in a military vein. Whether intended for ceremonial or actual military use, all weapons for the court were made in the palace workshops, which attracted some of the finest artisans in the empire. The Mughal style of this dagger's hilt decoration probably reflected imperial preference.

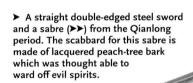

▶ A straight double-edged steel sword and a sabre (▶▶) from the Qianlong period. The scabbard for this sabre is made of lacquered peach-tree bark which was thought able to ward off evil spirits.

▼ The Qianlong emperor, who had particular success in conquering vast lands to the west, assumed the title 'Old Man of the Ten Great Victories'.

Key Campaigns

The Jinchuan Uprisings, 1747–49 and 1771–76
Minorities on the Sichuan/Tibet borderlands rebel, necessitating campaigns in mountainous terrain dominated by unassailable stone towers. Despite the defeat at Muguomu, the Qing eventually secure victory.

The Xinjiang Campaigns, 1755–59
The culmination of protracted series of wars instigated by Qianlong's grandfather, the Kangxi Emperor (1662–1722), these campaigns expand the empire and remove the nomadic threat to China's Central Asian borders.

Wars in Burma (1766–70), Vietnam (1788–89), and Taiwan
This sequence of campaigns serves to suppress potential rebels and rivals.

War against the Gurkhas in Tibet/Nepal, 1790–92
The two wars are a triumph of logistics. They also alert the Qing, under Fu Kang'an, to the British presence in India on the eve of British overtures to China.

Suppression of Uprisings, 1765–1799
Qianlong sends forces to deal with Muslim uprisings in Xinjiang (1765) and Gansu province (1781 and 1784), the Millenarian uprising under Wang Lun in Shandong province (1774), and the Miao uprisings in Yunnan and Hunan provinces (1790s).

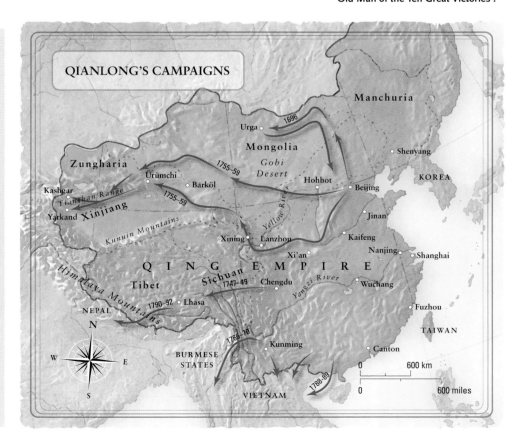

QIANLONG'S CAMPAIGNS

Manchuria

Urga 1696

Mongolia

Zungharia

Ürümchi 1755–59 Gobi Desert Hohhot

Shenyang

Kashgar

Tianshan Range Barköl

Yarkand Xinjiang 1755–59

Yellow River

KOREA

Beijing

Jinan

Kunlun Mountains

Xining Lanzhou

Kaifeng

Nanjing Shanghai

Xi'an

Himalaya Mountains

QING EMPIRE

Tibet Sichuan 1747–49 Chengdu

Yangzi River

Wuchang

1790–92 Lhasa

NEPAL

Kunming

1766–70

Fuzhou

TAIWAN

N
W E
S

BURMESE STATES

Canton

0 — 600 km

0 — 600 miles

VIETNAM

1788–89

'Only in war do we have no regard for expense, difficulty or danger; we are ready to try anything!'

QING IMPERIAL PRINCE TO
A JESUIT MISSIONARY AT
THE QIANLONG COURT

▲ Acutely conscious of art's political power, Qianlong had himself painted in many guises (Chinese emperor, Inner Asian khan, Tibetan bodhisattva, and so on) to impress authority upon his culturally diverse subjects. This portrait shows him in full winter-season court dress, seated upon a golden dragon-throne.

wars lasted longer and their armies travelled further than ever before. Not only were supply lines more effective, but firearms also played a decisive role. Often following Jesuit advice, Qianlong's armies built cannon that were lighter and more mobile than their own earlier models. Some were strapped to camels and transported to distant battlefronts, while others were built on the spot. Secondly, military expansion was underpinned by extensive institutional innovation, notably the consolidation of a Grand Council, originally founded to run military campaigns, into the highest agency of government. Thirdly, Qianlong's personal obsession with warfare kept military power at the forefront of policy. Qianlong paid the closest attention to campaign planning and execution, often staying awake all night awaiting battle reports, even though he never personally saw action.

▶ Each aspect of an imperial robe, such as this one belonging to the Qianlong emperor and similar to that in the painting above, carried meaning. Bright yellow was reserved for imperial use; narrow sleeves and 'horseshoe' cuffs were typical of Manchu equestrian styles; five-clawed dragons and the 12 symbols of ancient imperial authority express Qianlong's continuation of Chinese tradition and his wide-reaching power.

George Washington

Inspiring Rebel Commander and First American President

'I have not only grown gray but almost blind in the service of my country.'
GEORGE WASHINGTON

A Life in Brief

1732, 22 February
Born in Westmoreland County, Virginia

1775, 15 June
Appointed commander-in-chief of the Continental Army

1783, 23 December
Resigns his commission

1789, 30 April
Inauguration as President of the United States

1798, 13 July
Appointed lieutenant-general

1799, 14 December
Dies at Mount Vernon, Virginia

▶▶ Charles Willson Peale's 1779 painting *George Washington at Princeton* depicts the triumphant American commander, with captured enemy flags at his feet and his hand resting on a captured cannon, in the midst of the great winter campaign of 1776–77 in which he saved the Revolution and secured his place as its most important figure.

▼ This gold watch, made in London by the renowned firm of James McCabe in 1793–94, was carried by George Washington during his second term as president.

Of all the men who contributed to the success of the American War of Independence and the effort to provide the United States of America with an effective system of governance, none was as important as George Washington. As commander of the Continental Army and the nation's first president, he towered over a generation of military and political leaders whose accomplishments have rarely, if ever, been equalled in world history.

Born and raised in Virginia, Washington entered adulthood with military ambitions, inspired by the exploits of his older half-brother who served the British crown as a Marine officer. Washington's first opportunity to gratify these came in 1754 when he led troops into the Ohio Valley to assert Virginia's claim to that land. Although Washington demonstrated considerable personal courage and ability as a leader of men in the course of this campaign, his lack of tactical skill was evident at the battle of Great Meadows (July 1754), which ended with his surrender at Fort Necessity. When the British government dispatched troops to America to drive the French from the Ohio Country, Washington accompanied them. He was present at their defeat at the battle of the Monongahela (July 1755), where he once again demonstrated considerable bravery and leadership ability. Nonetheless, Washington was subsequently unable to secure a much-desired commission in the British regular army during the French and Indian War (1754–63).

Washington spent the decade following the conflict managing his plantation at Mount Vernon and supporting the growing colonial resistance movement. In June 1775 he was appointed commander-in-chief of the army the Continental Congress was organizing for the war with Britain, and it quickly became evident that he had matured into a far wiser commander than had been the case during the French and Indian War. Although instinctively aggressive, Washington would demonstrate throughout his tenure of command of the Continental Army that he also appreciated prudence and the importance of discipline – both in himself and his army. Upon taking command, Washington immediately undertook efforts to organize and train his army along European lines. At the same time, he was sensitive to the political anxieties his assumption of military power had created, and adopted the practice of explicitly deferring to civil governments at all levels.

Although Washington was able to force the British to evacuate Boston in March 1776, a few months later his army was routed by a British force under Sir William Howe at the battle of Long Island. Washington and his army were then chased out of New York and New Jersey after engagements at Harlem Heights, White Plains, Fort Washington and Fort Lee. Having crossed the Delaware River into Pennsylvania in early December 1776, Washington faced a crisis, with enlistments in his army expiring and Patriot morale at its lowest ebb. He responded with bold, daring action. On 25 December he led his army back across the Delaware and, adopting 'victory or death' as the password for the operation, executed a well-conceived attack against an enemy outpost at Trenton that ended with the capitulation of the garrison. The victory at Trenton and one at Princeton shortly thereafter compelled the British to abandon their outposts in New Jersey, and provided a critical boost to Patriot morale.

Key Battles and Campaigns

The Battle of the Great Meadows, 3 July 1754
As commander of a force of Virginia militia, Washington ambushes a small French party at Jumonville Glen in western Pennsylvania. A punitive expedition by French forces under de Villiars then pursues Washington's command and forces its surrender at Fort Necessity. These events spark a major war between Great Britain and France that will result in the expulsion of the latter from much of North America.

The Battle of Long Island, 27 August 1776
In the first major battle of the War for Independence, Washington and his army are outmanoeuvred and routed by a British force under William Howe. The British go on to take New York.

The Christmas Campaign (26 December 1776–3 January 1777)
After being chased out of New York and New Jersey, the Continental Army is on the point of falling apart and the cause of American independence hangs by a thread. Washington responds by crossing the Delaware River to attack British outposts at Trenton and Princeton. His capture of the garrison at the former, and victory over British forces under William Howe at the latter, effectively saves the American Revolution.

The Siege of Yorktown, 28 September–17 October 1781
Assisted by French land and naval forces, Washington compels the surrender of the British army commanded by Charles Cornwallis after a brief siege. After Yorktown, the British government abandons its effort to regain its former colonies, and recognizes the independence of the United States of America.

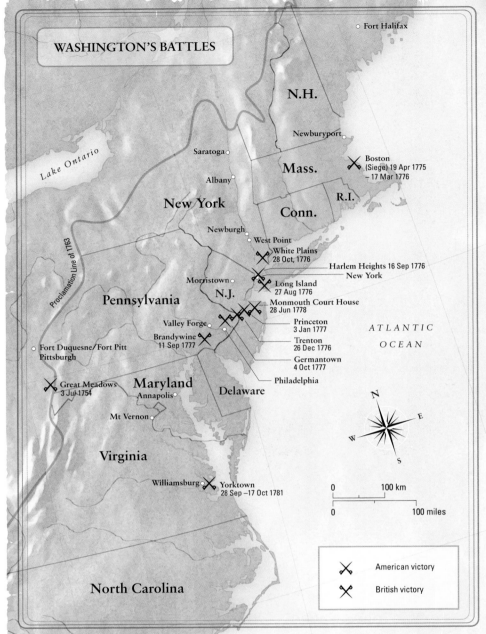

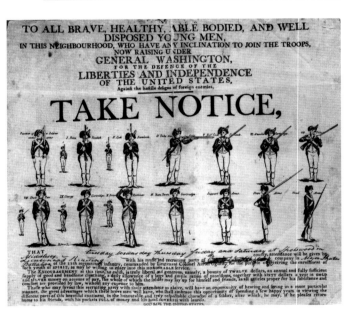

▲ Recruiting poster for the Continental Army. The initial enthusiasm for the American Revolution faded significantly by the end of its first year. Consequently, finding enough 'brave, healthy, able bodied, and well disposed young men' to maintain the strength and efficiency of the Continental Army proved a constant challenge for Washington for the rest of the war.

◄ Washington's campaigns demonstrated his ability to overcome low soldier morale with a combination of military boldness and soundly conceived tactics. He transformed his army into a highly professional force.

Washington suffered tactical defeats in 1777 at Brandywine Creek and Germantown, and could not keep the British from taking Philadelphia. He was, however, able to preserve his army, which held far greater significance than control of the capital. The arrival of Prussian officer Baron von Steuben at the Continental Army's subsequent winter encampment at Valley Forge, combined with changes in the composition of the army, facilitated Washington's efforts to transform it from the enthusiastic but ill-disciplined force of 1775–76 to a tough, well-drilled professional one. In 1778 Washington initiated an engagement at Monmouth Court House; it did not achieve as much as he hoped, but did demonstrate that Washington's natural aggressiveness had not been dulled by earlier defeats, and that his ability as a battlefield tactician and the proficiency of his army were both growing.

After Monmouth, Washington posted his army near New York City. When a French army commanded by Comte de Rochambeau arrived in 1781, he began making plans to drive the British from New York, though these were subsequently dropped. Having learnt of a favourable opportunity to attack a British force operating in Virginia, he led his and Rochambeau's forces south. In October 1781 Washington conducted a well-executed siege of a British army at Yorktown, and forced its surrender.

Washington and his army then returned to encampments along the Hudson River. It was here in 1783 that the Newburgh Conspiracy spread among officers angered by the failure of Congress to pay the army; the talk among some was of using force to settle their grievances. Washington successfully countered the conspiracy by personally appealing to his subordinates, during a meeting with them in March, to abandon their proposed course of action. Two months later, Washington submitted to Congress (at its request) his 'Sentiments on a Peace Establishment', but his suggestions on how to develop the nation's military institutions were not put into practice.

After learning that the Treaty of Paris (3 September 1783) had ended the war, Washington made a triumphal return to New York City, before resigning his commission that December. As the new nation struggled with deep economic and political problems, Washington assumed leadership of a faction of men whose efforts resulted in the writing and ratification of a new constitution for the United States. He then served two terms as the first President of the United States under the Constitution. Washington's determination to strengthen the power and prestige of the national government while in office is evident in his suppression of the 1794 Whiskey Rebellion, and successful prosecution of a war against Native American tribes in the Ohio Territory. In international affairs, Washington steered a neutral course through the European wars that erupted during his administration, and urged his successors to follow his lead in their dealings with other nations. However, the administration of his successor brought an undeclared war with France (known as the 'Quasi' or 'Half War', 1798–1800), during which Washington once again assumed command of the US army. When Washington died in 1799, the lieutenant-general's rank he held died with him, and would not again be authorized by the US Congress until 1864. To ensure Washington would always hold supreme rank, though, in 1976 Congress promoted him retroactively to the rank of General of the Armies of the United States.

Without Washington, it is difficult to see how the Americans could have been as successful as they were in securing their independence and establishing an effective functioning government for their republic. That Washington suffered many tactical defeats as a commander is true; however, these were largely attributable to the obstacles the society he served often placed in the way of his efforts to foster and maintain the physical strength and technical proficiency of the Continental Army. Washington was able to overcome these challenges because he possessed a clear strategic vision, an unwavering dedication to his goals, and a keen appreciation of the means necessary to achieve them – as well as the political skills to maintain good civil–military relations and the strength of character to hold his army and country together. These qualities enabled Washington not only to win the war and secure the peace, but to inspire in the people of the United States a sense of a common purpose and destiny. Rarely has a country been as blessed in having the right man, in the right place, at the right time. Washington fully merits recognition as the 'Father of his Country', one of history's outstanding captains, and a truly great man.

▲ Gilbert Stuart's iconic *Unfinished Portrait*, one in a series of paintings Stuart produced of Washington during his presidency, appears on the US one dollar bill and is undoubtedly the best-known portrait of the great American general and statesman.

▲ Washington accomplished all that he did despite suffering dental problems throughout his adult life: by the time he became president in 1789 he had lost all but one of his teeth. He tried several different sets of dentures, including this one (none of these, contrary to myth, were made of wood), in hopes of finding a means to alleviate his intense discomfort and distress but never found one.

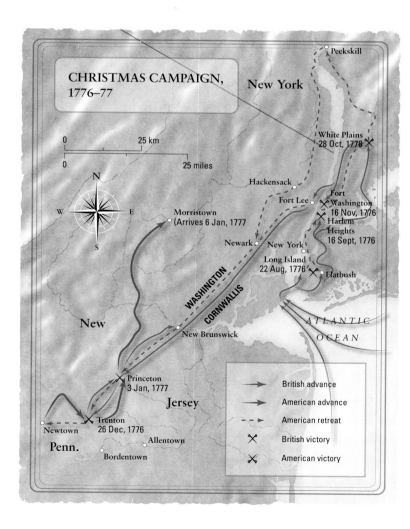

CHRISTMAS CAMPAIGN, 1776–77

New York

Peekskill

0 — 25 km
0 — 25 miles

White Plains
28 Oct, 1776 ✕

Hackensack

Fort Lee

Fort Washington
16 Nov, 1776 ✕

Harlem Heights
16 Sept, 1776

Morristown
(Arrives 6 Jan, 1777)

Newark

New York

Long Island
22 Aug, 1776 ✕

Flatbush

WASHINGTON

CORNWALLIS

New Brunswick

ATLANTIC OCEAN

New

Princeton
3 Jan, 1777 ✕

Jersey

Trenton
26 Dec, 1776 ✕

Newtown

Allentown

Penn.

Bordentown

→ British advance
→ American advance
--► American retreat
✕ British victory
✕ American victory

◄ 'Necessity,' Washington proclaimed in December 1776, 'dire necessity, will, nay must justify my attack.' With his army on the verge of collapse after being chased out of New York and New Jersey, Washington led his men across the icy Delaware River on a miserable Christmas night. He then launched a skilfully conceived three-prong attack against Trenton that ended with the surrender of the garrison, then followed it up with a hard-fought victory at Princeton. When Washington's army subsequently went into winter quarters in Morristown, the British abandoned their advanced outposts in New Jersey. Thanks to Washington and his army, the Revolution had survived the great crisis that one revolutionary figure proclaimed 'the times that try men souls'.

Charles Cornwallis (1738–1805)

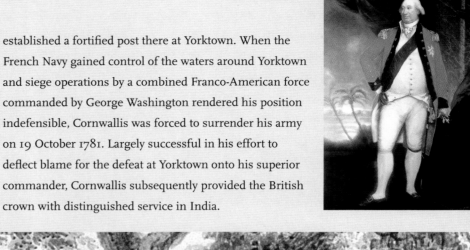

In 1780, the accomplished and highly regarded Cornwallis assumed command of the British war effort in the south. He promptly routed one American force at Camden, and then chased another commanded by Nathanael Greene out of the Carolinas. His inability decisively to defeat Greene, however, combined with setbacks at King's Mountain and Cowpens, ultimately doomed the effort to restore loyal governments in the southern colonies. Cornwallis subsequently took his army to Virginia and eventually established a fortified post there at Yorktown. When the French Navy gained control of the waters around Yorktown and siege operations by a combined Franco-American force commanded by George Washington rendered his position indefensible, Cornwallis was forced to surrender his army on 19 October 1781. Largely successful in his effort to deflect blame for the defeat at Yorktown onto his superior commander, Cornwallis subsequently provided the British crown with distinguished service in India.

'Discipline is the soul of an army.... It makes small numbers formidable, procures success to the weak, and esteem to all.' GEORGE WASHINGTON

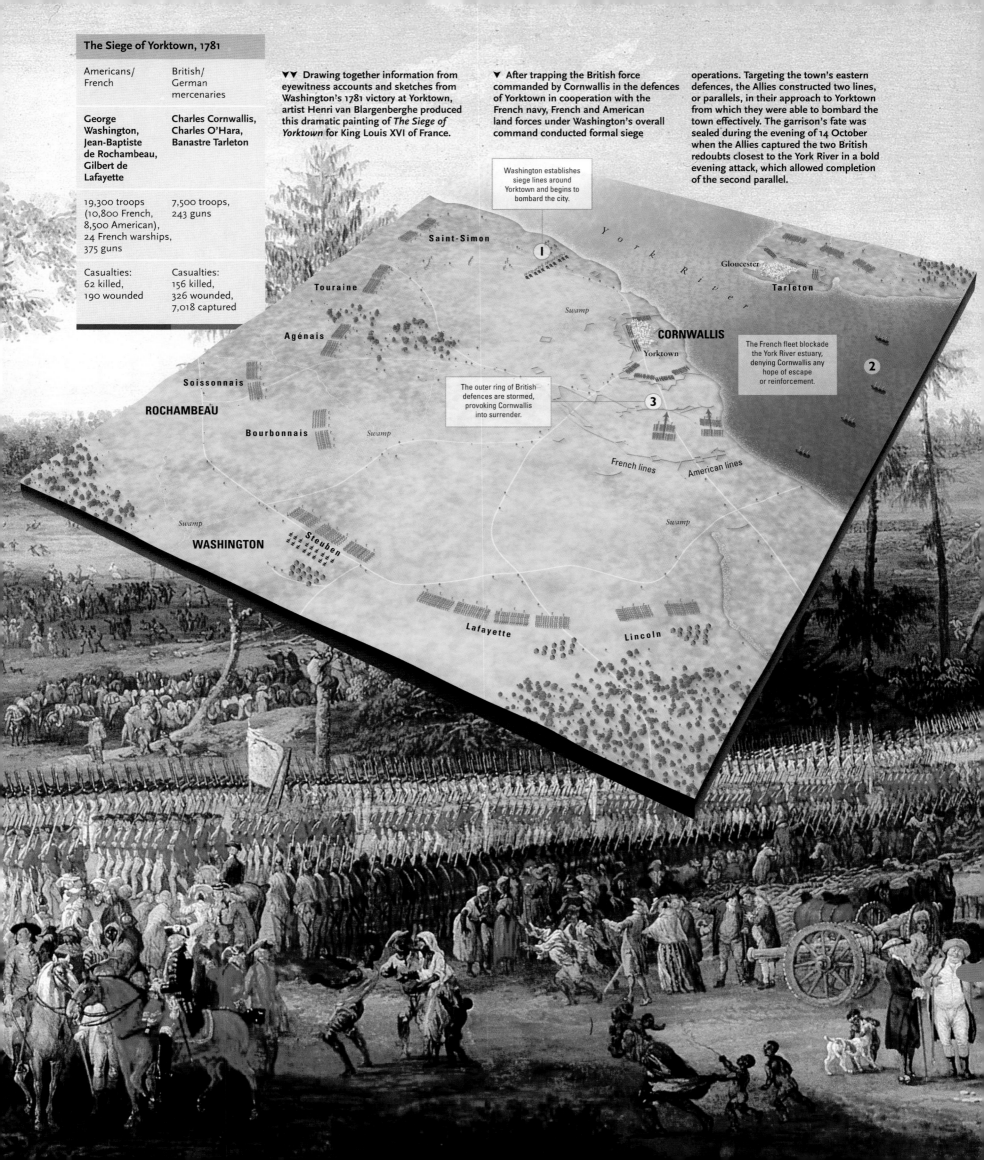

The Siege of Yorktown, 1781

Americans/French	British/German mercenaries
George Washington, Jean-Baptiste de Rochambeau, Gilbert de Lafayette	Charles Cornwallis, Charles O'Hara, Banastre Tarleton
19,300 troops (10,800 French, 8,500 American), 24 French warships, 375 guns	7,500 troops, 243 guns
Casualties: 62 killed, 190 wounded	Casualties: 156 killed, 326 wounded, 7,018 captured

▼▼ Drawing together information from eyewitness accounts and sketches from Washington's 1781 victory at Yorktown, artist Henri van Blargenberghe produced this dramatic painting of *The Siege of Yorktown* for King Louis XVI of France.

▼ After trapping the British force commanded by Cornwallis in the defences of Yorktown in cooperation with the French navy, French and American land forces under Washington's overall command conducted formal siege operations. Targeting the town's eastern defences, the Allies constructed two lines, or parallels, in their approach to Yorktown from which they were able to bombard the town effectively. The garrison's fate was sealed during the evening of 14 October when the Allies captured the two British redoubts closest to the York River in a bold evening attack, which allowed completion of the second parallel.

Washington establishes siege lines around Yorktown and begins to bombard the city.

The French fleet blockade the York River estuary, denying Cornwallis any hope of escape or reinforcement.

The outer ring of British defences are stormed, provoking Cornwallis into surrender.

Saint-Simon

Touraine

Agénais

Soissonnais

ROCHAMBEAU

Bourbonnais

WASHINGTON

Steuben

Lafayette

Lincoln

York River

Gloucester

Tarleton

CORNWALLIS

Yorktown

French lines

American lines

Swamp

Napoleon

Emperor of France and Conqueror of Much of Europe

'Power is my mistress. I have worked too hard at her conquest to allow anyone to take her away from me.'
NAPOLEON

A Life in Brief

1769, 15 August
Born in Ajaccio, Corsica

1796–97
Commander-in-Chief, Army of Italy

1798
Commander-in-Chief, Army of the Orient

1804, 2 December
Crowned Emperor of the French

1814, 11 April
Abdicates and is sent into exile on Elba

1815, 15 October
Exiled by the British to St Helena in the South Atlantic Ocean

1821
Dies on St Helena

Napoleon was the father of modern warfare and one of the greatest military captains in western civilization. His rapid conquest of Europe (1805–07) was the product of diplomatic opportunism, economy of force, expert and veteran leadership, manoeuvre and coordination of armies and corps on the strategic and operational level. He favoured the strategy of the central position – attacking his enemy piecemeal before he could unite – and the *manoeuvre sur la derrière*, the strategic or operational envelopment of his army. Napoleon sought decision on the battlefield, followed by the destruction of the enemy.

Napoleon's military education began aged 9 at Brienne-le-Château. It was one of several new academies opened in the 1770s to educate a new generation of French officers from the lesser nobility and middle class. At 16, Napoleon entered the École Militaire in Paris, and was commissioned a year later as a lieutenant of artillery. He spent several years on leave in Corsica and Paris, before being posted in 1793 to the Army of Italy and receiving his baptism of fire at Dego (near Genoa) in 1794. A few months later he joined the army before Toulon. The city had rebelled against Revolutionary authority, and was under siege. Napoleon, a mere captain, requested permission to direct the siege. Within a month the city fell, and Napoleon was promoted General of Brigade. From Toulon he returned briefly to Italy, and then in 1795 to Paris, where he defended the government against a Royalist coup by a judicious use of artillery. He was promoted Commander-in-Chief of the Army of Italy in 1796, a move that would bring about a dramatic transformation in this awkward 26-year-old.

THE YEARS OF CONQUEST

Napoleon conducted a brilliant lightning campaign in Italy in 1796–97, breaking the Austro-Sardinian forces at Montenotte and Millesimo and forcing the Kingdom of Sardinia to surrender after Mondovi. Pursuing the Austrians, he outflanked their position on the Milanese border, culminating in the battle of Lodi. Four Austrian attempts to recapture Lombardy ended in their defeat at Lonato, Castiglione, Arcola and Rivoli. Napoleon then invaded Austria in 1797 from Italy, ending the War of the First Coalition (1792–97). He was rewarded for his victory with command of the Army of the Orient, and sailed for Egypt in 1798.

Napoleon captured Alexandria and defeated a Mamluk army outside Cairo in the dramatic Battle of the Pyramids (Giza). In 1799 he marched north,

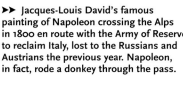

▶ One of Napoleon's many swords. Its gilded bronze, gold and pearl inlay reflects its use as a ceremonial accoutrement, as opposed to a weapon of war.

▶▶ Jacques-Louis David's famous painting of Napoleon crossing the Alps in 1800 en route with the Army of Reserve to reclaim Italy, lost to the Russians and Austrians the previous year. Napoleon, in fact, rode a donkey through the pass.

▲ **Napoleon's invasion of Egypt lent itself to exotic imagery, enhancing the young general's reputation. His decisive victory over Mamluk forces at Giza in the so-called Battle of the Pyramids in 1798 provided him with such an opportunity.**

▲▼ **The sabre worn by Napoleon during the coup of 18 Brumaire is actually similar to the scimitars he saw during his campaign in Egypt. His use of this sabre/scimitar during the coup reflects his purposeful attempt to identify himself as the conqueror of Egypt. The telescope is also said to have belonged to Napoleon.**

entered Jerusalem and laid siege to the Turkish-held fortress at Acre. Failing to take the city, Napoleon withdrew to Egypt, from where, in the autumn, he returned to France to participate in a coup d'état.

Now First Consul of France, Napoleon contended with a Second Coalition against him (1798–1802), as Austrian armies overran Italy and ranged in Germany. Leading the Army of Reserve over the Alps, Napoleon narrowly defeated the Austrians at Marengo on 14 June 1800. In February 1801 the Austrians signed the Peace of Luneville, concluding hostilities. Only Britain remained an enemy of France, but lacking Continental allies, she concluded a treaty at Amiens in 1802.

Napoleon consolidated his domestic political power and expanded his influence in Western Europe. He brokered the restructuring of the Holy Roman Empire, and annexed Piedmont and Genoa. He became president of the Italian Republic, a French satellite, and violated his agreements with Austria and Britain. His aggressive policies led to war with Britain in 1803, and the formation of a Third Coalition (of Britain, Russia and Austria) against him.

Napoleon, now Emperor of the French, allied with Spain against Britain, but was unable to invade England before the coalition threatened France. Napoleon turned his Grande Armée from the Channel coast to south Germany, where in October 1805 it forced the surrender of the Austrian army at Ulm. Napoleon seized Vienna, then advanced against the Russians and Austrians in Moravia. On 2 December

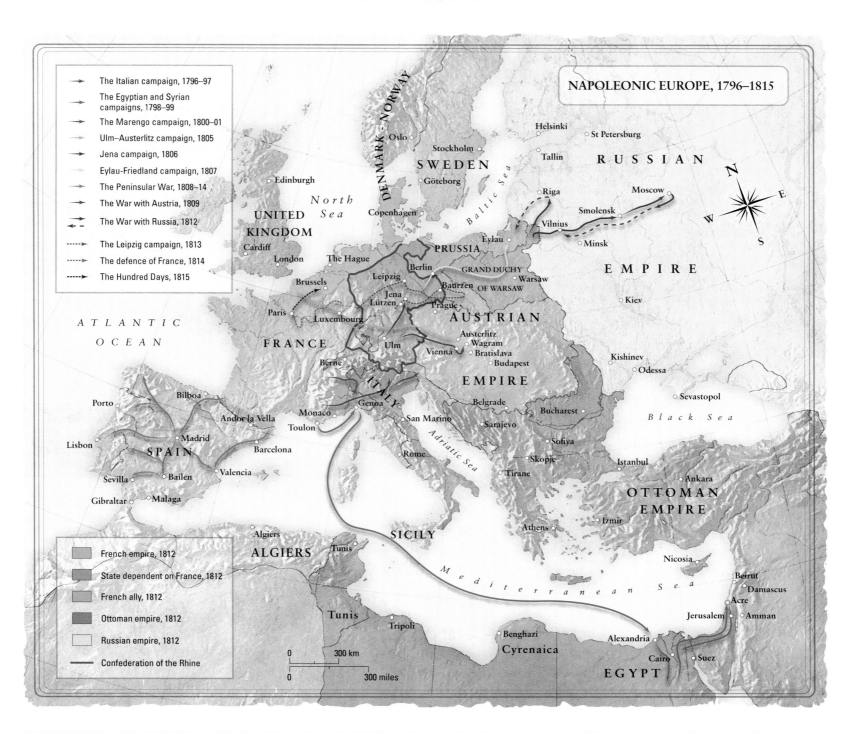

The Italian campaign, 1796–97
The Egyptian and Syrian campaigns, 1798–99
The Marengo campaign, 1800–01
Ulm–Austerlitz campaign, 1805
Jena campaign, 1806
Eylau–Friedland campaign, 1807
The Peninsular War, 1808–14
The War with Austria, 1809
The War with Russia, 1812
The Leipzig campaign, 1813
the defence of France, 1814
The Hundred Days, 1815

NAPOLEONIC EUROPE, 1796–1815

French empire, 1812
State dependent on France, 1812
French ally, 1812
Ottoman empire, 1812
Russian empire, 1812
Confederation of the Rhine

0   300 km
0   300 miles

Key Campaigns

**The Italian Campaign,
April 1796–January 1797**
Though badly equipped and heavily
outnumbered by the Austrians,
Napoleon gains a decisive triumph,
conquering northern Italy.

**The War of the Second Coalition,
1798–1801**
The Allies are defeated by France,
which becomes newly energetic under
Napoleon. His victory at Marengo (14
June 1800) is a key triumph.

The Egyptian Campaign, 1798–1801
Napoleon's expedition to Egypt is
intended to open a route to India.
Despite early successes on land, his
plan is wrecked by British sea power,
especially Nelson's victory at the Battle
of the Nile (1–2 August 1798). In 1801
the British push the French out of Egypt.

**The Wars of the Third and Fourth
Coalition, 1805–07**
In high-tempo campaigning, Napoleon
outmanoeuvres the Austrians at Ulm
(1805) before advancing to defeat
Austria and Russia at Austerlitz (1805).
Prussia follows at Jena (1806), although
the Russians mount a more successful
resistance.

The Peninsular War, 1808–14
In order to impose the Continental
System on the Iberian Peninsula,
Napoleon invades Portugal, then Spain.
The Spanish people revolt; Britain enters
the war and eventually the French are
driven from Iberia by Wellington.

The War with Austria, 1809
Emboldened by the French
concentration on Spain, Austria tries
to liberate Germany from French rule.
Due to Napoleon's vigorous response
(notably at Wagram, 5–6 July), the
Austrians soon seek an armistice.

The War with Russia, 1812
Tsar Alexander of Russia, France's only
major continental rival, is persuaded
by Britain to renounce the Continental
System, a serious economic blow
to France. Napoleon invades
Russia, carries the field at Borodino
(7 September) and reaches Moscow.
However, the retreat in the harsh winter
of 1812 inflicts heavy casualties.

The Leipzig Campaign, 1813
The Allies unite to end Napoleon's grip
on Europe, with Prussia and Austria
joining Russia and Britain. Despite
a crushing defeat at Leipzig (16–19
October), Napoleon refuses peace terms
offered by the Allies.

The Hundred Days, March–June 1815
Escaping from exile on the island of
Elba, Napoleon returns to Paris, musters
an army and marches north to invade
Belgium. On 18 June, he is defeated by
the Allied armies at Waterloo.

▲ Accorded the respect of his enemies,
even Wellington is known to have believed
Napoleon the greatest general 'in any age'.
Yet Napoleon saw his legacy as lying away
from the battlefield, in the dissemination
of the French Revolution's political
ideals: 'My true glory is not to have won
40 battles. Waterloo will erase the memory
of so many victories. But what nothing
will destroy, what will live forever, is my
Civil Code.'

*'War justifies
everything.'*
NAPOLEON

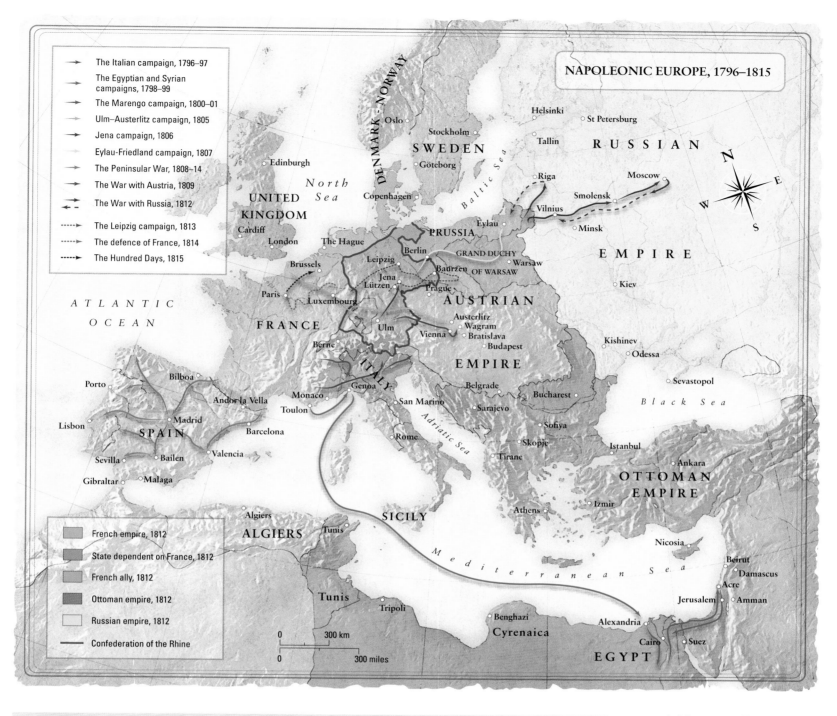

Key Campaigns

NAPOLEONIC EUROPE, 1796–1815

Legend:
- The Italian campaign, 1796–97
- The Egyptian and Syrian campaigns, 1798–99
- The Marengo campaign, 1800–01
- Ulm–Austerlitz campaign, 1805
- Jena campaign, 1806
- Eylau-Friedland campaign, 1807
- The Peninsular War, 1808–14
- The War with Austria, 1809
- The War with Russia, 1812
- The Leipzig campaign, 1813
- The defence of France, 1814
- The Hundred Days, 1815

- French empire, 1812
- State dependent on France, 1812
- French ally, 1812
- Ottoman empire, 1812
- Russian empire, 1812
- Confederation of the Rhine

The Italian Campaign, April 1796–January 1797
Though badly equipped and heavily outnumbered by the Austrians, Napoleon gains a decisive triumph, conquering northern Italy.

The War of the Second Coalition, 1798–1801
The Allies are defeated by France, which becomes newly energetic under Napoleon. His victory at Marengo (14 June 1800) is a key triumph.

The Egyptian Campaign, 1798–1801
Napoleon's expedition to Egypt is intended to open a route to India. Despite early successes on land, his plan is wrecked by British sea power, especially Nelson's victory at the Battle of the Nile (1–2 August 1798). In 1801 the British push the French out of Egypt.

The Wars of the Third and Fourth Coalition, 1805–07
In high-tempo campaigning, Napoleon outmanoeuvres the Austrians at Ulm (1805) before advancing to defeat Austria and Russia at Austerlitz (1805). Prussia follows at Jena (1806), although the Russians mount a more successful resistance.

The Peninsular War, 1808–14
In order to impose the Continental System on the Iberian Peninsula, Napoleon invades Portugal, then Spain. The Spanish people revolt; Britain enters the war and eventually the French are driven from Iberia by Wellington.

The War with Austria, 1809
Emboldened by the French concentration on Spain, Austria tries to liberate Germany from French rule. Due to Napoleon's vigorous response (notably at Wagram, 5–6 July), the Austrians soon seek an armistice.

The War with Russia, 1812
Tsar Alexander of Russia, France's only major continental rival, is persuaded by Britain to renounce the Continental System, a serious economic blow to France. Napoleon invades Russia, carries the field at Borodino (7 September) and reaches Moscow. However, the retreat in the harsh winter of 1812 inflicts heavy casualties.

The Leipzig Campaign, 1813
The Allies unite to end Napoleon's grip on Europe, with Prussia and Austria joining Russia and Britain. Despite a crushing defeat at Leipzig (16–19 October), Napoleon refuses peace terms offered by the Allies.

The Hundred Days, March–June 1815
Escaping from exile on the island of Elba, Napoleon returns to Paris, musters an army and marches north to invade Belgium. On 18 June, he is defeated by the Allied armies at Waterloo.

▲ Accorded the respect of his enemies, even Wellington is known to have believed Napoleon the greatest general 'in any age'. Yet Napoleon saw his legacy as lying away from the battlefield, in the dissemination of the French Revolution's political ideals: 'My true glory is not to have won 40 battles. Waterloo will erase the memory of so many victories. But what nothing will destroy, what will live forever, is my Civil Code.'

'War justifies everything.'
NAPOLEON

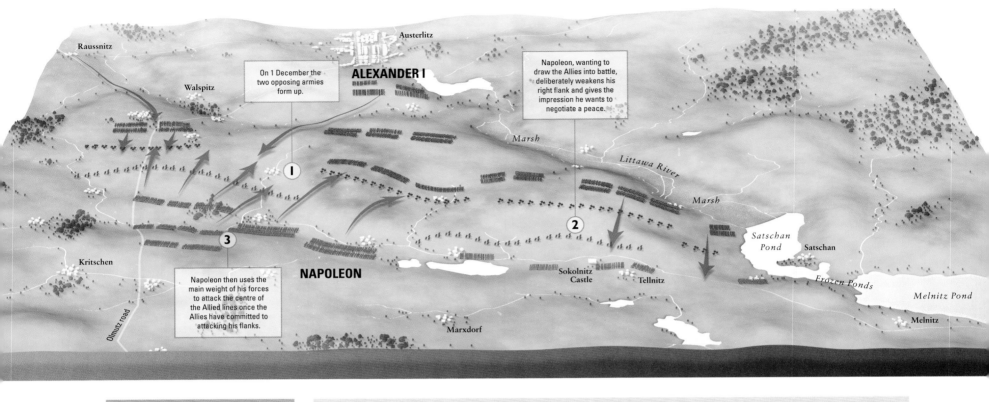

On 1 December the two opposing armies form up.

Napoleon, wanting to draw the Allies into battle, deliberately weakens his right flank and gives the impression he wants to negotiate a peace.

Napoleon then uses the main weight of his forces to attack the centre of the Allied lines once the Allies have committed to attacking his flanks.

The Battle of Austerlitz, 1805	
French	Russians/Austrians
Napoleon	**Alexander I**
72,000 troops	86,000 troops (71,000 Russian, 15,000 Austrian)
Casualties: 1,305 killed, 6,340 wounded, 573 captured, 1 lost	Casualties: 15,000 killed or wounded, 12,000 captured, 200 lost

▲◄ The battle of Austerlitz was Napoleon's most decisive and dramatic victory. He set the Russian army, including Tsar Alexander I, to flight, leaving their Austrian allies to sue for peace. The battle sealed the fate of the Third Coalition.

Davout (1770–1823)

Louis-Nicholas Davout was perhaps Napoleon's most able marshal. He fought with the armies of the North and Rhine during the War of the First Coalition, and accompanied Bonaparte to Egypt in 1798. In 1804, he attained the rank of Marshal of France, thirteenth in seniority. In 1805 Davout led I Army Corps, shoring up Napoleon's right flank at Austerlitz, and in 1806 he commanded the venerated III Army Corps, defeating the main Prussian army at Auerstädt. He organized the army of the Grand Duchy of Warsaw between 1807 and 1808, and commanded the Army of Germany after Napoleon's departure for Spain. In 1809, Davout's actions at Teugn-Hausen (Thann) delayed Archduke Charles's army long enough for Napoleon to threaten envelopment at Eggmühl, and at Wagram he turned the Austrian left flank. During the Russian campaign, Davout led I Army Corps at Borodino and was initially responsible for the rearguard during the retreat from Moscow. From December 1812 to March 1813

Davout held the strategic centre of the French army in Poland. In spring 1813 Napoleon posted him to Hamburg, which he defended successfully from Russian attacks until April 1814. Napoleon appointed him Minister of War upon his return from Elba in February 1815. After the restoration, Davout spent three years in internal exile, until elevated to the Chamber of Peers in 1818.

'What my enemies call a general peace is my destruction. What I call peace is merely the disarmament of my enemies. Am I not more moderate than they?' NAPOLEON

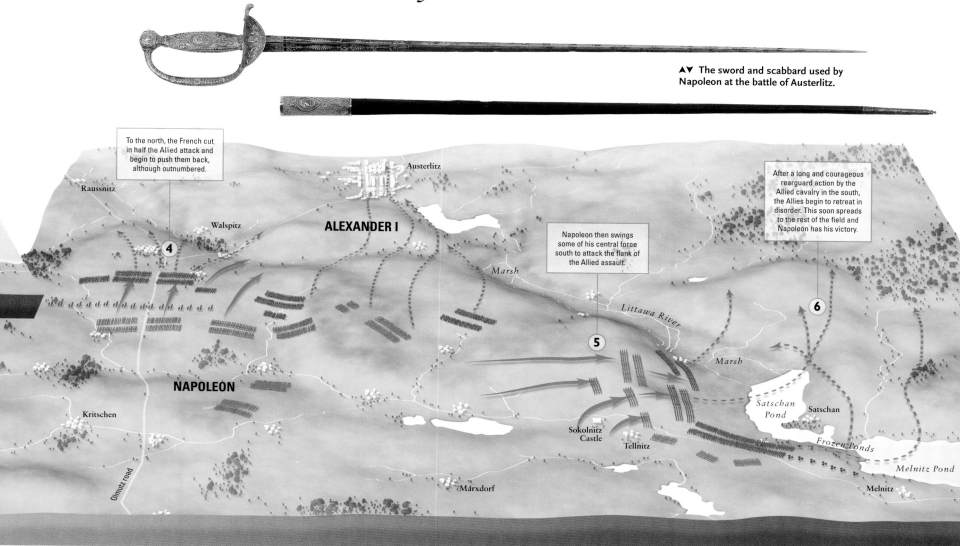

▲▼ The sword and scabbard used by Napoleon at the battle of Austerlitz.

To the north, the French cut in half the Allied attack and begin to push them back, although outnumbered.

After a long and courageous rearguard action by the Allied cavalry in the south, the Allies begin to retreat in disorder. This soon spreads to the rest of the field and Napoleon has his victory.

Napoleon then swings some of his central force south to attack the flank of the Allied assault.

Raussnitz

Austerlitz

Walspitz

ALEXANDER I

4

Marsh

5

6

Littawa River

Marsh

NAPOLEON

Satschan Pond

Satschan

Kritschen

Sokolnitz Castle

Tellnitz

Frozen Ponds

Olmutz road

Marxdorf

Melnitz Pond

Melnitz

1805, Napoleon decisively defeated the Russo-Austrian army at Austerlitz, ending the War of the Third Coalition.

Napoleon transformed the Holy Roman Empire in 1806 into the Confederation of the Rhine, with the allied German princes contributing 100,000 men to his armies. Prussia, however, remained outside of the Confederation, and tensions with France culminated in war. On 14 October 1806 the French armies crushed the Prussians at Jena and Auerstädt. Napoleon moved against Russian armies in Poland, fighting an indecisive engagement at Eylau in February 1807. In the spring, Napoleon decisively defeated the Russians at Friedland, compelling Tsar Alexander to sign a treaty at Tilsit, effectively making Russia a French ally.

Despite his success on the Continent, Napoleon was unable to achieve results at sea. The greatest prospect of a Franco-Spanish alliance against Britain failed miserably at Trafalgar in 1805. In response, he established an embargo on English goods to the Continent in 1806 (the Continental System), hoping it would have a critical impact on Britain. It ultimately led to the invasion of Portugal, to the betrayal of his Spanish ally, and the draining and distracting Peninsular War.

The Austrians moved against Napoleon in 1809. Archduke Charles invaded Bavaria with a large army, while a second advanced into Italy. With only 60,000 French immediately available, Napoleon turned to the Rheinbund until reinforcements could be sent. A month after the invasion, Napoleon caught the Archduke at Eggmühl in Bavaria, and the Austrians retreated into Bohemia and towards Vienna. Napoleon captured the Austrian capital, and in May stormed

▶▶ Typical of European representations of victorious commanders between the 16th and 19th centuries, this painting of Austerlitz by François Gerard shows Napoleon on a white horse receiving news of his triumph from his subordinates, who bring him captured enemy standards.

▲ A pistol possessed by Napoleon at the battle of Wagram. The battle followed Napoleon's first defeat at the hands of the Archduke Charles at Aspern-Essling.

▲▲ The battle of Wagram, here represented in a contemporary painting by Johann Lorenz Rugendas II, was the largest European battle to date, until 1813. Napoleon's victory over Charles led to the conclusion of the 1809 campaign.

across the Danube at Aspern-Essling, but was repulsed. After six weeks of preparation, Napoleon attacked again, at Wagram, defeated the Austrians and effectively ended the war.

Master of Europe, Napoleon turned his attention towards Russia. In June 1812, his army of 600,000 men invaded. In a bloody battle at Borodino, 70 miles west of Moscow, Napoleon forced the Russian armies to withdraw, and he entered the capital a week later. Tsar Alexander refused to negotiate, and, with winter coming and supplies low, Napoleon had little choice but to withdraw from Russia. The retreat was a debacle, and fewer than 120,000 troops returned.

The Russians pursued the French into Poland, and convinced the Prussians to join a (sixth) coalition against France in March 1813. Napoleon rebuilt his

shattered army and returned to Germany, where he gave the coalition armies a drubbing at Lützen and Bautzen. An armistice was agreed upon through August 1813. Austria now joined the coalition, and the Allies' overwhelming numbers effectively gave them advantage over the French. Napoleon's German allies gradually defected to the coalition, and his marshals' inability to capitalize on their spring victories led to virtual encirclement at Leipzig. The October 1813 'Battle of the Nations', as it is known, led to the collapse of Napoleonic Germany, and the coalition crossed the Rhine into France at the end of December.

The 1814 campaign in France restored Napoleon's energy, and despite the poor strategic situation, he achieved several remarkable victories over the Prussians at Brienne-le-Château, Champaubert,

> *'In war, men are nothing,*
> *one man is everything.'* NAPOLEON

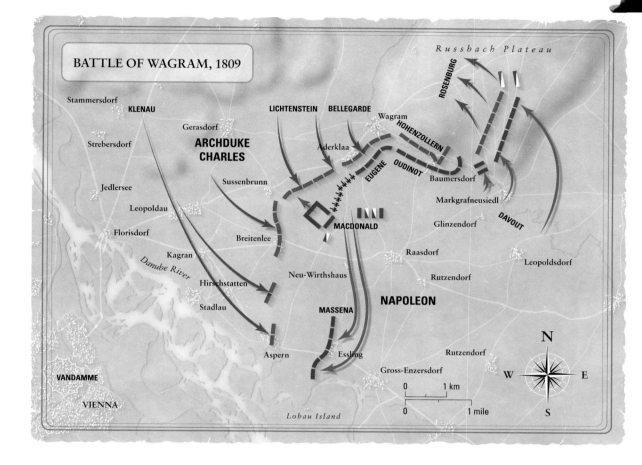

BATTLE OF WAGRAM, 1809

▲ The Duke of Wellington once quipped 'Napoleon's hat was worth 50,000 men on the battlefield.' He often removed it on the battlefield when inspiring soldiers.

◄ Napoleon was to defeat his Austrian opponents at Wagram and bring the War with Austria to a conclusion. The victory was, however, won with heavy losses. Having formed a semicircle, Napoleon ordered an attack on the Austrian centre that was poorly coordinated and finally repulsed. The following day, shown here, saw Charles issue a general attack, intending to draw reserves from the French right whilst simultaneously moving in on the left. The attempt was unsuccessful, with Davout's forces stopping the assault in the east, and Massena's forces stabilizing the situation to the south.

Montmirail and Vauchamps. These battles, however, were not decisive, and the coalition's numerical superiority led to Napoleon's defeat at Arcis-sur-Aube and the capture of Paris.

Napoleon went into brief exile on the island of Elba, but escaped to France in spring 1815 and reclaimed the throne. The Hundred Days (March–June 1815) witnessed the restoration of the coalition, and the culmination of events at Waterloo in Belgium. Using the strategy of the central position, Napoleon kept apart the British (at Quatre-Bras) and the Prussians (at Ligny). The latter were defeated but not pursued, and two days later, when Napoleon engaged the Duke of Wellington at Waterloo, he found the Prussians rallied and on his flank. Napoleon's defeat led to his final exile on the island of St Helena.

NAPOLEON'S ART OF WAR

Napoleon was an innovator. His method of waging war shows clear influences of Bourcet, Guibert and

Du Teil, military reformers who influenced French military thought prior to 1789. Bourcet advocated the employment of a divisional command structure to march armies along parallel but mutually supporting routes. Guibert stressed tactical flexibility to achieve advantage on the battlefield. Finally, Du Teil advocated artillery as a separate branch of the army, not merely a supportive arm.

Although the French army already utilized the divisional system, Napoleon expanded it to create army corps composed of two or more infantry divisions, a cavalry brigade or division, and artillery. Corps numbered 20,000–30,000 men, except during the Russian campaign, where their strengths effectively doubled. A corps was a self-contained fighting unit, able to maintain itself in combat for a day until reinforcements arrived. Napoleon employed corps with great skill, deploying his armies on a broad strategic front and then concentrating them rapidly in the operational theatre.

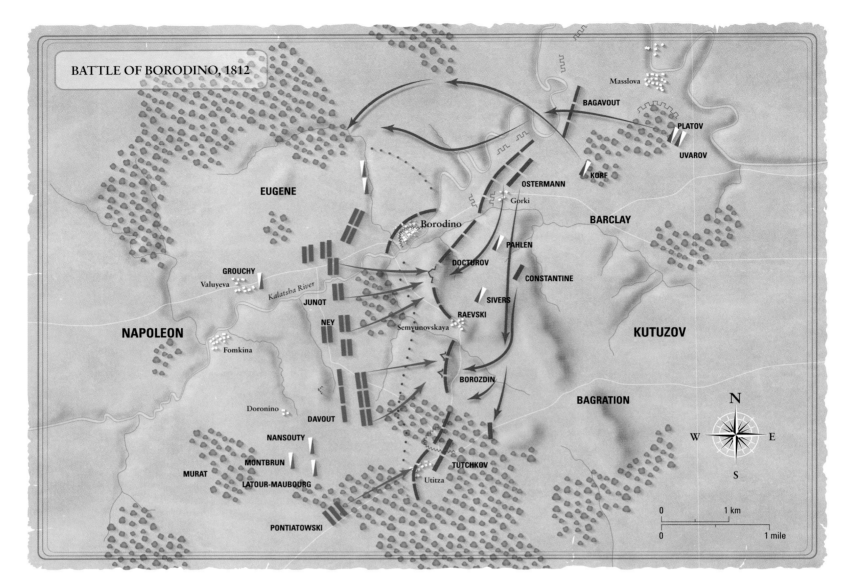

BATTLE OF BORODINO, 1812

Masslova

BAGAVOUT

PLATOV

UVAROV

KORF

OSTERMANN

Gorki

BARCLAY

EUGENE

Borodino

PAHLEN

DOCTUROV

CONSTANTINE

GROUCHY

Valuyeva

Kalatsha River

SIVERS

JUNOT

RAEVSKI

NEY

Semyunovskaya

NAPOLEON

KUTUZOV

Fomkina

BOROZDIN

Doronino

BAGRATION

DAVOUT

NANSOUTY

MONTBRUN

MURAT

LATOUR-MAUBOURG

TUTCHKOV

Utitza

N
W   E
S

0   1 km
0   1 mile

PONTIATOWSKI

▲ The battle of Borodino, fought 70 miles west of Moscow, led to the abandonment of the capital city by Alexander and the Russian army. The battle cost Napoleon and the Russians 50,000 casualties. It began with a successful but costly frontal assault by the French, eventually stalled by Russian reserves. Anticipating the continuation of battle the following day, Napoleon held back his Imperial Guard and a Russian counterattack was defeated with artillery. At nightfall, both sides disengaged and Kutuzov made the decision with his officers to retreat.

Kutuzov (1745–1813)

Mikhail Illarionovich Golenishchev-Kutuzov was the most famous Russian general of the Napoleonic Wars, often referred to as the 'Fox of the North'. During the War of the Third Coalition, he arrived on the Bavarian frontier too late to save the Austrian army at Ulm. Retreating north of Vienna to unite with Tsar Alexander and Buxhowden's army, Kutuzov pleaded with the sovereign to avoid battle at Austerlitz, and was made a scapegoat after the defeat there. Only in 1811 did the Tsar see fit to return him to command, during the Russo-Turkish War. Kutuzov had secured decisive victory by June 1812, forcing the Ottomans to sign the Treaty of Bucharest. Almost immediately, Napoleon's 600,000 troops invaded Russia, and Alexander appointed Kutuzov commander-in-chief of the Russian armies. Kutuzov denied Napoleon battle, making use of Russia's vast spaces. Forced by the Tsar and generals to give battle at Borodino, Kutuzov

lost a third of his army, and Moscow was captured. However, the French winter retreat did represent a critical success for Kutuzov's cautious tactics. The Tsar wanted to pursue the French into central Europe; Kutuzov argued that the army was in no condition to continue its campaign, but was again overruled. He died from illness in Silesia (Poland) in April 1813.

▲ French generals shelter within an infantry square on the left, while more infantry mass on the right for an assault on the Russian-held heights in the middle distance in Louis François Lejeune's painting of Borodino, 7 September 1812.

The corps system, and Napoleon's willingness to rely upon the expert leadership of his marshals and generals, allowed him to position his army and maintain a significant central reserve (which frequently included his Imperial Guard, an additional infantry corps, and a cavalry corps). Napoleon held the reserve until the enemy line wavered at a particular point, and then committed them as a *masse du rupture*. The breaking of the enemy line was followed by a pursuit, hoping to turn a retreat into a rout.

An artillerist by trade, Napoleon understood its critical significance on the battlefield. He attached artillery batteries to each infantry division, and established corps and army reserves. Napoleon often concentrated his corps and army artillery into grand batteries of 70-plus heavy guns to focus their fire on a particular point in the enemy line, as at Wagram, Borodino and Waterloo.

◄ Napoleon possessed many horses during his military career. Marengo was his horse of choice during the Waterloo campaign. Captured after the battle, the horse's skeleton is on display at the British Army Museum in Chelsea, London.

Horatio Nelson

British Naval Hero against France

'My disposition cannot bear tame and slow measures.'
HORATIO NELSON

➤ Rear Admiral Sir Horatio Nelson as depicted by the English portrait painter Lemuel Abbot in 1800. Among the many medals he displays is a 'chelengk' in his hat: this was presented to Nelson by the Ottoman sultan after the battle of the Nile, with the 13 diamond-encrusted sprays representing the French ships at that battle.

Horatio Nelson holds a unique position among naval leaders. He has an iconic status among many navies as the ideal of professional dedication. In part he owes this to the circumstances of his death at the battle of Trafalgar (1805) and the popular impression of the significance of that battle. However, recent scholarship has confirmed that Nelson exercised qualities of aggressive leadership that, by the end of his life, raised him far above his contemporaries.

NELSON'S EARLY CAREER

The son of the Rector of Burnham Thorpe, Norfolk, Nelson was imbued with a strong Christian faith, which demanded submission to duty and fate. He always believed in a God-given order of society and that, whatever he did, his fate lay in the hands of an all-powerful God. He joined the Royal Navy aged 12 under the patronage of his uncle, Captain Maurice Suckling. Suckling ensured that Nelson had the opportunities to learn the duties of an officer quickly by sanctioning his dispatch on voyages to the West Indies (1771–72), the Arctic (1773) and to the East Indies (1774–76). The long voyages gave Nelson not only a thorough grounding in seamanship and navigation, but also an understanding of the logistical requirements of managing ships far from home.

After returning from the East Indies and passing his lieutenant's examination in April 1777, he joined the frigate *Lowestoffe*, bound for the West Indies under Captain William Locker, who became his professional mentor. From Locker, he learned the importance of aggression – the frame of mind that put attacking the enemy with confidence in victory at the head of the professional virtues. It was a lesson he put into practice commanding small vessels, assisting land operations and suppressing smuggling in the West Indies between 1778 and 1787.

In June 1787 Nelson returned to England. Although he had proved an extremely capable and dedicated officer, his virtues were not universally recognized. Most important, further employment was blocked by the king's poor opinion of him. To a man of Nelson's temper, fiercely dedicated to his God and king, this was not just a professional setback, but a devastating blow. It may have contributed to his determination to ensure that, in future, his true merits were always faithfully recorded and even proclaimed to the public.

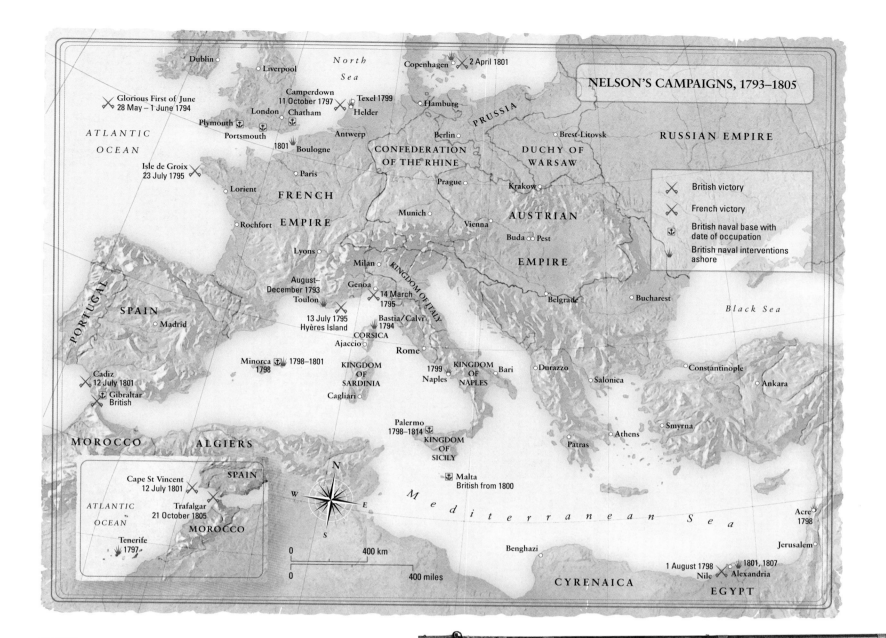

NELSON'S CAMPAIGNS, 1793–1805

Dublin
Liverpool
North Sea
Copenhagen ⚔ 2 April 1801
Glorious First of June
28 May – 1 June 1794
Camperdown
11 October 1797 ⚔ Texel 1799
Hamburg
London Chatham Helder
PRUSSIA
Brest-Litovsk
RUSSIAN EMPIRE
Plymouth ⚓ Portsmouth
Antwerp
Berlin
1801 Boulogne
CONFEDERATION
OF THE RHINE
DUCHY OF
WARSAW
ATLANTIC OCEAN
Paris
Isle de Groix
23 July 1795 ⚔
Lorient
FRENCH
Prague
Krakow
EMPIRE
Rochfort
Munich
AUSTRIAN
Lyons
Vienna
EMPIRE
Buda ⚬ ⚬ Pest
Belgrade
Bucharest
Black Sea

	British victory
⚔	French victory
⚓	British naval base with date of occupation
	British naval interventions ashore

Milan
KINGDOM OF ITALY
August–
December 1793
Toulon
Genoa
14 March
1795
13 July 1795
Hyères Island
Bastia/Calvi
1794
CORSICA
Ajaccio
Rome
KINGDOM
OF
SARDINIA
Cagliari
1799
Naples
KINGDOM
OF
NAPLES
Bari
Durazzo
Salonica
Constantinople
Ankara

PORTUGAL
SPAIN
Madrid
Cadiz
12 July 1801 ⚔
Gibraltar
British ⚓
Minorca ⚓ 1798–1801
1798

Palermo
1798–1814 ⚓
KINGDOM
OF
SICILY
Athens
Smyrna
Patras

MOROCCO   ALGIERS

Cape St Vincent
12 July 1801 ⚔
ATLANTIC OCEAN
SPAIN
Trafalgar
21 October 1805 ⚔
MOROCCO
Tenerife
1797

Malta
British from 1800

N
W E
S
Mediterranean Sea
Acre
1798
Jerusalem

0   400 km
0   400 miles

Benghazi
1 August 1798 ⚔ 1801, 1807
Nile ⚔ Alexandria
CYRENAICA
EGYPT

Key Battles

The Battle of the Nile, 1 August 1798
Brueys's squadron of 16 French warships lies at anchor in line at Aboukir Bay, Egypt. Nelson attacks at dusk, with some ships penetrating to the landward side of the French line to catch them by fire on both sides. The French are overwhelmed, losing 14 of the 16 ships.

The Battle of Copenhagen, 2 April 1801
Nelson attacks Fischer's Danish ships and floating batteries protecting Copenhagen. A hard-fought action ensues, in which British gunnery finally reduces the Danish fire, forcing them to accept the truce that Nelson offers.

The Battle of Trafalgar, 21 October 1805
The weakened Franco-Spanish fleet of 33 ships (under Villeneuve and Gravina) comes out of Cadiz for the Mediterranean, but is caught by Nelson's far more efficient squadron of 27 ships. The Combined Fleet forms line to await the British force, which approaches from windward in two columns. After a feint toward the enemy van, which fixes that part of their force in place, Nelson concentrates his two lines on the centre and rear of the enemy, forcing a melee in which more than 20 enemy ships are taken or burned.

▲▲ Over a period of 21 years Nelson fought campaigns and battles across Western Europe, in Scandinavia, North Africa and in the Canary Islands.

▲ A late 18th-century Turkish rifle which belonged to Nelson, adorned with silver, gilt brass and mother-of-pearl decoration. The rifle may have been a gift from the Sultan of Turkey.

The Rewards of Aggression

In January 1793 Nelson was given command of the *Agamemnon* and ordered to the Mediterranean with Admiral Lord Hood's squadron. Nelson served on detached duties and cooperated with the army in landings on Corsica in 1794. His great confidence contrasted with the soldiers' extreme caution. Nelson's wish to make a frontal assault on the town of Bastia was rejected by a council of war. Instead, the town fell after a blockade and formal siege of about five weeks, with few losses to the attackers. The attack on the town of Calvi followed a similar pattern. Nelson commanded the seamen serving batteries attacking the town. It was here, on 12 July, that stones thrown up by a French shot, struck Nelson in the face, permanently depriving him of sight in the right eye. The town fell on 10 August, but Nelson was dissatisfied with the reports in London as he felt they did not recognize his part in the conquests adequately.

> *'First gain the victory and then make the best use of it you can.'*
>
> HORATIO NELSON

► The explosion of the French flagship *L'Orient*, during the Battle of the Nile, dramatically represented in 1800 by Philip James de Loutherbourg. The famous event, which was observed as far away as Alexandria, has been depicted several times.

▼ The Battle of the Nile. Nelson saw the French fleet at anchor at about 14.30 and immediately fell upon them, rather than waiting for the next day. Action commenced at 18.15. Captain Foley in the *Goliath* saw the gap between the head of the French line and the shore, and led the way through, enabling the British to put the French squadron under fire from both sides. Only two French ships of the line and two frigates escaped the annihilation of the squadron.

Nelson continued to serve in the Mediterranean under the command of Admiral Hotham. He did not hide his frustration with Hotham, who, he thought, did not pursue the French vigorously enough in two actions in March and July 1795.

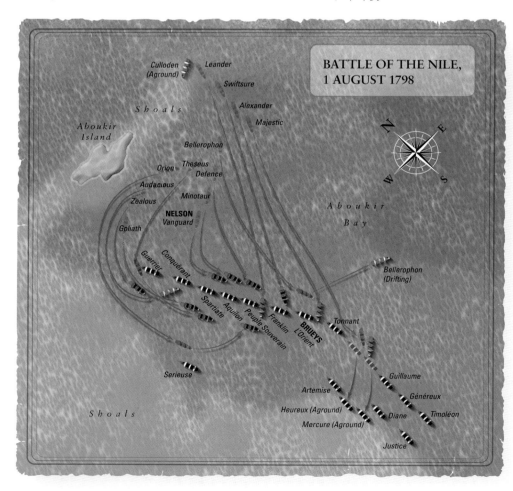

BATTLE OF THE NILE,
1 AUGUST 1798

In November 1795 Hotham was replaced by Admiral Sir John Jervis. Jervis recognized Nelson's abilities and allowed him to act independently on the Italian coast. On 14 February 1797 Jervis's squadron met a Spanish one off Cape St Vincent. The Spanish squadron was sailing in two parts, and Nelson, commanding the *Captain*, fully understood Jervis's intention of getting between them to defeat them in detail. He left the line of battle to cut off the movements of the Spanish ships closing the gap. After a fierce exchange of gunfire, he laid the *Captain* against the *San Nicholas* and led a boarding party, which took the vessel. The prize lay next to the *San Josef*, and Nelson advanced across to take that ship as well. Nelson had played a great part in a major victory, and made sure that his own account of the action was published. He was gratified with public acclaim, flag rank and a knighthood. Jervis then sent Nelson to capture Santa Cruz, Tenerife. However, Nelson's confidence in his own ability in shore actions proved to be misplaced. The well-organized defence resisted the first landing attempt, and when Nelson commanded a second attempt on 24 July 1797, it was driven off with heavy casualties. Among these was Nelson, whose shattered right arm had to be amputated. Despite the failure, Nelson was received in London with great acclaim. After his recovery he was sent to rejoin Jervis (now Earl St Vincent) at Gibraltar.

It was from this point that his quality as a squadron commander became evident.

PUBLIC ACCLAIM

In May 1798 St Vincent sent Nelson with a squadron of 13 ships into the Mediterranean to seek out an expeditionary force rumoured to be assembling in Toulon. The French made it out of Toulon, but Nelson found them at anchor in Aboukir Bay in Egypt on the evening of 1 August. Nelson's squadron was small, and he ensured that each captain had understood his intentions. He immediately attacked, and the French force was devastated in what became known as the Battle of the Nile. Only two out of 16 French ships escaped.

The news made Nelson an unparalleled hero at the time. The Royal Navy was undoubtedly the most powerful naval force in the world. Victories had been won, but this victory was an annihilation of the enemy, which no other commander had achieved. In January 1801 he was appointed second-in-command of an expedition to the Baltic to prevent that sea being closed to British traffic by the armed neutrality of Denmark, Sweden and Russia. The battle of Copenhagen (2 April 1801) was an extremely hard-fought action in shoal waters around that city, but, as their line crumbled, the Danes were forced to accept a truce. Nelson was appointed commander of the squadron to continue the voyage into the Baltic to prevent Russian and Swedish interruption of British trade. However, the murder of Tsar Paul I ended the armed neutrality before Nelson had to engage with them.

Nelson's popularity was now so high that when he returned to Britain he was put in command of the forces in the Channel facing the ports from which France could mount an invasion. His attempts to burn the shipping in Boulogne failed, but his presence was enough to reassure the British public until the Peace of Amiens was signed in October 1801.

SQUADRON COMMAND

With the renewal of war in May 1803 Nelson was appointed commander of the Mediterranean squadron. Here, he demonstrated exemplary squadron command.

The Battle of Trafalgar, 1805	
British	French/ Spaniards
Horatio Nelson	**Charles Silvestre de Villeneuve**
27 ships of the line plus 6 others	France: 18 ships of the line plus 8 others; Spain: 15 ships of the line
Casualties: 449 dead, 1,246 wounded	Casualties: France: 2,218 dead, 1,115 wounded; Spain: 1,025 dead, 1,383 wounded; 21 ships captured, 1 ship destroyed

▲ The British fleet (here shown in the traditional order of sailing) approached the Combined Fleet in two columns; Collingwood, leading the windward column, came into contact with the Combined Fleet line at approximately 12.15 – and the battle of Trafalgar commenced. Nelson, leading the leeward column, came into contact with the enemy line at 12.30. Action continued till around 17.30.

▼ Nelson's uniform undress coat is preserved at the National Maritime Museum in London.

195

HMS *Victory*, Nelson's ship at Trafalgar, now sits preserved in dry dock in Portsmouth, England.
▲ A stateroom on the quarter deck, looking aft to Nelson's cabin.
▼ Cannons in place on one of the gundecks.

For about two years he had to maintain a large force in a condition to move quickly in response to news of French movements. He had to keep up an intelligence network across the Mediterranean to allow him the best chance of anticipating French moves. Most of all he had to ensure that his captains were able and willing to carry out his orders at the time of battle. For this the system of discipline and service at sea certainly prepared them, but understanding the admiral's intentions as the line approached the enemy was beyond the capability of contemporary signalling systems. Nelson did not have with him a unified group of officers that had served under him for years. At Trafalgar (see below) only ten of the 27 captains had served with him before, but he used regular briefings of a changing core of officers to spread the message.

After the French squadron broke out of Toulon in March 1805, Nelson followed the combined Franco-Spanish force across the Atlantic to the West Indies and back. Although he failed to catch up with them

before they reached Corunna in Spain, his squadron was in far better shape for battle than his enemy. By the time the fleets met off Cape Trafalgar on 21 October 1805, Nelson and his officers were clear about his plan of attack. Confident of his own force, he intended to bring on a melee, concentrating on the centre and rear of the enemy to destroy them in detail. The complete destruction of the Franco-Spanish squadron remains one of the outstanding naval victories in history.

Nelson's death at the point of victory cemented his reputation for posterity. His focus on the destruction of the enemy as his primary purpose marks him out. He was sustained in the drive to destroy his enemy by his complete faith in divine providence and by an urgent desire for secular adoration. Fortunately, these psychological factors were matched by practical competence in ship and squadron command, and a clear understanding of his own strengths and the weaknesses of his enemies. Nelson possessed the weapons, the will and ability to achieve great things.

'Duty is the great business of a sea officer; all private considerations must give way to it, however painful it may be.'
HORATIO NELSON

▲ *The Death of Nelson*, an 1807 painting by Arthur Devis. Nelson's supposed last words, 'Kiss me, Hardy', have passed into English folklore — but, although he did speak these words shortly before his death, his actual last words according to conflicting accounts of those present were either 'Thank God I have done my duty' or 'Drink, drink. Fan, fan. Rub, rub' (a request to alleviate his pain).

◄ A 19th-century scene of the battle of Trafalgar (by Auguste Meyer), showing what is possibly the battleship *Redoubtable* in the action of sinking an enemy vessel.

Duke of Wellington

British Victor over Napoleon

'All the business of war, and indeed all the business of life, is to endeavour to find out what you don't know by what you do; that's what I called "guessing what was at the other side of the hill".' DUKE OF WELLINGTON

Empires & Revolutions

Duke of Wellington

A Life in Brief

1769, 1 May
Born Arthur Wellesley in Dublin, Ireland

1805
Knighted

1809
Becomes Viscount Wellington

1812
Field Marshal and Marquis

1814
Becomes Duke of Wellington

1818–27 and 1834–35
Cabinet minister

1828–30
Prime Minister

1852, 14 September
Dies at Walmer Castle, England

➤ A pair of boots once owned and worn by Wellington. Such footwear was as practical as it was elegant and was widely used by officers in European armies of the period, notably by those commanding infantry and light cavalry units.

➤➤ As one of the most prominent members of British society whose fame extended across much of the world, Wellington was a popular subject for portrayal by some of the leading artists of his era, including the celebrated Spanish master Francisco de Goya. Here he is depicted in an 1814 portrait by Thomas Phillips.

With the possible exception of Nelson (pp. 192–97), whom he once met, Wellington remains the most famous military commander that Britain has ever produced. More widely, his record of martial success has seldom been matched. Although one of his siege operations (Burgos, 1812) had to be abandoned, he never lost a battle in the open field. He also emerged victorious from one of history's most celebrated clashes, Waterloo, whereby, together with his Prussian allies, he conclusively defeated Napoleon (pp. 180–91).

While serving in the Low Countries in 1794, where he first saw shots fired in anger, this rather unpromising young officer had complained that none of his colleagues had known 'anything of the management of an army' and that he had thereby 'learnt what one ought not to do'. Thereafter, he rededicated himself to his chosen profession, demonstrating a remarkable flair for it. Certainly, his subsequent campaigns in India (1803–05) and the Iberian Peninsula (1808–14) underscore his mastery of logistics as much as his exceptional *coup d'oeil*, his foresight, courage, patience and remarkable stamina, his careful accumulation and analysis of intelligence, and his fearsome ability to turn the environment to his advantage. Whereas his own mother had sensed he would prove 'food for powder and nothing more', he was to evince a keen understanding of the men under his command and those they opposed, as well as both the weaknesses and strengths of the weaponry they had at their disposal.

FROM INDIA TO IBERIA

Having first joined the army in 1787, Arthur Wellesley (as he then was), exploiting his influential family's wealth and political connections, obtained rapid promotion, becoming a lieutenant-colonel in just six years. He also became MP for Trim in Ireland, the first of several parliamentary seats he was to hold during his career. In 1797, he went with the 33rd Foot to India, of which his brother, Richard, was appointed governor-general the following year. Arthur was given a command in Mysore and subsequently became governor of Seringapatam. When hostilities with the Marathas re-ignited in 1803, Wellesley led an expedition through the Deccan. At Assaye, on 23 September, he assailed a far larger force of enemy troops and put it to flight. Pushing on, he secured another impressive victory at Argaon on 28 November, and captured Gwalior in mid-December.

Further British successes led to an uneasy peace, and Wellesley eventually returned to England, acquiring a knighthood and a new parliamentary seat. Besides serving in the Duke of Portland's administration, he led forces in homeland defence and during the Copenhagen expedition of 1807, earning the 'Sepoy General' still more respect among his peers. It was his exploits in the Peninsular War that were destined to raise his reputation to that of a Marlborough (pp. 158–63), however. As first the Portuguese and then the Spaniards began turning openly against Napoleon, London resolved to establish

◄ This splendid gold cross was awarded to Wellington in recognition of his exploits in the Peninsular War, each of the bars recording one of his victorious campaigns. Besides the honours conferred upon him by the British Crown, he was also granted titles by the Portuguese and Spanish kings, grateful for his services in saving their dynasties and lands from Napoleon.

▼ Wellington's European campaigns were concentrated in the Iberian Peninsula; after victory there the field of operations moved to northern France.

a foothold on the European mainland from which to menace the French empire. Wellesley was duly sent to Portugal with a small army in 1808. He comfortably defeated the French at Vimeiro, but, obliged to surrender his command to more senior officers who arrived at the fighting's climax, was unable to exploit his victory. A pact was concluded with the French, whereby they obtained safe passage home. An official enquiry exonerated Wellesley – soon to be Viscount Wellington – and he rejoined the garrison in Portugal.

Meanwhile, in 1808 Sir John Moore had led most of Britain's disposable forces into Spain, only to be chased off by a huge French army. Nevertheless, his daring thrust had distracted the enemy, giving Moore's colleagues time to consolidate their grip on Portugal. Although he had doubted whether the British toehold there could be maintained, Wellington was persuaded that it could be, provided the Portuguese were willing and enabled to support his Redcoats. Extraordinarily close collaboration ensued, whereby the Portuguese effectively placed their country under his control. Countless labourers helped construct the Lines of Torres Vedras – awesome defences that, arcing from the Tagus to the Atlantic, guarded Lisbon's landward side – while British officers raised, equipped and trained Portuguese soldiers who more than doubled the size of Wellington's army.

Much of this host, together with Lisbon's beleaguered civilian population, were kept supplied with food and *matériel* imported by sea. This mammoth undertaking highlights Wellington's logistical talents. His triumph in the arid peninsula is largely attributable to his success in keeping his forces much better supplied than his opponents frequently were. In seeking to make good any shortfalls, the French endeavoured to live off the land – but to do this effectively, units had to be dispersed, making them easy prey. Moreover, requisitioning often alienated the populace, exacerbating the guerrilla conflict that plagued Napoleon's occupying forces. Although Wellington's own relations with the Spaniards were occasionally tense, his diplomacy, coupled with that of his brother Henry, London's ambassador, proved sufficient to maintain the Anglo-Spanish partnership.

Wellington's peninsular strategy was categorized into two phases, the first of which was essentially defensive and attritional. After an abortive attempt to collaborate with Spanish armies in 1809, he 'rolled with the punch', executing a fighting withdrawal to the Lines. The enemy's attempts to starve him out proved counterproductive, with the French

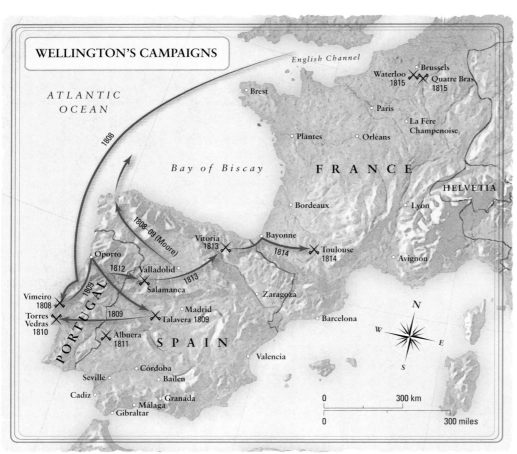

WELLINGTON'S CAMPAIGNS

ATLANTIC OCEAN

English Channel

Brest

Bay of Biscay

FRANCE

HELVETIA

Paris

La Fère Champenoise

Plantes

Orléans

Bordeaux

Lyon

Bayonne

Vitoria 1813

Toulouse 1814

Avignon

Oporto

1812

Valladolid

Salamanca

Zaragoza

Barcelona

Vimeiro 1808

Torres Vedras 1810

Madrid

Talavera 1809

Albuera 1811

SPAIN

Valencia

PORTUGAL

Córdoba

Bailen

Seville

Cadiz

Granada

Málaga

Gibraltar

Brussels
Waterloo 1815
Quatre Bras 1815

1808

1808-09 (Moore)

1809

1809

1813

1814

N
W   E
S

0   300 km

0   300 miles

Key Battles

The Battle of Assaye, 23 September 1803
In India, during the Second-Anglo Maratha War, Wellesley pursues the Maratha force, and encounters Sindhia's far larger army on the banks of the River Kaitna. Wellesley elects to attack and fords the river near the village of Assaye. In what he called 'the bloodiest fighting for the number that I ever saw', Wellesley's forces eventually routed the Marathas.

The Battle of Vitoria, 21 June 1813
Wellington advances across northern Spain in search of a climactic battle with the main French army under King Joseph Bonaparte. His subsequent victory at Vitoria all but sweeps the French from the Iberian Peninsula and coincides with the crumbling of Napoleon's empire in Central Europe.

The Battle of Waterloo, 18 June 1815
Defending the ridge of Mont St Jean, Wellington's polyglot army thwarts Napoleon's attacks. Meanwhile, Blücher's Prussians envelop Napoleon's army's right flank, sealing his downfall.

▲ Wellington is shown visiting the site of Waterloo in this painting by Haydon.

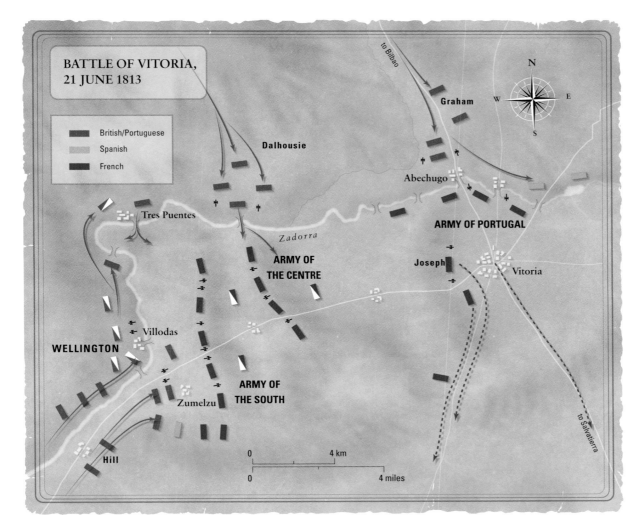

BATTLE OF VITORIA,
21 JUNE 1813

British/Portuguese
Spanish
French

Tres Puentes

Zadorra

Dalhousie

Graham

Abechugo

ARMY OF PORTUGAL

ARMY OF
THE CENTRE

Joseph

Vitoria

to Bilbao

Villodas

WELLINGTON

Zumelzu

ARMY OF
THE SOUTH

Hill

to Salvatierra

0   4 km
0   4 miles

◄ Together with Waterloo, Vitoria is widely regarded as the most spectacular of Wellington's triumphs over Napoleon's armies. The victory that secured Wellington the rank of field marshal, it cleared the French from all but a few enclaves in the Iberian Peninsula, and exposed southern France to invasion by the allied powers. Key to Wellington's success at Vitoria was his discovery of the unguarded bridge at Tres Puentes, which light infantry were able to seize with little difficulty, being concealed by high ground. With British and Portuguese forces already attacking from the north, the French found themselves under attack from several directions and were sent into retreat.

abandoning Portugal for good. The second, offensive phase commenced in 1812; Wellington seized the key fortresses of Badajoz and Ciudad Rodrigo with operations in which he traded some lives for time, so as to preclude any effective response by the French field armies. He subsequently assailed the northernmost of these at Salamanca, compelling his adversaries to relinquish territory in order to muster their strength. After falling back once again, he returned to the attack, routing the French at Vitoria in 1813 and thrusting as far into southern France as Toulouse.

WELLINGTON'S ART OF WAR

In most of his battles, including Waterloo, Wellington's tactics were essentially defensive: his opponents would exhaust themselves in fruitless attacks and then be swept aside by a timely riposte. As they could both take and hold ground, Wellington valued his infantry units the most; any cavalry and cannon usually acted in their support. Once, when asked whether he could ultimately prevail over Napoleon's legions, he pointed at a passing Redcoat, saying, 'It all depends upon that article... Give me enough of it, and I am sure.' British infantry were for the most part exceptionally well

drilled and stoically courageous. Wellington habitually deployed them just two deep, so as to maximize their frontage and, thus, firepower. He had a superb eye for ground and, wherever possible, used it to shield his forces from fire and observation. A thick sheath of skirmishers further helped mask and protect his main infantry formations until he was ready to unleash them. Time and again, French commanders were bewildered by his dispositions, and found that their guns were effectively neutralized by his use of terrain and shallow formations, that their horsemen could make no headway against his unshaken heavy infantry and that their own skirmishers were kept at bay by his numerous light troops. When, at Waterloo, muddy ground and dense, tall crops – which hampered both movement and visibility – compounded these problems, even Napoleon himself succumbed to defeat.

WATERLOO AND BEYOND

The Allied invasion of France in 1814 had secured Napoleon's abdication, but, within months, he had escaped from exile and, in a bloodless coup, toppled France's restored Bourbon monarchy. Europe's great

► Although, on battlefields increasingly dominated by firepower, the scope for employing manual weapons was increasingly limited, swords remained the cardinal arm of European cavalrymen; light horsemen normally carried a sabre, whereas heavy cavalry were armed with long, straight blades. All officers possessed swords, however, if only as emblems of rank and for ceremonial purposes. As is the case with this one, the blades would often be decoratively engraved.

'It is not the business of generals to shoot one another.' WELLINGTON

Duke of Wellington

Empires & Revolutions

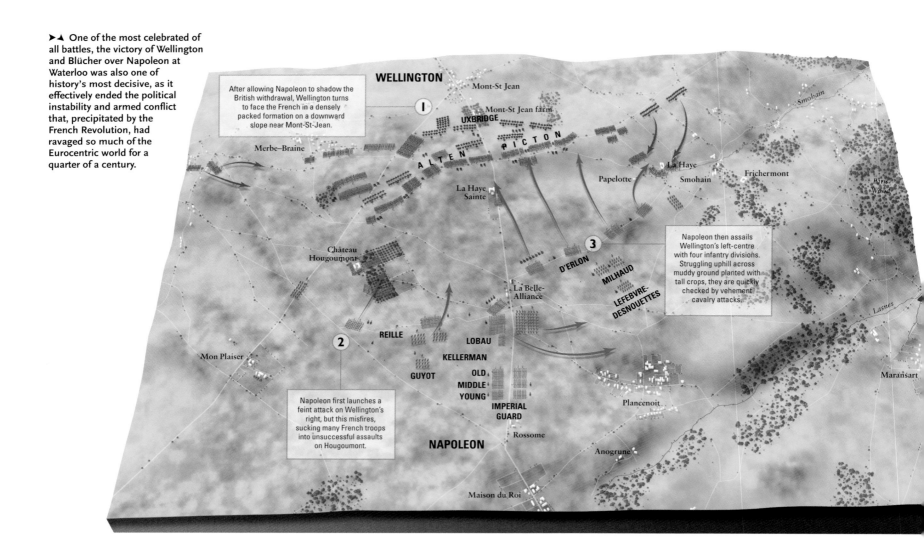

► ▲ One of the most celebrated of all battles, the victory of Wellington and Blücher over Napoleon at Waterloo was also one of history's most decisive, as it effectively ended the political instability and armed conflict that, precipitated by the French Revolution, had ravaged so much of the Eurocentric world for a quarter of a century.

WELLINGTON

Mont-St Jean

After allowing Napoleon to shadow the British withdrawal, Wellington turns to face the French in a densely packed formation on a downward slope near Mont-St-Jean.

1

Mont-St Jean farm

UXBRIDGE

ALTEN   PICTON

Smohain

Merbe–Braine

La Haye
Sainte

Papelotte   La Haye
Smohain   Frichermont

Pars
Wood

Château
Hougoumont

D'ERLON   3

Napoleon then assails Wellington's left-centre with four infantry divisions. Struggling uphill across muddy ground planted with tall crops, they are quickly checked by vehement cavalry attacks.

MILHAUD

LEFEBVRE-DESNOUETTES

La Belle-
Alliance

Lasnes

Mon Plaiser

REILLE   LOBAU

2   KELLERMAN

GUYOT   OLD
MIDDLE
YOUNG

Plancenoit

Maransart

Napoleon first launches a feint attack on Wellington's right, but this misfires, sucking many French troops into unsuccessful assaults on Hougoumont.

**IMPERIAL
GUARD**

NAPOLEON   Rossome

Anogrune

Maison du Roi

The Battle of Waterloo, 1815	
British, Prussians and Allies	French
Duke of Wellington, Gebhard von Blücher	**Napoleon**
67,000 Anglo-Allies, 60,000 Prussians	73,000
Casualties: 23,000 killed or wounded (15,000 Anglo-Allies, 8,000 Prussian)	Casualties: 25,000 killed or wounded, 7,000 captured and 15,000 missing

► Some of Wellington's orders for Waterloo. His subordinates had general instructions to fight a defensive engagement, but unit commanders were given some scope for mounting limited counterattacks on their own initiative. Wellington in any case had a knack for being in the right place at the right time – something he suggested contributed substantially to his overall success – and took control personally wherever and whenever real danger threatened.

powers responded by amassing huge armies to retake France. The foremost of these – an Anglo-Dutch-German force of 112,000 under Wellington and 130,000 Prussians under Field Marshal Blücher – were assembling in Belgium when Napoleon, reasoning that attack was his best defence, crossed the Sambre with 123,000 troops, seeking to prise his opponents apart and defeat each of them in turn. On 16 June, while his army's left wing pinned Wellington down at Quatre Bras, Napoleon assailed Blücher at Ligny, inflicting a severe defeat. With the Allies retreating northwards – the Prussians towards Wavre, Wellington towards Brussels – Napoleon now shifted his weight against Wellington, detaching a third of his remaining troops to contain Blücher. However, this force followed, rather than intercepted, the Prussians, leaving all but their rearguard free to rejoin their allies.

Assured that he would be supported by at least one Prussian army corps, Wellington turned to fight near Waterloo on 18 June. Barely had Napoleon's attack begun when the foremost Prussians reached the battlefield's eastern edge. Already struggling to make inroads into Wellington's strong defensive position, ever more of Napoleon's forces had to be diverted into warding off this threat. By evening, the Allies had twice as many troops on the field as the French, whom they routed with converging attacks. Within days, Napoleon had abdicated again, ending the war he had so recklessly revived.

Thereafter, Wellington was to play a major role in his country's internal politics, briefly serving as prime minister. Too accustomed to giving orders, however, he found the compromises of parliamentary democracy irksome, and his resistance to electoral reform in particular made him so unpopular that he had to have metal shutters fitted to the windows of his London home to shield them from stone-throwing critics. Similarly, his conservatism had a stultifying effect when he became the administrative head of Britain's army from 1842, leaving that force ill-prepared for the Crimean War (1853–56).

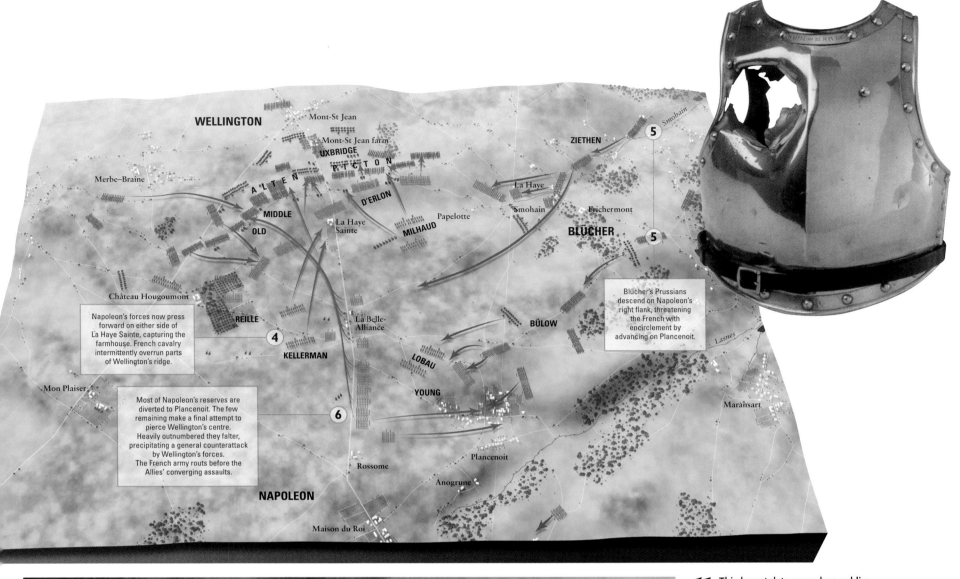

WELLINGTON

Mont-St Jean

ZIETHEN · 5 · Smohain

Mont-St Jean farm

UXBRIDGE

PICTON

Merbe–Braine

A L T E N

La Haye

MIDDLE

D'ERLON

Smohain

Frichermont

OLD

La Haye
Sainte

Papelotte

MILHAUD

BLÜCHER · 5 ·

Château Hougoumont

REILLE

La Belle-
Alliance

BÜLOW

Blücher's Prussians
descend on Napoleon's
right flank, threatening
the French with
encirclement by
advancing on Plancenoit.

Napoleon's forces now press
forward on either side of
La Haye Sainte, capturing the
farmhouse. French cavalry
intermittently overrun parts
of Wellington's ridge.

· 4 ·

KELLERMAN

LOBAU

Lasnes

Mon Plaiser

Most of Napoleon's reserves are
diverted to Plancenoit. The few
remaining make a final attempt to
pierce Wellington's centre.
Heavily outnumbered they falter,
precipitating a general counterattack
by Wellington's forces.
The French army routs before the
Allies' converging assaults.

· 6 ·

YOUNG

Maransart

Rossome

Plancenoit

NAPOLEON

Anogrune

Maison du Roi

▼◄ This breastplate, worn by a soldier
of the Second Carabinier Regiment and
pierced by a cannonball at Waterloo, is
typical of the body armour worn by French
heavy cavalry. Pigeon-breasted, such a
cuirass was capable of resisting not only
sword-cuts but also pistol- and musket-
balls fired from a distance. Cannon-shot
was another matter, however, as the
damage to this one demonstrates.

◄ This dramatic oil painting of Waterloo
by Denis Dighton is the artist's impression
of the closing stages of battle. Wellington
is pictured in the bottom right-hand
corner, directing the general counterattack
of his Anglo-Dutch-German troops against
the recoiling French.

*'Next to a lost
battle, nothing is
so sad as a battle
that has been
won.'* WELLINGTON

4

The
Modern
Age

◄◄ American infantry wade in: the 165th Infantry Assault Wave attack the Gilbert Islands in November 1943. Coral bottom waters and Japanese machine gun fire from the right flank made progress slow. Admiral Nimitz was the strategic director of this offensive in the Central Pacific. These were difficult assaults on well-prepared and highly motivated defenders, but American successes in the Gilberts helped prepare the way for operations against the Marshall Islands.

▼ Trench scene with British troops, 1916. In that year there was an ambitious ground plan for a series of concerted assaults by the Allies on all major German fronts. Designed to inflict sufficient all-round damage on the German army, not least by forcing them to use up their reserves, to permit follow-up attacks that would achieve the long-awaited breakthrough, this strategy was derailed by the pre-emptive German assault on French-held Verdun in February 1916. This obliged the British to take a greater share in the eventual Anglo-French attack on the Somme in July 1916. The attack was poorly prepared, both in the sense of inadequate supporting firepower and in the definition of attainable objectives.

Military command became more complex from the 19th century as the scale and complexity of war increased, in part a consequence of the new technology of conflict. The example of Chester Nimitz (pp. 274–79), the commander of the American fleet in the Pacific during World War II who had to face the unprecedented challenge of carrier warfare, is a pertinent one. Prior to the outbreak of war between Japan and the USA, no two powers had fought each other using aircraft carriers, and it was thus a matter of learning on the job. Indeed, until that point it had been assumed that the conflict would be largely contested by battleships.

Technology had also advanced in areas other than military systems, notably communications, in the form of railways, steamships, the telegraph and radio, and surveillance, particularly radar. Moltke the Elder (pp. 214–17) owed his effective command of the Prussians during the Wars of German Unification (1864–71) to his understanding of how to make best use of the new rail and telegraph systems;

his aim was to enable Prussia to mobilize and deploy its troops rapidly, and in doing so to provide force multipliers that could be used for operational purposes. Indeed, Moltke encouraged the development of these systems to this end, and as a result ensured the enhancement of Prussian strategic power.

The increases in military range and capabilities applied not only to air power over both sea and land, but also to submarine warfare and, from the 1940s, to the use of long-range missiles. This further stretched command skills, particularly at the strategic level, and not least in the challenge to combine the advantages of these varied means of warfare and to distribute resources to each accordingly. These skills were in part those associated with the management of large-scale military coalitions. Thus, in World War II George C. Marshall (p. 264), the US chief-of-staff, played a key role in helping reconcile different views and interests within the branches of service, and directing them to ensure the furtherance of strategic goals. These problems were even greater when the alliances involved were between different powers, and overcoming them was part of the skill of Eisenhower (pp. 258–67). Like George Washington (pp. 174–79), he was a supremely political general, and in the best of senses, able to contain contrasting views, not least those of difficult and competing generals.

Operational skills remained an important aspect of military command. They were seen, for example, in the

very different campaigning of Ulysses S. Grant (pp. 218–25) during the American Civil War (1861–65), and Georgy Zhukov (pp. 268–73), the most effective Soviet general during the war with Germany between 1941 and 1945. Grant was particularly important because he displayed a new style of Union generalship. Under his predecessors, very bloody battles had been fought, such as Antietam (1862) and Gettysburg (1863), but these had been interspersed with periods in which there was singularly little main-force conflict. In contrast, Grant introduced to the crucial eastern theatre a high tempo of operations in which the Army of the Potomac made repeated attacks on the Confederates. This helped make the war more attritional, which ensured that the advantages the Union possessed (namely greater resources) were effectively brought to bear. Grant thus combined operational acuity and strategic insight

Zhukov showed another characteristic shared by many leading commanders, that of effectiveness against more than one opponent. The defeat he inflicted on the Japanese in 1939 helped encourage the latter to turn against Britain and the USA, which was of great advantage to the Soviet Union when Germany attacked in 1941. In the latter war, Zhukov proved able to combine mobility and firepower adeptly, and showed himself to be a master of the combination of manoeuvre operations with attritional tactics and strategy; this led to victory over Germany. Zhukov subsequently became Soviet Minister of Defence, proving that he was more than simply an effective commander in the field.

Future conflict is likely to continue to demand the skills previously discussed. However, if there is high-spectrum warfare between major powers, it will probably result in a more rapid operational tempo than has been the case until now.

▲ Ulysses S. Grant, shown here in a contemporary painting flanked by his generals, helped bring a new relentlessness to the strategy of the Union forces in the American Civil War. Although the term 'total war' was not employed, the practice of Grant, Sherman and others is seen as important. Moreover in field command in 1864–65, Grant added a strategic purposefulness and impetus to Union military policy. In the Overland Campaign, Grant subordinated the individual battle to the repeated pressure of campaigning against the confederates.

▼ A German soldier on the Eastern Front in World War II. The Germans were eventually outfought as a result of improvements in Soviet warmaking, especially operational technique.

Shaka Zulu

Leader who Forged a New Force in Southern Africa

'See that the gate of my kraal is closed properly and let none of Zwide's young bulls escape.' SHAKA ZULU, AT THE BATTLE OF GQOKLI HILL

A Life in Brief

c. 1787
Born in KwaZulu, South Africa

1828, 22 September
Assassinated near Dukuza, South Africa

Shaka remains a controversial and repeatedly reinterpreted military leader to this day, but it is clear that he was a commander of outstanding ability. An able tactician, strategist and statesman, he changed the nature of warfare in southern Africa. In addition, through the creation of new political and military structures, he developed and expanded the Zulu kingdom.

▶ Shaka, King of the Zulus. In this, his only contemporary portrait, Shaka poses majestically in war dress. Rising from obscurity, Shaka created the most powerful military state in southern Africa and his memory remains a potent political force in the region even now.

◀ Shaka's 'Stick of Authority'. Chiefs and men of distinction often carried staffs as symbols of their high rank. Shaka's ornately carved personal staff marked him as ruler over all the various clans he had amalgamated to form the Zulu state.

It is difficult to achieve a balanced reconstruction of Shaka's life and achievements. His early years can be glimpsed only through oral tradition, much of it enshrouded in heroic myth, while his later years were first chronicled by European outsiders who blatantly sought to vilify him. Through the 20th century, historical interpretations diverged widely, some casting him as a great military innovator and empire builder and others emphasizing his alleged psychoses and ferocity. More recently, revisionists have argued that Shaka's reputation has been almost entirely shaped by contemporary South African power struggles, with some even offering an essentially demilitarized view of him. Beneath these veneers of distortion and exaggeration, however, one still perceives a gifted military commander whose significance to military history is considerable.

Rejected by his father, a minor chief, Shaka spent a difficult childhood as an outcast in the KwaZulu/Natal region, in which, for various reasons, competition for pastoral resources had become acute by the early 19th century. Frequent clashes encouraged the emergence of politico-military coalitions, with one of the strongest led by Dingiswayo of Mthethwa. In his service Shaka built a reputation as a skilled warrior, and ascended to the chieftaincy of the small Zulu clan. In 1818 he defeated Dingiswayo's main rivals, the Ndwandwe of Chief Zwide, at Gqokli Hill. After the death of Dingiswayo, Shaka gained command of Mthethwa and Zulu forces.

While his military innovations have been wildly exaggerated in some accounts, Shaka does appear to have realized that short stabbing spears and enveloping tactical formations could be used to deadly effect in face-to-face confrontations, and moved away from the more tentative combat of earlier warfare. He also converted a system of age-based regiments into a standing army of 15,000 men. Relentlessly employing his well-trained and disciplined troops to win decisive victories, he altered the very mode of southern African warfare. His regimental system also promoted centralized control over his expanding, well-ordered state, while at the same time increasing a sense of corporate identity among his people and facilitating the incorporation of outsiders. Having broken Ndwandwe power at the battles of Mhlatuze and Ndolowane, Shaka entrusted field command of further territorial expansions to lieutenants, resulting in an over-extension of his power. Although again exaggerated in some accounts, Shaka's growing political ruthlessness contributed to his being assassinated by his half-brothers in 1828.

Overcoming tremendous odds, Shaka transformed himself from outsider to political centralizer and created the most powerful warrior nation in southern Africa. His memory remains a potent force in political and ethnic struggles that still continue in South Africa.

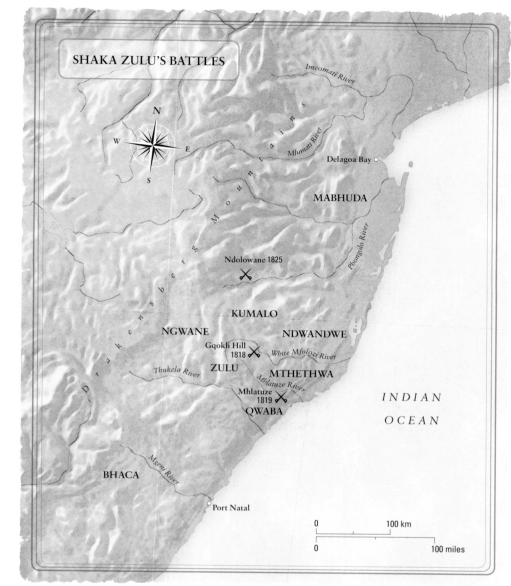

SHAKA ZULU'S BATTLES

Incomati River

Mlumati River

Delagoa Bay

MABHUDA

Phongolo River

Ndolowane 1825 ⚔

KUMALO

NGWANE · NDWANDWE

Gqokli Hill 1818 ⚔ · White Mfolozi River

Thukela River · ZULU · MTHETHWA

Mhlatuze River

Mhlatuze 1819 ⚔

QWABA

INDIAN OCEAN

BHACA

Mgeni River

Port Natal

0   100 km
0   100 miles

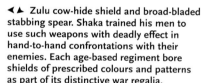

◄▲ Zulu cow-hide shield and broad-bladed stabbing spear. Shaka trained his men to use such weapons with deadly effect in hand-to-hand confrontations with their enemies. Each age-based regiment bore shields of prescribed colours and patterns as part of its distinctive war regalia.

▲ Shaka's world: a map of the Zulu/Natal region of southern Africa showing the territories of ethnic groups with whom Shaka was allied and against whom he campaigned. Eventually he would bring the entire area under his control.

Key Battles and Campaigns

The Battle of Gqokli Hill, 1818
In his first major battle, Shaka intercepts and defeats Zwide's army as it crosses the White Mfolozi River.

The Mhlatuze Campaign, 1819
Shaka wages a guerrilla campaign against Ndwandwe attacks under Zwagendaba and Soshangane, culminating in a major victory at Mhlatuze.

The Battle of Ndolowane, 1825
Shaka decisively crushes Zwide's son and successor, Sikhunyana, destroying Ndwandwe power.

◄ Although dating from many years after Shaka, these Zulu warriors display costumes and arms quite similar to those in use during Shaka's time. Their shields, feathers and furs constitute the specific 'uniform' of their particular age-regiment. Shaka converted such regiments into a highly effective standing army that would fundamentally alter the mode of warfare in southern Africa.

Simón Bolívar

Hero of the Latin American Wars of Independence

'Those who serve a revolution plough the sea.'

SIMÓN BOLÍVAR

A Life in Brief

1783, 24 July
Born in Caracas, Venezuela

1797
Serves as a cadet in the colonial militia

1811, 23 July
Fights his first battle at Valencia

1813, 14 October
Granted the title Captain-General and Liberator of Venezuela

1814, 27 November
Named General-in-Chief by the New Granadan government

1824, 24 February
Named dictator of Peru

1828, August
Becomes de facto dictator of Colombia

1830, January
Renounces power and, in frustration, plans to enter voluntary exile

1830, 17 December
Dies near Santa Marta, Colombia

◀ **Portrait of Bolívar by the Peruvian soldier and artist José Gil de Castro, 1825.**

◀◀ **Bolívar campaigned widely in South America, liberating a huge area.**

▶▶ **Simón Bolívar and Francisco de Paula Santander travelling to Bogotá with the army of the 'Liberator' after the battle of Boyacá, 10th August 1819, as depicted by the 19th-century artist Francisco de Paula Alvarez.**

Bolívar has been referred to as 'the Spanish-American George Washington'. He commanded an army that liberated an area of South America equal to that which Napoleon had conquered in Europe. He crafted a union of three entities (Venezuela, New Granada and Ecuador) into Colombia, and articulated a plan for Spanish-American continental union. Though reviled by many at the time of his death, in modern Latin America Bolívar is considered the most significant of Spanish-American military commanders and statesmen in the wars of independence.

Save for a brief stint in the Spanish colonial militia, Bolívar had no formal military training. However, in the early years of the Spanish-American Wars of Independence (1810–25), he fiercely opposed the notion that autonomy rather than outright independence was the best way of preserving the political, and especially the social, privileges of Venezuela's white Creole (American-born Spaniards) elite, the class to which he belonged. When the first Venezuelan republic collapsed in July 1812, he blamed its failure on its federalist structure and in May 1813 led an army of New Granadans in the 'Admirable Campaign' to recover Caracas. To inspire the patriot cause (and to impress the British) he declared that Creoles would be spared even if neutral or guilty of aiding the royalists but Spaniards, even if neutral, would be killed. Nonetheless, the second Venezuelan republic failed after the Spaniards mustered slaves and coloured people into a guerrilla army that ravaged the countryside and invaded Venezuela's cities. From late 1814 to late 1816 Bolívar was an exile.

In his effort to recapture Venezuela, Bolívar sought Haitian aid, pledging to give freedom to any slave who fought for the revolution. From early 1817 onwards, his war strategy and tactics changed, and he was determined to move to the offensive. He resolved to win the war in the countryside and strengthen his ranks with coloured and black soldiers, many of them from the defiantly independent people of the Venezuelan plains. His Creole friends warned about the dangers of using a liberating force of coloured troops, reminding Bolívar of the race war unleashed during the Haitian revolution. Bolívar responded by saying that if whites did most of the dying, then only people of colour would remain to rule over the new republics.

In 1818 European (mostly British) veterans from the Napoleonic Wars arrived to provide a disciplined core to Bolívar's remodelled army. He liberated New Granada and carried the war south into Ecuador and Peru, achieving final victory in 1824.

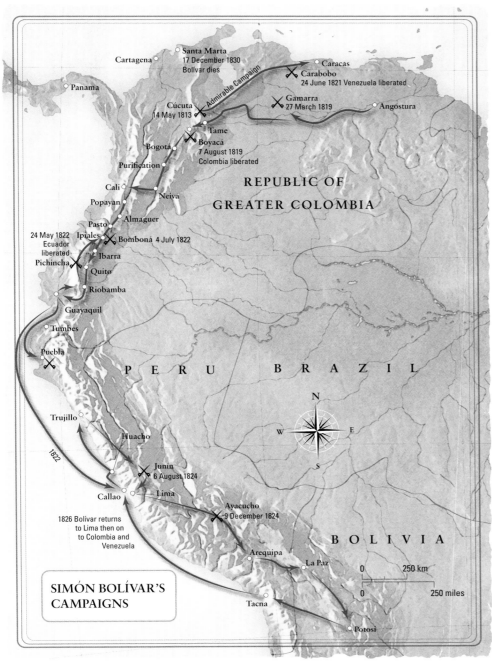

Map labels (SIMÓN BOLÍVAR'S CAMPAIGNS)

Cartagena
Panama
Santa Marta
17 December 1830
Bolívar dies
Caracas
Carabobo
24 June 1821 Venezuela liberated
Cúcuta
14 May 1813
Gamarra
27 March 1819
Angóstura
Admirable Campaign
Tame
Boyacá
7 August 1819
Colombia liberated
Bogotá
Purification
Cali
Popayan
Neiva
Almaguer
Pasto
24 May 1822
Ecuador
liberated
Ipiales
Bombona 4 July 1822
Pichincha
Ibarra
Quito
Riobamba
Guayaquil
Tumbes
Puebla

REPUBLIC OF
GREATER COLOMBIA

PERU
BRAZIL
BOLIVIA

Trujillo
Huacho
1822
Junín
6 August 1824
Callao
Lima
1826 Bolívar returns
to Lima then on
to Colombia and
Venezuela
Ayacucho
9 December 1824
Arequipa
La Paz
Tacna
Potosí

0   250 km
0   250 miles

SIMÓN BOLÍVAR'S
CAMPAIGNS

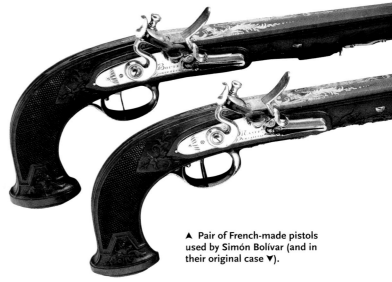

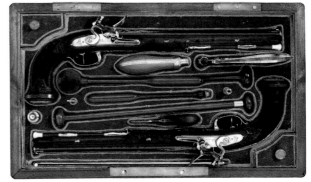

▲ Pair of French-made pistols
used by Simón Bolívar (and in
their original case ▼).

Key Battles and Campaigns

Venezuelan War of Independence, 1811–23
Bolívar leads the 'Admirable Campaign' (May–August 1813),
and retakes Caracas from the Spanish-backed royalist forces.
After the second republic collapses, he conducts campaigns
in Venezuela between January 1817 and February 1818.

The Battle of Boyacá, 7 August 1819
Following his invasion of New Granada (Colombia), Bolívar
defeats the Spanish at Boyacá, capturing 1,800 prisoners,
including the royalist commander. The victory leads to the
taking of Bogotá three days later.

The Battle of Junín, 6 August 1824
Between April 1822 and December 1824, Bolívar marches into
Ecuador and Peru, the last bastion of Spain's empire in South
America. At Junín, Peru, his men defeat the Spanish using
sabres and lances.

Giuseppe Garibaldi

Flamboyant Nationalist General in the Wars of Italian Unification

'I do not reject any enterprise, no matter how hazardous, when it comes to fighting the enemies of our country.' GIUSEPPE GARIBALDI

A Life in Brief

1807, 4 July
Born in Nice

1833, April
Meets Giuseppe Mazzini, proponent of Italian unification, and pledges to dedicate his life to the liberation of his homeland

1882, 2 June
Dies on the island of Caprera

▶ Giuseppe Garibaldi, here in his late 40s, travelled widely and led a life that epitomized the romantic libertarianism of his age.

Garibaldi first came to prominence as the leading military figure of the Risorgimento, the Italian national unification movement of the mid-19th century that sought to bring together the different states of the Italian peninsula. A talented and flamboyant leader of men, feted by his red-shirted followers, he fought for the independence of several other countries, and personified the romantic ideals of liberty and valour.

Garibaldi spent his early professional life as a merchant captain. His political interest was already strong, and he was soon involved in a failed uprising in Piedmont in 1834. Garibaldi fled to Latin America, and during his time in Brazil and Uruguay, where he adopted various independent causes, he absorbed local guerrilla warfare techniques. During his time in Uruguay, in 1842, he founded the Italian Legion, and it was here that his troops adopted their famous red shirts.

Following the outbreak of the First Italian War of Independence in 1848, Garibaldi returned to Italy. He arrived too late to play a significant role in the campaign, but the following year went to the aid of the newly declared Roman Republic, formerly part of the Papal States. The French sent an expeditionary force to quash the republic which Garibaldi defeated. When the Republic collapsed on 30 June 1849, he made a brilliant withdrawal through Central Italy.

Garibaldi fled Italy once more, and spent time in New York and South America, before heading back to Italy. In 1859 the Second Italian War of Independence broke out, and now a regular brigade commander, his heavily outnumbered troops defeated the Austrians twice at Varese and San Fermo.

Garibaldi's finest hour came in May 1860, when he landed in Sicily with 'the Thousand' in an attempt to liberate it from Bourbon control. He captured Palermo and other key towns, before crossing the Straits of Messina. He entered Naples on 7 September, and defeated the Bourbon army at the battle of Volturno in early October. The unification of Italy was now assured, and Garibaldi retired to the island of Caprera. In 1862, he attempted a further march on Rome, but Garibaldi's passage was challenged by regular Italian troops, resulting in his arrest and detention.

In 1866, during the Third Italian War of Independence, his regular-army force campaigned in Trentino province, defeating the Austrians six times in 18 days, notably at Bezzecca. In 1867 he led a further march on Rome with 6,000 volunteers, but pro-papal French troops defeated him at the battle of Mentana on 3 November, and Garibaldi spent a brief period in captivity before being released. His final campaign came in 1870–71, when he fought with the Army of the Vosges in defence of the newly declared French Third Republic against German invaders.

Key Battles

The Defence of Rome, April–June 1849

Garibaldi's volunteers come to the aid of the nascent Roman Republic. His troops man the walls of the city and repel determined French attacks under General Charles Oudinot. However, Garibaldi's men are forced to leave the city.

The Battle of Milazzo, 20 July 1860

During the expedition of the Thousand on Sicily, Garibaldi attacks the Bourbon-loyal city on 20 July. The Bourbon troops put up a stiff defence, but reinforcements fail to reach them, and Garibaldi's 5,000-strong force takes the city.

The Battle of Bezzecca, 21 July 1866

During the Third Italian War of Independence, which led on from the outbreak of the Franco-Prussian War, Garibaldi's force invades Trentino province in an attempt to drive the Austrians from northeast Italy. His men recapture the city of Bezzecca using artillery fire and an infantry assault.

'Rome or death!'

GIUSEPPE GARIBALDI

▼ *Garibaldi with the Red Shirts in the Battle of Calatafimi*, a late 19th-century depiction by Remigio Legat. The site of the battle is today marked by a grandly conceived obelisk monument.

▶ The unification of Italy in 1860, after the defeat of the Bourbons in Sicily, was the crowning moment of Garibaldi's illustrious career. Much of what he learned of warfare came from his experiences fighting alongside guerrilla troops in South America, where he aided several independent causes.

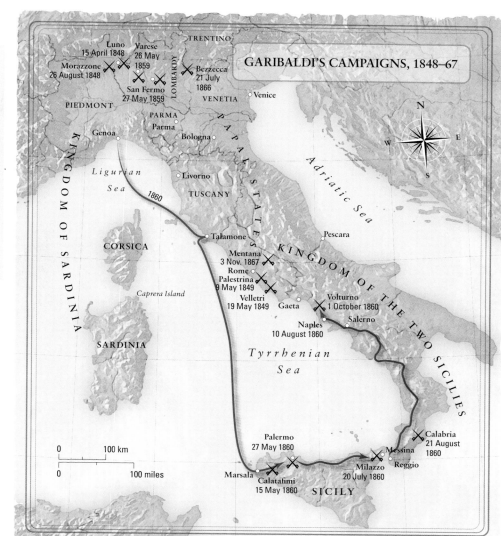

GARIBALDI'S CAMPAIGNS, 1848–67

Luno 15 April 1848 · Varese 26 May 1859 · TRENTINO · Morazzone 26 August 1848 · San Fermo 27 May 1859 · LOMBARDY · Bezzeca 21 July 1866 · VENETIA · Venice · PIEDMONT · PARMA · Parma · Bologna · Genoa

Ligurian Sea · 1860 · Livorno · TUSCANY · PAPAL STATES · Adriatic Sea · Pescara

KINGDOM OF SARDINIA · CORSICA · Talamone · Mentana 3 Nov. 1867 · Rome · Palestrina 9 May 1849 · Velletri 19 May 1849 · Gaeta · Volturno 1 October 1860 · Salerno · Naples 10 August 1860 · KINGDOM OF THE TWO SICILIES

Caprera Island

SARDINIA · *Tyrrhenian Sea*

Calabria 21 August 1860 · Messina · Milazzo 20 July 1860 · Reggio

Palermo 27 May 1860 · Marsala · Calatafimi 15 May 1860 · SICILY

0 — 100 km
0 — 100 miles

Moltke the Elder

Key Prussian General in the Wars of German Unification

'In the long run, luck is awarded to the efficient.'
MOLTKE THE ELDER

A Life in Brief

1800, 26 October
Born in Parchim, in the state of
Mecklenburg-Schwerin, Germany

1857
Becomes Chief of the Prussian
General Staff

1866
Field Marshal

1891, 24 April
Dies in Berlin

▶ **General Field Marshal Helmuth Count
von Moltke as depicted by Franz Seraph
von Lenbach in 1890, a year before his
death. Moltke masterminded Prussian
victories over Austria in 1866 and France
in 1870–71.**

◀◀ **Map showing Moltke's three
campaigns that paved the way for
Bismarck's unification of Germany.**

▼ **Prussian Balloon Musket, designed,
at the request of Moltke, to shoot down
observation balloons.**

Count Helmuth Karl Bernhard von Moltke (known as
Moltke the Elder, to distinguish him from his nephew
Helmuth Johann Ludwig von Moltke) is an example
of a great commander whose contribution focused
on organization, rather than leadership on the field
of battle, although he had considerable experience
of the latter. His victories over the Danes (Danish-
Prussian War, 1864), Austrians (Austro-Prussian War,
1866) and French (Franco-Prussian War, 1870–71)
contributed greatly to the Prussian reputation
for military genius, which endured well into the
20th century.

Initially trained in the Danish army, Moltke
switched to its Prussian counterpart in 1821, joining
the Prussian general staff in 1833. Sent to help advise
the Ottoman army in Armenia in 1835, he entered
the sultan's service, and fought the Egyptians
in 1839.

Rejoining the general staff, Moltke became
its chief in 1857 and greatly reorganized it in the
period 1858–59. He adapted Napoleonic ideas of
the continuous offensive to the practicalities of
the industrial age, incorporating the advantages in
communication and movement that railways brought.
In place of frontal attack, which he decried in 1864
in his *Remarks on the Influence of Improved Rifles on
the Attack*, Moltke sought to envelop opposing forces
and to oblige them to mount such attacks themselves
in an effort to regain freedom of manoeuvre. In this
way, the benefits that rifled weapons and the scale of
conflict had given the defence could be countered.
Moltke aimed for a rapid conclusion to any war
through decisive victory in battle, which would destroy
the ability of the enemy forces to continue effective

resistance. Moltke noted the preference for battle over
conquest in his *Instructions for Large-Unit Commanders*,
which appeared in 1869.

The Prussians developed a system of general
staff work and training at a dedicated academy, and
it was this body that was given much of the credit for
victory over Austria in 1866 and France in 1870–71.
The training of staff officers gave the Prussian army
a coherence its opponents lacked, and the academy's
graduates knew their place in a coordinated command
system. The system of joint responsibility between
field commanders and staff officers provided not only
a necessary coherence, but also a means to ensure
the high level of forward planning that was valuable
in order to maintain the effectiveness of offensive

Modern Age   **Moltke the Elder**

214

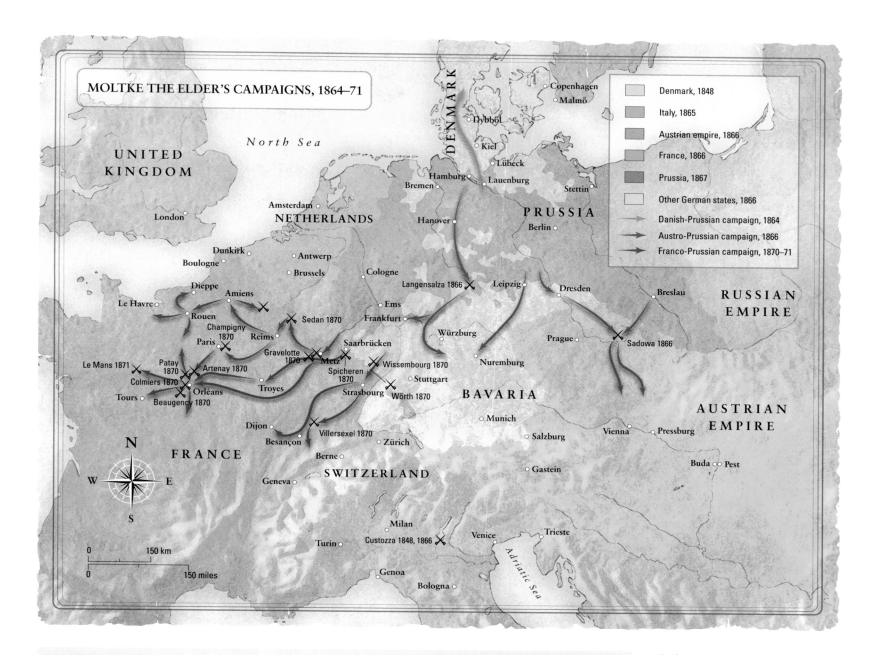

MOLTKE THE ELDER'S CAMPAIGNS, 1864–71

North Sea

UNITED KINGDOM

DENMARK

Copenhagen
Malmö
Dybbøl
Kiel
Lübeck
Lauenburg
Stettin

Hamburg
Bremen
Hanover
Amsterdam
NETHERLANDS
London
Berlin
PRUSSIA

Dunkirk
Boulogne
Dieppe
Amiens
Antwerp
Brussels
Cologne
Langensalza 1866
Leipzig
Dresden
Breslau

RUSSIAN EMPIRE

Le Havre
Rouen
Champigny 1870
Reims
Sedan 1870
Frankfurt
Würzburg
Prague
Sadowa 1866

Paris
Gravelotte 1870
Metz
Saarbrücken
Nuremburg

Le Mans 1871
Patay 1870
Artenay 1870
Spicheren 1870
Wissembourg 1870
Stuttgart
Colmiers 1870
Orléans
Troyes
Strasbourg
Wörth 1870
BAVARIA
AUSTRIAN EMPIRE
Tours
Beaugency 1870

Dijon
Villersexel 1870
Zürich
Munich
Salzburg
Vienna
Pressburg
Besançon

FRANCE
Geneva
Berne
SWITZERLAND
Gastein
Buda Pest

N
W E
S

Milan
Venice
Trieste
Turin
Custozza 1848, 1866
Adriatic Sea
Genoa
Bologna

0   150 km
0   150 miles

Legend:
- Denmark, 1848
- Italy, 1865
- Austrian empire, 1866
- France, 1866
- Prussia, 1867
- Other German states, 1866
- → Danish-Prussian campaign, 1864
- → Austro-Prussian campaign, 1866
- → Franco-Prussian campaign, 1870–71

Key Battles

The Battle of Sadowa (Königgrätz), 3 July 1866
In the decisive battle of the Austro-Prussian War, the Austrians, under Lajos von Benedek, are unable to take advantage of their interior position, and are outmanoeuvred by the Prussians at Sadowa (Czech Republic) near the River Elbe. The Prussian units possess a flexibility in attack that their opponents lack, and this ensures that the Austrian positions are caught in the flank and hit by crossfire.

The Battle of Wörth, 6 August 1870
In the opening stages of the Franco-Prussian War, the Prussian Third Army defeats the greatly outnumbered French I Corps under Patrice MacMahon, outflanking the defenders near the village of Wörth in Alsace. The French entrenchments prove an easy target for the superior Prussian artillery.

The Battle of Gravelotte, 18 August 1870
Moltke's 188,000 Prussians attack 113,000 French troops under François Bazaine who are holed up in good defensive positions around the village of Gravelotte in Lorraine. The French inflict heavier casualties, but the Prussians retain the initiative; under pressure, the French fall back.

The Battle of Sedan, 1 September 1870
Trapped by rapidly advancing Prussian forces at Sedan, the French – under first Patrice MacMahon and then Auguste-Alexandre Ducrotin – lack the foresight to occupy the surrounding hills. These are seized by the Prussians, which gives their artillery a dominating position; the subsequent French attempts to capture the hills are driven back. The French are once again encircled, lose heavily and surrender. The French emperor Napoleon III is captured.

The Blockade of Metz, 3 September–23 October 1870
Following his defeat at Gravelotte, François Bazaine's Army of the Rhine retreats to Metz, where it is besieged by the Prussians. Bazaine fails to break out and surrenders on 23 October.

'No battle plan survives contact with the enemy.'
MOLTKE THE ELDER

▼ A selection of Prussian uniforms modelled by, amongst others, Wilhelm I (centre) and Bismarck (centre right), as illustrated in a contemporary book.

► Moltke convinced his master, King Wilhelm I of Prussia, to attack the much larger Austrian army under Lajos von Benedek at Sadowa, confident that he could hold out long enough for two further Prussian armies to converge on the field and turn the enemy flanks. Thanks to superior firepower and organization, this risky plan largely worked and the war was won.

▼▼ The Prussian firing line holds firm in the face of fierce Austrian attacks at Sadowa, in this painting by Carl Röchling (1855–1920), one of 19th-century Germany's foremost military artists. Prussian infantry used superior breech-loading rifles known as needle guns, which allowed them sometimes to fire lying down from concealed positions.

▼ A *Pickelhaube*, or German spike helmet, first adopted by the Prussian military in 1842. Made from boiled leather, the original design proved unwieldy, frequently falling forward under its combined height and weight to block the wearer's vision. Nevertheless, a more practical design was not introduced before 1856.

SADOWA, 3 JULY 1866

MOLTKE

Sadowa
Benatky
Chlum
Nederlist
Lochenitz
Rozberice
Ysestary
LAJOS VON BENEDEK
Briza
B O H E M I A
Bistritz
Sterzey
Kukleny
Königgrätz

0   1 km
0   1 miles

that contrasted markedly with the French practice of 'muddling through'.

The hard work and organizational skills of the Prussian general staff ensured that the country's large numbers of troops and reserves could be mobilized successfully. This was achieved in 1866 and 1870, in part thanks to an effective exploitation of the railway network in order rapidly to achieve the desired initial deployment and thus gain the strategic initiative. Through the use of planned rail movements, which Moltke greatly encouraged, the Prussians made mobilization a predictable sequence and greatly eased the process of concentration of forces. The railways, and telegraph communications, did not solve all problems, though, and were of very limited value on the battlefield. However, they were a considerable improvement over the means that had previously been available.

The Prussian general staff also ensured that their forces were better able to contain mistakes and to prevent them from overthrowing the overall strategic and tactical plans. In short, they managed risk and error. Moltke did encounter problems with opponents

operations. Prussian operational art provided generally informed responsiveness under pressure, and therefore an ability to achieve victory despite all the fog and friction of war. It was also central to a self-conscious, intellectual professionalization of war. Moltke's system ensured a degree of effectiveness

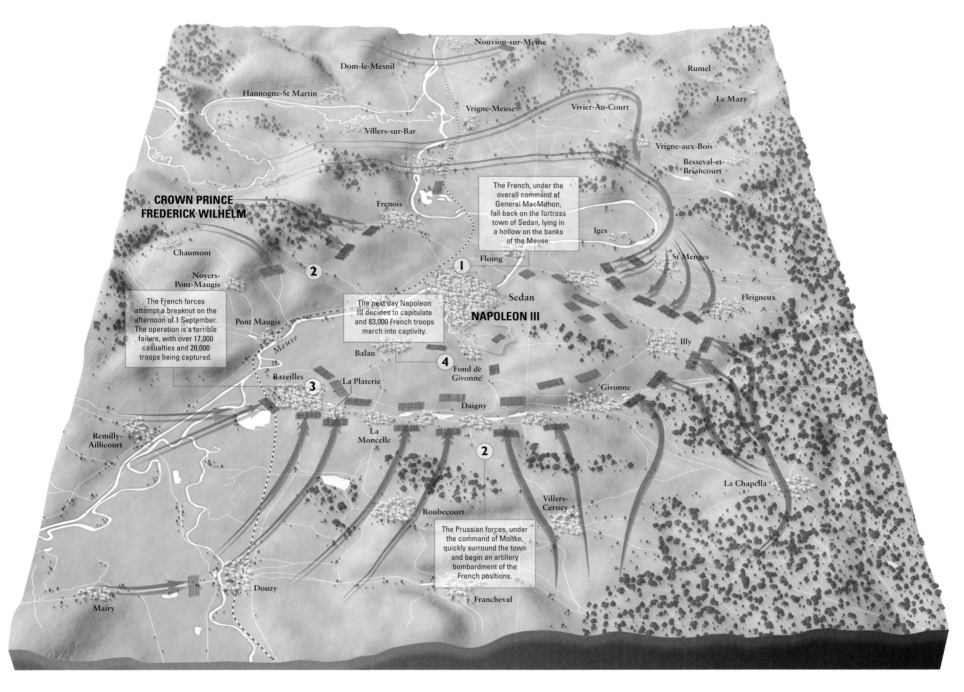

CROWN PRINCE
FREDERICK WILHELM

The French forces
attempt a breakout on the
afternoon of 1 September.
The operation is a terrible
failure, with over 17,000
casualties and 20,000
troops being captured.

The next day Napoleon
III decides to capitulate
and 83,000 French troops
march into captivity.

The French, under the
overall command of
General MacMahon,
fall back on the fortress
town of Sedan, lying in
a hollow on the banks
of the Meuse.

The Prussian forces, under
the command of Moltke,
quickly surround the town
and begin an artillery
bombardment of the
French positions.

Sedan
NAPOLEON III

failing to move as anticipated, but, in the circumstances of 1866 and 1870, he was better able to understand, think through and control the consequences. In 1866, Prussia and Austria faced each other with broadly comparable numbers, providing an opportunity for Prussia to demonstrate the superior quality of her army. The Prussians gained the initiative, taking the Austrians by surprise with the speed of the main Prussian advance (thanks to Moltke's more effective mobilization and deployment plan), and were outmanoeuvred by Prussian armies using Moltke's strategy of exterior lines of communication (where an army operates from several bases against an enemy, with each of these bases referring back to a central base or headquarters). Whereas Napoleon had used separately operating corps within his army, Moltke employed independently operating armies – much larger forces. Furthermore,

unlike Napoleon, who concentrated his forces prior to battle, Moltke aimed for a concentration of his armies during the battle.

Moltke himself warned of the hazards of extrapolating from his victories. While arguing that it was preferable to fight on the territory of one's opponent, he was increasingly sceptical about the potential of the strategic offensive because of increases in defensive firepower and the size of armies. Furthermore, in 1866 and 1870 deficiencies in leadership and strategy on the part of Austria and France played into Moltke's hands, enabling him to outmanoeuvre his opponents. Prussia had also gained through attacking its opponents sequentially rather than simultaneously. Moltke retired from active service in 1888, his nephew Moltke the Younger succeeding him as chief of the general staff in 1906.

The Battle of Sedan, 1870	
Prussians and Bavarians	French
Helmuth von Moltke, Wilhelm I, Ludwig Freiherr von der Tann	Napoleon III, Patrice MacMahon, August-Alexandre Ducrot
200,000 troops, 774 cannon	120,000 troops, 564 cannon
Casualties: 2,320 killed, 5,980 wounded, 700 missing	Casualties: 3,000 killed, 14,000 wounded, 21,000 captured, 82,000 surrendered

▲ The battle of Sedan in 1870 resulted from a series of brilliant manoeuvres whereby Moltke trapped the much smaller main French army and pounded it with his artillery. Napoleon III's decision to surrender not only ended his Second Empire, but also represented the greatest French military disaster prior to 1940.

Ulysses S. Grant

Victorious Union General in the American Civil War

'The art of war is simple enough. Find out where your enemy is. Get at him as soon as you can. Strike him as hard as you can, and keep moving on.' ULYSSES S. GRANT

A Life in Brief

1822, 27 April
Born at Point Pleasant, Ohio

1843
Graduates from West Point

1863, June
Assumes command of Army of the Tennessee

1864, March
Appointed Lieutenant General and General-in-Chief of the Union armies

1866, 25 July
Appointed first full general in United States history

1869, 4 March
Inaugurated President of the United States

1885, 23 July
Dies at Mt McGregor, New York

▶▶ 'The concentration of all that is American,' was how one Union officer described Grant the day this photo was taken near Cold Harbor, Virginia, in June 1864. At the time, Grant was preparing to cross the James and attack Petersburg. It was Grant's possession of a rare combination of skill and determination (the latter quality so effectively captured in this photo) that made him a great commander.

◀ A Union officer's sword, scabbard and belt. Part of Grant's appeal to his countrymen was his modesty: content to wear a common soldier's uniform, he rarely carried a sword while in the field.

Grant was the finest Union commander of the American Civil War, and one of the truly great commanders in all American military history. While determination and aggressiveness certainly distinguished his generalship, Grant brought many other essential qualities to his military endeavours. Among these were his skill as a manager and logistician, his flair for boldly planned and executed manoeuvres, his ability to work well with the navy, and his talent for clearly visualizing and coordinating the activities of multiple combat elements in complex operations.

Grant was born Hiram Ulysses Grant. Whilst attending the US Military Academy, a clerical error led to his evermore being known as Ulysses S. Grant. After graduating in the middle of the class of 1843, Grant demonstrated considerable ability as an officer, especially during the Mexican War (1846–48), and by the time he left the army in 1854 could boast of attaining the rank of captain faster than most of his classmates. Civilian life, however, brought financial hardship, and in 1860 Grant had been reduced to working as a clerk at his family's leather goods shop in Illinois.

When the Civil War began in 1861, Grant returned to the army and, after a few months commanding troops in Illinois and Missouri, was promoted to Brigadier General and given command of the critical river town of Cairo, Illinois. Grant became a national hero in February 1862 when he collaborated with a naval force in the capture of Fort Henry and Fort Donelson, and insisted, in negotiating the surrender of the latter, that he would give the trapped garrison 'no terms except unconditional and immediate surrender.' Unfortunately, communication breakdowns then developed between Grant and his immediate superior, Major General Henry W. Halleck. Furious and somewhat jealous over his subordinate's new fame, Halleck relieved Grant from command and notified Washington that reports indicated Grant had 'resumed his former bad habits' – a thinly veiled allusion to stories that alcoholism had been the cause of Grant's earlier resignation from the army. There was, however, no evidence to substantiate these charges, so Halleck was forced to restore Grant to command.

Grant then proceeded to Pittsburg Landing on the Tennessee River, with instructions to hold his forces there to await the arrival of another army commanded by Don Carlos Buell. On 6 April 1862 a Confederate army commanded by General Albert Sidney Johnston initiated the battle of Shiloh by launching a massive surprise attack on Grant's army. The timely arrival of Buell's command enabled Grant's army to survive the carelessness of its commander, who launched a counterattack on 7 April that drove the Confederates from the field. Shortly thereafter, Halleck removed Grant from field command.

Key Battles and Campaigns (see also Robert E. Lee's entry)

The Fort Henry and Fort Donelson Campaign, February 1862
In cooperation with naval forces, Grant captures two key Confederate defensive positions on the Tennessee and Cumberland Rivers and over 15,000 troops. These are the first major Union victories of the Civil War in the West, and open the heartland of the Confederacy west of the Appalachians to invasion.

The Battle of Shiloh, 6–7 April 1862
The Confederate attack on Grant's unprepared army drives the Federals from their initial camps before the Union commander, aided by the timely arrival of reinforcements, manages to patch together a strong defensive line that holds out against determined enemy attacks the rest of the day. Receiving further reinforcements during the night, Grant counterattacks the next day and drives the Confederates away.

The Vicksburg Campaign, December 1862, March–July 1863
In one of the great campaigns in modern military history, Grant outmanoeuvres and outfights two Confederate armies en route to forcing one to surrender itself and the town of Vicksburg after a month-long siege. The capture of Vicksburg gives the North possession of the Mississippi River, accomplishing one of the Union's most important strategic objectives.

The Petersburg Campaign, June 1864–March 1865
Over the course of a nine-month campaign, Grant gradually secures control of the supply lines that support Lee's army, then breaks its lines, forcing it to abandon Petersburg and the Confederate capital of Richmond.

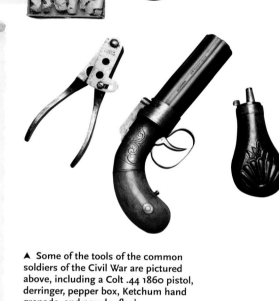

▲ Some of the tools of the common soldiers of the Civil War are pictured above, including a Colt .44 1860 pistol, derringer, pepper box, Ketchum hand grenade, and powder flask.

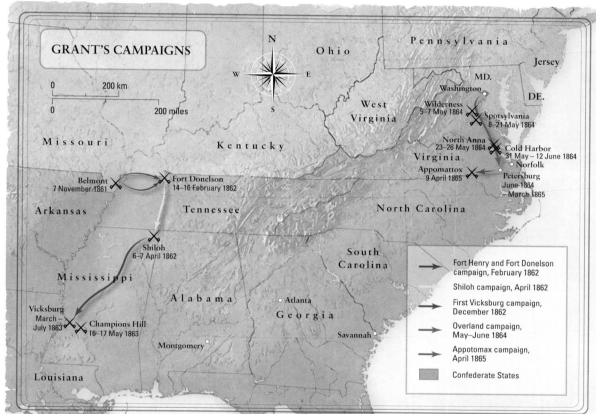

GRANT'S CAMPAIGNS

Fort Henry and Fort Donelson campaign, February 1862

Shiloh campaign, April 1862

First Vicksburg campaign, December 1862

Overland campaign, May–June 1864

Appotomax campaign, April 1865

Confederate States

◄ Grant's American Civil War campaigns, including among them the victory at Vicksburg in 1863, made him a national hero and ensured the confidence of President Abraham Lincoln.

When Halleck was called to Washington in June 1862 to become Commanding General of all the Union armies, Grant once again assumed command of Union forces in west Tennessee and northern Mississippi, with the mission of consolidating Federal control over the region and preparing an offensive against the town of Vicksburg on the Mississippi River. The former task proved difficult due to the hostility of the local population, and as a result Grant began taking a much tougher stance towards Southern civilians and their property during the summer of 1862. In the autumn, Grant conducted operations against Confederate forces in northern Mississippi that produced battles at Iuka and Corinth, but did little to advance either side's strategic interests.

Grant then turned his attention to Vicksburg, which stood in the way of the North's regaining control of the entire Mississippi River. After his first attempt to take the town failed in December 1862, Grant spent several months trying a number of schemes in cooperation with naval forces, before conceiving and implementing a brilliant campaign of manoeuvre in April and May 1863. After crossing the Mississippi south of Vicksburg, Grant pushed inland. He then drove off an army the Confederate government had sent to assist Vicksburg's defenders before turning west to win engagements at Champion's Hill and the Big Black River and to force Lieutenant General John C. Pemberton's Confederate army to take refuge in the fortifications of Vicksburg. On 4 July 1863,

◄◄ As Grant's forces left the battlefields of Spotsylvania in May 1864, photographer Timothy O'Sullivan was able to secure a perch in Massaponax Church from which he captured a remarkable series of images of Grant, his staff, and Army of the Potomac commander George Meade as they held a 'council of war'. Grant is the officer seated with his legs crossed directly in front of the two trees who is smoking a cigar.

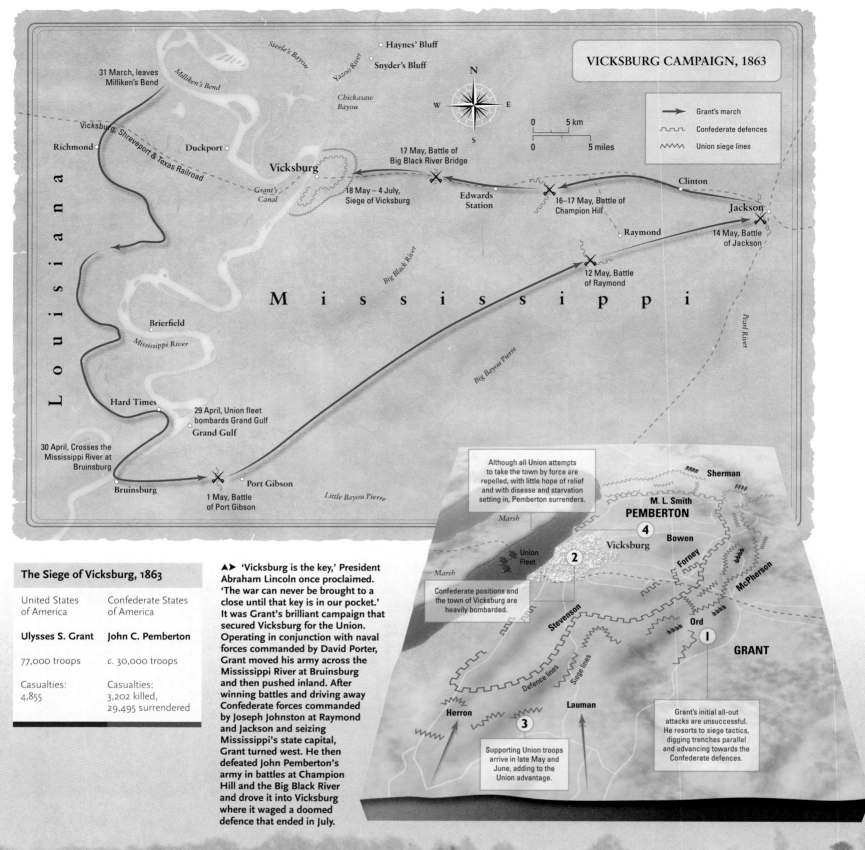

VICKSBURG CAMPAIGN, 1863

31 March, leaves Milliken's Bend

Vicksburg, Shreveport & Texas Railroad

Haynes' Bluff

Snyder's Bluff

Steele's Bayou

Yazoo River

Chickasaw Bayou

Milliken's Bend

Richmond

Duckport

Vicksburg

Grant's Canal

17 May, Battle of Big Black River Bridge

18 May – 4 July, Siege of Vicksburg

Edwards Station

16–17 May, Battle of Champion Hill

Clinton

Jackson

14 May, Battle of Jackson

Raymond

M i s s i s s i p p i

Big Black River

12 May, Battle of Raymond

Pearl River

Brierfield

Mississippi River

Big Bayou Pierre

L o u i s i a n a

Hard Times

29 April, Union fleet bombards Grand Gulf

Grand Gulf

Little Bayou Pierre

30 April, Crosses the Mississippi River at Bruinsburg

Bruinsburg

Port Gibson

1 May, Battle of Port Gibson

Legend:
- Grant's march
- Confederate defences
- Union siege lines

0   5 km

0   5 miles

Although all Union attempts to take the town by force are repelled, with little hope of relief and with disease and starvation setting in, Pemberton surrenders.

Confederate positions and the town of Vicksburg are heavily bombarded.

Sherman

M. L. Smith

PEMBERTON

Vicksburg

Bowen

Forney

McPherson

Marsh

Union Fleet

Marsh

Stevenson

Ord

Defence lines

Siege lines

GRANT

Herron

Lauman

Supporting Union troops arrive in late May and June, adding to the Union advantage.

Grant's initial all-out attacks are unsuccessful. He resorts to siege tactics, digging trenches parallel and advancing towards the Confederate defences.

The Siege of Vicksburg, 1863

United States of America	Confederate States of America
Ulysses S. Grant	**John C. Pemberton**
77,000 troops	c. 30,000 troops
Casualties: 4,855	Casualties: 3,202 killed, 29,495 surrendered

▲▶ 'Vicksburg is the key,' President Abraham Lincoln once proclaimed. 'The war can never be brought to a close until that key is in our pocket.' It was Grant's brilliant campaign that secured Vicksburg for the Union. Operating in conjunction with naval forces commanded by David Porter, Grant moved his army across the Mississippi River at Bruinsburg and then pushed inland. After winning battles and driving away Confederate forces commanded by Joseph Johnston at Raymond and Jackson and seizing Mississippi's state capital, Grant turned west. He then defeated John Pemberton's army in battles at Champion Hill and the Big Black River and drove it into Vicksburg where it waged a doomed defence that ended in July.

▲ Crossed cannon were the insignia of artillerymen on both sides in the Civil War. The North's great quantitative and qualitative superiority in artillery played a significant role in Grant's ability to achieve victories at places like Vicksburg and Petersburg.

◄ These guns were part of the 'Last Line' Grant established near Pittsburg Landing on 6 April 1862. They helped the Union army recover from the terrible beating it took that morning at Shiloh and provided the foundation from which Grant launched the counterattack on the seventh that transformed a battle that had begun with the Confederates overrunning Grant's unprepared front line into a Union victory.

◄ Lee's success in blocking Grant's attempt to cut the Confederate army off from its capital by seizing Spotsylvania Court House led to two weeks of bloody fighting between the two armies. Vowing to 'fight it out on this line if it takes all summer', Grant launched multiple attacks against Lee's strong defensive position. Although a few managed to penetrate the Confederate defences, Grant was ultimately fought to a stalemate in heavy fighting that cost both armies heavily.

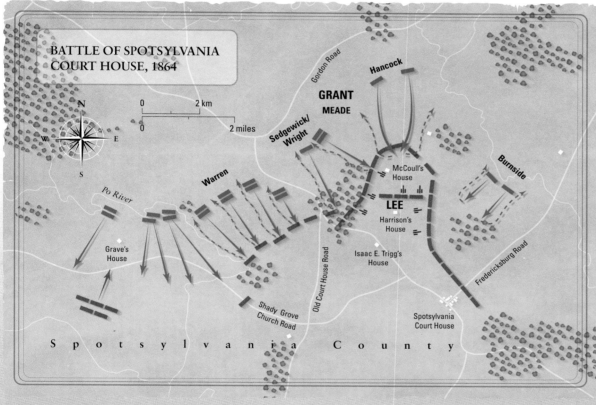

BATTLE OF SPOTSYLVANIA
COURT HOUSE, 1864

Gordon Road

Hancock

GRANT
MEADE

Sedgewick/
Wright

McCoull's
House

Warren

LEE

Burnside

Po River

Harrison's
House

Grave's
House

Isaac E. Trigg's
House

Fredericksburg Road

Old Court House Road

Shady Grove
Church Road

Spotsylvania
Court House

S p o t s y l v a n i a   C o u n t y

0   2 km
0   2 miles

'Lee's army is the objective point... and to capture that is all we want.' ULYSSES S. GRANT

▼ Men and guns belonging to Battery B, Pennsylvania Light Artillery, one of the units whose service under Grant's direction during the Overland and Petersburg Campaigns helped save the Union.

William T. Sherman (1820–91)

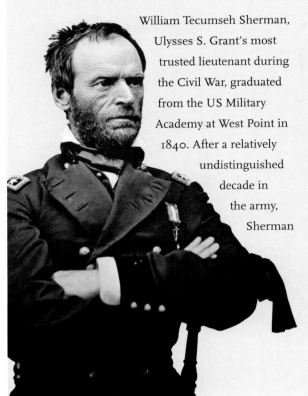

William Tecumseh Sherman, Ulysses S. Grant's most trusted lieutenant during the Civil War, graduated from the US Military Academy at West Point in 1840. After a relatively undistinguished decade in the army, Sherman resigned his commission and was serving as superintendent of the Louisiana Military Seminary in 1861. Sherman subsequently volunteered his services to the Union and, after leading a brigade at the battle of First Manassas (or Bull Run, 21 July 1861), took command of Union forces in Kentucky, but was removed from that post amid rumours that the stress of command had driven him insane. Sherman's road to redemption began at the April 1862 battle of Shiloh, where he performed well in his first engagement under the command of Grant, with whom he quickly forged a close personal and professional relationship. Their relationship was further cemented in the course of their service together during the 1862–63 Vicksburg Campaign and 1863 battle of Chattanooga.

When Grant became commanding general of all the Union armies in 1864, he made Sherman the principal Union commander in the West. Sherman subsequently conducted a successful campaign that resulted in the capture of Atlanta and then won Grant's support for a plan to conduct a massive raid from Atlanta to the Atlantic Coast. As intended, 'Sherman's March to the Sea' inflicted massive material and moral damage on the Confederacy, and was followed by a similarly destructive march north through the Carolinas. Shortly after reaching North Carolina in early 1865, Sherman accepted the surrender of the main Confederate army in that state. When Grant became president in 1869, Sherman took his place as Commanding General of the army and oversaw the conduct of a number of conflicts with the western Indians, while vigorously pushing initiatives to improve the level of professionalism in the US army.

Grant accepted Pemberton's surrender of his army and Vicksburg.

Vicksburg once again made Grant a national hero and won for him the full confidence of President Abraham Lincoln, who also appreciated the zeal with which Grant implemented policies attacking slavery in 1863. Grant solidified his status as the North's outstanding commander by winning the battle of Chattanooga in November 1863. Upon the request of his superiors in Washington, Grant then submitted a proposal for operations east of the Appalachians that called for sending 60,000 troops by sea to southern Virginia and then having them conduct a massive raid into North Carolina. However, his bold and inspired concept was rejected by the Lincoln administration.

Nonetheless, in March 1864 Grant became the first man since George Washington (pp. 174–79) to hold the rank of Lieutenant General in the US army. On assuming his new rank and the office of Commanding General of all the Union armies, Grant developed a strategy that called for simultaneous advances in 1864 by a force commanded by Major General William T. Sherman in Georgia and four armies in Virginia. The most important of the Virginia armies was the Army

▲ **Members of Battery M, 5th US Artillery in a captured Confederate fort just outside Atlanta shortly after the town's surrender to Sherman's command in September 1864.**

▼ **Civil War soldier's shoes.**

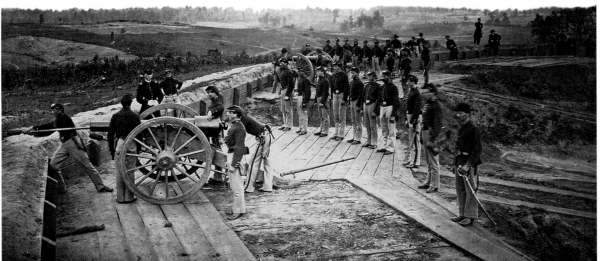

Ulysses S. Grant
William T. Sherman

of the Potomac, which was to operate against General Robert E. Lee's Army of Northern Virginia under Grant's direct supervision, although it technically remained under the command of Major General George Meade.

The Army of the Potomac waged a brutal campaign against Lee in May and April 1864, highlighted by the battles of the Wilderness, Spotsylvania, the North Anna, and Cold Harbor, in which Grant's efforts to outmanoeuvre Lee were consistently thwarted. Grant then moved his army across the James River in a brilliantly conceived and executed operation, only to see his bid to capture quickly the transportation hub of Petersburg fail due to the exhaustion of his troops and problematic frontline leadership. Grant then conducted a nine-month campaign against Richmond and Petersburg that culminated in a series of successful Union assaults in April 1865. When Lee evacuated Petersburg and Richmond, Grant conducted a vigorous pursuit operation that forced the Confederate commander to surrender his army at Appomattox Court House on 9 April 1865. While Grant operated against Lee's forces at Richmond and Petersburg, Sherman captured Atlanta and then applied the operational method he and Grant had developed (comprising army-size raids to destroy Southern resources and morale) in epic marches through Georgia and the Carolinas.

Grant initially advocated a lenient policy towards defeated Confederates, but came to champion more rigorous use of military power to protect the freedmen

and ensure the authority of the federal government was respected in the South. This brought him into conflict with President Andrew Johnson and eventually led him to accept the Republican Party's nomination for President of the United States in 1868. After serving two terms in that office, Grant engaged in various business enterprises that ruined him financially. He then turned to writing and, battling throat cancer, managed to finish his military memoirs, which were a financial success and are widely considered among the finest ever written.

▲ Grant on the porch of the cabin on Mt. McGregor in upstate New York, where he completed work on his memoirs just before his death in 1885. Grant's memoirs provide perhaps the greatest study of generalship and the Civil War ever written and one of the seminal works in all military history.

▼ General-in-chief Ulysses S. Grant with his staff. This photo was taken in front of the modest cabin at City Point, Virginia, from which he directed the campaign against Richmond and Petersburg and coordinated the operations of all the armies of the United States from 1864–65.

Robert E. Lee

Masterful Confederate Commander of the Army of Northern Virginia

'Duty is the most sublime word in our language. Do your duty in all things. You cannot do more. You should never wish to do less.' ROBERT E. LEE

A Life in Brief

1807, 19 January
Born at Stratford Hall, Virginia

1829
Graduates from US Military Academy

1861, April
Appointed Commander of Virginia military forces

1861, August
Appointed General in the Confederate army

1862, March
Appointed military adviser to President Davis

1862, June
Assumes command of the Army of Northern Virginia

1865, 31 January
Appointed General-in-Chief of the Confederate armies

1865, 9 April
Surrenders at Appomattox Court House

1870, 12 October
Dies at Lexington, Virginia

▶ General Robert E. Lee in Richmond shortly after the surrender of his army at Appomattox in April 1865. Despite his brilliance as a commander, Lee was ultimately doomed to failure in his effort to win enough victories to secure Confederate independence and compelled to, in his words, 'yield to overwhelming numbers and resources'.

Robert Edward Lee was by far the best and most important man to lead the armies of the Confederate States of America in the American Civil War. He is also seen by many as a good man who brought lasting dignity to the South's cause, while others point to his close contact with slavery. However, it is clear that Lee deserves his reputation as one of the most admired commanders in history.

The son of a distinguished hero of the American War for Independence (Henry Lee), the young Robert compiled an outstanding record as a cadet. On graduating from the US Military Academy at West Point in 1829, he forged a distinguished record of service in the antebellum army, highlighted by widely praised exploits during the Mexican War (1846–48) and a brief tenure as superintendent at West Point. In 1861, Lee resigned from the US army after learning of Virginia's secession from the Union. After undistinguished performances in western Virginia and the Carolinas, and a stint as military adviser to Confederate president Jefferson Davis, Lee took command of the main Confederate army in Virginia in June 1862.

Within a few months of assuming command of the Army of Northern Virginia, Lee had established a strong claim to recognition as one of history's outstanding captains. Brilliantly executing a bold offensive strategy, he transferred the war in Virginia from the doorstep of his own capital to the gates of Washington by winning victories in the Seven Days Battles and Second Manassas Campaign – the latter one of the most brilliant examples of manoeuvre warfare in the Civil War. He then led his army across the Potomac River into Maryland hoping that by maintaining the operational initiative and building on the momentum gained by his earlier victories, he might persuade the North to quit the war. However, his effort was thwarted by Union forces commanded by George B. McClellan, and after suffering defeats at South Mountain and Antietam, Lee was compelled to return to Virginia.

Despite the setback in Maryland and the heavy casualties his army

Key Battles and Campaigns

The Seven Days Battles, 25 June–1 July 1862
Less than a month after assuming command of the Army of Northern Virginia, Lee drives the Union army commanded by George B. McClellan from the gates of the Confederate capital. The series of bloody battles dashes hopes for a quick Northern victory in the war.

The Battle of Second Manassas (Second Bull Run), 28–30 August 1862
In a spectacular campaign in central and northern Virginia, Lee outmanoeuvres a Union army commanded by John Pope, and then wins a smashing tactical victory that drives it from the field.

The Maryland Campaign, September 1862
Although able to capture a large Federal garrison at Harpers Ferry, Lee's bid for a victory north of the Potomac ends with his army driven out of Maryland after defeats at South Mountain and Antietam by McClellan.

The Battle of Fredericksburg, 11–15 December 1862
Lee wins his easiest victory of the war at Fredericksburg by repulsing a series of poorly executed attacks by Union forces commanded by Ambrose Burnside.

The Battle of Chancellorsville, 30 April–6 May 1863
Lee responds to an initially impressive manoeuvre by a vastly superior Federal army by boldly seizing the tactical offensive. He drives Joseph Hooker's forces back across the Rappahannock River through skilful manoeuvres and determined fighting.

The Battle of Gettysburg, 1–3 July 1863
Lee s greatest effort to win a decisive victory on Northern soil is foiled at Gettysburg. After routing elements of George G. Meade's Army of the Potomac on the first day of battle, Lee launches a series of attacks over the following two days against the Union flanks and centre, but these are decisively and bloodily repulsed.

The Overland Campaign, May–June 1864
In a great clash between two of the finest commanders the United States has ever produced, forces commanded by Grant and Lee wage a brutal campaign highlighted by the battles of the Wilderness, Spotsylvania, the North Anna, and Cold Harbor. Lee is forced back into the defences of Richmond and Petersburg.

The Petersburg Campaign, June 1864–March 1865
Over the course of a nine-month campaign, Lee continually thwarts efforts by Grant to either break his lines around Richmond and Petersburg or secure control of the transportation network. Nonetheless, the campaign ends with Lee forced to abandon Petersburg and Richmond.

The Appomattox Campaign, 29 March–9 April 1865
After abandoning Richmond and Petersburg, Lee makes a desperate attempt to reach North Carolina with his army, but is prevented from doing so and forced to surrender by pursuing forces commanded by Grant at Appomattox Court House. This ends the Civil War in Virginia and ensures the defeat of the Confederacy.

> *'It is well that war is so terrible; we should grow too fond of it.'* ROBERT E. LEE

LEE'S BATTLES

✗ Victory
✗ Defeat

Pennsylvania

Gettysburg 1–3 Jul 1863

Antietam 17 Sep 1862

New Jersey

South Mountain 14 Sep 1862

West Virginia

Baltimore

Maryland

Delaware

ATLANTIC

Washington D.C.

Second Manassas 28–30 Aug 1862

Chancellorsville 30 Apr – 6 May 1863

Fredericksburg 11–15 Dec 1862

Wilderness 4–6 May 1864

Spotsylvania 8–21 May 1864

Chesapeake Bay

OCEAN

Richmond

Seven Days 25 Jun – 1 Jul 1862

Appomattox Court House 9 Apr 1865

Petersburg Jun 1864 – Mar 1865

Yorktown

Virginia

Norfolk

0   100 km
0   100 miles

►► Dramatic advances in weapons technology during the decades prior to the Civil War were among the factors that made it such a brutal and deadly conflict. Due in part to the extensive use of modern small arms like the .58 calibre rifle musket pictured above, more Americans died in the Civil War than in all other American wars combined prior to Vietnam. Edged weapons, such as this Model 1850 'Foot' Officer's sword, right, played an increasingly minor role.

◄ Lee's brave campaign during the American Civil War ended in surrender.

▼ General Lee atop Traveller, his favourite mount during and after the war. The most famous warhorse in American history, Traveller's remains rest only yards away from his master's in Lexington, Virginia.

Thomas 'Stonewall' Jackson (1824–63)

One of the finest commanders of the American Civil War, Thomas Jonathan Jackson was an 1846 graduate of West Point who had fought with distinction in the Mexican War and was serving on the faculty of the Virginia Military Institute when Virginia seceded from the Union. He immediately won fame and the nickname 'Stonewall' for his performance at the 1861 battle of First Manassas on the Confederate side. Then, in the spring of 1862, Jackson conducted one of the truly outstanding campaigns in American military history in the Shenandoah Valley. His initial defeat at Kernstown and subsequent victories at McDowell, Front Royal, Winchester, Cross Keys, and Port Republic gave Robert E. Lee the opportunity to attack successfully

a powerful Union army that was operating against the Confederate capital. However, in the Seven Days Battles, in which Lee drove the Federals from the gates of Richmond, Jackson performed poorly. He more than redeemed himself, though, by skilfully leading a wing of Lee's army in the subsequent Second Manassas and Maryland campaigns.

In late 1862, Jackson officially became Commander of the Army of Northern Virginia's II Corps and performed well at the battle of Fredericksburg. He once again demonstrated tactical brilliance at the May 1863 battle of Chancellorsville, successfully manoeuvring his command to deliver a powerful blow that overwhelmed the enemy's flank. However, while

conducting a personal reconnaissance in search of an opportunity to exploit his success, Jackson was accidentally shot by some of his own men. While recuperating from his wounds, he contracted pneumonia and died. Whether the loss of Jackson doomed the Confederacy to defeat is debatable, but there is little doubt that Grant was fortunate not to have to face Jackson when he battled Lee's army in 1864–65.

▶ A contemporary sketch by Alfred R. Waud vividly portrays the routed Federal army fleeing from the 'Old Bull Run battleground' on 30 August 1862.

▼ A scene from the hard-fought battle of Second Manassas.

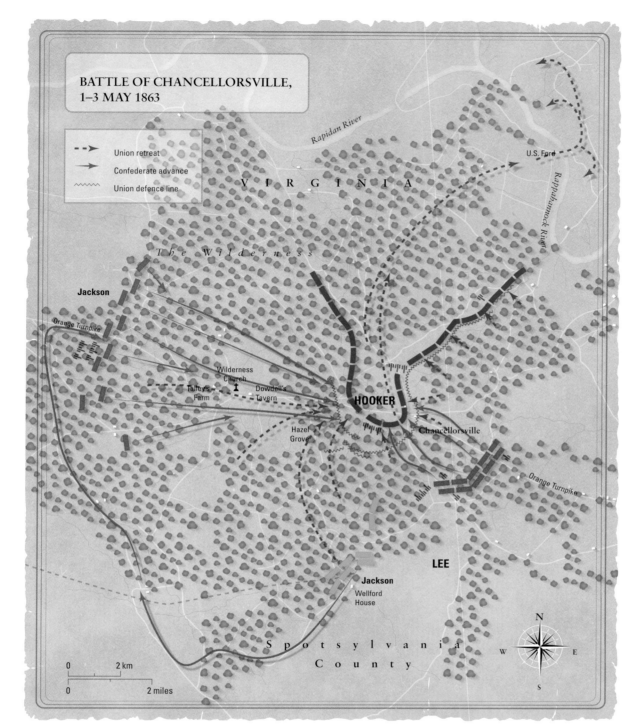

BATTLE OF CHANCELLORSVILLE, 1–3 MAY 1863

- - → Union retreat
— → Confederate advance
〜〜〜 Union defence line

Rapidan River

Rappahannock River

V I R G I N I A

U.S. Ford

The Wilderness

Jackson

Orange Turnpike

Wilderness Church

Talley's Farm

Dowdall's Tavern

HOOKER

Chancellorsville

Hazel Grove

Orange Turnpike

LEE

Jackson
Wellford House

S p o t s y l v a n i a
C o u n t y

0   2 km
0   2 miles

N / E / S / W

▲ This contemporary sketch by Arthur Lumley is of one of the more infamous episodes in the war, the December 1862 'Sack of Fredericksburg' by Federal troops. Two days later, they went on to suffer perhaps their worst defeat of the war at Lee's hands at the battle of Fredericksburg.

◄ A bold flank march by Stonewall Jackson's corps and hard fighting by the entire Army of Northern Virginia enabled Lee to overcome a skilful opening manoeuvre by his opponent and two to one disadvantage in manpower to win a brilliant, but costly victory at the battle of Chancellorsville.

had sustained since his assumption of command, Lee was able to easily win a defensive victory at the battle of Fredericksburg in December 1862. Then, a few months later at Chancellorsville, Lee brilliantly manoeuvred his army to defeat a force more than twice as large as his own, in one of the great tactical masterpieces in American military history. Lee followed up this victory by leading his army north across the Potomac, but his ambition for an offensive victory on northern soil was once again frustrated at the epic three-day battle of Gettysburg. After returning to Virginia, Lee engaged in a war of manoeuvre with the Federals throughout the autumn of 1863 that produced no decisive results.

With his army badly depleted by two years of hard fighting and his opponent possessing overwhelming advantages in numbers, Lee was compelled to fight primarily on the defensive in 1864. He did so with magnificent skill, and inflicted brutal punishment on his opponent in the Overland and Petersburg campaigns of 1864–65, but could not overcome the North's great superiority in manpower and *matériel*. Nonetheless, even when managed with great skill and determination by Ulysses S. Grant (pp. 218–25), these advantages did not bring about Union victory until April 1865. After surrendering his army at Appomattox Court House, Lee spent most of his remaining years as the successful president of a small Virginia college.

'We cannot afford to be idle, and though weaker than our opponents in men and military equipment, must endeavour to harass, if we cannot destroy them.' ROBERT E. LEE

Robert E. Lee

Modern Age

Menelik

Ethiopian Ruler who Repulsed an Italian Invasion

'I have no intention at all of being an indifferent spectator, if the distant powers hold the idea of dividing up Africa.' MENELIK

A Life in Brief

1844, 17 August
Born in Ankober, Ethiopia

1889–1913
Emperor of Ethiopia

1913, 12 December
Dies at Addis Ababa, Ethiopia

▲ The votive crown of Menelik symbolizing his status as Negusa Nagast ('King of Kings') over the states he brought under his control through relentless military campaigns to form a reinvigorated Ethiopian empire.

▶ Menelik posing majestically in coronation robes and crown at the height of his power. Having repulsed the Italian invasion, unified his country, modernized his army and greatly expanded his territory, Menelik became an inspiration for Africans and people of African descent throughout the world.

Menelik was a gifted military leader on all levels. His unique victory over the Italians in 1896 preserved Ethiopian independence into the 20th century and beyond, and served as the foundation for later Pan-African movements. A military and civil modernizer and skilled diplomat who played European powers off against one another, his later campaigns of territorial expansion doubled the size of the Ethiopian empire.

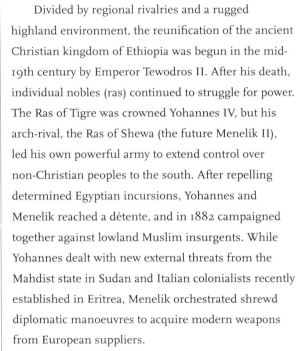

Divided by regional rivalries and a rugged highland environment, the reunification of the ancient Christian kingdom of Ethiopia was begun in the mid-19th century by Emperor Tewodros II. After his death, individual nobles (ras) continued to struggle for power. The Ras of Tigre was crowned Yohannes IV, but his arch-rival, the Ras of Shewa (the future Menelik II), led his own powerful army to extend control over non-Christian peoples to the south. After repelling determined Egyptian incursions, Yohannes and Menelik reached a détente, and in 1882 campaigned together against lowland Muslim insurgents. While Yohannes dealt with new external threats from the Mahdist state in Sudan and Italian colonialists recently established in Eritrea, Menelik orchestrated shrewd diplomatic manoeuvres to acquire modern weapons from European suppliers.

After Yohannes was killed fighting the Mahdists, Menelik ascended the throne in 1889 and entered into a bitter dispute with the Italians concerning the recently signed Treaty of Wuchale. The Italians interpreted the treaty as a concession of Ethiopian sovereignty, while Menelik held that it did not dilute his independence. Avoiding the arms embargo placed on the rest of tropical Africa by the Brussels Conference of 1890, Menelik continued to stockpile arms. In 1896, with the European 'scramble for Africa' reaching its peak, the Italians dispatched an invasion force of 20,000 men to occupy Ethiopia. Menelik tapped into a burgeoning sense of Ethiopian patriotism, born from an age-old determination to defend their unique

Key Battles

The Battle of Embabo, 6 June 1882

Making good use of modern firearms and the mobility of a strong cavalry force, Menelik shatters the army of the rival state of Gojjam, capturing the Gojjami Ras, Tekla Hayimanot. The victory paves the way Menelik's further conquests in southern and western Ethiopia.

▼ **Menelik's Ethiopian forces overwhelm the final resistance of Italian imperial troops at Adwa.**

The Battle of Adwa, 1 March 1896

This is the most decisive victory over invading European colonialists during the 'scramble for Africa'. Having defeated flank attacks by Italian and allied African forces, Menelik concentrates his army against the Italian centre, overwhelming two more brigades. While some Italian troops initially fall back in good order, the retreat soon turns into a rout, and the invading army is annihilated.

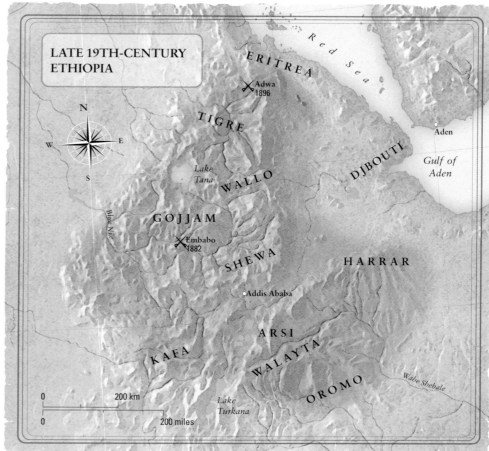

Christianity against outsiders, to mobilize an army of 100,000, many equipped with up-to-date weapons and even artillery. Bedevilled by fatal overconfidence and faulty maps, uncoordinated Italian attacks were overwhelmed by Menelik's troops at Adwa. Having suffered the loss of half their force, the Italians retracted their claims.

Entrusting operational command to lieutenants, Menelik then became the only African leader to participate in the 'scramble', doubling the size of his country through a series of conquests. He devoted much attention to his army, which became the most powerful in Africa. He made organizational and tactical changes to maximize the firepower of his modern weapons and laid plans to establish a domestic arms industry. He effected a closer unification of Ethiopia than his predecessors had done, though regional tensions, which would eventually erupt into horrific civil wars, remained. Unable to rule effectively after a debilitating stroke in 1906, he died in 1913.

▲ The extent of the Ethiopian empire at the end of the 19th century. After defeating the Italians in 1896, Menelik became the sole African leader effectively to participate in the 'scramble for Africa', conquering many neighbouring territories through a series of military campaigns to create a vast imperial state.

◄ High-ranking Ethiopian warriors (in c. 1889) displaying both the traditional weapons and modern firearms they would use in defeating imperial intrusions and conquering new territories in Menelik's campaigns. Menelik's diplomatic skills allowed him to avoid the embargo on firearms importation imposed on the rest of tropical Africa by European powers.

Garnet Wolseley

Key General of British Imperialism

'To see England great is my highest aspiration, and that I might have a leading part in contributing to the attainment of that greatness, is my only real ambition.' GARNET WOLSELEY

A Life in Brief

1833, 4 June
Born in Dublin

1852, 12 March
Commissioned into the army

1882, 18 November
General and peer

1885, 19 August
Viscount

1894, 26 May
Field Marshal

1895, 1 November
Commander-in-Chief of the British army

1913, 25 March
Dies at Menton, France

Immortalized by Gilbert and Sullivan as the 'very model of a modern major-general', Garnet Joseph Wolseley was known to the British public as 'Our Only General'. Though he failed to reach Khartoum in time to save Charles Gordon in 1885, Wolseley went on to lay the foundations for a modern British army, and was the leading soldier of his generation.

When many commissions were still purchased, Wolseley advanced without benefit of money through sheer courage. In the Second Anglo-Burmese War (1852–53), he received a thigh wound that troubled him all his life. In the Crimea (1854–56), he lost the sight of his left eye. After further service in the Indian Mutiny (1857) and the Third China War (1860), Wolseley emerged a brevet lieutenant-colonel after just eight years' service. Stationed in Canada, he consolidated his reputation as a leading reformer in 1869 with a practical manual on soldiering, *The Soldier's Pocket Book*. Chosen to quell a rebellion in the Canadian Northwest, Wolseley forged through the wilderness to re-occupy Fort Garry on the Red River in 1870.

Knighted and promoted, Wolseley was then chosen to throw back an Asante (or Ashanti) invasion of the Gold Coast in West Africa in 1873. Gathering a group of ambitious young officers, Wolseley advanced through disease-ridden forests to defeat the

 Wolseley (►) served in many different theatres of war, particularly in Africa. His reputation as an able and efficient leader led to the coining of a popular phrase at the time, 'All Sir Garnet', meaning that 'everything is under control'.

Key Battles

The Battle of Amoaful, January 1874
During the Second Asante War (1873–74), the troops of Wolseley's punitive expedition target the Asante capital of Kumase. At Amoaful, they encounter Amankwatia's numerically superior Asante warriors, and advance in loose square formation through thick bush. They fight off successive enveloping attacks for over four hours, before emerging victorious.

The Battle of Tel-el-Kebir, 13 September 1882
During the conquest of Egypt, Wolseley's forces execute a risky night march across the desert, before launching a surprise dawn assault on the entrenched Egyptians under Arabi Pasha. The British carry the position in not much more than an hour.

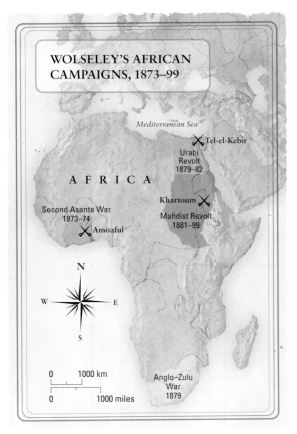

WOLSELEY'S AFRICAN CAMPAIGNS, 1873–99

Mediterranean Sea

Tel-el-Kebir

Urabi Revolt 1879–82

AFRICA

Second Asante War 1873–74

Amoaful

Khartoum

Mahdist Revolt 1881–99

Anglo–Zulu War 1879

0 1000 km
0 1000 miles

Asante and occupy Kumase. In 1875 he was sent to administer Natal in South Africa and then to occupy Cyprus in 1878. In 1879 Wolseley and his 'Ashanti Ring' of adherents were despatched to retrieve the situation in Zululand, though the Zulu were defeated before Wolseley reached the front. Completing the subjugation of the Zulu, Wolseley became successively quartermaster-general and adjutant-general despite the opposition of conservatives, who resented his championship of reform and their exclusion from his well-publicized campaigns. When a nationalist revolt threatened the Suez Canal in 1882, Wolseley destroyed the Egyptian army at Tel-el-Kebir, being rewarded with a peerage. Two years later, during the Mahdist revolt in the Sudan, Wolseley was despatched belatedly to relieve General Gordon: his troops reached Khartoum just two days too late.

Wolseley became commander-in-chief in Ireland in 1890 and commander-in-chief of the army as a whole in 1895. Unfortunately, his health was declining and he had inherited a post stripped of its former powers. Nonetheless, swift mobilization at the start of the South African (Boer) War in 1899 owed much to Wolseley, even if subsequent early defeats illustrated how much more reform was yet required. However, by the time of his retirement in 1900, he had laid the foundations for further professionalization.

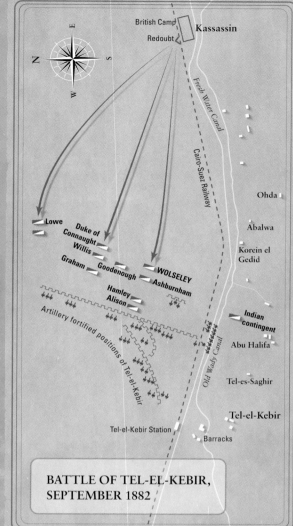

BATTLE OF TEL-EL-KEBIR, SEPTEMBER 1882

▲ The Bronze Star, awarded to all British soldiers taking part in the Egyptian campaigns between 1882 and 1885.

▼ 'Bird's eye' views of colonial battles, such as this depiction of Tel-el-Kebir, were popular in Victorian Britain. Some of the best-known battle artists of the day produced versions, including Lady Butler and Alphonse de Neuville.

▼ The Black Watch during the dawn assault on the Egyptian lines at Tel-el-Kebir in September 1882 as depicted by Henri-Louis Dupray. The Highland Brigade, which led Wolseley's advance, was lionized by the British press. It suffered most of the 57 British dead.

▲ Wolseley's force advanced in two main columns, led respectively on the left flank by Sir Archibald Alison's Highland Brigade and on the right flank by Sir Gerald Graham's Guards Brigade, while Sir Drury Lowe's Cavalry Brigade also moved up on the right flank to conduct the pursuit once the Egyptian line gave way.

Admiral Togo

Japanese Commander who Destroyed the Russian Fleet

'The fate of the Japanese empire rests upon this one battle; let every man do his utmost!' ADMIRAL TOGO

➤ Catapulted to international hero status as a result of his stunning victory at the battle of Tsushima, Admiral Togo remained an icon to the Japanese nation and received the title of *koshaku* (marquis) shortly before his death in 1934. Shown here in his dress white uniform, Togo positioned himself above politics following the Russo-Japanese War.

Over a span of just 24 hours in May 1905, at the battle of Tsushima, Admiral Togo Heihachiro and the Japanese Combined Fleet not only changed the course of the Russo-Japanese War (1904–05) but, in the words of US president Theodore Roosevelt, 'saved the Japanese empire'. Togo's annihilation of the Russian Baltic Squadron conferred an air of divinity on him in his native Japan, and gave the nation its first internationally recognized hero.

Born into a samurai family, Togo originated from Satsuma, the feudal domain that supplied many of Japan's naval officers after the 1868 Meiji Restoration, which brought an end to the Tokugawa shogunate. While his pedigree gave Togo's career a head start, his education laid its foundations proper. He began his formal study of English in 1869 and one year later served as a cadet on the training vessel *Ryujyo*. Demonstrating ability in naval science and English, Togo was selected for further study in Britain at the Thames Nautical Training College, an education that culminated with a circumnavigation of the globe on HMS *Hampshire* in 1875.

Togo returned to Japan in 1878 as a lieutenant on the warship *Hiei*. This began an 18-year period

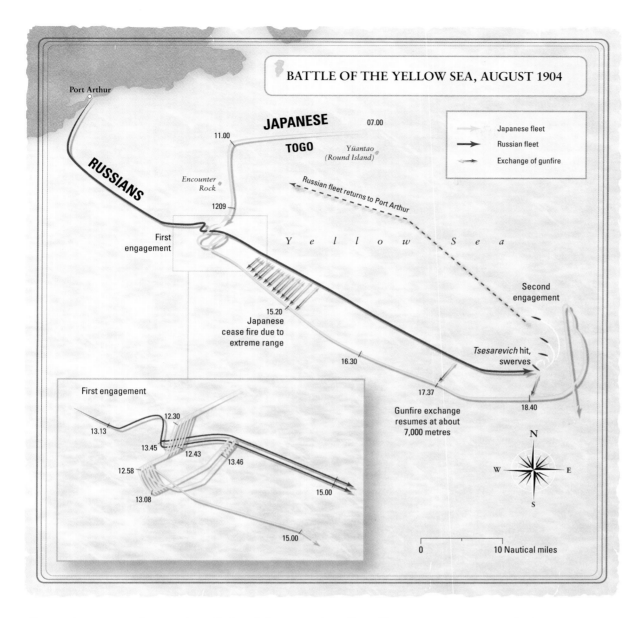

BATTLE OF THE YELLOW SEA, AUGUST 1904

JAPANESE
TOGO
07.00
11.00

Port Arthur

RUSSIANS

Yüantao
(Round Island)

Encounter
Rock

Russian fleet returns to Port Arthur

1209

First
engagement

Y e l l o w   S e a

Japanese fleet
Russian fleet
Exchange of gunfire

15.20
Japanese
cease fire due to
extreme range

Second
engagement

16.30

Tsesarevich hit,
swerves

17.37

18.40

Gunfire exchange
resumes at about
7,000 metres

N

First engagement

12.30
13.13
13.45
12.43
13.46
12.58
13.08
15.00
15.00

W   E

S

0   10 Nautical miles

Key Battles and Campaigns

The Battle of Port Arthur, 8–9 February 1904
Togo orders a surprise destroyer attack on Admiral Oskar Stark's Russian Pacific Fleet in the opening move of the Russo-Japanese War. Togo withholds his capital ships from the initial night attack, fearing their exposure to Russian coastal artillery. The attack is inconclusive, and the next day, following a brief skirmish, Togo withdraws to avoid being trapped.

The Battle of the Yellow Sea, 10 August 1904
After the initial attack in February, the Japanese blockade Port Arthur. The Russian First Pacific Squadron under Admiral Vitgeft attempts to break out, but Togo allows them to exit and then places his ships between the Russians and the port. In the ensuing battle, the Japanese ships cause disarray in the Russian order of sail, but Togo breaks off contact at night and the Russian ships limp back to Port Arthur.

The Battle of Tsushima, 27–28 May 1905
From the *Mikasa*, Togo directs the outmanoeuvring, outgunning and complete annihilation of the Russian Baltic Squadron, commanded by Admiral Zinovy Rozhestvensky. The Japanese sink or capture 34 of Russia's 38 warships for the loss of only three torpedo boats. It is, in the words of naval historian Sir Julian Corbett, 'the most decisive and complete naval victory in history'.

▼ After breaking the blockade at Port Arthur, Admiral Vitgeft's First Pacific Squadron exchanged fire with Togo's battle fleet at the battle of the Yellow Sea. Togo repeatedly attempted to cap Vitgeft's 'T' but did so at extreme range making it impossible for Japan to secure victory. Suffering considerable damage to his flagship, the *Mikasa*, and not wishing to risk significant losses, Togo withdrew his capital ships and enabled the Russians to return to Port Arthur.

▼ The locations of Admiral Togo's two major battles.

of sea assignments and promotions. Onboard the battle cruiser *Naniwa*, Togo received his first combat experience in 1894 during the First Sino-Japanese War (1894–95). Ironically, Togo's first engagement took place against a British-flagged vessel, the *Kowshing*, which had been chartered by China to ferry troops to Korea. Operating within the confines of maritime law, Togo's warships sank the vessel. The skilled manner in which Togo dealt with the brief fallout from this incident was met with greater acclaim than his other achievements against Chinese naval forces at the Battle of the Yalu (September 1894) and the capture of the Chinese port of Weihaiwei (February 1895). In 1895, Togo attained the rank of rear admiral and spent the next nine years in command positions onshore.

As war between Japan and Russia became increasingly likely, the navy minister Yamamoto Gonnohyoe appointed Togo as commander-in-chief of the Combined Fleet in 1903. When asked years later why he had selected Togo, Yamamoto replied that Togo had, since birth, been blessed with good fortune and that luck was needed to defeat the much larger Russian

military. Yamamoto was correct on both counts. As commander, Togo was given three responsibilities: to eliminate the Russian Far Eastern Squadron at the start of the war; to protect troop transports from Japan to Korea; and to destroy the Russian Baltic Squadron if it joined the conflict. Initially, Togo's caution – which some view as overcautiousness – lost Japan the opportunity of a quick naval victory. On 9 February 1904, Togo refused to send his main

Gulf of Chinli
Korea Bay
Pyongyang
Sea of Japan
Port Arthur
Seoul
Yellow Sea 10 Aug 1904
KOREA
Pusan
Yellow Sea
Hiroshima
Tokyo
JAPAN
Tsushima Strait
Tsushima 27–28 May 1905
CHINA
East China Sea
PACIFIC OCEAN
N   W   E   S

235

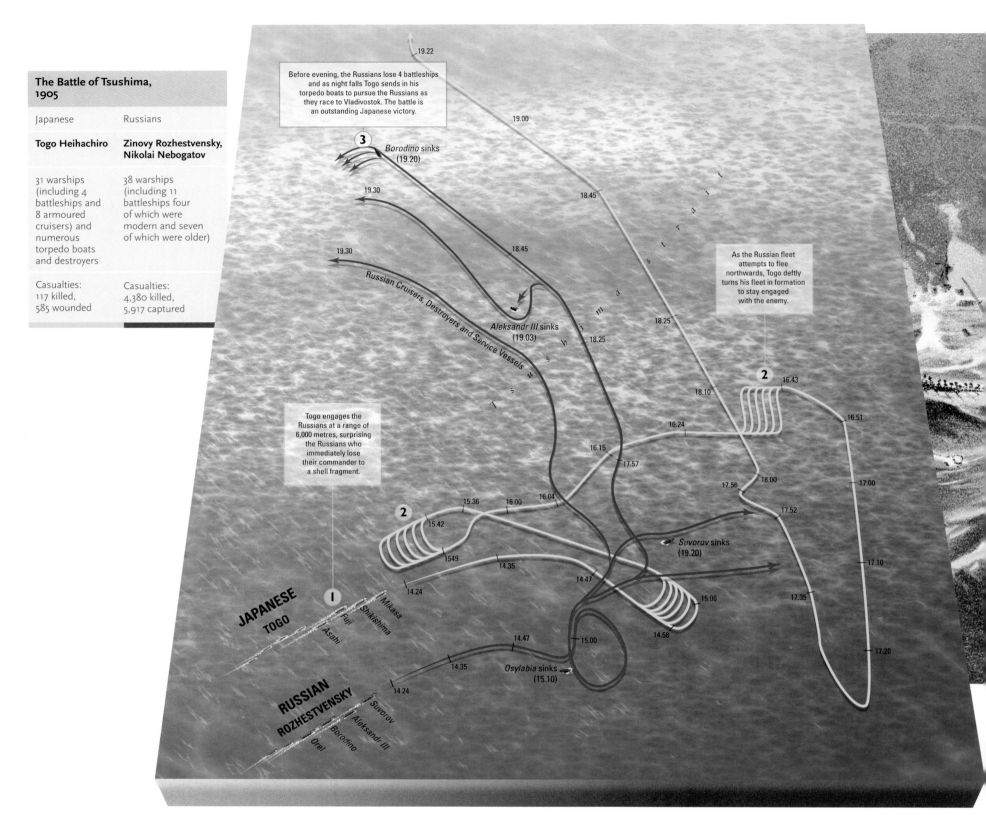

The Battle of Tsushima, 1905

Japanese	Russians
Togo Heihachiro	Zinovy Rozhestvensky, Nikolai Nebogatov
31 warships (including 4 battleships and 8 armoured cruisers) and numerous torpedo boats and destroyers	38 warships (including 11 battleships four of which were modern and seven of which were older)
Casualties: 117 killed, 585 wounded	Casualties: 4,380 killed, 5,917 captured

Before evening, the Russians lose 4 battleships and as night falls Togo sends in his torpedo boats to pursue the Russians as they race to Vladivostok. The battle is an outstanding Japanese victory.

3 *Borodino* sinks (19.20)

19.22

19.00

19.30

18.45

19.30

18.45

As the Russian fleet attempts to flee northwards, Togo deftly turns his fleet in formation to stay engaged with the enemy.

Russian Cruisers, Destroyers and Service Vessels

Aleksandr III sinks (19.03)

18.25

18.25

18.10

2 16.43

16.51

Togo engages the Russians at a range of 6,000 metres, surprising the Russians who immediately lose their commander to a shell fragment.

16.24

16.15

17.57

16.04

16.00

15.36

15.42

2

1549

14.35

14.47

Suvorov sinks (19.20)

17.56

18.00

17.52

17.00

17.10

14.24

15.06

15.00

14.58

17.35

17.20

JAPANESE TOGO

Mikasa
Shikishima
Fuji
Asahi

1

14.47

15.00

Osylabia sinks (15.10)

14.35

14.24

RUSSIAN ROZHESTVENSKY

Suvorov
Aleksandr III
Borodino
Orel

◀ Simply the most important and also the most lopsided naval battle since the battle of Trafalgar in 1805, Togo's decisive victory at the battle of Tsushima destroyed Russia's naval power and forced Tsar Nicholas II to accept a negotiated peace that ended the Russo-Japanese War. At a cost of only three torpedo boats, Togo's fleet sank or captured 34 of Russia's 38 warships. Tsushima also helped make the Japanese navy popular, linking it with views on the national destiny, as well as encouraging politicians to associate themselves with the navy, which, in turn, helped secure its expansion.

fleet against an anchored Russian naval squadron that a Japanese destroyer squadron had attacked the previous night. When Togo reversed this decision and attacked at midday, the regrouped Russian warships provided a stronger than expected response that necessitated Togo's retreat. Although the Russian fleet remained, initially, blockaded at Port Arthur (Lushun, China), they broke out in August and engaged Togo's fleet. At the Battle of the Yellow Sea in August 1904, Togo's over-cautious approach again cost him a decisive victory. He would not make the same mistake for a third time.

Togo was given a final opportunity to secure decisive victory when Tsar Nicholas II ordered the Russian Baltic Squadron to the Far East. For Japan to win the war, destruction of this fleet was essential. A Japanese defeat here would not only embolden Russian forces to push on with their increasingly successful land war against the Japanese in Manchuria, but would also allow Russian warships to launch attacks against mainland Japan. As the Baltic Fleet steamed towards the Sea of Japan, Togo implemented a rigorous training programme that emphasized gunnery, communications, torpedo attacks and specific

manoeuvres geared towards giving the Combined Fleet unparalleled tactical advantage over the voyage-weary Russian squadron. It worked. On the morning of 27 May 1905, Togo's fleet annihilated the Russians at the battle of Tsushima. His achievements ended Russian hopes of overall victory and secured Japan's position as a regional power in northeast Asia and the Western Pacific until 1945.

News of this impressive victory spread quickly. With it, worldwide calls for a negotiated peace grew strong, which both countries accepted in September 1905. In a series of well-choreographed naval pageants – which, not without coincidence, coincided with the 100-year anniversary of the victory of Nelson (pp. 192–97) at Trafalgar – Togo was welcomed home by a grateful nation.

Though Togo served as Chief of the Navy General Staff between 1905 and 1909, the remaining years of his life were spent in positions where neither his near divinity nor hero status could easily be tarnished. In 1911 he attended the coronation celebrations of King George V in London followed by an extended tour of Britain and the United States. In both countries, Togo met politicians, journalists and the public, and impressed nearly everyone with his reserved and dignified presence – but most of all his silence. Togo remained throughout his life a man of few words.

Shortly before his death in 1934, Togo received the title of *koshaku* (marquis). He was afforded a state funeral that included a naval review attended by representatives and warships from America, Britain, China, France, Italy and the Netherlands. The Togo Shrine was opened in 1940 in Harajuku, Tokyo; along with the Mikasa Warship Memorial in Yokosuka, it remains a fitting tribute to Japan's greatest military hero.

▲ A popular print of the battle of Tsushima. The battle entered public consciousness as the battle that saved the Japanese empire.

▼ The battleship *Mikasa*, one of the most powerful and technologically advanced warships when launched in 1902, was Admiral Togo's flagship during the Russo-Japanese War.

Marshal Foch

French General and Commander of Allied Forces in World War I

'I am not waging war for the sake of waging war. If I obtain through the armistice the conditions that we wish to impose on Germany, I am satisfied.' MARSHAL FOCH

A Life in Brief

1851
Born at Tarbes, southwest France

1870
Volunteers for service during the Franco-Prussian War

1908
Commander of the *École supérieur de guerre*, Paris

1913
Commander of the elite XX Corps

1917, May
Chief of Staff of the French army

1918, March
Commander-in-chief of Allied forces on the Western Front

1918, August
Marshal of France

1929, 20 March
Dies in Paris

Ferdinand Foch began World War I as one of France's most aggressive corps commanders. His hard charging and offensive tactics cost France tremendous casualties in 1914 and 1915, but, unlike many other generals of his age, Foch learned to adapt to the new style of warfare. He was at his best when working at the grand strategic level. In 1918 he became commander-in-chief of the Allied armies on the Western Front, and successfully orchestrated the various national armies into a single, more coherent coalition capable of defeating the Germans.

In the years before World War I, Foch became famous for his determined advocacy of offensive infantry tactics. He also built close links with the British army, helping to decide how British and French forces might work together on the Continent to meet a future threat from Germany.

When war broke out, Foch was in command of the elite French XX Corps. His early offensives conformed to his ideas of war, but ended in bloody failure. Nevertheless, he played a central role at the First Battle of the Marne in command of an improvised Ninth Army, leading a risky but ultimately successful charge. Throughout 1915 he advocated more offensives, most of which failed, although they did convince him to develop new ideas based around modern technologies and doctrines that were more sparing of French lives. Using such methods, he led the relatively successful French portion of the battle of the Somme in 1916, but a new French government, anxious to limit troop losses, largely relegated him to lesser duties in the winter of 1916/17.  (➤ p. 243)

➤ Ferdinand Foch pictured shortly after the war in his capacity as military adviser to the Paris Peace Conference. The diplomats and politicians routinely disregarded his advice, leaving Foch bitter and angry at what he saw as a flawed peace treaty that did not adequately provide for France's security. In a final gesture of defiance, he refused to attend the signing ceremony at Versailles.

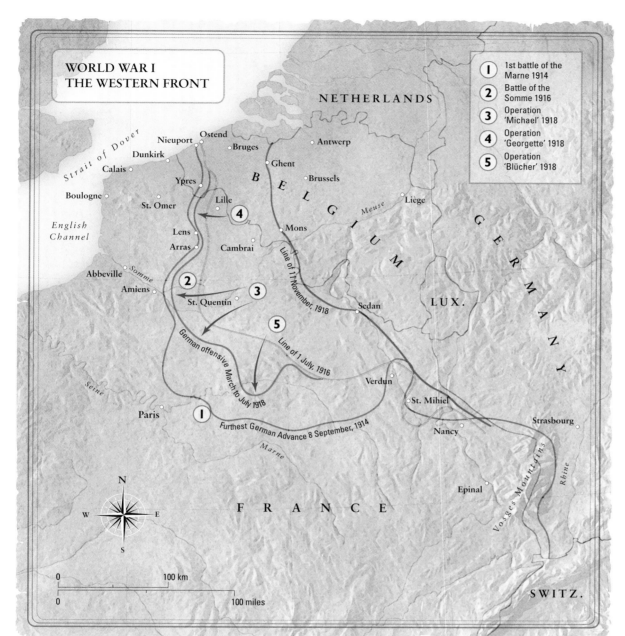

WORLD WAR I THE WESTERN FRONT

1. 1st battle of the Marne 1914
2. Battle of the Somme 1916
3. Operation 'Michael' 1918
4. Operation 'Georgette' 1918
5. Operation 'Blücher' 1918

NETHERLANDS

Strait of Dover

Nieuport • Ostend
Dunkirk • Bruges
Calais • Ghent • Antwerp
Boulogne • Ypres • Brussels
St. Omer • Lille **4** • Liège
English Channel • Lens • Mons
Abbeville • Arras • Cambrai
Amiens **2** • St. Quentin **3**
5
Paris **1**
Seine
Furthest German Advance 8 September, 1914

BELGIUM
GERMANY
LUX.
Meuse
Sedan
Verdun • St. Mihiel
Nancy • Strasbourg
Line of 11 November, 1918
Line of 1 July, 1916
German offensive March to July 1918
Marne
Epinal
Vosges Mountains
Rhine

F R A N C E

SWITZ.

0 ___ 100 km
0 ___ 100 miles

Key Battles

The First Battle of the Marne, 1914
Foch takes over an improvised army and leads it into a gap in the German lines near a swamp. He charges, breaking up a German offensive.

The Somme, 1916
Using more complex tactics and facing lighter opposition, Foch's French forces advance further than the British units to their north, but are unable to achieve meaningful operational results.

The Second Battle of the Marne, 1918
Foch oversees a massive redirection of forces; this enables his army commanders to launch the offensive that turns the tide of the war.

▶ Sword of honour awarded to Foch by the Ville de Paris. Foch helped to save Paris twice, in 1914 and again in 1918. In the latter case, he advised his wife to stay in the city even as the French government left for the safety of Bordeaux.

◀ An overview of the Western Front in World War I. Foch maintained an aggressive style of military leadership throughout his career, but the human cost of his early offensive tactics led him to adapt to the realities of modern warfare. Operations 'Michael', 'Georgette' and 'Blücher' were all part of the 1918 German offensive.

Marshal Henri-Philippe Pétain (1856–1951)

Pétain represented much of what was good and bad about France in the era of the two world wars. He vaulted to national prominence as commander of Army Group Centre during the titanic battle of Verdun in 1916. He developed a system called 'noria' (after a type of waterwheel), that rotated units in and out of the battle, and kept the supply lines open. He received the lion's share of the credit for the French ability to withstand the German attack there. Unlike Foch, Pétain's approach to war emphasized the power of the defensive and the need to limit counterattacks.

In 1917 Pétain became commander of the French army in the wake of a series of mutinies that followed the disastrous Nivelle Offensive. Pétain took a firm hold, rebuilding trust with his men and modernizing both doctrine and equipment. These reforms helped the French army recover from its losses and play a critical role in the final offensives of 1918. Pétain's perpetual pessimism cost him the job of Allied commander-in-chief, which went to Foch. The latter never fully trusted Pétain, whose grasp of the tactical and operational realities of modern war suited France well.

Pétain became a great French hero after 1918, but in 1940 he was brought out of retirement to negotiate an armistice with the Germans – a role that has made him the most controversial of France's World War I generals.

▲ French soldiers on the Marne in 1914. Within a few months all French soldiers would wear metal helmets and would be armed with large numbers of modern machine guns, artillery pieces, and, later in the war, tanks.

◀ ▶ The First Battle of the Marne, in which French and British forces repelled the advancing Germans who were within 30 miles of Paris. Foch is claimed to have reported to his generals: 'My centre is giving way and my right is in retreat. Situation excellent. I shall attack.' The French army are shown here taking advantage of the gap opened up in the German line by Von Kluck's turning to meet the French attack on his right. With the threat of complete encirclement evident by 9 September, the Germans went into retreat.

▼ Some of the men transported by taxi from Paris railway stations to the front lines. This episode formed a central part of the 'Miracle of the Marne' mythology that developed after the battle.

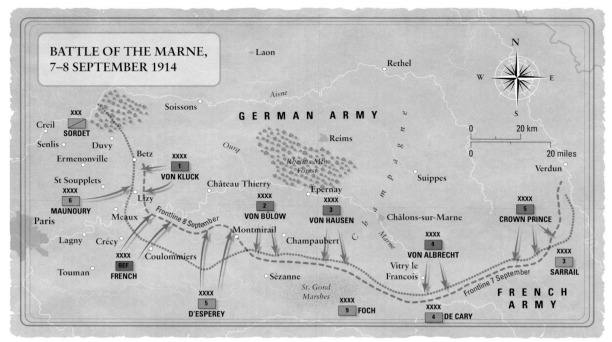

BATTLE OF THE MARNE, 7–8 SEPTEMBER 1914

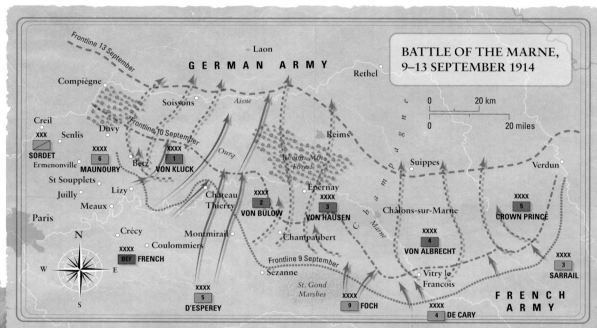

BATTLE OF THE MARNE, 9–13 SEPTEMBER 1914

Marshal Joseph Joffre (1852–1931)

In 1911 Joffre was a compromise choice for the role of Chief of Staff of the French army, chiefly due to his superior understanding of the military uses of railways. He wrote Plan XVII, the French war plan, which emphasized a concentration of forces in eastern France. It proved a poor choice in 1914, but Joffre reacted to the crisis calmly and professionally. He oversaw the gathering of forces that helped the Allies win the First Battle of the Marne, thereby saving Paris. He then began a ruthless process of firing dozens of officers who had not performed well,

although he continued to support Foch, whom he made commander of an army group at the end of the year.

Joffre and Foch's 1915 offensives were exceedingly bloody without producing the promised results. Joffre, a moderate republican, had also developed antagonistic relationships with several important French politicians. His failure to plan and prepare for the massive German assault at Verdun in 1916 led to a serious crisis in confidence in his leadership. Still regarded as a hero by the public, the French

government promoted Joffre to Marshal of France before forcing his retirement in December 1916. He then headed a critical French mission to the United States after America's entry into the war in 1917.

Field Marshal Sir Douglas Haig (1861–1928)

Douglas Haig came from a wealthy Scottish family and developed close ties to the British royal family and to King George V himself. He was a British corps commander at the outbreak of the war and performed well in the opening months. In 1915 Haig helped to design two battles that he believed Britain would have won if he had been given more resources. The resultant 1915 'shell scandal' led to the sacking of Sir John French as commander of the British Expeditionary Force, and Haig's promotion to that job.

Haig bears primary responsibility for the unrealistic goals and defects in planning that characterized the Somme campaign of 1916. His dour

nature often made people think he was not intelligent, and he soon developed contentious relations with British Prime Minister David Lloyd George, who sought unsuccessfully to replace him.

Haig came to appreciate the need for modern staff arrangements and weapons, such as tanks and airplanes, yet he proved to be unimaginative and stubborn, evidenced most starkly by his poor performance during the Passchendaele campaign in 1917. Political pressure mounted on him, but he remained dedicated to modernizing the British army and keeping the government focused on the Western Front as much as possible. In 1918, Haig agreed to

support Foch's appointment as commander-in-chief of Allied armies in the hope that French reinforcements might help to bolster British positions in Flanders and near the crucial English Channel ports. Haig remains the subject of intense historical debate, admired and reviled in equal measure.

▼ A British tank advances on the Somme, 1916. Foch commanded the French portion of the Somme offensive. His troops generally gained more ground than did the British under Haig. Foch, however, refused to criticize Haig's conduct of the campaign, even when pressed by British Prime Minister David Lloyd George.

▲ US troops cross a pontoon bridge over the Marne in the Second Battle of the Marne, 1918. During the battle Foch oversaw the integration of untried American divisions into veteran French corps. After the battle, he supported the formation of an independent American First Army with its own sector of the Western Front.

The Second Battle of the Marne, 1918

Allied Forces	Germans
Marshal Foch	**Crown Prince Wilhelm**
460,000 troops	505,000 troops
Casualties: 110,000	Casualties: 160,000

▼ The Second Battle of the Marne was Foch's masterpiece. He coordinated the efforts of French, British and American forces to win a critical victory. The battle stopped the German offensives and made Allied victory in 1918 possible.

▼ Amongst the ruins of a cathedral near the Marne, French troops drive back the Germans with machine guns, 1918.

Just before midnight on 27 May the German offensive begins.

The German advance continues, although in places the Allied forces are well prepared.

On 18 July a massive Allied counterattack begins in the direction of the critical rail junction of Soissons.

By mid-July the Germans are only halted by the barrier of the River Marne and repeated counterattacks by the French.

Admiral John Rushworth Jellicoe (1859–1935)

John Jellicoe was commander-in-chief of the highly regarded British Grand Fleet in 1914. Although the resources at his disposal were large, so too were his duties. He had the dual responsibility of keeping Britain's coastline secure from invasion and the empire's immediate lines of supply safe from German interference. Churchill famously called him 'the only man who could lose the war in a single afternoon'. The British government also expected him to deal with the German High Seas Fleet in a manner akin to Lord Nelson's annihilation of the French at Trafalgar in 1805. Jellicoe, however, thought such a feat beyond the Royal Navy's capability.

His chance to deal with the German navy came in June 1916 at the battle of Jutland (he is shown here on board a battleship on 31 May 1916). Although sailors of the Royal Navy handled their ships with skill and ultimately chased the German fleet back to Germany, in the eyes of many Jellicoe had failed to win a massive victory. He took a great deal of criticism for his caution at Jutland, although others understood that he had achieved the important goal of forcing the Germans back to their home ports. As recognition of his accomplishments, Jellicoe was promoted to First Sea Lord, the senior admiral in the fleet, at the end of the year. However, he was pessimistic about Britain's chances to defeat the German U-boat blockade, and his inability to deal with the German submarine threat in particular led to him being dismissed on 24 December 1917.

General John Pershing (1860–1948)

Pershing commanded the American Expeditionary Force during World War I. He insisted on training his men in offensive, open-warfare tactics that bore little resemblance to the realities of warfare in 1917 and 1918.

He also stubbornly resisted all attempts by European commanders, including Foch, to place American soldiers under European command. When the great German offensive of 1918 began in March, however, he agreed to meet the emergency by placing American divisions under French corps commanders. This policy proved to be a sensible compromise and the performance of American troops sufficiently impressed Foch and others to lead to the creation of a separate American First Army and a dedicated American section of the Western Front shortly after the Second Battle of the Marne. Pershing then supervised the two, great, distinctly American battles of the war: the reduction of the Saint-Mihiel salient and Meuse–Argonne Offensive (at the time, the largest battle ever fought by an American force).

'I have only one virtue. I have forgotten everything I once knew.' MARSHAL FOCH

In May 1917, Foch returned to prominence as Chief of Staff of the French army. Anticipating a German offensive in the spring of 1918, he was a firm advocate of placing one officer in charge of all Allied efforts on the Western Front and creating a combined multi-national reserve. When the German offensive did indeed begin in March, he emerged as the obvious candidate for the job of Allied commander-in-chief. In this role, Foch acted more as a coordinator than a commander, although he was successful in synchronizing strategy amongst the British, French and American armies.

In July 1918, Foch was one of the first Allied commanders to realize the opportunities that a strike against the German salient in the Marne Valley might provide. He was also almost alone in divining that the next German move would be east towards the rail centre of Reims, rather than west towards Paris. He directed the massive Allied counteroffensive known as the Second Battle of the Marne, which changed the momentum of the war. He was the first senior commander to realize that if the Allies moved quickly and efficiently, they could win the war in 1918. By November 1918 he had overseen a series of Allied offensives that had slowly pushed German forces back and made clear to the German high command that Germany could not win the war.

▼ The Allied commanders (left to right: Joffre, Foch, Haig, Pershing and Pétain) in jubilant moods at the victory celebration, Paris, 14 July 1919. During this period, Foch was awarded the titles of Honorary Field Marshal of Great Britain and Poland. Foch attended Haig's funeral in London in 1928 and died in Paris the following year.

Erich Ludendorff

Leading German General of World War I

'Total war involves the active participation of the whole population.'
ERICH LUDENDORFF

A Life in Brief

1865, 9 April
Born in Kruszewnia (Poland)

1877
Enters cadet school at Plön

1896
Captain

1906–08
Instructor in tactics and military history at the Kriegsakademie, Berlin

1907
Lieutenant-colonel

1911
Colonel

1914, August
Chief of Staff, Eighth Army

November 1914
Chief of Staff, Supreme Command East

1916
First General Quartermaster

1937, 20 December
Dies in Tutzing, Germany

◀ **Taking over a German army shattered by a failed offensive at Verdun and by a merciless Entente offensive on the Somme, Erich Ludendorff's extraordinary skills as an organizer allowed the German army to hold out through another two years of punishing warfare.**

Erich Ludendorff represented a new generation of Prusso-German officers who owed their positions less to the established political and social order of Imperial Germany and more to their abilities. His organizational and tactical skills made him the power behind the throne of the titular head of the German army, Paul von Hindenburg, from 1916 until 1918. Ludendorff is credited with introducing reforms that created a tactically efficient army, paving the way for blitzkrieg warfare.

Unlike many other officers, Ludendorff came from a humble background. Having served his time in line and marine infantry regiments, in 1890 he took a step that changed his career and arguably the course

of German history – he passed the entrance examination for the Kriegsakademie (War Academy) and began training as a General Staff officer. Ludendorff took full advantage of the opportunities this offered him, and worked very closely first with Alfred von Schlieffen and then from 1906 Helmuth von Moltke (the Younger). However, Ludendorff fell foul of high political forces in a row over army expansion and was assigned to a brigade command in a small provincial city in 1913.

Only the coming of war in August 1914 saved Ludendorff's flagging career. He won special recognition for his efforts in the capture of the Belgian fortress of Liège in 1914. On 22 August, he was appointed Chief of the General Staff of Eighth Army, which had been performing badly against the Russians. The combination with his commander, Paul von Hindenburg, proved to be one of the most fruitful of the war. Hindenburg provided authority and charisma as commander, while Ludendorff's keen mind planned and worked out operations behind the scenes. The two men arrived on the Eastern Front to find a demoralized Eighth Army facing a larger, advancing Russian force, and they acted quickly to re-establish order. At the battle of Tannenberg, German units converged on the Russian Second Army and almost annihilated it. The Eighth Army then trounced the Russian First Army to the north in what became known as the First Battle of the Masurian Lakes. These two victories removed the Russian threat to eastern Germany, and Hindenburg and Ludendorff were hailed as heroes.

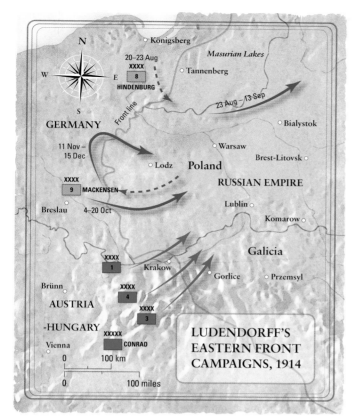

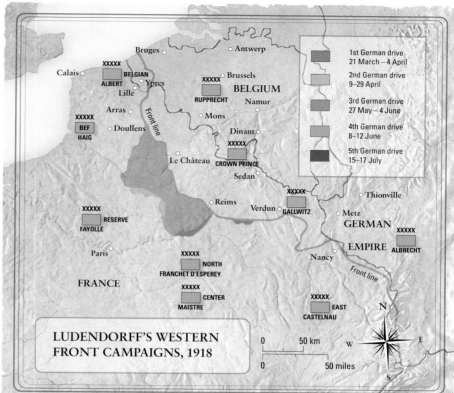

Key Battles

The Battle of Tannenberg, 26–31 August 1914
The German Eighth Army under the command of Paul von Hindenburg, with Ludendorff as his chief of staff, uses its superior rail transport to concentrate against the flanks of Alexander Samsonov's Second Army before it can unite with Paul von Rennenkampf's First Army to the north. The Russian Second Army is virtually surrounded in a classic battle of encirclement, and loses 140,000 of its 150,000 men, including Samsonov, who commits suicide.

The Somme Offensive, 21 March–5 April 1918
Using new infantry and artillery tactics, three German armies (Second, Seventeenth and Eighteenth) rip a 60-mile hole in the lines of the British Third and Fifth Armies and advance almost 50 miles. However, the advance is costly to German small-unit leaders, upon whom the new tactics depend, and the Germans have difficulties bringing up artillery and supplies. German casualties are nearly as great as those of the British and French, who lose around 240,000 dead, wounded or missing.

▶ The battle of Tannenberg and the battle of the Masurian Lakes a few days later stopped the Russian invasion of eastern Germany in its tracks. At the same time, a major contrast between German success and Austrian failure further south became apparent. Although these battles achieved a great deal and the Russians suffered heavy casualties, ultimately they were merely setbacks for the Russians and not the 'decisive' battles hoped for. The Russians were able to make good their losses and continue the war for another 3 years.

▲ The offensives of 1918 were Germany's last gamble to produce a battlefield victory that would end World War I before American troops could reach Europe. Although, like Tannenberg, they produced stunning tactical successes and inflicted heavy casualties on the Entente forces, the Germans were too weak to deliver the knock-out battlefield success needed to end the war. By the end of the offensives, the German army had been weakened to such an extent that it was incapable of defending against the Entente counterattacks. Thus, what was meant to provide a German victory ultimately brought a German defeat.

Paul von Hindenburg (1847–1934)

Hindenburg and Ludendorff formed one of the most effective command teams of World War I. The older Hindenburg provided authority and leadership, while the younger Ludendorff brought energy and intelligence. Recalled from retirement in August 1914, Hindenburg was dispatched to the Eastern Front to take command of the failing Eighth Army. Under his command, Eighth Army annihilated two superior Russian armies in August and September 1914, freeing Germany from the threat of invasion and gaining Hindenburg a popular following. Hindenburg used this to achieve his and Ludendorff's political goals, particularly after he was named Chief of the General Staff of the German army in August 1916. The two men effectively functioned as a dictatorship from 1916 to the end of the war. Under Hindenburg's command, Ludendorff made the German army fit for modern warfare: tactics were updated, older personnel were replaced and industrial mobilization brought new weapons. These steps were not enough, however, to prevent defeat by the Allies. Hindenburg oversaw the dissolution of the Hohenzollern monarchy, but remained a popular figure and was elected President of the Weimar Republic in May 1925, a post he held until his death in 1934.

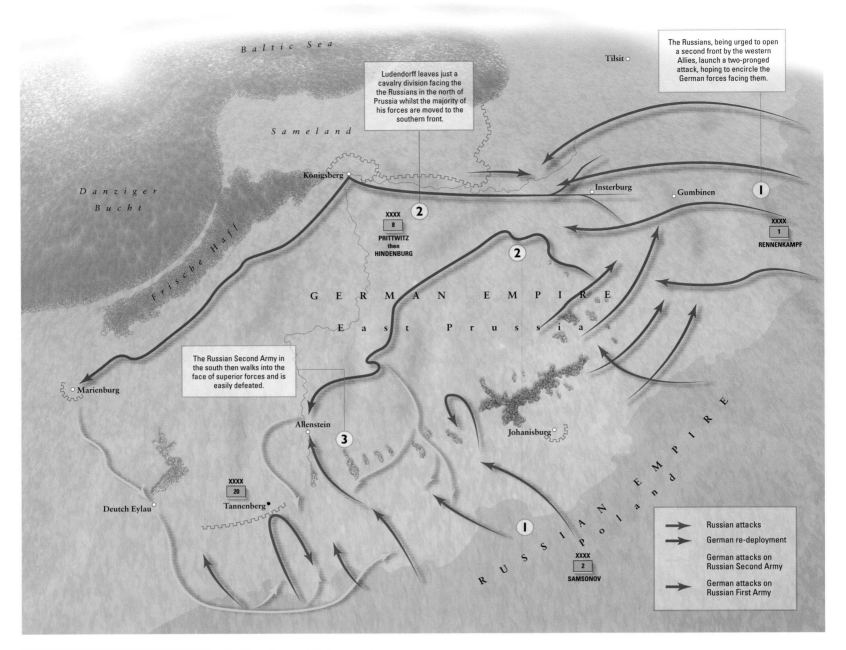

The Russians, being urged to open a second front by the western Allies, launch a two-pronged attack, hoping to encircle the German forces facing them.

Ludendorff leaves just a cavalry division facing the the Russians in the north of Prussia whilst the majority of his forces are moved to the southern front.

The Russian Second Army in the south then walks into the face of superior forces and is easily defeated.

XXXX 8 PRITTWITZ then HINDENBURG

XXXX 1 RENNENKAMPF

XXXX 20

XXXX 2 SAMSONOV

→ Russian attacks

⇒ German re-deployment

German attacks on Russian Second Army

→ German attacks on Russian First Army

Baltic Sea

Sameland

Danziger Bucht

Frische Haff

Königsberg

Tilsit ○

Insterburg

Gumbinen

G E R M A N   E M P I R E

E a s t   P r u s s i a

Marienburg

Allenstein

Johanisburg

Deutch Eylau

Tannenberg

R U S S I A N   P o l a n d   E M P I R E

Erich Ludendorff

Modern Age

The Battle of Tannenberg, 1914

Germans	Russians
Paul von Hindenburg (Chief of Staff: Erich Ludendorff)	Alexander Samsonov
100,000 troops	150,000 troops
Casualties: 12,500 killed or wounded	Casualties: 30,000 killed or wounded, 95,000 captured

▲ Superior staff work, bold German leadership and timid Russian commanders allowed the German Eighth Army to concentrate its units on the Russian Second Army and carry out a classic battle of encirclement. Cut off from outside assistance and pounded from all sides, the men of the Russian Second Army had little choice but to surrender or to die.

➤ Here, German infantrymen advance across an open field under Russian artillery fire during the battle of Tannenberg. In the open, infantrymen were extremely vulnerable to the effects of enemy artillery. Consequently, 1914 saw extremely high casualties on all sides. To provide some protection from enemy fire, trenches were dug. In the west, this led to four years of stalemate.

➤➤ During the battle of Tannenberg, German and Russian soldiers fought desperate actions in the villages and towns of East Prussia, leaving many, such as this one, in ruins.

These successes laid the foundation for Hindenburg and Ludendorff to be appointed to the German High Command in August 1916, where they effectively functioned as a 'silent dictatorship'. During this period, Ludendorff made his greatest mark on the German army. He introduced sweeping changes to both defensive and offensive tactics, often termed storm-troop tactics, emphasizing decentralized command and control of the infantry and combined arms. These changes allowed small-unit commanders to take advantage of fleeting opportunities on the battlefield without having to wait for authorization, and increased the cooperation between infantry and artillery.

The new defensive tactics allowed the German army to absorb tremendous blows inflicted by the Western Allies in the Second Battle of the Aisne (16 April–9 May 1917) and Passchendaele (31 July–

Alexei Brusilov (1853–1926)

Brusilov was one of Imperial Russia's most successful generals. Promoted to command of the Southwest Army Group in early 1916, he put his ideas of deception and surprise into wider practice during the so-called 'Brusilov Offensive' of June 1916 in which his army captured 25,000 square kilometres from and inflicted some 1.5 million casualties on the Austro-Hungarian army.

6 November 1917) at relatively low cost to itself. The German offensives against the Russians at Riga (1–3 September 1917) and the Italians at Caporetto (24 October–10 November 1917) proved that storm-troop tactics could succeed, and Ludendorff planned to use them to inflict a decisive blow against the Western Allies in spring 1918 before US troops could arrive in large numbers. Marshalling all available German forces and resources, Ludendorff launched this new Somme offensive on 21 March. The initial results were better than anyone could have hoped for and were unique for the Western Front. However, it proved difficult to bring artillery and supplies forward over badly damaged battlefields, and the great offensive soon ran out of steam. Between April and July, Ludendorff launched four other offensives in an effort to finish off the Western Allies, but each of these met the same fate as the first. Recognizing that the German army was exhausted and victory out of reach, Ludendorff called for an armistice in early October 1918. The German army was too weak and the Allied forces too strong for Ludendorff's simple battlefield approach to succeed.

After the German collapse, Ludendorff fled to Sweden to avoid revolution at home and a vindictive Allied force. He returned in late 1919, and for the remainder of his life worked to shift blame for the German defeat onto others, most notably the Jews and Social Democrats, and to overthrow the Weimar Republic. He participated in Hitler's 1923 Beer Hall Putsch and served as a representative of the Nazi Party in the Reichstag from 1924 to 1928, but fell out with the Nazis before his death in 1937.

▲ New offensive tactics allowed the German army to break the deadlock of the trenches in the spring of 1918. Relying on small teams of soldiers armed with a wide range of weapons (known as 'stormtroops'), German units sliced through Allied lines and were only stopped when they outran their own artillery protection. In this photo, a stormtroop makes attacks through a French position at Villers-Bretonneux in April 1918.

▼ The Hindenburg-Ludendorff team was one of the most effective command teams of World War I. The aristocratic Hindenburg functioned as a 'replacement emperor' for Germany between 1916 and 1918, while Ludendorff worked largely behind the scenes. Here, the two men review German officers.

Mustafa Kemal

Great Turkish Nationalist Leader

'Freedom and independence define my character.'

MUSTAFA KEMAL

A Life in Brief

1881, 19 May
Born in Salonika, Macedonia

1915
Commands the 19th Division at Gallipoli

1916
Commands XVI Corps in the Caucasus

1917–18
Commander of Seventh Army, and Lightning Group, in Syria/ Palestine

1921
Appointed commander-in-chief by the National Assembly

1923
Becomes first president of Turkey

1938, 10 November
Dies in Istanbul

◄ **This medal is the Gallipoli Star, awarded to veterans of the Gallipoli campaign. Victories in the defensive naval campaign in 1915, and then in the campaign on Gallipoli, raised the prestige and morale of the Ottoman forces.**

◀ **Mustafa Kemal, pictured around 1916. He had left the Gallipoli campaign in December 1915 after serious disagreements with Liman von Sanders and Enver Pasha. But his obvious talents saw him command a Corps and then an Army in 1916.**

The man born plain Mustafa (his schoolteacher added 'Kemal' to his name) first rose to prominence in the 1915 Gallipoli campaign, where he organized the successful defence of the peninsula during the Allied landings. Later, he enjoyed success in the 1916 Caucasus campaign, and as army commander in 1917–18. His greatest achievement, though, was as commander-in-chief during the Turkish War of Independence (1919–22), which led to the creation of modern Turkey and the granting of the name Atatürk ('father of the Turks').

Mustafa Kemal was both a politician and a soldier. As a nationalist, he acted against the sultan's Ottoman regime, and strongly objected to German military influence. As a soldier, he proved an aggressive commander when needed, but often advocated defensive strategies. In the 1911–12 Cyrenaica Campaign against the Italians, Kemal was primarily a staff officer. In Gallipoli in 1915, Kemal acted decisively to defend against the Australian and New Zealand landing on 25 April, when he rapidly ordered his division forward and coordinated the defence. Later, Kemal assumed overall command in the vital Chunuk Bair area, and on 10 August 1915 launched a mass attack at dawn, which turned back the crucial Allied positions on the high ground, and ultimately forced the Allied withdrawal.

Rising in rank, Kemal commanded XVI Corps in the Caucasus in 1916, where he both attacked and retreated as the situation demanded. Appointed to an army command in Syria/Palestine in 1917–18, Kemal advocated a purely defensive strategy and argued against the plans of the German commanders. By then the Ottoman army was in disarray, and Kemal conducted a retreat until the armistice.

Kemal became as much a politician as a soldier during the ensuing political-military war against his Ottoman opponents, and against the Allied occupiers, especially the Greeks. As commander-in-chief, Kemal directed a defensive strategy of the 'inner sanctuary' of Anatolia, in which the Greek army would be used up in a Turkish defence in depth of the whole country; his plan succeeded. Kemal did not command the army personally, except at the battle of Dumlupinar (26–30 August 1922), which concluded the war, but he set overall strategy. During the battle, Kemal commanded Turkish forces in the south and west, which led the main attack, and ordered the pincer movement that encircled the Greek army and led to its rout. Kemal then went on to reform Ottoman society radically and create modern Turkey, as Atatürk.

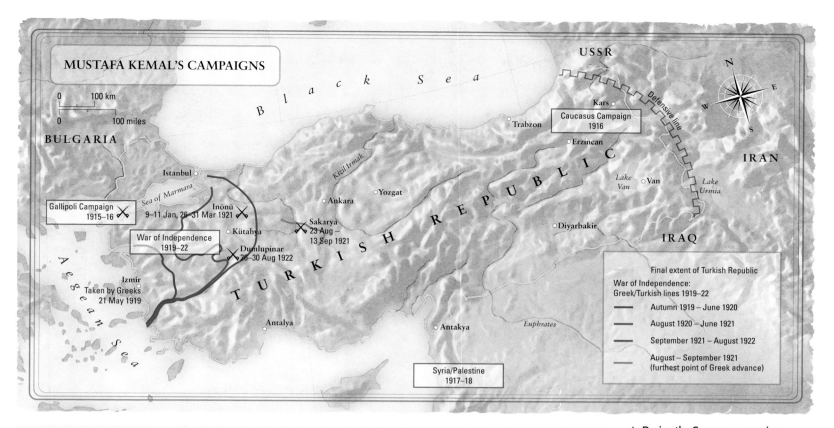

MUSTAFA KEMAL'S CAMPAIGNS

0   100 km
0   100 miles

BULGARIA

Black Sea

USSR

Trabzon

Caucasus Campaign
1916

Kars

Defensive line

Erzincan

IRAN

Istanbul

Sea of Marmara

Inönü
9–11 Jan, 26–31 Mar 1921

Gallipoli Campaign
1915–16

Kızıl Irmak

Ankara

Yozgat

Lake
Van

Van

Lake
Urmia

War of Independence
1919–22

Kütahya

Sakarya
23 Aug –
13 Sep 1921

T U R K I S H   R E P U B L I C

Diyarbakir

IRAQ

Dumlupinar
26–30 Aug 1922

Izmir
Taken by Greeks
21 May 1919

Aegean Sea

Antalya

Antakya

Euphrates

Final extent of Turkish Republic
War of Independence:
Greek/Turkish lines 1919–22

Autumn 1919 – June 1920

August 1920 – June 1921

September 1921 – August 1922

August – September 1921
(furthest point of Greek advance)

Syria/Palestine
1917–18

▲ During the Caucasus campaign
Kemal commanded XVI Corps. Later
he commanded Seventh Army and the
Lightning Group in Syria/Palestine.
Then Kemal assumed overall strategic
command in the War of Independence
in Anatolia (battle sites shown).

Key Battles

**The Gallipoli Campaign,
April 1915–January 1916**
British and French forces
land on Gallipoli, but
cannot advance. Kemal
is instrumental in halting
the Allied attacks in April
and August 1915. After a
long campaign, the Allies
are eventually forced
to withdraw.

**The Caucasus Campaign,
1916**
On the disputed borders
between the Russian and
Ottoman empires, Kemal
emerges as a capable corps
commander in both attack
and defence, notably during
the battle of Bitlis.

**Syria/Palestine,
1917–18**
Overwhelming British forces
advance north and force
the Ottomans to capitulate
in October 1918. Kemal's
retreat preserves Ottoman
arms, equipment and
manpower.

**The War of Independence,
1919–22**
In the wake of the Greek
capture of Izmir in 1919,
Turkish troops win the battles
of First and Second Inönü,
Sakarya, and Dumlupinar
against the Greeks. Kemal is
chief strategist, and military
commander at Dumlupinar.

◄ Around 1922 Kemal reviews troops
during the War of Independence,
largely fought against Greek forces. His
defensive strategy coupled with aggressive
counteroffensives won the day for Turkish
forces, leading to overall Turkish victory,
and to Kemal's leadership of modern
Turkey as Atatürk.

*'You can be sure
that when he
is made pasha,
he will want to
become sultan,
and that if he
became sultan,
he would want
to be God.'*

ENVER PASHA ON KEMAL

Erich von Manstein

Ablest of Hitler's Generals

'The confidence of the man in the ranks rests upon a man's strength of character.' ERICH VON MANSTEIN

A Life in Brief

1887, November 17
Born in Berlin, adopted by childless Prussian noble family

1906
Commissioned as a Prussian Guards officer

1913
Attends War Academy

1914, November
Severely wounded on Western Front

1920
Company commander

1935
Head of Operations, Army General Staff

1936
First Quartermaster, Army General Staff

1939
Chief of Staff, Army Group South

1940
Chief of Staff, Army Group A

1941, June
Commander, LVI Corps

1941, September
Commander, Eleventh Army

1942
Commander, Army Group Don

1943
Commander, Army Group South

1944, March
Dismissed by Hitler

1973, June 12
Dies at Irschenhausen, Bavaria

◀ Manstein (foreground) confers with his staff officers about dispositions and deployments over a map board sometime during 1942–43.

Manstein was one of the key operational commanders of World War II, and an outstanding staff officer. However, he was not a frontline commander who commanded loyalty and affection from his troops, and he shared the lack of strategic vision of many other German generals. His accomplishments as a commander are also often exaggerated, notably in his own memoirs.

Manstein's military career began in the Prussian Guards. In 1913 he attended the War Academy for aspiring staff officers. Badly wounded in November 1914, he served for the rest of World War I as an operations officer. After Germany's defeat he joined the Frontier Guard service before becoming a company commander in the interwar army. Hitler's rise to power

Key Battles and Campaigns

Operation Case Red, France, June 1940
Due to his differences with Halder, Manstein commands XXXVIII Corps (part of Günther von Kluge's Fourth Army) during the invasion of France, and is only involved in Operation Case Red, the second stage of the campaign to take France. His corps spearheads the advance from the River Somme to the River Loire, and is the first German unit to cross the Seine.

The Crimea, September 1941–July 1942
Manstein ably commands the Eleventh Army during the conquest of the Crimea (September–October 1941); only the port-city of Sevastopol holds out against the German onslaught. Between December 1941 and April 1942 he defends German gains against a surprise Soviet counteroffensive on the Kertsch Peninsula, but the eastern Crimea is lost. He is fortunate to keep his command after this setback, and in May 1942 launches a swift counteroffensive,

which routs the Red Army and recaptures the eastern Crimea in just two weeks. In June, Manstein renews his assault on, and finally conquers, Sevastopol. Hitler rewards him by promoting him to field marshal.

The Attempted Relief of Stalingrad, December 1942
Manstein takes command of Army Group Don and endeavours, unsuccessfully, to rescue Friedrich Paulus's Sixth Army encircled at Stalingrad, in Operation Winter Storm. Fourth Panzer Army makes some headway to the beleaguered Axis forces, but is forced to withdraw by enveloping Soviet forces to the north.

The Third Battle of Kharkov, February–March 1943
In a desperate effort to evade being encircled and annihilated by the Soviet advance on Rostov, Manstein effects a strategic withdrawal from the Caucasus into the eastern Ukraine. On 21 February, Manstein launches a stunning counteroffensive, spearheaded by the Leibstandarte Adolf Hitler division, that routs the Red Army. Kharkov is recaptured on 14 March. Hitler rewards Manstein with the Oak Leaves for his Knight's Cross.

▶▶ Manstein devised the plans for the southern advance on Warsaw in September 1939 during the Polish Campaign as well as the penetration through the Ardennes in June 1940. In 1941 he commanded the advance through the Baltic States, the Ukraine, and the Crimea. In 1942 he stormed Sevastopol but failed to relieve the beleaguered Sixth Army at Stalingrad during the following winter. He recaptured Kharkov in March 1943; participated in the failed 'Citadel' offensive at Kursk in July; and rescued part of the forces encircled in the Cherkassy Pocket in February 1944.

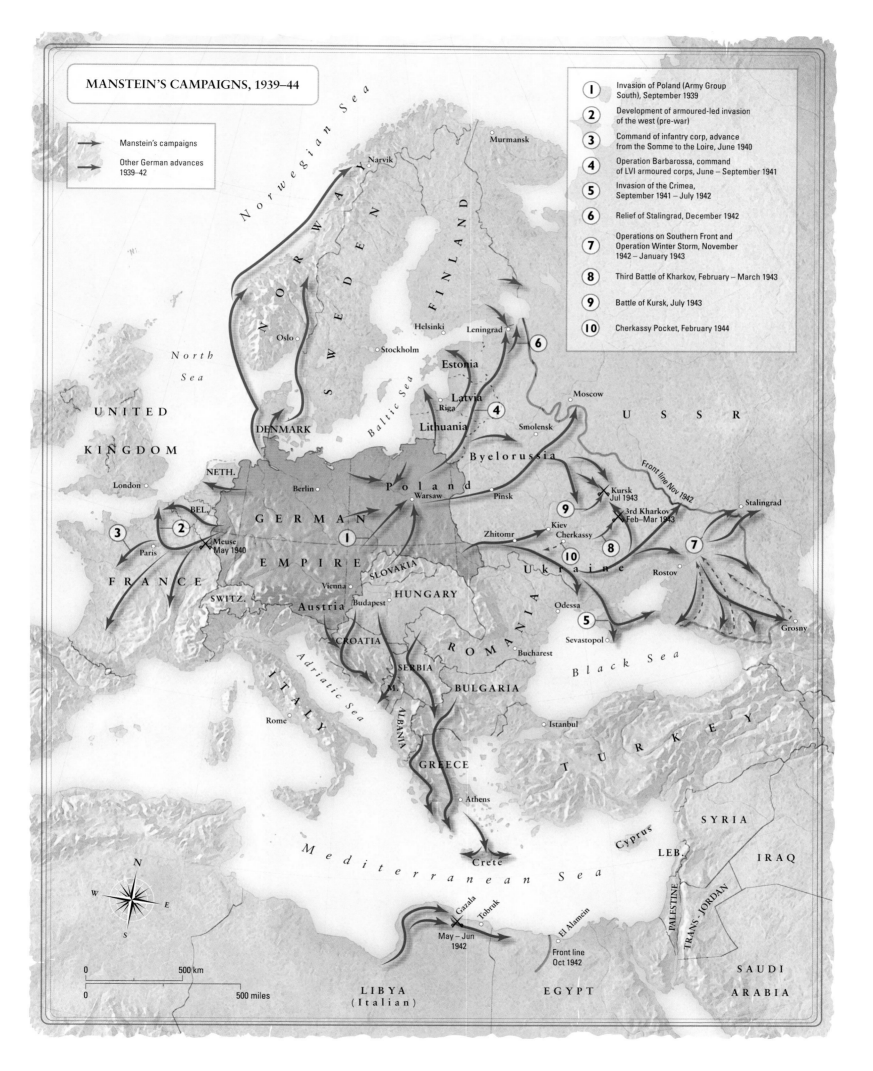

MANSTEIN'S CAMPAIGNS, 1939–44

Manstein's campaigns

Other German advances
1939–42

1. Invasion of Poland (Army Group South), September 1939
2. Development of armoured-led invasion of the west (pre-war)
3. Command of infantry corp, advance from the Somme to the Loire, June 1940
4. Operation Barbarossa, command of LVI armoured corps, June – September 1941
5. Invasion of the Crimea, September 1941 – July 1942
6. Relief of Stalingrad, December 1942
7. Operations on Southern Front and Operation Winter Storm, November 1942 – January 1943
8. Third Battle of Kharkov, February – March 1943
9. Battle of Kursk, July 1943
10. Cherkassy Pocket, February 1944

Norwegian Sea

Murmansk

Narvik

NORWAY

SWEDEN

FINLAND

North Sea

Helsinki

Leningrad

Oslo

Stockholm

Estonia

Baltic Sea

Latvia

Riga

Moscow

U S S R

DENMARK

Lithuania

Smolensk

UNITED

KINGDOM

NETH.

Berlin

Byelorussia

London

Poland

Warsaw

Pinsk

Front line Nov 1942

Stalingrad

BEL.

Kursk
Jul 1943

GERMAN

Kiev

3rd Kharkov
Feb–Mar 1943

Meuse
May 1940

Paris

EMPIRE

Zhitomr

Cherkassy

Ukraine

Rostov

7

FRANCE

SLOVAKIA

SWITZ.

Vienna

HUNGARY

Austria

Budapest

ROMANIA

Odessa

Sevastopol

Black Sea

Grosny

CROATIA

Bucharest

SERBIA

Adriatic Sea

M.

BULGARIA

ITALY

ALBANIA

Rome

Istanbul

GREECE

T U R K E Y

Athens

Cyprus

SYRIA

LEB.

IRAQ

Mediterranean Sea

Crete

PALESTINE

TRANS-JORDAN

N

W   E

S

Gazala

Tobruk

El Alamein

May – Jun
1942

Front line
Oct 1942

SAUDI

0   500 km

0   500 miles

LIBYA
(Italian)

EGYPT

ARABIA

Heinz Guderian (1888–1954)

Guderian was a military theorist and self-proclaimed father of the German armoured force of World War II. In the 1930s he advocated the employment of concentrated tank forces to restore offensive power to the battlefield. He contributed to the creation of independent Panzer divisions and was a daring operational field commander in Germany's blitzkrieg victories early in the war.

Guderian led the XIX Motorized Corps in the 1939 Polish campaign, crossing the Polish Corridor and advancing deep into the enemy rear. During May 1940 he effected the penetration through the Ardennes and forced the River Meuse, leading to the isolation and evacuation of the British Expeditionary Force from Dunkirk. He then led a Panzer group deep into the French rear in June 1940 to complete the defeat of France (he is shown here in a command vehicle in 1940, with an Enigma coding machine in the foreground). The next summer he led the Second Panzer Group in dramatic encirclements

of Soviet forces at Minsk, Smolensk and Kiev during Operation Barbarossa, the Axis invasion of the Soviet Union. As his spearheads neared the outskirts of Moscow in early December, the advance stalled. Driven back during the Soviet winter counteroffensive, Guderian was dismissed by Hitler on 26 December.

In the wake of disastrous defeats at Stalingrad and on the Don, Hitler recalled Guderian on 1 March 1943 as Inspector General of Armoured Forces, in an effort to revitalize the tank arm. Yet he proved unable to reverse Germany's mounting defeats. After the failed 20 July 1944 assassination plot on Hitler, Guderian was elevated to acting chief of the Army General Staff, where he attempted to halt the Soviet advance on Germany. He masterminded the brief spoiling attack at Arnswalde in February 1945 that delayed the final Soviet offensive on Berlin. Increasing disagreements led the Führer to force convalescence leave on Guderian in mid-March.

▾▸ **The battle of the Meuse.** The forces of Heinz Guderian's XIX Panzer Corps launched six assault crossings of the Meuse north of Sedan on 13 May 1940 under heavy artillery and Stuka dive bomber fire support. In the picture below, a German light tank stands before a badly damaged bridge. After heavy fighting in the face of fierce resistance, three bridgeheads were established and, having reinforced the lodgements, the Germans were able first to consolidate them together, repulsing heavy French counterattacks, and then break out towards both the west and the south.

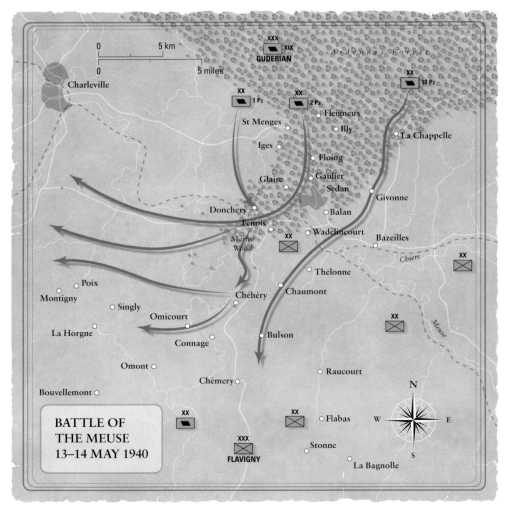

BATTLE OF
THE MEUSE
13–14 MAY 1940

provided unprecedented opportunity for promotion and in July 1935 Manstein became Head of the Operations Branch in the Army General Staff. In 1938 he received a coveted field command of an infantry division, and as war approached he became Chief of Staff of Army Group South.

THE YEARS OF CONQUEST

In his role as Chief of Staff, Manstein helped devise the plan for a concentrated armoured thrust from Silesia into Poland and on to Warsaw (Operation Case White). The invasion of Poland was launched on 1 September 1939, and was a great success for the new blitzkrieg tactics.

During spring 1940, Manstein, now Chief of Staff of Army Group A, proffered a more audacious plan for the invasion of France than the original 'Case Yellow' proposed by Franz Halder, head of the Army General Staff. Halder's plan essentially replicated the failed Schlieffen Plan of 1914, which sought to defeat the French army quickly by an advance through Belgium, before concentrating all resources on defeating Russia in the east. After intense debate, and despite much opposition, a modified version

of Manstein's 'cut of the sickle' plan was adopted in February. Manstein envisaged concentrated armoured forces negotiating the hilly, forested Ardennes and forcing the River Meuse, thereby penetrating the Allied front and isolating the British Expeditionary Force from the bulk of the French army. His plan worked; it achieved strategic surprise, and correctly predicted Allied intentions of advancing into Belgium to thwart a renewed Schlieffen Plan, leaving them exposed to envelopment. However, Manstein made enemies while advancing his ideas: Halder struck back by posting him to command a second-wave infantry corps that only participated late in the campaign. Hitler, however, promoted Manstein to full general and awarded him the Knight's Cross for devising the plan.

In June 1941 Manstein led a corps in the drive on Leningrad during Operation Barbarossa, the German invasion of the Soviet Union. His success led to promotion in September to command the Eleventh Army, tasked with conquering the Crimea. His forces broke through the Perekop Isthmus during October and by mid-November had subdued the peninsula, with the exception of the fortified port-city of Sevastopol. Manstein's first attempt to capture Sevastopol failed,

▲ A German Panzer III tank with superstructure removed. Such vehicles were used as tractors or to carry supplies and equipment, particularly for assault engineers. This vehicle is advancing in the vicinity of Grodno on 26 June 1941 during the opening days of Operation Barbarossa, the German invasion of the Soviet Union.

◄ A photo reconnaissance image shows German armour supported by armoured personnel carriers transporting mechanized infantry engaging Soviet forces at long range during the retreat from Orel on 12 August 1942. The German strategic withdrawal was occasioned by their defeat at Kursk during Operation Citadel the previous month. Several hit vehicles can be seen on fire.

Erich von Manstein

Modern Age

Erwin Rommel (1891–1944)

Rommel was a dynamic and courageous leader who was loved by his troops and admired by his enemies. In 1929 he became a military instructor, and his popular text *Infantry Attacks!* led to appointments as commander of Hitler's personal escort in 1938 and the 7th Panzer Division in 1940. Rommel led the latter with distinction in the 1940 French campaign, penetrating the country's defences and repulsing the Allied counterattack at Arras during May, before advancing to Cherbourg in June. In February 1941 Hitler entrusted Rommel with a small force (which later became the Afrika Korps) to bolster Italian forces in Libya. Rommel pursued an aggressive defence that routed British and Commonwealth forces in two major advances during 1941–42. He broke through at Gazala in May 1942 and stormed Tobruk on 21 June – a feat for which Hitler promoted

him to field marshal – before advancing to El Alamein. Montgomery's Eighth Army wore down Panzer Army Afrika during the Second Battle of El Alamein, while Rommel was on sick leave, and then drove Axis forces back to Tunisia. Rommel returned to thwart the Allied attempt to overrun Tunisia during Operation Torch (November 1942), but could not prevent the Axis collapse in Tunisia in May 1943.

In July 1943 Hitler appointed Rommel commander of Army Group B, which assumed the defence of northern France and Belgium in November. He energetically prepared to stop the Allies on the beaches and annihilate them with a rapid armoured counterthrust. However, Rommel failed to repulse the June 1944 invasion and

was seriously injured during an air attack. The involvement of his staff in the 20 July assassination plot against Hitler placed him under suspicion. Hitler gave him the choice of being tried for treason or committing suicide. Rommel took his own life on 14 October 1944, and was buried with full military honours.

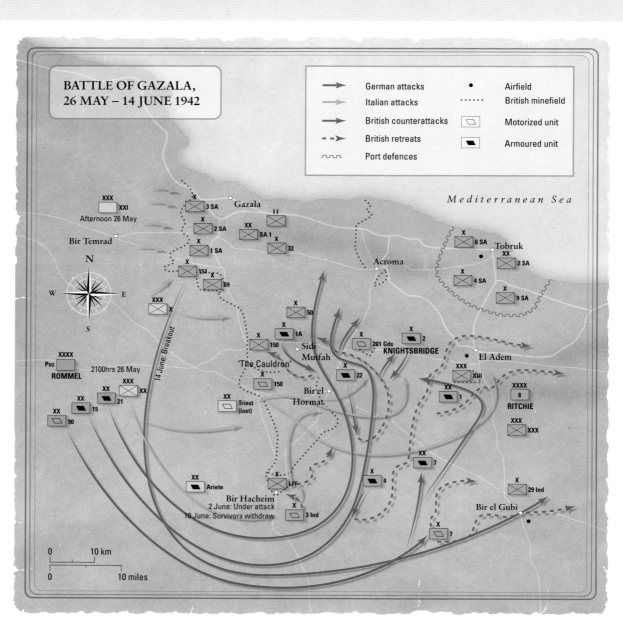

BATTLE OF GAZALA, 26 MAY – 14 JUNE 1942

German attacks
Italian attacks
British counterattacks
British retreats
Port defences
Airfield
British minefield
Motorized unit
Armoured unit

▲▲ Night-time image showing a German armoured car in action during the siege of Tobruk in North Africa during June 1942.

▲ A German artillery piece continues the onslaught during daytime against the besieged defenders of Tobruk.

➤ The battle of Gazala and the fall of Tobruk. Rommel, after his infantry divisions had pinned the Allied front line in the defences of the Gazala Line, took his armour round the southern bastion of Bir Hacheim, repulsed repeated British armoured counterattacks at Bir el Gubi and advanced to the coast, before reversing direction to strike northwestwards along the coast to storm Tobruk.

'The German generals of this war were the best-finished product of their profession — anywhere.'
BASIL LIDDELL HART

and he had to suspend his second in late December when Soviet forces landed at Kerch and recaptured the Eastern Crimea. Caught unawares by the Soviet counteroffensive, he was fortunate that the divisional commander who failed to hold the isthmus became the scapegoat.

In May 1942 Manstein launched a new offensive that ejected the Red Army from the Eastern Crimea within two weeks, paving the way for a lavishly supported assault on Sevastopol. There was little finesse to the capture of the port-city, though, it being accomplished by overwhelming firepower. Organized Soviet resistance ceased on 4 July: however, pockets remained for months after this and the price of victory

proved high. Hitler was pleased by his success, and subsequently dispatched Manstein to capture Leningrad, which had been under siege since September 1941. Here, he thwarted repeated Soviet attempts to relieve the city, but Soviet spoiling attacks interfered with his plans for a decisive assault on the city.

THE TIDE TURNS IN THE EAST

On 21 November 1942 Hitler appointed Manstein to command the newly formed Army Group Don, tasked with rescuing the encircled Sixth Army at Stalingrad. His relief effort came within 30 miles of the trapped army, but Manstein waited too long and failed to rescue it; part of it might possibly have escaped if he had ordered the army to break out earlier. Moreover, the Soviet

▶▲ Romanian troops support Manstein's final assault on Sevastopol, codenamed Operation Stoerfang, on 7 July 1942. Depicted is a late war version of the Mauser Karabiner 98. This became the standard German rifle of World War II. A modified version of the original Mauser Gewehr 98, over 14 million were produced between 1935 and 1945 and saw service in every theatre.

255

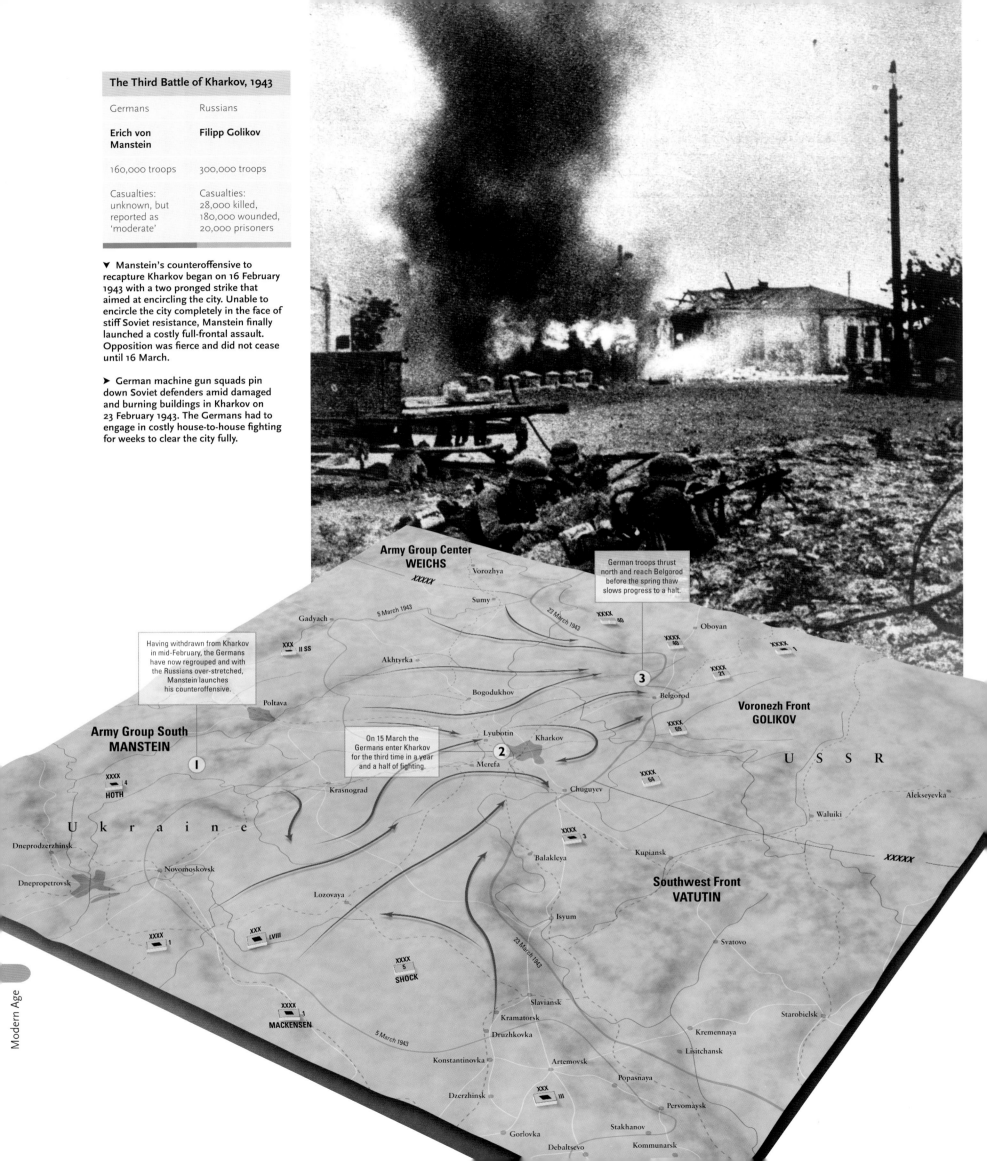

The Third Battle of Kharkov, 1943

Germans	Russians
Erich von Manstein	**Filipp Golikov**
160,000 troops	300,000 troops
Casualties: unknown, but reported as 'moderate'	Casualties: 28,000 killed, 180,000 wounded, 20,000 prisoners

▼ Manstein's counteroffensive to recapture Kharkov began on 16 February 1943 with a two pronged strike that aimed at encircling the city. Unable to encircle the city completely in the face of stiff Soviet resistance, Manstein finally launched a costly full-frontal assault. Opposition was fierce and did not cease until 16 March.

➤ German machine gun squads pin down Soviet defenders amid damaged and burning buildings in Kharkov on 23 February 1943. The Germans had to engage in costly house-to-house fighting for weeks to clear the city fully.

Army Group Center
WEICHS

Army Group South
MANSTEIN

Voronezh Front
GOLIKOV

Southwest Front
VATUTIN

Having withdrawn from Kharkov in mid-February, the Germans have now regrouped and with the Russians over-stretched, Manstein launches his counteroffensive.

On 15 March the Germans enter Kharkov for the third time in a year and a half of fighting.

German troops thrust north and reach Belgorod before the spring thaw slows progress to a halt.

U k r a i n e

U S S R

HOTH

MACKENSEN

SHOCK

Vorozhya
Sumy
Gadyach
Oboyan
Akhtyrka
Bogodukhov
Belgorod
Poltava
Lyubotin
Kharkov
Merefa
Krasnograd
Chuguyev
Alekseyevka
Waluiki
Dneprodzerzhinsk
Novomoskovsk
Balakleya
Kupiansk
Dnepropetrovsk
Lozovaya
Isyum
Svatovo
Slaviansk
Starobielsk
Kramatorsk
Druzhkovka
Kremennaya
Lisitchansk
Konstantinovka
Artemovsk
Dzerzhinsk
Popasnaya
Pervomaysk
Stakhanov
Gorlovka
Debaltsevo
Kommunarsk

5 March 1943
23 March 1943
5 March 1943
23 March 1943

Modern Age

Gerd von Rundstedt (1875–1953)

A staff officer throughout World War I, Rundstedt's willingness to serve as one of Hitler's senior generals in the interwar years helped the Nazis win the loyalty of the Prussian officer corps. Rundstedt retired after the 1938 annexation of the Sudetenland but Hitler recalled him as Commander of Army Group South for the Polish campaign. He then led Army Group A in the West, where he implemented the deep penetration of the Ardennes, devised by his chief of staff Erich von Manstein. Hitler rewarded Rundstedt with promotion to field marshal and gave him command of Army Group South during Operation Barbarossa. Rundstedt's retreat from Rostov, however, led to his dismissal on 1 December 1941.

In March 1942 Hitler appointed Rundstedt as Commander-in-Chief West, but the Führer's distrust of Rundstedt's conservatism ultimately led him to appoint Erwin Rommel as his subordinate. Hitler increasingly backed Rommel in the controversy over the counter-invasion strategy and dismissed Rundstedt on 2 July 1944, following his failure to defeat the Allies at Normandy. However, his seniority and respectability ensured that Hitler could never entirely dispose of his services. Rundstedt was appointed to head the honour court that dismissed army officers complicit in the 20 July assassination plot, and he was recalled as Commander-in-Chief West on 4 September 1944. He oversaw the December 1944 Ardennes offensive, but increasingly became a mere conduit for the Führer's orders. Hitler, pictured here examining a map of the Soviet Union with von Rundstedt, retired him permanently on 11 March 1945 in the wake of capture of the bridge over the River Rhine at Remagen by US troops. Arrested in May by US troops, he remained in custody until 1949, but evaded war-crimes prosecution due to ill health. He died four years later in Hanover.

thrust towards Rostov forced Manstein to abandon his relief effort and to effect a strategic retreat from the Caucasus.

During February 1943, Hitler gave Manstein operational freedom to arrest the continuing Soviet advance in the Ukraine. Conducting a delaying defence on his threatened northern flank, he withdrew forces from his southern front and launched a devastating counterattack northwards on 21 February that shattered the Soviet Southwestern Front and recaptured Kharkov three weeks later, temporarily stabilizing the situation. Manstein styled this operational technique *rochade*, after the chess move where a player castles his king. It was his greatest major battlefield accomplishment – yet he would never repeat this feat.

Lacking strategic vision, Manstein believed he could turn around the war on the Eastern Front with similar operational counterstrikes. He supported Hitler's ill-conceived Operation Citadel offensive in July 1943 to pinch off and annihilate Soviet forces astride Kursk. Thereafter, Manstein's forces were steadily pushed back beyond the River Dnieper. During February 1944 he rescued only some of the forces isolated in the Cherkassy Pocket. Disenchanted with Manstein, Hitler relieved him during late March, appeasing him with the award of the Swords to his Knight's Cross. Manstein anticipated being recalled and continued to believe that his military genius could change the strategic situation sufficiently to allow a negotiated peace; however, he failed to see that the brutality of the Nazi regime made political negotiation highly unlikely. He was never recalled to service, and at war's end was arrested in Germany by British troops.

LATER YEARS

In 1949, having escaped the post-war Nuremberg trials, Manstein was convicted of violations of the laws of war by a British military tribunal in Germany, and he served three years in prison. On his release, he became a military adviser to the West German government. In 1955 he published *Lost Victories*, which would become one of the most widely read World War II memoirs.

▲ Knight's Cross with Oak Leaves. Introduced in June 1940, the Oak Leaves were awarded for repeated acts of outstanding heroism and independent initiative to previous recipients of the coveted Knight's Cross and Iron Cross. Only 853 soldiers received the award. Further outstanding acts of heroism were rewarded with the addition of Swords, Diamonds, and the ultimate award, Golden Oak Leaves, which was awarded just once in 1945.

▼ The Gewehr 1943 self-loading rifle was a response to the German infantryman's demands for increased firepower. Designed by Walther, this rifle was an improved version of the Gewehr 1941 that incorporated technology replicated from the captured Soviet Tokarev SVT 40 semi-automatic rifle.

Dwight D. Eisenhower

Supreme Allied Commander During World War II

'Humility must always be the portion of any man who receives acclaim earned in blood of his followers and sacrifices of his friends.'

DWIGHT D. EISENHOWER

A Life in Brief

1890, 14 October
Born in Denison, Texas

1915
Second Lieutenant, US army

1916
First Lieutenant

1917
Captain

1920
Major

1936
Lieutenant Colonel

1941
Colonel

1941
Brigadier General

1942
Major General

1942
Lieutenant General

1943
General

1944
General of the Army

1945–48
Chief of Staff, US army

1948–50
President of Columbia University

December 1950–May 1952
Supreme Commander NATO

20 January 1953–20 January 1961
President of the United States

1969, 28 March
Dies in Washington, DC

Dwight D. Eisenhower is generally regarded as one of the great commanders of World War II, and one of the most influential men of the 20th century – yet he never led or commanded troops in action, and never saw combat throughout a long and successful military career. Eisenhower led the Anglo-American forces in Tunisia and Sicily to their first combined victories in 1943. He later oversaw Operation Overlord (1944) and the subsequent campaign in northwest Europe to defeat Nazi Germany. In the post-war period, he served as Supreme Commander of NATO and became the 34th President of the United States.

In the summer of 1942 Eisenhower was selected by General George Marshall as the Supreme Allied Commander Mediterranean. In this capacity he commanded the Operation Torch landings in November 1942, the first Anglo-American assault on Hitler's Reich. Eisenhower's inexperience as a commander was starkly revealed in the North African campaign, when the Allied advance to Tunis stalled, and the Axis forces were able to rally themselves. The political deal struck with Admiral Darlan, the Vichy French commander in North Africa, proved controversial, and nearly led to

► Eisenhower at the wheel of a jeep in December 1944. He was normally driven by Kay Summersby, a British Mechanized Transport Corps driver, who stayed with him throughout the war.

Viscount Montgomery of Alamein (1887–1976)

Bernard Law Montgomery was both the most successful British general of World War II and the most controversial. His abrasive personality made relations with superiors and allies consistently difficult, but he was admired by those who served under him and was an efficient and effective battlefield commander.

Montgomery first saw combat in 1914, and was severely wounded at the First Battle of Ypres. He continued his military career in the inter-war years, and after the tragic death of his wife in 1936, devoted his life to his profession. He commanded a division during the British Expeditionary Force's retreat to Dunkirk in 1940, but it was his selection for command of the Eighth Army in 1942 that saw him rise to prominence. He defeated Rommel at the Second Battle of El Alamein, and recorded further victories in North Africa and Tunisia. The 1943 Sicilian campaign saw a personal rivalry develop between Montgomery and US General George Patton, which lasted for the rest of the war. Montgomery continued to command Eighth Army in the subsequent Italian campaign, but was brought home for the forthcoming invasion of France.

As overall land commander, Montgomery planned and executed the Normandy campaign that followed the 6 June 1944 invasion. He was heavily criticized

by American generals and British airmen for his slow rate of progress, notably around Caen, but the German forces were eventually routed. Montgomery was given the opportunity to prove his 'narrow thrust' strategy in the Arnhem campaign; however, the overly ambitious and hastily planned operation – uncharacteristic of Montgomery's more generally cautious approach – led to the destruction of the British 1st Airborne Division. In late 1944 Montgomery clashed with Eisenhower once again, criticizing American commanders during the German counteroffensive in the Ardennes. In 1946, Montgomery was granted the title Viscount Montgomery of Alamein, and served as Chief of the Imperial General Staff.

In the picture above (taken in 1944), Montgomery briefs King George VI in his map lorry, part of the spartan headquarters known as 'Monty's caravans'.

'I think sometimes that I am a cross between a one-time soldier, a pseudo-statesman, a jack-legged politician and a crooked diplomat. I walk a soapy tight-rope in a rain storm with a blazing furnace on one side and a pack of ravenous tigers on the other.'

EISENHOWER COMMENTING ON HIS ROLE IN NORTH AFRICA

▼ Selected as Supreme Allied Commander Mediterranean in the summer of 1942, Eisenhower's campaigns in North Africa were to expose his relative inexperience. Nevertheless, it was during this period that he would learn how best to act as the war continued.

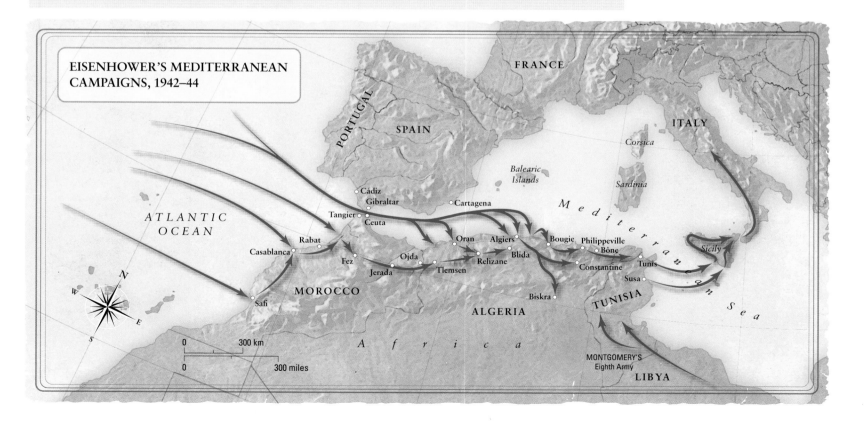

EISENHOWER'S MEDITERRANEAN CAMPAIGNS, 1942–44

Admiral Sir Andrew Cunningham (1883–1963)

Andrew Browne Cunningham (Viscount Cunningham of Hyndhope) was arguably Britain's finest fighting admiral of World War II. With a lifetime of experience of service in the Mediterranean, he was the ideal commander for the Mediterranean Fleet in 1940. Imbued with an aggressive Nelsonian spirit, Cunningham took the fight to the Italian Navy from the moment that Italy entered the war in June 1940. He scored remarkable victories at Taranto in November 1940, proving the effectiveness of carrier-borne torpedo attacks on ships in harbour, and brought on a daring night action at Cape Matapan in April 1941. Cunningham worked his men and ships very hard – especially so during the battle for Crete in April 1941, which saw heavy losses and damage to his fleet. After a brief stint in Washington, Cunningham returned to operational command as Eisenhower's naval commander for both the Tunisian campaign and the invasion of Sicily. Eisenhower relied heavily upon Cunningham's undoubted experience in these amphibious invasions. Appointed First Sea Lord in 1943, Cunningham worked tirelessly both for his navy and for the Allied cause for the rest of the war.

▲▲ American troops, crammed into a landing craft, approach the North African shore during Operation Torch on 8 November 1942. Anglo-French relations had deteriorated to such an extent that the landings were primarily made by flag-flying American troops in the hope that the defending French troops would not resist.

▲ A large American flag is again prominent as troops land on the beaches at Surcouf, 20 miles east of Algiers.

▼ Landing supplies and equipment on the beach at Oran in Algeria, 1 December 1942. As Operation Torch progressed, the Allied supply lines became increasingly stretched and this became a major reason for the Allied failure to win the 'race for Tunis' in December 1942.

Eisenhower's removal. However, as the campaign and the war developed, he progressively learnt how best to act.

In his role as Supreme Allied Commander, Eisenhower had to hold together the alliance of the United States and Great Britain and ensure that his headquarters promoted a spirit of practical cooperation based on honesty and mutual respect. In working towards this goal, even Eisenhower's critics – such as General Alan Brooke – came to realize his importance to the Allied war effort.

By the end of the hard-fought Tunisian campaign, Eisenhower had proved his determination and ability in surmounting considerable obstacles. The planning for the next step – the invasion of Sicily (Operation Husky) – went badly adrift, as Eisenhower adjusted to working with three influential British commanders under him: Air Marshal Tedder, Admiral Cunningham

◄◄ US paratroopers of the 82nd Airborne Division making their first combat jump from their C47 aircraft during the invasion of Sicily. The paratroopers were badly scattered by high winds and anti-aircraft fire but still played an important role during the subsequent fighting.

◄ Black smoke pours from an Allied ship hit by Axis air attack during the Allied invasion of Sicily, near the town of Gela, 10 July 1943. Heavy Axis air attacks were experienced by the Allied fleets off Sicily in the early days of the invasion and this led to a tragic friendly fire incident when planes carrying more paratroop reinforcements were shot down on 11 July 1943.

▼ American soldiers debarking from their landing craft, 21 July 1943. The US forces on Sicily executed a number of amphibious 'end-runs' in an attempt to envelop the German defence of the island but they were foiled by fierce resistance.

Field Marshal Sir Alan Brooke (1883–1963)

Alan Francis Brooke (Viscount Alanbrooke) was perhaps Britain's finest strategist of World War II. He developed a formidable reputation as an artillery officer in World War I and commanded a corps in the British Expeditionary Force during 1939–40. He became Commander-in-Chief, Home Forces in the summer of 1940 and worked strenuously to ensure that, even with the meagre resources at his disposal, Britain was ready for the expected German invasion. In December 1941 Brooke was appointed Chief of the Imperial General Staff, and thus became the principal strategic adviser to the Cabinet and

Prime Minister. His predecessor, Sir John Dill, had been unable to control Churchill's often wild mood swings and mercurial approach to strategy, but Brooke quickly learned how to cope with this. He worked constantly behind the scenes to maintain the focus of British strategy.

Brooke also had to work closely with the chiefs of the American armed forces on the Combined Chiefs of Staff committee, the remarkable Allied organization, which coordinated the combined resources of the American and British war efforts on a global scale. Although there was little warmth between

Brooke and his American counterparts (such as Marshall), his talent, intelligence and clear strategic thought came to be respected.

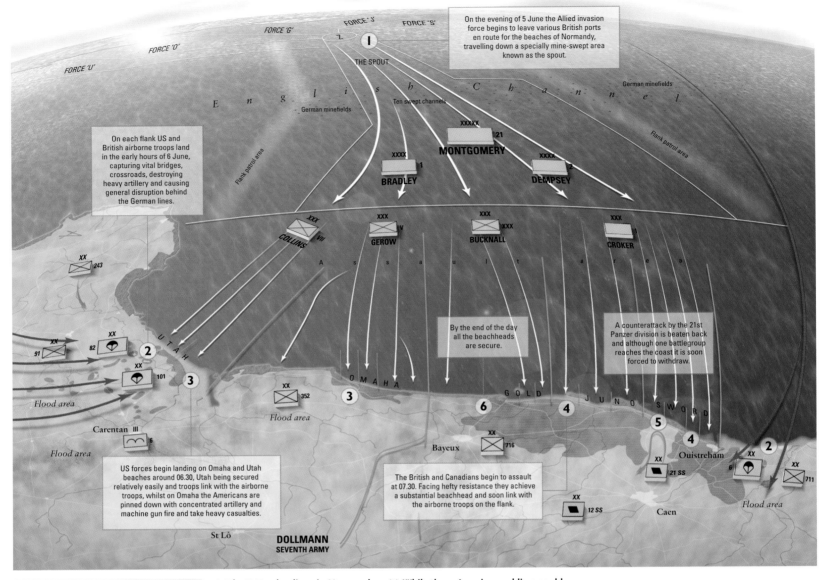

The Normandy Campaign, 1944

Allies	Germans
Eisenhower, Montgomery	Rundstedt, Rommel, Dollmann
1,450,000 troops (by 25 July)	380,000 troops (by 23 July)
Casualties: United States: 29,000 killed, 106,000 wounded; United Kingdom: 11,000 killed, 54,000 wounded; Canada: 5,000 killed, 13,000 wounded; France: 12,200 civilian killed and missing	Casualties: 23,019 killed, 67,060 wounded, 198,616 missing or captured

▲ The D-Day landings in Normandy in June 1944 marked the start of combined Allied efforts to liberate mainland Europe from the occupying German forces. Over 11,000 sorties flown by Allied air forces that day had a major impact, as did the largely British supporting navy.

▼ While these American soldiers could come ashore at Utah beach with relative ease, it was a different story down the coast at Omaha beach. There, the men of the 1st and 29th US Infantry Divisions met with fierce resistance and suffered 3,000 casualties. The heavy fighting meant that it took nearly all day to secure the beach and begin the drive inland at Omaha.

General Henry 'Hap' Arnold (1886–1950)

Henry 'Hap' Arnold was the first commanding general of the US Army Air Forces, and presided over the creation of the largest and most powerful air force ever assembled. Arnold began his army career in the infantry, but soon transferred to the new aeronautical division of the Signal Corps. He was a keen advocate of air power throughout the inter-war years and became Chief of the Army Air Corps in 1938. His vision and foresight led to vital programmes of research and development, industrial cooperation, aircrew training and the construction of new airbases. Arnold put his personal weight behind many new projects, including the B-29 bomber programme; despite numerous setbacks, it became a formidable weapon against Japan. After the reorganization of the army in early 1942, Arnold became a full member of the Joint Chiefs of Staff and the Combined Chiefs of Staff. He developed a close working relationship with George Marshall, even though Marshall disagreed with Arnold's view that strategic bombing might make a ground invasion of Europe unnecessary. Arnold's achievement in creating and managing this formidable instrument of airpower were recognized by his promotion to General of the Army and, later, by his promotion to General of the Air Force.

and the often difficult General Montgomery. The 1943 campaign was ultimately successful, but less decisive than had been hoped. Eisenhower directed the opening stages of the Italian mainland campaign before returning to Britain to oversee the plan for Operation Overlord, the invasion of Hitler's 'Fortress Europe'.

Although the majority of the detailed planning for Overlord was undertaken by his subordinates, most notably Montgomery and Admiral Sir Bertram Ramsay, the final responsibility for the invasion rested with Eisenhower. In the early hours of 5 June 1944, he took one of the most difficult decisions in military history when, after uncertain weather reports and one postponement already, he gave the go-ahead for the greatest amphibious invasion ever launched.

◄ American soldiers wait in foxholes at Utah Beach on 6 June 1944 for the order to move inland against German fortifications. The beach was still under sporadic German artillery fire throughout the day. The 4th US Infantry Division landed at Utah Beach and encountered relatively light resistance as it pushed inland to link up with the paratroops of 82nd and 101st Airborne Divisions.

Key Campaigns

The North African Campaign (Operation Torch),
8 November 1942–13 May 1943
Eisenhower commands the Anglo-American invasion of
French North Africa, which ends with the capture of Tunis
and over 200,000 Axis troops in May 1943.

The Invasion of Sicily (Operation Husky),
10 July 1943–17 August 1943
Eisenhower's Anglo-American invasion brings about the
downfall of Mussolini's Fascist government. However,
fierce Axis resistance allows the majority of the German
forces on the island to escape to the Italian mainland.

Operation Neptune, 6 June 1944
Eisenhower orders the beginning of the assault landing
in Normandy, the opening phase of Operation Overlord.
By the end of the first day, the Allies have established a
beachhead in Hitler's 'Fortress Europe'.

The Northwest Europe Campaign (Operation Overlord),
6 June 1944–8 May 1945
The Allies fight a tough campaign in Normandy before
finally breaking out across France. Resistance stiffens along
the German frontier, and Hitler launches the Ardennes
offensive in December 1944. In early 1945 the Western
Allies cross the Rhine and push deep into Germany.

➤ Eisenhower's importance during the
Allied campaigns in western Europe rested
on his ability to maintain the cooperation
and spirit of trust between United States
and British forces.

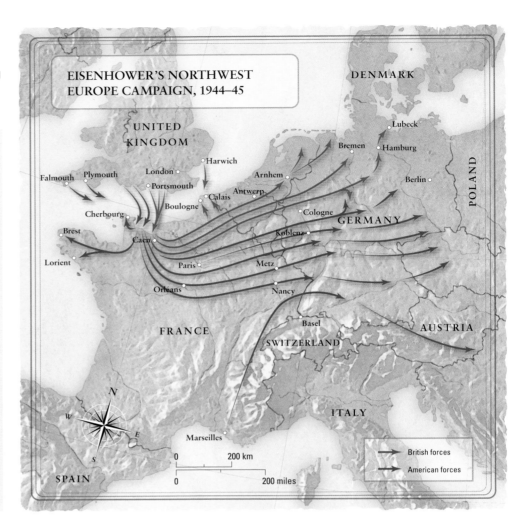

EISENHOWER'S NORTHWEST
EUROPE CAMPAIGN, 1944–45

0   200 km

0   200 miles

→ British forces

→ American forces

General George C. Marshall (1880–1959)

George Catlett Marshall can be considered the true
architect of US victory in World War II, although
he has never achieved the wider recognition
he deserves. He spent the war in Washington,
principally because Roosevelt refused to let him
leave: he had made himself indispensable.

Marshall first came to prominence as a member
of Pershing's headquarters staff during World War I.
In the inter-war years he became a key figure in
the War Department, and was promoted to Army
Chief of Staff on 1 September 1939. Marshall then
presided over the greatest-ever expansion of US
armed forces, and ensured that these military
resources were utilized effectively in the various
theatres of war, leading Churchill to dub him the
'organizer of victory'. His position on the US Joint
Chiefs of Staff and the Allied Combined Chiefs of
Staff committees was critical, and his friendship
with Sir John Dill ensured that the alliance remained
on course. Despite crossing swords with his British
opposite numbers on several occasions, Marshall

worked to ensure that Allied strategy was as efficient
and effective as possible, and the advice and support
he gave to Eisenhower was vital. After the war,
he formulated the famous 'Marshall Plan' for the
post-war reconstruction of Europe.

Eisenhower's role in the subsequent Normandy campaign was limited, as Montgomery initially held the post of Allied Land Commander. However, Eisenhower took on this role from 1 September 1944, and immediately found himself plunged into controversy – particularly with Montgomery. The arguments between the two men revolved around the best approach to invading Germany. While Montgomery favoured what became known as a 'narrow thrust towards the Ruhr', Eisenhower preferred a broad front that would allow the Allied armies to exert pressure all along it while taking opportunities to advance

wherever they presented themselves. Nonetheless, Eisenhower gave Montgomery the resources he needed to mount Operation Market Garden, the over-ambitious attempt to seize an early crossing over the Rhine. When this failed badly, the campaign began to follow Eisenhower's plan, except for the serious interruption of the German counteroffensive in the Ardennes in December 1944. Eisenhower's rapid reaction to this crisis showed his true stature, as well as his hard-won skill and experience as the Supreme Allied Commander. He subsequently demonstrated his mettle as a theatre commander in the final advance

▲ The crew of a 'Quad Fifty' (M51 Multiple .5 Calibre Machine Gun) are silhouetted against the sky streaked with vapour trails from Allied and German planes engaged in a dogfight on Christmas Day 1944, near Puttendorf, Germany. While the Allied armies had developed efficient anti-aircraft systems for the invasion of Europe, the dominance of Allied airpower meant that the Luftwaffe's ability to intervene in the land battle was severely limited.

Dwight D. Eisenhower   Modern Age

General George Patton (1885–1945)

George Smith Patton was one of the most remarkable US army commanders of World War II. Famous for his pearl-handled revolvers, his theatrical profanity and explosive temper, he was respected by friend and foe as one of the best armour commanders of the war, who fought with drive and dash.

Patton had served with the US cavalry prior to World War I, but gained fame as one of the first American commanders of a tank battalion during the Meuse-Argonne Offensive in late 1918. He returned to the cavalry after the war but never forgot the role and importance of armour. Patton's opening experiences of World War II came as one of the task force commanders during the November 1942 Allied invasion of North Africa. After the shock of the Kasserine Pass battles, which revealed shortcomings in American training and tactics, Eisenhower placed Patton in command of the II US Corps and he led it to its first solid successes in battle. Patton's drive on Palermo during the Sicilian campaign made headlines, but his career was nearly destroyed when he reprimanded and slapped two shell-shocked soldiers in field hospitals on the island. He was protected by Eisenhower, thanks to his fighting talent and their previous friendship. Patton returned to command the Third US Army after the breakout from Normandy, and soon his troops were pushing across France in one of the most remarkable advances in military history. Held up on the German frontier, as much by lack of fuel as enemy action, Patton became increasingly frustrated, but showed his true mettle again when he drove his army to the relief of Bastogne during the Battle of the Bulge (Ardennes Offensive). Peace saw Patton out of step again, with increasing criticism of his occupation policies in Germany. He was killed in a car accident in December 1945 in Germany.

into Germany while orchestrating the movements of nine Allied armies, seven of which were American.

Eisenhower's decisions in the last months of the war were also controversial. Following President Roosevelt's policies, he made no attempt to reach Berlin before the Soviets, despite being pressed to do so by his subordinates. The Western Allies were shut out of eastern Germany, the consequences of which became apparent as the Cold War developed.

Eisenhower might properly be described as a political general. He never developed the sure touch of battlefield command, but his role as Supreme Allied Commander made him one of the key figures of the alliance. His insistence on cooperation and honesty between the British and Americans meant that their combined efforts became more than the sum of their parts, and ultimately achieved the victory that both powers desired.

▲ Soldiers of the 101st Airborne Division march out of the town of Bastogne, Belgium after their epic resistance during the Battle of the Bulge in December 1944. The division was completely surrounded at Bastogne for eight days. The soldiers likened their position to the 'hole in the doughnut' but when called upon to surrender by the Germans, General McAuliffe, the deputy commander of the division, simply replied 'Nuts!' The division was relieved by elements of Patton's Third Army on 26 December 1944.

▶ The Battle of the Bulge (also known as the Ardennes Offensive) was the single most costly to human life of all those experienced by US forces during World War II. Aiming to divide the Allied line in half and capture Belgium, the Germans achieved a surprise offensive, but were ultimately forced to retreat by the swift response of the Allied forces.

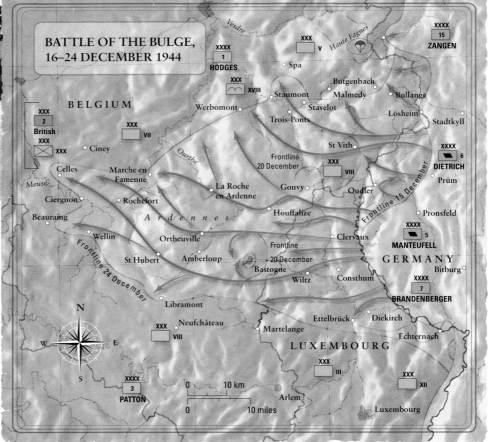

'Every gun made, every warship launched, every rocket fired signifies, in the final sense, a theft from those who hunger and are not fed, those who are cold and are not clothed…. This is not a way of life at all…. Under the cloud of threatening war, it is humanity hanging from a cross of iron.'

EISENHOWER'S 'CHANCE FOR PEACE' ADDRESS, 16 APRIL 1953.

◄ Prime Minister Winston Churchill shares a drink with General William H. Simpson, commander of the US Ninth Army, Field Marshal Sir Alan Brooke and Major General Alvan C. Gillem of the 13 US Corps in the citadel of Julich, Germany while Field Marshal Bernard Montgomery, a teetotaller, sits outside and takes notes. This photo was taken on 6 March 1945; the US 30th Infantry Division had captured Julich on 23 February 1945 after its successful crossing of the Rur River.

Georgy Zhukov

Greatest Soviet General of World War II

'I asked myself how and with what should the Soviet people repay the enemy…. With the sword and with the sword alone… was the only answer.' GEORGY ZHUKOV

A Life in Brief

1896, 1 December
Born to a peasant family in the village of Strelkovka, Kaluga Province, Russia

1923–30
Commander, cavalry regiment

1930
Commander, cavalry brigade

1931–33
Serves on staff of Cavalry Inspectorate of the Red Army

1933–37
Commander, cavalry division

1937–38
Commander, cavalry corps

1938–39
Assistant Commander of the Byelorussian Military District

1939, June–August
Commander of LVII Special Corps at battle of Khalkin Gol

1940, May–December
Commander of the Kiev Special Military District

1941, January–September
Chief of the General Staff, member of Military Council of USSR

1941, June
Deputy Supreme Commander of the Armed Forces

1945, May–1946, June
Commands the Soviet army of occupation in eastern Germany

1946, June–1953, March
Commander of the Odessa Military District

1953, March–1957, October
Minister of Defence

1974, 18 June
Dies in Moscow

◀ **Marshal Zhukov in full dress uniform. The topmost medal over his left breast is the gold star of the Hero of the Soviet Union.**

Marshal Georgy Zhukov is the most acclaimed and iconic figure in Soviet military history, and is credited with being the saviour of Moscow in 1941 and the architect of victory in the offensives at Stalingrad and Berlin. One of the few Soviet generals who had the courage to stand up to Stalin, Zhukov's foremost talent was his ability to plan and orchestrate large-scale offensive operations using the combined efforts of massed armour, artillery, infantry and tactical airpower, backed with abundant logistical support.

Zhukov began his military service in 1915 as a conscript cavalryman in the Imperial Russian Army. From the beginning, he showed leadership by example at the tactical level, earning two St George crosses for heroism in combat during World War I. Following the October Revolution, Zhukov, as a non-commissioned officer, was required to join the new Red Army. He did so in 1918 (the same year he joined the Communist Party), and fought against the Whites in the civil war until 1921. His talent for small-unit leadership propelled him from platoon to cavalry squadron command by the war's end. Between 1922 and 1939 Zhukov attended several advanced courses of military instruction, impressing his superiors with his organizational ability, energy, strong will and operational–tactical knowledge. Zhukov made up for his lack of formal instruction (he did not attend staff college) with intensive independent study of the writings of the USSR's best military theorists. He also took a keen interest in the development of military technology – armour in particular – and strove to learn the advantages these new developments could bring to Soviet strategy and tactics.

THE EMERGING LEADER

In June 1939 Zhukov exercised combat command once again, leading LVII Special Corps in the battle of Khalkin Gol against units of the Japanese Kwantung army. The Japanese had attacked and driven back weak and poorly led Soviet and Mongolian forces. Stalin appointed Zhukov on the advice of several of his top military and political advisers, who had high opinions of Zhukov by that time. On assuming command Zhukov began to organize the battle

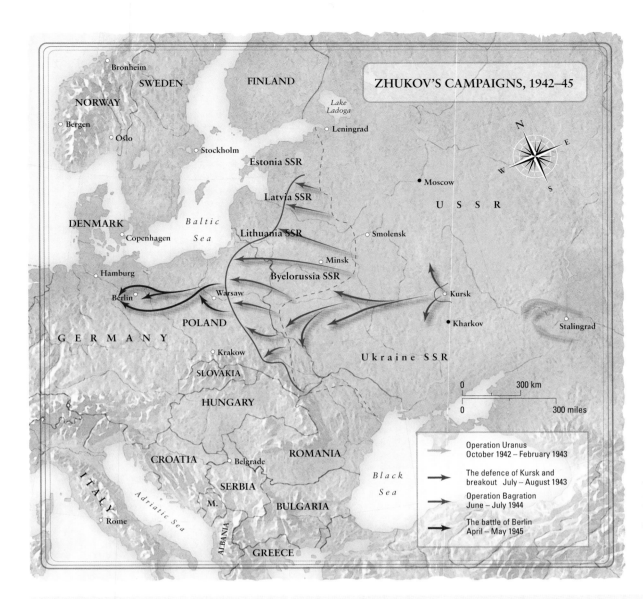

ZHUKOV'S CAMPAIGNS, 1942–45

Operation Uranus	October 1942 – February 1943
The defence of Kursk and breakout	July – August 1943
Operation Bagration	June – July 1944
The battle of Berlin	April – May 1945

◄ This map illustrates Zhukov's most significant contributions in pushing the Germans out of the USSR to the capture of Berlin from November 1942 to May 1945. The counteroffensive at Stalingrad is at shown on the right of the map, the battle of Kursk in the centre-right, Operation Bagration in the centre, and finally the lengthy assault on Berlin on the left.

Key Battles and Campaigns

The Defence of Moscow, October–December 1941
Zhukov supervises the defensive battles for Moscow and subsequent winter counteroffensive, in which the Germans are stopped at the gates of Moscow and then thrown back dozens of kilometres. The latter conforms to Stalin's desire to attack the Germans on a broad front, hoping to break through the weakest point. Although Moscow is saved, the counteroffensive fails to destroy Army Group Centre as hoped, in part because the broad front prevents the Soviets from employing critical mass at decisive points.

Operation Uranus, October 1942–February 1943
The Stalingrad counteroffensive is one of Zhukov's greatest achievements. The Red Army breaks through on the weakly defended northern and southern flanks of the German Sixth Army, and then drives deep into their rear. Sixth Army is entirely cut off in Stalingrad by this double envelopment, and by the end of February has been destroyed.

Operation Mars, November–December 1942
Coinciding with the Stalingrad counteroffensive, this is arguably Zhukov's greatest failure. The Red Army attempts to eliminate the Rzhev salient, pushing the Germans further from Moscow, but the defences are far more formidable and the German response far more effective than Zhukov has anticipated. However, Zhukov insists that the Soviet forces keep up the attack for three weeks, by which time they are utterly shattered.

Operation Bagration, June–July 1944
In one of the largest and best-coordinated offensives executed by the Red Army during the war, the German Army is pushed out of Byelorussia and back to the River Vistula in Poland. The fighting, which involves four Soviet army groups, demonstrates the progress made by the Red Army in strategic planning, tactics and logistical support. The operation succeeds in destroying the German Army Group Centre in the process, something that Stalin had tried but failed to do in the 1941–42 winter offensive.

The Battle of Berlin, April–May 1945
Although a less sophisticated operation than the battles of Stalingrad and Operation Bagration, relying less on manoeuvre and skill, Zhukov captures the German capital before the Western Allies can reach it. The Red Army overwhelms defenders with men, artillery, tanks and aircraft, crushing them in only a few short weeks, but it suffers more casualties than it inflicts in the process.

area, first in response to the situation created by the enemy, and then with the aim of seizing the initiative. He demonstrated effective command by gathering complete, accurate and timely information on enemy activity – personally, if possible, by visits to the front – and amassing the human and material resources he thought necessary for the job. He asked Moscow for an additional three infantry divisions, two artillery regiments, a tank brigade and several fighter and bomber units, and the necessary combat supplies.

Zhukov always sought maximum material support, and the more successful he was the more willing Stalin was to grant him this.

One of the chief characteristics of his command style was his impatience with inept subordinates. If Zhukov thought a man had failed to perform, he would be summarily relieved, with no second chances. Also, he openly allowed units under his command to suffer heavy casualties, if this brought success more quickly than alternative methods. When necessary, Zhukov

▲ Soviet infantry sortie against German positions outside Leningrad, summer 1942.

'Where there is Zhukov, there is victory!'
ANONYMOUS WORLD WAR II
RED ARMY SAYING

went to elaborate lengths to deceive the enemy as to his intentions, and thus achieve surprise. He was also a thoroughly modern commander, as shown at Khalkin Gol in his use of combined arms (comprising air bombardment, artillery fire, and infantry and armour assaults) in both offence and defence. Furthermore, he sought to turn the enemy's flank and encircle him whenever possible, but was not above resorting to massed frontal attacks that relied on strength of numbers.

Success in the Great Patriotic War

In the course of the Soviet war against Germany (the Great Patriotic War, 1941–45), Zhukov served primarily on the staff of the Supreme High Command (Stavka) as Stalin's deputy, and therefore as the highest-ranking military officer in charge of the armed forces.

At first, Zhukov was instructed to take control of emergencies and critical situations, such as stopping the German advance east of Smolensk in July 1941, the defence of Leningrad in October, and the defence of Moscow in November. His success in the December counteroffensive before Moscow probably encouraged Stalin to put him in charge of the Stalingrad campaign in autumn 1942, despite his hand in the failed battle of Kharkov that spring. Following the triumph at Stalingrad, from late winter 1943 onwards Zhukov was responsible for planning the major offensives designed to drive the Germans out of the USSR and achieve final victory. Zhukov, however, was not free to devise strategy independently: Stalin established the major parameters within which Zhukov had to work. The most significant of these was that Soviet men and *matériel* would be spread across the entire front

Konstantin Konstantinovich Rokossovsky (1896–1968)

A veteran of the cavalry of the Russian Imperial Army in World War I, and a Red officer in the Russian Civil War, Rokossovsky was a general at the time of the German invasion. In June 1941, he commanded a mechanized corps in the Kiev Military District in the direct line of German advance, which fought well, but failed to slow or stop the enemy. Subsequently he took command of Sixteenth Army, with the mission of blocking the German attack on Moscow on the Smolensk–Moscow highway. In the impressive battle of Elnya (August 1941), Rokossovsky succeeded in fighting the Germans to a temporary standstill. For the rest of the war Rokossovsky was mostly directly or indirectly under the command of Zhukov, who respected his abilities. What set Rokossovsky apart from most of his peers was his mastery of combined-arms operations, including use of tactical air support, and his ability to consider each battlefield in the context of an overall campaign. Like Zhukov, Rokossovsky had the courage to argue his points with Stalin. Successful in the battle of Moscow, he subsequently commanded the Don Front in the battle of Stalingrad (shown above), which broke through the north side of the Axis defences to encircle the German Sixth Army. He commanded the Central Front in the battle of Kursk in July 1943, where he thwarted the German offensive and inflicted serious losses on the enemy, although his forces also suffered heavily. In the summer of 1944 Rokossovsky was promoted to marshal and commanded a front in the successful campaign in Byelorussia to destroy Army Group Centre. In the final campaign of the war he commanded the Second Byelorussian Front, which was the right wing of the final offensive against Berlin. In recognition of the role he played in this, Stalin allowed him to lead the victory parade in Moscow in June 1945.

rather than concentrated along one or two main axes of advance. Nevertheless, Zhukov consistently sought to make military considerations paramount and earned a reputation for standing up to Stalin and arguing his points vociferously.

As the military leader of Stavka, Zhukov assembled a team of exceptionally talented officers, most prominently marshals Alexander Vasilevsky and Boris Shaposhnikov, whose input, when heeded, had a marked effect on Zhukov's success. Zhukov made good use of his study of the works of such strategic thinkers as Alexander Svechin, Vladimir Triandafilov and Mikhail Tukhachevsky. Particularly evident from

1942 onwards was his use of Tukhachevsky's concepts of combined-arms warfare and the battle in depth, which focused on breaking through the enemy's front and driving deep into his rear with mechanized forces supported by tactical aviation.

At the end of the war Zhukov commanded the Soviet army of occupation in Germany for a year before being transferred to the less important post of Commander of the Odessa Military District. After Stalin's death in March 1953, Nikita Khrushchev appointed him Minister of Defence. He held this post until October 1957 when he was dismissed by Khrushchev, who feared his political ambition.

▼ The Mosin-Nagant M1891/30 bolt-action sniper rifle in 7.62 x 54 mm was highly accurate and deadly in the hands of Soviet snipers. More than 300,000 of the sniper variant were produced prior to and during the war. The non-sniper variant, lacking the scope, was the mainstay of the Red Army in both rifle and carbine form. Soviet factories, between 1930 and the end of 1945, produced nearly 17,000,000 of these rifles.

▼▲ The PPSh-41 submachine gun, introduced in large numbers to the Red Army in 1942, gave Soviet infantry the edge they needed for close-in fighting. Fully automatic, firing the 7.62 x 25 mm pistol cartridge with a drum magazine holding 71 rounds, or a stick magazine of 35 rounds, a squad armed with the PPSh-41 could overwhelm the enemy with a hail of bullets at close quarters. Armed with the PPSh-41, Soviet soldiers, below, take aim at the Germans defending the Red October plant in Stalingrad.

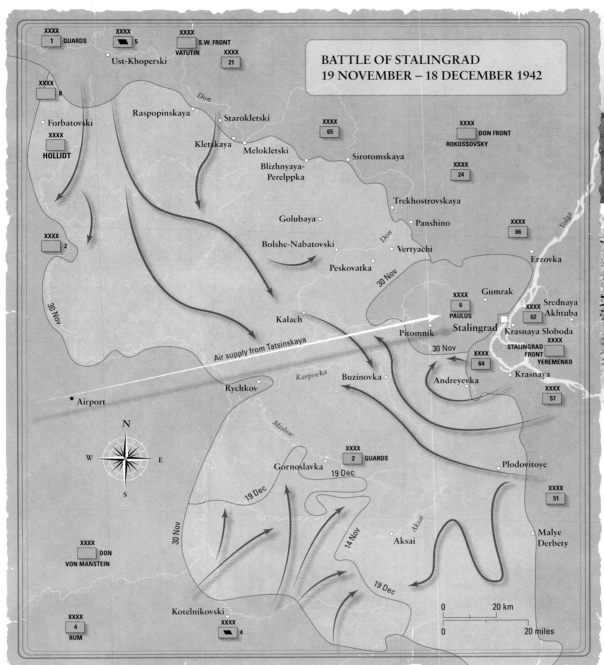

BATTLE OF STALINGRAD
19 NOVEMBER – 18 DECEMBER 1942

XXXX 1 GUARDS
XXXX 5
XXXX S.W. FRONT VATUTIN
XXXX 21
XXXX 8
XXXX HOLLIDT
Ust-Khoperski
Don
Raspopinskaya
Staroletski
Kletskaya
Melokletski
Forbatovski
XXXX 65
XXXX DON FRONT ROKOSSOVSKY
Sirotomskaya
XXXX 24
Blizhnyaya-Perelppka
Trekhostrovskaya
Golubaya
Panshino
XXXX 66
Volga
XXXX 2
Bolshe-Nabatovski
Don
Vertyachi
Erzovka
Peskovatka
30 Nov
30 Nov
XXXX 6 PAULUS
Gumrak
XXXX 62
Srednaya Akhtuba
Kalach
Pitomnik
Stalingrad
Krasnaya Sloboda
Air supply from Tatsinskaya
30 Nov
XXXX 64
STALINGRAD FRONT YEREMENKO
Karpovka
Buzinovka
Andreyevka
Krasnaya
Rychkov
Airport
Misbov
XXXX 57
N
W E S
Gornoslavka
19 Dec
XXXX 2 GUARDS
Plodovitoye
19 Dec
Aksai
XXXX 51
30 Nov
14 Nov
Aksai
Malye Derbety
XXXX DON VON MANSTEIN
19 Dec
0   20 km
0   20 miles
Kotelnikovski
XXXX 4 RUM
XXXX 4

▲▲ A Soviet counterattack northwest of Stalingrad using Lend-Lease American tanks. In the foreground is an M5 Stuart tank armed with a 37 mm gun. In the background are M3 Sherman tanks armed with short-barrelled 75 mm guns.

▲ Soviet soldier examining an unexploded German artillery shell of extremely large calibre, possibly from a rail-mounted cannon.

◄ This map illustrates the Soviet counteroffensive against the German Sixth Army at Stalingrad. Soviet forces north and south of Stalingrad broke through weakly held German and other Axis positions to sally deep behind the enemy lines, link up and seal off Stalingrad. They then successfully fought off German attempts to break the encirclement and crushed the German Stalingrad pocket.

▼ With the tide of battle turning, Red Army soldiers attack the ever-shrinking German positions in Stalingrad proper.

Admiral Nimitz

Successful Commander of American Naval Forces against Japan

'God grant me the courage not to give up what I think is right, even though I think it is hopeless.'

ADMIRAL NIMITZ

▶ Admiral Chester W. Nimitz leans out of the cockpit of a B29 Super Fortress bomber named in his honour at Guam, 21 June 1945. The ability to combine air and sea power was a major factor in his victories over the Japanese.

A master of naval warfare, Chester Nimitz was a key American leader in the Pacific Theatre of Operations during World War II. He oversaw the tactical development of carrier warfare, in particular cooperation between carriers and other surface warships. The pressures of campaigning across the Pacific were immense, yet Nimitz overcame them with great success. In the post-war period, he served as Chief of Naval Operations (1945–47) and then as special assistant to the Secretary of the Navy.

Nimitz attended the American Naval Academy at Annapolis between 1901 and 1905. He spent time on the China Station, before beginning a career in the embryonic submarine branch in 1909; between 1912 and 1913 he commanded the Atlantic Submarine Flotilla. During World War I, Nimitz was chief of staff to the commander of the Atlantic Fleet's submarine

division. Post-war staff appointments led to promotion, and at the close of 1941 he became an admiral and Commander-in-Chief, US Pacific Fleet (CINCPAC).

CORAL SEA AND MIDWAY, 1942

As CINCPAC, Nimitz had to respond to the initial Japanese raids and territorial advances, and then lead the counterattack. Despite the lack of a single American commander for the Pacific, Nimitz played a key role in developing close tri-service cooperation. The battles of the Coral Sea (7–8 May 1942) and Midway (2–6 June 1942) were key successes against the Japanese. The victories showed how Pearl Harbor had failed to destroy American naval power and the extent to which Nimitz had stiffened American resolve.

Nimitz made particularly good use of intelligence information at Coral Sea, where the Americans had intercepted and decoded Japanese messages and were waiting for the Japanese invasion fleet. Although the US navy suffered serious losses in the battle, particularly the carrier *Lexington*, the Japanese were hit equally hard, losing many aircraft; crucially, they desisted from their naval advance on Port Moresby in New Guinea. Prior to Midway, Allied code-breakers were again able to inform Nimitz of Japanese intent and their task force disposition.

The Japanese planning and preparation prior to Midway were flawed: they underestimated the strength of the US fleet, and their tactical plan and resultant deployment were overly complex. Admiral Yamamoto also exaggerated the role of battleships in any encounter with Nimitz's fleet. Failures alone, however, do not explain battles. Although there were serious deficiencies in the US force – for example, problems with the torpedoes carried by their bombers – American preparation was superior, and Nimitz deserves much of the credit for this. The sinking of four Japanese heavy carriers at Midway, and the loss of many Japanese aircraft and pilots, shifted the balance of naval power in the Pacific to the Americans. The initiative was taken away from the Japanese, and the arithmetic of carrier warfare began to count against them. Nimitz exploited this shift by launching the Solomon Islands campaign in August 1942, which saw bloody fighting at Guadalcanal.

Key Battles and Campaigns

The Battle of the Coral Sea, 7–8 May 1942
The first battle fought entirely between carrier groups, and one in which the ships of Nimitz and Admiral Shigeyoshi never make visual contact with each other. The Americans suffer serious losses, including the carrier *Lexington*, but the Japanese advance on Port Moresby is thwarted.

The Battle of Midway, 2–6 June 1942
The Japanese Admiral Yamamoto seeks a decisive battle with Nimitz's fleet. However, all four heavy Japanese aircraft carriers engaged in the battle are sunk. The battle provokes a major shift in the balance of naval power in the Pacific.

The Battle of Guadalcanal, August 1942–February 1943
The Japanese seize Guadalcanal in the Solomon Islands on 7 July 1942, but on 7 August the Americans land. Control of the island is settled by American naval success in the naval battle between 12 and 16 November 1942, which compromises the ability of the Japanese to support their force on the island.

The Battle of Tarawa, November 1943
The Americans capture the key atolls of Makin and Tarawa in the Gilbert Islands in November 1943, although only after difficult assaults on well-prepared and highly motivated defenders. Tarawa alone costs 3,000 American dead and wounded.

The Mariana Islands and Palau Campaign, 1944
The overrunning of the Mariana Islands in 1944 marks a decisive advance into the Western Pacific. The resolve of the Japanese defenders is shown on the island of Saipan (a vital bomber base), where almost the entire garrison of 27,000 men dies resisting attack.

The Battle of Leyte Gulf, 24–25 October 1944
One of the largest naval battles in history, fought over a vast area of deployment nearly the size of the British Isles, Leyte Gulf ends in terrible defeat for the Imperial Japanese Navy. In Operation Sho, the Japanese seek to intervene in the American invasion of the Philippines, and succeed in threatening the landing fleet. However, they fail to push home their effort, and, in the end, lose four carriers and three battleships.

The Battle of Okinawa, March–June 1945
The island is targeted to provide airbases for the invasion of Japan. Okinawa proves a vicious conflict in which the Americans lose 7,613 men and the Japanese 110,000.

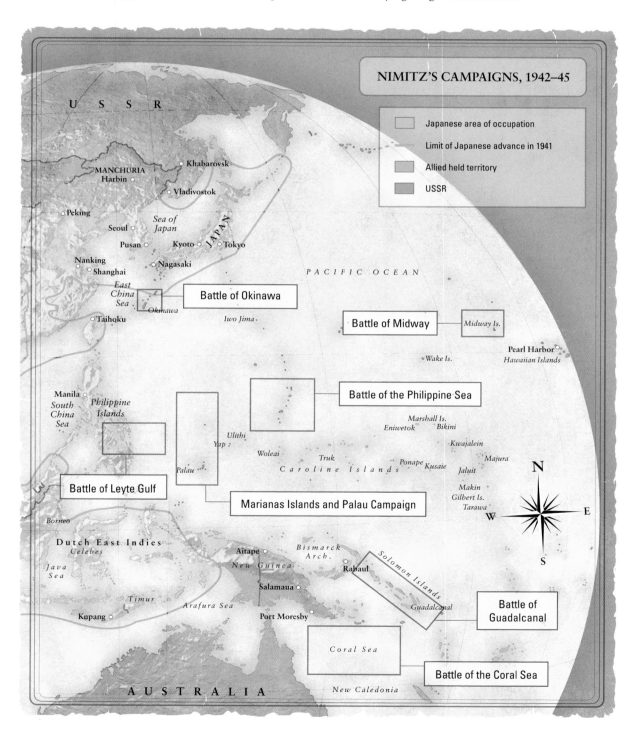

NIMITZ'S CAMPAIGNS, 1942–45

Japanese area of occupation

Limit of Japanese advance in 1941

Allied held territory

USSR

◄ Nimitz can be credited with having stiffened American military resolve after the bombings at Pearl Harbor. The success of United States naval forces during the Pacific campaigns of World War II was brought about by excellent preparation and effective use of intelligence information under his leadership.

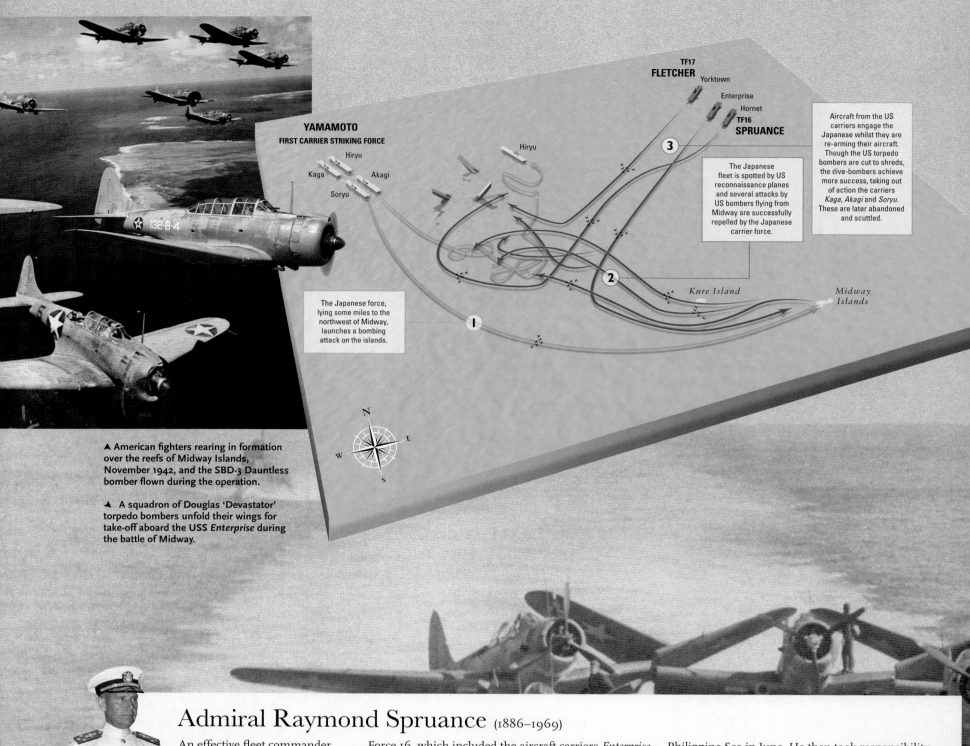

YAMAMOTO
FIRST CARRIER STRIKING FORCE

Hiryu
Kaga   Akagi
Soryu

Hiryu

TF17
FLETCHER   Yorktown
Enterprise
Hornet
TF16
SPRUANCE

3

1

2

Kure Island

Midway Islands

The Japanese force, lying some miles to the northwest of Midway, launches a bombing attack on the islands.

The Japanese fleet is spotted by US reconnaissance planes and several attacks by US bombers flying from Midway are successfully repelled by the Japanese carrier force.

Aircraft from the US carriers engage the Japanese whilst they are re-arming their aircraft. Though the US torpedo bombers are cut to shreds, the dive-bombers achieve more success, taking out of action the carriers *Kaga*, *Akagi* and *Soryu*. These are later abandoned and scuttled.

N
NE
E
SE
S
SW
W
NW

▲ American fighters rearing in formation over the reefs of Midway Islands, November 1942, and the SBD-3 Dauntless bomber flown during the operation.

▲ A squadron of Douglas 'Devastator' torpedo bombers unfold their wings for take-off aboard the USS *Enterprise* during the battle of Midway.

Admiral Raymond Spruance (1886–1969)

An effective fleet commander in the Pacific, Raymond Spruance was a key figure at the operational level. His career reflected shifts in American naval power. Prior to World War II, he served on battleships and destroyers, and at the outbreak of war found himself in charge of a cruiser division. Due to Vice Admiral William 'Bull' Halsey's illness, Spruance was given command of Task Force 16, which included the aircraft carriers *Enterprise* and *Hornet*. This was despite Spruance having no experience of carrier warfare. He was active in that role from the battle of Midway in 1942, where his command of the two carriers contributed greatly to the victory. Spruance then became Nimitz's chief of staff, followed by deputy commander of the Pacific Fleet and Pacific Ocean, and then, in 1943, commander of the Central Pacific Area and Force. As such, in the winter of 1943/44, Spruance directed operations against the Gilbert and Marshall Islands. Promoted to admiral in 1944, Spruance took the war into the Mariana Islands, smashing a Japanese fleet at the Battle of the Philippine Sea in June. He then took responsibility for the naval aspect of the attacks on Iwo Jima and Okinawa, and for carrier raids on Japan. He also took part in the planning for the proposed November 1945 invasion of Japan (Operation Downfall), which was cancelled through fear of excessive casualties. Spruance briefly succeeded Nimitz as commander of the Pacific Fleet in late 1945, before becoming President of the Navy War College. He retired from the US navy in 1948, and was the US ambassador to the Philippines between 1952 and 1955. He is buried in Golden Gate National Cemetery, California, next to Admiral Chester Nimitz.

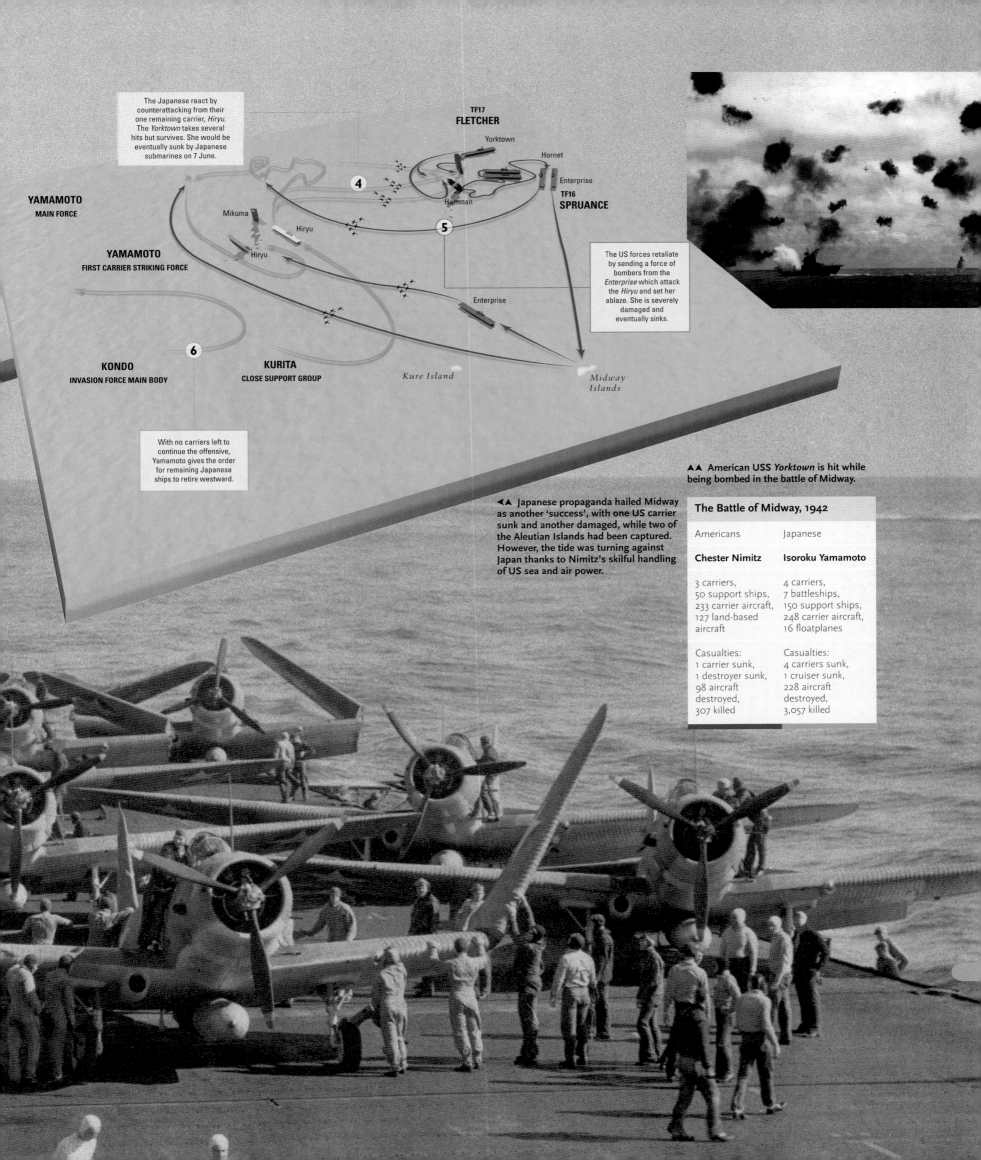

The Japanese react by counterattacking from their one remaining carrier, *Hiryu*. The *Yorktown* takes several hits but survives. She would be eventually sunk by Japanese submarines on 7 June.

TF17
FLETCHER

Yorktown

Hornet

Enterprise
TF16
SPRUANCE

Hamman

YAMAMOTO
MAIN FORCE

Mikuma

Hiryu

Hiryu

4

5

The US forces retaliate by sending a force of bombers from the *Enterprise* which attack the *Hiryu* and set her ablaze. She is severely damaged and eventually sinks.

YAMAMOTO
FIRST CARRIER STRIKING FORCE

Enterprise

6

KONDO
INVASION FORCE MAIN BODY

KURITA
CLOSE SUPPORT GROUP

Kure Island

Midway Islands

With no carriers left to continue the offensive, Yamamoto gives the order for remaining Japanese ships to retire westward.

◄▲ American USS *Yorktown* is hit while being bombed in the battle of Midway.

◄▲ Japanese propaganda hailed Midway as another 'success', with one US carrier sunk and another damaged, while two of the Aleutian Islands had been captured. However, the tide was turning against Japan thanks to Nimitz's skilful handling of US sea and air power.

The Battle of Midway, 1942

Americans	Japanese
Chester Nimitz	**Isoroku Yamamoto**
3 carriers, 50 support ships, 233 carrier aircraft, 127 land-based aircraft	4 carriers, 7 battleships, 150 support ships, 248 carrier aircraft, 16 floatplanes
Casualties: 1 carrier sunk, 1 destroyer sunk, 98 aircraft destroyed, 307 killed	Casualties: 4 carriers sunk, 1 cruiser sunk, 228 aircraft destroyed, 3,057 killed

▲▲ Pilots clamber out of cockpits on **USS**
Lexington following a raid on Tawara in the
Gilbert Islands.

▲ Despite losing half of his aircraft,
and with its hydraulic system destroyed
by a direct hit flying over Palau, Pilot
R. Black performed a remarkable landing
and emerges here from the cockpit,
19 May 1944.

◄ The Japanese found the decisive fleet
engagement they had long sought at Leyte
Gulf in the Philippines, 23–25 October
1944, but the result was a disaster that
destroyed their navy's offensive capacity
in the largest battle in naval history. The
Japanese heavy cruiser under aerial attack
sank shortly after this picture was taken.

The 1943–44 Campaigns

Once resources became available, Nimitz's next focus
for operations was in the Central Pacific area. Key
atolls, notably Makin and Tarawa in the Gilbert Islands,
were captured in November 1943 – although Tarawa
cost 3,000 American dead and wounded. Successes
in the Gilberts helped prepare the way for operations
against the Marshall Islands in early 1944. This axis,
pressed for by Nimitz, represented the shortest route
for an advance on the Philippines. The US army
wanted a southern drive, the navy a central Pacific
one. There were sufficient resources to do both, but
the strategic choice was also important; Japanese naval
and air power may have been grower weaker, but there
were a large number of Japanese island bases, and
an effective plan was required to take them without
wasting time or lives. Under Nimitz's oversight,
America's land, sea and air forces gained cumulative
experience in successful and closely coordinated
amphibious operations.

There was also an increased success in submarine
warfare against Japan. American submarines benefited
from good surface speed and range, the ability to
decipher Japanese signals, and a clear determination

to attack. Unrestricted submarine warfare had been
ordered after Pearl Harbor. The attack on Japanese
trade stymied Japan's attempts to increase the
production of munitions: her industry was heavily
dependent on the import of raw materials from
the empire.

The campaigning in 1944 saw the collapse of the
Japanese empire in the Pacific. Without air superiority
Japanese naval units were highly vulnerable, and
logistical decline severely affected Japanese strategic
capability. Nimitz could decide where to make
attacks and could neutralize bases, such as Truk in
the Caroline Islands, by 'leapfrogging' them. Such
manoeuvring maintained the pace of the advance,
lessened the extent of brutal conflict, and reflected the
degree to which the Americans held the initiative.

Nimitz's advances were cumulative; gains,
such as the Marshall Islands in early 1944, provided
bases that made it easier to strike at Saipan, Tinian
and Guam in the Mariana Islands. Victory in the
Battle of the Philippine Sea (19–20 June 1944)
enabled the Americans to overrun the Marianas.
This provided not only sites for airfields but also an
important forward logistical base for the navy and for

◄ **Admiral Chester W. Nimitz,
photographed in October 1945 on his
arrival in Washington DC. For his service
as Commander-in-Chief, he was presented
with a Gold Star by President Truman.**

amphibious operations. After that, Nimitz cooperated
in the invasion of the Philippines.

THE FINAL CAMPAIGNS

Promoted to Fleet Admiral in December 1944, Nimitz
oversaw the seizure of the islands of Iwo Jima and
Okinawa in early 1945. However, they would come at
a heavy cost. Despite massive air and sea support, the
difficulty of capturing these islands was immense, with
heavy casualties among both the attacking US Marines
and the entrenched and fanatical Japanese defenders.
Nimitz's style was to concentrate on the strategic
dimension, leaving operational details to others.
This was of the utmost importance: an incoherent

set of attacks would have failed to exert appropriate
cumulative impact.

Aside from the focus on the islands, Nimitz
also oversaw the naval pressure on Japan. This grew
stronger in 1945. Although the Japanese still occupied
large areas in East and Southeast Asia, these forces
were isolated. American submarines operated with
few difficulties in the Yellow and East China seas and
the Sea of Japan. Carrier-borne planes attacked Japan,
dominated its air space and mined its waters, while
warships bombarded coastal positions.

American naval power had proved crucial to
victory in the conflict for control of the Pacific, and this
looked towards America's post-war naval dominance.

Vo Nguyen Giap

North Vietnamese General who Defeated the French and Americans

'Inheriting and continuing our nation's tradition of fighting against foreign invasion, our people have defeated a large force with a smaller one.'

VO NGUYEN GIAP

A Life in Brief

1911, 15 August
Born in An Xa, Quang Binh Province, central Vietnam

1946
Senior general of the VPA and Minister of Defence

1991
Relieved of all government posts

➤ **General Vo Nguyen Giap, senior general of the Vietnam People's Army and minister of defence of the Democratic Republic of Vietnam.**

➤➤ **Map showing French positions and Viet Minh attacks during the 1954 battle of Dien Bien Phu, a bold stroke by Giap and one of the 20th-century's most important battles. The resounding French defeat here allowed the politicians to shift blame for the Indo-China debacle to the military and to extricate the nation from Indo-China.**

Vo Nguyen Giap commanded Vietnamese forces that fought the Japanese, French and Americans. Giap was a brilliant strategist who successfully combined guerrilla warfare and conventional military operations. Following his retirement from public life in 1991, he was designated a 'national treasure'.

A Vietnamese nationalist, Giap joined the Indochinese Communist Party (ICP) in 1937. In 1940 the Vietnamese nationalist leader Ho Chi Minh sent him to northern Tonkin to organize military opposition to the French and Japanese by the Vietnam Independence League (Viet Minh) – despite his lack of formal military training. In December 1944, Giap formed the first brigade of what would become the Vietnam People's Army (VPA).

In 1945 Giap became minister of the interior in Ho Chi Minh's new Democratic Republic of Vietnam (DRV). In 1946 he was made senior general in the VPA (until 1972) and the DRV minister of defence (until 1986). When the fragile peace with the French collapsed, Giap led the Viet Minh in the long Indo-China War (1946–54). Initially outnumbered, Giap took to the jungle and waged guerrilla war, but slowly built up a 300,000-strong army. In 1950 he secured Route Coloniale 4 in northern Vietnam, allowing ready access to China. His forces suffered heavy losses, however, during the pitched battles aimed at capturing Hanoi.

When the French established a blocking position at Dien Bien Phu in 1954, Giap accepted the challenge. He assembled five divisions and more artillery than the French. His anti-aircraft guns proceeded to drive off the limited French air support, and Giap won the most important battle of the war.

Giap directed VPA forces in the fighting in South Vietnam in the 1960s and 1970s. He opposed the January 1968 Tet Offensive, but carried it out on orders from the senior DRV leadership. A major military defeat for the VPA, the Offensive did not spark the intended general uprising in the south against the Americans, but it did bring a sharp change in public opinion in the United States. In 1972, Giap was again pressurized to order a massive conventional invasion of South Vietnam across the Demilitarized Zone (the Eastertide Offensive). When the offensive was blunted, Giap's reluctance was vindicated.

Sharp disagreements within the DRV leadership led to Giap being stripped of his command of the VPA later that year, although he retained the post of minister of defence. His protégé, General Van Tien Dung, directed the final offensive in 1975 that resulted in the defeat of South Vietnam.

Key Campaigns

The Indo-China War (1946–54)
September–October 1950, Giap defeats the French in the battle for Route Coloniale 4, securing the border with Communist China and ending the possibility of a French victory. At Hoa Binh (November 1951–February 1952), in an attempt to control the Red River Delta, the French inflict heavy casualties on the VPA. At Dien Bien Phu (March–May 1954), a French and allied force is surrounded by Giap's superior numbers, and eventually overrun.

The Vietnam War (1962–75)
The multiple uprisings of the Tet Offensive (January–June 1968) result in 50 per cent losses among the 80,000 VPA troops committed, but the operation turns US public opinion against the war. The March–October 1972 Eastertide Offensive sees the VPA troops pour over the border into South Vietnam, but US air power and rallying South Vietnamese ground forces halt the offensive.

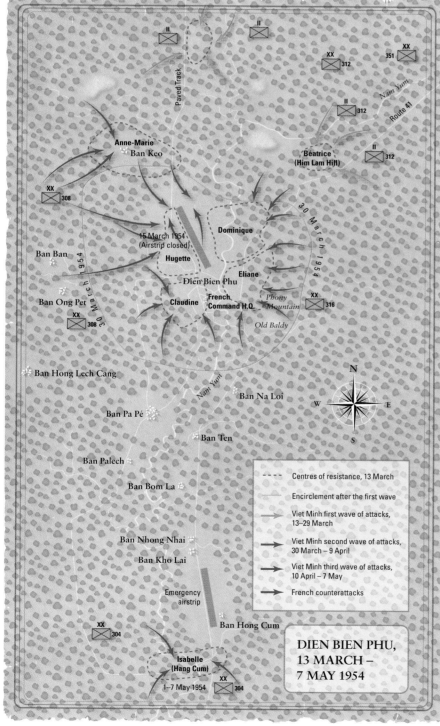

DIEN BIEN PHU, 13 MARCH – 7 MAY 1954

Centres of resistance, 13 March
Encirclement after the first wave
Viet Minh first wave of attacks, 13–29 March
Viet Minh second wave of attacks, 30 March – 9 April
Viet Minh third wave of attacks, 10 April – 7 May
French counterattacks

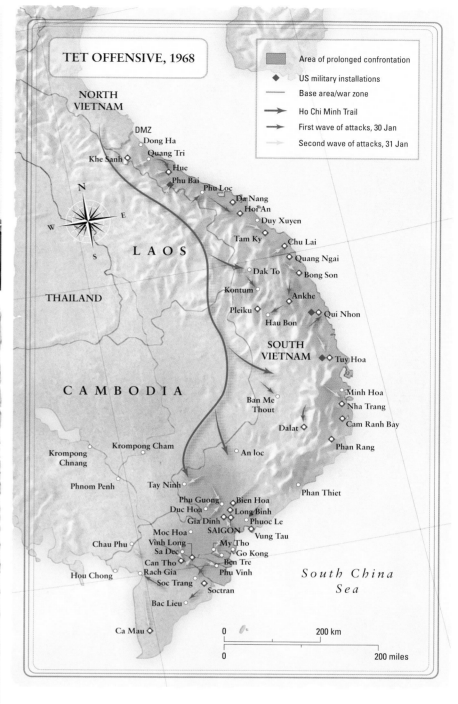

TET OFFENSIVE, 1968

Area of prolonged confrontation
US military installations
Base area/war zone
Ho Chi Minh Trail
First wave of attacks, 30 Jan
Second wave of attacks, 31 Jan

▲ Map showing locations struck during the Communist Tet Offensive of January 1968. Communist forces attacked 36 of 44 provincial capitals, 5 of 6 autonomous cities, 64 of 242 district capitals, and about 50 hamlets. This offensive, ordered by the North Vietnamese leadership over Giap's objections, failed to achieve its stated aims but was nonetheless a turning point in the Vietnam War.

▲▼ Fighting in Cholon, Saigon, during the Tet Offensive. Over two divisions were used for the attacks in and close to Saigon, but these attacks were largely contained and overcome within several days.

Vo Nguyen Giap

Modern Age

Great Military Leaders A to Z

Abbas I (1571–1629) – see pp. 132–33

Agrippa, Marcus (63–12 BC) – see p. 46

Akbar (1542–1605) – see pp. 120–23

Alaric the Goth (AD 370–410)
King of the Visigoths (r. AD 395–410). Alaric was a provincial leader within the Germanic provinces of the Roman empire, but after the battle of Frigidus (September, AD 394) he revolted, and twice invaded the Italian peninsula and sacked Rome. Unable to take Constantinople, he ravaged Greece. He was checked by a Roman army at Pollentia (AD 402) and Verona (AD 403), but he returned and besieged Rome in AD 407 and then again in 410. Despite negotiations, the city fell. Alaric's ambitions to lead the empire cut short by his death from fever.

Alaungpaya (1714–60)
Founder of the Third Burmese empire and Konbaung dynasty. Born Aung Zeya, as a tribal chief he resisted the invasion of Burma by the Pegu kingdom in 1752, which proved so popular that thousands flocked to his side. When his king was slain in 1754, Alaungpaya continued the resistance, until Pegu was overrun. It is alleged he ordered the massacre of Europeans who had assisted his enemies, but there is little evidence to support the claim. He died from wounds he sustained on campaign against the neighbouring Ayutthaya.

Alba, Duke of (1507–82) – see p. 115

Alexander, Harold (1891–1969)
Highly decorated British field marshal. In World War I, Alexander rose rapidly to command the Irish Guards on the Western Front, being twice decorated for gallantry and twice wounded. In World War II, he assisted in the successful extraction of the BEF from France in 1940, and served briefly in Burma, the Middle East and then North Africa. He played a key role in the battle of El Alamein with Montgomery (q.v.) against Rommel (q.v.) and went on to command Fifteenth Army in Italy. He was greatly respected not only by his men, but also by senior Allied officers.

Alexander the Great (356–323 BC) – see pp. 18–23

Alfred the Great (AD 849–99)
Leader of the West Saxons and King of Wessex. Alfred conducted a successful defence against the Danish Viking invasions of England from his base in the marshlands of Somerset. According to folklore, Alfred was so engrossed in planning his guerrilla campaigns against the Danes that he was once scolded by his safe-house hosts for burning some cakes. He fought at least nine successful actions in AD 870 alone, finally crushing the

Danes at Ethandun in AD 878. He launched a protracted counterattack, taking London (c. AD 885), whilst clearing the West Country and the southeast of England. He also constituted the first Saxon navy and perfected a system of reservists for rapid mobilization.

Allenby, Edmund, 1st Viscount (1861–1936)
Field marshal, and one of the most successful British commanders of World War I. Nicknamed 'The Bull', Allenby commanded troops in the Second Boer War, on the Western Front, and, most famously, in Palestine against the Ottoman Turks in 1917–18. Emphasizing discipline and efficiency, Allenby inspired confidence in his men, and he led them to take Jerusalem in 1917. British imperial forces helped him overcome manpower shortages and gave him the opportunity to carry out a brilliant flanking attack at Megiddo in 1918, which broke the back of Ottoman Turk resistance in the war.

Anson, George, 1st Baron (1697–1762) (▲)
British admiral, and later First Lord of the Admiralty. During the War of the Austrian Succession (1740–48), Anson's determination to fulfil his mission – to harass the Spaniards in South America – in fact led to a circumnavigation of the globe. Although storms and sickness reduced his flotilla and crews, he continued to attack the port of Paita in Peru, crossed the Pacific and then captured a galleon near the Philippines, before returning to England in triumph. In May 1747, he commanded the fleet that defeated the French at the First Battle of Cape Finisterre.

Arminius (16 BC–AD 21) – see p. 45

Arnold, Henry 'Hap' (1886–1950) – see p. 263

Ashoka the Great (304–232 BC)
One of India's greatest rulers. The son of a Mauryan emperor, Ashoka was schooled in military and political science, and he managed to quell an uprising in Takshashila (Taxila) in Sindh by his presence alone. He subsequently carried out a brutal court coup, and then conquered several neighbouring states. When one of his generals

was checked in Kalinga, he personally commanded one of the greatest Indian armies ever assembled and laid waste to the region. The devastation nevertheless affected him deeply, and he converted to Buddhism.

Attila the Hun (AD 406–53)
Notorious expander of the Hunnish empire. As Khan of the Huns from AD 434, Attila controlled much of central and eastern Europe. The Huns perfected their horsemanship and use of the composite bow to conquer all the land between the Rhine and the Volga. Attila's mounted armies raided the Balkans twice (AD 441–43 and 447), devastating its economy. Although defeated at Chalons (France, also known as the Catalaunian Fields) in AD 451, he nevertheless drove the Western Roman emperor from Ravenna in AD 452. Attila's forces proved adaptable, employing siege weapons to take several Danubian cities, but he was unable to bring about the decisive defeat of the Western Romans.

Augustus (63 BC–AD 14) – see pp. 42–47

Babur (1483–1530) – see pp. 116–19

Baquedano González, Manuel Jesús (1823–97)
Commander-in-chief of the Chilean army during the War of the Pacific (1879–84). His military career in the 1850s and 1860s was marked with demonstrations of loyalty to the prevailing governments in a period of unrest, but in the War of the Pacific against Peru, his resolute leadership gave him the chance for senior command. He led the Chilean forces to victory at Chorrillos and Miraflores in 1881 and was popular with the public, a fact that led to his subsequent nomination for the presidency, which he declined. However, he formed a caretaker administration during political unrest in the 1890s.

Basil II, the Bulgar-Slayer (AD 958–1025)
Byzantine ruler who expanded the empire to its greatest extent. When he came to power in AD 976, he was compelled to crush revolts at Skleros (AD 979) and Phokas (AD 989) and did so by forging an alliance with the Rus'. He drove the Arabs back from Syria in a series of battles from AD 995 and then, after mixed fortunes, retook Bulgaria in a series of campaigns that culminated in the battle of Kleidion (AD 1014). It is alleged that he blinded thousands of his Bulgarian prisoners here, earning his famous epithet. Basil went on to take the Crimea, Armenia and southern Italy.

Bayezid (1354–1403)
Ottoman sultan, nicknamed 'The Thunderbolt' for his brutal retributions. When his father Murad I was murdered shortly after the First Battle of Kosovo Field (1389), Bayezid ascended to the throne. He captured Bulgaria and northern Greece (1389–95) and laid siege to Constantinople between

1391 and 1398. He intercepted and defeated a crusader army in 1396 at the battle of Nicopolis, and crushed a Turkish army at Karaman the following year. However, at the battle of Ankara in 1402, Bayezid was captured by Timur (q.v.) and subsequently died in captivity.

Belisarius (AD 500–65) – see pp. 52–53

Blake, Robert (1599–1657)
Famous admiral, and one of the most outstanding British officers of his generation. A Somerset merchant and Member of Parliament, Blake rose to prominence during the English Civil Wars (1642–51). He combined religious zeal and pragmatism in his defence of Taunton (1644–45) against the Royalists. In 1649 he was made general-at-sea and spent two years destroying the remaining Royalist strongholds and fleets. He defeated the Dutch in the First Anglo-Dutch War (1652–54) and smashed a Turkish pirate fleet in 1655. He went on to defeat a Spanish fleet off Tenerife in 1657, but died of fever on his return voyage to England.

Blücher, Gebhard von (1742–1819)
Prussian marshal who played a key part in the final defeat of Napoleon (q.v.). A soldier from the age of 16, Blücher nevertheless spent much of his youth drinking, gambling and courting. He was twice wounded in action against Napoleon's armies (1806 and 1813) and, although defeated, he managed to secure a victory over the French at Katzbach (1813). He led part of the invasion of France in 1814, where he was again beaten by Napoleon (at Champaubert, Vauxchamps and Montmirail), but in 1815 he confronted the French emperor at the head of an army of 120,000 men. At Ligny (1815), he was pinned by his dead horse and his army was rolled back, but his refusal to abandon his Anglo-Dutch allies, led by Wellington (q.v.), meant that he was able to combine forces and defeat Napoleon at Waterloo in 1815.

Bohemond, Prince of Taranto and Antioch (1058–1111)
Crusading Norman leader from southern Italy. Bohemond led a Norman army against Byzantine Thessaly in 1080, inflicting several defeats on Alexius I. Returning to Italy, his Adriatic possessions were overrun and he only secured southern Italy with papal support. In the ensuing First Crusade (1096–99), Bohemond led inspired Norman forces back across Thessaly and into Asia Minor, taking Antioch in 1098. Despite harbouring ambitions to create a great principality in the east, he was captured by his enemies, defeated on the Euphrates in 1104, and checked by the Byzantines and Venetians in 1108.

Bolívar, Simón (1783–1830) – see pp. 210–11

Boscawen, Edward (1711–61)
Cornish-born British admiral, noted for his aggression in battle. At Cartagena in 1741 Boscawen demonstrated his preference for leading by example by taking a party of seamen to capture a shore battery. He personally captured a French frigate in 1744 and was in the midst of the action at the First Battle of Cape Finisterre (1747). During the Seven Years' War, he intercepted and captured a French squadron in 1755, assisted in the taking of the fortress of Louisburg on Cape Breton Island, and then, in 1759, crucially smashed an invasion fleet at the battle of Lagos, off Portugal.

Brooke, Alan, 1st Viscount (1883–1963) – see p. 261

Bruce, Robert (1274–1329) – see pp. 88–89

Brusilov, Alexei (1853–1926) – see p. 247

Byng, Julian, 1st Viscount of Vimy (1862–1935)
British field marshal who served with distinction during World War I. In the Second Boer War (1899–1902), Byng commanded an irregular cavalry unit with success. On the outbreak of World War I, he was deployed to lead a cavalry division, then the entire cavalry corps, in France. He was sent to Gallipoli to evacuate forces from Suvla Bay before taking command of the Canadian corps back in France. He was largely responsible for the taking of Vimy Ridge in 1917, a brilliant set-piece operation that reflected all the lessons learned during the war to that date. He went on to command the Third Army, and was a strong advocate of tank warfare; the latter led to the initial success of Cambrai (1917), although a lack of reserves and resources resulted in setbacks later in the action. Enduring the German offensives of 1918, he led his formation through the Hundred Days campaign of 1918, which broke the Kaiser's forces on the Western Front.

Caesar, Julius (100–44 BC) – see pp. 36–41

Campbell, Colin, 1st Baron Clyde (1792–1863)
British commander of the 'Thin Red Line' at the battle of Balaclava (1854). Campbell began a full career of active service in the Peninsular War (1808–14), where he distinguished himself as a young officer. He went on to command during the First Opium War (1839–42), and in the First Anglo-Sikh War (1845–46). In the latter, his sangfroid under fire proved inspirational at the battles of Chillianwala and Gujarat, and he demanded the same self-discipline from his men, as demonstrated by the events at Balaclava in the Crimea. He captured the public imagination in Britain when he led a relief column to Lucknow during the Indian Mutiny in 1857, and crushed the uprising in central India.

Carnot, Lazare (1753–1823)
Great organizer and reformer of the French Revolutionary Army. Carnot established an understanding of conflict that was to have a profound influence on the 20th century, namely the concept of total war. An engineer in the pre-Revolution era, he realized that, with invasion looming on every front, France needed to exploit its resources to the full. He amalgamated the old army and the Revolutionary volunteers, reorganized the supply of munitions, established a war industry and mobilized the public. In the autumn of 1793, he assisted in the defeat of the Austrians at the battle of Wattignies. Although out of favour, he defended Antwerp for France in 1814 and became war minister under Napoleon (q.v.).

Chandragupta (350–293 BC) – see pp. 24–25

Charlemagne (AD 742–814) – see pp. 58–61

Charles V, Holy Roman Emperor (1500–58) – see pp. 112–15

Charles X, King of Sweden (1622–60)
Scandinavian ruler who fought Poland and Denmark. In the Second Northern War (1655–60) Charles overran Poland, and, despite serious national resistance against him and a protracted retreat to avoid converging enemy armies, he defeated John II's larger forces at Warsaw in 1656. In the subsequent fighting against Denmark, Charles's army drove through Jutland and then, taking advantage of an exceptionally cold winter, he made a series of precarious crossings of the frozen Belts between the Danish islands. The sudden arrival of the Swedish forces compelled the Danish to make peace.

Charles XII, King of Sweden (1682–1718) (▲)
Roving commander of the Great Northern War (1700–21). Opinions are divided on Charles XII: he is regarded as a military success in tactics and organization, but his reign ended in the chaotic decline of Swedish power. When Poland, Denmark and Russia declared war in 1700, Charles embarked on a successful amphibious campaign against Denmark and also defeated the Russians at Narva. The Poles and Saxons were defeated in a series of battles between 1702 and 1706. However, his invasion of Russia in 1708 ended in disaster at Poltava in 1709 and Charles was forced to take refuge in Turkish Bessarabia. Despite military reforms, on his return to Sweden Charles was unable to defeat the combination of powers ranged against him and he was killed in action at Frederiksten (Norway) in 1718.

Charles of Austria, Archduke (1771–1847)
Austrian field marshal of the Napoleonic era. In the French Revolutionary Wars (1792–1802), Charles proved a competent general; he beat the French at Wetzlar, Amberg and Würzburg in 1796, stopping a French advance on Austria, and in 1799 defeated the French again at Stockach (1800). Charles checked Napoleon (q.v.) at Aspern-Essling in 1809 and was only defeated at Wagram two months later at enormous cost. Charles proved a more cautious and conservative commander than Napoleon, but he improved the Austrian army.

A to Z Great Military Leaders

Chen Yi (1901–72)
Chinese communist military commander. Chen began his career as a guerrilla, but commanded the New Fourth Army in the operations against the Japanese between 1937 and 1945. In the Chinese Civil War (1945–49), Chen led the Shandong counteroffensive, defeated the Kuomintang at Huai-Hai and captured the lower Yangtse in 1948–49. He went on to become foreign minister, but he was purged as part of the Cultural Revolution in 1967.

Chuikov, Vasily (1900–82)
Marshal and Hero of the Soviet Union. Chuikov enlisted in the Red Army during the Russian Revolution and served in Poland and Finland in 1939 and 1940. After a brief spell in China as a military adviser, he returned to the Soviet Union to command the 62nd Army, which made a fighting withdrawal to Stalingrad. The 62nd's epic defence of the city earned it the new title of 8th Guards Army. Chuikov led the counterattack on the Byelorussian front and the advance through Poland, and he commanded the 8th Guards as it fought its way through Berlin. In this great advance, Chuikov's forces covered large distances, up to 40 miles a day, often over difficult ground. He was eventually promoted to commander-in-chief of Soviet ground forces in the 1960s.

Clark, Mark (1896–1984)
Flamboyant and controversial US general of World War II. As commander of Fifth Army, Clark demonstrated his skill and determination in the fighting in North Africa, during Operation Torch (1943) and Italy, particularly at Anzio, Salerno and Cassino (1944). However, he was criticized for claiming the limelight and his decision to enter Rome, rather than encircle the German Tenth Army as ordered, possibly prolonged the Italian campaign in 1944. However, he was promoted and commanded during the later stages of the operations there. In the post-war period, Clark commanded UN forces in Korea from May 1952 until the 1953 armistice.

Claude, Duke of Villars (1653–1734) – see p. 163

Clive of India (1725–74)
Key figure in securing British control of the Indian subcontinent. Originally a clerk of the East India Company, Robert Clive took command of a small force that seized Arcot from Chandra Sahib, an ally of France, in 1751, and then subsequently withstood a siege unsupported for 53 days. Promoted to lieutenant-colonel, he took command of another small force that was attacked by Suraj ud-Dowlah, the Nawab of Bengal, at Plassey (1757). Preserving his powder during a thunderstorm, Clive's 39th Foot assaulted the Indian guns, whilst Suraj's 'allies', whom Clive had been subverting prior to the battle, melted away. His victory gave the East India Company control of Bengal.

Cochrane, Thomas (1775–1860)
Dashing and maverick British admiral. Known to the French as the 'Sea Wolf', Cochrane was a master of deception and daring, and an accomplished fighting seaman. He tricked pursuers, raided French bases and captured the warship *Gamo* even though he was outnumbered five to one. He frequently fell out with his superiors and was suspended from the Royal Navy, only to command the Chilean and Brazilian navies with great success against Spain and Portugal. He was brilliant in capturing ships and ports, raiding and evading, but his subsequent political career was a failure.

Collingwood, Cuthbert (1748–1810)
Admiral and contemporary of Nelson (q.v.). Collingwood served his entire life in the Royal Navy, seeing action from 1797 onwards. He blockaded Spain and France and reported the gathering of the Franco-Spanish fleets in 1805, which led to the victory at Trafalgar. During the latter, Collingwood's ship *Royal Sovereign* was the first into action, and although hemmed in, he sank the *Santa Ana* and disabled several other enemy vessels. When Nelson was killed, Collingwood took over, and he went on to command the Mediterranean fleet. He was deeply respected by his political masters and by ordinary sailors alike.

Collins, Michael (1890–1922)
Irish revolutionary leader and first commander-in-chief of the national army. Collins joined the Irish Republican Brotherhood, and, with the Irish Volunteers, took part in the failed Easter Rising against British rule in Dublin in 1916. The debacle influenced him profoundly and he spent his time in internment planning to revive the Republican cause using both political and guerrilla tactics, which were to become hallmarks of Irish insurgency techniques for decades. On his release, he launched his irregular campaign and became director of IRA (Irish Republican Army) intelligence. However, by 1921 he felt the time had come to negotiate a settlement with the British. The opposition of other republicans led to the Irish Civil War (1922–23), in which Collins used artillery to shell his opponents in Dublin and acted ruthlessly. He was killed in 1922 in an ambush whilst trying to make contact with an opposition leader.

Condé, Prince de (1621–86) – see p. 140

Constantine I (AD 280–337)
The first Christian Roman emperor. Originally the caesar (sub-emperor) of Britain and Gaul, Constantine defeated Frankish rebellions and controlled tribes across the Rhine with punitive campaigns. He crushed his two leading rivals in a series of operations, winning decisive victories at the Milvian Bridge (AD 312) to secure Rome, and Chalcedon (AD 324) to secure the eastern provinces. Constantine reunited the empire, expropriated his rivals' realms to finance his army and court and established Christianity as the imperial religion. He set up an elite mobile force to augment the limited auxiliaries along the frontier, professionalized the officer corps and increased the number of men from the provinces in the army.

Córdoba, Gonzalo Fernández de (1453–1515)
Spanish leader of the Reconquista. During the latter, Córdoba distinguished himself in the sieges of Tajara, Íllora and Monte Frio, where he was the first man to scale the walls. In 1495, he led an expedition to Sicily against the French, supported by his Venetian allies who controlled the seas. His initial setback did not deter him and he took Atella (in Campania), before going on to relieve Rome. In 1500, he led a Spanish–Venetian force against Turkish-held Cephalonia. He defeated the French in the battle of Cerignola (1502) using arquebus and cannon fire. At Garigliano (1503), in a night attack, he outmanoeuvred a larger force using a pontoon bridge. On the battlefield, Córdoba successfully combined the use of infantry firepower and pikemen in the tercio, along with artillery and light cavalry, but he was also a renowned siege specialist.

Cornwallis, Charles (1738–1805) – see p. 178

Cortés, Hernándo (1484–1547) – see pp. 98–101

Crazy Horse (1840–77) (▲)
Courageous and aggressive chief of the Lakota Sioux. Crazy Horse (Tasunca-uitco in Lakota) epitomized the mounted Native American warrior. He played a key role in the resistance to white American annexations, fighting on the Bozeman Trail campaign (1865–68), and he deceived and then massacred the Fetterman Column (1866). The climax of his career came when he joined other Plains Indians tribes to protect lands around the Black Hills in 1876. Crazy Horse inflicted a defeat on George Crook at Rosebud, and, when attacked by Custer at Little Big Horn, he orchestrated a rapid envelopment of a 7th Cavalry detachment and wiped them out. However, Washington committed more resources to the destruction of the Plains Indians that winter, and Crazy Horse was murdered in Nebraska.

Cromwell, Oliver (1599–1658) – see pp. 142–47

Cunningham, Sir Andrew (1883–1963) – see p. 260

Currie, Sir Arthur (1875–1933)
Commander of the Canadian Expeditionary Force during World War I. Currie's Canadian Corps, which fought as a composite force in the second half of the war, earned a reputation for aggression and skill. He commanded a brigade in 1915 at Second Battle of Ypres, was promoted to general

and led the attack on Vimy Ridge in 1917. His attention to detail, meticulous preparation and willingness to devolve command to platoon level ensured that this crucial ridge was carried for relatively light losses. Although he disagreed with Haig (q.v.) at times, he led the Canadians through a series of successful operations in the final year of the war.

Cyrus the Great (598–528 BC) – see pp. 16–17

Daun, Count Leopold Josef von (1705–66) – see p. 167

Davout, Louis-Nicholas (1770–1823) – see p. 184

Dayan, Moshe (1915–81)
Israeli military leader during the post-war Arab–Israeli conflicts. Dayan joined the Haganah (militia) aged 14, hoping to emulate the British officer Orde Wingate (q.v.). In 1941, whilst fighting in Syria alongside Australian forces against the Vichy French, he was hit by a sniper's bullet and lost an eye. With a reputation for courage, charisma and resilience, he led operations in the Jordan Valley and on the central front in the Arab-Israeli War (1948), and through the Suez Crisis (1956). His overconfidence after the Six Day War (1967), partly led to the early setbacks during the Yom Kippur War (1973). He advocated withdrawal, but was overruled, and this misjudgement ended his military career.

Dewey, George (1837–1917)
American admiral best known for his victory in the battle of Manila Bay (1898). A veteran of the American Civil War (1861–65), Dewey led his squadron to Manila Bay at the outbreak of the Spanish-American War. He utterly destroyed the Spanish Pacific fleet, without losing any of his men (save one who died of a heart attack). His victory encouraged President McKinley to consider the occupation of the Philippines. His threat to shell the Filipinos ensured that landings took place, although it cost good relations with these former allies.

Dönitz, Karl (1891–1980)
Commander-in-Chief of the German navy from 1943. Dönitz joined the Kriegsmarine in 1911, and served as a U-boat officer in World War I. His own vessel was sunk in 1918 and he was taken prisoner. In the inter-war years, he gained experience of both surface and submarine service, but at the outbreak of World War II he was pessimistic about the ability of U-boats to operate successfully against British countermeasures. Nevertheless, he believed that 'wolf packs' of submarines could defeat the British convoy system and that a campaign against British logistics would force them to capitulate. He lobbied hard for more U-boats, but Erich Raeder (the Commander-in-Chief until January 1943) and Hitler put their faith in an enhanced surface fleet. Despite considerable successes in the Battle of the Atlantic (1940–43), his codes were blown and his U-boat campaign was defeated. A committed Nazi, he succeeded Hitler in 1945, and was subsequently tried and imprisoned by the Allies.

Dowding, Hugh, 1st Baron (1882–1970)
Head of Fighter Command during the critical months of the Battle of Britain (1940). Dowding served with the Royal Flying Corps during World War I, and was promoted to air marshal in 1933. In this role he championed the integration of radar, raid plotting and radio control of fighter squadrons. During the Battle of Britain, he resisted attempts to throw too many pilots into the campaign, always maintaining a reserve, and refused to accept the introduction of larger 'big wing' fighter formations. However, his distant personality alienated some senior colleagues and he was retired from command as soon as the crisis of 1940 was over.

Drake, Sir Francis (*c.* 1542–96)
English privateer and architect of the defeat of the Armada. A fervent Protestant, Drake joined his cousin, John Hawkins, on expeditions to Africa in the 1560s. The Spaniards reacted violently to English smuggling activities in the Americas, and Drake seized the opportunity to attack Spanish shipping in the Atlantic, before circumnavigating the globe (1577–81). Royal approval for his raiding followed, and he made destructive attacks in the Caribbean (1584–85), attacked the Spanish fleet in Cadiz ('singeing the King of Spain's beard') and was a leading officer in the defeat of the Armada (1588). Despite unsuccessful attacks on Portugal and the Caribbean, his reputation remained intact. Legend has it that, in time of national emergency, Drake's shipboard drum will beat to resurrect his spirit.

Edward I (1239–1307) – see pp. 84–87

Edward III (1312–77)
Long-reigning English monarch during the Hundred Years' War (1337–1453). During his campaign against the Scots in the 1330s, Edward learnt how to handle dismounted men-at-arms and longbowmen. From 1337 he was at war with France, and, whilst he was unsuccessful in the Low Countries, he defeated the French fleet at Sluys in 1340. On land, he and his able commanders were victorious over the French in a series of campaigns, notably at Crécy in 1346 where English archers inflicted heavy casualties. Calais fell the following year, but Edward failed to capture Reims as planned in 1359, and in the latter years of his reign most of his French provinces were lost.

Edward, the Black Prince (1330–76)
Executor of a brilliant campaign through France during the Hundred Years' War. According to Froissart's account of Crécy (1346), the Black Prince was denied reserves for relieving his hard-pressed troops by his father Edward III (q.v.), so that he might 'win his spurs'. The Black Prince's French campaign included a raid on the Languedoc in 1355, and then a decisive action at Poitiers (1356). He went on to lead forces in Spain, winning the battle of Nájera (1367), and suppressed a revolt in his province of Aquitaine in 1370. However, his later years were marked by ill health.

Eisenhower, Dwight D.
(1890–1969) – see pp. 258–67

El Cid (*c.* 1040–99)
Castilian nobleman who led the early campaigns against the Moors in the Reconquista. Born Rodrigo Díaz de Vivar, in his early career he fought the Aragonese alongside the Moors at the battle of Graus (1063), where he established a reputation for bravery. He frequently consulted his men on the tactics to be used, made great use of deception and psychological operations and had a humility in command that many respected. At Cabra (1079), El Cid inspired his men to rally, turning the battle around and routing the Emir of Granada. However, his subsequent exile from Castile meant he became a mercenary officer fighting for both Christians and Muslims, holding Saragossa through several sieges and conquering Valencia in 1094.

Epaminondas (*c.* 418–362 BC)
Theban general who defeated Sparta. At the battle of Leuctra (371 BC), Epaminondas and his Boeotian confederates ended the 300-year supremacy of the Spartan phalanx in a decisive engagement. Massing his best troops in depth on his left, he targeted the elite Spartan formations and broke their lines, killing their king in the process. He was able to command vast numbers of men thanks to his political system, but he ensured the fall of Sparta by freeing their helots and dispersing their allies. He also championed combined light infantry–cavalry tactics. Epaminondas was killed at the moment of victory in the battle of Mantineia (362 BC) against a Spartan-led coalition.

Eugene, Prince of Savoy (1663–1736) – see p. 162

Fairfax, Sir Thomas (1612–71) – see p. 145

Faisal bin al-Hussein (1883–1933) (▲)
Leader of the Arab Revolt (1916–18) against Ottoman rule. During the revolt, Faisal and T. E. Lawrence knew that raids by lightly armed and mobile fighters, used in conjunction with regular British forces, comprised the most successful tactical option. Faisal led the raids on the Hejaz railway and the attack on the port of Aqaba in 1917, which enabled British and allied forces to be landed and cut off the Arabian Peninsula from Ottoman control. With gathering strength, Faisal commanded at Tafila (1918) and broke a regular Ottoman Turkish column before dashing on to Damascus for the armistice.

Fisher, Sir John 'Jackie', 1st Baron Kilverstone (1841–1920)
British admiral who presided over the transformation of the Royal Navy from wooden hulls and sails to steel and steam. As First Sea Lord, Fisher introduced HMS *Dreadnought* in 1906, a revolutionary design that rendered all other vessels obsolete. He also introduced light armoured cruisers to patrol Britain's far-flung maritime sea lanes, and anticipated the threats of submarine warfare and air power to the supremacy of surface fleets. Despite his vision, he made few allies amongst naval and political colleagues.

Foch, Ferdinand (1851–1929) – see pp. 238–43

Foix, Gaston de, Duke of Nemours (1489–1512)
Executor of a six-month campaign in Italy (1511–12) during the War of the League of Cambrai. Known as the 'Thunderbolt of Italy', Gaston arrived in Italy aged only 21. He animated the French forces and scattered the army of the Holy League at Bologna. Marching south, he compelled the Papal–Spanish army to fight at Ravenna (1512) and, flanking their entrenchments, won a decisive victory at the cost of his own life.

Franco, General Francisco (1892–1975)
Nationalist leader of Spain from 1936 to 1975. Franco's early military experiences came as a cavalry officer in North Africa and as commander of the Spanish Foreign Legion in Morocco in 1923 during the Third Rif War (1920–26). However, he took a hard line against the Asturian miners during their 1934, and was removed to the Canary Islands when he advocated emergency powers against the political left. He orchestrated the airlift of troops from North Africa to initiate the Spanish Civil War (1936–39), managed his German and Italian allies and defeated the Soviet-backed forces of the left – often ruthlessly. His victory led to 40 years of undisputed political control of the country as generalissimo.

Frederick I, Barbarossa (1122–90) – see pp. 72–75

Frederick II (1194–1250)
Hohenstaufen Holy Roman emperor. Although crowned in Germany and in Sicily, Frederick spent much of his early reign involved in conflicts with the Papal States or on the Crusades. Even though he managed to secure Jerusalem by negotiation and enjoyed a large Christian following, he was excommunicated. Frederick was forced to suppress a Lombard rising in 1237, and captured papal cities between 1239 and 1241, but was unable to secure Rome itself. Innocent IV went on a counterattack against Frederick and his allies in 1245, and the decisive moment came outside Parma in 1247 when Frederick's imperial forces were defeated.

Frederick the Great (1712–86) – see pp. 164–67

Frunze, Mikhail (1885–1925)
Successful and energetic Bolshevik commander. Frunze joined the communists after being sent to Siberia by the Tsarist regime, working as an agitator within the Russian army. His observations of different fronts in World War I proved a valuable education. After the Revolution, Frunze set up a soviet in Minsk and disrupted General Kornilov's attempts to seize Petrograd, took part in the October coup and crushed anti-communist revolts. In the Russian Civil War (1917–22) he fought Kolchak, and spread communist control in Central Asia, before defeating White forces in southern Russia at Perekop (1920). His achievements rivalled those of Trotsky. After the Civil War he reformed the Red Army, and introduced much of its doctrine, strategy and tactical thinking.

Garibaldi, Giuseppe (1807–82) – see pp. 212–13

Godfrey of Bouillon (1060–1100)
Flemish warrior knight and leader of the First Crusade. Leaving his estates in Lorraine, Godfrey raised an army of knights and retainers and marched to Constantinople, and then subsequently to Jerusalem in 1099. Godfrey and his men assisted in the siege of Antioch and other actions, but his legendary appeal was confirmed when he and his followers were amongst the first to scale the walls of Jerusalem. Although he rejected the title of king, he was an imposing figure and was the undisputed master of the city. Myths were later created about his prowess and singular leadership.

Gordon, Charles George (1833–85)
British major-general, immortalized as 'Gordon of Khartoum'. As an officer of the Royal Engineers, Gordon saw active service in the Crimean War (1854–56) and the Second China War (1858–60). He remained in the Chinese empire to reorganize the army and led Chinese forces to victory over the Taiping rebels. After a series of commands, he was given responsibility for the evacuation of Egyptian personnel from Khartoum in the face of a Mahdist rebellion in 1884. Believing his government was losing the opportunity to restore authority in the Sudan, he defended the city, but a relief column arrived two days too late to prevent its fall. A devout Christian, his stubborn defence and sacrificial death captured the British public's imagination.

Grant, Ulysses S. (1822–55) – see pp. 218–25

Greene, Nathanael (1742–86)
Gifted Patriot organizer and strategist of the American War of Independence (1775–83). A self-taught militiaman before the war, Greene rose from private to major general in the Continental Army. He was given command of forts when the fighting broke out, and, in the early battles, he won the trust and respect of Washington (q.v.). He was appointed to command a demoralized force in the southern states, where he handled a strategic retreat with skill. Although twice defeated by Cornwallis (q.v.), he kept his forces in the field and drew British forces after him.

Guderian, Heinz (1888–1954) – see p. 252

Guesclin, Bertrand du (1320–80)
Breton military commander of the Hundred Years' War. As Constable of France, du Guesclin enjoyed a reputation as a skilled commander, despite his short stature and alleged ugliness. He fought for Duke Charles of Blois in the Breton Civil War (1341–64) and defended Rennes against the English using guerrilla tactics (1356–57). He defeated the Anglo-Navarrese at Cocherel (1364) before being beaten and captured at Auray (1364). He fought as a mercenary captain in Spain in 1366–67, although he was again defeated at Nájera. He later fought the English in northern France and won the battle of Pontvallain (1370). He fought two campaigns to regain control of Brittany in 1373–74. A soldier all his life, du Guesclin was a loyal, disciplined and admirable tactician.

Guiscard, Robert (*c.* 1015–85)
Norman ruler of southern Italy and Sicily. Following his half-brothers to the south of Italy, Robert's aim was to take Calabria from the Byzantines. In a few years he had raised a force capable of defeating a combined Byzantine–Papal army (1053), seized Apulia (1057), instructed his brother to take Sicily from the Arabs and then consolidated his hold over all of the south of the peninsula. He crushed a rival faction of Lombards, and then assembled an allied fleet to defeat a Venetian–Byzantine force. He was distracted by the need to rescue the Pope from the Holy Roman Emperor in 1084, and died before he could march on Constantinople and take the Byzantine crown.

Gustavus Adolphus (1594–1632) – see pp. 134–37

Gwanggaeto the Great of Goguryeo (AD 374–413)
Expander of the Gorguryeo kingdom of Korea. Under Gwanggaeto's rule, Goguryeo became the largest of the three kingdoms of Korea, with an empire stretching across most of the Korean peninsula into northern China, Mongolia and maritime Russia. To achieve this, he defeated the dominant Korean kingdom of Baekje by building a cavalry-based army and a new navy. Between AD 392 and 394, his 50,000-strong mounted force took key cities, before making an amphibious assault on his rival's capital in AD 396. By AD 410 he controlled what is now Manchuria, defeating minor states en route. Recently, disputes have arisen over his proper ethnic origin, leading to several nations claiming him as a hero.

Hadrian (AD 76–138) – see p. 50

Haig, Sir Douglas (1861–1928) – see p. 241

Hannibal (247–183 BC) – see pp. 32–35

Henry V (1386–1422)
Inspirational English king, immortalized by Shakespeare. Henry gained valuable experience – particularly in suppressing guerrilla forces, maintaining logistics and siege warfare – in crushing the revolt of the Welsh fighter Owen Glendower. As king, he invaded France and besieged Harfleur, winning a decisive victory at Agincourt in 1415 using longbowmen supported by dismounted armoured infantry. He recommenced the campaign in 1417, sustaining operations through the winter, taking Caen, Rouen and Meaux by 1420, and imposed a peace settlement on France. Henry had a pragmatic understanding

of military affairs, not least the motivational power of leadership, and the employment of the latest artillery technology.

Hill, Ambrose Powell (1825–65)
Confederate commander during the American Civil War. Identifiable by the red hunting shirt he wore in battle, Hill's best martial qualities were aggression and devotion. Promoted to divisional command, he distinguished himself during the Seven Days Battles (1862), and his forced march to Antietam from Harper's Ferry in 1863 helped Lee turn the tide of the battle. At Gettysburg, he suffered from sickness, but led his corps in action regardless. Although illnesses continued to plague him, he commanded his forces through several actions in 1864, including the Wilderness, Spotsylvania and Cold Harbor. In 1865, he was killed at Petersburg whilst rallying his men after the Union forces had broken through.

Hindenburg, Paul von (1847–1934) – see p. 245

Hone Heke (c. 1810–50)
Maori warrior chief who fought British colonial rule. Hailing from the northern tip of New Zealand's North Island, Hone Heke grew disenchanted with the white settlers despite having supported the 1840 Treaty of Waitangi. He cut down the flagstaff that marked British territory, initiating the First New Zealand War (1845–46). He drove out the settlers and checked the attack of British forces on his pa fortification. He then assaulted a neighbouring, pro-British tribe. When the British attacked his pa at Ruapekapeka on a Sunday, the devout Hone Heke and his followers were at church; he was unable to retake the pa and his forces were dispersed. He was subsequently reconciled to the British before his death, but had demonstrated that the paheka (whites) could be checked, providing inspiration for further Maori resistance in 1860.

Hunyadi, János (1407–56) – see pp. 92–93

Husain ibn Ali (AD 626–680)
Grandson of the Prophet Muhammad. As son of the caliph Ali, Husain claimed the caliphate through hereditary succession and the 'divine light'. The Umayyad Arab caliph Yazid I and his confederates condemned this claim and demanded Husain's submission. His refusal and rebellion in AD 680 ultimately led to the schism of Arab Sunnis and Persian Shi'a, but in the short term, Husain was only able to muster a small number of 'companions' to fight against an army of several thousand at Karbala (AD 680). A moated encampment offered scant advantage and Husain appears to have sallied forth knowing the outcome was inevitable. This act of self-sacrifice has continued to inspire similar acts of martyrdom up to the present day.

Jackson, Thomas 'Stonewall' (1824–63) – see p. 228

Jellicoe, John Rushworth (1859–1935) – see p. 243

Joan of Arc (1412–31)
French national heroine. The 'maid of Orléans' asserted that, guided by visions from God, she aimed to recover territory lost to England during the Hundred Years' War. She was sent to assist in the relief of the siege at Orléans, inspired veteran commanders to action, and consequently achieved success. Despite success in several other minor actions, she was hampered by intrigue at the royal court. Wounded in action outside Paris, she was captured near Compiègne. She was tried for heresy by the English, burnt at the stake and later canonized.

Joffre, Joseph (1852–1931) – see p. 241

Kangxi Emperor of China (1654–1722) (▲)
Longest-reigning Chinese emperor. Kangxi ruled all of China from 1661 until his death. A Manchu Qing, he cleared the population from the coast of southern China to fight his rebellious enemies. When the Zunghar (western) Mongols attacked feudatory allies, Kangxi personally commanded the three armies against them, winning a decisive victory at Zuunmod (1696). However, the Zunghars remained a threat, capturing Tibet in 1717. Much of Kangxi's later career was taken up with suppressing revolts, trying to impose discipline on his warlord commanders and preventing coups.

Kemal, Mustafa (1881–1938) – see pp. 248–49

Kesselring, Albert (1885–1960)
German Luftwaffe commander of World War II. Kesselring joined the German army in 1904 and served in staff appointments in World War I. At the outbreak of World War II in 1939, he commanded the 1st and 2nd Air Fleets in Poland and France, and fought the RAF in the Battle of Britain (1940). In 1941, he took command of the German air forces in the Mediterranean. However, with Axis forces in retreat in 1943, he was assigned to defend the Italian peninsula. Whilst he authorized reprisals against Italian partisans, he gained respect for trying to avoid the physical destruction of historic monuments, particularly in Rome and Siena. In 1945, he was transferred to Germany, and, after Hitler's suicide, he was responsible for the defence of southern Germany. He was later imprisoned for the massacre of Italian civilians.

Khalid ibn al-Walid (AD 592–642)
Arab general of the Muslim conquests. Originally from Mecca, Khalid ibn al-Walid joined Muhammad as a cavalry commander and participated in several actions against other Arabs in the early Islamic conquests. After Muhammad's death, he led the forces of Abu Bakr through several further campaigns, including the defeat of the Persian empire (AD 633). He also seized the Arab state of the Ghassanids from Roman Syrian control. He continued to hold high rank in the wars against the Byzantines, capturing Damascus (AD 635) and defeating the Byzantine forces decisively at the battle of Yarmuk (AD 636), which opened up the Levant.

Khan, Chingiz (1162–1227) – see pp. 76–79

Khan, Kublai (1215–94) – see p. 79

Khan, Ögedei (1186–1241)
Son and successor to Chingiz Khan (q.v.) who expanded the Mongol empire to its greatest extent. Ögedei was a charismatic, pragmatic and successful cavalry commander. He and his subordinates waged war in China over 45 years, finally annexing the entire region. He made Korea a vassal state, consolidated Mongol rule in Persia and invaded Russia, Hungary and Poland. He made excellent use of his generals and they achieved victories at Liegnitz and Mohi (both 1241), but his death prevented the further westward expansion of his forces.

Kitchener, Herbert, 1st Earl (1850–1916)
Irish-born field marshal, immortalized in a series of World War I recruiting posters. Kitchener's early career was marked by service in Egypt and the Sudan, particularly the expedition to relieve Charles Gordon (q.v.). From 1896 to 1898, he commanded an Anglo-Egyptian–Sudanese force that defeated the Mahdists. The decisive action at Omdurman (1898) was made possible by his meticulous planning and logistical support, as well as superior firepower. In the Second Boer War (1899–1902), he assisted in the defeat of the Boer conventional forces at Paardeberg (1900) and then fought the guerrillas to a standstill in a controversial campaign of land clearances and detention camps. He subsequently reformed the British-Indian army, and in World War I predicted that a long war would need a massive mobilization of manpower, leading him to raise Britain's largest volunteer force. Kitchener was lost at sea in 1916 after the warship he was travelling on was sunk by a German mine.

Konev, Ivan (1897–1973)
Hero of the Soviet Union, and brutal suppressor of the 1956 Hungarian uprising. An artilleryman in the Russian Civil War (1917–22), Konev used his favoured status under Stalin to advance his career in the 1930s, but his qualities were demonstrated in the fighting retreat he conducted against Nazi forces in 1941 (and by his subsequent counteroffensive in 1944–45). He checked German thrusts towards Moscow in 1941 and was given command of the Ukrainian Front in 1943. In 1944, his armies drove the Germans from Ukraine and Byelorussia into Poland. He assisted the Slovak partisans in their uprising against the Nazis, and he supported Zhukov's (q.v.) drive towards and into Berlin.

Kutuzov, Mikhail (1745–1813) – see p. 190

Lake, Gerard, 1st Viscount (1744–1808)
British general who played a key role in the subjugation of the Subcontinent. An officer of the Foot Guards of the British army in the American Revolutionary War (1775–83), Lake gained further experience in the Flanders campaign of 1793. He then took independent command of 20,000 men in Ireland to confront the rebellion there in 1798. He won the decisive victory of Vinegar Hill (1798) and believed that stern measures were needed to suppress the unrest. He also contained the French invasion of that year. In 1799 he was made commander-in-chief in India, and he took the field against the Marathas in 1803. He won the battles of Ally Ghur and Laswari, and took the fortress of Aligarh, then Delhi and Agra. He then defeated the Maratha confederate Holkar at Farrukhabad (1804) to conclude that war in 1805. His contemporary Wellington (q.v.) praised Lake's energy, ability and valour.

Lannes, Jean (1768–1809)
Brave and dashing French marshal, whom Napoleon (q.v.) regarded as his 'best friend'. In a short but brilliant career, Lannes epitomized the audacity of the officer corps of Revolutionary and Napoleonic France. He had joined as a volunteer during the Revolution in 1792, but, in just two years' fighting in Spain, was promoted to colonel. In Italy, he exhibited energy and courage such that Napoleon made him a general. He fought in Egypt in 1798, and in 1800 he led Napoleon's advance guard into Italy. He performed well as a corps commander in the Austerlitz campaign (1805), winning actions at Saalfeld, Jena and Auerstädt (1806) and Friedland (1807). In Spain, he brought to an end the gruelling siege of Saragossa in 1808 before returning to central Europe. At Ratisbon (Regensburg), he himself scaled the walls in an impetuous attempt to prevent a long siege, but he was fatally wounded at Aspern-Essling in 1809.

Lee, Robert E. (1807–70) – see pp. 226–29

Leonidas I (c. 520–480 BC)
King of Sparta and leader of 'the 300' at Thermopylae. During the invasion of Xerxes I of Persia (q.v.) into northern Greece, Leonidas was determined to hold the vital pass at Thermopylae at all costs. For two days, Leonidas's band, supported by 1,600 allies, held off 20,000 Persians. When a Greek traitor led the Persians on a route to outflank the Spartans, Leonidas sent away all but his immediate bodyguard, but refused to abandon his post. He and his 300 men were cut down, defiant to the last.

Lima e Silva, Luís Alves de, Duke of Caxias (1803–80)
Successful Brazilian military commander. At the time of Brazil's independence in 1822, Alves was an officer in the army. He helped establish the Imperial Guard, fought against a revolt in Bahia (1823), participated in the Argentina-Brazil War (1825–28), pacified Maranhão (1837) and was instrumental in bringing to an end the unrest known as the War of Tatters (1835–45). Between 1866 and 1869,

he fought the Paraguayans in the War of the Triple Alliance (1864–70), famously crossing the Paraguayan Chaco; his inspirational leadership, notably in the battle of Itororó (1868), contributed to overall victory.

Lin Biao (1907–71)
One the most successful Chinese communist guerrilla leaders of the Mao era. Graduating from the Whampoa Military Academy in 1925, Biao fought the northern warlords, and then organized resistance to Chiang Kai-shek's Kuomintang party from 1928. In 1934 he led a guerrilla campaign that culminated in the occupation of Yan'an. Advocating the same techniques, Biao achieved success against the Japanese in 1937 and the Kuomintang in the Chinese Civil War (1945–49), particularly at the battles of Lien Shen and Pin Jin. Despite his loyalty to Mao, his victory in the Sino-Indian War (1962) and his support for the Cultural Revolution, he was accused of plotting a coup and died while trying to flee China in 1971.

Lockwood, Charles A. (1890–1967)
Successful submarine force commander who hastened Japanese defeat in World War II. Lockwood had gained valuable experience of submarines in the Asiatic Fleet during World War I. In 1943 he was appointed as commander of all American submarine forces in the Pacific. Known for his attention to the welfare of his men, particularly those who endured long voyages, he was nicknamed 'Uncle Charlie'. However, his insistence on improved vessels and better torpedo design proved equally as important. By constantly moving his bases further forward, Lockwood was able to place a stranglehold blockade on Japanese shipping that contributed to Japan's capitulation in 1945.

Longstreet, James (1821–1904)
Dependable Confederate commander of the American Civil War (1861–65). Nicknamed by Robert E. Lee (q.v.) 'Old War Horse', Longstreet was condemned for allegedly delaying Pickett's charge at the battle of Gettysburg (1863), which was the turning point of the war. However, like 'Stonewall' Jackson (q.v.), Longstreet understood that infantry assaults could only succeed when Federal forces had been outmanoeuvred. He demonstrated this with his decisive attacks at Second Battle of Manassas (1862) and Chickamauga (1863). At Fredericksburg (1862) he compelled the Union army to make repeated and costly attacks when his own men occupied a strong position. Despite wounds sustained in the battle of the Wilderness (1864), he continued to serve throughout the final stages of the conflict.

Ludendorff, Erich (1865–1937) – see pp. 244–47

Lyautey, Louis-Hubert (1854–1934)
One of France's most successful colonial officers. Serving in Indo-China in 1894, he was strongly influenced by Joseph Gallieni and saw military pacification as an opportunity to harmonize the 'civilizing mission' of colonialism, French nationalism and economic development. In 1900, he espoused the idea that the colonial officer was not only a soldier but an administrator, engineer and

farmer. He believed that working with local elites better guaranteed a pacified and successful colony. In 1903, Lyautey transferred to Algeria to apply his tache d'huile (spot of oil) through economic penetration via trading posts. However, the locally recruited goums (irregular soldiers) had mixed success and he was forced to return to using razzia (raiding) tactics. Economic inequalities meant he was unable to prevent the Rif rebellion of 1925, but he was ahead of his time in realizing that counter-insurgency required more than military solutions.

Lysander (d. 395 BC)
Commander of the Spartan fleet who defeated the Athenians at Aegospotami and captured their city. At Ephesus, he established a thriving dockyard, and, using Persian support, he ensured loyalty through better wages. In 406 BC, when the Athenian fleet tried to lure him into an ambush, Lysander turned the tables and inflicted a defeat on his rivals. Raiding Athenian cities, he encouraged oligarchic regimes to replace them. At Aegospotami (405 BC), the Athenians failed to bring Lysander to battle, but, whilst they were dispersed and resting at night along the coast, he mounted a ferocious attack. The Athenians were utterly defeated. Finally, in 404 BC, he besieged Athens; and its capitulation brought the Peloponnesian War (431–404 BC) to an end. His attempts to have himself crowned ended in the break up of his network of patronage and his death.

MacArthur, Douglas (1880–1964) (▶)
Controversial American military leader of World War II and the Korean War (1950–53). Whilst many considered MacArthur to be determined and iconic, others accused him of being an insubordinate self-publicist. He had served in World War I, where he often led from the front, before being dispatched to the Philippines during the inter-war years. The Japanese attacks in 1941 overwhelmed his forces there, but his vow 'I will return' became a hallmark of a determined attitude that captured the public imagination. During the Korean War, MacArthur outflanked the North Koreans in a daring amphibious landing at Inchon (1950), but when attacked by Chinese forces in November 1950, he advocated the use of nuclear strikes. A heroic figure to the American public in World War II, he was sacked for refusing to accept the directives of the United States government to limit operations during the Korean War.

Mackensen, August von (1849–1945) (▲)
Successful German field marshal who fought
on the Eastern Front and in Serbia and Romania
during World War I. Mackensen began his career
in the Wars of German Unification (1864–71),
but he gained senior command in the fighting in
East Prussia in 1914 under Paul von Hindenburg
(q.v.). He demonstrated great skill in the operations
around Lodz and Warsaw, and in 1915 he captured
two cities in Galicia. In October of that year, he led
a German–Austro-Hungarian force to complete
the destruction of Serbia's army, and in 1916
he conducted a successful campaign against
Romania. Although in command of a multinational
army, he continued to win almost every action
through 1916–17, but was unable to stem the
defeat of 1918.

Manekshaw, Sam (b. 1914)
Distinguished Indian army officer who commanded
troops though four decades and five conflicts. As
a captain in World War II, he was wounded in
action whilst leading an attack against Japanese
machine guns, and was decorated in the field with
the Military Cross. Later in the campaign he was
wounded again. He led a brigade in the First Indo-
Pakistani War (1947–48), and was Chief of the
Army Staff during the third war in 1971, helping
to overwhelm Pakistan's forces in the nascent
Bangladesh. He was overruled and his advice was
ignored during the disastrous 1962 Sino-Indian
War, but he was honoured by the conferring of the
rank of field marshal in 1973.

Mannerheim, Carl Gustaf (1867–1951)
Finnish commander-in-chief and president. In
the Russo-Japanese War (1904–05), whilst serving
as a cavalry officer of the Imperial Russian army,
Mannerheim was promoted for his bravery at
the battle of Mukden (1905). He took part in
World War I, but during the Russian Civil War
(1917–22) Mannerheim took command of the
Finnish cavalry against the revolutionaries. When
the Soviets attacked Finland in the Winter War
of 1939–40, Mannerheim acted as commander-
in-chief and fought the USSR to a standstill. In
the Continuation War (1941–44), Mannerheim
maintained Finland's freedom of action despite
cooperation with the German forces. As president
of Finland, in 1944 he negotiated a settlement
with the Soviets.

Manstein, Erich von (1887–1973) – see pp. 250–57

Marius, Gaius (157–86 BC)
Republican Roman general who reformed the army.
A rival of Sulla (q.v.), Marius had commanded
forces successfully in Asia Minor and was therefore
selected (over Sulla) to lead the army in Mauretania
in 107 BC. Sulla later claimed the credit for the
victories, but Marius's changes to the recruitment
regulations, which allowed the poorest Romans
to serve in the legions, were of greater lasting
significance. Rome now lay poised to expand its
armies and its territories. First, Marius had to deal
with the invasion of the Cimbri and Teutons and
their Gallic allies. As three vast columns approached
the Italian peninsula, Marius defeated two of them
at Aquae Sextiae (Aix-en-Provence, 102 BC) and
Vercellae (101 BC), and the third turned back. Marius
was active in the defeat of the Italian rebels in the
Social War (91–88 BC), but he was unable to hold
Rome against Sulla.

Marlborough, Duke of
(1650–1722) – see pp. 158–63

Marshall, George C. (1880–1959) – see p. 264

Martel, Charles (AD 686–741) – see p. 60

Maurice of Nassau (1567–1625)
Prince of Orange, and victor of the battles
of Turnhout (1597) and Nieuwpoort (1600).
As stadtholder during the Dutch Revolt
(1568–1648), Maurice was appointed captain-
general of the army in 1587 and immediately
set about organizing the resistance. He made
an intellectual study of tactics, logistics and
siegecraft and was regarded as a great strategist.
He captured Breda, Steenwijk and Geertuidenberg,
won a significant victory in the cavalry action
at Turnhout (1597) and another at Nieuwpoort
(1600). He opposed a peace settlement with Spain,
which merely gave his adversaries time to regroup,
but he was effectively the ruler of the Dutch
Republic from 1618. When the war with Spain
resumed, he continued to offer resistance until
his death in 1625.

Mehmed II (1432–81)
Ottoman sultan who captured Constantinople and
brought the Byzantine empire to an end. Mehmed's
1453 siege of Constantinople was marked by the
extensive use of artillery and the immense effort
of hauling ships overland to bombard the city's
more vulnerable defences. Mehmed also invaded
Anatolia, capturing the Greek exclave of Trebizond.
Having secured these places, Mehmed was free
to concentrate his efforts against Europe. He laid
siege to Belgrade in 1456, and defeated Vlad III
of Wallachia in 1462, although he achieved only
a pyrrhic victory against Stephen the Great of
Moldavia at Valea Alba (1476) and was forced
to retire. In 1480 he invaded Italy, intending to
reunite the Roman empire, but he was unable
to hold on to Otranto, and rebellion in Albania
halted his advance.

Menelik (1844–1913) – see pp. 230–31

Minamoto no Yoshitsune (1159–89)
General of the Minamoto clan who excelled during
the Genpei War (1180–85). In 1159 Yoshitsune's
father and eldest brothers were killed, leaving him
to be brought up by the Fujiwara clan. However,
in 1180 he heard that his brother, Yorimoto, had
assumed the leadership of the Minamoto clan,
and Yoshitsune rejoined him to take part in his
campaigns against the rival Taira. Yoshitsune
defeated them at the battles of Ichi-no-Tani (1184),
Yashima (1185) and Dan-no-ura (1185), with the
latter a decisive victory. However, after the Genpei
War, Yoshitsune sided with Emperor Go-Shirakawa
against his brother. He took refuge again with the
Fujiwara, but was betrayed and was compelled to
commit suicide.

Moltke the Elder (1800–91) – see pp. 214–17

Monash, Sir John (1865–1931)
Australian commander of World War I. Monash led
a brigade at Gallipoli (1915) and earned a reputation
for independent decision-making and thorough
organization, although he was unable to capitalize
on the capture of Hill 971 or Hill 60 as hoped. In
France, he was able to command an Australian
division through Messines and Passchendaele (1917)
although casualties were heavy. As Commander
of the Australian Corps, he embraced the new
thinking about combined-arms operations and
contributed to the decisive defeat of Germany in the
summer and autumn of 1918. He enjoyed a loyal
following largely through his man-management
and innovations.

Montecuccoli, Count Raimondo (1609–80)
Roving Italian commander, regarded by many as the
foremost officer of his age. Montecuccoli combined
a distinguished military career with an intellectual
analysis of the art of war, producing, posthumously,
his famous *Memorie della Guerra* (1703). He began
his active service as a private soldier in the Low
Countries in the 1620s and commanded troops at
Breitenfeld (1631), Lützen (1632) and Nördlingen
(1634). At the siege of Kaiserslautern (1635) he led
a spectacular cavalry charge through the breach.
He served in Austria, Italy, Hungary, Silesia and
Transylvania in senior command appointments,
defeating the Poles, Swedes and Ottoman Turks,
and outmanoeuvred Turenne (q.v.) and Condé (q.v.)
on the Rhine in the 1670s.

Montgomery of Alamein (1887–1976) – see p. 259

Moore, Sir John (1761–1809)
British commander in the Peninsular War
(1808–14), killed at Corunna. Moore set up a
new training establishment for light infantry at
Shorncliffe in 1803, basing his innovations on his
experiences in America and the Mediterranean.
He constructed a series of strongpoints and a
military canal on the south coast of England, with
a mobile reserve, that could resist French invasion.
He had a reputation for the humane treatment of
soldiers, which ensured a great loyalty from his
men. Deployed to Spain, he conducted a brilliant
fighting withdrawal to Corunna and Vigo, but was
mortally wounded in the final battle on the coast.

Munnich, Burkhard Cristoph von
(1683–1767) – see p. 157

Nader Shah (1688–1747) – see pp. 168–69

Napier, Sir Charles (1782–1853)
British general who conquered Sind. Credited with the shortest and most pithy operational dispatch in British military history, it is alleged that Napier, having conquered the trans-Indus province of Sind contrary to orders, signalled simply 'peccavi' ('I have sinned'). Napier had served with Sir John Moore (q.v.) in the Light Brigade in the Peninsular War (1808–14) and strongly supported his light infantry training. After the war, he governed the island of Cephalonia with a benign despotism, and he confronted Chartist unrest in the north of England with a sympathetic but firm style. He was sent to India in 1842 and defeated the emirs of Sind at Miani (1843). He was subsequently appointed commander-in-chief in India, but resigned over disagreements with the governor general. He dressed in an unorthodox fashion and combined his interest in political radicalism with a firm conviction in strong leadership.

Napier, Robert, 1st Baron of Magdala (1810–90)
British general who defeated Emperor Tewodros of Abyssinia. Napier fought in the Sikh wars (1845–46, and 1848–49), on the North-West Frontier of India, in the Indian Mutiny (1857) and in China, but he achieved his crowning triumph in Abyssinia in 1867. Entrusted with the rescue of British hostages and the punishment of the Abyssinians, Napier conducted a model expedition over hundreds of miles of mountainous terrain. He organized, in advance, a great complexity of logistics, which enabled him to move into the country and inflict a decisive defeat on Emperor Tewodros II at Arogi, and then to extract his men with minimum loss.

Napoleon (1769–1821) – see pp. 180–91

Narses (AD 480–574)
Byzantine eunuch best known for his operations in Italy and southeastern Europe against the Goths, Vandals and Franks. Narses was first blooded in quelling rioting that threatened to engulf Constantinople in AD 532. He also engaged in a round of bloody street fighting when posted to Alexandria to support an unpopular bishop there. Soon after his arrival in Italy in AD 538 he lifted the Gothic siege of Arminium (Rimini), but soon ran into disputes with his superior. In AD 545 he led the Heruli against raiders in Thrace before returning to Italy to defeat the chieftain Totila at Busta Gallorum (AD 552) and capturing Rome. In AD 553 he won the battle of Mons Lactarius. He laid siege to several settlements held by the Goths, but was forced to fight an invasion of Vandals and Franks, defeating them all in AD 554. In AD 562, he finally crushed the invading hordes.

Nelson (1758–1805) – see pp. 192–97

Nevsky, Alexander (1220–63)
Russian national hero who repelled German and Swedish invaders. Born to a royal family, Alexander was appointed as prince of Novgorod in 1236 to defend the province from a Swedish invasion. As soon as the Swedes reached the River Neva, Alexander's smaller army made a surprise attack and defeated them so completely that the invasion was halted. Alexander 'of the Neva' was soon recalled from a temporary exile to confront a second German invasion led by the crusading Livonian Knights. His spear-wielding infantry defeated the German cavalry on the ice at Lake Chudskoe (1242), once again ending any chance of occupation.

Ney, Michel (1769–1815)
Courageous French marshal who served Napoleon (q.v.) in all his major imperial campaigns. Nay rose through the ranks of the cavalry in the French Revolutionary Army, and went on to serve Napoleon in the German states, Spain and Russia. During the latter, in the disastrous retreat from Moscow in 1812, he earned the epithet 'the bravest of the brave' for the distinction of being the last French soldier to step out of the Russian empire. There is some speculation that Ney began to suffer from combat stress because of a series of poor judgements after this date, but he continued to exhibit his customary reckless courage in the period 1813 to 1815. He was unable to beat Wellington at Quatre Bras or Waterloo (1815), and only narrowly survived Napoleon's denouement. He was shot by firing squad on the restoration of the old monarchy.

Nimitz, Chester (1885–1966) – see pp. 274–79

Nogi Maresuke (1849–1912)
Japanese hero of the capture of Port Arthur. In the Sino-Japanese War (1894–95), Nogi commanded an infantry brigade that penetrated the Chinese defences of Port Arthur in just one day and he led an amphibious invasion of Taiwan. For these reasons he was selected to lead the Japanese Third Army in the Russo-Japanese War (1904–05) and tasked with the capture of Port Arthur from the Tsar's forces. The defence was stubborn, and Nogi was compelled to make costly attacks over five months. Through sheer determination he took the city, and went on to fight at Mukden (1905). He later committed suicide, partly to atone for the heavy losses he had caused.

Nzinga, Queen of Ndongo and Matamba
(1583–1663)
Southwest African ruler who fought Portuguese colonists and slave-traders. When the Portuguese drove Nzinga from the island of Kidonga, she initially recaptured it but was subsequently forced out. At this point she turned her attention to the conquest of the neighbouring kingdom of Matamba instead (1631). She led her troops into battle personally, and was skilled in diplomacy, using her alliance with the Dutch to defeat the Portuguese at Ngoleme (1644). She was defeated in turn at Kavanga (1646) but she again routed the Portuguese in 1647. A Portuguese–Brazilian assault on Luanda forced her to retire to Matamba, where she continued to fight until 1657.

Oda Nobunaga (1534–82) – see p. 125

Osman Pasha (1832–1900) (▲)
Ottoman defender of Plevna (Pleven) against the Russians in the war of 1877–78. Osman Pasha's stubborn defence of the Bulgarian town was made possible by outstanding field defences and his cool leadership, and it almost turned the tide of the war in the Ottomans' favour. His entrenchments denied the Russians the opportunity of a coup de main, and the Tsar's troops were forced into a prolonged investment. When Osman's supplies and munitions ran out, he led the final great sortie, but was wounded by shell fragments and subsequently captured. Honoured by the Russians themselves, he was acclaimed by the Ottoman public.

Otto the Great (AD 912–73) – see pp. 62–63

Patton, George S. (1885–1945) – see p. 266

Pellew, Edward, 1st Viscount Exmouth (1757–1833)
Long-serving British admiral. In the American War of Independence (1775–83), Pellew took command of a ship when senior officers were hors de combat, and earned a reputation for great courage in action. He fought French privateers in the 1780s even though he was outnumbered. At the outbreak of the French Revolutionary War in 1792, he was back in action, fighting and capturing a French warship so swiftly that he seized intact its codebooks. He personally saved many lives in a grounding incident in 1796, and defeated the French warship *Droits de l'homme* the following year, despite being outgunned. In 1816, he led the bombardment of Algiers to free 1,000 Christian slaves, and was elevated to the peerage.

Pershing, John (1860–1948) – see p. 243

Pétain, Henri-Philippe (1856–1951) – see p. 239

Peter the Great (1672–1725) – see pp. 152–57

Philip II of Macedon (382–336 BC) – see p. 19

Piłsudski, Józef (1867–1935)
Dictator of Poland 1926–35. Piłsudski started out as a Polish nationalist revolutionary, eager to throw off Russian imperial rule, forming combat teams to carry out shootings and bombings. He persuaded Austria to allow him to form a paramilitary force in her territory, which fought alongside the Habsburgs in World War I. In 1917, he withdrew his support for the Central Powers and organized

his own Polish military–political force, which fought the Ukrainians and then the Bolsheviks. He then produced a daring plan for the defeat of the Red Army as it advanced towards Warsaw in 1920, with the key combat role assigned to himself and a small brigade of selected fighters. His plan worked to a tee, and ended hopes for a communist 'world revolution'. Piłsudski later seized power in a coup, and ruled in an authoritarian manner.

Pizarro, Francisco (1478–1541) – see pp. 102–03

Plumer, Herbert (1857–1932)
Field marshal, and one of the most successful British commanders of World War I. Although trained as an infantry officer, Plumer led mounted Rhodesians in the Second Boer War (1899–1902). During World War I, he was a corps commander in 1914 and commander of the Second Army in 1915; well liked by his men, he was nicknamed 'Daddy' because of his paternalism and appearance. In June 1917 he led the meticulous and successful operations at Messines and made some gains despite the appalling conditions at Passchendaele. In late 1917, he was despatched to Italy after the Italian collapse at Caporetto, before returning to the Western Front to stabilize the line against Ludendorff's (q.v.) 1918 offensive. He was methodical and economical with his men's lives, knowing that these were the expectations of a citizen army.

Pompey (104–48 BC) – see p. 39

Qianlong Emperor (1711–99) – see pp. 170–73

Radetzky, Josef (1766–1858)
Austrian general who served his nation for over 70 years. Radetzky's career began with great distinction; he led cavalry through enemy lines at Fleurus (1794), and was noted for his personal courage in action at Trebbia and Novi (1799). At Marengo (1800), he was seriously wounded, but survived. He fought Napoleon (q.v.) at Wagram (1808) and helped design the Allied battle plan at Leipzig (1813) and for the campaign of 1814. He was also an advocate of army reform, but was unable to persuade the conservatives of the need for this, with the consequence that the Austrian army was less efficient after the war. In the 1848–49 revolutions in Italy, he was initially compelled to fall back to the Quadrilateral fortress complex (Legnago, Mantua, Peschiera and Verona) and to rely upon manoeuvre, until he had sufficient forces to deal a decisive blow to the army of Piedmont-Sardinia at the battle of Novara (1849).

Ramesses II (*c*. 1303–1213 BC)
Egypt's greatest pharaoh, who fought the Hittites at Kadesh in 1274 BC (one of the earliest recorded battles). Early in his reign, Ramesses lured the Sherden sea pirates onto the Egyptian coast and defeated them with pre-positioned and carefully coordinated attacks, later incorporating them into his own forces. He made several incursions into the Near East and reorganized the army. In the war with the Hittites, Ramesses was himself

tricked into believing that his adversaries were 200 miles distant by spies at Kadesh, but he recovered from the ambuscade and the arrival of his third brigade helped turn the tide. Later, he advanced on Jerusalem and Jericho, but was unable to secure his conquests despite some successes on the battlefield.

Ramsay, Sir Bertram (1883–1945)
British admiral who commanded naval forces at Dunkirk and D-Day. Ramsay was mentioned in dispatches for his role in the 1918 Zeebrugge Raid and was given the same recognition in World War II for defending British waters off the Channel coast in 1940. He was responsible for the successful evacuation of the British Expeditionary Force from Dunkirk that year, and he was able to develop his amphibious operations expertise whilst in command of the naval forces during the Allied landings in Operation Torch (North Africa, 1942), Operation Husky (Sicily, 1943) and Operation Neptune (Normandy, 1944), all of which were great successes.

Richard the Lionheart (1156–1199) – see p. 70

Ridgway, Matthew (1895–1993)
American general who restored the United Nations' military fortunes in the Korean War (1950–53). In World War II, Ridgway had commanded the 82nd Airborne Division in Italy and he was known for his skill in training and innovation. In Normandy in 1944 he accompanied his parachutists into action and was later given command of XVIII Airborne Corps for the invasion of Germany. He assumed command of the US Eighth Army in Korea in 1950 during its demoralizing retreat, instilling an offensive spirit and insisting on better leadership at all levels. He helped turn the tide against Chinese communist forces and eventually took over supreme command from MacArthur (q.v.).

Roberts, Frederick, 1st Earl (1832–1914)
British general, immortalized as 'Bobs' by Rudyard Kipling, who defeated the Boers. As a young officer, Roberts was awarded the Victoria Cross in the Indian Mutiny (1857) and he took part in several colonial campaigns. In the Second Anglo-Afghan War (1878–80), he led the Kurram column, and then marched on Kabul. However, the defeat of a smaller British contingent at Maiwand (1880) compelled him to make a forced march from Kabul to Kandahar without logistical support. He defeated the Afghans at Kandahar (1881). He was recalled to active service after the initial setbacks of the Second Boer War (1899–1902), and led a large formation to crush the Afrikaners at Paardeberg (1900) before seizing their two capitals.

Rodney, George, 1st Baron (1719–92)
Outstanding 18th-century British naval commander. Rodney led the bombardment of Le Havre in 1759 and blockaded the French coast in 1760, destroying many potential invasion vessels. In 1762 in the Caribbean, he took Martinique, St Lucia and Grenada, and his marines and sailors served as a land force in action against Fort Royal. In 1780 he seized a Spanish convoy and defeated a Spanish fleet at Cape St Vincent, and the following year took

St Eustatius from the Dutch. In 1782, he won the decisive Battle of the Saintes (Dominica), which disabled the French fleet and saved Jamaica.

Rokossovsky, Konstantin (1896–1968) – see p. 271

Rommel, Erwin (1891–1944) – see p. 254

Rumyantsev-Zadunaisky, Peter (1725–96)
Russian general and military writer. Rumyantsev first served in the Russo-Swedish War (1741–43), and, as a colonel, distinguished himself in the Seven Years' War at Gross-Jägerndorf (1757) and Kunersdorf (1759). He captured the Prussian fortress of Kolberg in 1761, which enabled the Russian army to advance on Berlin. Under Catherine the Great, Rumyantsev defeated the Ottomans decisively at Larga and Kagula and crossed the Danube into Romania, which compelled the Ottomans to sue for peace at Kuchuk Kainarji (1774). His success generated jealousy in others and he resigned his command during the second war with the Ottomans. He was reduced to a nominal figurehead in the Polish campaign of 1794.

Rundstedt, Gerd von (1875–1953) – see p. 257

Rupert, Prince of the Rhine (1619–82) – see p. 146

Ruyter, Michiel de (1607–76) (▲)
Famous 17th-century Dutch admiral. De Ruyter was a merchant sailor who gained naval command through his seamanship. Under Tromp (q.v.), he served as a squadron commander in the First Anglo-Dutch War (1652–54), but established his reputation fighting corsairs off the Barbary Coast and in the Baltic against Sweden in the 1650s. He raided English colonies in the Caribbean in 1664–65 and then commanded the Dutch fleet in the Second Anglo-Dutch War (1665–67), with mixed success until he raided the Medway in 1667 and destroyed the English flagship. In the Third Anglo-Dutch War (1672–74), he won victories at Solebay (1672), Schoonveld and Texel (1673). However, he failed to capture Martinique in 1674 and was killed in action in 1676.

Saladin (1138–1193) – see pp. 68–71

Samori Touré (1830–1900)
Warrior chief who founded the Islamic Wassoulou empire in West Africa. Samori established an efficient and well-organized fighting force of

infantry and cavalry formations. The French clashed with this expansionist warlord and slaver, but he made use of European firearms and attacked vulnerable lines of communication to force their withdrawal in 1882 and 1885. By 1887, he commanded *c.* 40,000 men, but the French exploited unrest in his empire, and, despite a few minor victories over isolated columns, he was unable to halt the conquest of his realm. He turned to a scorched-earth policy and fought on into 1898, but he was eventually captured and died in captivity.

San Martín, José de (1778–1850)
Argentine general who fought for South American independence from Spain. San Martín learnt the craft of war during the Peninsular War (1808–14) alongside the Spanish army. He returned to Argentina in 1812 to join the United Provinces of the South. He trained his own brigade in the techniques of European warfare, and won a skirmish at San Lorenzo in 1813. He went on to create a second brigade, the Army of Cuyo, in 1814 with which he made a gruelling crossing of the Andes. At Chacabuco (1817) he won a significant victory, but he was checked at Cancha Rayada (1818). In Peru, he gradually isolated the royalists until, in 1821, he marched into Lima, thereby completing the liberation of southern South America. The following year, he appeared to make a private treaty with Simón Bolívar (q.v.), and entered retirement.

Sargon II (r. 722–705 BC)
King of the Assyrians, under whom the empire reached its greatest extent. Between 720 and 717 BC he defeated the Egyptians, took possession of Syria and Gaza and conquered the upper Euphrates. Moving into the eastern Caucasus, he transported his entire army over the mountains. He crushed the Uratians and laid waste to much of their land. In 711 BC he took Ashdod after a Philistine rebellion, and he waged war against the nomadic Cimmerians and the neighbouring state of Elam, scoring a number of victories. Sargon also crushed the kingdom of Israel, exiling many of its inhabitants and thus giving rise to the legends of the 'lost tribes'.

Saxe, Maurice de (1696–1750)
French marshal, and author of the military memoir *Mes Rêveries*. As a boy, Maurice had accompanied Eugene of Savoy on campaign, and whilst only 14 he had taken part in an engagement with such ferocity that he was admonished for rashness. Under Peter the Great (q.v.), Saxe fought the Swedes, and in 1712 he accompanied his father the King of Poland in the siege of Stralsund. By 17, he was in command of his own regiment. His coup de main to seize Prague at night in 1741 during the War of the Austrian Succession (1740–48) was stunning, and he went on to take the fortress of Eger. Promoted to marshal, he laid siege to Tournai and defeated a British force at Fontenoy (1745). He won further victories at Rocoux (1746) and Lawfeldt (1747), capturing Maastricht in 1748.

Schwarzkopf, H. Norman (b. 1934)
American general nicknamed 'Stormin' Norman' for his quick temper. Schwarzkopf led the coalition forces against Iraq during operations Desert Shield and Desert Storm in 1991. He had been a relatively junior officer in the Vietnam War (1965–75), advising a Vietnamese airborne division. He was decorated for bravery for his part in the rescue of troops caught in a minefield, but he also earned a reputation for toughness combined with a strong sense of welfare for his men. He brought these values to bear in the 1991 Gulf War, but also demonstrated his charismatic appeal with his regular media briefings. As a strategist, his deception plan and deployment of overwhelming force brought the conflict to a swift conclusion.

Scipio Africanus (236–*c.* 183 BC) – see p. 35

Scott, Winfield (1786–1866)
Long-serving US army general. Although remembered chiefly for his service in the Mexican-American War (1846–48) and the American Civil War (1861–65), Scott had also served in the War of 1812 and in campaigns against the Native Americans. Nicknamed 'Old Fuss and Feathers', he was an authority on tactics and had personal experience of command in action to back his theories. In the Mexican-American War, he advocated and executed an amphibious operation to outflank the enemy, winning a series of battles in 1847. He became Union commander-in-chief at the beginning of the American Civil War, advocating a long-term strategy of blockade (the Anaconda Plan), and occupation of the Mississippi, ports and the seizure of Atlanta, which played a key role in delivering a Union victory.

Selim I (1465–1520) – see pp. 104–07

Sennacherib (r. 705–681 BC)
King of the Assyrians, and son of Sargon II (q.v.). Sennacherib inherited a large empire from his father and immediately faced a serious rebellion by the Chaldaeans, Aramaeans and Elamites. He crushed the revolt, captured Babylon and swept the southern marshes. However, he was forced to repeat the operation in 700 and 694 BC. In the latter campaign, he led a riverine force against the Elamites and Chaldaeans on the coast of the Persian Gulf. However, whilst fighting in the south, he was outflanked to the north. He was forced to fight his way up the Tigris until he defeated the Babylonian rebels decisively at Nippur (693 BC). In 701 BC, Sennacherib had also fought a rebellion in Judah, where he failed to take Jerusalem but defeated the rebels' Egyptian allies, thus claiming victory.

Shaka Zulu (1787–1828) – see pp. 208–09

Shamyl, Imam (1796–1871)
Leader of the Daghestani fighters resisting Russian imperial expansion in the Caucasus. Born to Avar tribesmen, Shamyl imbibed a traditional Islamic education and emerged as a committed guerrilla leader. In 1834 he was recognized as an inspiring imam, and set up an Islamist political system across the region. He led raids by his murids (fighters) against Russian columns and checked their southern advance on several occasions. Nevertheless, after the Crimean War (1853–56)

Alexander II's armies tightened the net around him. His domain gradually contracted and Chechnya was pacified, compelling him to sue for peace. He was treated magnanimously in defeat.

Sherman, William T. (1820–91) – see p. 224

Shi Huangdi (259–210 BC) – see pp. 26–31

Skobelev, Mikhail (1843–82)
Brilliant, impetuous and flamboyant Russian general, known as the 'Garibaldi of the Slavs'. In 1874, Skobelev distinguished himself as a commander in the war against the Khanate of Khiva, and the following year he fought against the Khanate of Kokand. At Makram, he defeated a far larger enemy force, and then scattered a pursuing mounted force at Andijan (Uzbekistan) with a handful of horsemen. In the Russo-Turkish War (1877–78), he animated those around him during the desperate fighting at Plevna. In the final stage of that campaign, he led a brilliant ride to defeat the Turks at the Shipka Pass (1878) capturing 36,000 men. He ended his career with a decisive, bloody campaign against the Turkmen in 1882.

Slim, William, 1st Viscount (1891–1970) (▲)
British field marshal who reversed the fortunes of Fourteenth Army in Southeast Asia during World War II. Slim took great care of the welfare provision for his men and placed considerable emphasis on maintaining the morale of his troops. He was wounded twice in World War I and was awarded the Military Cross for his outstanding performance in Mesopotamia. In World War II, he initially served in East Africa. Against the Japanese, Slim focused on enabling his forces to operate independently of their lines of communication in boxes, thus neutralizing enemy infiltration and envelopment tactics. He encouraged offensive patrolling and all-arms cooperation. Having blunted every Japanese thrust towards India in 1944, he counterattacked into Burma. By 1945, he had retaken Meiktila, Mandalay and Rangoon.

Smuts, Jan C. (1870–1950)
Boer commando leader, and later British field marshal. During the Second Boer War (1899–1902) Smuts led a daring campaign deep into Cape Colony. Reconciled to Britain, he was given command of South African forces in World War I, taking German South-West Africa and containing the German operations in East Africa. He went on to serve in

the British War Cabinet, and did so again during World War II (practically as Churchill's deputy). An intellectual, politician and philosopher, he was one of the 20th century's outstanding soldier-statesmen.

Sobieski, Jan (1629–96) – see pp. 148–51

Soult, Nicolas (1769–1851)
Marshal of France under Napoleon (q.v.) and the restored monarchy. Originally a private soldier, Soult distinguished himself in his early career with episodes of exemplary personal courage. In 1805 he was appointed by Napoleon to command a corps, and he played a key role in the victory at Austerlitz. He was subsequently deployed to Spain, where he defeated the Spanish at Burgos (Gamonal, 1808) and took Oporto from Portugal (1809). Although driven from Oporto by Wellesley (the future Wellington, q.v.), he won a significant victory at Ocaña (1809), took Andalusia and the strategic city of Badajoz. He briefly served in the 1813 campaign in central Europe, and did his best to stem the invasion of southern France by Wellington, but he was ill suited to the role of chief of staff in 1815, and his late political career was a failure.

Spaatz, Carl A. (1891–1974) (▲)
Director of the US strategic bombing campaigns against Germany and Japan in World War II. Briefly a pilot in World War I, in 1942 Spaatz was given command of the Eighth Air Force in Europe, and gained experience in North Africa and Italy between 1942 and 1943. In 1944, he commanded the US Strategic Air Forces in Europe and ordered daylight missions against Germany's oil and industrial installations. Although criticized for the heavy losses this generated, Spaatz enjoyed the confidence of Eisenhower (q.v.), and the relentless bombing undoubtedly shortened the war in Europe.

Spartacus (*c.* 120–70 BC)
Slave rebel who defied Rome. In 73 BC, Spartacus (who had probably received some military training and was a gladiator) and 70 others escaped captivity and took refuge near Vesuvius. Having defeated a militia sent against him, his defiance acted as a magnet for many other escaped slaves and rebels. For three years, Spartacus defeated the forces sent against him, including Rome's legionaries. It appears he marched the length of the Italian peninsula, his forces swelling, before eventually returning to southern Italy. He was intercepted

by Pompey (q.v.) at Silarus, and his army was routed. His body was never found.

Spruance, Raymond (1886–1969) – see p. 276

Stilicho (AD 359–408)
Roman soldier who took control of the eastern half of the empire. In the 380s AD, Flavius Stilicho was made a general and tasked with securing the borders against the incursions of the Visigoths, a mission he fulfilled for 20 years. He took part in the battle of Frigidus (AD 394) for Emperor Theodosius, and was later rewarded with command of the armies in the west. However, he was superb in his defence of Italy during the joint invasion by the Visigoths under Alaric (q.v.) and Radagaisus's Ostrogoths. Relieving Milan, he defeated Alaric at Pollentia (AD 402) and Verona (AD 403). Radagaisus led a vast German force against Florence but Stilicho defeated him at Fiesole. Stilicho was later arrested and executed by plotters in AD 408.

Sudirman (1916–50)
Military commander during Indonesia's struggle for independence. Sudirman came to prominence in 1945 when he was elected by fellow Javanese officers to lead the pro-independence forces. Known as the bapak-tentara (father of the army), he was respected for his traditional Muslim values, his absence of any taint of collaboration with the Dutch colonial authorities and his use of Japanese-trained militias. He argued that the army was the embodiment of the state, and had to be kept above political divisions. In 1948, the Dutch attack on Yogyakarta practically extinguished the political will to continue resistance, but Sudirman, although sick, raised a guerrilla force in the hills. His relentless campaign persuaded the Dutch to negotiate. He opposed any compromise, but agreed to terminate the campaign for the sake of national unity.

Suffren, Pierre André de (1729–88)
Energetic and combative French admiral. Gaining experience against pirates and against the British during the Seven Years' War (1756–63), his greatest achievement came late in his career. He attacked a British squadron off the Cape coast in 1781 and then sailed into the Bay of Bengal to fight a series of engagements in 1782. He managed to drive the British off the coast of Trincomalee (Sri Lanka), forcing its garrison to surrender. Short-tempered but determined, he kept French resistance alive in the theatre until recalled in 1783.

Süleyman the Magnificent
(1494–1566) – see pp. 108–11

Sulla (138–78 BC)
Dictator of Rome. Early in his career, Lucius Cornelius Sulla captured the Numidian king by persuading his rival to betray him, and he went on to defeat the Germanic tribes that invaded Italy at Vercellae in 101 BC. In 92 BC he repulsed the Armenians and then achieved fame by crushing the Italian Socii in the Social War (91–88 BC). Soon after, during unrest in Rome, he marched on the capital and imposed a new political order. He defeated Athens in the First Mithridatic War (91–85 BC) after

a prolonged siege, and then went on to smash the more numerous Pontic armies at Chaeronea and Orchomenos (86 BC). Nevertheless, continual intrigue led him to march on Rome again and he installed himself as dictator.

Sun Tzu (*c.* 400–320 BC)
Author of the world's oldest work of military theory. Sun Tzu is thought to have been a general at the time of the Warring States in the 4th century BC. His remarks appear to have been based on practical experience, although some seem to be more philosophical. He espoused the use of direct and indirect warfare, the latter including information war, deception, psychological operations and irregular campaigning. He drew attention to certain principles, doctrine and purposes in war. His suggestion that armies should move 'like water', and his emphasis on unconventional techniques, had a profound influence on Mao and Vo Nguyen Giap (q.v.).

Suvorov, Alexander (1729–1800)
Russian general who never lost a battle. Suvorov's early career was spent in service against the Poles and Swedes, and he won a significant victory against the Ottomans at Kozludji in the Russo-Turkish War of 1768–74. He won several actions in the Russo-Turkish War of 1787–92 including Ochakov, Focsani and Rimnik. In 1790 he took the fortress of Ismail in Bessarabia and then served in Poland, where he stormed Warsaw in 1794. In the war against Revolutionary France, he conducted a brilliant, if gruelling, strategic withdrawal across the Alps in winter (1799). A generalissimo of Russia, he never lost the common touch and he inculcated the values of dash, self-sacrifice and stoicism that became hallmarks of the Russian army. His pragmatic leadership inspired not only the soldiers of his era, but also those of subsequent generations.

Taksin the Great (1734–82)
King of Siam from 1768 to 1782. When the Burmese besieged Ayutthaya in 1767, Taksin, a provisional governor of Tak and Kamphaeng Phet, assisted in the organization of its defence. He was one of several commanders who eventually drove the Burmese from the country, before defeating his rivals and reuniting the country as king. In 1770 he launched a war against the Nguyen of Cambodia, and his joint Siamese–Cambodian forces achieved victory in 1772. Despite his military successes, he was declared insane and was killed in a coup d'état in 1782.

Taylor, Zachery (1784–1850)
Twelfth president of the United States of America. Nicknamed 'Old Rough and Ready' because of his unkempt appearance, Taylor was a long serving officer in the American army before becoming president. In the War of 1812, he successfully defended Fort Harrison against a Native-American attack, and he went on to fight in the Black Hawk War (1832) and the Second Seminole War (1835–42). Taylor was deployed to the Rio Grande in 1846 and was attacked by Mexican forces, prompting the outbreak of the Mexican-American War (1846–48). Taylor's victories at Monterrey and Buena Vista made him a household name across the United States.

Templer, Sir Gerald (1898–1979)
British commander who defeated the guerrilla rebels during the Malayan Emergency (1948–60). Templer gained combat experience in France and Italy in World War II. He understood that counter-insurgency required more than military operations; as a result, in Malaya he integrated intelligence, military action and civil policing, made use of civilian resettlement to isolate communist guerrillas, and sent deep jungle patrols to neutralize the insurgents' bases. Air power kept the latter supplied and enabled small patrols to be redeployed rapidly. Templer's counter-insurgency techniques, particularly during the most intense phase of the Emergency (1952–54), were profoundly influential.

Theodoric the Great (AD 454–526)
King of the Ostrogoths, and ruler of the Visigoths and of Italy. Theodoric absorbed ideas about the Roman army from his time in Constantinople as a young man, and, on his return to his native Ostrogothic kingdom, he agreed to act as an agent of the Emperor Zeno. It was decided that he should invade Italy to reduce the power of King Odoacer, the ruler who had overthrown the Western empire in AD 476. Theodoric won the battles of Isonzo (AD 489) and Verona (AD 490) and he captured Ravenna in AD 493. At the peace conference banquet between the two monarchs, Theodoric killed Odoacer. Between AD 506 and 523 he fought the Franks as regent for the Visogothic king and defended his own realm, leading to a much mythologized reputation in German culture.

Thutmose III (r. 1479–1425 BC)
Pharaoh who built up an extensive empire through almost constant campaigning. Thutmose won the battle of Megiddo (1457 BC, the earliest battle for which we have a detailed description of the military strategy employed) against the kingdom of Kadesh by striking through a mountain pass to appear behind his enemies, and he waged war against the peoples of southern Syria with great ruthlessness. His chroniclers claimed he crossed the Euphrates and defeated the state of Mitanni by a clever deception. Whilst campaigning against rebels in Syria, he struck rapidly north and east and ferried his men across the river using reed boats carried by his troops. Mitanni, unprepared for any attack, quickly succumbed to the Egyptian onslaught. However, Thutmose spent years suppressing rebellions throughout his empire.

Tiglath-Pileser III (r. 745–727 BC)
King of Assyria. Seizing the throne in the midst of a civil war, Tiglath-Pileser became one of the most successful military leaders of the Assyrian empire. He annexed Babylonia in 745 BC and defeated Urartu (Armenia–northern Iraq) soon after. He then subjugated the neighbouring states, including Judah and Philistia. His military reforms essentially allowed for foreigners to be incorporated into his infantry, whilst native Assyrians were retained in the cavalry and the chariots. This gave Tiglath-Pileser far larger forces than his enemies, and enabled him to dominate greater areas than his predecessors.

Tilly, Count von (1559–1632) – see p. 136

Timur (1336–1405) – see pp. 80–83

Tippu Sultan (1750–99)
Ruler of Mysore from 1782. Known as the 'Tiger of Mysore', Tippu fought the British and their Indian allies on three occasions. He was adept at manipulating religious emotions and the arts of diplomacy, but he was also an able and courageous soldier, defeating small British–Indian forces at Pollilur (1780) and Annagudi (1782). However, when outnumbered, as in the Fourth Anglo-Mysore War (1798–99), he was unable to prevent an assault on his own capital, Seringapatam. Tippu had developed an older idea of rocket batteries in his forces, and these made such an impression on his British adversaries that they were briefly incorporated into their armed forces. Tippu was killed in action defending a breach in the walls of Seringapatam.

Tito, Josip Broz (1892–1980)
Partisan leader and president of Yugoslavia. In World War I, Tito had been conscripted to fight Russia. He was wounded and captured, and imprisoned until liberated by Russian revolutionaries. He joined the Red Guards in the Russian Civil War (1917–22). An active communist in the inter-war years in Yugoslavia, the German occupation of 1941 prompted him to create guerrilla bands. A skilled leader, Tito fought not only the Germans but also the non-communist guerrilla movement, and his defeat of the latter enabled him to become the post-war dictator. In the post-war period, he took tough action against those that had collaborated with the Germans.

Titus (AD 39–81)
Roman emperor and conqueror of the Jews. At the outbreak of the Jewish-Roman War in AD 66, Titus, an experienced officer, joined the 60,000-strong force in Judaea. He distinguished himself during the campaign, and was left in command when his father Vespasian (q.v.), the new emperor, departed for Rome in AD 69. Titus laid siege to Jerusalem, skilfully permitting pilgrims to enter but not leave, thus denying the defenders sufficient rations to hold out. The outer walls were then breached, and enemy deserters were crucified to terrorize his opponents. The final assault carried the city, which was then sacked. Titus eventually succeeded his father as emperor.

Togo Heihachiro (1848–1934) – see pp. 234–37

Tokugawa Ieyasu (1543–1616) – see p. 128

Toyotomi Hideyoshi (1537–1598) – see pp. 124–31

Trajan (AD 53–117) – see pp. 48–51

Tromp, Maarten (1598–1653)
Dutch admiral. As a youth, Tromp was twice captured by pirates and enslaved, but his skill in seamanship and gunnery won him his freedom; later, he would use these talents against privateers. In 1637 he became, in effect, the commander of

the Dutch fleet and two years later defeated a large Spanish force at the Battle of the Downs (1639), which denied them naval supremacy. In the First Anglo-Dutch War (1652–54), Tromp led the Dutch at the battles of Dungeness, Portland, the Gabbard, and Scheveningen, where he was killed by a sharpshooter.

Trotsky, Leon (1879–1940) (▲)
Communist revolutionary who had been a war correspondent and had no previous military experience. As Soviet People's Commissar for War, Trotsky invigorated the nascent Red Army with his own brand of revolutionary zeal soon after the Bolshevik coup d'état in October 1917. Abandoning the revolutionary attacks on hierarchy and its democratized selection of officers, Trotsky employed former Tsarist 'specialist' leaders (voyenspets) who had experience and reintroduced elite regiments. He intervened personally to restore the fragmenting eastern front during the Russian Civil War (1917–22), but, for all his great oratory, he was pragmatic in his strategy and rejected the zealots' calls for a hopelessly utopian 'proletarian' style of warfare.

Turenne (1611–75) – see pp. 138–41

Vasilevsky, Alexander (1895–1977)
Coordinator of the Soviet armed forces in the 1943–45 counteroffensives. Vasilevsky had served as a junior officer in World War I, and fought in the Russian Civil War (1917–22) and the Polish–Soviet War (1919–21). Enjoying good relations with Stalin, he was promoted in the inter-war years, and, despite the setbacks of 1941, he inspired a positive attitude amongst the senior officers and was the lynchpin in the defence of Moscow and Stalingrad. He assumed command of the Soviet counteroffensive after the German defeat on the Volga in 1943. Although sometimes hamstrung by Stalin's interference, he conducted operations on the Don, and in the Donets Basin, the Crimea, Ukraine, Byelorussia and the Baltic States, taking Königsberg (Kaliningrad) in April 1945. In August 1945, he executed the attack on Japanese forces in east Asia (the battle of Manchuria), defeating his enemy in just 24 days.

Vatutin, Nikolai (1901–1944)
Soviet general who liberated Kiev. Vatutin fought in the Russian Civil War (1917–22) against Nestor Makhno's Ukrainians. In 1939 he took part in

operations against Poland, and seized Bessarabia from Romania. Although he forced Manstein (q.v.) to halt his advance on Leningrad, his inexperience led to huge Soviet losses and he was forced to withdraw. In 1942, his preference for encirclement and tactical innovations almost worked at Demyansk, and he conducted a desperate defence at Voronezh. In 1943 he assisted in the defeat of the Germans at Stalingrad, but was checked again at Kharkov. At Kiev and Korosten, he used decoy forces to deceive Manstein and drove the Germans backwards. Vatutin was ambushed and killed by Ukrainian partisans in 1944.

Vauban, Sébastien le Prestre de (1633–1707) – see p. 141

Vercingetorix (d. 46 BC) – see p. 38

Vespasian (AD 9–79)
Roman emperor from AD 69, and founder of the Flavian dynasty. Vespasian's military career began as a tribune in Thrace in AD 36. He was appointed to command the II Legion 'Augusta' by Claudius in AD 41, and led it in the Roman invasion of Britain (AD 43), subduing the hill forts in the southwest. He was subsequently awarded a triumph in Rome. Having served as consul, he became governor of the province of Africa, before leading two legions to Judaea to suppress the Jewish revolt (AD 66). In the wake of the Roman civil wars of AD 68, Vespasian was proclaimed emperor by his troops, and despite numerous plots against him, his reign was predominantly peaceful. In AD 78, he entrusted Agricola with consolidating Roman rule in Britain; his campaign pushed the empire's northern frontier into Caledonia (Scotland).

Vo Nguyen Giap (b. 1911) – see pp. 280–81

Wallenstein, Albrecht von (1583–1634) – see p. 137

Washington, George (1732–99) – see pp. 174–79

Wellington, Duke of (1769–1852) – see pp. 198–203

William III (1650–1702)
Victor of the Battle of the Boyne (1690). William (Prince of Orange) was a stadtholder of the provinces of the Netherlands who became king of England in a largely bloodless coup d'état in 1688 (the Glorious Revolution). In 1672 the Dutch were occupied by the French; William restored their confidence, arguing they should defend their country 'to the last ditch'. Following the success of Ruyter (q.v.) at sea against England, William managed to parry the French long enough for them to make peace (1678). Invited to take power in England as champion of Protestantism and constitutional monarchy, William became king, although in Scotland and Ireland he encountered resistance. The Scots were subdued, and William himself defeated the Jacobite cause at the Battle of the Boyne in Ireland. In the Netherlands, his forces and their allies fared less well against France until the peace of 1697.

William of Orange (1533–84) – see p. 113

William the Conqueror
(c. 1027–1087) – see pp. 64–67

Wingate, Orde (1903–44)
Controversial commander who specialized in irregular warfare. In the inter-war years, Wingate served in the British administration in Palestine as an intelligence officer, during which time he organized Jewish counter-insurgency squads. At the outbreak of World War II, he established Gideon Force in Ethiopia to harass the Italians. He was identified by Archibald Wavell as an officer with a talent for operations behind enemy lines, and, as a result, in February 1943 Wingate led his Chindit force on Operation Longcloth, a penetration deep inside Japanese-occupied Burma. The Chindits harassed the Japanese lines of communications and enjoyed some success, although the gruelling conditions depleted their effectiveness. Wingate was killed in an air crash on the second Chindit deployment in 1944.

Wolfe, James (1727–59) (▲)
British general who took Canada from the French. Wolfe's career was short but brilliant. He began active service at the battle of Dettingen (1743) and he gained further experience during the Jacobite Rising of 1745–46 and in Germany during the War of the Austrian Succession (1740–48). On the outbreak of the Seven Years' War (1756–63), Wolfe distinguished himself in the attack on Rochefort and the siege of Louisbourg, and he was given responsibility for the assault on Quebec in 1759. His daring attack involved his force scaling cliffs on the St Lawrence River, which brought them onto the Plains of Abraham. The French garrison sallied out but Wolfe's troops won the action, and with it control of Quebec and Canada. However, as the French began to give way, Wolfe was mortally wounded.

Wolseley, Garnet (1833–1913) – see pp. 232–33

Wrangel, Pyotr (1878–1928)
The most successful White general of the Russian Civil War (1917–22). As an officer in the Tsarist army, Wrangel took part in the Russo-Japanese War (1904–05), operations in the Baltic provinces during the unrest of the 1905 Russian Revolution, and led a cavalry unit in World War I. On the outbreak of the 1917 Revolution, Wrangel commanded a cavalry formation and eventually the entire southern Volunteer Army of White forces, capturing Tsaritsyn

(subsequently renamed Stalingrad and Volgograd) from the Bolsheviks in 1919. He was a successful administrator in the territories he controlled and enjoyed a strong following in the Crimea. When his White army was overwhelmed he offered his men a choice: to evacuate, or to endure Bolshevik rule. Many joined him in exile in 1920 and he became a prominent anti-Bolshevik figurehead until his premature death.

Yamashita Tomoyuki (1885–1946)
Japanese general, known as the 'Tiger of Malaya', who captured Singapore. In contrast to many other senior officers before World War II, Yamashita was opposed to a conflict with the Western allies; consequently, he was given command of a counter-insurgency campaign in northern China between 1937 and 1938 – an appointment without prestige. However, in December 1941 he led 30,000 combat troops against British Malaya and the much-vaunted island stronghold of Singapore. The Japanese landings, infiltration and thrusts in depth caused confusion and demoralization, and, once isolated, the Singapore garrison could offer no effective resistance. Yamashita assumed command of the Philippines too late to organize an effective defence against the American landings in 1945, and was forced to surrender eight months later. He was executed by the Allies, who considered him responsible for the excesses of his men.

Yi Sun-Shin (1545–98) – see p. 127

Zhu De (1886–1976)
Co-founder of the Chinese Red Army. Zhu was a serving army officer when he took part in the 1911 Revolution, but he became a warlord and opium addict. However, in 1920 his exposure to the ideas of communism transformed him. He joined the Kuomintang party in 1926, but when the United Front split, he had no hesitation in forming a communist militia. Although he was frequently forced to withdraw, he persevered, enabling the resistance to continue. In 1931, he organized the Fourth Counter-Encirclement campaign, and, whilst he suffered heavy casualties in the Long March, he rebuilt his army in Yan'an. He offered resistance to the Japanese during World War II and then assisted in the final takeover of the country in 1949. Although he organized the 'volunteers' of the People's Liberation Army in the Korean War (1950–53), he fell victim to the purges of the Cultural Revolution in 1966. He was reinstated in 1971, largely on the basis of his successful military career.

Zhukov, Georgy (1896–1974) – see pp. 268–73

Žižka, Jan (c. 1360–1424) – see pp. 90–91

The Ancient World

Cyrus the Great

Mallowan, M., 'Cyrus the Great (558–529 BC)', in I. Gershevitch (ed.), *The Cambridge History of Iran*, vol. 2: *The Median and Achaemenian Periods* (Cambridge, 1985)
Olmstead, A. T., *History of the Persian Empire* (Chicago and London, 1948)
Potts, D. T., 'Cyrus the Great and the Kingdom of Anshan', in V. S. Curtis and S. Stewart (eds.), *Birth of the Persian Empire*, vol. 1: *The Idea of Iran* (London, 2005)

Alexander the Great

Arrian, *The Campaigns of Alexander*, trans. J. R. Hamilton (Harmondsworth, 1971)
Bosworth, A. B., *Conquest and Empire: the Reign of Alexander the Great* (Cambridge, 1988)
Engels, D. W., *Alexander the Great and the Logistics of the Macedonian Army* (Berkeley and London, 1978)
Hammond, N. G. L., *Alexander the Great: King, Commander and Statesman* (Park Ridge and London, 1981)
Lane Fox, R., *Alexander the Great* (Harmondsworth, 1973)
Wiesehöfer, J., *Ancient Persia* (London and New York, 2001)

Philip of Macedon

Cawkwell, G. L., *Philip of Macedon* (London, 1978)

Chandragupta

Boesche, R., 'Kautilya's Arthasastra on War and Diplomacy in Ancient India', *The Journal of Military History*, 67:1 (2007), pp. 9–37
Coningham, R. A. E. and M. J. Manuel, 'South Asian Warfare from the Indus Civilisation to AD 530' in P. De Souza (ed.) *The Ancient World at War*, pp. 229–42 (London and New York, 2007)
Kulke, H. and D. Rothermund, *A History of India* (London and New York, 1990)
Mookerji, R. K., *Chandragupta Maurya and his Times* (New Delhi, 1986)
Rangarajan, L. N. (trans.), *Kautilya's Arthasastra* (New Delhi, 1992)

Shi Huangdi

Cotterell, A., *The First Emperor of China* (London and New York, 1981)
Guisso, R. W. L., D. Miller and C. Pagani, *The First Emperor of China* (Toronto, 1989)
Hsu, C., *Ancient China in Transition* (Stanford, 1965)
Sima Qian, *Records of the Grand Historian: Qin Dynasty*, trans. B. Watson (Hong Kong and New York, 1993)
—— *Historical Records*, trans. R. Dawson (Oxford, 1994)

Hannibal

Daly, G., *Cannae: the Experience of Battle in the Second Punic War* (London and New York, 2002)
Goldsworthy, A., *The Punic Wars* (London, 2000)
Goldsworthy, A., *The Complete Roman Army* (London and New York, 2003)
Livy, *The War with Hannibal*, trans. A. Selincourt (Harmondsworth, 1965)
Polybius, *The Rise of the Roman Empire*, trans. I. Scott-Kilvert (Harmondsworth, 1989)

Scipio Africanus

Scullard, H. H., *Scipio Africanus: Soldier and Politician* (London and New York, 1970)

Julius Caesar

Caesar, *The Civil War*, trans. J. Gardner (Harmondsworth, 1976)
—— *The Conquest of Gaul*, trans. S. A. Handford and J. Gardner (Harmondsworth, 1982)
Goldsworthy, A., *The Complete Roman Army* (London and New York, 2003)
—— *Caesar: the Life of a Colossus* (London, 2007)
Keppie, L., *The Making of the Roman Army: from Republic to Empire* (London and New York, 1998)

Vercingetorix

Martin, P. M., *Vercingétorix : le Politique, le Stratège* (Paris, 2000)

Augustus

Augustus, *Res Gestae Divi Augusti: the Achievements of the Divine Augustus*, ed. and trans. P. A. Brunt and J. M. Moore (Oxford, 1967)
Cassius Dio, *The Roman History: the Reign of Augustus*, trans. I. Scott-Kilvert (Harmondsworth, 1987)
Goldsworthy, A., *The Complete Roman Army* (London and New York, 2003)
Keppie, L., *The Making of the Roman Army: from Republic to Empire* (London and New York, 1998)
Shotter, D., *Augustus Caesar* (London and New York, 2005)

Arminius

Wells, P. S., *The Battle that Stopped Rome: Emperor Augustus, Arminius and the Slaughter of the Legions in the Teutoburg Forest* (New York, 2003)

Marcus Agrippa

Reinhold, M., *Marcus Agrippa: a Biography* (Michigan, 1933)

Trajan

Bennett, J., *Trajan: Optimus Princeps* (London and New York, 2000)
Goldsworthy, A., *The Complete Roman Army* (London and New York, 2003)
Rossi, L., *Trajan's Column and the Dacian Wars* (London and New York, 1971)

Hadrian

Birley, A., *Hadrian: the Restless Emperor* (London and New York, 2004)

Belisarius

Cameron, A., B. Ward-Perkins and M. Whitby (eds.), *The Cambridge Ancient History*, vol. XIV: *Late Antiquity, Empire and Successors, AD 425–600* (Cambridge, 2000)
Evans, J. A. S., *The Age of Justinian: the Circumstances of Imperial Power* (London, 1996)
Martindale, J. R. (ed.), *The Prosopography of the Later Roman Empire*, vol. IIIa: AD 527–641 (Cambridge, 1992)

The Medieval World

Charlemagne

Becher, M., *Charlemagne*, trans. D. S. Bachrach (New Haven, 2003)
Collins, R., *Charlemagne* (Basingstoke, 1998)
King, P. D., *Charlemagne: Translated Sources* (Lancaster, 1987)
Notker the Stammerer, *Charlemagne*, trans. L. Thorpe (Harmondsworth, 1969)

Charles Martel

Fouracre, P., *The Age of Charles Martel* (Harlow, 2000)

Otto the Great

Bachrach, B. S. and D. Bachrach, 'Saxon military revolution, 912–973? Myth and reality', *Early Medieval Europe*, 15:2 (2007), pp. 186–222
Bowlus, C. R., *The Battle of Lechfeld and its Aftermath, August 955: the End of the Age of Migrations in the Latin West* (Aldershot, 2006)
Leyser, K., *Medieval Germany and its Neighbours 900–1250* (London, 1982)

William the Conqueror

Bates, D., *William the Conqueror* (Stroud, 2001)
Douglas, D. C., *William the Conqueror* (London, 1964)
Gillingham, J., 'William the Bastard at War', in *Studies in Medieval History Presented to R. Allen Brown*, ed. C. Harper-Bill, C. Holdsworth and J. Nelson (Woodbridge, 1989)
Lawson, M. K., *The Battle of Hastings 1066* (Stroud, 2002)
Morillo, S. (ed.), *The Battle of Hastings* (Woodbridge, 1996)

Saladin

Baha' al-Din Ibn Shaddad, *The Rare and Excellent History of Saladin*, trans. D. S. Richards (Crusade Texts in Translation series, London, 2001)
Ehrenkreutz, A. S., *Saladin* (New York, 1972)
Gibb, H., Sir, *The Life of Saladin: from the Works of Baha ad-Din and Imad ad-Din* (London, 2006)
Gibb, H. and Y. Ibish (ed.), *Saladin: Studies in Islamic History* (Beirut, 1974)
Lyons, M. C. and D. E. P. Jackson, *Saladin: The Politics of Holy War* (Cambridge, 1982)
Regan, G., *Saladin and the Fall of Jerusalem* (London, 1988)

Richard the Lionheart

Gillingham, J., *Richard the Lionheart* (London, 1978)
—— *Richard Coeur de Lion: Kingship, Chivalry and War in the Twelfth Century* (London, 1994)
Turner, R. V. and R. R. Heiser, *The Reign of Richard Lionheart: Ruler of the Angevin Empire, 1189–1199* (The Medieval World series, London, 2000)

Frederick Barbarossa

Gravett, C., *German Medieval Armies 1000–1300* (London, 1997)
Haverkamp, A. and H. Vollrath (eds.), *England and Germany in the High Middle Ages* (Oxford and London, 1996)
Munz, P., *Frederick Barbarossa: a Study in Medieval Politics* (Ithaca, 1969)
Otto of Freising, *The Deeds of Frederick Barbarossa*, trans. C. C. Mierow (New York, 2004)

Chingiz Khan

May, T., 'Jamuqa and the Education of Chinggis Khan', *Acta Mongolica* 6 (2006), pp. 273–86
—— 'The Training of an Inner Asian Nomad Army in the Pre-Modern Period', *The Journal of Military History*, 70:3 (2006), pp. 617–35
—— *The Mongol Art of War* (London, 2007)
Morgan, D., *The Mongols* (2nd ed., Cambridge, MA, 2007)
Rachewiltz, Igor de (ed. and trans.), *The Secret History of the Mongols* (Leiden, 2004)
Ratchnevsky, P., *Genghis Khan: his Life and Legacy* (Cambridge, MA, 1992)

Kublai Khan

Allsen, T., *Culture and Conquest in Mongol Eurasia* (Cambridge and New York, 2001)
Rossabi, M., *Khubilai Khan – his Life and Times* (Los Angeles and Berkeley, 1988)
Polo, M. *The Travels*, ed. and trans. R. Latham (London and New York, 1958)

Timur

Arabshah, A., *Tamerlane or Timur the Great Amir* (Lahore, 1936)
Clavijo, G., *Embassy to Tamerlane* (London, 1928)
Grousset, R., *The Empire of the Steppes*, trans. Naomi Walford (New Brunswick, 1970)
Hookham, H., *Tamburlaine the Conqueror* (London, 1962)
Manz, B. F., *The Rise and Rule of Tamerlane* (Cambridge and New York, 1991)

Edward I

Morris, J. E., *The Welsh Wars of Edward I* (Oxford, 1901)
Prestwich, M., *Edward I* (New Haven and London, 1998)
Taylor, A. J., *The Welsh Castles of Edward I* (London, 1986)
Watson, F., *Under the Hammer: Edward I and Scotland 1286–1306* (East Linton, 1998)

Robert Bruce

Barrow, G. W. S., *Robert Bruce and the Community of the Realm of Scotland* (4th edition, Edinburgh, 2005)
Brown, M., *The Wars of Scotland 1214–1371* (Edinburgh, 2004)
Duncan, A. A. M. (ed.), *John Barbour, The Bruce* (Edinburgh, 1997)

Jan Žižka

Heymann, F. G., *John Zizka and the Hussite Revolution* (Princeton, 1955)
Kaminsky, H., *A History of the Hussite Revolution* (Berkeley, 1967)
Macek, J., *The Hussite Movement in Bohemia* (Prague, 1958)

János Hunyadi

Engel, P., *The Realm of St Stephen: a History of Hungary, 895–1526* (London and New York, 2001)
Held, J., *Hunyadi: Legend and Reality* (New York, 1985)
Muresanu, C., *John Hunyadi: Defender of Christendom* (Portland, 2001)

The Age of Empires and Revolutions

Hernando Cortés

Díaz del Castillo, B., *The Conquest of Mexico*, trans. J. M. Cohen (Harmondsworth, 1963)
Hassig, R., *Mexico and the Spanish Conquest* (Norman, 2006)
Pagden, A. (ed.), *Hernán Cortés: Letters from Mexico* (New Haven, 1986)
Restall, M., *Seven Myths of the Spanish Conquest* (New York and Oxford, 2003)
Thomas, H., *Conquest: Montezuma, Cortés, and the Fall of Old Mexico* (New York, 1995)

Francisco Pizarro

Cieza de León, P., *The Discovery and Conquest of Peru*, ed. and trans. A. P. Cook and N. D. Cook (Durham, NC, 1998)
Hemming, J., *The Conquest of the Incas* (New York, 2003)
Lockhart, J., *The Men of Cajamarca: a Social and Biographical Study of the First Conquerors of Peru* (Austin, 1972)
Restall, M., *Seven Myths of the Spanish Conquest* (New York and Oxford, 2003)

Zarate, A., *The Discovery and Conquest of Peru*, trans. J. M. Cohen (Harmondsworth 1968)

Sultan Selim I
Allouche, A., *The Origins and Development of the Ottoman–Safavid Conflict, 906–962/1500–1555* (Berlin, 1983)
Hess, A. C., 'The Ottoman Conquest of Egypt (1517) and the Beginning of the Sixteenth-Century World War', *International Journal of Middle East Studies*, 4:1 (1973), pp. 55–76
Kan, M., 'Selim I's Iranian and Egyptian Expeditions', *Revue Internationale d'Histoire Militaire*, 46 (1980), pp. 71–91
Petry, C. F., *Twilight of Majesty: the Reigns of the Mamluk Sultans al-Ashraf Qaytbay and Qansuh al-Ghawri in Egypt* (Seattle and London, 1993)

Süleyman the Magnificent
Atil, E., *Süleymanname: the Illustrated History of Süleyman the Magnificent* (New York, 1986)
Fodor, P., 'Ottoman Policy towards Hungary, 1520–1541', *Acta Orientalia Academiae Scientiarum Hungaricae*, 45: 2–3 (1991), pp. 271–345
Kunt, M. and C. Woodhead, *Süleyman the Magnificent and his Age: the Ottoman Empire in the Early Modern World* (White Plains, 1995)
Labib, S., 'The Era of Süleyman the Magnificent: Crisis of Orientation', *International Journal of Middle East Studies*, 10: 4 (1979), pp. 435–51
Szakály, F. 'The 1526 Mohács Disaster', *New Hungarian Quarterly*, 18: 65 (1977), pp. 43–63

Emperor Charles V
Alvarez, M. F., *Charles V* (London, 1975)
Brandi, K., *The Emperor Charles V* (New York, 1939)
Tracy, J., *Charles V: Impresario of War* (Cambridge, 2002)
Rodríguez Salgado, M. J., *The Changing Face of Empire* (Cambridge, 1988)

William of Orange
Swart, K. W., *William of Orange and the Revolt of the Netherlands* (Aldershot, 2003)
Wedgwood, V. *William the Silent* (New Haven, 1944)

Fernando Álvarez de Toledo, Duke of Alba
González de León, F., *The Road to Rocroi* (Leiden, 2008)
Maltby, W. S., *Alba* (Berkeley, 1983)

Babur
Babur, Z. M., *The Baburnama: Memoirs of Babu, Prince and Emperor*, trans., ed., and annot. Wheeler M. Thackston (New York, 1996)
Dale, S. F., *The Garden of the Eight Paradises: Babur and the Culture of Empire in Central Asia, Afghanistan and India* (Leiden, 2004)
Gommans, J., *Mughal Warfare: Indian Frontiers and High Roads to Empire, 1500–1700* (London, 2002)
Khan, I. A., *Gunpowder and Firearms: Warfare in Medieval India* (Delhi, 2004)
Richards, J. F., *The Mughal Empire* (New Cambridge History of India series, Cambridge, 1993)
Robinson, F., *The Mughal Emperors and the Islamic Dynasties of India, Iran and Central Asia 1206–1925* (London and New York, 2007)

Akbar
Fazl, A., *The Ain-i Akbari*, trans. H. Blochmann, ed. D. C. Phillot (2nd ed., Calcutta, 1939)
—— *The Akbar Nama*, trans. H. Beveridge (reprint, Delhi, 1993)

Gommans, J., *Mughal Warfare: Indian Frontiers and High Roads to Empire, 1500–1700* (London, 2002)
Khan, I. A., *Gunpowder and Firearms: Warfare in Medieval India* (Delhi, 2004)
Richards, J. F., *The Mughal Empire* (New Cambridge History of India series, Cambridge, 1993)
Robinson, F., *The Mughal Emperors and the Islamic Dynasties of India, Iran and Central Asia 1206–1925* (London and New York, 2007)

Toyotomi Hideyoshi
Berry, M. E., *Hideyoshi* (Cambridge, MA, 1982)
Hall, J. W., K. Nagahara and K. Yamamura (eds.), *Japan before Tokugawa: Political Consolidation and Economic Growth, 1500–1650* (Princeton, 1981)
Hall, J. W. (ed.), *The Cambridge History of Japan*, vol. 4: *Early Modern Japan* (Cambridge, 1991)

Oda Nobunaga
Lamers, J. P., *Japonius Tyrannus: the Japanese Warlord Oda Nobunaga Reconsidered* (Leiden, 2000)
Hall, J. W. (ed.), *The Cambridge History of Japan*, vol. 4: *Early Modern Japan* (Cambridge, 1991)

Yi Sun-Shin
Hall, J. W. (ed.), *The Cambridge History of Japan*, vol. 4: *Early Modern Japan* (Cambridge, 1991)

Tokugawa Ieyasu
Ikegami, E., *The Taming of the Samurai: Honorific Individualism and the Making of Modern Japan* (Cambridge, MA, 1995)
Hall, J. W. (ed.), *The Cambridge History of Japan*, vol. 4: *Early Modern Japan* (Cambridge, 1991)

Shah Abbas I
Eskandar Beg Monshi, *History of Shah Abbas the Great*, trans. R. Savory, 2 vols. (Boulder, 1978)
Newman, A., *Safavid Iran: Rebirth of a Persian Empire* (London, 2006)
Savory, R., 'Abbas I', *Encyclopaedia Iranica* (www.iranica.com, 2007)

Gustavus Adolphus
Asch, R. G., *The Thirty Years War: the Holy Roman Empire and Europe, 1618–48* (Basingstoke and London, 1997)
Frost, R. I., *The Northern Wars, 1558–1721: War, State and Society in Northeastern Europe, 1558–1721* (Harlow, 2000)
Glete, J., *War and the State in Early Modern Europe: Spain, the Dutch Republic and Sweden as Fiscal-Military States, 1500–1650* (London and New York, 2002)
Glete, J., 'Amphibious Warfare in the Baltic, 1550–1700', in M. C. Fissel and D. J. B. Trim (eds.), *Amphibious Warfare, 1000–1700: Commerce, State Formation and European Expansion* (Leiden, 2006), pp. 123–147
Parker, G., *The Thirty Years' War* (London and New York, 1984)
Redlich, F., *The German Military Enterpriser and his Workforce: a Study in European Economic and Social History*, vol. 1 (Wiesbaden, 1964)
Roberts, M., *Gustavus Adolphus: a History of Sweden 1611–1632*, 2 vols. (London and New York, 1953–58)

Johann Tserclaes, Count von Tilly
Sadler, R., *Reichsgraf Johann T. Serclaes von Tilly. Chronik über Leben und Laufbahn* (Altötting, 2007)

Albrecht Wenzel Eusebius von Wallenstein
Mann, G., *Wallenstein: His Life Narrated* (London, 1976)

Turenne
Bérenger, J., *Turenne* (Paris, 1987)
Cate, C., 'The Making of a Marshal', *MHQ: The Quarterly Journal of Military History*, 5:3 (1993), pp. 26–35
Lynn, J. A., *Giant of the Grande Siècle: the French Army 1610–1715* (Cambridge, 1997)

Condé
Godley, E., *The Great Condé* (London, 1915)

Vauban
Duffy, C., *Fire and Stone: the Science of Fortress Warfare 1660–1800* (London, 1996)

Oliver Cromwell
Coward, B., *Oliver Cromwell* (London, 1991)
Cromwell, O., *The Writings and Speeches of Oliver Cromwell*, ed. W. C. Abbott, 4 vols. (Oxford, 1988)
Gentles, I., *The New Model Army in England, Ireland and Scotland, 1645–1653* (Oxford, 1992)
Morrill, J. S. (ed.), *Oliver Cromwell and the English Revolution* (Harlow, 1990)

Sir Thomas Fairfax
Wilson, J., *Fairfax* (London, 1985)

Prince Rupert of the Rhine
Darman, P. M., 'Prince Rupert of the Rhine: a Study in Generalship, 1642–1646', MPhil thesis (University of York, 1987)
Morrah, P., *Prince Rupert of the Rhine* (London, 1976)

Jan Sobieski
Barker, T. M., *Double Eagle and Crescent: Vienna's Second Siege and its Historical Setting* (Albany, 1967)
Brzezinski, R., *Polish Armies 1569–1696* (Osprey Men-at-Arms series nos. 184 and 188, London, 1988)
Frost, R. I., *The Northern Wars, 1558–1721: War, State and Society in Northeastern Europe, 1558–1721* (Harlow, 2000)
Stoye, J., *The Siege of Vienna* (London, 1964)

Peter the Great
Englund, P., *The Battle of Poltava* (London, 1992)
Fuller, W. C., *Strategy and Power in Russia 1600–1914* (New York, 1992)
Hughes, L., *Russia in the Age of Peter the Great* (New Haven, 1998)
Konstam, A., *Peter the Great's Army* (Osprey Men-at-Arms series nos. 260 and 264, London, 1993)

Burkhard Christoph von Münnich
Cassels, L., *The Struggle for the Ottoman Empire, 1717–1740* (London, 1966)
Duffy, C., *Russia's Military Way to the West* (London, 1981)

Duke of Marlborough
Black, J. M., *European Warfare in Global Context, 1660–1815* (London, 2007)
Chandler, D., *Marlborough as Military Commander* (London, 1973)
—— *The Art of Warfare in the Age of Marlborough* (London, 1976)
Jones, J., *Marlborough* (Cambridge, 1993)
Murray, G. (ed.), *The Letters and Dispatches of John Churchill, First Duke of Marlborough* (London, 1845)
Snyder, H. (ed.), *The Marlborough–Godolphin Correspondence* (Oxford, 1975)

Eugene, Prince of Savoy
McKay, D., *Prince Eugene of Savoy* (London and New York, 1977)

Claude, Duke of Villars
Sturgill, C., *Marshal Villars and the War of the Spanish Succession* (Lexington, KY, 1965)

Frederick the Great
Anderson, M., *The War of the Austrian Succession, 1740–1748* (Harlow, 1995)
Duffy, C., *The Army of Frederick the Great* (London, 1974)
—— *Frederick the Great: a Military Life* (London, 1988)
Showalter, D., *The Wars of Frederick the Great* (Harlow, 1996)

Count Leopold Josef von Daun
Duffy, C., *Instrument of War: the Austrian Army in the Seven Years War* (Chicago, 2000)

Nader Shah
Axworthy, M., *Sword of Persia: Nader Shah, from Tribal Warrior to Conquering Tyrant* (London, 2006)
Lockhart, L., *Nadir Shah* (London, 1938)
Tucker, E., *Nadir Shah's Quest for Legitimacy in Post-Safavid Iran* (Gainesville, 2006)
—— 'Nader Shah', *Encyclopaedia Iranica* (www.iranica.com, updated 29 March 2006)

Qianlong Emperor
Chang, M., *A Court on Horseback: Imperial Touring & the Construction of Qing Rule, 1680–1785* (Cambridge, MA and London, 2007)
Dai Yingcong, 'A Disguised Defeat: the Myanmar Campaign of the Qing Dynasty', *Modern Asian Studies*, 38 (2004), pp. 145–89
Perdue, P. C., *China Marches West: the Qing Conquest of Central Eurasia* (Cambridge, MA and London, 2005)
Waley-Cohen, J., *The Culture of War in China: Empire and the Military under the Qing Dynasty* (London, 2006)

George Washington
Abbott, W. W. et al (eds.), *The Papers of George Washington, 1748–1799*, 52 vols. to date (Charlottesville, 1976–)
Ellis, J. J., *His Excellency: George Washington* (New York, 2004)
Ferling, J. E., *The First of Men: a Life of George Washington* (Knoxville, 1988)
Freeman, D. S., *George Washington: a Biography*, 7 vols. (New York, 1948–57)
Higginbotham, D., *George Washington and the American Military Tradition* (Athens, GA, 1985)

Charles Cornwallis
Billias, G. A. (ed.), *George Washington's Generals and Opponents: their Exploits and Leadership* (New York, 1994)
Wickwire, F. and M., *Cornwallis: the American Adventure* (Boston, 1970)

Napoleon
Esdaile, C., *The Peninsular War: a New History* (London, 2003)
Leggiere, M., *Napoleon and Berlin: the Franco-Prussian War in North Germany, 1813* (Norman, 2002)
—— *The Fall of Napoleon: Volume 1, the Allied Invasion of France, 1813–1814* (Cambridge Military Histories series, Cambridge, 2007)
Rothenberg, G. E., *The Art of Warfare in the Age of Napoleon* (Bloomington, 1980)
—— *Napoleon's Great Adversary: the Archduke Charles and the Austrian Army, 1792–1814* (Staplehurst, 1995)
—— *The Napoleonic Wars* (New York, 2005)
Schneid, F. C., *Napoleon's Conquest of Europe: the War of the Third Coalition* (Westport, 2005)

Davout
Charrier, P., *Le Maréchal Davout* (Millau, 2005)

Kutuzov

Mikaberidze, A., *The Russian Officer Corps in the Revolutionary and Napoleonic Wars, 1792–1815* (El Dorado, 2005)

Horatio Nelson

Cannadine, D. (ed.), *Admiral Lord Nelson: Context and Legacy* (Basingstoke, 2005)

Hayward, J., *For God and Glory: Lord Nelson and his Way of War* (Annapolis, 2003)

Knight, R., *The Pursuit of Victory: the Life and Achievement of Horatio Nelson* (London, 2005)

Lambert, A., *Nelson: Britannia's God of War* (London, 2004)

White, C., *Nelson the Admiral* (Stroud, 2005)

Duke of Wellington

Gates, D., *The Spanish Ulcer: a History of the Peninsular War* (London, 2002)

James, L., *The Iron Duke: a Military Biography of Wellington* (London, 1992)

Weller, J., *Wellington in India* (London, 1993)

The Modern Age

Shaka Zulu

Hamilton, C. A., 'The Character and Objects of Chaka', *The Journal of African History*, 33 (1992), pp. 37–63

—— *The Mfecane Aftermath: Reconstructive Debates in Southern African History* (Johannesburg, 1995)

Knight, I. J., *Warrior Chiefs of Southern Africa* (New York, 1995)

Morris, D. R., *The Washing of the Spears* (London, 1966)

Omer-Cooper, J. D., *The Zulu Aftermath* (London, 1966)

Ritter, E. A., *Shaka Zulu* (London, 1955)

Simón Bolívar

Bushnell, D., *Simón Bolívar: Liberation and Disappointment* (New York and London, 2004)

Lynch, J., *Simón Bolívar: A Life* (New Haven, 2006)

Masur, G., *Simón Bolívar* (Albuquerque, 1968)

O'Leary, D. F., *Bolívar and the War of Independence: Memorias del General Daniel Florencio O'Leary*, trans. and ed. R. F. McNerney, Jr. (Austin and London, 1970)

Slatta, R. and J. DeGrummond, *Simón Bolívar's Quest for Glory* (College Station, 2003)

Giuseppe Garibaldi

Garibaldi, G., *Memorie* (Turin, 1975)

Lipira, B. S., *Giuseppe Garibaldi: a Biography of the Father of Modern Italy* (London, 1998)

Paoletti, C., 'Latin American Warfare and Garibaldi's Tactics', in *Acta of the XXIV ICMH Annual Conference* (1998)

Paoletti, C., *Gli Italiani in armi: cinque secoli di storia militare nazionale 1494–2000* (Rome, 2001)

Ridley, J., *Garibaldi* (London, 2001)

Moltke the Elder

Blackbourn, D., *The Long Nineteenth Century: a History of Germany, 1780–1918* (New York, 1998)

Hughes, D. J. (ed.), *Moltke on the Art of War: Selected Writings* (New York, 1996)

von Moltke, H. K. B., *The Franco-German War of 1870–71* (London, 1907, reprinted 1992)

Ulysses S. Grant

Fuller, J. F. C., *The Generalship of Ulysses S. Grant* (New York, 1929)

Grant, U. S., *Personal Memoirs of U.S. Grant*, 2 vols. (New York, 1885)

Simon, J. Y. (ed.), *The Papers of Ulysses S. Grant*, 28 vols. to date (Carbondale, 1967–)

Simpson, B. D., *Ulysses S. Grant: Triumph over Adversity, 1822–1865* (Boston, 2000)

Smith, J. E., *Grant* (New York, 2002)

William T. Sherman

Marszelak, J. F., *Sherman: a Soldier's Passion for Order* (New York, 1993)

Sherman, W. T., *Memoirs of W. T. Sherman*, 2 vols. (New York, 1875)

Robert E. Lee

Dowdey, C. and L. H. Manarin (eds.), *The Wartime Papers of R. E. Lee* (Boston, MA, 1961)

Freeman, D. S., *R. E. Lee*, 4 vols. (New York, 1934–35)

Gallagher, G. W. (ed.), *Lee the Soldier* (Lincoln, NE, 1995)

Thomas 'Stonewall' Jackson

Henderson, G. F. R., *Stonewall Jackson and the American Civil War*, 2 vols. (London, 1900)

Robertson, J. I., *Stonewall Jackson: the Man, the Soldier, the Legend* (New York, 1997)

Menelik

Berkeley, G., *The Campaign of Adowa and the Rise of Menelik* (London, 1935)

Caulk, R., 'Firearms and Princely Power in Ethiopia in the Nineteenth Century', *The Journal of African History*, 13 (1972), pp. 609–30

Dankwah, R. H. K., *Shewa, Menelik and the Ethiopian Empire* (London, 1975)

Dunn, J., 'For God, Emperor, Country! The Evolution of Ethiopia's Nineteenth Century Army', *War in History*, 7 (1994)

Marcus, H., *The Life and Times of Menelik II* (New York and London, 1975)

Rubenson, S., *The Survival of Ethiopian Independence* (London, 1976)

Garnet Wolseley

Beckett, I. F. W., *The Victorians at War* (London, 2003)

Bond, B. (ed.), *Victorian Military Campaigns* (London, 1967)

Kochanski, H., *Sir Garnet Wolseley: Victorian Hero* (London, 1999)

Lehmann, J., *All Sir Garnet: a Life of Field Marshal Lord Wolseley* (London, 1964)

Maurice, J. F., *The Campaign of 1882 in Egypt* (Portsmouth, 1887, reprinted 1973)

Symons, J., *England's Pride: the Story of the Gordon Relief Expedition* (London, 1965)

Admiral Togo

Aizawa, K., 'Differences Regarding Togo's Surprise Attack on Port Arthur,' in D. Wolfe et al, *The Russo-Japanese War in Global Perspective: World War Zero*, vol. 2 (Leiden and Boston, 2007)

Bodley, R. V. C., *Admiral Togo: the Authorized Life of Admiral of the Fleet, Marquis Heihachiro Togo, O.M.* (London, 1935)

Evans, D. and M. Peattie, *Kaigun: Strategy, Tactics, and Technology in the Imperial Japanese Navy, 1887–1941* (Annapolis, 1997)

Nakamura, K. (ed.), *Admiral Togo: the Hero of the World, a Memoir* (Tokyo, 1934)

Marshal Foch

Liddell Hart, B. H., *Foch: Man of Orléans* (Boston, 1932)

Neiberg, M., *Foch: Supreme Allied Commander in the Great War* (Dulles, 2003)

Marshal Henri-Philippe Pétain

Bruce, R., *Pétain: Verdun to Vichy* (Dulles, 2007)

Marshal Joseph Joffre

Doughty, R., 'French Strategy in 1914: Joffre's

Own', *The Journal of Military History*, 67:2 (2003), pp. 427–54

Field Marshal Sir Douglas Haig

Wiest, A., *Haig: Evolution of a Commander* (Dulles, 2005)

Admiral John Rushworth Jellicoe

Bacon, R., *The Life of John Rushworth, Earl Jellicoe* (London, 1936)

General John Pershing

Smythe, D., *Pershing: General of the Armies* (Bloomington, 1986)

Erich Ludendorff

Kitchen, M., *The Silent Dictatorship: the Politics of the German High Command under Hindenburg and Ludendorff, 1916–1918* (London, 1976)

Lee, J., *The Warlords: the Campaigns of Hindenburg and Ludendorff* (London, 2005)

Ludendorff, E., *Ludendorff's Own Story*, 2 vols. (London, 1919)

Ludendorff, M., *My Married Life with Ludendorff* (London, 1930)

Parkinson, R., *Tormented Warrior: Ludendorff and the Supreme Command* (London, 1978)

Paul von Hindenburg

Asprey, R., *The German High Command at War: Hindenburg and Ludendorff and the First World War* (New York, 1991)

Hindenburg, P. von., *Out of My Life* (London, 1920)

Wheeler-Bennett, J., *Hindenburg: the Wooden Titan* (London, 1967)

Mustafa Kemal

Erickson, E. J., *Ottoman Army Effectiveness in World War I: a Comparative Study* (Abingdon Park and New York, 2007)

Macfie, A. L., *Ataturk* (London, 1994)

Mango, A., *Ataturk* (New York, 2002)

Travers, T., *Gallipoli 1915* (Stroud and Charleston, 2001)

Erich von Manstein

Manstein, E. von, *Lost Victories: the War Memoirs of Hitler's Most Brilliant General*, trans. A. G. Powell (Chicago, 1958)

Paget, R. T., *Manstein: his Campaigns and his Trial* (London, 1957)

Stein, M., *Field Marshal Von Manstein, a Portrait: the Janus Head* (Solihull, 2007)

Heinz Guderian

Guderian, H., *Achtung-Panzer! The Development of Tank Warfare* (London, 1999)

—— *Panzer Leader* (Harmondsworth, 2000)

Erwin Rommel

Liddell-Hart, B. H. (ed), *The Rommel Papers* (Cambridge, MA, 1982)

Rommel, E., *Infantry Attacks* (London, 2006)

Gerd von Rundstedt

Blumentritt, G., *Von Rundstedt: the Soldier and the Man*, trans. C. Reavely (London, 1952)

Messenger, C., *The Last Prussian: a Biography of Field Marshal Gerd Von Rundstedt* (London, 1991)

Dwight D. Eisenhower

Ambrose, S. E., *Eisenhower: Soldier, General of the Army, President-Elect, 1890–1952* (London, 1984)

D'Este, C., *Eisenhower: a Soldier's Life* (London, 2003)

Eisenhower, D. D., *Crusade in Europe* (Baltimore, 1997)

Chandler, A. D., *The Papers of Dwight David Eisenhower: the War Years*, 5 vols. (Baltimore, 1970)

Viscount Montgomery of Alamein

Montgomery, B. L., *The Memoirs of Field Marshal the Viscount Montgomery of Alamein* (London, 1958)

Hamilton, N., *Monty: Master of the Battlefield, 1942–1944* (London, 1985)

Admiral Sir Andrew Cunningham

Cunningham, A. B., *A Sailor's Odyssey: the Autobiography of Admiral of the Fleet Viscount Cunningham of Hyndhope, KT, GCB, OM, DSO* (London, 1951)

Simpson, M. A., *A Life of Admiral of the Fleet Andrew Cunningham: a Twentieth Century Naval Leader* (London, 2004)

Field Marshal Sir Alan Brooke

Danchev, A. and D. Todman (eds.), *War Diaries, 1939–1945: Field Marshal Lord Alanbrooke* (London, 2001)

Fraser, D., *Alanbrooke* (London, 1982)

General Henry 'Hap' Arnold

Coffey, T. M., *Hap: the Story of the US Air Force and the Man who Built It, General Henry "Hap" Arnold* (New York, 1982)

Diso, D. A., *Hap Arnold and the Evolution of American Airpower* (Washington, DC, 2000)

General George C. Marshall

Cray, E., *General of the Army: George C. Marshall, Soldier and Statesman* (New York, 1990)

General George Patton

D'Este, C., *A Genius for War: a Life of General George S. Patton* (London, 1995)

Patton, G. S., *War as I Knew It* (Boston, 1995)

Georgy Zhukov

Cheney, O. P., *Zhukov* (Norman and London, 1996)

Spahr, W. J., *Zhukov: the Rise and Fall of a Great Captain* (Novato, 1993)

Zhukov, G. K., *Georgi Zhukov: Marshal of the Soviet Union. Reminiscences and Reflections*, trans. V. Schneierson (Moscow, 1985)

—— *Marshal Zhukov's Greatest Battles*, trans. T. Shabad (New York, 1969)

Konstantin Konstantinovich Rokossovsky

Rokossovsky, K. K., *A Soldier's Duty*, trans. and ed. R. Daglish (Moscow, 1985)

Woff, R., 'Konstantin Konstantinovich Rokossovsky', in H. Shukman (ed.), *Stalin's Generals* (New York, 1993), pp. 177–96

Admiral Nimitz

Alexander, J. H., *Storm Landings: Epic Amphibious Battles in the Central Pacific* (Annapolis, 1997)

Potter, E. B. and C. W. Nimitz (eds.), *The Great Sea War: the Story of Naval Action in World War II* (Englewood Cliffs, 1960)

Potter, E. B., *Nimitz* (Annapolis, 1976)

Admiral Raymond Spruance

Buell, T. B., *The Quiet Warrior: a Biography of Admiral Raymond A. Spruance* (Classics of Naval Literature series, Annapolis, 1987)

Vo Nguyen Giap

Currey, C. B., *Victory at Any Cost: the Genius of Viet Nam General Vo Nguyen Giap* (Washington, DC, 1997)

Macdonald, P., *Giap: the Victor in Vietnam* (New York, 1993)

Tucker, S. C., *Vietnam* (Lexington, KY, 1999)

Vo Nguyen Giap, *Unforgettable Days* (Hanoi, 1978)

List of Contributors

Jeremy Black is Professor of History at the University of Exeter. Graduating from Cambridge with a Starred First, he did postgraduate work at Oxford and then taught at Durham, eventually as Professor, before moving to Exeter in 1996. He has lectured extensively in Australia, Canada, Denmark, France, Germany, Italy, Japan, the Netherlands, New Zealand and the USA, where he has held visiting chairs at West Point, Texas Christian University and Stillman College. A past council member of the Royal Historical Society, Black is a fellow of the Royal Society for the Encouragement of Arts, Manufactures and Commerce, a senior fellow of the Foreign Policy Research Institute and a trustee of Agora. He was appointed to the Order of Membership of the British Empire for services to stamp design. He is, or has been, on a number of editorial boards, including the *Journal of Military History*, the journal of the Royal United Services Institute, *Media History* and *History Today*, and was editor of *Archives*. In 2008 he was awarded the Samuel Eliot Morison prize by the Society for Military History for services to military history.

His many books include *War and the World, 1450–2000* (2000), *Maps and History* (2000), *The British Seaborne Empire* (2004), and *European Warfare in a Global Context, 1600–1815* (2006). **Introduction and section openers; Saladin; Duke of Marlborough; Frederick the Great; Moltke the Elder; Admiral Nimitz**

Gábor Ágoston is Associate Professor in the Department of History, Georgetown University, Washington. His most recent publication is *Guns for the Sultan: Military Power and the Weapons Industry in the Ottoman Empire* (2005). **János Hunyadi**

Niall Barr is Reader in Military History at the Defence Studies Department, King's College, London, based at the Joint Services Command and Staff College. His many publications include *Pendulum of War: The Three Battles of El Alamein* (2004). **Dwight D. Eisenhower**

Ian Beckett is Professor of History at the University of Northampton and Chairman of the Army Records Society. He has published extensively on the British army between 1870 and 1918. **Garnet Wolseley**

Charles R. Bowlus is Professor Emeritus at the University of Arkansas at Little Rock, where he taught for 30 years. He continues to publish books and articles on medieval German history. **Otto the Great**

Niccolò Capponi divides his time between teaching and freelance writing. Born and raised in Florence, he has written extensively on a number of historical topics, with a focus on Renaissance warfare. **Sultan Selim I; Süleyman the Magnificent**

Robin Coningham is Professor of Archaeology and Head of Department at Durham University and has conducted fieldwork throughout South Asia. He is currently working in the Anuradhapura region of Sri Lanka and on the Tehran Plain of Iran. **Chandragupta**

Simon Coningham is completing an MA in the History of Warfare at King's College, London, prior to undertaking research into imperial policing. **Chandragupta**

Petr Čornej is Professor of Czech History at Charles University in Prague. His work on the 15th-century Czechs includes *The Mystery of the Czech Chronicles* (new edition 2003) and *The Great History of the Czech Crown Lands, Vol. V: 1402–1437* (2000) and *Vol. VI: 1437–1526* (2007). **Jan Žižka**

David Drew is an archaeologist and author who has worked for 30 years in Latin America, principally in Peru. He has written books and articles and made documentary films on both Andean and Maya archaeology. **Francisco Pizarro**

Robert Foley is a senior lecturer in modern military history at the University of Liverpool. He is author of *German Strategy and the Path to Verdun* (2005) and *Alfred von Schlieffen's Military Writings* (2004). **Erich Ludendorff**

John France is Professor of History and Director of the Callaghan Centre for the Study of Conflict at Swansea University. His latest book is *The Crusades and the Expansion of Catholic Christendom, 1000–1714* (2005). **Charlemagne; Frederick Barbarossa**

David Gates, of the Defence Studies Department, King's College, London, is the author of *Warfare in the Nineteenth Century* (2001) and *The Spanish Ulcer: A History of the Peninsular War* (2002). **Duke of Wellington**

Jan Glete is Professor of History at Stockholm University. His recent works include *Warfare at Sea, 1500–1650* (2000) and *War and the State in Early Modern Europe* (2002). **Gustavus Adolphus**

Fernando González de León is Associate Professor of History at Springfield College, Massachusetts and works on Spanish military history among other fields. His forthcoming book *The Road to Rocroi* studies the Army of Flanders. **Emperor Charles V**

Richard Harding is Professor of Organisational History at the University of Westminster. He is author of *Amphibious Warfare in the Eighteenth Century* (1991) and and *Seapower and Naval History* (1999). **Horatio Nelson**

Russell A. Hart is Associate Professor of History at Hawai'i Pacific University. He is the author of *Clash of Arms: How the Allies Won in Normandy* (2001) and *Guderian: Panzer Pioneer or Mythmaker?* (2006). **Erich von Manstein**

Rob Johnson is a lecturer in International Security Studies and Head of Academic Development at the University of Bath. His work on conflict includes *Oil, Islam and Conflict* (2007) and *Spying for Empire* (2007). **Great Military Leaders A to Z**

John Lamphear is a Professor Emeritus from the University of Texas where he specialized in African military history. His publications include *The Scattering Time* (1992) and an edited collection of essays on African Military history (2007). **Shaka Zulu; Menelik**

Lester D. Langley is Research Professor Emeritus, University of Georgia. He is the author of *The Americas in the Age of Revolution, 1750–1850* (1996). **Simón Bolívar**

Timothy May is Assistant Professor of History at North Georgia College & State University. He is the author of *The Mongol Art of War* (2007). **Chingiz Khan; Timur**

Michael S. Neiberg is professor of history and co-director of the Center for the Study of War and Society at the University of Southern Mississippi. He is the author of several works including *Fighting the Great War: A Global History* (2005) and *The Second Battle of the Marne* (2008). **Marshal Foch**

Andrew J. Newman is Reader in Islamic Studies and Persian at the University of Edinburgh. He is the author of *Safavid Iran: Rebirth of a Persian Empire* (2006). **Shah Abbas I; Nader Shah**

Ciro Paoletti is a military historian and director of the Associazione Studi Storici. His work in Italian spans some 100 books; in English he has published many scholarly articles as well as *A Military History of Italy* (2007). **Giuseppe Garibaldi**

Charles A. Peterson taught premodern Chinese history at Cornell University where in 2006 he was named Professor Emeritus. His publications include much specialist literature as well contributions to the *Cambridge History of China*. **Shi Huangdi**

Nigel Pollard is an ancient historian and archaeologist in Swansea University's Department of Classics, Ancient History and Egyptology. He is the author of *Soldiers, Cities and Civilians in Roman Syria* (2000). **Hannibal; Julius Caesar; Augustus; Trajan**

Michael Prestwich has retired from his professorship of history at Durham University. His work includes *Edward I* (1988), *Armies and Warfare in the Middle Ages: the English Experience* (1996), and *Plantagenet England 1225–1360* (2005). **William the Conqueror; Edward I; Robert Bruce**

Ethan S. Rafuse is an associate professor of military history at the US Army Command and General Staff College. He is the author of five books and over 100 essays, articles, and book reviews. **George Washington; Ulysses S. Grant; Robert E. Lee**

Roger Reese is Professor of History at Texas A&M University. He is author of *Stalin's Reluctant Soldiers* (1996), *The Soviet Military Experience* (2000) and *Red Commanders* (2005). **Georgy Zhukov**

Matthew Restall was educated at Oxford and UCLA. He is Edwin Erle Sparks Professor of Colonial Latin American History at Pennsylvania State University and editor of *Ethnohistory* journal. *Invading Guatemala* (2007) is his ninth book. **Hernando Cortés**

Francis Robinson is Professor of the History of South Asia in the Department of History, Royal Holloway, University of London. His recent works include *Islam, South Asia and the West* (2007) and *The Mughals and the Islamic Dynasties of India, Iran and Central Asia* (2007). **Babur; Akbar**

J. Charles Schencking is Senior Lecturer in Japanese History at the University of Melbourne. He has published widely on the history of the Imperial Japanese Navy including *Making Waves: Politics, Propaganda, and the Emergence of the Imperial Japanese Navy, 1868–1922* (2005). **Admiral Togo**

Frederick C. Schneid is Professor of History at High Point University. His most recent publications are *Napoleon's Conquest of Europe: The War of the Third Coalition* (2005) and *Warfare in Europe, 1792–1815* (2007). **Napoleon**

Nicholas Sekunda studied at Manchester and now works for Gdańsk University, Poland. He is the author of a number of books on ancient warfare, including *The Army of Alexander the Great* (1984). **Cyrus the Great**

Shinko Taniguchi is a history lecturer at Waseda University in Japan. She is the author of *Law and Norms of Early Modern Japan* (2005), *The Real Image of Chushingura* (2006) and *The Use of Japanese Samurai Forces* (2007). **Toyotomi Hideyoshi**

Tim Travers is Professor Emeritus at the University of Calgary. His works include *The Killing Ground* (1987), *How the War Was Won* (1992), *Gallipoli 1915* (2001), *World History of Warfare* (co-author, 2002) and *Pirates: A History* (2007). **Mustafa Kemal**

Spencer C. Tucker retired from teaching in 2003 as holder of the chair of Military History at the Virginia Military Institute. He is the author or editor of 27 books and encyclopedias treating military and naval history. **Vo Nguyen Giap**

Joanna Waley-Cohen is Professor of History at New York University and author most recently of *The Culture of War in China: Empire and the Military under the Qing Dynasty* (2006). **Qianlong Emperor**

Michael Whitby is Professor of Classics and Ancient History at the University of Warwick. He specializes in Late Roman History, and is co-editor of *The Cambridge History of Greek and Roman Warfare*. **Alexander the Great; Belisarius**

Peter H. Wilson is G.F. Grant Professor of History at the University of Hull. His books include *German Armies: War and German Politics, 1648–1806* (1998) and *From Reich to Revolution: German History, 1558–1806* (2004). **Turenne; Oliver Cromwell; Jan Sobieski; Peter the Great**

Sources of Illustrations

t: top; b: bottom; c: centre; r: right; l: left
All maps, battle plans and reconstructions: Red Lion Prints
© Thames & Hudson Ltd, London

1 Musée de l'Armée, Paris; 2–3 akg-images; 4 © Araldo de Luca/Corbis; 5 Tapestry Museum, Bayeux; 6 Palazzo Pitti, Florence. Photo Bridgeman Art Library; 7 © Corbis; 8 akg-images; 9 British Library, London. Photo © British Library Board. All Rights Reserved/Bridgeman Art Library; 10 Private Colletion. Photo Bridgeman Art Library; 11 AFP/Getty Images; 12–13 © Araldo de Luca/Corbis; 14 Metropolitan Museum of Art/Art Resource/Scala, Florence; 15 Photo Art Archive/Museo Nazionale Terme, Rome/Gianni Dagli Orti; 16 Photo Art Archive/Gianni Dagli Orti; 17t British Museum, London; 17c © The Gallery Collection/Corbis; 18l Acropolis Museum, Athens; 19tl Archaeological Museum, Thessaloniki; 19tr Archaeological Museum, Thessaloniki; 20t Museo Archeologico Nazionale, Naples; 22b Turkish National Museum, Istanbul; 25tl Wheeler Archive, Faculty of Oriental Studies, Cambridge University; 25b © Adam Woolfitt/Corbis; 26 Xia Juxian, Guo Yan; 27c Xia Juxian, Guo Yan; 27tr Xia Juxian, Guo Yan; 27cr Xia Juxian, Guo Yan; 27br Xia Juxian, Guo Yan; 28 © Keren Su/Corbis; 29t Xia Juxian, Guo Yan; 29bl Xia Juxian, Guo Yan; 29bcl Xia Juxian, Guo Yan; 29bc Xia Juxian, Guo Yan; 29bcr Xia Juxian, Guo Yan; 29br Xia Juxian, Guo Yan; 30–31 © Keren Su/Corbis; 32l British Museum Images, London; 32r akg-images; 33tr Museo Archaeologico Nacional, Madrid; 34tl Bardo Museum, Tunis, Tunisia; 35t Photo Art Archive/Museo Capitolino, Rome/Gianni Dagli Orti; 36 Museo Pio-Clementino, Vatican Museums; 38 Photo Roger Wilson; 38bl Cabinet des médailles de la Bibliothèque Nationale de France, Paris; 38br Cabinet des médailles de la Bibliothèque Nationale de France, Paris; 39t Musée du Louvre, Paris; 39b Archaeological Museum, Venice; 40b © Araldo de Luca/Corbis; 41 Théâtre antique d'Orange, Orange, France; 42 Kunsthistorisches Museum, Vienna; 43 Museo Chiaramonti, Vatican Museums; 44b Musée du Louvre, Paris; 45tl British Museum, London. Photo © Scala, Florence/HIP 2004; 45tr © Mimmo Jodice/Corbis; 45b Teutoburg Forest, Detmold, Germany; 46t © Charles & Josette Lenars/Corbis; 46b Musei Pontificie, Vatican Museums; 47t Museo dell'Ara Pacis, Rome. Photo The Art Archive/Gianni Dagli Orti; 47b Museo dell'Ara Pacis, Rome; 48 Photo The Art Archive/Musée du Louvre, Paris/Gianni Dagli Orti; 49br British Museum, London. Photo © Scala, Florence/HIP 2003; 50l Photo The Art Archive/Gianni Dagli Orti; 50c © Werner Forman/Corbis; 50r Photo The Art Archive/Jarrold Publishing; 51 Trajan's Forum, Rome. Photo © Scala, Florence, courtesy of the Ministero Beni e Att. Culturali 1990; 52 San Vitale, Ravenna. Photo © Scala, Florence 1990; 53tr Fitzwilliam Museum, University of Cambridge. Photo Bridgeman Art Library; 53b Photo courtesy Professor Michael Whitby, University of Warwick; 54–55 Tapestry Museum, Bayeux; 56 Bibliothèque Nationale de France, Paris; 57l Narodni Museum, Prague. Photo akg-images; 57r British Library, London. Photo Bridgeman Art Library; 58 Musée du Louvre, Paris. Photo © Scala, Florence 1995; 59tr Photo akg-images/Erich Lessing; 59br Muenzkabinett, Staatliche Museen zu Berlin, Germany. Photo © Karin Maerz/Scala, Florence/Bildarchiv Preussischer Kulturbesitz, Berlin; 60l Photo RMN/Peter Willi; 60r © Archivo Iconografico, S.A./Corbis; 61t akg-images/Erich Lessing; 61c Musée de l'Armée, Paris. Photo RMN; 62 akg-images/Schütze/Rodemann; 63tl Wuttembergische Landesbibliothek, Cod. Bibl.2.23; 64t akg-images/British Library, London; 64b British Library, London. Photo © Scala, Florence/HIP 2003; 65l © Jonathan Blair/Corbis; 66–67 akg-images/A.F. Kersting; 67t Tapestry Museum, Bayeux; 68l akg-images/British Library, London; 68c Bodleian Library, University of Oxford, MS. Huntington 264, f.117; 68r Bodleian Library, University of Oxford, MS. Huntington 264, f.102v; 69l © Kevin Fleming/Corbis; 70c akg-images/Erich Lessing; 70b akg-images/Erich Lessing; 72 akg-images; 74 Palazzo Pubblico, Siena.Photo Bridgeman Art Library; 75t Photo The Art Archive/Museum der Stadt, Vienna/Gianni Dagli Orti; 75b akg-images; 76 National Palace Museum, Taipei, Taiwan. Photo Bridgeman Art Library; 77b British Museum, London; 78b © The Board of Trustees of the Armouries, UK; 79 National Palace Museum, Taipei, Taiwan; 80 Gur-e Mir Mausoluem, Samarkand, Uzbekistan; 81b State Hermitage Museum, St Petersburg; 82b Topkapi Sarayi Armoury, Istanbul; 83l © Christine Osbourne/Corbis; 83r Private Collection; 84 akg-images/British Library, London; 85br © Richard T. Nowitz/Corbis; 85bc © Dave G. Houser/Corbis; 86t akg-images/British Library, London; 87 Reproduced by permission of the Syndics of Cambridge University Library MS.Ee.3.59, f.32; 88 National Library of Scotland, Edinburgh, Ms.Acc.9309; 89tl British Library, London, Ms. Add.47682, fol.40; 89br British Library, London, Ms.Add.47682, fol.40; 90l Photo The Art Archive; 90r akg-images/Erich Lessing; 91b akg-images/Erich Lessing; 92 British Library, London. Photo © Scala, Florence/HIP 2003; 93br Hungarian National Museum, Budapest; 94–5 Palazzo Pitti, Florence. Photo Bridgeman Art Library; 97 Photo © Musée d'Orsay, Paris/Giraudon/Bridgeman Art Library; 98 Photo © Scala, Florence, courtesy of the Ministero Beni e Att. Culturali 1990; 99t Photo © Christie's Images Ltd 2008; 100tl © Corbis; 100b © Archivo Iconografico, S.A./Corbis; 101 Photo © Christie's Images Ltd 2008; 102l Museo del Ejercito, Madrid. Photo Bridgeman Art Library; 102r akg-images; 103t Kunstbibliothek, Staatliche Museen zu Kunst, Berlin. Photo © Scala, Florence/Bildarchiv Preussischer Kulturbesitz, Berlin 2005; 103br © Hubert Stadler/Corbis; 104 Topkapi Sarayi Museum, Istanbul; 105 Topkapi Sarayi Museum, Istanbul. Photo Bridgeman Art Library; 106b Topkapi Sarayi Museum, Istanbul; 107l Topkapi Sarayi Museum, Istanbul; 107c Topkapi Sarayi Museum, Istanbul; 107r Topkapi Sarayi Museum, Istanbul; 108 Gemäldegalerie, Kunsthistorisches Museum, Vienna; 109 Historisches Museum der Stadt Wien, Vienna; 110b akg-images/Cameraphoto; 111tl Topkapi Sarayi Museum, Istanbul; 111tr Topkapi Sarayi Museum, Istanbul; 112 Museo di San Martino, Naples; 113b Rijksmuseum, Amsterdam; 114l Kunsthistorisches Museum, Vienna; 114r Museo del Prado, Madrid; 115t © Massimo Listri/Corbis; 116 Trustees of the British Museum, London, 1921, 1011.0.3; 117l British Library, London. Photo © Scala, Florence/HIP 2003; 119l National Museum, New Delhi; 119r Edward Binney 3rd Collection of Turkish Art at the Los Angeles County Museum of Art, M.85.237.28. Photo © 2007 Museum Associates/LACMA; 120t Chester Beatty Library, Dublin; 120b British Museum, London. Photo © Scala, Florence/HIP 2004; 122bl Victoria & Albert Museum, London; 122br Victoria & Albert Museum, London; 123l Victoria & Albert Museum, London; 123r Victoria & Albert Museum, London; 124 Courtesy Osaka Castle Museum, Japan; 125 Courtesy Osaka Castle Museum, Japan; 126tl Courtesy Osaka Castle Museum, Japan; 126b Courtesy Osaka Castle Museum, Japan; 127b © Bohemian Nomad Picturemakers/Corbis; 128tl TNM Image Archives, http://TNMArchives.jp; 128tr © Craig Lovell/Corbis; 128cl TNM Image Archives, http://TNMArchives.jp; 128br Tosho-gu Shrine; 129r TNM Image Archives, http://TNMArchives.jp; 130–31 Courtesy the Osaka Castle Museum, Japan; 132 The Trustees of the British Museum, London, 1920, 0917, 0.13.2; 133t Photo The Art Archive/Palace of Chihil Soutoun Isfahan/Gianni Dagli Orti; 134 akg-images; 135c © Board of Trustees of the Armouries, UK; 135b © Board of Trustees of the Armouries, UK; 136t akg-images; 136br akg-images; 137tl Photo © Ann Ronan/HIP/Scala, Florence 2005; 137b akg-images; 139 Musée de château de Versailles; 140b Musée Conde, Chantilly. Photo Giraudon/Bridgeman Art Library; 141tl Min. Defense-Service Historique de l'Armee de Terre, France. Photo Griaudon/The Bridgeman Art Library; 141tr Min. Defense-Service Historique de l'Armée de Terre, France. Photo Flammarion/Bridgeman Art Library; 141b Pushkin Museum, Moscow. Photo Giraudon/Bridgeman Art Library; 142 Courtesy Cromwell Museum, Huntingdon, UK; 143 Private Collection. Photo © Christie's Images Ltd 2008; 144b Photo © Ashmolean Museum, University of Oxford, UK/Bridgeman Art Library; 145tl British Library, London; 145tr © The Board of Trustees of the Armouries, UK; 145c Courtesy the Cromwell Museum, Huntingdon; 146c © The Board of Trustees of the Armouries, UK; 146bl © The Board of Trustees of the Armouries, UK; 146br Photo National Portrait Gallery, London; 147 © Bettman/Corbis; 148l akg-images/Erich Lessing; 148r Palazzo Pitti, Florence; 149c Wavel State Art Collection, Cracow. Photo Lukasz Schuster/Bridgeman Art Library; 150–51 Photo The Art Archive/Museum der Stadt Wien/Gianni Dagli Orti; 152 The Royal Collection © Her Majesty Queen Elizabeth II; 153bc The Lenin Library, Moscow; 153cr Photo © Scala, Florence 1991; 153br akg-images/Erich Lessing; 154–55 Peterhof Palace, Petrodvorets, St Petersburg. Photo Bridgeman Art Library; 156tl Chateau de Versailles. Photo Giraudon/Bridgeman Art Library; 157t Pushkin Museum, Moscow. Photo Bridgeman Art Library; 157b Bildarchiv der Österreichischen Nationalbibliothek, Vienna; 158 © Arte & Immagini srl/Corbis; 159b Courtesy the Council of the National Army Museum, London; 160t Blenheim Palace, Oxfordshire, UK. Photo Bridgeman Art Library; 160–61 © Archivio Iconografico, S.A./Corbis; 162t Musee Municipal, Cambrai, France. Photo © Austrian Archive/Scala, Florence 2006; 163t Photo © Christie's Images Ltd 2008; 163b Image copyright Blenheim Palace. Reproduced by kind permission of His Grace the Duke of Marlborough, Blenheim Palace Image Library; 164 Photo The Art Archive/Musée des Beaux Arts Nantes/Gianni Dagli Orti; 165b Neue Galerie, Kassel. Photo © Museumlandschaft Hesseen Lassel/Bridgeman Art Library; 165tr akg-images; 166t Imagno/Getty Images; 167 © Stapleton Collection/Corbis; 168 Museum of Fine Arts, Boston; 169bl Private Collection; 169br State Hermitage Museum, St Petersburg; 170 Palace Museum, Beijing; 171 Palace Museum, Beijing; 172tl Palace Museum, Beijing; 172tr Musée National des Arts Asiatiques Guimet, Paris; 172cl Palace Museum, Beijing; 172cr Palace Museum, Beijing; 173t Palace Museum, Beijing; 173c Palace Museum, Beijing; 173r Palace Museum, Beijing; 174 Courtesy Mount Vernon Ladies' Association; 175 Photo © Metropolitan Museum of Art/Art Resource/Scala, Florence 2007; 176l Photo The Art Archive/Culver Pictures; 177t Museum of Fine Arts, Boston; 177c Courtesy Mount Vernon Ladies' Association; 178t British Library, London. Photo © Scala, Florence/HIP 2005; 178–79 Photo The Art Archive/Musée de Château de Versailles/Gianni Dagli Orti; 180 akg-images; 181 Kunsthistorisches Museum, Vienna. Photo Austrian Archive/Scala, Florence; 182t Photo © Ann Ronan/HIP/Scala, Florence 2003; 182b akg-images; 184b akg-images; 185t Musée de l'Armée, Paris. Photo RMN/Pascal Segrette; 186–87 akg-images/Erich Lessing; 188t Musée de l'Armée, Paris. Photo RMN/Photographe inconnu; 188b Courtesy Historical Image Bank, www.historicalimagebank.com; 189t Giovanni Caselli Library; 190b State Historical Museum, Moscow. Photo RIA Novosti/Bridgeman Art Library; 191t akg-images/Erich Lessing; 191b Courtesy the Council of the National Army Museum, London; 192 Photo © National Maritime Museum, London; 193b Photo © National Maritime Museum, London; 194t Photo © Art Media/HIP/Scala, Florence 2005; 195tr Photo © National Maritime Museum, London; 196tl © Adam Woolfitt/Corbis; 196cl © Adam Woolfitt/Corbis; 196–97 akg-images; 197tr Photo © National Maritime Museum, London; 198 Walmer Castle, Kent, English Heritage, London. Photo © Scala, Florence/HIP 2003; 199 Photo © Christie's Images Ltd 2008; 200t Apsley House, The Wellington Museum, London. Photo Bridgeman Art Library; 200br Photo © Royal Hospital Chelsea, London. Photo Bridgeman Art Library; 201r © The Board of Trustees of the Armouries, UK; 202b Apsley House, The Wellington Museum, London. Photo Bridgeman Art Library; 203tr Musée de l'Armée, Paris; 203b Private Collection. Photo Bridgeman Art Library; 204–05 © Corbis; 206 Photo Art Archive/Imperial War Museum, London; 207t National Portrait Gallery, Smithsonian Institution, Washington, D.C. Photo © National Portrait Gallery, Smithsonian/Art Resource/Scala, Florence 2008; 207b Photo Cody Images; 208l Collection Amafa Heritage KwaZulu Natal; 208r Courtesy Ian Knight; 209l Courtesy Ian Knight; 209bl Courtesy Ian Knight; 209br Hulton Archive/Getty Images; 210 Private Collection. Photo Bridgeman Art Library; 211tr © Christie's/Handout/Reuters/Corbis; 211cr © Christie's/Handout/Reuters/Corbis; 211b Photo The Art Archive/Museo Nacional Bogota/Gianni Dagli Orti; 212 Hulton Archive/Getty Images; 213b © Archivo Iconografico, S.A./Corbis; 214l © Corbis; 214r Hamburger Kunsthalle, Hamburg. Photo © Elke Walford/Scala, Florence/Bildarchiv Preussischer Kulturbesitz, Berlin 2008; 215b Photo The Art Archive/Musée Carnavalet, Paris/Gianni Dagli Orti; 216b akg-images; 219 Photo Library of Congress, Washington, D.C.; 220 © Corbis; 221r © Tria Giovan/Corbis; 222–223 Photo © Metropolitan Museum of Art/Art Resource/Scala, Florence 2007; 223tl © Corbis; 224t © Hulton-Deutsch Collection/Corbis; 224bl © Tria Giovan/Corbis; 224br © Corbis; 225b © Corbis; 225t © Corbis; 226 © Corbis; 227c Gettysburg National Military Park; 227r US Army Military History Institute; 227br © Corbis; 228t © Corbis; 228c © Corbis; 228b MPI/Getty Images; 229r © Corbis; 230l © Werner Forman/Corbis; 230r akg-images; 231tl Photo Mary Evans Picture Library; 231b Photo Mary Evans/Rue Des Archives; 232l © Hulton-Deutsch Collection/Corbis; 233 Courtesy the Council, National Army Museum, London/Bridgeman Art Library; 233tr Private Collection; 233cr Private Collection. Photo © Malcolm Innes Gallery, London, UK/The Bridgeman Art Library; 234 © Bettmann/Corbis; 237t Photo The Art Archive; 237b Hulton Archive/Getty Images; 238 Hulton Archive/Getty Images; 239tr Musée de l'Armée, Paris. Photo RMN/Pascal Segrette; 239b Photo © Ann Ronan/HIP/Scala, Florence 2005; 240tl Hulton Archive/Getty Images; 240b ND/Roger Viollet/Getty Images; 241t © Bettman/Corbis; 241c © Hulton-Deutsch Collection/Corbis; 241b Photo The Art Archive/Imperial War Museum; 242tl Hulton Archive/Getty Images; 242b © Corbis; 243t Photo Imperial War Museum, London; 243c © Bettmann/Corbis; 243b akg-images; 244 Photo Mary Evans Picture Library; 245b akg-images; 246bl Hulton Archive/Getty Images; 246br akg-images; 247tl akg-images; 247tr © Bettmann/Corbis; 247b © Bettmann/Corbis; 248r Keystone/Getty Images; 249b General Photographic Agency/Getty Images; 250 akg-images; 252t Photo The Art Archive; 252bl akg-images/Ullstein Bild; 253l Mansell/Time & Life Pictures/Getty Images; 253r © Corbis; 254cl Photo The Art Archive; 254bl Photo The Art Archive; 254t © Hulton-Deutsch Collection/Corbis; 255t akg-images; 256t Keystone/Getty Images; 257t © Corbis; 257c akg-images; 258 © Hulton-Deutsch Collection/Corbis; 259t Public Record Office, London. Photo © Scala, Florence/HIP 2003; 260tl Eliot Elisofon//Time & Life Pictures/Getty Images; 260tlb akg-images/Ullstein Bild; 260tr Photo Imperial War Museum, London; 260b Photo Imperial War Museum, London; 261 © Bettmann/Corbis; 261tl Keystone/Getty Images; 261tr J.R. Eyerman/Time & Life Pictures/Getty Images; 261b Photo Imperial War Museum, London; 262 © Bettmann/Corbis; 263t © Corbis; 263b © Bettmann/Corbis; 264b © Bettmann/Corbis; 265 Photo The Art Archive/National Archives Washington, D.C.; 266t © Bettmann/Corbis; 266bl © Corbis; 267 Fred Ramage/Keystone/Getty Images; 268 © Bettmann/Corbis; 270 © Hulton-Deutsch Collection/Corbis; 271 akg-images; 272b Hulton Archive/Getty Images; 273tr © Bettmann/Corbis; 273trb Victor Temin/Slava Katamidze Collection/Getty Images; 273b Georgi Zelma/Slava Katamidze Collection/Getty Images; 274 Keystone/Getty Images; 276t © Bettmann/Corbis; 276tc National Air and Space Museum, Smithsonian Institution, Washington, D.C.; 276bl US Navy/Time & Life Pictures/Getty Images; 276–77 © Bettmann/Corbis; 277tr © Corbis; 278tl © Corbis; 278bl Keystone/Getty Images; 278r © Corbis; 279 Thomas D. Mcavoy/Time & Life Pictures/Getty Images; 280 Central Press/Getty Images; 281tl © Catherine Karnow/Corbis; 281bc © Tim Page/Corbis; 281br © Tim Page/Corbis; 282 National Maritime Museum, London; 283 Royal Army Museum, Sweden; 285 Imperial War Museum, London; 287 National Palace Museum, Beijing; 288 © Bettmann/Corbis; 289 © Corbis; 290 © Chris Hellier/Corbis; 291 National Maritime Museum, London; 292 National Army Museum, London; 293 © Corbis; 294 Imperial War Museum, London; 295 McCord Museum, McGill University, Montreal

Index